JUN 1 - 2015

EAST MEADOW PUBLIC LIBRARY

W9-AMB-790

Unfinished Business:

Social Action in Suburbia – Long Island, NY

1945-2014

East Meadow Public Library
1886 Front Street, East Meadow, NY 11554
(516) 794-2570
www.eastmeadow.info

By
Paul M. Arfin

Unfinished Business: Social Action in Suburbia – Long Island NY
1945-2014 © 2015 Paul M. Arfin
All rights reserved.

Second printing

No part of the book may be reproduced or transmitted in any form whatsoever without prior written permission from the author except in the case of brief quotations.

The information in this book is true and complete to the best of the knowledge of the author.

Edited by Nancy Schmidtmann, M.A., M.L.S.

Interior book design by Bob Houston eBook Formatting

Table of Contents

Foreword

Ruth A. Brandwein, Ph.D., MSW

Dr. Brandwein is Professor Emerita and former Dean, School of Social Welfare at Stony Brook University and former Commissioner, Suffolk County Department of Social Services

I was born and raised in Brooklyn, but when I first came to Long Island in late 1980, after having lived in Seattle, Boston and Iowa City, my first two thoughts were "there is no there there" and William Butler Yeats' line "the center does not hold." L.I. had no center. It seemed like a long line of shopping centers, crowded highways and strip malls. I arrived after the height of the civil rights and women's movement struggles so missed the opportunity to join the struggle with so many featured in this book. I had been recruited to become the second Dean of the still new School of Social Welfare at Stony Brook, after having spent two years at the University of Iowa as Director of its School of Social Work. Although I had been raised in Brooklyn and lived after college for a few years in Manhattan, I experienced real culture shock. People interrupted, spoke loudly and were often rude. Quite a change from Iowa City!

Several years later, when Patrick Halpin became Suffolk County Executive, his deputy, Evelyn Roth, asked me to become chair of the newly formed Task Force on Family Violence. There I got to know many of the county and nonprofit leaders in the fields of child, partner and elder abuse. Then, when I became social services commissioner for Suffolk County I had the opportunity to get to know many more leaders of human service organizations, particularly in Suffolk County. After four years I returned to Stony Brook, but had left the deanship while retaining my tenured, full professor position. I became Director of the School's Social Justice Center and worked on advocacy issues with Long Island-wide organizations such as the Long Island Progressive Coalition (LIPC), the Health and Welfare Council and Catholic Charities, interacting with many more of Long Island's leaders in human services and human rights.

I wish I had had a book like this one when I entered the fray. Long Island's human services network is a complex, interlinking tapestry with an important history that this book begins to unravel. It is a great Who's Who on Long Island, a primer of the cast of characters who have struggled for social justice over decades and also provides a chronological catalogue of the many social service agencies that developed on Long Island. The period Arfin covers is the critical period of growth of such programs.

Long Island is an entity, but it is composed of two very different sub-parts. Although Suffolk County had been settled in the 17th century, it had remained rural, with little New England like towns and villages of farmers and fisher folk. Nassau saw its heyday of development post World War II and with its proximity to NYC and migrants fleeing to the suburbs; it developed its social services system before Suffolk. Nassau faces New York City, with many commuting there for employment. Many in Eastern Suffolk have never even visited New York City. It is a foreign, somewhat forbidding place to them. Nassau was redlined early in its post-war construction boom, resulting in severe segregation both in race and class. Suffolk County also has enclaves of African American and Hispanic residents but also has two small Indian reservations, the wealthy Hamptons and many white, working class villages. Geographically Nassau is smaller than one Suffolk town, Brookhaven while Suffolk extends from the Nassau border to the North and South forks 60 miles away. Today much of Eastern Suffolk is still agricultural, having switched from potato farms and duck raising to turf farms and vineyards. Unlike Nassau, which saw the development of much of its social service system in the 1950s and early '60s, Suffolk was still guided by a philosophy of local control and meager services provided by the towns and a distrust of government from the federal down to the county level. The establishment of Stony Brook's School of Social Welfare in the 1970s had a profound influence in the professionalization of social services in Suffolk County with many of its graduates assuming leadership positions in county agencies. Its focus on social justice and mission of empowerment of the vulnerable has made a small dent in the culture.

To attempt to capture in one book the complexity of this sprawling place known as Long Island, and to do it through so many years is a major accomplishment. Arfin has done a prodigious job in compiling an enormous array of information about people, programs and policies over more than half a century, a time of great changes and upheavals. By framing the chapters in a national context, we are helped to understand what was happening on Long Island within the political and economic currents of national social movements that were occurring at the time.

This book will be a valuable guide to those new to Long Island; it will be an excellent text for social work, human service, public administration, political science and history students. Most of all, it will be an invaluable reminder to those of us who lived through some or all of the struggles described. We will meet or reconnect with old friends and colleagues, we will understand better what motivated people to do what they did. For me, learning the "back stories" of so many of my colleagues who had worked and struggled in Long Island well before I arrived on the scene is invaluable,-- I just wish I had this book when I arrived. It could have saved me from making many mistakes and would have helped me be more effective in my efforts.

Santayana said that those who do not learn from history are doomed to repeat it. History never quite repeats in the same way, but that understanding can help us learn from the past to work for a better future.

I left Long Island four years ago and reading this manuscript has been a bittersweet experience of reacquainting myself with so many people I worked with for almost 30 years, in areas of homelessness, domestic violence, welfare reform, social work education, legislative advocacy, mental health and child welfare. It has also helped me see that Long Island does have a "there there." It is in the hearts and souls and passions of all those who have given their lives to make life better for others, and for all of us.

Acknowledgements

I want to express a special debt of gratitude to my three lunch buddies, Richard Dina, Rick Van Dyke, and Tom Williams. Our lunches at Major's in Woodbury over the past several years have enriched my life and inspired me to tackle what often appeared to be a monumental job. Each of my buddies has energized me since we first met in the late 1960s as idealistic 30 year olds. Their substantial accomplishments on Long Island are a lasting testimony to a commitment to an equitable and caring society. Their friendships and encouragement while I struggled with this project propelled me on. Without their advice, I could not have completed it.

I have been very been fortunate to work on Long Island during the historical period covered in this book and am especially grateful for the opportunity to get to know the many dedicated lay and professional people in the Island's nonprofit sector. They always impressed me as focused on trying to do what is best for the people that their organizations served.

I am deeply appreciative of being able to meet the people whom I profile. Without their willingness to remember and reflect, the book would simply have been a chronological account of activities by individual and organizations. Some of them, well into their ninth and 10th decades of life, moved me with stories of the genesis of social services and social action on Long Island after World War II. I am especially inspired by these individuals who are 10 to 20 years older than I and continuing their public service as educators, consultants and nonprofit board members. Their enthusiasm for life and their lifetime involvement in social change gave my writing a greater sense of urgency and importance.

I benefited tremendously from the skilled copy editing assistance of Nancy Schmidtmann. Other colleagues also reviewed the material and chimed in with helpful advice. They include: Ruth Brandwein, Peggy Brown, Dick Dina, Lucy Gluck, Norman Goodman, Bob Keeler, Nancy Marr, Marge Rogatz, Evelyn Roth, Tom Williams, and Rick Van Dyke

Karl Grossman, an award-winning journalist and longtime friend, provided invaluable advice and encouragement about resources that helped me move the project forward, despite my many doubts and uncertainties. As a prolific reporter and author, Karl shared his substantial knowledge of Long Island, opening doors that otherwise might have been closed.

I also want to thank Kristin Nyitray, head of Special Collections and Archives at the Frank Melville, Jr. Memorial Library of Stony Brook University, and her staff for her assistance in assembling some of the material contained in these pages. Mark Rothenberg, senior reference specialist for the Suffolk Cooperative Library System and the Patchogue/Medford Library, helped me with records contained in historical editions of Long Island's weekly newspapers. Natalie A. Naylor at Hofstra University was very helpful providing historical information about the role of women in Long Island's past.

I also benefited from the demographic research contributed by Seth Forman, director of the Suffolk County Planning Department, as well as the inestimable advice and suggestions from Christopher Neidt, academic director of the National Center for Suburban Studies at Hofstra University, as I labored to write my first historical book.

My friend José Avila's technical assistance and helpfulness while I was writing and organizing were priceless. He was always patient with my limited computer skills and helped me find the right solutions to my dilemmas, even when I was frustrated. Bob Houston's assistance in formatting the book was invaluable in shepherding the book toward my submission to CreateSpace. Acknowledgement is also made to Sara Ann Zola, Senior Publishing Consultant at CreateSpace and the rest of the staff, for their professionalism and skills in the self-publication process.

I am also extremely thankful for the financial support provided by my patrons especially the assistance of Lillian McCormick who appreciated the book's potential to inspire others to action. Besides their generosity, their belief in the importance of telling the stories of Long Island's social service and social action pioneers drove me to continue to write.

My daughters Sari and Liza, my son-in-law Jeremy and my dear friends Jeff and Joan Bloomberg were always there for me when the project seemed overwhelming.

Last but far from least, I express my unconditional love and appreciation to my dear wife, Karen. For 47 years, she has always been encouraging and supportive. Without her encouragement, advice and support, I could not have completed the project.

Introduction

"Never doubt that a small group of thoughtful, committed people can change the world. Indeed, it is the only thing that ever has." Margaret Mead, Anthropologist

"Those who cannot remember the past are condemned to repeat it." George Santanyana, Spanish philosopher, essayist, poet and novelist

"True compassion is more than flinging a coin to a beggar; it comes to see that an edifice which produces beggars needs restructuring" Martin Luther King Jr.

"I am a man. No, I am not a spook like those who haunted Edgar Allan Poe; nor am I one of your Hollywood-movie ectoplasms. I am a man of substance, of flesh and bone, fiber, and liquids – and might even said to possess a mind. I am invisible, understand, simply because people refuse to see me. Like the bodiless heads you see sometimes in circus sideshows, it is as though I have been surrounded by mirrors of hard, distorting glass. When they approach me they see only my surroundings, themselves, or figments of their imagination- indeed, everything and everything but me." Ralph Ellison, Invisisble Man

In early 2014, when I told friends, colleagues, and relatives about my decision to write this historical account of Long Island, many wondered why I wanted to spend part of my retirement in such an ambitious endeavor. I had some of the same feelings. Several years ago, I had written my personal memoirs, including stories of my nonprofit career, *"Portrait of a Peace Corps Gringo."* Move on, I thought. Thinking about my half-century career in nonprofit work was rewarding but was sure to also generate memories of struggles, pressure, frustrations, misgivings and regrets. Move on. Leave the past behind you. Smell the flowers.

There have been so many momentous times since 1945. The Korean War. The Cold War. The McCarthy Hearings. The Space Race. The Nuclear Threat. The Cuban Missile Crisis. The Assassination of a President. The Military Draft. The Vietnam War. The Civil Rights Struggles in the South and North. The Countercultural Movement. The Women's Movement. The Disability Rights Movement. The Murders of the Rev. Dr. Martin Luther King Jr. and Malcolm X. The Watergate Scandal. The Reagan Revolution. 9-11. Global Warming. The Emergence of the Tea Party. The Stalemated Congress. And more.

So, you ask, why did I write this book? In good part, I wanted to document the important work done by people whose contributions to their communities have gone virtually unrecognized and unheralded. Late last year, I read Doris Kearns Goodwin's book "The Bully Pulpit." I was particularly struck by the book's accounts of what is called the Progressive Era when *McClure's Magazine*, its publisher and muckraking reporters Ida Tarbell, Lincoln Steffens and Ray Stannard Baker helped President Theodore Roosevelt break up monopolies and trusts and enact significant social legislation.

It struck me that books should also be written about people in local communities such as Long Island who challenge establish norms, advocate for unpopular causes and neglected people and influence powerful political forces, even though the issues they believe in lack the national significance and influence that McClure and his staff had on national affairs. It did not seem right that the stories about post-World War II Long Island's social advocates should be left to the records of the organizations and movements that they worked so hard to establish, and to their obituaries. In like manner, it did not seem right that the many struggles for civil rights fought by black, white, Latino and Native Americans should go virtually ignored. The stories of Long Island battles for freedom and independence from the British during the Revolutionary War are graphically portrayed in our history, as they should be. But the Island's more-recent history of social advancements since 1945 remains virtually untold.

I recognize that part of the reason that the "social heroes" of whom I speak are of the mind that their personal work should be implemented without fanfare, not in the headlines. The professionals among them believe that their work was to identify and mobilize local people to lead community organizations to advance the common good, and that history must be left for another author to document.

I have provided the reader with an overview of the 70-year span in which international and national events and policies played important roles in post-World War II Long Island, often billed as "America's first suburb." These events briefly introduce each chapter's Long Island story. The overviews chronicle the civil rights movement, youth movement, the environmental movement, the women's movement, the anti-war movement and the disability rights movement. They describe the development and evolution of progressive social action on Long Island and the lay leaders and social service professionals who worked to convince local, state and federal officials to provide sufficient public support to address the problems resulting from Long Island's rapid and extreme population growth following World War II.

The book describes the political climate in which organizations came into being and grew, as well as the constraints that limited their development. It tells the story of the struggle to demonstrate that poverty and social problems, especially racism, existed amid Long Island's communities. It discusses the challenges facing many Long Islanders, regardless of income, who experienced individual and family problems that they were unable to handle themselves.

I chose to write this information in chronological order rather than by subject categories, preferring to provide readers with what social welfare issues were being addressed during different historical periods. Those who wish to explore any particular social welfare category can review the subject headings in the index to learn about particular people or organizations.

The book has four purposes: first, I hope to inspire today's social action and social service leaders to continue the struggle for social justice and a responsive social service delivery system; second, I want to chronicle the people and the times in which tremendous social progress was made; third, I want to share the lessons I learned as I reviewed the gathered material in hopes that they will prove useful to current and future activists; fourth, I hope the book serves as a call to action for Long Island's leaders to continue to pursue the legacy of progressive social action embodied in the people described in the book.

Ultimately, the book represents one person's description of history. I conducted this research myself, so I take total responsibility for any misstatements or misunderstandings. I made my best efforts objectively to describe the period from 1945-2014.

The book integrates stories about organizations and individual volunteers and professionals, both in the civil rights and social justice struggles as well as those organizations and individuals who developed social work programs. It seemed apparent that social justice and social work programs are inextricably intertwined. Indeed, many of the people described worked in both arenas, simultaneously addressing racism and social work programs.

By decade, it is the story of:

1950s

-- A Grumman executive, Leon "Jake" Swirbul, and a public relations professional, Paul Townsend, who launched a major fund-raising campaign in behalf of Long Island's voluntary hospitals which were facing rapid population growth. Their work led to the development of the United Way of Long Island.

-- David Kadane, a distinguished Hofstra University law professor and former Peace Corps volunteer and Long Island Lighting Co. attorney, who led efforts to establish the Nassau County Youth Board and a variety of nonprofit organizations.

--Caroline Veatch, a Plandome woman who established a multimillion-dollar fund to provide hundreds of nonprofits with support for organizing poor and disenfranchised people.

1960s

-- Sadie Hofstein, a passionate advocate for people with mental illnesses, who fought tremendous public and political resistance to establish the first group home on Long Island.

--A nameless former Suffolk County welfare worker who, just prior to her retirement, provided county executive H. Lee Dennison with the documentation to prove the county's complicity in funding slum housing for welfare recipients.

--John L. Kearse, a determined Nassau County anti-poverty leader, who fought to establish employment and training opportunities for people living in Nassau's poorest communities.

--Earl Jordan, minister of the Bethel African Methodist Episcopal (AME) Church in Huntington, who befriended Helen McIntyre, an intelligent and compassionate Dix Hills resident, were able to use their influence to establish a summer camp program at Oyster Bay Cove's exclusive East Woods School for the preschool children of Huntington Station's low-income families.

--Joyce Spencer Insolia, a passionate advocate for civil rights, who rallied citizens against housing discrimination and helped organize a march on Huntington Town Hall led by Bayard Rustin that highlighted unsanitary conditions and the plight of black families blocked from securing better rental housing.

1970s

--John J. Foley, a Suffolk County legislator who, with Priscilla Redfield Roe, Phyllis Vineyard, Joyce Moore Turner, and Marilyn Shellabarger, a group of community activists, worked tirelessly over many years to establish health clinics throughout Suffolk County.

--Anthony Cotto, a youth worker who fought community resistance to his efforts to establish a social service agency for Latinos in Patchogue.

--Bessie Smith, a Southold Town resident, whose efforts to establish an anti-poverty organization helped area migrant workers and low-income families.

1980s

--Joan Saltzman, the wife of Arnold Saltzman, a U.S. ambassador, who saw the need for group homes for those with emotional problems and successfully launched a campaign to establish Nassau County's first group home

--Eleanor Kirk, Janet Walerstein and Gloria Wallick, concerned about the lack of affordable, quality child day care, established an Island-wide child-care advocacy and information and referral program.

--Dorothy Weiss, a Syosset woman who, through persistence and belief in the importance of serving the frail elderly, established one of Long Island's first adult day care centers.

I tried to provide a representative sampling of Long Island's nonprofit and social action organizations that were founded during the 1945-2014 period. Thus, the book is not a comprehensive description of every Long Island nonprofit organization of yesterday or today. It does not discuss every problem or every social ill faced by Long Islanders. In like manner, it does not recognize thousands of very special people who persevered -- often against great odds--to make Long Island better for future generations.

In addition, the book does not profile the work of the thousands of civic organizations that were developed to enrich Long Island, groups like the Chambers of Commerce, Lions Clubs, Kiwanis Clubs, Rotary Clubs, and fraternal organizations. In like manner, the book does not discuss boards of educations, PTAs and other school organizations, libraries, historical societies, sports leagues or business associations like the LIA, ABLI, LIMBA, and others. This important work is left to others to complete.

I wrote some of the book's Exemplary Community Leader and Grassroots Organizer profiles and organizational stories from my oral interviews. I wrote others based on archival sources. Still others were written by colleagues and contributors, which I greatly appreciate. Mostly, people who lived through these often-turbulent times tell the book's stories. Fortunately, I was able to contact many who are now well into their 9th and 10th decades. However, many of the people I wanted to interview are deceased and are recognized on the In Memoriam pages. Fortunately, I was able to reach some of their survivors to recount their remembrances.

I also tried to provide a geographic cross-section of nonprofits, both large and small; those providing mental and health services; disability services; services for children, youth and families, as well as those operating anti-poverty programs; social justice programs; juvenile and criminal justice education and diversion programs.

Besides discussing direct-service organizations, I describe the work of such groups as the League of Women Voters, the Long Island Progressive Coalition and other good government groups. I also recount the work of the two major community councils, the Health & Welfare Council of Long Island and the Suffolk Community Council, Inc., as well as the emergence of the United Way of Long Island as the Island's largest unified giving program. In addition, I depict the emergence of four charitable organizations during the period: the Long Island Community Foundation, the Unitarian Universalist Veatch Program at Shelter Rock, The Rauch Foundation, and the Hagedorn Foundation.

I believe that the individuals and organizations described in the following pages created many policies and programs that have withstood the test of time. In many cases, these programs were pioneered on Long Island and have been replicated in other parts of the nation. They are recorded in Part V.

History suggests that social and economic change operates in cycles. What seems impossible to accomplish one year sometimes becomes possible the following year. What divides in one season unites in another season.

Social action and social service leaders of Long Island's past focused on their missions and, motivated by idealism and commitments to the greater good, offer inspiration and practical advice to the activists of today and tomorrow.

Notes to Readers:

1. Since the book is organized by chronological periods, it does not portray in one place the development of an organization nor does it portray the work of any individuals. Readers interested in following the course of a particular organization or individual are encouraged to refer to the Index for these purposes. If you would like to understand the dramatic demographic changes that occurred on Long Island, Appendix titled "Long Island Demographic Profile Charts."

2. From time-to-time throughout the book, the author's personal reflections appear as framed stories.

3. Demographic "factoids" depicting Long Island growth appear at the beginning of each chapter. In addition, the Appendix includes a demographic overview, by decade during the period covered in the book.

4. A list of common Long Island nonprofit organizational acronyms is found in the Appendix.

Part I

Chapter I: Historical Background

While this book is principally about Long Island charitable and social organizations from the mid-20th to the early 21st century, it is important to understand that there were people inhabiting Long Island well before the European settlers arrived.

When Long Island was first discovered by the white man, it was occupied by thirteen tribes or groups of Indians, who inhabited the north and south shores of the Island. On the south side, from west to east, were the Canarsee, the Rockaway, the Merric, the Marsapeague, the Secatogue, the Unkechaug, the Shinnecock, and the Montauk tribe who lived on the eastern end of the Island on the south fork. On the north shore in the same order were the Matinecock, the Nissequog, the Setalcott, and the Corchaug (Cutchogue) tribes. The Manhassets inhabited Shelter Island. [1]

In addition, African American, slaves, brought from Barbados as early as the 1650s, lived on Long Island. McManus tells us that these slaves first arrived on Shelter Island. Slavery was widespread with 40 percent of Long Island households having one or more slaves in the late 1600s. The population of blacks was 15 percent of the total Suffolk County population by 1723. [2]

It is also important to have a sense of how charity was handled by the European settlers. Life on Long Island did not begin when William Levitt developed Levittown following World War II to house white Americans pursuing the American Dream of home ownership.

Early settlers addressed social welfare issues principally through the work of individual and church charity as well as local towns that had Overseers of the Poor who discharged their responsibilities by paying individuals or families to take in indigent people.

The first recorded evidence of a Long Islander freeing a slave occurred when Quaker Alice Crabb freed Tom Gall in her 1685 will as an individual act of charity. The Oyster Bay freeholders gave him several acres of land in 1697 further evidence of charitable acts. [3]

During the Revolutionary War period, some Long Island women joined their husbands serving in the military, providing medical and other services and received rations. Quakers on Long Island pioneered antislavery efforts during the war when 17 percent of Long Islanders were enslaved. Quakers also started a charity society in 1794 to educate free blacks. [4]

Later, in the 19th century the institutionalization of the indigent began with almshouses, orphanages, charities established by Catholic nuns and other charitable organizations. After the Civil War, women returned to domestic roles and charity work through their churches' missionary societies, raising funds for religious and benevolent causes through fairs, donation parties, dinners and cookbooks. [5]

- In the last third of the 19th century," Naylor reports that "women expanded their activities well beyond churches and into other organizations serving their communities. Wealthy women, most of whom had country homes on Long Island, were philanthropists who provided significant sums to worthy causes" while some got personally involved in causes of special interest to them. They organized women's clubs, self-improvement activities, community service projects, women's suffrage activities, and engaged in the work of the Red Cross, especially during wartimes. The wealthiest supported the development of hospitals, almshouses, relief for the poor, libraries and colleges. Other, less wealthy women along with nuns in Catholic religious orders, those involved with women's organizations and individual women, contributed to development of a humanitarian, benevolent and social services infrastructure that serves as an inspiration to those that followed. Among the most notables:
- Margaret Olivia Slocum Sage (1828-1918) who was the "lady bountiful" of Sag Harbor contributing funds to public education, the local library, the fire department, and public parks and financed an industrial school for immigrants in Inwood.
- Louisine Waldron Elder Havemeyer (1855-1929), an art collector, was active in the women's suffrage movement, sponsoring exhibits of her art collections with the proceeds benefiting suffrage work. Later, she donated her collection to the Metropolitan Museum of Art.
- Martha Cowdin Bacon (1860-1940) raised millions for the American Ambulance Service hospital in France and hosted benefits for Nassau Hospital. She also donated land, a building and an endowment for the Robert Bacon Memorial Children's Library in Westbury.
- Kate Mason Hofstra (1860-1933) donated land in Hempstead and funds for "public, charitable, benevolent, scientific, or research purposes" with the result that Hofstra University was established to develop educational and social welfare programs.
- Alice Throckmorton McLean (1886-1968) from St. James organized the American Voluntary Services in 1940 to aid the war effort.

- Dorothy Bigelow Melville (1894-1989) was a nurses' aide during World War I in New York City hospitals and with the Red Cross in World War II. She was co-founder and for many years, president of what today is the Long Island Museum of American Art, History, & Carriages and the Ward Melville Heritage Organization in Stony Brook. [6]

After the Great Depression in the 1930s, Long Island's population grew dramatically in the 1940s especially in Nassau County and western Suffolk County. There were few social action and social agencies in existence. Those that did exist were primarily affiliates of state, national, and international organizations. There was no school of social work on Long Island until Adelphi College established its school in 1949. Public welfare for the poor was handled by poorly trained welfare officers appointed by local town politicians who made decisions on which poor families should receive public aid. There were no family counseling agencies to address the needs of a rapidly-growing population of young families.

The majority of Long Island hospitals were founded by their communities as nonprofit hospitals in the early part of the 20th century. Eleven were established after the population explosion that followed World War II. The oldest hospital, Winthrop University Hospital, was founded as a medical dispensary where soldiers from the Spanish-American War were cared for.

Hospitals were ill-prepared to provide emergency or inpatient care. Outpatient care did not exist at all. Few psychiatrists, psychologists, or clinical social workers functioned on Long Island. Families that needed these services had to travel to New York City to obtain them often paying prohibitive fees. Long Island hospitals continued to evolve in their current locations, expanding their buildings, floors and wings, and emergency departments. Only after World War II did Long Island see the development of smaller physician-owned, proprietary hospitals. Today, there are no for-profit acute care hospitals, all have closed or converted to nonprofit sponsor. [7]

Naylor describes the philanthropic and benevolent work of wealthy women, like the women described earlier, during the late 19th century as having a significant impact on Long Island communities. Their work, along with the work of nuns in Catholic religious orders, was vital to the development of social welfare infrastructure of Long Island. [8]

In the late 19th century and early 20th century, volunteer citizen organizations contributed greatly to Nassau County's child welfare programs. Organizations like the State Charities Aid Association, the Local Visiting Committee, and the Nassau County Association insisted on the right of citizens to have a say in how public monies were expended, especially in child welfare programs. The State Charities Aid Association demonstrated the importance of enlisting high profile, influential people to work for the cause, people who are not easily brushed aside or put off, and who can use their contacts to open doors that otherwise would be slammed shut. In addition, the concept of friendly visiting, denuded of its social control/class superiority aspects, suggested that it could contribute to improving child welfare services. [9]

Some social welfare agencies existed prior to the period which is the focus of the book (1945-2014). Following are some of these nonprofit organizations, listed by year of founding. The majority of them focused on medical care, services to people with disabilities and crisis assistance to the poor. Many were operated by church organizations and associations. They were funded primarily through the benevolence of wealthy people living on the North Shore of Nassau County and western Suffolk County who owned country homes on Long Island. Most of the organizations they established are still functioning, either continuing as nonprofit organizations or becoming agencies of government. Their lay and professional leaders laid the groundwork for what was to follow. It is chronicled here so that future leaders may understand that their work will also be remembered and passed to those that follow.

Pioneering Social Agencies on Long Island

St. Johnland (1866)

Reverend William Muhlenberg established St. Johnland in Kings Park as a rural "Christian industrial community" for poor "crippled boys, orphaned girls and old men, with a school and farm." [10]

Dominican Sisters (1867)

The Dominican Sisters received the donation of an 87 acre farm in North Amityville where they established their Motherhouse, a novitiate, orphanage and old age home. [11]

Madonna Heights Services (1868)

"Mother Euphrasia spearheaded the establishment of the House of Good Shepherd in Brooklyn where five sisters ran Madonna Heights, a home for girls. The home remained in Brooklyn until 1954 when the sisters purchased the Herman Baruch estate in Dix Hills and moved the program there." [12]

Suffolk County Farm and Education Center and the Suffolk County Almshouse (1870)

Suffolk County government financed the institution with the aid of the Charities Aid Society, a voluntary nonprofit. Its board composed of benevolent individuals from different parts of the county, was established for the purpose of visiting the Alms House, overseeing its management, and assisting in caring for and ministering to the wants of its inmates. The board arranged for occasional religious services in the house to be conducted by volunteers from neighboring churches. The board made regular visits and evaluated the cleanliness of the place, and the care given to all – the able-bodied, the old and infirm and the mentally ill.

In 1929, a new public welfare law was passed. It abolished the term "Almshouse or Poorhouse" and the institution became known as the Suffolk County Home. Old Age Assistance (OAA) came into being and, through the medium of cash grants, many aged poor persons were cared for in their own homes. By 1930, the population at the county home was made up largely of homeless and chronically indigent persons. In 1935, plans were drawn for a new home and infirmary. The old buildings were slated for demolition upon their completion.

By 1938, most of the people residing at the home were the homeless or infirm, and they had the reputation of receiving the best care available. The infirmary served not only those residing in the house; many welfare surgeries were performed there too.

The people who resided in the home were for the most part not ill but rather families whose homes had been burnt, clammers and baymen who had no winter homes, and the very poor. Many of the residents secured jobs within the home; working in the kitchen, laundry and performing general cleaning duties. When the new county home opened in 1937, the farm came under the administration and operation of the county Department of Public Welfare whose Commissioner stated that "the farm has continued to show evidence of being one of the country's most prudent investments." The farm supplied approximately 80 percent of all food consumed in the Suffolk County Jail, the Children's Shelter, the Suffolk County Infirmary and Home, and the Honor Farm Annex itself. Residents of the Home were no longer forced to work on the farm; rather those who chose to did so continued on a voluntary basis until 1940. Residents of the town of Yaphank were employed during harvest and many of the women of Yaphank were employed for the purpose of canning the many vegetables grown.

Yearly, the farm typically produced milk, cream, beef, pork, chicken and turkey. Food crops included potatoes, onions, cabbage, tomatoes, beets, carrots and turnips together with strawberries. Over the years, the farm supplied most, if not all, of the meat and vegetables to the county home and infirmary, the county jails in Riverhead and Yaphank, the Holtsville sanitarium, the Hauppauge juvenile jail and various children's welfare camps. In addition to the successful production of food, the farm participated in local fairs and entered livestock in shows to be judged. It soon became an educational resource. [13]

Ladies Committee for Relief of the Poor (1869)

"Sara Ann Barnum was Long Island's leading civic activist in the nineteenth century. She helped the poor by facilitating the purchase of land for the establishment of a new almshouse near Oceanside. Barnum later oversaw the almshouse as chair of the visiting committee. The land was named "Barnum Island." [14]

YMCA of Long Island (1870)

In 1870, there is evidence that the YMCA movement reached Long Island. Activities first began stirring in the city of Glen Cove. But the recorded formal origins of the YMCA of Long Island, Inc. go back to 1916, when a group of local volunteers met in the Garden City Hotel, and voted the organization into existence. Its headquarters was in a small building near the Mineola train station. A general secretary was hired and set out with a $40,000 budget – pledged by the community. Ambitious plans were laid which included widespread training of volunteer leaders to develop, conduct, and promote scouting and other boys' activities. These activities included camps, bible study, lectures, athletics, religious work, health and recreation, educational and vocational classes, and an employment service. Unfortunately, all these plans were set aside when the United States was drawn into World War I a few months later.

For the duration of World War I, the YMCA of Long Island devoted its full attention to the needs of young men and boys involved in the war effort. Two canteens were established to serve Camp Mills, an enormous Army installation then located in Garden City. The YMCA was also active in farm camps on eastern Long Island. It was not until May 1919, that a formal certificate of incorporation was drawn and approved, and the Young Men's Christian Association of Nassau and Suffolk Counties was born. At the time, Long Island was a rural area where farming was the main occupation and people looked to a few large villages and hamlets for social and cultural leadership. The fledgling YMCA found an immediate demand for its services and was soon active in forty-one Long Island communities primarily offering swimming, camping, and character-building programs." [15]

Regarding the history of the YMCA, Tom William, a dear friend and colleague of the author, recalls a story that was common to many young men in Europe during the latter 19th century.

My grandfather, John Nabersberg, was born in Germany and immigrated to the United States in 1858. In a family chronicle, my great aunt wrote that in Düsseldorf he joined the YMCA and made it a practice from then on to make a connection with the organization wherever he lived for any length of time. These contacts were of immense value to John for they brought companionship with congenial young men but above all he profited by the excellent evening courses which offered a variety of college-level subjects taught by educators and scientists of superior attainments. [16]

Southampton Fresh Air Fund (1877)

The Fresh Air Fund, an independent nonprofit organization, was created with one simple mission – to allow children living in low-income communities to get away from hot, noisy city streets and enjoy free summer experiences in the country. [17]

Sea Side Children's Hospital (1880)

William K. Vanderbilt and his wife Alva had a country home in Great River, Idle Hour. Alva built and financially supported Sea Side Children's Hospital in Great River and donated $100,000 to Nassau Hospital. After divorce and remarriage to Oliver H.P. Belmont, Alva "built and was the primary financial supporter of Hempstead Hospital." "She was also a major supporter of women's suffrage." [18]

The Long Island Home (1882)

The organization was founded in Amityville as a private health care facility. In the months following the attack on Pearl Harbor, the fear of the bombing of U.S. cities was a real threat. Fourteen employees of The Long Island Home volunteered to serve as air raid wardens and until the end of the war rotating shifts of employees kept watch at the hospital around the clock. Despite the grimness of the war years, employees continued their tradition of socializing with one another as a 'family.' [19]

Children's House (1884)

The agency started when small groups of dedicated people stood up for the downtrodden and forgotten. They built and maintained what was known as The Temporary Home for Friendless Children. It was located in Mineola, then a part of Queens County of New York City. The agency served abused and neglected children. Children's House, was later named Nassau House. Children's House's originators were famous Long Island names like the Hicks and Christ families. Up until the mid-1980's, Children's House existed entirely as a residential agency – a classic orphanage for abused and neglected children." [20]

MercyFirst (1894)

MercyFirst was founded as sister orphanages by the Sisters of Mercy, St. Mary's of the Angels Home in Syosset and Angel Guardian Home in Brooklyn. [21]

SCO Family of Services (1895)

SCO began in 1895 when "a group of kind women whose hearts had been stirred by the frightful suffering of delicate infants in New York tenement houses" established the Country Home for Convalescent Babies in Upstate New York. The Country Home admitted "sick and suffering small children, whom hardly anyone else can take" after they were released from the hospital following an acute illness, and before they were returned home to their families. The children recuperated at the home for several weeks. Two years later, a new home was built on fourteen acres in Sea Cliff. The Bakers, Carnegies, Morgans, Phipps and Whitneys, in addition to many other prominent New York families, supported the facility. During World War II, the home closed briefly and then reopened in 1947 under the auspices of the Diocese of Brooklyn, when it was renamed St. Christopher's Home. [22]

The Garnet Memorial Fresh Air Home (1895)

The home, located in Westbury, was the result of a group of African American women living in Manhattan who wanted to establish what they called a "fresh air home for working women and girls, a place where they could resort and find rest, quiet and a fresh invigorating atmosphere." The home was named in memory of Reverend Henry Highland Garnet who was regarded as an outstanding African American abolitionist and religious leader who died in 1892 while serving as the United State Minister to Liberia. [23]

Glen Cove Boys & Girls Club (1903)

The Glen Cove Boys & Girls Club at Lincoln House was established to serve underprivileged youth and families in the greater Glen Cove Community since. Known as the Lincoln House Settlement, it moved to its current location in 1925 utilizing a small, five-room building. [24]

The Five Towns Community Center (1907)

The center was established as the Margaret Sage Industrial School for immigrants in Inwood. [25]

Parker Jewish Institute (1907)

The Institute began as a shelter for twenty-five indigent men and women. [26]

Daughters of Wisdom (1907)

The Daughters of Wisdom opened a Port Jefferson home for homeless Brooklyn children with disabilities. Nine months later the Brooklyn Home for Handicapped Children was established to provide support, care, education, and medical and surgical treatment of blind and handicapped children. By 1910, a three-story structure designed to accommodate 250 children was built on Fairview Hill and was dedicated as St. Charles Hospital. [27]

Peninsula Counseling Center (1913)

The agency was established as the Relief Association of Lawrence. [28]

Cornell Cooperative Extension (CCE) of Nassau County (1914)

The Land Grant Act was signed into law on July 2, 1862, by President Abraham Lincoln, provided grants of federal lands to states and territories to help establish colleges to offer practical education for all citizens. The Smith-Lever Act of 1914 recognized the value of this early work in New York and other states, as it established the formal relationship among federal, state, and local governments to support extension work that continues today. In 1914, through New York State County Law 224, Nassau County began its Cooperative Extension program under the leadership of community citizens who formed the first Board of Directors. [29]

Suffolk County Girl Scout Council (1915)

The Council's first troop in Suffolk County and Long Island and the first of twelve in the nation was organized in 1915. Birdsall Otis Edey, a noted environmentalist from Bellport, became the first and only Long Islander elected president of Girl Scouts of the USA. Seven councils were established. [30]

Cornell Cooperative Extension (CCE) of Suffolk County (1917)

CCE was established as a nonprofit community education agency. [31]

Nassau County Girl Scout Council (1917)

The organization started as a nonprofit organization. [32]

American Red Cross: Nassau and Suffolk Chapter (1916-1918)

According to the Nassau Chapter's 50th anniversary publication, the motivation for establishing the Chapter was related to the United States' entry into World War I. In the early years of the American Red Cross, there were often groups that organized locally in the name of the Red Cross, but were not unified or recognized by the national Red Cross. According to the 50th anniversary publication, small groups in Nassau County had developed in the name of the Red Cross, but it was not until America entered the war that they felt the need to consolidate into a single, more effective group. The Nassau Chapter's founder and first Chairman was Mrs. Henry P. Davison of Locust Valley. Her husband raised millions of dollars during World War I for the American Red

Cross. Early Chapter activities included home service, production, and first aid.

Home service often provided relief including communication and financial support to military families while their husbands or sons were overseas. Services were provided to migratory families, a reference to military wives who migrated to Nassau County to be close to their recently-returned husbands recovering at Camp Mills. The chapter fabricated items for hospitals and soldiers/sailors. Products included hospital garments and linens, gauze, front line parcels, and comfort bags. First aid classes were provided by the chapter beginning in 1918. Regarding actual disaster relief, the chapter's first efforts were to raise funds for victims of Midwest flooding in 1951. Nassau County was expected to raise $25K as contribution to the $5M that the president asked the American Red Cross to raise.

The Suffolk Chapter did not exist until 1963 as it was a consolidation of five existing Suffolk Chapters. The Babylon Chapter was recognized in 1935; the Hampton Chapter in 1916; the North Fork Chapter in 1931; the North Suffolk Chapter in 1931; the South Suffolk Chapter in 1917. These chapters provided support for the World War I effort; assistance during an influenza epidemic; a train derailment; and aid to a U.S. military ship that went ashore on Fire Island in 1919. [33]

The League of Women Voters (LWV) (1920)

The LWV was founded by Carrie Chapman Catt during the convention of the National American Woman Suffrage Association. The convention was held just six months before the 19th amendment to the U.S. Constitution was ratified, giving women the right to vote after a 72-year struggle. The league began as a "mighty political experiment" designed to help 20 million women carry out their new responsibilities as voters. It encouraged them to use their new power to participate in shaping public policy. From the beginning, the LWV has been an activist, grassroots organization whose leaders believed that citizens should play a critical role in advocacy. It was then, and is now, a nonpartisan organization. LWV founders believed that maintaining a nonpartisan stance would protect the fledgling organization from becoming mired in the party politics of the day. However, LWV members were encouraged to be political themselves, by educating citizens about, and lobbying for, government and social reform legislation.

Helen Pratt was elected first President of the Nassau Chapter. She was a founder of the Lincoln Settlement House in Glen Cove. The Chapter's committees were involved in child welfare and labor, education, the legal status of women and women in industry among other subjects. [34]

The Long Island Council of Churches (early 1920s)

The Long Island Council of Churches was active in both counties as an ecumenical ministry. It began to serve migrant farm workers and their families on the East End. As the number of people served continued to increase and the population became more diverse, the organization expanded its services to include emergency food and social services, housing, transportation, prescription and eyeglass assistance, fuel, gas and electricity assistance, predatory lending prevention/personal financial education, interfaith education, and advocacy for the poor. [35]

Family Service League (FSL) (1926)

Huntington Village was changing anew following World War I. The downtown business district was booming – and spreading. Soldiers from World War II found work with new businesses or were starting their own enterprises. New homes were being built, more movement from farms to the village was occurring, and there was some migration from New York City.

With this change came new concerns about social problems - orphans, poverty, teens with nothing to do, unemployment and family stability. It was the summer of 1924 when several Huntington families were camping when the moms began discussing these concerns. They were inspired by a woman who ran a soup kitchen in the downtown village during the 1890s. Around the camp fire in the evening, the adults convinced each other that something had to be done. They resolved bring their concerns to business leaders, clergy and Town officials when they returned home. As a result over the next two years, a number of public meetings were held with the community becoming more and more involved.

FSL held its first meeting as a group of Huntington town women who came together to help teens and unemployed people in the community. They opened a recreation center which fast became a gathering place. Soon it became clear that a real need existed for one-on-one attention to family problems. By 1927, FSL hired Helen Bauer, its first social worker whose job was to go from home to home, visiting families. In the 1930's, FSL focused on aiding the unemployed and became involved in a Works Projects Administration (WPA) project to build the Village Green Park in Huntington. During World War II and for years after, Family Service League became a loosely knit organization providing direct services, including food baskets, to needy families in the community.

During World War II, FSL had a large storefront right off Main Street where a variety of services were provided including temporary work, various groups, a place where the Girl Scouts met, and a small boxing area to keep adolescent boys off the streets. In addition, FSL spearheaded the development of various group activities for teens. FSL remained a loosely knit organization, providing direct services such as food baskets at Thanksgiving, to needy families in the community, recreation services for youth, and aid to families. [36]

Harriet Tubman Community Club (1928)

Verini Harris Morton-Jones, the first African American woman physician in Hempstead was among the women who organized the club and served as director of the settlement house for six years organizing Girls Scout, Boy Scout and other cultural and recreational clubs and organizations for children and adults. [37]

Little Flower Children and Family Services of New York (1929)

Little Flower was founded as a nonprofit charity serving children, families and developmentally disabled adults across New York City and Long Island. In 1929, the New York State Board of Charities approved the incorporation of Little Flower House of Providence for Homeless Colored Children, a residential center for orphaned, abandoned, and neglected children, founded by Father Bernard J. Quinn. John Fagan, a sophomore at Cathedral College, joined Little Flower's Camp Claver as a counselor, serving as a lifeguard and cottage parent for 20 boys. Father Fagan went on to become the agency's Executive Director." [38]

Five Towns Community Chest (1931)

A number of local men pondered how they could be of service to their neighbors. They took great pride in their respective communities of Inwood, Lawrence, Cedarhurst, Hewlett and Woodmere and the growing number of social agencies providing services for their residents. In February 1932, the first annual meeting of the newly named Community Chest of Hewlett, Woodmere, Cedarhurst, Lawrence and Inwood was formed. The objective was simple as outlined in their constitution: 'The object of this organization shall be to solicit, collect and otherwise raise money for charitable, philanthropic, and benevolent purposes and to expend and disburse of the same to the needy by directly furnishing them with relief, and indirectly by making contributions to other agencies whose purpose it is to furnish shelter and relief to the needy.' [39]

Suffolk Community Council (SCC) (1933)

Although the Council began in 1933 largely as a voluntary group of individual members, they soon complemented their group by professionals active in many fields of health and human services. Social workers, educators and concerned citizens came together to form a voluntary association of professional and community people concerned about improving health and welfare services in Suffolk County, particularly for those hardest hit by the Great Depression. Serving as first a "Community Service Council," the group focused study on identifying problems, advocating for and then participating in the development of services to meet emerging needs, with the council often serving as a sponsor or host for fledgling organizations and agencies.

They met originally as separate East End and West End groups and, several times a year, in Riverhead as one council. The West End group was developed by Mary Levermore who chaired the Family Service League in Huntington. The East End group was affiliated with Temporary Emergency Relief Authority (TERA), a predecessor of Social Security, the Board of Cooperative Educational Services (B.O.C.E.S) Suffolk County Board of Health, Suffolk County Board of Children's Welfare and Family Services, all parts of the county department of welfare.

Throughout the 1930s and 1940, SCC was linked to the New York State Charities Aid Association's statewide information sharing and training networks. [40]

Planned Parenthood of Nassau County (PPNC) (1933)

"PPNC began to provide preventive health services, education and counseling." [41]

Self Help Community Services (1936)

In 1936, a group of German émigrés joined forces to help newly-arriving European Jewish refugees fleeing from Nazi persecution establish themselves in America. They believed that with basic support, new arrivals would be able to use their skills, experiences and strengths to build independent, dignified and productive lives. Thus, on November 10, 1936 in New York City, Self Help was born.

In its early years, Self Help worked with successive waves of refugees providing personalized, direct services. Immigrants were guided through the confounding maze of bureaucratic paperwork, helping them find housing and financial assistance. While men prepared to re-enter their established professions or refocus their skills, their wives and sisters were assisted in finding jobs, such as practical nursing and homemaking that built on their household skills. In 1945, Self Help initiated programs serving the elderly, forerunners of today's home care and training programs. [42]

Part I Notes

1. Thomas R. Bayles, "The Long Island Indians," www.longwood.k12.ny.us/history/index.htm.
2. Edgar J. McManus, A History of Negro Slavery in New York, (Syracuse University Press, 1966).

3. Lynda R. Day, Making a Way to Freedom: A History of African Americans and Long Island, (Empire State Books, 1997).
4. Edgar J. McManus, A History of Negro Slavery in New York
5. Alice Ross, "Long Island Women and Benevolence: Changing Images of Women's Place, 1880-1920,) Long Island Women: Activists and Innovators, ed. Natalie A. Naylor and Maureen O. Murphy, Empire State Books, 1998).
6. Natalie A. Naylor, Women in Long Island's Past: A History of Eminent Ladies and Everyday Lives, (History Press, 2012).
7. "Findings of the Regional Advisory Committee," (Commission on Health Care Facilities, October 2006). Information obtained from the following website: www. www.nyhealthcarecommission.org.
8. Natalie A. Naylor, Women in Long Island's Past: A History of Eminent Ladies and Everyday Lives, (History Press, 2012).
9. Ruth Shackelford, "Early Child Welfare in Nassau County," (Long Island Historical Journal 17, 2004-2005).
10. Information obtained Long Island Historical Journal 17, 2004-2005)from agency's website: www.stjohnland.org
11. Information obtained from agency's website: http://www.amityvilleop.org/index.php/about-us/mission-statement
12. Information obtained from agency's website: www.sco.org/madonna-heights.com.
13. Barbara Rivadeneyra and Kathleen DeMarco, Suffolk County Farm and Education Center Master Plan 1999 (Cornell Cooperative Extension of Suffolk County, Kermit Graf Executive, Robert Gaffney, Suffolk County Executive).
14. Information obtained from YMCA of Long Island's website: www.ymcali.org
15. Tom Williams, interview of January 29, 2014.
16. Natalie A. Naylor, Women in Long Island's Past: A History of Eminent Ladies and Everyday Lives, (History Press, 2012).
17. Information obtained from agency's website: http://www.freshair.org/history-and-mission.
18. Natalie A. Naylor, Women in Long Island's Past: A History of Eminent Ladies and Everyday Lives, (History Press, 2012).
19. Information obtained from agency's website: www.longislandhome.org.
20. Information obtained from agency's website: www.familyandchildrens.org.
21. Information obtained from agency's website: www.mercyfirst.org
22. Information obtained from agency's website: www.sco.org.
23. Judith A. Burgess, "The Garnet Memorial Home: An African American Fresh Air Home in Westbury, Long Island 1895-1954" Long Island History Journal 16, 2003-2004.
24. Information obtained from agency's website: www.glencovebgc.org.

25. Information obtained from agency's website: www. fivetownscommunityctr.org.
26. Information obtained from agency's website: wwwparkerinstitute.org
27. Natalie A. Naylor, Women in Long Island's Past: A History of Eminent Ladies and Everyday Lives, (History Press, 2012).
28. Information obtained from agency's website: www.pccli.org.
29. Information obtained from agency's website: www.cccenassau.org.
30. Information obtained from agency's website: www.gssc.us.
31. Information obtained from agency's website: www.ccesuffolk.org.
32. Information obtained from agency's website: www.gsnc.org.
33. Information obtained from agency's website: www. redcross.org/ny/mineola.
34. Information obtained from agency's website: www.lwv-suffolkcounty.org.
35. Information obtained from agency's website: www.liccdonate.org
36. Information obtained from agency's website: www.fsl.li.org.
37. Natalie A. Naylor, Women in Long Island's Past: A History of Eminent Ladies and Everyday Lives, (History Press, 2012).
38. Information obtained from agency's website: www.redcross.org/ny/mineola.
39. Information obtained from agency's website: www.littleflowerny.org
40. Information obtained from agency's website: www. fivetownscommunitychest.org.
41. File Boxes of Suffolk Community Council (Special Collections and University Archives at Stony Brook University).
42. Information obtained from agency's website: www.selfhelp.net.

PHOTOGRAPHS OF NONPROFIT EXECUTIVES,

ELECTED AND APPOINTED OFFICIALS,

JOURNALISTS, AND CIVIL RIGHTS LEADERS

FROM 1960-1985

Sal Ambrosino

Joseph Barbaro

Gregory Blass

Ruth Brandwein

Nora Bredes

Frances Brisbane

Robert Detor

Jane Devine

Richard Dina

Thomas Downey

Steve Englebright

Barbara Faron

Sandy Feinberg

Rene Fiechter

John J. Foley

Marianne Garvin

Marilyn Goldstein

Karl Grossman

Janet Hanson

Palast, in July 1983, with State Assemblyman Paul Harenberg, sponsor of the legislation that would put LILCO, the nuclear power company out of business. The photo was taken just after Cuomo's office requested I secretly help the Governor kill the bill.

Paul Harenberg

John Imhof

Pearl Kamer

David Kapell

John L. Kearse

Robert Keeler

Jean Kelly

Lee Koppelman (r)

Lawrence Levy

Abraham Lurie

Nancy Marr

James Morgo

May Newburger

Diana O'Neill (c)

Catherine Papell

Jill Rooney

Evelyn Roth

Louise Skolnik   **Marcia Spector**

David Starr   **Walter Stockton**

William Tymann

Reinhardt Van Dyke

Janet Walerstein

Thomas Williams

Part II

Chapter I: 1945-1949

Overview

World War II ended in 1945, first in Europe and then in Japan after the bombs were dropped on Hiroshima and Nagasaki changing our world forever. President Franklin Delano Roosevelt died after completing an unprecedented four terms and was followed by President Harry Truman who made the decision to use the bomb. Truman also served as President during the Korean War and signed the legislation that integrated the troops serving in the military, ending hundreds of years of segregation. Problems during the period included what to do with 'Rosie the Riveter' now that the men were home; how to treat the blacks such as the Tuskegee Airmen and other returning black GIs; and making room for GIs returning to GI mortgages and free school and wanting a better life for their young families in the suburbs.

In 1948, Truman signed an executive order stating: 'It is hereby declared to be the policy of the President that there shall be equality of treatment and opportunity for all persons in the armed forces without regard to race, color, religion or national origin. [1]

Change was in the air after World War II had been won. The troops returned home committed to settle down to a job, marriage, and a home. Government had demonstrated an effectiveness to solve problems. The troops supported tax-supported programs to create jobs and educate its citizens. In *The Fourth Turning,* Strauss and Howe portray a post-World War II America as positive and upbeat. Under President Dwight Eisenhower the economy grew with plentiful jobs in the defense, auto, and consumer goods' industries as well as in building the nation's interstate and local highways and other infrastructure. In 1945, former British Prime Minister Winston Churchill said that 'America stands at the summit of the world.' His remark recognized America's strong military power and its booming economy. Certainly, there was a nascent civil rights movement brewing and a crusade against communism at home and abroad but, overall, America was the most powerful nation in the world. [2]

There was a common belief and confidence, that if you worked hard, you could accomplish anything and have a standard of living that was better than ever existed before, living in a nice house, owning a car, and sending your children to college. Some called this period: "Pax Americana," "Good Times," the "Best Years," "Happy Days," and the "American High." The middle-class grew as did worker productivity while the gap between the rich and poor narrowed. Suburban life was the preferred order of the day for millions of young American families.

Many of the men and women who fought in World War II were entitled to federal aid to purchase homes and pursue higher education under the G.I. Bill. These primarily 30-40 year olds often had two-three children in their households. They purchased cars, refrigerators, dishwashers, washing machines and driers, and television sets. They opened bank accounts and began to save money for their children's education.

Demographic Factoid

Long Island's 1945 population was 776,894. Of this total, Nassau had 520,519 residents and Suffolk, a land area that is three-times larger than Nassau County's, had 256,375 residents. [3]

Author's Reflections

Long Island's post-World War II political leaders set out to design local governments to control every aspect of public life virtually with one-party control. The result is 709 different governmental units that make it extremely difficult for residents either to have a sense of community or to know where to turn when they need information or services or want to correct a grievance. These governmental units represent villages, cities, and towns, school districts, postal districts, water districts, zip codes, census districts, statistical planning areas, and fire districts that often do not coincide with one another. Reform measures are, therefore, difficult to undertake since, without a sense of community, residents are less likely to show concern for their neighbors' welfare or for who represents them as elected officials. And, with so many governmental districts to pay for, it is no surprise that Long Island is one of the most heavily- taxed regions in the nation.

As I grew up in Mineola, our family often visited our Brooklyn-dwelling relatives on weekends. The traffic on the Belt Parkway on Sunday evenings heading east was bumper-to-bumper. We listened and laughed at comedian Jack Benny and the Fibber McGee and Molly show on the car radio. Our family enjoyed time at the Jolly Roger Amusement Park, Lollipop Farm, and eating hot dogs at McGinnis' and one of the twenty-eight flavors of ice cream at Howard Johnson restaurants. On summer weekends, our family drove to Jones Beach, Sunken Meadow, Heckscher State Parks or Lake Ronkonkoma to picnic and swim. Most of our neighbors methodically tended their lawns. Mothers most often did not work outside the home. Fathers commuted to work in New York City either on the Long Island Rail Road or by car on the newly-constructed Long Island Expressway or one of the two parkways.

Living in Mineola was like living in "Andyhardysville." I rode my bicycle to nearby Herricks to go fishing with friends at Perkins Pond where we camped overnight in the woods cooking hot dogs and Heinz baked beans and toasting marshmallows. When it rained, we sheltered ourselves under an overpass of the privately-owned Vanderbilt Motor Parkway. I earned spending money selling empty beer and soda bottles I collected at the many local housing construction sites. I joined Little League and Babe Ruth baseball teams and a Cub Scout troop. As a teenager, I enjoyed time at drive-in movies, bowling centers, or ice skating and roller skating rinks. On Sundays, most families on our block attended church services. Our neighbors were mostly Italian and Irish. In the small minority, were Jews who chose to live primarily in the Five Towns, Great Neck, or parts of central Nassau and hamlets in western central Suffolk County. Other minorities were German, Portuguese, Polish, African American, and Hispanic/Latino. In junior high school I recall anti-Semitic remarks made by some of my neighbors and classmates and an incident where rocks were thrown through the window of the synagogue where I was studying for my Bar Mitzvah. Nevertheless, there was hope, confidence, and optimism in the air with a deep belief that if you worked hard, you could find work, enjoy a middle class life, and be better off than your parents, in effect, the American Dream.

Long Island's new residents were often civically active, joining or forming volunteer ambulance squads, emergency medical services, PTAs, church and synagogue religious education programs, Boy and Girl scout troops, veterans organizations, police auxiliaries, fraternal organizations such as Masons, Knights of Pythias, Knights of Columbus and ethnic mutual aid societies, as well as business groups such as Lions, Kiwanis, Rotary, and Chambers of Commerce. For the more politically-minded, they primarily joined the Republican Party whether their party affiliation in the city was Republican or Democratic. It became well-known and accepted that if you wanted a summer job for your teenager or a street pot hole filled quickly, you needed to join the Republican Party.

Not all of these post-World War-II suburbanites could afford the aforementioned middle class life style. These individuals could not afford the mortgages, cars, and appliances common to others. Their housing choices were, therefore, extremely limited often requiring rental apartments located in commercial and business districts. If you were white and poor, you could buy a home according to your ability to afford the mortgage. If you were African American, your housing choices were further limited by overt and covert racism and limited to housing in the Hempstead/Roosevelt area, the city of

Glen Cove, Central Islip, Brentwood, Wyandanch, North Amityville, Gordon Heights, New Cassel, and Riverhead.

Returning World War II veterans spurred a population and housing boom driven in part by benefits from the GI bill. The economic demands of the post-war boom and the burgeoning Civil Rights movement led to conflicts over discrimination in housing, jobs and education. The Federal Housing Administration (FHA), which instituted policies that reinforced patterns of segregation, routinely denied low-interest loans to non-whites. The experience of fighting for freedom in Europe and then returning to a country where discrimination and opportunities were limited fostered discontent for many returning black GIs. The legacy of post-war economic discrimination contributed to the wealth gap between whites and non-whites that we see today. One of the most important factors that contributed to the wealth gap was the federal housing policy. This policy, endorsing redlining and discrimination in sales, financing and homeowners insurance, is reflected in the unequal rates of home ownership even today.

In the U.S., African Americans, Mexicans, Chinese and Japanese immigrants were targets of discrimination in employment and property ownership. Blacks lost their homes through foreclosures during the 1930s and 40s, many of them victims of fraud and deception. In the South, many blacks were victims of exploitative tenant-sharecropper systems that kept them in perpetual debt. Since Chinese Americans were effectively denied citizenship until the 1950s, their access to jobs was limited, and they were prohibited by law from owning property. Although Japanese Americans were able to buy property, much of their wealth was confiscated during World War II when they were forced into internment camps. For Mexican Americans, opportunities for employment were largely limited to guest worker programs. The *bracero* program, which began in 1942 and officially ended in 1964, allowed them temporary entry into the U.S. as migrant workers in farms throughout California and the Southwest.
[4]

The ultimate manifestation of institutional racism occurred in Levittown, often regarded as America's first planned suburban community. In Levittown, African Americans were prohibited from purchasing homes regardless of their incomes or military service. Brokers were prohibited from selling to blacks. Levittown served as a model for post-WWII suburban development that began in 1947 with housing for 17,000 families.

The owner agrees not to permit the premises to be used or occupied by any person other than members of the Caucasian Race but the employment and maintenance of other than Caucasian domestic servants shall be permitted. [5]

For a more in-depth account of racism on Long Island, go to Part VIII.

Historically, evidence exists of anti-Semitism on Long Island after World War II. Jews were not permitted to purchase homes in some communities including Levittown. Evidence of anti-Semitism was recorded in *Newsday* articles. *See Chapter II for further discussion*

News Stories

Newsday reported in **"Jews Pledge $25,000 to Combat Intolerance Spread," (January 2, 1945)**. According to the article, the pledged fund was established to "combat insidious un-American propaganda" and was pledged by Five Towns and Far Rockaway representatives of four national Jewish organizations. The article reports that these organizations were the American Jewish Congress; the Jewish Labor Committee; the American Jewish Committee; and the Anti-Defamation League, sponsored by the B'Nai B'rith. In the article, Dr. Irving Miller, spiritual leader of Congregation Shaaray Tefila said: "Jewish people must not only combat anti-Semitism, by anti-'anything' where the political rights of any person are endangered."

In **"Heyday for Hate on Long Island," (July 12, 1960)**, *Newsday* reporter John Cummings, describes about the activities of Fritz Kuhn and other leaders of the German-American Bund which met and marched at Yaphank's Camp Siegfried in the 1930s. Cummings reported that "the hate that died when the last deluded American storm trooper left Yaphank is being revived by America's new self-appointed 'fuehrer,' George Lincoln Rockwell, another admirer of Hitler and his twisted ideas."

David Starr, the long-time editor of the Long Island Daily Press as well as the national editor of the Newhouse News, recounts his acquaintance with Robert Moses, a major figure in Long Island's development.

I met Robert Moses in the early 1960s. It happened through one of his chief lieutenants, Sid Shapiro.

Moses was the autocrat of five empires, and he had one chief lieutenant in charge of each. One was the New York State Park Commission, which he had persuaded New York State Governor Al Smith to create in the late 1920s. Another was the New York City Parks Department. The third was the State Power Authority. The fourth was the oversight of all Federal funding for construction projects in New York City, especially highways and bridges and the fifth was the Long Island State Park Commission which managed the state beaches, state parks and state highways in Nassau and Suffolk Counties. Shapiro's title was chief engineer of the commission. He was its boss.

We became good friends. Sid was one of those plain-spoken, to-the-point, no-nonsense managers, highly intelligent, utterly practical, widely-read---devoted entirely to the man he always called RM. We shared base beliefs in birds and bees and flowers and parks and beaches and conservation and environmental purity and the management thereof.

When Moses wanted something done on Long Island which could be done easier and better with press endorsement, it was Sid who paved the way with me. He would propose something. If I liked it, he would arrange for me to meet with Moses. We had design a campaign together.

That is how, in 1970, we accomplished one of the greatest conservation feats in state history---the ceding of 50,000 acres of town-owned wetlands in Great South Bay to the state, forever wild.

Moses had learned that town politicians were turning over wetlands to builders for housing development. The builders dredged sand from the bay bottom, dumped it on the wetlands and then added foundations for houses. Whether bribes were being passed was unknown, but not unimaginable.

Saving the wetlands was crucial. They were the birthplace of all kinds of flora and fauna, a veritable factory for the production and protection of fish, amphibians, birds and mammals.

Moses knew that we could never wrest control of the wetlands from the politicians just by asking for it, so we devised a campaign. *The Long Island Press* would assign a reporter and photographer to uncover how the wetlands were being desecrated. We would then run a series of editorials demanding that the politicians stop. And finally, we would recommend that the wetlands be taken out of the jurisdiction of the towns and placed under state control, forever wild. State control, of course, meant under the control of the head of the state park system, Robert Moses.

It worked like a charm. I assigned Lenny Victor, a brilliant writer who was also a wonderful photographer, to write the series. *Newsday*, of course, foolishly ignored the whole question because it did not want to recognize its competitor's good work. But the politicians could not ignore or argue with the evidence or the crusading newspaper that revealed it, so one by one, each of the townships in Nassau and Suffolk ceded its wetlands to the state.

For my role in saving the 50,000 acres of wetlands, I was chosen that year to receive the first award of the newly-founded New York State Conservation Society, a handsome statue of a mountain lion. It stands on the shelf of newspaper memorabilia in my office still. And no, I never divulged that Moses deserved the medal as much as I did.

Moses was one of the most impressive men I ever met. He was a brilliant thinker, utterly rational, decisive, curious about everything and devilishly impatient. He knew how to get things done---but getting done only his way. He would not---could not---brook discussion, let alone opposition, once he had made his mind up.

At one of our meetings about the wetlands, I and Congressman Otis Pike, who represented Suffolk County, met with Moses at the Arsenal in Central Park, where he hung out when in New York City. We were discussing an aspect of the enterprise, and Otis was pressing Moses to do something. Moses resisted and his face started to get red, and he stood up, talking louder and louder. Sid Shapiro passed me to note to relay to Otis. It read 'Do you want to give RM a heart attack?' Otis stopped.

Moses too easily showed his disdain, if not his contempt, for people, including people who had elected or delegated power. Al Smith had given him a lot of authority when he was a young man, and Mayor Fiorello LaGuardia had continued to give him power. As a result, of course, RM was respected, feared, obeyed, kowtowed to, but not beloved. Many politicians also scorned him as a bleeding-heart-do-gooder. Privately, they referred to him as a 'Boy Scout.' But they could not ignore him.

He made enemies.

One of them was Nelson Rockefeller. Moses foolishly thought that Nelson was just a rich kid whom he could handle the way he did New York State Governors Al Smith, Herbert Lehman, Averill Harriman and New York City Mayors LaGuardia, Bill O'Dwyer and Bob Wagner. But he could not. Nelson resented him and that was the beginning of the downfall. The first sign was Rockefeller's cancellation of Moses' plan to build a bridge from Oyster Bay to Rye in Westchester over the Long Island Sound.

I was a part of that project. Moses had planned it long, long before, when he built the Wantagh/Bethpage Parkway. That eased traffic North-to-South in eastern Nassau County, but Moses from the beginning---ten years before---had envisioned extending that road to Rye.

Moses one day announced the grandiose plan, but not details of its route. Shapiro came to my office to show that to me. I took one look at the road from Jericho Turnpike to Oyster Bay, and I laughed out loud. I told Sid that the highway went right through Len Hall's living room. The plan promptly went back to the engineers for a little re-location.

The road was badly needed. It would have siphoned off some half of the traffic from Long Island that had to go all the way to the Bronx, to cross over the Sound over the Throngs Neck Bridge and up Interstate 95 North. It would have saved millions of dollars and time. But the bridge was vehemently opposed in the Rye area, where lots of high-ranking Republicans lived. It would have gone right through their grand estates. The Herald-Tribune vigorously opposed the plan---its publishers lived along the route. In addition, of course, Nelson thoroughly disliked Bob, and all that killed the plan. Not unusual. It is the way so much of public accomplishment is accomplished---or not. [6]

News Story

The first recorded history in *Newsday* of efforts of Long Island social agencies recorded by *Newsday* **March 26, 1941**). In the article, **"Arrange for Social Work Conference,"** it is reported that: "Representatives of all of the principal social agencies of Nassau and Suffolk County, both public and private, will participate in the regional conference on social work to be held at the Freeport Elks Club, April 3. The event is reported to be the ninth annual such gathering. Topics to be covered by guest speakers and an expert panel are: "Social Welfare Today and Tomorrow," "Community Problems and National Defense," and "Family Relationships and the Adjustment of the Individual."

After World War II ended, Nassau County political leaders and wealthier families began to focus some of their attention on the needs of the poor, the disabled, health care, higher education and the arts. According to some of the interviewed in this book, people like Martha B. Farish Gerry, Joan Saltzman, May Newburger, helped to establish and support nonprofit organizations.

The work of others prominent people is described in the following pages.

Social Agencies by Year

1945

Catholic Charities

The Brooklyn Diocese established two Catholic Charities rented offices, one in Mineola and one in Bay Shore. Mary O'Hagan, a trained social worker and dear colleague of the author, was assigned to work in the Mineola office. [7]

1947

Catholic Charities

The Reverend Charles E. Bermingham, former national director of the Catholic Youth Organization (CYO), was assigned to the position of director of Catholic Charities with the intention of extending Catholic Charities' programs into Suffolk County. Jane Cohen was appointed head of the Bay Shore office. [8]

Nassau County Welfare Forum

At a meeting of the Nassau County Welfare Forum, Lyman S. Ford of the New York Community Council addressed seventy representatives from county health, welfare and social groups. Lyman spoke of the advantages of having a community council to act as a clearinghouse to prevent duplication of services by various local welfare agencies. [9]

YMCA of Nassau and Suffolk Counties (to be later named The YMCA of Long Island)

The YMCA launched a successful fund raising campaign to expand the organization's character building programs throughout Long Island. Among campaign leaders were Long Island Lighting Company Vice President Robert O. Olmsted of Glen Head, Duncan M. Findlay of Huntington and Raymond Pierce of Glen Cove. [10]

Associated Boys Club of Locust Valley (renamed as the Grenville Baker Boys Club and later the Grenville Baker Boys and Girls Club)

The club was established by Milward W. (Pidge) Martin, Pepsi Cola's chief attorney and treasurer and Edith Hay Wykoff, editor of the *Locust Valley Leader*. Mrs. George P. Baker and her family donated and built the original clubhouse. It was named after Mrs. Baker's son, Grenville, a decorated Air Force captain who died in 1949. [11]

1948

Long Island Home

Long Island's reputation grew, the number of patients admitted each year steadily increased. To meet the needs of expanding patient census and staff, planning began for a new administration building. Griffing Hall (named for board member, Robert P. Griffing) was erected with offices for administration, doctors, social services, admissions and medical records. [12]

The Society of St. Vincent de Paul of Long Island

"The society was founded and comprised of fifty-four volunteer groups, three thrift stores, ten food pantries, and two temporary homes. The agency grew to serve over 200,000 people annually through a myriad of programs and services that help people overcome hardships." [13]

News Stories

Newsday reported in **"L.I. Villages Get State Aid for Youth" (June 24, 1948)** indicating that Over $25K in state aid had been allocated to twenty-two Nassau and Suffolk county municipalities by the New York State Youth Commission for community youth projects as part of the state's $2.1M program to assist communities operate recreation projects, education programs, and youth bureaus.

In 1949, *Newsday* reported on what appears to be Long Island's first effort at social agency planning. In **"Social Agencies to Organize County Council Tomorrow" (November 30, 1949)**, it is announced that a council to coordinate the work of public and private agencies in Nassau is being organized. Lewis L. Delafield served as chair of the organizing committee. The council planned to serve as an advisory board to coordinate planning of public health, welfare and recreational programs and avoid any overlapping or duplication of services. It planned to study community needs and seek to stimulate interest in social problems. Under the described arrangements, the council will not have any jurisdiction over member groups and will not raise funds for their programs.

1949

The Nassau County Women's Forum and Hofstra and Adelphi colleges sponsored a series of human relations workshops. At the ninth session, Mrs. Garda Bowman, coordinator of community councils of the New York State Commission Against Discrimination said: "Men and women are compelled by necessity to look at the facts and assume responsibility of building and maintaining our democracy. This work should be carried on by representative groups of individuals in the community. [14]

The Health and Welfare Council of Long Island

Delegates of thirty-two social agencies formed the County Council of Social Agencies to set up a unified program so that member organizations will function more effectively together than they do alone. Dr. John Miller, Superintendent of Great Neck schools was elected chairman. [15]

Council of Social Agencies of the Five Towns Community Chest

The council renewed its appeal to New York State Governor Thomas Dewey for state aid for day care centers for young children such as the Five Towns Cooperative Child Care Center. The council also studied mental hygiene clinics in neighboring counties and issued a report indicating that conditions were favorable to establish a Nassau clinic. The report said that there were 750 youngsters ranging in ages from two weeks to 18 years who were being cared for in 420 foster care with an urgent need for an additional 125 foster homes. [16]

Association for Help to Retarded Children of Nassau County (AHRC)

AHRC placed an ad in a community newspaper read "The Spastic Paralysis Society of Long Island will meet at Lynbrook High School. All those with similar problems are welcome to attend." Ten people showed up and marked the beginning of what today is known as the United Cerebral Palsy Association of Nassau County. This small group of parents had children with cerebral palsy, but little was known about the condition at that time and there was no appropriate education or treatment. Together, the families rented space, hired a teacher and a physician, and began a program which would ultimately receive international recognition for its innovative and outstanding services. Meanwhile, a major fundraising campaign was launched to build a facility for the children. The building opened in 1952 thanks to many contributors and volunteers who donated construction services. This was the first comprehensive treatment and rehabilitation center for people with cerebral palsy. As its reputation grew, so did its clientele.

Little help was available in Suffolk County for families of children with intellectual and other developmental disabilities. Not much was understood about their problems. There were few alternatives outside of full-time parental care. They were shunned by society and largely ignored by public education. And for the most part, professional assistance could only be found in institutions that were hardly more than warehouses, places of little help and less hope. But in 1949, a small group of parents came together to form what was later to be known as AHRC, an organization founded on the conviction that every person, regardless of their intellectual abilities, has the right to live with dignity, learn with pride and work to achieve their highest potential." [17]

Notes: Chapter I

1. Information obtained from agency's website: http://www.trumanlibrary.org
2. William Strauss and Neil Howe, The Fourth Turning, (Broadway Books, 1997)
3. United States Census Bureau: www.census.gov
4. Race: Are we so different? (The American Anthropological Association in collaboration with the Science Museum of Minnesota. RACE is the first national traveling exhibition to tell the stories of race from the biological, cultural, and historical points of view. Combining these perspectives offers an unprecedented look at race and racism in the United States. RACE Project of American Anthropological Association).
5. Terms of a lease agreement dated January 21, 1948 between the Levittown Corporation and a tenant applicant (Levittown Library Archives)
6. David Starr, "A Description of My Knowledge of Robert Moses" was submitted by email to the author on April 20, 2104.
7. Richly Blessed: The Diocese of Rockville Centre, (Walesworth Publishing Company, Diocese of Rockville Centre's Public Information Office, 1991).
8. IBID.
9. "Welfare Forum Told of Council Benefits" Newsday, September 25, 1947.
10. "Y Heartened by Response to Campaign," (Nassau Daily Review Star, December 4, 1947)
11. Information obtained from agency's website:www.gbbgc.org
12. Information obtained from agency's website: www.longislandhome.org
13. Information obtained from agency's website: www.svdpusa.org
14. "Says Building Democracy Via Civic Action" Newsday, February 18, 1949
15. "Form County Council of Social Agencies" Newsday, December 2, 1949.
16. "Mental Clinic Needed For Nassau, 5 Towns Group Told" Newsday, March 16, 1949.
17. Information obtained from agency's website: www.ahrc.org

Chapter II: 1950-1954

Overview

Presidencies of Harry S. Truman and Dwight David Eisenhower. The Korean War. The Cold War. The McCarthy Hearings. Brown v. Board of Education.

Demographic Factoid

In the five year period 1945-1950, Nassau's population grew by 152,246 or 29.3% to 672,765 while Suffolk's population grew by 19,754 or 7.7% to 276,129.[1]

News Stories

Fear of communism in America was very much in Long Island's air during the early 1950s. A *Newsday* article, **"Shun Red Bait, Stern Warns Urban League," (April 3, 1950),** reported on a speech made by Henry Root Stern, chairman of the State Board of Social Welfare. According to the article, Stern "warned minority groups that their efforts for social and economic equality might be defeated by their 'over-sensitivity' in their relations with majority groups and bigotry against other minorities."

In 1953, anti-Semitic attitudes were reported by *Newsday* in the article **"Anti-Semitism Poster Rouses North Shore," (March 17, 1953).** The article states that "angry citizens and police officials launched a probe into mysterious plans for a mass meeting in the Port Washington High School. A notice of the proposed meeting was pinned on one of the village's official bulletin boards. It was signed by "the North Shore anti-Semitic

---

World War II and the Holocaust had a tremendous effect on America's Jews. One major effect was to greatly increase support for the creation of Israel. Zionism, the belief that the Jewish people have the right to create a country in their ancient homeland, had not previously been very influential among Jewish Americans. Attitudes changed after learning of the Holocaust in which six million Jews were brutally murdered and hundreds of thousands were left as survivors in horrible displaced persons camps with nowhere to go. Both of these facts fueled support for Zionism.

World War II also impacted interactions between Jewish and non-Jewish Americans. Most Americans had never met a Jew before the war. During the war, more than 550,000 Jewish soldiers served. Interacting with Jews in the military challenged anti-Semitic ideas.

During the 1950s, barriers to Jewish participation in mainstream American life continued to shrink. Clubs and hotels began admitting Jews. University quotas limiting the number of Jewish students were removed. Businesses and banks became willing to hire Jewish individuals. America's acceptance of Jews both enabled and was reinforced by Jewish entertainers. Unlike earlier Jewish entertainers who tried to hide their Jewish identity, Jewish actors and comedians in the 1950s were identifiably Jewish. This shows an increased confidence among Jews regarding their acceptance in America.

These Jewish individuals further eroded anti-Semitism through their popularity and by exposing millions of Americans to Jewish culture and traditions. At the same time, elements of American Jewish culture began to disappear as Jews became more assimilated. Throughout Jewish American history, many Jews felt that sounding or looking different from their non-Jewish neighbors was an obstacle towards acceptance and success. The Eastern European Jews who immigrated in the late nineteenth and early twentieth centuries urged their children to become as American as possible. This often resulted in the loss of cultural elements such as the use of the Yiddish language that set Jews apart. The disappearance of Yiddish theater and literature was accelerated by the growth of the suburbs, since this destroyed the Jewish neighborhoods upon which these institutions depended. [2]

Author's Reflection

Growing up in Mineola on Long Island in the late 1940s and through the 1950s, I experienced anti-Semitism at school and in the community. Our family belonged to a temple, Beth Sholom where I completed my Bar Mitzvah studies and participated in youth group activities. During this period of my early adolescence, I recall schoolmates throwing rocks through the temple's windows while we studied. I remember childhood friends treating me differently as it became known that I was Jewish. I will never forget a football coach who treated me more harshly than he did other players. I remember overhearing anti-Semitic words and stereotypical remarks in school hallways and on the sports teams.

Social Agencies by Year

1950

The Family Consultation Service of the Episcopal Diocese of Long Island

"The agency began to work with youth at risk. The service later changed its name to the Youth Consultation Service." [3]

United Cerebral Palsy of Suffolk (UCP of Suffolk)

A group of parents looking for answers to their questions about cerebral palsy and services for their children, came together to form United Cerebral Palsy of Suffolk. They knocked on doors to raise money and awareness, and by the mid-1950s they had appointed a medical director and initiated an outpatient rehabilitation program at the "center for the physically handicapped" within the Brentwood School District. By the end of the decade they had secured the donation of property on Indian Head Road in Commack. By 1959, ground was broken for the Suffolk Rehabilitation Center. [4]

1951

North Shore Junior League (later to be named the Junior League of Long Island)

The organization was formed with the goal of developing exceptionally qualified civic leaders who would collaborate with community partners to identify a community's most urgent needs and address them with meaningful and relevant programs and initiatives that not only would improve lives, but also change the way people think. An exchange shop in Roslyn was established. [5]

Family Service League (FSL)

A small Huntington nonprofit captured the interest of a trained social worker, Jane Page Nichols who recognized that the organization needed a professional executive director and a structured counseling program. For the next ten years, the volunteer board of directors worked to develop Family Service League into a countywide counseling agency with a paid professional staff. She was J.P. Morgan's granddaughter and had access to people of influence and means. She was so inspired by the potential of FSL to help children and families in her growing community that she decided to become a trained social worker, enrolling in the graduate program of the New York (Columbia) School of Social Work. She recognized that FSL needed a professional executive director and a structured counseling program. Upon receiving her degree, she became the volunteer executive director of the agency. Under Jane Nichols' leadership, the volunteer board of directors worked to develop FSL into a counseling agency with a paid professional staff. [6]

Lutheran School for the Deaf

Mill Neck Manor had its beginnings in 1944 at the LCMS Saginaw Convention. A resolution was passed to raise funds commemorating the 50th anniversary of the Synod's ministry to the Deaf in order to establish a school for Deaf children. Money was raised for the cause for four years, and a group of pastors and laymen from the New York area began to meet and discuss setting up the school. In 1947 the group incorporated as the charitable, non-profit corporation Lutheran Friends of the Deaf. In 1956, the Board of Trustees received the "Absolute Charter" by the New York State Board of Regents. In 1949, Lutheran Friends of the Deaf purchased 86-acre 'Sefton Manor' from Lillian Sefton Dodge for $216,000. In 1951, four years after Lutheran Friends of the Deaf incorporated, Mill Neck Manor Lutheran School opened to nineteen deaf boys and girls. By 1956, Mill Neck Manor was fully accredited by New York State. [7]

Planned Parenthood Center of North Suffolk

Planned Parenthood Center of North Suffolk was established with private donations from residents of Oyster Bay and Huntington villages, along with a start-up loan of $500 from Planned Parenthood of Nassau County. In similar fashion, Planned Parenthood Nassau loaned $500 to a group in Patchogue and Bellport for the establishment of Planned Parenthood of East Suffolk in 1963. Planned Parenthood of North Suffolk and Planned Parenthood of East Suffolk merged in June 1979, and assumed the name of Planned Parenthood of Suffolk County (PPSC). [8]

Episcopal Diocese of Long Island

The diocese launched its first combined fundraising campaign to aid the Church Charity Foundation which sheltered more than 100 aged and blind persons in its homes and maintained St. John's Hospital, the Church Mission of Help, a social service agency, the Bishop's Call, and the Diocesan Home for Boys in Sayville, provided home care for needy convalescents and aided small missions. [9]

News Stories

The Long Island Industrial Fund

Between 1951 and 1959, *Newsday* wrote over twenty stories regarding the establishment of The Long Island Industrial Fund including: **"Airborne Stars Spark Industry Fund Rallies" (September 14, 1951); "New Unit Launches Charity Fund Study" (May 14, 1952); "Industry Maps Hospital Drive."**

The articles report that the fund was established to provide financial aid for Long Island hospitals. It was the result of the efforts of 400 Nassau and Suffolk county companies and the cooperation of Long Island's 110,000 industrial workers. The effort was led by radio and TV personality Tex McCrary, chairman of the North Shore Hospital. McCrary called the effort: "An idea that hospitals of a community must be supported, not just by a few wealthy people, but by everybody sharing the responsibility for them."

The Nassau Mental Health Association

The Association was originally based at Adelphi College, sponsored the premier of a play on conflict in the family, *And You Never Know,* produced by the American Theater Wing. According to Dorothy Robin, chairman of the association's projects planning committee, the success of previous plays in Nassau schools made this recent event possible. [10]

1952

Suffolk Community Council (SCC)

SCC's bylaws were adopted with the stated purpose of 'promotion of the general welfare of the community through such activities as the study of community needs and resources; the promotion of social improvement; cooperative planning for health, welfare, and educational services; and the creation of public opinion.' The year's focus was 'Mental Health.' A committee was launched and worked to establish the Mental Health Association of Suffolk which was formed sometime during 1951-52. The Council also conducted a survey of public schools as to the unmet needs of children for dental care.

"SCC projects for the year included researching the need for a vocational high school, a mental health clinic, youth community groups, and programs to prevent delinquency. The SCC established a sheltered workshop committee to consider vocational planning for persons with disabilities which, in 1954, became nonprofit "Skills Unlimited." [11]

News Stories

Investigating health care in Nassau County, on **April 6, 1953**, *Newsday* began a seven-part series **"Medical Care Lags in Booming Nassau,"** written by Madeline Ryttenberg about the state of health care on Long Island. The series chronicles the rapid growth of Long Island, especially Nassau County, in the post-World War II period. "Nassau's jet-propelled population increase is tied to a horse-and-buggy system of medicine that can mean serious trouble as the county continues to expand," wrote Ryttenberg.

The report, written by Dr. John Gorrell, head of the hospital administration department at Columbia's College of Physicians and Surgeons, presented statistical evidence that "the very poor leave Nassau County to get medical care and there are almost no outpatient facilities at voluntary hospitals to take care of people who need a doctor but not a bed and who cannot afford to pay the full cost of treatment." The Gorrell report was not well-received by the medical society and majority of private physicians took the position that clinics are open to abuse by people who can afford to pay fees.

News Stories, continued

The county's privately financed family service agencies had a different story to tell. These included Catholic Charities; Family Service Association of Lawrence; Family Service Association of Nassau County; Jewish Community Service of Queens-Nassau; Port Washington Community Services; and Manhasset Health Center. The agencies felt that a new survey needed to be done to discover what new facilities are needed; which existing ones should be expanded, which people need help, and what policies should be altered to assure that everyone who needed care could receive it.

The *Newsday* series had an impact just a week after its completion. The Hospital Council of Nassau issued a statement acknowledging the need for outpatient services through hospitals for the indigent and medically indigent of Nassau County.

South Oaks Hospital

"The hospital was established during the time of the introduction of psychotherapeutic drugs and when psychiatry entered a new phase. During this decade of major change in the treatment of mental illness, the hospital was also changing rapidly. The Long Island Home made the transition from a long-stay sanitarium to a progressive psychiatric hospital. At that time, the name of The Long Island Home was no longer fitting and South Oaks Hospital was born. In 1952, the Board of Directors, recognizing the need in the community for a facility for non-psychiatric patients, decided to convert Searle Cottage into a nursing home. This facility was renamed Broadlawn Manor Nursing Home. During the same year, a restaurant and the Hospitality Shoppe opened in the Main Building. The Hospitality Shoppe was intended to be used by friends and relatives of patients and staff, but was also open to the public. It soon became a favorite restaurant for people in the community. The menu included Broiled Lobster and fries for $3 and Prime Ribs of Beef with Whipped Potatoes for $1.50." [12]

1953

North Shore Child Guidance Association (NSCGA) (later to be named: North Shore Child and Family Guidance Center (NSCGC)

North Shore Child Guidance Association was officially incorporated after a year of community educational outreach by the Willets Road School's Parent Teachers Association's mental hygiene committee that was concerned about the lack of facilities to help youth at risk. The group began to consider the establishment of what would come to be NSCGCA. By 1953, the association was incorporated and spread adding new community boards of concerned and interested individuals. Membership grew to 700 by 1956 with fund raising activities producing $20,000. In 1956, NSCGA secured a state license becoming Nassau's first community-supported mental health clinic. As communities and families experienced mental health issues, they became aware of the center's existence and quality services, demand grew, as did the establishment of educational programs on mental health topics. Membership grew to 1,000 by 1964. [13]

News Story

In **"Nassau Mental Health Unit Seeks $75,000 (April 23, 1953),** *Newsday* reported that the newly-formed Mental Health Association, through its general chairman, State Assemblyman Joseph F. Carlino, that the newly-incorporated association started a drive to raise $75,000 to carry out its programs.

1954

News Story

According to a *Newsday* article **"Nassau Health Dept. Moves to Gain Control of Mental Health $," (January 29, 1954)** reporter Marty Arnold wrote that the department sought an amendment a bill that would give it control over its money rather than have it by a board appointed by the County Executive. Assemblyman Joseph F. Carlino had been working with Dr. David G. Salten on mental health legislation for over one year. Salten, the Superintendent of Long Beach's Schools and president of the Nassau Mental Health Association, hailed the bill as a "tremendous step forward in mental health. It places the entire facilities of the state at the disposal of the county. Its objectives are great."

New Story

In a *Newsday* article **"Juvenile Delinquency on the Rise; Authorities Differ on a Solution," (January 29, 1954)** "Nassau is planning to build a $1M addition to its present juvenile facilities." 'Suffolk's children are not so fortunate: the treatment of juveniles there is something like in the Ozark Mountains'" according to the Reverend Charles E. Bermingham, director of the Nassau-Suffolk branch of Catholic Charities.

The article reported that "juvenile delinquency is increasing every year and Nassau and Suffolk are no exception to the trend."

News Story

A *Newsday* article **"Ready Development Center for Retarded Children in Nassau," (March 16, 1954)**; reports that the first 'cradle-to-the grave' program for retarded children will be launched when the Nassau County Association for the Help of Retarded Children opens a coordination and development center in Nassau Hospital." According to the article, the entire program will be financed privately without state or federal aid. The staff will consist of thirty volunteers under Dr. Alan A. Jacques, a professional director.

Notes: Chapter II

1. United States Census Bureau: www.census.gov.
2. Information obtained from the agency's website: *www.icsresources.org/content/curricula/JewsInAmericaReading4.pdf.*
3. Information obtained from agency's website: www.dioceselongisland.org.
4. Information obtained from United Cerebral Palsy of Suffolk County website: www.ucp-suffolk.org
5. Information obtained from agency's website: www.jlli.org.
6. Rick Van Dyke, interview of March 26, 2014, Port Washington NY.
7. Information obtained from agency's website: www.millneckmanor.org
8. Email correspondence provided by agency's public affairs office, November 15, 2014.
9. "LI Episcopal Diocese to Seek $150,000" Newsday, May 21, 1951.
10. "Mental Health Unit to Sponsor Drama" Newsday, September 26, 1951.
11. Collections of the Suffolk Community Council, information gathered in the Special Collections and University Archives at Stony Brook University.
12. Information obtained from agency's website: www.south-oaks.org
13. Information obtained from agency's website: www. *Northshorechildguidance.org.*

Chapter III: 1955-1959

Overview

Montgomery Bus Boycott. Emmett Till Murdered. Hungarian Revolution. Suez Crisis. Sputnik I and the Space Race. The Nuclear Threat. The Ugly American. The Affluent Society. The Cuban Revolution. The Birth Control Pill.

News Stories

In a *Newsday* article, **"Need for Women in Government Puts Lawyer in Political Race,"** by Olivia Weil **(October 31, 1955***)* Bay Shore attorney Anne F. Mead of Sayville states her plans to run for justice of the peace in Islip Township running against a non-attorney. Mead went on to become a Deputy County Executive in Suffolk County under H. Lee Dennison, the county's first county executive.

Anti-Semitic attitudes were again revealed by *Newsday* reporter Frank Johnson in his article **"Villager Sees Bias if G'den City Bars Temple," (March 7, 1956).** Robert F. Welch told the zoning board of appeals that "failure to approve the petition will stigmatize this community as anti-Semitic...it will be a sad day for the U.S. if we become so uncharitable, if we prevent people from attending their churches because it inconveniences us." Witnesses opposed to the temple claimed that it would decrease property values, bring noise, parking problems, and traffic congestion.

"5 Youths Arrested in Kings Park as Police Avert Gang" (May 8, 1956) was the headline of a *Newsday* article concerning another event in Huntington town during 1955 showed further resident concern about the community's young people. One year after the event, five teenagers were arrested as part of a "vicious North Shore gang seeking revenge for beating some of its members suffered at the hands of a rival gang." Apparently, the incidence of gang activity had reached the suburbs and wasn't limited to commonly-regarded low income communities.

Long Island hospitals applied for federal funds for new buildings authorized by the Hall-Burton Act. Under the legislation, federal funds were to be allocated under state supervision to provide hospital facilities in population-boom areas like Nassau County. The Act, enacted into law in 1946, was intended to provide grants and guaranteed loads to America's hospitals which were required to demonstrate that they provided a reasonable amount of free care every year. The money required that state and local governments provide two-thirds of the construction costs. Because the states and localities were required to prove the solvency of the construction project in question, the poorest municipalities did not apply with the result that the majority of funding did not end up in these areas. And, for many years, there was no regulation in place to ensure that hospitals were providing any free care.

A group of six voluntary, nonprofit hospitals formed the Hospital Council of Nassau County, Inc. in 1955. In 1956, a seventh Nassau facility was admitted to membership and the Council's charter was expanded to include seven Suffolk facilities under a new name, The Nassau-Suffolk Hospital Council, Inc. The Hospital Council was born just as the baby boom generation flocked to Long Island. This population explosion and expansion necessitated the need for more hospital beds, more preventive and primary care services, and eventually, evermore advanced medical technology, treatment, testing and diagnostics. While this hospital growth and innovation was taking place, the Nassau-Suffolk Hospital Council was making a mark for itself, as the voice and representative of all the nonprofit and public hospitals in the region." [1]

1955

National Association of Social Workers (NASW)

NASW in New York State was established with chapters in both Nassau and Suffolk counties. Its purposes are to strengthen and unify the profession; promote the development of social work practice; and promote human well-being through social action. In later years, NASW established the New York State Political Action for Candidate Election (NYS PACE) committee as a separate and independent political arm endorsing candidates, disbursing voluntary contributions, and providing volunteers to candidates for public office who support legislation and policies consistent with those of NASW. [2]

News Story

Newsday published a five-part series titled **"Nowhere to Turn"** by Pat Herman (**March 13-15, 1955**) that describes social services in Nassau County. The article begins:

"Nassau, the fastest growing county in the country, and her sister Suffolk, are as slowly paced as backwoods communities in developing social services for their citizens." To find answers to her questions, Herman screened 38 social agencies and examined the institutional and hospital facilities available.. Her conclusions are that "special interest groups on the private and county levels have stalled the expansion of low-cost psychiatric clinics and outpatient facilities in hospitals; a county-wide, non-sectarian family agency, which professional social workers consider the key to keeping the home intact, does

---

not serve any of the 1,500,000 Long Island citizens; and, thirdly, the Island's approach to care of disturbed and delinquent children is antiquated."

A light in the darkness of Long Island health care occurred in 1956 when North Shore Hospital established outpatient facilities where a resident did not need a doctor's referral to receive treatment if he was unable to pay for treatment. The last article in Herman's series reflected two advances for Long Island's family services' scene. Part of the reason was the opening of the North Shore Child Guidance Center in 1956, the first privately-financed treatment center for children on Long Island.

1956

Middle Country Public Library

The library began serving the Selden and Centereach communities as a hub of comprehensive programs and services in the mid-1950s. Through grants and fundraising, is programs are able to provide leadership and training for libraries across Long Island and the nation. The library has been redefining the public library. Working in partnership with the business, social service, health, education, civic and philanthropic communities, the Middle Country Public Library evolved into a forward-thinking organization, whose leaders were willing to learn about and adopt concepts from other industries, and then integrate them within the public library setting. [3]

News Story

After Herman's five-part *Nowhere to Turn* series in March, *Newsday* reporter Tom Renner wrote **"Long Island's Blackboard Jungle" (June 13, 1956)** in which he recommended several actions in response to what he described as a crisis in teenage crime. In coming to his recommendations, Renner interviewed Children's Court Judge Franklin T. Voelker and County Attorney Lloyd Dodge as well as police, public officials, and spokesmen for citizens committees. The nine recommendations were: establish a county police department with a juvenile aid bureau like the one established in Huntington town last year; establish a Long Island rehabilitation institution to reduce the frequency of sending youthful offenders to state training schools in faraway Otisville and Warwick; build a detention center; increase availability of psychiatric care; provide more recreational facilities; seek greater community participation; establish more stringent laws that punish the parents of habitual offenders; provide higher pay to probation officers, and improve parental discipline through education.

News Story

In **"Nassau Group Organized to Fight Alcohol Problem,"** (December 6, 1956) *Newsday* reports that a special committee was formed to promote a better understanding of alcoholism and provide help for alcoholics. Seventeen prominent Nassau citizens were named to the group.

1957

Family and Children's Association (FCA) (*Later to be named Family and Children's Association)*

FCA was preceded by the Family Service Association (FSA) of Nassau County. FCA began in late 1957 as a family counseling resource in the population-burgeoning county as Long Island's first non-sectarian family counseling service. The organization grew rapidly handling many tragic cases from people with very serious problems who had been waiting for help while others came to the agency with marital trouble among young parents. Martha Farish Gerry, a board member, played an important role in the organization and served as trustee and benefactor to many major New York City charities. She was a recognized thoroughbred race horse owner.

From the 1960s to 1997, Salvatore Ambrosino served as the executive director of FSA. Ambrosino grew up in NYC. He joined the Merchant Marines in WWII, and earned his Social Work Degree from Brooklyn College after the war. He earned his Ph.D. in education from Teachers College, Columbia University in 1960. Ambrosino went to work at Family Service Association of Nassau County as executive director in 1960 and retired in 1997. He was a fierce advocate for the poor, developing unique educational services for children in poverty and preventive services for seniors living alone. He was known as the "Dean of Nonprofits" by his peers. He was instrumental as a board member of the Health and Welfare Council of creating the Nassau County Youth Board and Nassau County's Mental Health agency. Ambrosino was also one of the founders of the Nassau Agency Council and the Port Washington Group House. He also served as board member of the United Way of Long Island for many years. Robert Sunley, a social worker who conceptualized 'case-to-cause advocacy' served as Ambrosino's assistant executive director. In this capacity, Sunley helped incorporate 'case-to-cause' advocacy into FCA." [4]

The Mental Health Association in Suffolk County, Inc. (MHAS)

"The MHAS was founded as a nonprofit, charitable organization dedicated to improving the mental health of the community. Its core service was to provide information and referral services. MHA staff and volunteers receive thousands of telephone and email requests from individuals, families and professionals seeking mental health resources and supportive services. Key to the organization's founding was the work of attorney Anne Mead of Sayville. At the time, Mead was deputy county executive to Suffolk's first County Executive H. Lee Dennison. Gertrude Seeley of the Hamptons served as the association's director." [5]

Selden Centereach Public Library (later to be named the Middle Country Public Library (MCPL)

MCPL was incorporated as the Selden Centereach Public Library in 1957. At the time, the library consisted of two storefronts in Selden and Centereach. It began serving the community as a hub of comprehensive programs and services. Over the years, through grants and fund raising, the organization has provided leadership and training for libraries across Long Island and the nation. The library has been redefining the public library. Working in partnership with the business, social service, health, education, civic and philanthropic communities, MCPL evolved into a forward thinking organization, willing to learn about and adopt concepts from other industries, and then integrate them within the public library setting. In 1960, the library name was changed to Middle Country. [6]

Catholic Charities

As early as the beginning of the Rockville Centre Diocese in 1957, Bishop Walter P. Kellenberg, saw that there would be a growing demand for comprehensive programs designed to meet human needs from infancy to through adolescence into the years of adulthood and older age. At first there were two Charities' offices on Long Island, in Mineola and Bay Shore. They had been created by the Brooklyn Diocese which had begun family services in 1945 on Long Island using rented office space in Mineola with social worker Mary O'Hagan assigned to supervise this office. In 1947, the Reverend Charles E. Bermingham returned to the Brooklyn Catholic Charities from Washington, D.C., where he had been serving as the National Director of the Catholic Youth Organization (CYO). He was assigned to St. Joseph's Parish in Babylon with the intention of extending Charities' programs into Suffolk County. When quarters were rented in Bay Shore, Jane Cohen became the first staff member. In 1954, as demand for Charities' services grew, Catholic Charities appointed the Reverend James Green, a psychiatric social worker, to become director of the family service division in Suffolk County. Over the next four years, the division provided services out of offices from Lynbrook, Bay Shore, and Riverhead.

In 1957, Bishop Kellenberg appointed Father Bermingham as the first executive director of Catholic Charities for the new Diocese. Bermingham adopted a policy of collaboration with, and service to people of all faiths, a policy that was uncommon among dioceses. He also insisted on cooperation between Catholic Charities and public welfare agencies at all levels and promoted the importance of preventive services.

Bishop Kellenberg and the trustees could see that it was essential to raise funds to permit the agency's growth. Trustee members were Vincent Baldwin; Thomas Daly; the Honorable Thomas P. Farley; Jeremiah Burns; Eugene McGovern; Walter E. Van der Waag; and Joseph Virone. The trustees formed a Bishop's Committee of the Laity consisting of laymen from the various parishes. These laymen chaired Charities' annual fund raising appeals.

Bermingham recognized that middle class people saw the mental health centers as serving only the poor while he knew that mental health issues were faced by people of all socio-economic levels. Therefore, he established a sliding-scale fee schedule so that all people could utilize the mental health services and pay for services according to their incomes. Bermingham immediately hired Joseph Barbaro as executive secretary of Catholic Charities, the first time a layman was appointed to a top administrative position formerly open primarily to clerics. He was one of the very few laymen in such a capacity in the country. Barbaro had served on the faculty of Fordham University School of Social Services.

Barbaro grew up in Brooklyn one of six children raised by his widowed mother after his father died when Barbaro was two years old. From a very young age, he was, and remains, very close to the church. Barbaro graduated from St. John's University in 1941 with plans to go into merchandising. During his four years in college, Barbaro worked for Macy's Departments stores to pay his tuition. Upon graduation, Macy's invited Barbaro to enter a company training program. As he neared graduation, one of his parish priests, Father Landis, asked Barbaro why he did not go into social work to which Barbaro responded: 'What is that?' The priest had just been appointed as the director of the Italian Board of Guardians in the Brooklyn Diocese and asked Barbaro to join him there. It was at the Board of Guardians that Barbaro met Father Bermingham. During this period, Barbaro began to take social work courses in Fordham's School of Social Services.

In 1944, towards the end of World War II, Barbaro entered the Army where he was assigned to the medical corps because of his experience as a social worker. At that time, the Army was beginning to recognize social work's role as part of the army medical corps. Barbaro helped to establish the first army rehabilitation center on the west coast and went on to become chief social worker for the expanded center before his discharge in 1945. After military service, Fordham gave Barbaro credit for one year of social work field instruction for his social work in the military service. Upon his discharge, Barbaro took a job with the New York City Youth Board, heading what was called the 'gang project' where he supervised untrained social workers assigned to different gangs. After six years with the Youth Board, he went on to the Muscular Dystrophy Association in the position of Director of Social Work for two years.

In 1957, when Barbaro started at Catholic Charities its budget was $67,000 with 11 staff members in both counties. This was a period of tremendous growth. Charities quickly became the largest voluntary agency on Long Island. From its inception, Catholic Charities felt that psychiatric help was a necessary ingredient of its family services programs. Consequently, the St. Anthony Guidance Clinic was set up in Mineola receiving the first Nassau County contract for promoting mental health services. This was soon followed by the Catholic Mental Health Clinic in Bay Shore in Suffolk County. Catholic Charities also established a Health and Hospital Department to coordinate the work of the Catholic hospitals on Long Island.

Another important developmental step recalls Barbaro, was undertaken by Bermingham who mobilized people in the wealthier parishes into a Bishop's Committee of the laity. He recognized that the organization would require private funding to undertake its plans. This all-male committee, made of influential and wealthy individuals, known as the Bishop's Committee for Charity, became the fund raising arm of the new Catholic Charities. Their wives also got involved in what was called the "Regina Assembly" and developed the Regina Residence, a facility for unwed mothers-to-be in Port Jefferson. The facility replaced the need to utilize facilities provided by the Brooklyn Diocese and the Archdiocese of New York.

Other programs were soon developed including a program for the deaf and the blind by Father Martin Hall. The Catholic Youth Organization (CYO) was also established as a department. Upon the death of Father Michael Leavy, CYO's first director, the Reverend Gerald J. Ryan was appointed Director of CYO. Ryan was a Fordham student in Barbaro's social work administration class. Barbaro asked Ryan why he was taking social work courses. Ryan said that he felt that " it would make him a better parish priest." Under Ryan's leadership, summer camps were developed in Melville, and Mattituck. Ryan went on to become a Bishop in the Diocese. Years later, a parish outreach center at Our Lady of the Miraculous Medal Parish in Wyandanch was named the Gerald J. Ryan Outreach Center.

Monsignor Robert Emmett Fagan played a very important role at Catholic Charities. Barbaro recounts the story of Fagan's first assignment after completing graduate studies at Fordham's School of Social Work. Father Bermingham sent Fagan to the East End to calm a situation involving tensions between residents and migrant farm workers. 'It was baptism by fire in a highly-charged environment with racial overtones,' recalls Barbaro. Bermingham told him to "learn how to handle people." According to Barbaro,

Fagan felt that this advice became a cornerstone of his work at Catholic Charities for decades to come. Fagan was then asked to develop a Big Brothers program to help boys growing up in single parent homes without male role models. The program attracted many volunteers and grew to a point where Charities asked the county to take it over.

In 1972, Barbaro returned to work for Catholic Charities after serving as Nassau's Social Services Commissioner. He recalls Fagan, then head of the agency, developing Long Island first group home for what were then called 'retarded' children in a vacant, former Valley Stream convent. Amidst vocal community opposition, Fagan negotiated with local residents who opposed the project. Things got so heated at one point that Fagan was told that he would be shot dead if he allowed the project to proceed. He asked the community for one year in which to operate the program after which, if the community continued to oppose the project, Fagan would remove it. One year later, according to Barbaro, community opposition ceased due to the project's success. The feared disturbances and reduced property values did not result. Catholic Charities went on to develop several other such group homes as well as residences for retarded adults. Barbaro also recalls working to reorganize the service delivery system at Catholic Charities from one around the kinds of services offered, to one where each site offered a "department store-type" array of services.

Monsignor John Gilmartin's work in the 1980s was to develop a new direction for the agency called "Parish Community Human Services. The change came from a mandate from Charities' national office after the 'Cadre Study' was conducted calling for Charities to return to its roots in parishes. This decision, according to Gilmartin, was partly due to "influence of government funding that supported programs. Charities wanted to be parish based, not program based." Gilmartin, worked with several priests, --Monsignor John Cervini, Father Peter Garry, and Father Paul Rahilly, and Sister Eileen McKeon took steps to reconnect with parishes to providing training for staff and parish volunteers. The program came to be called "Parish Outreach." Gilmartin became the Diocesan Director of Parish Outreach and was later replaced by Dr. Paul Kirdahy. Later, Parish Outreach was renamed "Parish Social Ministry."

Over the following years, the agency's ministries grew to include affordable housing, services for seniors, food and nutrition programs for mothers, babies, and seniors, a HIV/AIDS ministry and housing, a residence for the mentally ill homeless and residential programs for children and teens with emotional disturbances. Programs were expanded for immigrant services, mental health, alcohol and substance abuse, support for the developmentally disabled, and advocacy for the poor.

The housing department opened its first affordable senior housing complex in Selden in 1978 with 200 units. Currently, the agency operates 1,329 units of senior housing. Catholic Charities is the largest provider of affordable senior housing on Long Island. Its housing programs are available to people without regard to their religious beliefs.

Gilmartin reports that Charities' board of trustees was very active during this growth period. Due to the generosity of board member Thomas Casey, a large bequest enabled the continued expansion of services to people in need. [7]

For further information, visit Part II, Chapter V, regarding Joseph Barbaro.

The Association for Children with Learning Disabilities (ACLD) (now named Association for Children and Adults with Learning Disabilities

"The agency began when a group of families came together to advocate for services for their children with disabilities." [8]

News Story

In **"Social Agency Group Asks for Youth Service Bureau," (December 13, 1957),** *Newsday* reporter Jim Hadjiin reported that the Nassau County Council of Social Agencies, a group formed by the Nassau Health and Welfare Council, voted to seek state aid to form a county youth bureau. The group felt that the youth bureau was needed due to the increase in the county's youth population and rising juvenile delinquency in the past two years. As reported in *Newsday,* **"Nassau Forms Youth Board to Stem Crime," (May 11, 1965),** it took eight years for the county board of supervisors to establish the agency.

The Episcopal Diocese of Long Island's Church Charity Foundation and its Youth Consultation Unit

The diocese and its youth consultation unit were active during the 1950s raising funds for its various programs and joining with the few other family agencies of the time to advocate for more services needed for Long Island's growing population. This included shelters for more than 100 aged and blind persons at its Home for the Aged and Blind; St. John's Hospital; the Church Mission of Help, a social service agency; the Bishop's Call which helped support a home for boys in Sayville, and a home care program for needy convalescents. The non-sectarian Youth Consultation Unit offered casework counseling to troubled youngsters and their parents. [9]

News Story

In a *Newsday* article, **"United Fund Eyed for LI Charities" (September 19, 1957),** a group of labor, industry, and business leaders announced that they were considering the establishment of a united effort to raise charitable funds rather than through the separate campaigns conducted by individual agencies. In the following year, *Newsday* reported that Leon (Jake) Swirbul, president of Grumman Aircraft of Bethpage would head the year's United campaign.

1958

News Story

Reports of anti-Semitism continued into the late 1950s. In **"Bomb Tossed at LI House; Blame Bias," (February 4, 1958),** *Newsday* reporter Allan Wallach gave an account of "a homemade oversized 'cherry bomb' thrown out of the darkness onto the porch roof of an expensive home in this fashionable North Shore village last night..." The homeowners reported "years of harassment" including remarks like "we do not want your kind around here." The homeowners had ignored rumors of hostility in Plandome to persons of the Jewish faith whose application to join an exclusive local club was ignored.

News Story

In **"Unit Maps Fight on Youth Crime,"** September 27, 1958), *Newsday* reported on plans for the creation of a county-wide youth bureau with state aid to prevent juvenile delinquency. The announcement was made by Sam Levine, chairman of the youth committee of the Nassau County Council of Social Agencies. According to the article, Arthur Katz of Adelphi School of Social Work will survey the county to determine existing services and what kinds of services are needed.

1959

Throughout the 1950s, the former city-dwelling newcomers to Long Island supported government programs to build roads, schools, libraries, parks and playgrounds, as well as for police protection. Before the new settlers arrived, Long Island government services were minimal, limited to small departments of public works, parks and recreation, police, public health and welfare. There were virtually no childcare centers, nursery schools, youth centers, or health or mental health centers. Private charity on Long Island before 1960 was extremely limited.

News Story

In the last of a *Newsday* four-part series **"How Nassau Can Unshackle Justice in Handcuffs," (April 15, 1959)** by Jane Gerard, Judge Robert C. Richter says "…times have changed…Nassau has grown to a big-city size and we definitely need some method to help us meet the problem." Richter was referring to the need more-efficient means to deal with family-related criminal matters through the establishment of a family court.

The Caroline Veatch Legacy and the Veatch Committee

The origins of the Veatch Program can be traced to the early years of the congregation when it was known as the North Shore Unitarian Society. At that time, Caroline Veatch was a homebound member of the congregation who had inherited royalty rights and stockholdings from her husband Arthur Veatch, a geologist and founder of North European Oil. Caroline Veatch joined the North Shore UU congregation in 1948. When she died in 1953 she left the congregation her royalty rights, plus $50,000 in cash and 35,000 shares of North European Oil stock.

Using the income that began coming to the congregation from Mrs. Veatch's bequeathed royalty rights, the congregation in 1957 began making loans to Metro New York Unitarian churches as well as making a grant in 1958 to the American Unitarian Association to recruit new ministers. In 1959, wishing to give guidelines and structure to how such funds were disbursed, the congregation approved the Veatch Resolution establishing the Veatch Committee.

In 1969, the Veatch Committee developed guidelines for making nondenominational grants. The committee's records show it interpreted the recently-revised Veatch Resolution to allow it to simultaneously consider making grants to "Unitarian/local, Unitarian/national, Unitarian/worldwide, and community programs of the local/metropolitan area. In 1973, a Veatch study group was appointed and, based on their recommendations, in 1974 the Veatch Program resolution was once again amended and the Veatch Board of Governors was formed. From 1975 forward, the Veatch Program's position was secured with the establishment of the Veatch Board. This signaled the congregation's commitment to expanding guidelines that permitted more nondenominational grants at a time when the royalty income was increasing dramatically." [10]

For further information, visit Part IV, Significant Changes Since 1985.

Notes: Chapter III

1. Information obtained from: www.hrsa.gov/gethealthcare/affordable/hillburton.
2. Information obtained from: www.naswnys.org.
3. Sandra Feinberg, Email correspondence of November 15, 2014.
4. Richard Dina and Rick Van Dyke, interviews of May 25, 2014 and August 6, 2014 respectively.
5. Davis Pollack, interview of April 1, 2014, Islip NY.
6. Sandra Feinberg, Email correspondence of November 15, 2014.
7. Richly Blessed: The Diocese of Rockville Centre (Walesworth Publishing Company) and interview with Joseph Barbaro of June 12, 2014, 1991.
8. Information obtained from agency's website: www.acld.org.
9. Information obtained from agency's website: www.dioceselongisland.org.
10. Report to the Veatch Board of Governors (Veatch Advisory Group, February, 2007 and updated by Ned Wight, Executive Director in November 2012).

Chapter IV: 1960-1964

Overview

First Televised Presidential Debates. Bay of Pigs and Cuban Missile Crisis. Military Draft. Berlin Wall Construction. Peace Corps. *The Other American.* Community Mental Health Act. Freedom Riders. Civil Rights Act. Food Stamps. Work Study. Title VII. Adolph Eichmann Trial. President Kennedy's Assassination. March on Washington. Dr. Martin Luther King, Jr.'s "I Have a Dream" Speech. The Beatles. Nelson Mandela's Imprisonment.

Demographic Factoid

Both of Long Island's counties experienced substantial population growth during the decade covering 1950-1960. Nassau County's population grew from 672,765 to 1,300,171 residents, representing a substantial growth rate of 93.3 percent. Meanwhile, Suffolk County's population grew from 276,129 to 670,213 residents, representing a 142.7 percent increase.[1]

The following account of the early 1960s is based on an interview with Dr. Lee Koppelman who served as director of planning under H. Lee Dennison, Suffolk County's first county executive.

According to Lee Koppelman, history was made with the election of H. Lee Dennison who became Long Island's and Suffolk County's first county executive. Dennison was a major figure in Long Island history. H. Lee Dennison, a life-long Republican when he first ran to become Suffolk County's first county executive, was fiscally conservative but socially liberal. Koppelman describes Dennison as a spiritual person with an innate social consciousness based on his Bible readings. "He was a man totally without prejudice," says Koppelman. Dennison had worked for Robert Moses, the president of the Long Island State Park Commission and creator of Long Island's parkways and many of its state parks. Dennison also served as superintendent of highways in Suffolk from 1925-1950. In 1950, as a reform-minded person, Dennison wrote a bombshell report tracing Suffolk County's 300-year history of road construction revealing that the county had never engineered a paved road. He wanted the county to professionalize its road construction rather than simply maintaining its crude road system. From 1950 to 1959, he struggled, unable to find work that interested him. During this period, he worked as a land surveyor while studying to earn a Degree as a Professional Engineer.

In 1959, the Brookhaven Town Democratic Party asked Dennison, still a Republican living in Port Jefferson Station, to run for Town Supervisor. Dennison refused, indicating that he would run but only for the new County Executive position. He had only $6,500 for his campaign. He refused to accept contributions over $100. *Newsday* supported Dennison with the result and he won the election by only three hundred votes.

Koppelman recalls that, in 1960, Dennison hired Anne Mead (who Dennison affectionately called 'Annie Wannie'). Mead was a Democratic attorney and was assigned primarily to prepare the legislation to be submitted to the county board of supervisors for action. Dennison was not an attorney so he did not know how to prepare and write legislation. He needed Mead's competent assistance in this critical area since he had many legislative resolutions to bring to the supervisors.

Koppelman tells a humorous story about a Smithtown resident named Ned Smith, who worked for him as in a civil defense-related job. He did not know that Ned Smith was part of the family that founded Smithtown. When Koppelman was doing his first open space study, he got a call from a Mrs. Smith who invited him to meet at her baronial home in St. James to discuss the study. He had assumed that the Smiths who dated back to the American Revolution were Republicans. Upon entering the living room, he noticed a photo of Ned Smith his friend and employee. He showed shock in his face and explained to Mrs. Smith his association with Ned. She revealed that Ned was her nephew, "Ned-boy.' Aghast, Koppelman said that he assumed that Smiths were Republicans, at which Mrs. Smith responded "What is your problem? Ned is a Democrat. Why does that surprise you? What could we Smiths be but Democrats? We would never be part of an *upstart* party that only started in 1860."

Dennison initiated Suffolk County's first public effort to address the social problems of the times especially affordable housing. He hired Koppelman, an apolitical person, as his planning director. With Koppelman at his side, Dennison conducted walking tours of Wyandanch and North Amityville to personally witness low income housing himself. He formed a Migrant Labor and Slum Housing Committee in his office. The committee consisted of clergymen. Koppelman served as staff to the committee.

Also in 1960, because Dennison was aware that the number of poor residents was growing dramatically, he formed what he called a 'flying squad of detectives,' consisting of three welfare officers, one a former police detective, a police officer, and a woman with a background as a town welfare officer. The flying squad would investigate welfare fraud based on 'tip-offs.' One of the squad's first investigations concerned a Riverhead farmer who was found to be sleeping with one of his migrant workers while she was claiming welfare aid. *Newsday* did an extensive investigation of the situation. The county board of supervisors responded to this public exposure by eliminating the short-lived Flying Squad of Detectives.

The board of supervisors objected to Dennison's active interest in the housing issue on the basis of "home-rule," that reviewed all issues coming under town control. At the time, land could be bought at extremely low prices with the result that there were a number of major land scandals in the late 1950s involving a group consisting of a court judge, a member of the original planning board, and several elected officials, who illegally purchased thousands of acres of land. Koppelman credits *Newsday* for exposing this tax scam where in which land could be bought for next to nothing. The League of Women Voters was also very active in bringing public attention to the scandal. It went so far that Governor Averell Harriman appointed New York State's Assistant Attorney General, who lived in Huntington, to lead a special investigation. As a result of the investigation, several indictments were issued, something that never happened before since Suffolk district attorneys never found reasons to indict members of their own parties.

According to Koppelman, the establishment of county housing authorities was considered in both Nassau and Suffolk. The state housing agency urged the counties to eliminate its slums by establishing a regional authority or one for each county. They foretold that slums would develop on Long Island without regional planning of housing codes and their enforcement with a policy of open occupancy and equal opportunity. County leaders, however, decided that the multiplicity of governmental units posed a major obstacle that would likely frustrate the initiative so it did not come to pass and was never instituted to this day. Koppelman, at Dennison's request, prepared a plan that included housing. The plan met with extremely negative responses from the county Board of Supervisors because it essentially acknowledged that most of the new residents were unemployed, disabled, or women heading households.

The Open Space Preservation Program was a major initiative undertaken by Koppelman during the Dennison years. It began in the early 1960s and involved the outright purchase of open space land by the county - much of it set aside as parkland. Through the decades, Suffolk County went on to amass more open space land than any other county in the United States, more than 20,000 acres.

Koppelman says his desire to help the needy as instinctual. In the third grade, his teacher asked the class what they would do if they had a million dollars. Koppelman's response was for a Utopian society where everyone had houses and jobs. [2]

According to Richard Amper, Executive Director of the Pine Barrens Society, Koppelman was hasty in his younger years, promoting development in excess of what was appropriate for Long Island. He was quite authoritative in his early years, and was hard to sway.' He told the *Stony Brook Press* reporter that Koppelman urged public officials to make land-use decisions and to plan for growth on Long Island in a way that protects for future generations the sole source aquifer that supplies the region's drinking water. Critics say that any measure of Koppelman's career has to take into account the reality of modern Long Island as a region beset by high taxes, a lack of affordable housing, strip malls and traffic jams." Koppelman told the *Stony Brook Press* that he views the biggest failure on the island as "the lack of affordable housing, especially of the elderly, the poor and single families. 3

News Story

A *Newsday* five-part series **"Long Island's Migrants" (August 28, 1961)** written by Harvey Aronson began with a description of the physical and economic conditions of Long Island's migrant farm workers. Aronson reported that migrant farm laborers are "vital to the agricultural economy of eastern Suffolk County but also live in the suburbanized western section of the county." He describes their housing as ranging from regulated and unregulated "functional-to-good housing, to board houses that are adequate, and hovels that are not."

Meanwhile in Nassau County in the early 1960s, civil rights activists like Hugh A. Wilson began to work on issues facing the poor. Wilson, born in Kingston, Jamaica is a retired professor of political science who graduated Howard University where he met Stokely Carmichael who was head of the Student Nonviolent Coordinating Committee. Wilson worked as a community organizer in Long Beach initially and later director of the welfare rights movement on Long Island as well as a union organizer.

1963 was a year of considerable civil rights struggle on Long Island as reflected in the following sampling of dozens of civil rights stories reported in *Newsday*.

In 1963, *Newsday* published a number of articles about civil rights issues on Long Island including:

News Stories

In **"Negro Housing Unfit In Moriches: NAACP,"(January 9, 1963)**, *Newsday* reporter Bob Uris notes that NAACP official W. Burghardt Turner "demanded that Suffolk County and Brookhaven town officials take immediate action to correct what he termed "horrible, demoralizing, and mentally debilitating conditions in which Negroes are living in parts of the Center Moriches-East Moriches area."

Newsday reported in **"LI Group Finds Realty Bias" (January 21, 1963)** that the Huntington Town Committee on Human Relations "sent Negro and white members posing as prospective home buyers to real estate brokers in this township over the weekend, charged yesterday that 19 of the 20 brokers tested discriminated against Negroes. The group said it would send its findings to state officials to seek disciplinary action." Joyce Insolia, co-chairman of the group, indicated that the testers also discovered discrimination against Jews in the town.

In **"Suffolk Votes Rights Unit But No Funds for It," (May 14, 1963)**, *Newsday* reporters Art Bergman and Don Smith report that the Suffolk Board of Supervisors approved creation of a human relations commission but failed to provide funds to put it in operation. According to the article, County Executive H. Lee Dennison said "It is a long overdue step but at last we have a commission.

Later in the year, *Newsday* reporter Kenneth Crowe and Ken Byerly in **"Plan Huntington Town Rights March" (September 18, 1963)** described protest actions against *de facto* segregation including: A march on Huntington Town Hall as part of a drive to register all Negro voters and focus attention on the needs of minority groups; protests in Malverne between the United Committee for Action Now and the NAACP Lakeview branch regarding the establishment of a freedom school; a mass rally, with Jackie Robinson and Congressman Adam Clayton Powell as speakers in Westbury to urge integration of the predominantly Negro New Castle school; a Manhasset court case concerning the integration of the Valley School; and an Amityville buying boycott of local merchants organized to bring pressure on the school board to integrate the predominantly Negro Northeast Elementary School.

Social Agencies by Year

North Shore Child Guidance Center (NSCGC)

In the early 1960s, NSCGC obtained its first drug and alcohol license and established 'The Place' in New Castle. Soon thereafter, the agency became the first agency in New York State to receive an OCDY license (Outpatient Chemical Dependency for Youth). This license enabled the agency to provide mental health services to its substance abuse population at the same site. Soon, a joint venture was established with Nassau County's Family Court, Probation Department and Department of Mental Health to divert high-risk youth away from the juvenile justice system and reduce the number of out-of-home placements. [4]

1960

Jewish Community Centers

Jewish community centers have been in existence since the early 1850s. They started on Long Island in the 1960 and grew in number and size over the years. Percy Abrams was the first fulltime executive director of the Mid-Island then in Wantagh and the only Jewish Y at the time. Abrams had the mission to provide services to the entire spectrum of Long Island's Jewish community regardless of affiliation, religious ideology, or age.

Abrams was visionary, directing his efforts both inside the Y and as a member of the broader social welfare community, to train future leaders, encourage the training of social workers in group work practice, expand the role of executive directors and strengthen boards of directors to raise the funds needed to enable program growth." [5]

1961

United Fund for Long Island (later to be renamed the United Way of Long Island (UWLI)

The United Fund for Long Island was first conceived as a committee of the Health and Welfare Council under the leadership of David Kadane who was the council's president. The committee studied fund raising on Long Island and recommended that all charities in both counties join forces into one group. [6]

Townwide Fund of Huntington

A group of Huntington residents came together with the goal of helping those in need in the town. Their mission was to raise funds within the community to assist local charities such as the Red Cross, YMCA, Family Service League, Boy and Girl Scouts, and Huntington Hospital. As a non-governmental agency, The Townwide Fund of Huntington bridges the gap between dwindling governmental support for local charities and the increasing needs of community residents. The Townwide Fund board is made up of volunteers from all parts of the Town. [7]

Suffolk Rehabilitation Center (later renamed: United Cerebral Palsy of Suffolk)

The Suffolk Rehabilitation Center opened and immediately began providing medical rehabilitation and physical and occupational therapy to children with cerebral palsy, muscular dystrophy, polio, spina bifida, hemophilia, cardiac anomalies and orthopedic disabilities. Then as now less than half of those served had cerebral palsy. In the early 1960s, specialty medical care in pediatrics, otolaryngology, orthopedics, neurology ophthalmology and psychology became available at the center, followed by an audiology center, the first in Suffolk County, offering evaluations, diagnosis and speech therapy. As the decade progressed, preschool and school age education programs were introduced, and both clinical and medical services were extended to adults. Camp Indian Head welcomed its first youngsters in the late 1960s and UCP began providing services to BOCES." [8]

Adelphi School of Social Work

Adelphi's School of Social Work was established in 1949 and remained Long Island's only social work school until 1970 when the School of Social Welfare at Stony Brook University was established. Thus, Adelphi played a very important role in Long Island's social service scene training thousands of social workers many of whom remained on Long Island to serve their communities providing casework, group work, and community organization services. The school also contributed to the quality of life on Long Island through a variety of educational programs addressing the changing nature of the Island's demographics.

Personal Story

Louise Skolnik, Ph.D.

Louise Skolnik, Ph.D., provides the following overview of the school's development. She earned a Master's Degree in social work at Adelphi in 1974 and became a faculty member at the School in 1976. During her 27 year tenure at the School, Skolnik served as the director of the Social Services Center and as the School's associate dean. From 2002-2009 she was a member of the administration of Nassau County Executive Thomas R. Suozzi where she played a leadership role in the "No Wrong Door" transformation of the Health and Human Services system. Currently, Skolnik is a Professor Emerita at Adelphi's School of Social Work and an adjunct faculty member at Fordham University's School of Social Services. She was a founder and consultant to the Oral History Project of the National Center for Suburban Studies at Hofstra University. Among her many publications is "Social Welfare Programs: Narratives from Hard Times" (2006) which features recipients' life stories in teaching social policy and social welfare practice.

Skolnik describes the 1960s as the "Golden Era" of social work nationally as well as at Adelphi where there was excitement and idealism encouraging innovation and creativity. Social work was even the subject of a nationally-televised series "East Side/West Side." From its inception, the School was committed to a dual mission to enhance the lives of individuals and to change social systems to better meet human needs. In the midst of the early civil rights battles in the South for political, economic, and social justice, the School sent students to Mississippi to participate in voter registration drives as well as to New York City. Social change was also made a part of student practicum through a requirement that all students have practical experiences in individual and social change.

In the 1960s, under the leadership of Dean Joseph Vigilante, Ph.D., and Associate Dean Beulah Rothman, Ph.D., a strong team of faculty members was recruited. They included Catherine Papell, Ph.D., a group work expert and Myron Blanchard, George Lockhart, and Jerry Tavel, community organization specialists. The faculty was committed to developing a practice curriculum that prepared students to engage in multi-modal practice and one that actualized the dual mission of the profession. Adelphi' innovative practice curriculum (then first termed 'generic' and then 'foundation') influenced the contemporary design of social work practice curricula (now labeled 'generalist'). Relatedly, the school also innovated the establishment of field instruction centers that integrated practice and teaching, providing all students with casework, group work, and community organization methods.

Responding to the needs of people working in human services who wanted to obtain Social Work Degrees, in 1967, the School developed the ANSWER Program. The program enabled human service workers to earn a Bachelor's Degree by granting life experience credit and field work credit while working for their agencies. It was at that time the only school in the New York metropolitan area to have such a program and one of the few in the nation.

The school also launched a part-time program targeted at women with family responsibilities to enable them to take nine courses before fully matriculating in the school. No other New York-area school had such a program.

In 1979, Dean Vigilante asked Skolnik to assume the leadership of Adelphi's clinic that primarily offered casework services to the community. The clinic was built into the School's charter by its founders who wanted the School to have a practice 'laboratory' as part of its design. Skolnik added group work practice and community organization work for all students interning at the clinic to more fully reflect the School's multi-modal curriculum. The clinic's name was changed to the Adelphi Social Services Center and was re-envisioned as a multi-faceted, University-based social agency with three objectives: 1) to develop, implement, and test models for field instruction; 2) to provide services to the campus and the community which fulfill unmet needs; and 3) to serve as an arena for demonstration and research regarding such areas as models of training, methods of service delivery, populations with unmet needs, practice methodology, and the interrelationship of policy and practice. Forty student field work placements at the Bachelor's, Master's and Doctoral levels were developed.

From the center's beginning, Skolnik wanted to make certain that the center did not step on anyone's 'turf' and only developed programs that were non-duplicative and that none of the community agencies wished to undertake. An advisory committee chaired by Sadie Hofstein, then the executive director of the Mental Health Association of Nassau County, guided the center on the 15 funded demonstration and research programs it developed and ensured the support of community-based organizations. Among the programs were the following: the Breast Cancer Support Program; the Refugee Assistance Program; the Adult Learning Disabled Program; the Sexual Assault Victims Hotline and Counseling Program; Services to Rape Victims Task Force; and the Program for the Hearing Impaired.

The center grew to have a full-time director, a part-time director of program development and evaluation research, and a team of part-time field instructors, consultants, project coordinators, and a psychiatric consultant. Many of these staff positions were filled by faculty members. Services were provided at Adelphi and at several community-based sites. The center was able to respond quickly to emerging community needs. After President Ronald Reagan fired the nation's air traffic controllers rather than negotiate a new contract with them, Skolnik reached out to local air traffic controllers. She offered them opportunities to find employment and training programs as well as advocacy and counseling support services during their unemployment. Some of them even went on to earn MSWs.

In 1990, then Adelphi President Peter Diamandopoulos implemented draconian cuts in the School despite its effective programs. The center ceased to operate. Some of the programs found new homes in community agencies. The Breast Cancer Support program was the only one continued at Adelphi and as of 2014 is still in operation.

In 2002, Skolnik left Adelphi when she was appointed as deputy commissioner of the Nassau County Department of Social Services by Thomas Suozzi, Nassau County's newly elected Count Executive. In 2004,Suozzi asked Skolnik to become the County's Director of Human Services so she could use her social work education and program development expertise to help redesign the eight health and human services departments into an innovative integrated health and human services system informed by social work's ethical and empathic perspectives. Skolnik describes her work at the county as 'the icing on the cake of her professional career' and an opportunity to 'practice what she had preached' during her years at Adelphi. For her program development and public service work, the NASW Foundation in 2011 recognized Dr. Skolnik as an NASW Social Work Pioneer.

Skolnik's belief is that when social workers are in positions to effect social changes they need to plant seeds even though there are no guarantees that the innovations that they initiated will last. "You have to change systems,' says

Skolnik. As deputy commissioner, she conducted staff training programs through the human services department that she established. During this period, Skolnik organized the "No Wrong Door" Program making it a great deal easier for those seeking human service assistance from the county to access social services, health, mental health, youth services, senior citizen services under one roof." [9]

Author's Reflection

Between 1968-1972, I was a student at Adelphi's School of Social Work. My wife of one year, Karen, worked in the Department of Social Services during this period while I obtained a grant from the National Institute of Mental Health. Between Karen's salary, the stipend, and my summer work, we lived well in a one-bedroom apartment in Huntington Village.

I enjoyed the field of study I had undertaken especially the community organization courses conducted by Jerry Tavel and Myron Blanchard. They helped me to conceptualize the work I was doing and to appreciate the importance of group, organizational, and community process. Tensions at the school were high as they were in the society at large where things were seen polarized whether they were with respect to the wealthy and the poor; blacks and whites; men and women; traditional values and countercultural values; political points of view; or in world affairs. There were student protests against the school when a professor showed racist attitudes; protests against the war in Vietnam; and protests against President Lyndon Baines Johnson. I joined some of these protests.

The recollections of other Adelphi School of Social Work faculty members were gathered in personal interviews to further reflect their perspectives on the role of social work education and the fields of social work practice during the decades.

Personal Story

Dr. Abraham Lurie, Professor, Adelphi School of Social Work and

School of Social Welfare at Stony Brook University

Abraham Lurie was at Adelphi College for four years as a part-time professor of Sociology before and during the period when the college established its School of Social Work in 1949. Lurie was asked by the college's president to be the school's first dean but chose not to accept the offer, preferring to continue his career teaching, doing research, and maintaining a private practice. Lurie graduated from the New York School of Social Work that became the Columbia School of Social Work when future-President Dwight Eisenhower was Columbia's president. Lurie is a charter member of the

National Association of Social Workers which was originally the result of a merger of several social work associations. At the time, he was acting-chair of the American Association of Psychiatric Social Workers one of the merged organizations while the chairman was ill. Columbia, where Lurie also taught as an adjunct was psychoanalytically-oriented. The other merged associations were more interested in community social action, public welfare, and administration resulting in debate about which types of coursework should be offered and emphasized in social work curriculum in the schools of social work. Some schools emphasized theory and practice while others the Reichian theory and practice. The struggle also manifested itself in the National Association of Social Workers (NASW) as to its orientation. Most social workers agreed that NASW should emphasize social policy.

This conflict also existed in the Council of Social Work Education (CSWE) the organization that accredits schools of social work. CSWE is a nonprofit national association representing individual members as well as graduate and undergraduate programs of professional social work education. Founded in 1952, this partnership of educational and professional institutions, social welfare agencies, and private citizens is recognized by the Council for Higher Education Accreditation as the sole accrediting agency for social work education in the United States.

In the 1950s, CSWE decided to review the curricula at the schools. Lurie chaired a committee to survey social work field educators around the nation concerning their thinking about social work education. The result was the decision to reduce the emphasis on a psychodynamic approach. According to Lurie, this period of social work development was intellectually stimulating. Lurie observes that, at this time, many seeking admission to schools of social work included middle-class women seeking to develop private psychotherapy practices rather than being employed as generic social workers who were employed in agencies where salary levels were poor. Many social work students received grants enabling them to continue graduate education particularly in mental health. These students exhibited less interest in the social action agenda being promoted by CSWE and NASW. Adelphi thrived during this period. According to Lurie, Adelphi attracted a number of excellent faculty members and some wrote well-regarded books and contributed critical thought and analysis to the professional literature."

Lurie has had an extensive and diverse social work career. Besides his role as a social work educator, he helped to establish the Variety Preschoolers Workshop (now named The Variety Child Learning Center) as its first Chairman and later served as a consultant to Judy Bloch, Variety's Executive Director. He also set up a program for the frail elderly in an apartment building in Floral Park. He helped found one of the first group homes in Nassau County along with Sadie Hofstein, the Executive Director of the Mental Health Association of Nassau County where he also served on the Board of Directors.

Lurie recalls clearly community residents' anger when the association sought community support for the establishment of Nassau's first group home. This included statements by a psychiatrist and psychiatric social worker who complained that dangerous people could become residents in the group homes.

Lurie reflects that Social Work has always tried to find a 'niche' for itself. It has undergone a great deal of change since the 1930s, when, in the midst of the Great Depression, family agencies were being asked by clients for 'cash' money they needed to pay for food, rent, and other basic necessities rather than therapy. The agencies were not able to provide these funds so they counseled clients to find the inner strength to survive. Social workers began to offer clients information and resources rather than psychotherapy, services that some believe are not those commonly regarded as professional in nature and could be provided by less professionally-trained people. However, today, many social workers have become 'system navigators' and are held in high regard by health care teams.

Lurie sees many social agencies today are not run by social workers. Thus, staff development that was a basic ingredient of social work agencies of the past is no longer present. Other disciplines began to offer these social services thus adding to the difficulty in defining social work. Lurie points to another concern that Doctorate Degrees in Social Welfare are very similar to doctorates in Psychology or Sociology. However, schools are requiring a doctorate to join a social work faculty and the only way to get tenure is through publishing and research leaving less time for direct practice and the research is primarily in social policy, administration and family dynamics, with less emphasis on clinical practice.

Lurie feels that the Social Work profession today is in a very difficult position. While the Bureau of Labor Statistics reports that employment of social workers is projected to grow 19 percent from 2012 to 2022, faster than the average for all occupations, it is not clear what their definition of social work is. Employment growth will be driven by increased demand for health care and social services, but will vary by specialty. Lurie's greatest disappointment with Social Work is that it has not been able to carve out a core of activities that can be clearly identified as social work, a uniqueness which other professions such as medicine or law can claim. [10]

Personal Story

Dr. Susan Bendor: Professor, Adelphi School of Social Work and School of Social Welfare at Stony Brook University

Bendor earned a Master's Degree in Social Work in 1962. She recalls this period as one of excitement and idealism in the social work field partly due to the positive climate created by young President John F. Kennedy and civil rights leader Dr. Martin Luther King on a national level and at Adelphi itself with the arrival in 1961 of Adelphi's new dean, Joseph Vigilante. Vigilante was energetic and enterprising and supportive of innovation at the school and social work's role in social action and social justice activities. He wanted to expose students to social inequities. This included sending a group of social work students to participate in voter registration drives in the South as well as to participate in civil rights demonstrations and visits to Riker's Island Correctional Facility in New York City during student orientation week. Bendor looks back fondly on Adelphi's generic social work education, feeling that the coursework in casework, group work, and community organization, prepared her well. She describes Dean Vigilante as a member of the "social work mafia," that included Adrian Cabral of the Health and Welfare Council and Salvatore Ambrosino of the Family and Children's Association. According to Bendor, this trio worked well together to get things done.

When asked how Vigilante viewed Nassau County's one-party control by Republicans, Bendor feels that Vigilante was not willing to appeal for Republican financial support for the school's programs because he knew that he could not accept the implicit conditions, namely for political contributions conformance with the party's platform. Bendor recalls Vigilante as leery of losing his independence as a social activist.

One of the important lessons that Bendor learned while at Adelphi was to engage people with influence. She tells the story of how she organized her fellow students to convince Dean Vigilante to use his influence to stop a threatened strike at the field work agency where she was placed. Vigilante, struck by Bendor's concern about potential disruptions in services to her clients, was able to convince the other area social work schools to join Adelphi to urge the agency to stop the strike.

While at Adelphi, Bendor played leadership roles in forming an outpatient mental health program (Walkabout) and Project Residential Experience in Adult Learning (REAL). After she left Adelphi, she became the Chief Psychiatric Social Worker at Meadowbrook Hospital, Nassau County's only public hospital. There, again, Bendor applied her generic social work skills. Faced with a situation where an elderly woman was lost and confused and refused hospital admission, Bendor drove the woman to Nassau County Executive Ralph Caso's home and convinced him to use his influence to admit the woman to the hospital. Bendor knew that you sometimes have to go to the top to get things done.

In reflecting over the period since her days at Adelphi, Bendor feels that social workers have been demonized by conservative forces. She observes that the role models that were present in the 1960s do not exist anymore, characters like Dr. Martin Luther King, Robert Kennedy, Caesar Chavez, Malcolm X, etc. Bendor is disillusioned at today's social work and its focus on licensure and veritable absence of advocacy in behalf of better social conditions. She feels that there is no funding to support advocacy. [11]

Personal Story

Jerry Tavel, Associate Professor, Adelphi School of Social Work

Tavel was an assistant professor in Adelphi's School of Social Work from 1966-1996. After earning a Master's in Social Work at New York University in 1959, Tavel worked with a number of casework and group work positions at a number of nonprofit and governmental agencies in the New York metropolitan area, including the YMHA in Washington Heights, Camp Hurley, and various psychiatric centers. Because of his group work experience and knowledge of community organizing in social welfare settings, Tavel was involved in designing the school's community organization methods curricula originally developed by Professor Myron Blanchard in the early 1960s.

In discussing social work education and practice prior to the 1960s, Tavel reflects on the early 20th century debate about whether social work is a profession, a debate that contrasted a traditional, scientific method focused on efficiency, effectiveness, and prevention in the disbursement of public and private charity with the approach taken by Jane Addams' settlement house movement in the late 19th and the establishment of community service centers to meet the needs of the mass migration of immigrant populations that needed to learn English, apply for citizenship, and acculturate in America. He also points to the influence of labor unions in the development of social work

Tavel describes his early years at Adelphi as ones in which the school primarily prepared the mostly-female students for careers as caseworkers and psychotherapists. The school, like most schools of social work at the time, saw casework as the major method of social work practice while group work had begun to be taught as well. The underlying view was that social work education should prepare people to help people to change in order to function better in society not to prepare students to alleviate underlying social problems. The school's dean at the time was Arthur Katz, a well-respected social worker with a strong background as an administrator and group worker not as a caseworker. Since the school viewed casework as the major method to be taught, faculty consisted primarily of individuals skilled in casework, including Beulah Rothman and Florence Hazelkorn. Its group work faculty was led by Catherine Papell and included Gary Rosenberg, both very well-respected academics and practitioners.

Tavel also describes social work education's interest in community organization during the mid-1960s evolving primarily from changes in the external environment particularly the War on Poverty program under the leadership of President Kennedy's brother-in-law, Sargent Shriver, and the civil rights movement. Both of these concerned the need for structural change in society. Group workers, particularly, with their affinity towards collective thinking, were responsive to a curriculum that includes a broader view of social work practice, a more generic one. Both they and the caseworkers felt that the profession had a responsibility to contribute to the alleviation of poverty, inequality, and health and mental health disparities. The dean of the School, Joe Vigilante, and its Assistant Dean, Beulah Rothman, were very supportive of this thinking as well and facilitated the development of coursework and field work as part of a generic social work model that was replicated at many other schools. The generic model included the study and practice of casework, group work, and community organization.

Because Adelphi encouraged students during this time period to understand and practice more than casework and group work methodology, community organization coursework included the study of power in American society and its sources. The writing of C. Wright Mills who had written *The Power Elite* in 1956, was one of two models of power discussed. According to Mills' 0-sum theory, power is finite with a power elite consisting of top leaders in the military, economic, and political life of the world, making the major decisions affecting the masses. Their decisions, and lack of them, had dramatic impact upon the world's inhabitants leaving it to the rest of society to function within the framework established by the power elite. The other conceptual framework depicted power as accessible to all levels of society at one point in time or another. Individuals, individually and in groups and associations, could cause dramatic social changes. This point of view was compatible with the principles of social work and the practice of community organization.

The student body at Adelphi had a heavy concentration of black, primarily male students who were employees at public agencies such as the New York City Department of Social Services, the Veterans Administration, and the New York State Office of Mental Health. Tavel recalls that, in the late 1960s and early 1970s, his community organization classes had high percentages of these students. These agencies had a good deal of federal state money to support social work education including full tuition payment and other expenses. These employees were also provided with seniority. This support was provided with the proviso that the employees would, after completing their MSW studies, would return to their agencies for at least four years thus helping their agencies to benefit from their social work educations. Tavel believes that many did not honor their pledges. [12]

Personal Story

Martin Seitz, Ph.D., Director of Admissions Adelphi School of Social Work

Seitz was Director of Admissions at Adelphi School of Social Work from 1969-1974 and taught at the school for twenty-two years. Seitz described the early 1970s period as a time when Adelphi was still a relatively new school but was able to assemble a fine faculty while tapping into available scholarship aid to attract a large volume of applications from a diverse group of candidates.

Schools were being encouraged by the federal government and the Council on Social Work Education to train social workers to address issues of poverty especially in urban centers as part of President Lyndon B. Johnson's Great Society programs and the civil rights struggles of the 1960s. At the same time, the Council of Social Work Education encouraged schools of social work to seek diversity in their student bodies. 'You could not get accredited if you did not do so,' recalls Seitz.

The federal funding enabled the school to be very selective in student enrollments and recruit a wide cross-section of students including blacks and Latinos. Seitz particularly recalls the enrollment of many bright black students from Harlem. Previously, Adelphi had very few students of color. During this period, one-in-four students were African American.

School policy at the time was to train students in three social work methodologies, a generic approach to social work that included coursework and field work in casework, group work, and community organization. The school could accept 100 students each semester at the time. It was decided to divide the students along methodological areas of their interest. During Seitz' tenure, the practice was to include 50 students who concentrated on clinical social work methodology; 25 students concentrating on group work methods; and 25 students concentrating on a newly-developed community organization practice. This was part of a push to train social workers to be "chief cooks and bottle washers."

Seitz recalls that community organization practice, in earlier years at the schools of social work, was the most exclusive methodology. Recruited to this area of practice were only experienced executive directors with years of experience in leadership positions, raising funds, writing grants, working with board of directors, and working in inter-groups with other organizations and disciplines. In the late 1960s, community organization training in the schools of social work changed to one more applicable to what is commonly known as grassroots community organizing as practiced by such people as Saul Alinsky, Richard Cloward and Frances Fox Piven of Columbia's School of Social Work.

At the time, there were many middle-class, white, suburban women, pursuing careers in clinical social work in their post-child rearing years. They had their sights on obtaining clinical positions in Long Island family agencies. As the only school of social work on Long Island at the time, it was only natural for these women to enroll at Adelphi. Many of these students were not pleased with the generic approach being offered. Some felt that the core of social work was the application of psychotherapeutic methodology with individuals, and that this was being watered down by spending time on group work, community organization coursework and field work. Others saw the core of social work as efforts to address the societal, causative factors that lead to personal and family dysfunction and conflicts especially among low-income populations, not unlike the work that settlement houses had done in previous decades. Psychotherapy, according to this point of view, was seen as a middle-class luxury at a time when social workers should focus on the root causes of America's social problems.

A further reality of the time had to do with the settings in which social workers practiced. The clinical people wanted their studies to lead to their development of private clinical practices where they could earn a higher income than they would through employment in social agencies that were famous for their poor salaries and benefits. Family agencies provided staff development programs for these workers. This was viewed as an important aspect of professional development with more-seasoned social workers mentoring and guiding the less-seasoned. "Field work instructors," Seitz recalls, "had status." The move towards private practice, according to Seitz, "…was an important change in the field, as was a movement to view what had been called "clients" to be renamed "patients." Seitz feels that this was a mistake.

Another controversial subject of the time was the establishment of the Bachelor's in Social Work Degree. Faculty felt that many low-income people, interested in social work careers in minority communities, felt that it was too much to expect aspiring social work candidates to enroll in two-year M.S.W. programs while they raised families and remained employed. They advocated the development of B.A. in Social Work Degree programs so that these individuals could take a step towards becoming part of the profession. Some felt that the B.A. Degree devalued the profession and led to diminishing standards and confusion about the role of M.S.W.-level practitioners. Seitz wonders if the profession's standards have diminished over the past thirty years.

Another change occurred that is presented concerns. In the 1970s and earlier, schools of social work faculties came from years of direct social work practice. No one had a Doctorate Degree. With the development of Doctoral programs, many felt undue emphasis was being placed on research and writing rather than direct practice. Obtaining a Doctorate necessarily reduced the time spent as a practitioner. More-and-more, the Council on Social Work Education judged schools of social work by their academic accomplishments in research and their contributions to the literature rather than on their knowledge and experience in direct practice.

Seitz feels that the movement towards psychotherapy and one-on-one private practice of social workers is based on the economic realities of the past thirty years. The social work job opportunities were and are in the clinical area. He wonders if we can train good psychotherapists in two years as generic practitioners when they will likely enter private practices afterwards without staff development and supervision.

Lastly, Seitz believes that the community organization and group work jobs may be lost to social work. Many are now filled by people from a wide variety of educational backgrounds including history, political science, health care administration, English, etc. Seitz wonders if social work has lost its credibility as the best source of education and training in these methods. Social work's emphasis on the importance of group work and community organization for social reform may have been forgotten in today's social work education." [13]

Social Agencies by Year

1962

Long Island Home

During the 1960s, Long Island Home began construction on a new modern facility to replace Greenwood Hall. In 1966, the new building, Valentine Hall (named for then Board President, Alfred Valentine) was dedicated. During this time, there was a growing worldwide interest in the potential use of LSD for the treatment of mental illnesses and addictions. Consequently, in 1965, South Oaks Foundation sponsored an International Conference on LSD and Psychotherapy, which was attended by more than 300 psychiatrists from the United States, Canada, and Europe. The hospital also helped the local community to organize and fund a low-cost, nonprofit community mental health clinic.[14]

The Rauch Foundation

The foundation was established to focus on areas where it felt it can have the greatest impact: Children and families, the environment, and regional leadership. A comprehensive approach to problem solving was adopted with organizational activities extending beyond traditional grant-making to include research and communications efforts. The foundation's work is guided by its entrepreneurial roots by Philip Rauch Sr., an automotive engineer and the inventor of the hose clamp, a small part that played a big role in the growth of the auto industry. His two sons, Philip Rauch Jr. and Louis Rauch, created the foundation to support a wide range of educational and social causes. [15]

For a more in depth picture of the foundation's work, see Nancy Rauch Douzinas's profile in Part III.

1963

> Lincoln Lynch, head of Long Island's CORE, leads a march in West Hempstead in 1963 to call for more jobs for minorities at local employers such as Sealtest Dairy and Meadowbrook National Bank

© January 8, 1966 Newsday LLC

Junior League of Long Island

The league changed its name to the Junior League of the North Shore of Long Island and was accepted as a member of Association of Junior Leagues International. [16]

1964

News Story

In **"Sit-ins Push for Rental of Apartment to Negro," (February 8, 1964)**, *Newsday* reporters John Clark and Ernie Volkman describe a civil rights sit-in by black and white picketers protesting the refusal of a Huntington apartment owner who refused to rent to a Negro woman. Joyce Insolia, representing the Huntington Committee on Human Rights, said that: "A formal complaint" would be made to the State Commission on Human Rights under provisions of the state's Metcalf-Baker Fair Housing Law.

Community Action Agencies (CAAs) were founded under the Economic Opportunity Act of 1964 to fight poverty by empowering the poor in the United States. CAAs were intended to promote self-sufficiency, depending heavily on volunteer work, from low-income communities and depend heavily on federal funding which comes primarily from the Community Services Block Grant (CSBG) program. Each CAA has a board consisting of at least one-third low-income community members, one-third public officials, and up to one-third private sector leaders. CAAs are engaged in a broad range of activities that include promoting citizen participation, providing utility bill assistance and home weatherization for low-income individuals, administering of Head Start pre-school programs, job training, and operating food pantries. While it is commonly remembered that the Economic Opportunity Act was established with the leadership of President Lyndon Baines Johnson and the advocacy of Dr. Martin Luther King, it is often forgotten that the actual act was written by New York Congressman Adam Clayton Powell. In 1964, Governor Nelson Rockefeller created the Office of Economic Opportunity to supervise the distribution of federal anti-poverty funds with the funds being distributed to the state department of social welfare, the department of mental hygiene, and the division for youth.[17]

The Economic Opportunity Commission of Nassau County (EOC of Nassau)

The EOC of Nassau County story is a story not only of social services but of social action as well.

In Nassau County, the first grant received under the Act was awarded in 1964 by Nassau County Executive Eugene Nickerson to the Nassau Health and Welfare Council (NHWC) which was instructed to establish a committee of leaders to develop Nassau's anti-poverty program consisting of one-third government appointees, one-third local agencies and one-third representatives of the poor. The plan called for organizing neighborhood service centers in the ten poorest communities. The NHWC hired Steven Angell, a social worker and NHWC's Executive Director, as the part-time Director of the Economic Opportunity Commission.

In measuring a locality's poverty rate, federal anti-poverty officials measured poverty by four criteria: the number of people under the poverty level; the number of people living in overcrowded housing conditions; the number of people over 25 years of age with less than an eighth-grade education; and the number of families living in poverty.

The Economic Opportunity Commission of Nassau County, Inc. (EOC of Nassau) is a community action agency devoted to facilitating and strengthening basic social relationships between individuals, groups, and social institutions in Nassau County. In discharging such responsibilities it adopted the following credo:

- EOC of Nassau will participate in the mobilization of the community for support in the fight for the elimination of poverty; and
- In organizing necessary services when indicated to achieve that end;
- And in involving the community in the planning and execution of these programs;
- EOC of Nassau must critically examine programs designed to eliminate poverty to insure that they do not limit or deny benefits to any impoverished person.
- EOC of Nassau shall educate and provide technical assistance to the poor and assist them to organize themselves; to raise strong articulate voices around issues that affect their lives; to understand that they do have the power to affect change through voting power; to exercise their franchise to participate in government by affecting the political decisions being made; and to participate from water, sewer and school district levels to the village, town, county, state and federal levels.
- EOC of Nassau will attempt to develop locally-owned and/or controlled industrial and commercial enterprises in the poverty target communities which will employ the people in those communities; assure that the economic life of that community continues beyond 5PM (close of business) and assure that profits and wages are recycled within the communities, thereby having an impact upon the social and physical life of those communities.
- Our primary focus will be to uphold the principle that those citizens who will benefit directly from programs should be realistically involved in the planning and operation. We will also urge that disadvantaged people's potential for contributing to programs formulated for them and the greater community, be recognized and accepted as a means of ending their isolation, economically, psychologically and physically, from the larger society.
- As a Community Action Agency, primarily concerned with Community Organization, EOC of Nassau has a special responsibility to motivate other community social agencies and institutions to enlist the participation of deprived and alienated members of Nassau County in plans and programs, for successfully dealing with social problems, and problems of poverty.
- The anti-poverty programs, under the Federal Economic Opportunity Act, have general been viewed by our citizens as the singularly responsible agency, in relation to poverty. We must work towards having that concern shared by leaders in every sector of the population, in order to effect lasting and permanent social change.

- We agree that the larger goals for the conquest of poverty in this country must be shared, and sought by its leaders. Not only in the federal government, but by state, city, county, and village government also.
- However, business industrial and citizen's leaders of each community must also share in this effort the change to be sure that it is making its maximum contribution to helping people attain a satisfying and useful life. EOC of Nassau must actively assist in the direction and nature of such change.

The basic EOC of Nassau purpose summarized in the above *Credo* was substantially lost in the Nixon and Reagan administrations. In fact, the very name of the federal program was changed from the Economic Opportunity Act to the Community Service Act which proved to be the death knell for the act repealed in 1981 by President Ronald Reagan as part of the Omnibus Reconciliation Act of 1981.

The EOC board, recognizing that poverty could only be eliminated if poor people could earn decent income, formed the Community Economic Development Corporation (CEDC) as the economic development arm of the organization as well as a chartered Federal Credit Union. Buildings were purchased to house full-service community centers, child development Head Start centers, a weatherization warehouse and distribution center and affordable housing through a program of renovation and new construction. A drug prevention program funded with federal and state was launched in 1971 and an energy pilot program was launched which became a nationwide weatherization program. In addition, EOC's Head Start program expanded from a part-time basis to a full-year, full-day program while thousands participated in a daily local feeding program. Each center had an emergency food pantry, programs for the elderly, and jobs programs. The advent of the HIV crisis saw the development of education and counseling programs.

In 1970, EOC hired John L. Kearse as its CEO. Kearse served the organization for over thirty years providing creative and inspirational leadership. During the late 1970s to late 1980s, a great deal was done to build the organization. Community-controlled boards of directors were established for both the EOC and its credit union and a Dr. Martin Luther King, Jr. Scholarship Fund were established as was the Luenetta E. Miller Retirement Plan for EOC Nassau staff members. A Community Action Agency Insurance Group was established as an employee health plan. EOC and its delegate affiliates became the first drug-free program in Nassau County. [18]

News Story

Newsday reporter Adrian J. Meppen wrote **"Form United Fund in Nassau, Suffolk," (May 14, 1964)** discussing the official launch of an effort "to combine all Nassau and Suffolk health and welfare appeals into a single annual joint drive." David Kadane, a member of the United Fund's organizing committee indicated that the fund "could raise from $12M to $17M a year compared with $7.5M raise now in individual drives." Meppen indicates that the Long Island Fund was first conceived in April 1962 by a committee of the Health and Welfare Council.

Economic Opportunity Council of Suffolk County (EOC of Suffolk)

Suffolk County began its War on Poverty program in 1964. After the federal Office of Economic Opportunity accepted Suffolk County as a local planning and action region eligible to receive funding, the county board of supervisors passed the necessary legislation. County Executive H. Lee Dennison appointed a county-wide committee to launch and oversee any programs that might be approved by OEO. EOC of Suffolk soon became an independent nonprofit agency working with local people to establish community action programs each with its own opportunity center. Joyce Turner was EOC of Suffolk's first elected chairperson.

Once EOC of Suffolk was established as a legal entity, it was required to work with relevant county departments to identify what became known as 'poverty target areas,' based on socioeconomic and demographic criteria. A prime federal requirement was that the "maximum participation of those served" be assured with "the goal of producing lasting institutional change." OEO's concerns were in the development of community organization, job and manpower development, education, legal aid, housing, and health.

Funding was appropriated to provide children from low-income families with a preschool experience to give them an equal opportunity for success in the public school system. The first Head Start programs operated for approximately six weeks during summer times. They were located in Riverhead, Greenport, East Hampton, Southampton, Central Brookhaven, Amityville, Wyandanch, Bay Shore and Brentwood and were considered "pilot projects". The programs were so successful, that funding was appropriated for full year programs.

EOC of Suffolk's first federally-funded Head Start program in Brookhaven town was established due to the initiative of town supervisor Charles Dominy who had been approached Patchogue attorney, Victor Yannacone. Yannaccone had an early childhood development proposal that he had secured from a program operating in Maryland. The EOC of Suffolk asked the Board of Cooperative Educational Services (BOCES) to prepare the proposal for submission to OEO. A grant was approved to support the Brookhaven town Pre-Kindergarten program, the first Head Start grant funded agency. This center became EOC of Suffolk's model to replicate in its other community action agencies. By 1968, there were twelve Head Start programs and summer programs. [9]

Yours Ours Mine (YOM)

YOM is a Levittown-based, multi-service organization that began with the legal name the "Youth Direction Council of Levittown and Island Trees." Since the organization is based in what is commonly-known as America's first suburb, it is important to trace Levittown's history of social action and social services.

The Levittown housing complex welcomed its first residents in 1947 and grew rapidly. The story of racism in Levittown is described in Chapter II. According to a number of articles published in 1951 by a local newspaper, residents were active in community affairs through the development of a Youth Commission partially funded by a referendum approved by Levittown taxpayers that also funded the Levittown Psychological Center as part of the school district's adult education program.

Another newspaper, published by the Levitt Corporation, was distributed to resident families. The paper chronicled community events for many years but it did a lot more than that editorially. Naturally, it also had a vested interest in promoting Levittown as a great place to live. In 1951, *The Eagle* wrote several articles about the need for new recreational programs for young people. Levitt's paper wrote strong criticisms regarding The *Eagle's* description of recent events concerning youth in the community, saying "what seems evident is that William Levitt was fearful that the stories cast a negative image of Levittown. We realize that Bill Levitt has an investment to protect in Levittown. So do we. It is going a little too far, however, for his paper, through innuendo and lifting sentences out of context, to change the meaning and intent of our careful analysis of a problem of recreation, not delinquency.

By 1956, the school district's adult education program had begun a recreational and educational program for older residents in the district. In 1964, Yours Ours Mine was incorporated as a nonprofit, membership corporation to provide multi-faceted human service organization. It replaced The Youth Direction Council. In 1969, YOM hired James Edmondson, a former caseworker at the county human rights commission, youth worker at the county shelter, and director of the Roosevelt Youth Center and the Martin Luther King Center in Long Beach. Over the following years, through securing of county and state funding opportunities and growing community support, Edmondson established the YOM community center and substantially expanded YOM services to include children's and adult day care, substance abuse treatment, a marriage and family counseling center, and senior nutrition and transportation. Edmondson retired in 1999. [20]

Notes: Chapter IV

1. United States Census Bureau: www.census.gov.
2. Lee E. Koppelman, interview of March 7, 2014, Stony Brook NY.
3. Information obtained from agency's website: www.pinebarrens.org.
4. Information obtained from agency's website: www. Northshorechildguidance.org.
5. Information obtained from organization's website: www.discoverjcc.com.
6. "Form United Fund In Nassau, Suffolk" *Newsday*, May 14, 1964.
7. Information obtained from agency's website: www.townwidefund.org.
8. Information obtained from agency's website: www.ucp-suffolk.org.
9. Louise Skolnik, telephone interview of March 26, 2014.
10. Abraham Lurie, interview of April 10, 2014, Floral Park, NY.
11. Susan Bendor, telephone interview of April 30, 2014.
12. Jerry Tavel, telephone interview of April 28, 2014.
13. Martin Seitz, interview of April 10, 2014, Great Neck, NY.
14. Information obtained from agency's website: www.longislandhome.org.
15. Information obtained from agency's website: www.rauchfoundation.org.
16. Information obtained from organization's website: www.jlli.org
17. Information obtained from U.S. Government Printing Office website: www.gpo.gov.
18. Leone Baum, interview of January 29, 2014, Hempstead NY.
19. Collection of the Suffolk Community Council, (Special Collections and University Archives at Stony Brook University and November 19, 2014 interview with Joyce Moore Turner).
20. Collection of Yours Ours Mine, (Special Collections of the Levittown Public Library).

Chapter V: 1965-1969

Overview

Vietnam War. Civil Rights Struggles. Counter Cultural Movement. Women's Movement. Disability Rights Movement. Medicare and Medicaid. Equal Employment Opportunity Commission. Older Americans Act. Kerner Commission. Assassination of Dr. Martin Luther King, Jr.

1965 saw the development of the Nassau-Suffolk Regional Planning Board which was partly the result of considerable advocacy by members of the League of Women Voters (LWV) who were concerned about the late 1950 land scandals discussed in Chapter III. The League issued a 125-page report on the situation that included a recommendation that Suffolk's charter be re-written to establish an elected, full-time executive and legislative branches of government. The report emphasized the importance of planning and urged the establishment of an independent, professional, planning function. Town leaders strongly opposed the report's recommendations but *Newsday's* forceful daily coverage of the situation convinced the public to overwhelmingly support the charter revision's plans in 1959. At that time, a coordinator was appointed by the Board of Supervisors to fill the executive function described in the LWV report. [1]

News Story

A sign of the times with regards to political attitudes towards public assistance is suggested in a1965 *Newsday* story **(March 1, 1965)** in which the welfare commissioner is asked by John V.N. Klein, a member of the county board of supervisors to hire investigators to expose welfare fraud. Commissioner DiNapoli indicated that such investigators were not necessary because the number of cheats was infinitesimal. Klein also criticized the county's new anti-poverty program saying that it should be first directed to unemployed white collar workers.

The following four feature stories describe part of the Long Island cultural and social service/social action scene in the mid-late 1960s. One was written by a former deputy county executive; two were written by former social service commissioners; and one written by a community organizer and admission director at the School of Social Welfare at Stony Brook University.

The first story is told by Evelyn Roth, former Suffolk Deputy County Executive in the Patrick Halpin administration and director, Federation Employment Guidance Services (FEGS)/Long Island Division.

Evelyn Roth was raised in the Bronx at a time when women did not pursue careers other than in teaching, nursing, or secretarial work. Her father told her that education was the only career for a woman. She recalls watching Yankee games from her bedroom apartment until they built an outfield wall preventing her view which was a big disappointment to her.

Roth graduated from high school in 1959 at age 16 from City College of New York with a Degree in Education . She then took a teaching job in Harlem. She acquired her interest in politics at City College. Roth quit the substitute teaching job after three days confirming that she really did not want to teach. Today, she thinks that she was probably rebelling against her father who said that teaching was the only career for a woman. Being a good writer and wanting to be a career woman, Roth found work at a public relations firm. She soon married and had her first child, a son, after which the family moved to the suburbs into the Westbury section of Levittown.

In thinking about the politics of Nassau County in 1969 after she left New York City, Roth could not believe how much control the Republican Party had. She attended a civic association meeting when Fran Purcell was county executive with the former county board of supervisors. She recalls being shocked at Purcell's attitude at the civic association gathering. Basically, Roth recalls, Purcell said that "things work so well in Nassau County because everyone lives where they want to be, the whites with the whites and the blacks with the blacks. It is just fine and dandy." County employees were required to give 1% of their annual salaries to the Republican Party. Everything was determined by the county board of supervisors which was controlled by the Republican Party.

The following story is told by Joseph Barbaro, the former director of the Nassau County Department of Social Services from 1965-1971. It paints a vivid picture of the nature of politics and social welfare during this period.

In 1965, Joseph Barbaro, then head of Catholic Charities, was invited to a meeting with then-county executive Eugene Nickerson and Democratic leader Jack English. Nickerson was Nassau's first Democratic County Executive. Barbaro was offered the position of commissioner of the county's department of social services. Barbaro made it clear that if he accepted the job, he would professionalize the department and not be swayed by political influences. They offered him the job and he accepted it. Nickerson honored the agreement.

Upon accepting the position, Barbaro met with its top staff. One of them was the director of the A. Holly Patterson Home where he was provided with a home and many conveniences. Barbaro could see that these circumstances made him a political target but nonetheless he remained director of A. Holly Patterson Home throughout his term at the home.

Barbaro then asked the deputy director, a political appointee, if he wanted to become social service commissioner to which the deputy claimed he did not. Barbaro, knowing from his clinical experience that this wasn't a truthful answer, responded by saying that, if he did not want his job, he did not want him as his deputy. Barbaro was aware that his deputy had close contacts with politicians and had been hiring based on patronage decisions. After Barbaro, made it clear to the deputy that he, the commissioner would make all hiring decisions, the deputy went on to serve Barbaro well, handling day-to-day operations.

In his first week as social services commissioner, the Children's Shelter became a hot potato in the press when a shelter staff member was alleged to have had sex with one of the children. The district attorney, a Republican used the incident to take shots at democrat Nickerson. At the time, the shelter's director reported directly to Nickerson so Barbaro met with the county executive and urged him to place the Shelter under the social services department as was the case in many jurisdictions. Barbaro told Nickerson that he would professionalize the shelter which would protect his from incidents of this nature. Nickerson supported Barbaro's recommendation. Barbaro took other steps to improve conditions, policies, and procedures at the shelter.

Barbaro, recognizing the importance of hiring top-notch deputies for the department as a whole, brought in Irene Dwyer to manage many day-to-day staff issues and hired an black attorney in the peak of the black revolution, Barbaro wanted a black person on his top staff so he hired John Gregory, a future professor of law, to become an expert in welfare law. Gregory was respected by the black community and provided Barbaro with good insights about the black community and the black power activities against the department taking place in the mid and late 1960s.

Barbaro was an active member of the New York State Public Welfare Association. All of the upstate commissioners were political appointees who had little regard for social service recipients. He recalls that one commissioner had guard dogs protecting them in their offices. During this period, the name of the departments throughout the state was changed from "welfare department" to 'social services department.' Barbaro made a point of becoming an expert in welfare law spending many evening hours reading and learning the regulations. He became known as the 'liberal' in the commissioner group. With his knowledge of social service law and issues, Barbaro advised many democrats on current and future issues and became the president of the New York State Welfare Association.

Two other reforms that Barbaro undertook in the late 1960s and early 1970s were the establishment of a recipients' advisory committee and the cessation of the institutionalization of people with cerebral palsy at A. Holly Patterson facility. Barbaro loaned hospital furniture to a cerebral palsy, nonprofit group that enabled them to provide needed care.

Barbaro recalls that the department was often picketed by demonstrators during this period in one case they took over his office. This upset him knowing that he was instituting reforms that often went unappreciated. Frequently, there were demonstrations in the department's lobby and, on one occasion, his office. He arranged for policemen to be present. When he found out that many of the picketers were students at Adelphi's School of Social Work, Barbaro called Joe Vigilante, Adelphi's dean to express his frustration but, naturally, no action was taken to stop the students protesting. With the police present, picketers never took over his office again.

Barbaro's five-year term ended in 1971 so he sought other opportunities outside of government. He was approached by Lou Milone, the director of the county probation department, to find out if he wanted to remain as commissioner when Ralph Caso, the recently-elected Republican county executive came into office. Milone said that he should 'simply have a conversation with county Republican leader Joseph Margiotta.' Barbaro told him he wasn't interested in having such a conversation and returned to a position with Catholic Charities."

The following story is told by James Kirby, the commissioner of the Suffolk County Department of Social Services from 1965-1983.

James Kirby was raised in Kings Park by his Scottish father and English mother. His father immigrated to America in 1924 as a soccer player after years working in Scottish coal mines. His mother and father moved to Kings Park and took jobs in Kings Park State Mental Hospital. Kirby earned average grades as a student and a three-star athlete at Kings Park High School. His father was active in community affairs and served as a Democratic committeeman. Kirby was an altar boy at St. Joseph's R.C. Church. He worked part-time in grocery stores while in school. Upon graduation, Kirby considered a career as a physical education teacher but decided to join the Navy for two years after graduation in 1945.

Upon leaving the Navy, Kirby entered a three-year registered nursing program at Pilgrim State Hospital and later took courses in health care administration at Adelphi College where he earned a B.S. Degree in 1959. In 1963, he accepted a position at the Suffolk County Home and Infirmary for the Aging in Yaphank as deputy commissioner of public welfare in Suffolk County. In this position, he was responsible for the County Infirmary and Children's Shelter.

Kirby served in the deputy position for two-and-a-half years after which time, the commissioner, Richard Di Napoli, was elected as a State Assemblyman. Kirby, with his administrative experience running the Infirmary and the Shelter, and his B.A. Degree, became the likely heir to the commissioner position. However, Suffolk County Executive H. Lee Dennison wanted to appoint his first deputy, Anne Mead, to the post, a position that Mead very much wanted. At the time, the county had a board of supervisors whose approval Dennison needed to approve the appointment. The board was controlled by Republicans so, despite Dennison's wishes, the position was given to Kirby. Kirby sees politics as a 'give-and-take situation.'

Becoming commissioner in 1965, Kirby reported directly to Mead which was initially awkward but Mead and Kirby respected one another. As commissioner, Kirby was on call on a seven-day week basis. Initially, Kirby felt some resistance to his leadership upon the part of some of the social workers in the department who had been there for many years and wanted a commissioner with a Social Work Degree. He feels that this resistance dissipated as he demonstrated his administrative abilities and his efforts to provide good services to the department's clients.

Soon after assuming the commissioner position, Kirby appointed Mary Gordon, Director of Family Services and a highly-regarded professional social worker, as his deputy. Kirby describes Gordon as 'extremely loyal and dedicated. She only used half a sick day in her 45 years of public service. Mary was my right arm in the daily operation of the department. She was so knowledgeable,' says Kirby.

At the time, each of the ten town welfare offices made their own decisions about residents' eligibility for the home relief program while the county administered the program called Aid to Dependent Children (ADC) program. Seeing inevitable conflict in this situation, one of Kirby's first actions was to meet with each of the town supervisors to understand how their welfare offices functioned. The local Departments of Social Services recommended changes in the social services' law with the result that the counties took over the home relief program entirely.

Kirby became commissioner during a time of great conflict and upheaval in American life. It was a period of confrontations between youth and "the establishment," racial confrontations, anti-war protests as well as protests against governmental institutions including the department of social services. Picketing, demonstrations, and confrontations were almost daily occurrences at the department sometimes involving police protection of the commissioner and departmental staff. Kirby recalls that protesters also picked in front of his home with signs and banners.

Groups like People for Adequate Welfare, consisting of welfare recipients, community activists, and social workers were upset with the department's policies and the way clients were treated. More establishment groups under the auspices of The Suffolk Community Council vocally pleaded with Kirby and legislators for expanded benefits and services. Kirby was viewed as the 'enemy' to many public assistance recipients and advocates. Kirby acknowledges that it wasn't an easy time for him.

It was also a time when the federal government established the Medicare and Medicaid Programs requiring local social service departments to implement policies and procedures to implement the new programs. Under instructions from County Executive John V.N. Klein, Kirby was tasked with decentralizing the department of social services which would result in the removal of public assistance decisions from caseworkers and into a separate division of its own. Under decentralization, caseworkers focused on client services. Many social workers felt that public assistance decisions should remain under their domain and unsuccessfully fought for the continuation of current policies.

Day care services for working people were always one of Kirby's highest priorities but found considerable resistance from the county board of supervisors. He advocated before the board to establish county-run day care centers in Wyandanch, North Bellport, and Riverhead to enable mothers on welfare to hold full-time jobs. Kirby indicated that the centers might mean a reduction in the welfare budget. He felt that the centers were especially needed in Wyandanch, North Amityville, Riverhead, and North Bellport and that the state would pay 50% of the costs. He indicated that there were 5,600 widowed, divorced, or abandoned mothers on welfare. Kirby recalls attending the dedication of the Wyandanch Day Care Center where he met Rachel Robinson, the widow of baseball icon Jackie Robinson, one of Kirby's favorite baseball players.

Another critical issue facing the county in the 1970s was the deinstitutionalization of the three state psychiatric hospitals located in Suffolk County, Pilgrim State, Kings Park, and Central Islip. Kirby was very concerned about the situation and arranged to visit The Bay Bright Hotel in Bay Shore along with the press. Kirby was so upset by the filth and depravity he witnessed that he vomited. Kirby continued to try to convince state officials to slow the removal of patients until proper planning and structures were in place.

When asked if there was political interference when he needed to hire top-level staff, Kirby reported that he was usually able to hire people based on their credentials but there were times when political the pressure was great. In one instance, a top social services official and political referral, representing Kirby who was out of town, was quoted in the press, upon the tragic death of a social services client: "You have to die some time." Kirby fired the person the next morning and was supported by County Executive Klein.

Later in his tenure, Peter Fox Cohalan was elected county executive and soon asked for the resignation of all of his department heads. Kirby, as commissioner of social services, by state law had a five-year term, so he sent a nice letter to Cohalan, informing of the situation. According to Kirby, Cohalan delegated a great deal to his Deputy County Executives Howard De Martini and Frank Jones, who were "hard-nosed" political operatives. Kirby did have an ally in the Cohalan administration with John Gallagher, Cohalan's Chief Deputy.

In 1983, Kirby retired after a seventeen-year term which remains the longest term for a social service commissioner in Suffolk County. During his tenure, Kirby served as a member of Kings Park Psychiatric Center, the Suffolk County Charter Revision Commission, and the Suffolk County Mental Health Board. He is past president and director of Transitional Services of New York for Long Island, past president and director of the New York Public Welfare Association, a past chairman of the Advisory Board for the Handicapped for the Town of Smithtown, and a past member of the Community Advisory Board of St. John's Episcopal Hospital.

Kirby is married with two children and lives in Smithtown where he was engaged in many civic and community activities including the Smithtown Fire Department, the Father Seyfried Council of Knights of Columbus, the Smithtown Booster Club, and Smithtown Elks."

The following story is told by Tom Williams. Williams' experiences as a community organizer and director of admissions at the School of Social Welfare at Stony Brook University, portray the thinking and activities of many socially-concerned people from the late 1960s who pursued a distinguished career in public and private social welfare agencies

"As a young person growing up on Long Island I was not particularly aware of social problems here. My father worked at Brookhaven National Laboratory and we lived in the Village of Bellport, a pretty enclave on the South Shore. We went to Vermont to live with my grandmother for the summer and I was raised under idyllic circumstances.

"Some measure of social awareness was there however. My parents did not join the 'Old Inlet Club' on Fire Island because they had exclusionary policies. I knew students that lived in North Bellport, on the 'other side' of the railroad tracks although I did not know them well; we were two separated communities within the same school district. My parents always approached issues with fairness and understanding. My father as a scientist always looked at both sides of things. He always wanted to understand what made things work.

"I was sent away to private school and then to Williams College where I graduated with a Bachelor's Degree in Biology in 1961. The 'Science of Life' it was called, and yet I was not sure that I was cut out to be a scientist. So I applied for and got a job with the New York City Department of Welfare as a caseworker. My first assignment was in Harlem in the St. Nicholas Welfare Center. In New York in that job I saw and experienced the life of the very poorest of the poor, people who could not easily pull themselves out of poverty. So I became more dedicated to helping as I could.

"I joined Social Work Action for Welfare Rights and the Welfare Rights Organization and we organized to make the Welfare system more humane to the people it was supposed to be helping. I was part of a demonstration where we were arrested and jailed for the day and I was seeing a world which I had not known before.

"I enjoyed working in the field so much that I decided to go for a Degree in Social Work and focus in community organizing. After participating in social action within the school and helping to organize a student strike against the school (because the curriculum was not relevant to the needs of the people we were supposed to be helping) I got my degree in 1969.

"While at school I organized the InterSchool Council, a coalition of all seven of the schools of social work in New York. The mission of the ISC was to; 'Use student opinion and power as a positive force. The application of this force can stimulate change and help the students as well as the schools themselves, and the city as a whole, deal more effectively with the complex problem in today's society.' We were able to increase student participation in community action and focus the efforts of student placements on important and timely issues.

"My first job after graduation was a summer intern position with the National Institute for Mental Health (NIMH). I became part of a youth team that would look at 'increasing NIMH responsiveness to Youth Programs, Problems and Potentials.'

"We visited many youth mental health programs across the country to gather information for NIMH and its mental health programs. Many groups we spoke with did not want to have their names in a government report. The government was seen as 'the enemy of community development.' There was a feeling prevalent in many communities, that if one 'deviates from the norm he will be termed sick and be shut away.' Our report suggested that NIMH change its approach to communities and community mental health and seek appropriate representation from those communities and listen to what they felt were their mental health needs.

"The report surveyed over 100 community-based mental health agencies most of which were grassroots efforts to help children youth and families. Some of the most successful were intergenerational serving older adults as well. The report was successful in getting NIMH to take a closer look at their funding and how such a large federal bureaucracy could be more effective in delivering mental health services.

"Graduating with a Master's Degree in Social Work (MSW) I believed strongly in the mission of social work. To quote from the National Association of Social Workers: 'The primary mission of the social work profession is to enhance human well-being and help meet the basic needs of all people, with particular attention to the needs of those who are vulnerable, oppressed and living in poverty.' I wanted to do that. I thought that since there were few social services on Long Island but many in the City I would move back and see what I could do to work in the field.

"The year after I got my Degree in Social Work there was a 'race riot' in Bellport High School that closed it down for about three weeks. Black students wanted to have a club that addressed their concerns. The school resisted, posters of Malcolm X were put up by students, fights broke out and no one knew what to do; the police were called and the school was closed. This was one event among other thoughts that suggested that there was much to be done in the 'idyllic' suburbs of Long Island to make things better for people.

"During the heady days of developing the School of Social Welfare I also helped to organize and join a committee that was looking at the need for youth services in Suffolk County. Chaired by Anne Mead, director of the Suffolk Community Council and former deputy to the first Suffolk County Executive H. Lee Dennison, the Youth Services Coordinating Committee met for several years to see what could be done to alleviate the lives of the many young people living in the burgeoning Long Island suburbs. Members of the committee included Walter Stockton (now director of IGHL), Paul Arfin who worked in the Huntington Youth Development Association and the YMCA of Long Island, Tony Tramantano (4H Youth Development for Cornell Cooperative Extension), Dick Dina (Catholic Charities and subsequently director of Family and Children's Association), Jim Golbin from the Suffolk County Probation Department, Martin Timin of the School of Social Welfare, Mildred Kuntz, Joann Fogg, Tina Hamilton, and Barbara Strongin, of the Suffolk Girl Scout Council, Carol Tweedy, the director of Seabury Barn and other folks concerned about youth in the suburbs.

"The American dream of leaving New York City and living in the idyllic country side of Long Island did not work out for many families. Often having to work two jobs to make a living, not having many of the services they were used to in the city, poor public transportation; families were not always able to care for their children well.

"The committee determined that there were many youth needs not being met. News articles noted that 28 adolescents were found in a mass grave in Texas noting the need to deal with the problem of runaway and homeless youth. In response to this the Huntington Youth Bureau, the first municipal youth bureau in the County, established the Sanctuary Program for Runaway and Homeless Youth. Andy Casazza was a leader in the field of youth development and delinquency prevention and influential on my own thinking as well as supporting the development of a county youth bureau. Ed King and Paul Lowery as members of his staff were influential in the development of youth services in Suffolk.

"Child abuse and neglect cases were being reported in increasing numbers by the county department of social services. County Executive Peter Cohalan established the Suffolk County Task Force to Prevent Child Abuse and Neglect. He appointed Dr. Vincent Fontana, a national voice for abused and neglected children and the longtime medical director of the New York Foundling Hospital as the chairman of the Task Force and Bob Keeshan (Captain Kangaroo on television) as the vice chairman. The task force worked to establish a greater awareness of the problem and brought together the police, social services and various agencies to develop a more comprehensive approach to the problem. Paul Mc Crann, the assigned staff person from the Department of Social Services and director of the Child Protective Services Bureau, was instrumental in the workings of this task force. Cindy Pierce Lee, from Child Abuse Prevention Services was a volunteer who was also influential.

"Teen age pregnancy was identified as a problem and a blue ribbon task force was created to address this concern among youth. From this task force the Suffolk Network on Adolescent Pregnancy (SNAP) was created under the leadership of Marcia Spector. The agency brought together many individuals and groups to bring a comprehensive program to fight the problem. Today, SNAP has been merged with the EOC and continues to provide services to pregnant and parenting teens.

"The committee worked to create a county youth bureau that would coordinate youth services in the county and develop programs to comprehensively address the needs of youth in Suffolk County. Successfully prodding the county legislature to create a youth bureau, efforts were then made to develop Youth Bureaus in the towns as well to create a more comprehensive network of services.

"As part of the committee I worked to develop a youth bureau in Brookhaven Town. While the town did have a department of recreation it did not feel that other services were needed. At one Town Board meeting when presented with a request to put a stop sign at an intersection to provide a safer neighborhood, it was suggested that the parents tie their child to a tree so they would not go into the road.

"In the aftermath of the Watergate scandal there was a change in the political leadership of the town of Brookhaven and there was receptiveness to establishing a Youth Bureau to serve the wider needs of children youth and families. And as a new, young parent I became aware of the kinds of pressures on families from a new perspective that made me more committed to helping.

"The new supervisor of the town, John Randolph, created a youth task force and I became the chairman. After extensive interviews with agencies, schools, community groups and many others I wrote a report that made the case for a youth bureau in the town of Brookhaven. To quote from that report: 'The number of juvenile delinquency arrests as well as the arrest rate in Brookhaven is the highest for the county. There are many young people involved in drug and alcohol use and abuse. There is an alarming rise in the rate and number of teen age pregnancies, divorce figures, child abuse, the rising number of single parent homes, and out of wedlock births are all indications of the difficult time children are facing in their family situations... the lack of employment opportunities, vocational education are common throughout the town.'

"Having served on the town's task force to determine the need for a youth bureau I applied for the job and was appointed as the first director in the town of Brookhaven. Two new council members, Karen Lutz and Reggie Seltzer were very supportive of the new effort. Joel Lefkowitz a holdover Republican council member was also supportive and subsequently became town supervisor and supported the youth bureau in his tenure as supervisor. Over the years we developed programs based on the youth development model that built on the strengths of youth and families and worked to create community resiliency and self-sufficiency.

"Programs that worked were based on openness and cooperation. We worked hard to coordinate with other agencies and schools. It was important to address the needs of all youth not just those in poor communities. Providing services throughout such a large township was important since the whole community was contributing to support the youth bureau.

"Discovering that often agencies worked at cross purposes we developed a coordination program for child abuse cases called the Together Project. That project brought together probation, police, mental health, social services, schools and youth agencies to bring light on cases that were so complicated that no one knew the extent of the problems facing these abused children. Coordination and cooperation were keys to bringing successful solutions to these families.

"I believe my work in the child abuse sector has been very productive and helped to bring together many agencies and individuals to increase coordination and provide a better mosaic of services to children suffering from abuse and neglect. I served for twenty-five years on the child abuse prevention task force that morphed into the Task Force for the Prevention of Family Violence whose efforts resulted in the establishment of the Child Advocacy Center that coordinates reports of sexual abuse against children so that they do not have to repeat their story to many agencies and law enforcement personnel.

"I was a member of the Suffolk County Legislative Committee for Child Protection for over 25 years and chairman for most of that time. We helped coordinate programs for hospitals and medical services. We developed public service programs that raised the awareness of the problem, increased reporting and worked to provide help to parents, children and youth suffering from abuse and neglect. One of the key efforts was called 'silence breeds violence.' Keeping silent was not an option, agencies, politicians and the public needed to recognize the problem and deal with it. I think we helped with all that.

"After leaving the youth bureau after twenty-two years, I became the director of the Suffolk Community Council a coordinating agency for the nonprofit community. The council was formed in 1933 in response to the creation of the national Social Security program. At that time, many agencies wondered what their role should be after the federal government stepped in with many new programs. The council served as an information and advocacy agency for the many nonprofit social service agencies in Suffolk. It was instrumental in voicing the needs of the poor and underserved as well as to advocate for the need to support both politically and financially the agencies that served them.

"In response to the federal efforts the council, helped agencies focus their efforts on specific areas of need. Often the council would create a task force or committee that would address a specific need such as Teen Pregnancy (SNAP) and then create an agency to deal with that problem. The Suffolk Network on Adolescent Pregnancy was such a program as was the Retired Senior Volunteer Program (RSVP).

"When I left the council it was a fading organization. Coordination and advocacy were not well-funded and the Health and Welfare Council from Nassau County had made inroads to the Suffolk nonprofit community. It seemed like a merger of the two organizations would be a good idea but there were territorial issues that could not be overcome. For many years, the council had published a directory of community services that had been both an advocacy tool as well as a resource for agencies, municipalities and other community groups. However, the Middle Country Public Library had developed an online system for a Community Resource Data Base and it gradually replaced the hard copy directory.

"My final full-time position was with Cornell Cooperative Extension of Suffolk County. CCE is an agency that serves the agricultural community as well as providing programs for children youth and families. 4-H youth development, family services and many other programs were developed under the auspices of the National Land Grant College program and the extension system.

"I was interested in the idea of connecting the land with the people. There was a great deal of interest in local farming that was emerging at the time and making people more aware of where their food came from. Many children only knew that you went to the supermarket to get food. They knew little about farming and the earth. A book had come out around 2005 called *The Last Child in the Woods* by Richard Louvre, lamenting that children through their computers might know about an environmental problem across the world but did not know how to enjoy and learn from the outdoors in their own backyard. 'nature deficit disorder' it was called.

"One of my favorite projects started at CCE was called SOAR (Stewards of Our American Resources) and it provided a setting where youth referred to us from Probation Department could get an education through outdoor, experiential learning. Kids would go into a marshland, take water samples and do scientific measurements and learn science, math, and history all at the same time. We had them at the Suffolk County Farm and Education Center where they learned about growing food, raising animals and the role of agriculture on Long Island.

"Bringing children and youth together with the land was a very satisfying endeavor. It also provided an alternative education program for students who experienced trouble in the traditional classroom. Cornell Cooperative Extension offered many such alternative programming for children, youth and families.

"In retirement, I still work in the field of social work, teaching and supervising students from schools of social work in the area, through their field placements, about the profession of social work and social change. Working for the Economic Opportunity Council, it is satisfying to see young students becoming professionals and learning about the social service system of today.

"I also continue to be involved in land preservation and trying to lessen the alienation between the suburbs and the environment. Through work with the Post-Morrow Foundation in Brookhaven hamlet and the Peconic Land Trust serving all of Long Island and working to preserve farmland and open space, it continues to be a satisfying life.

"Working in the political world was sometimes treacherous and difficult. There were always budget battles to be fought and so it was important to develop community support for programs. With the support of parents, schools and communities the town and the county were convinced that there was a constituency there to support these programs and it was worth their while to continue to fund them.

"It is discouraging today to see the lack of confidence in government-supported programs to meet the needs of children, youth and families. The days in the 1960s, 1970s and 1980s saw a great growth in these programs and tremendous involvement of community support that made them successful. Coordination, cooperation and education were keys to that success."

Long Island's State Mental Hospitals and their Deinstitutionalization

Amidst Long Island's white sand beaches, productive farmland, Nassau County's Gold Coast, and Levittown-cookie cutter/shopping malls, there were three state hospitals housing over 30,000 human beings. These hospitals were Pilgrim State Hospital, Central Islip State Hospital, and Kings Park State Hospital. They housed people since the late 19th century. Conditions at these three facilities are painted in Lucy Winer's film "Kings Park."

> "On June 21, 1967, at the age of 17, Lucy Winer was committed to the female violent ward of Kings Park State Hospital following a series of failed suicide attempts. Over 30 years later, now a veteran documentary filmmaker, Lucy returns to Kings Park for the first time since her discharge. Her journey back sparks a decade-long effort to face her past and learn the story of the now abandoned institution that once held her captive. Her meetings with other former patients, their families, and the hospital staff reveal the painful legacy of our state hospital system and the crisis left by its demise.

> "They were very much alike - forbidding buildings and massive brick complexes - out of ear shot and hidden from view. These are the state hospitals where individuals deemed 'mentally ill' were compelled to live out their lives. Established in 1885 and closed in 1996, Kings Park State Hospital on Long Island, New York, warehoused over 9,000 patients at its height in the 1950s.

> "Stories are shared of the often brutally executed 'emptying out' of the hospital, and we follow Lucy in her effort to see how mental health care has changed since the hospital's close. Scenes shot at small mental health care centers, committed to the recovery of their members despite limited resources; let us see the kind of progress that is being made. In contrast, footage shot at the local jail reveals a very different reality - where the penal system has replaced the state hospital as the default 'provider' for people with serious mental illness." [2]

Author's Reflections

In 1965, I returned from two years living and working as a Peace Corps volunteer in Colombia South America as part of a rural community development project. Upon my return, I saw America through very different eyes and wanted to enter a career serving the community addressing issues of poverty. After a one-year job in Washington DC with an international youth development organization, I returned to Long Island to find employment. My reading during the period was about social issues including books by Malcolm X, Franz Fanon, and Eldridge Cleaver.

I felt that there was plenty of poverty and social problems on Long Island so that I did not need to relocate to do the kind of work I wanted to do. I accepted the position of director of a new youth center in Huntington and got involved with youth and family service and human rights organizations. I participated in the many local protest activities and attended the Poor Peoples' Campaign in Washington DC in 1967. I enjoyed the camaraderie I found with like-minded people who wanted to be part of the social change and countercultural movement of the times. I thought everything was possible despite the fact that I, and others like me, were viewed as unrealistic "do-gooders" who did not appreciate the economic opportunities that could be there is for the taking. My father often asked me "when are you going to get a real job?" I was treated by my relatives and many white friends as a liberal "do-gooder" who did not understand how things worked. While attending demonstrations to protest discrimination in housing, I was told by counter-protesters to "go back where you came from." Many viewed social workers having one agenda, protecting their jobs.

Social Agencies by Year

1965

Nassau/Suffolk Law Services (NS/LS)

"Nassau/Suffolk Law Services was established as the first legal service corporation program in the state. The nonprofit organization was incorporated by the Nassau County Law Services Committee to administer the legal aid services. The new corporation worked closely with the county's Economic Opportunity Commission to secure federal anti-poverty funds. NSLS began to provide free legal services as well as legal support to church, agency and grass roots organizations that work with the poor. NSLS' mission is to provide quality legal services in civil and criminal matters in a manner that respects the individual dignity of low income and disabled individuals and helps insure that they are afforded the full protection and benefits of the law. The staff is comprised of attorneys, paralegals, social workers and support staff. A social work component was established as a unique feature of the program and is based on the recognition that some of clients may need special support and services to manage and deal effectively with the legal system." [3]

<u>EOC of Suffolk</u>

The following description of the early days of EOC of Suffolk was recorded by Priscilla Redfield Roe in "The genesis of neighborhood health centers in Suffolk County: 1965-1968." Joyce Moore Turner, EOC's first chairperson added her recollections to the story in a 2014 interview.

"With regard to the development of community health centers, the challenge was how to bring affordable, comprehensive primary health care to the residents of the target areas. Alan Gartner, EOC's executive director inquired at the OEO about application requirements for demonstration grants and learned that an existing health service agency experienced in medical management and having the participation of a back-up hospital were required. EOC's health committee working closely with Dr. George Leone, Suffolk's health commissioner, Dr. Edith Forsythe, director of maternal and child health, and Mary O'Connell, a social worker, learned of an impressive Tufts Medical School program one that provided family-oriented, ambulatory primary care. Gartner proceeded to apply for available federal funding to develop the health centers.

"County Executive Dennison's next steps were to appoint a task force on hospitals & related services including his deputy Anne Mead. Joyce Turner, EOC's chairperson and Priscilla Redfield Roe were appointed to join the task force representing consumers who joined the representatives of public and private agencies. Plans were soon developed for a hospital-based program in Riverhead to provide care for seasonal farm laborers as well as a free-standing center in Wyandanch where an energetic and vocal CAP operated.

"Roe, serving as chairman of both EOC's health committee and the county task force on hospitals and related services, worked closely with county health department officials to fulfill its overall responsibility to provide health care to county residents. Roe lead efforts to identify the targeted poverty areas and engage indigenous people to join the local community action agencies, and develop the anti-poverty programs.

"The health center plan faced a challenge by the Suffolk County Medical Society that opposed the plan since it fixed fees for medical services would be set for patients. The society also disagreed with the maximum income level for consumer participation seeing it as too high and, thus, likely to reduce the number of consumers utilizing the services of private physicians.

"Fortunately, local community action agencies, especially the one in Wyandanch, were well organized. Claretha Ward, a CAP board member, used her organizing skills to mobilize residents to convince the county board of supervisors to move forward with proposed plan for health centers. This effort was aided by a tragic, catalytic event: the assassination of Dr. Martin Luther King, Jr. The county board of supervisors affirmatively approved the EOC/County Health Department/Good Samaritan Hospital plan. After the approval, Deputy County Executive Mead played an indispensable role in finding unused county funds at mid-year to carry out the necessary building conversions and drawing up the contracts between the hospital and the county.

"The task force moved forward immediately to establish a working committee. It asked Mead to identify federal and state aid. Joyce Turner, EOC's chairman, wanting to develop a way assure an ongoing county commitment to the health centers, analyzed the county's existing budget to find funds that could be transferred to support the health centers. Assistance was also secured through Dr. Edmund Pellegrino, head of the Health Sciences Center at Stony Brook University who assigned Dr. Peter Rogatz, the director pro-tem of the University Hospital and Edmund Ross to assist the task force along with Edmond Ross, a community organization specialist.

"The story of the development of Suffolk County's community health centers is testimony to the power of effective community organizing. It demonstrates how people of goodwill, despite cultural, political, and economic differences can find common purpose and accomplish lasting changes. The story demonstrates the effective collaboration of consumers and providers of health care and careful planning that they did together to work with politicians on both sides of the aisles.

"EOC of Suffolk had its problems in the early years. It experienced a number of periods in the 1960s and 1970s when there were gaps in leadership and complaints by federal officials requiring that the agency tighten its fiscal and administrative controls sometimes threatening to terminate funding to the agency's six community action centers. Such funding would leave it up to county and town officials to make up the difference with some of their revenue-sharing funds. EOCs around the nation felt that this effort would lead to the end of community action programs. They, therefore, organized their constituents and staff to oppose revenue-sharing.

"In the 1970s, threats also loomed to eliminate funding to the agency as part of efforts by the Nixon administration to abolish OEO funding of outreach programs to the poor. Threats also existed that funding for EOC's Head Start services, drug counseling, family planning, foster grandparent program, and summer free lunch program might be made part of a new revenue-sharing program, and thus, subject to year-to-year uncertainties."

The following personal story is told by John Gallagher, former Chief Deputy Suffolk County Executive and Police Commissioner. Gallagher represented the

County Executive on the EOC of Suffolk board of directors in its formative years.

Personal Story

John Gallagher

"Membership on the EOC of Suffolk board of directors, representing the county executive, afforded me a county-wide perspective that the need for job creation had to be aligned with life skills training in both minority and low-income white communities. Project Encourage, which I co-founded at Suffolk County Community College, showed that kids disadvantaged by their home environment could hope for a better future through education."

"The War on Poverty defined government's view of its role in the struggle to give equal opportunity to all citizens with health and human service needs. The federal level alone had access to resources vast enough to put a dent in a culture of poverty and discrimination that marked some communities. The Johnson initiatives are often given less credit than they deserve. Federal dollars DID improve people's lives in these decades and did help reduce the number of folks living below the poverty line, but they eventually came with a price – stifling bureaucracy. Interference in managing those programs eventually weakened their effectiveness."

Long Island's struggles affording equal rights and opportunities to blacks continued as evidenced by the following 1965 stories published in *Newsday*.

Community Action for Southold Township (CAST)

Gail Horton grew up in Southold on the North Fork of Long Island. Her father was a veterinarian with a diverse group of friends. Her North Fork childhood was filled with enjoyable experiences with both black and white children so she had not been exposed to racism. There were no black children in her school. A particular incident that she remembers is viewing an ambulance arriving near her dorm to pick up a black man who needed emergency care. She saw the ambulance driver refuse to take the injured black man to the hospital, insisting that he would have to wait for the black peoples' ambulance to arrive. This, and other similar experiences, disturbed her and left a deep impression on her.

After graduating from college in the early 1960s, Horton returned to Southold where she noticed that many of the black families who had been living in Southold for many years had moved to Greenport. At the time, Greenport had a mixed-race population one of the few such populations on Long Island. The blacks moved there because Greenport had affordable housing available after job losses occurred in the fishing and boat building industries. The exit of these workers resulted in the availability of low income housing. Some of this housing was owned by Oscar Golden, the Greenport mayor who did not maintain it well causing many problems for his tenants.

Housing was also available due to the closing of the nearby Warners' duck plants that had employed many black workers. The duck plants also employed many migrant workers who arrived seasonally from the South. Local residents were aware of the deployable living conditions present at these plants but building and health officials ignored them. The arrival of low-income blacks into Greenport, according to Horton, destabilized Greenport's middle class black community who had stable jobs and were upset with the arrival of the poor blacks with their many social problems and poor housing. Many whites also resented the new black residents.

In the mid-1960s, an elderly white couple convened a meeting at their home to discuss the arrival of the poor black families and how to help them. Reverends Ben Burn and Arthur Bryant were two of the organization's founding members. Bryant was heavily involved in the 1960s as an advocate for migrant farm workers. The group ultimately decided to form a community action organization that later affiliated with EOC of Suffolk. Horton first got involved with CAST in 1969 after she married and moved to Greenport. She got involved as a volunteer aide in the Head Start Program when Doris Wilson, a longtime Greenport resident, served as CAST's director. Horton joined the CAST board of directors as a representative of the village board at the invitation of the board, the only white person on the board. One of the issues that Horton focused on was family day care that would enable women to care for children in their homes earning needed income by operating family day care businesses. The other issue Horton that worked on was the relationship of CAST with the Eastern Farm Workers. According to Horton, they appeared to feel that CAST was usurping their place so there was friction. UFW workers disrupted some of CAST's meetings. During the late 1960s, Greenport saw its share of racial tensions especially with respect to the way that black students were treated in the schools. She feels that the faculty had little understanding of cultural differences. She discussed her concerns with school officials. According to Horton, they were steered into non-college bound courses. As a way of helping these students, an afterschool tutoring program was established by CAST.

CAST became one of EOC of Suffolk's local community action sites in the early 1970s. Bessie Swann worked for CAST as a community service worker in 1967 and in 1971 joined the Head Start program. After working at Head Start, Swann worked for the Eastern Suffolk Migrant Project and the Eastern Suffolk Federal Credit Union. Bessie Swann became CAST's director in 1979 and continued as director until around 2000 with Horton working closely with her.

Horton describes Swann as a natural leader who was respected by the community both of blacks and whites. "Bessie was smart and firm and believed in bringing people up," says Horton, "I learned a lot from her. People trusted her." Horton recalls Bessie calling her in the middle of the night to go with her downtown to try to quell racially-charged fights. Fortunately, the police chief at the time was a fair person who believed in community policing.

In one racially-charged situation in the late 1970s, Swann got caught in the middle between the U.S. Department of Justice, the NAACP, and the county human rights commission who wanted a tough stance against the school district who refused to adopt an affirmative action plan and black residents who wanted her advocacy to end. "I am a conciliator and I am neutral. But I personally feel that if Greenport's lack of racial progress keeps on, there will be some kind of explosion," said Swann in a 1981 *Newsday* article.

Besides operating the Head Start program, CAST sponsored a number of other programs during this early period including a day care program, a summer lunch and recreation program, and conducted community needs surveys. It had a number of Volunteers in Service to America (VISTA) staffers who helped the paid staff.

CAST's major initiative was the establishment of the Greenport Housing Alliance (now called the North Fork Housing Alliance) with a community development grant from the New York State Division of Housing and Renewal to undertake a series of housing rehabilitation projects. CAST also developed the Lakeside Gardens that constructed mixed use, new housing units on a former dump site. David Kapell, a future Greenport Mayor, was the community development worker at the time. CAST also managed the Section 8 low income housing program. The Housing Initiative did a great deal of good work rehabilitating deplorable housing conditions.

In the 1981 *Newsday* article, Swann said: "The black community is better informed and is beginning to realize that it must take a bigger role in the education of its children. More black kids are enrolling in academic programs and more parents are coming to CAST for assistance and the schools let CAST serve as a conduit for complaints about school activities. CAST now has courtesy notification of school and village job openings. The village drafted an affirmative action plan and hired a black woman as the second black on the village payroll." The *Newsday* article reports that Swann's organizing increased black voter registration from 87 to 290 in a two-year period.

Today, Greenport is primary populated by newcomers with second homes in the community. There has been a huge growth in the Latino community. Horton feels that CAST should be helping Latinos through advocacy and services to deal with acculturation issues that they face especially in the schools.

CAST is a very different organization concentrating on distributing food and clothing to the poor and operating a parent/child program. Community organization work and activism of the 1960s is no longer practiced. There is no political activism and CAST is not affiliated with EOC of Suffolk. [4]

News Stories

"Form Group to Aid Poor in Court Cases" (December 12, 1965) and "Legal Aid: Long Road for the Poor" by Frank Lynn **(November 19, 1965)** were *Newsday* stories describing the creation of Nassau County Law Services to provide legal counsel for poor defendants in both criminal and civil cases. The articles announced the formation of the new nonprofit organization and its plans to apply for federal funds to employ attorneys to help the poor. Adrian Cabral, associate director of the anti-poverty program indicated that they plan to launch the program early during the following year.

Family Service League (FSL)

Under the leadership of Robert Berglund from the mid-50s to the mid-60s, Jerry Edelstein from the mid-60s until 1969 and Jesse Nemtzow from the late 60s until 1985, there was a steady expansion in FSL's services and geographical spread to the East End and the South Shore. It was during this period that services were extended to the East End. Stepping Stones was developed as the first 'continuing treatment program,' a model on Long Island for mentally ill adults being discharged from Suffolk's large institutions for the mentally ill. It was in 1968 that a group of residents from the East End gathered to petition FSL to extend counseling services to the North Fork. In 1977, The West Islip Committee met with the FSL board to request help in establishing a counseling service in the South Shore. This effort resulted in a new FSL office providing individual, marital and family counseling located in the Westminster Presbyterian Church in West Islip." [5]

Community Development for Youth (CDY)

Under the leadership of Richard Shoenfeld, president of the Pickwick Organization was concerned about youth needs in the growing town. Shoenfeld was also a member of FSL's board. He spoke to FSL's executive director Robert Berglund who moved forward to secure the services of Columbia School of Social Work to conduct a study of youth needs and problems in the town and recommend a course of action. The survey results demonstrated a dramatic growth of the under-21 Township population, with 44 percent of the town's current population under age 20 and an estimated rise to 47 percent by 1970. Concern was also indicated that the rise in population could lead to increased juvenile crime. FSL decided to create a totally-separate nonprofit organization under the name, Community Development for Youth

(CDY) that was launched with Anthony Romeo as its executive director. FSL sought grant support from the Town of Huntington's supervisor and town board.

In 1966, the town of Huntington awarded a $15,635 grant to CDY using New York State Division for Youth matching funds. In early 1967, Romeo hired Paul Arfin as center director of a youth center located in a former auto dealership building in Halesite. Later that year, Romeo was dismissed by the CDY board because of differences with Romeo regarding his psychoanalytic approach to serving young people. Andrew Casazza, a School Social Worker at the Board of Cooperative Educational Services, was employed to fill the position. Casazza's employment began a series of dramatic of changes that influenced the future of youth services in Suffolk County.

Casazza was a non-traditional Social Worker with little respect for the popular Freudian approach to diagnosing individual problems. He, therefore, supervised Arfin to identify the root of problems and identify strategies to address them using community resources. He also decided that it was important to diversify CDY's programming to serve a much broader swath of Huntington's youth, not concentrating on serving the handful of acting-out youth that had made the Halesite center their haven and refuge. Casazza wanted to serve the needs of two other segments of the youth population; those who were unhappy with social conditions and wanted to serve their communities; and those that were increasingly involved in the youthful counter culture taking root in my communities with its "anti-establishment," drug using behavior, language, and political protests. Casazza understood that the town board would not continue funding CDY to serve a small group of alienated youth.

Two new initiatives were launched. A Teen Volunteer Corps was established to engage young people in summer volunteer assignments. Two hundred young people participated in summer 1967 helping the blind at the Burrwood Home, those with developmental disabilities at the Suffolk Center for Retarded Children, tutoring children at the Freedom Center. They also created new programs such as one where volunteers taught English to seasonal workers employed in the Townships nurseries and farms. These volunteers also published a weekly newspaper, The Bridge that chronicled TVC's work as well as providing opportunities for young people to express their ideas and concerns about their communities.

Under Casazza's leadership, CDY entered into an agreement to take over the Freedom Center in Huntington Station. CDY provided social work supervision to Mary Gravely, the center's longtime director and her staff. Other programs launched were a youth employment program 'YES,' and a Sunday night coffee house based in the Halesite building called 'Chicago Mollies Last Resort and Sitz Bath.' Furnished with tables made of large round wooden spools donated by LILCO and chairs, Sunday nights became a very popular venue for young people to 'hang-out,' converse, listen to folk music, discuss what was on their minds in an accepting, non-judgmental atmosphere.

Funding for CDY was eliminated in 1970 when the Town of Huntington Youth Bureau (HYB) and its related agencies and programs were established by Town Supervisor Jerome Ambro. Thus, the youth board evolved from small, CDY's pioneering youth service efforts. The youth board was established to promote the growth, development and well-being of youth and families throughout Huntington town, concentrating on those issues and problems challenging youthful residents: drugs and alcohol, juvenile delinquency, runaway and homelessness and secondary school dropouts. Programs were designed to build educational and work skills, strengthen families, and develop the sense of pride and self-worth that young people needed to thrive and succeed. HYB grew to have six local youth development centers scattered throughout the town. It became the model for town-sponsored youth services throughout Suffolk County. [6]

News Story

A *Newsday* article **"LI Readies 3 New Poverty Plans,"** (**April 15, 1965**) reported that officials in Nassau and Suffolk have developed anti-poverty plans under President Lyndon Johnson's Economic Opportunity Act. They included funding for a Neighborhood Youth Corps, a remedial education program, and Operation Head Start. Angelo Melillo, executive director of the youth services committee, a state and county-financed arm of the Nassau Health and Welfare Council, indicated that the plan was drawn up by his committee with the cooperation of the federal government and the county's economic development commission.

1966

Patrolman Donald Hagen with a cross that was burned on the grounds of Malverne High School in 1966. In the next year, Malverne implemented a school integration plan.

© August 16, 1979 Newsday LLC

Economic Opportunity Council of Suffolk

The 43- member Suffolk Economic Opportunity Commission selected Alan Gartner to become the first fulltime head of the county's anti-poverty program replacing Lou V. Tempera, the county labor commissioner who had filled the position on a part-time basis since the program was established in 1965.

Gartner, a history teacher, had been active in the civil rights movement since 1952 as a student at Antioch College. While at Antioch, he helped organize the first sit-in in the state of Ohio. He later served as aide to former national chairman of the Congress of Racial Equality, James Farmer. In that position, Gartner helped organize civil rights demonstrations in the South. [7]

The Long Island Home

A new building, Valentine Hall (named for then-board president, Alfred Valentine) was dedicated. During this time, there was a growing worldwide interest in the potential use of LSD for the treatment of mental illnesses and addictions. Consequently, South Oaks Foundation sponsored an International Conference on LSD and Psychotherapy, which was attended by more than 300 psychiatrists from the United States, Canada, and Europe. The hospital also helped the local community to organize and fund a low-cost, nonprofit community mental health clinic. Since that time Sunrise Clinic has continued to help thousands of Long Island's residents. [8]

Adelante of Suffolk County

A group of local Hispanic citizens realized a need for a stronger cultural presence. The organization's mission was to "inspire forward movement in the lives of the diverse people of the community, by promoting a deeper understanding and respect for cultural differences and similarities; by empowering young people to realize their unlimited potential; and by protecting seniors, and those with special needs, while improving their quality of life. For many years, the organization sponsored an annual parade in Brentwood that engaged all sectors of the community. Over the years, funded by contracts with county government, the organization grew as a provider of services for seniors, youth and persons with special needs." [9]

Variety Child Learning Center (VCLC)

Judith Bloch, founder of VPLC, is a pioneer and activist in the field of child development and one of the first professionals in the nation to recognize the need for early intervention in the field of special education. Bloch started VCLC with a small group of children that had been excluded from typical preschool. She established the first therapeutic pre-school for children with learning, language and behavior problems, with programs for families. She oversaw every step of the school's expansion and growth, from its one classroom beginning in Garden City to its current full service Learning Center in Syosset, providing services to thousands of children with developmental disabilities, their families and professionals, on- and off-site. She has been an advocate for national public policy changes that address the needs of children with developmental disabilities and their families." [10]

The Suffolk Community Council (SCC)

The council hired its first executive director, Anne F. Mead, an attorney and former deputy county executive under H. Lee Dennison. SCC formed a county-wide anti-poverty liaison committee to increase communication and coordination among local community agencies and also worked with other agencies to advocate for a county youth board. The council also conducted a study defining the need for a group home for youth which resulted in a home being established in Commack in 1967." [11]

1967

Economic Opportunity Commission of Suffolk County (EOC of Suffolk)

The Suffolk County Board of Supervisors voted to demand the suspension of Alan Gartner, the Suffolk Opportunity Commission's executive director and Bettye McKenzie, a commission staff member. The board also voted to conduct an investigation of Gartner and McKenzie who was accused of urging welfare recipients to demonstrate, distribute "radical literature" and defile the welfare department's headquarters building in Bay Shore. County Executive H. Lee Dennison and Joyce Turner, the commission's chairman, refused to take any action against Gartner or McKenzie. Board of Supervisors' chairman Gilbert Hanse of Babylon threatened to override a Dennison veto should he act on his pledge to do so. Due to the board of supervisors' actions, federal anti-poverty program officials warned that the entire Suffolk poverty program could be imperiled since it could be interpreted in Washington as interference by the board with the commission's legal authority. Later in the year, the Economic Opportunity Commission voted unanimously to dissolve itself and form a private nonprofit corporation so that it could function without interference by the county board of supervisors and thus free the anti-poverty program from political control and political controversy." [12]

During the late 1960s and early 1970s, *Newsday* followed the struggle by Long Island welfare recipients for better benefits and more-humane treatment by both counties' social service offices.

News Stories

In, **"The Welfare Movement: Not Dead But Exhausted,"** (1973) *Newsday* summarizes articles of October 25, 1967 when six welfare mothers sat in at the Nassau Department of Social Services' office in Mineola to protest inadequate housing; On August 7, 1969, the newspaper reported that Mrs. Luenetta Miller, a gray-haired, anti-poverty worker, lies down in the path of Governor Nelson Rockefeller's limousine during a demonstration by a Nassau welfare rights' group in Hempstead; and in February 1973, it was reported that Suffolk's welfare rights group, People for Adequate Welfare (PAW) was reorganizing after a one-year's inactivity searching for a less-militant image. In **"CORE Attacks Supes in Poverty Row," (February 13, 1967)**, *Newsday* reporter John Cummings states that CORE "charged the Suffolk Board of Supervisors with political interference in the county's antipoverty program and demanded that the board withdraw its requests for suspension of the program's executive director Alan Gartner." In another *Newsday* article regarding Suffolk poverty, **"Union Seeks LI Migrant Workers," (July 11, 1967)**, reporter Ray Larsen indicates that Cesar Chavez, president of the AFL-CIO's United Farm Workers Organizing Committee plans "to start signing up migrant workers throughout New York State this summer with particular emphasis on Suffolk County."

Then, after the riots in Newark, New Jersey occurred, *Newsday* reporters Joel Kramer and Dick McCord wrote **"Negroes Hear New Tune: Keep Long Island Cool," (July 24, 1967)** about an assembly of 700 people responded to a plea from the NAACP economic opportunity councils, urban renewal programs, human rights commissions and the Nassau County Police Department. Harold Russell, executive secretary of the Long Beach Human Relations Commission told the crowd: "We wanted to stress vote power and due process of law, and we wanted to reassure them that a lot of people do care about the poverty and discrimination in their lives."

1968

Literacy Nassau

Since its inception when it was known as Literacy Volunteers of America, Literacy Nassau has had a single and unwavering mission: to promote and foster literacy in Nassau County among adult learners in need of improved skills in Basic Literacy and English for Speakers of Other Languages. Through trained volunteer tutors in one-to-one and small group learning experiences students are matched with tutors to achieve the educational, economic and social goals they and their tutors have identified as important to them. Students are referred to Literacy Nassau by family, friends, local libraries and other community-based organizations. Volunteers are recruited from all over Nassau County. Tutors are trained, certified and supported by Literacy Nassau throughout the year." [13]

The Smithaven Ministries

During the 1960s, while Suffolk County underwent rapid population growth, major centers such as the State University at Stony Brook, Brookhaven National Laboratory, Grumman Aerospace and many more attracted employees while housing developers built large developments of single-family houses for these families. However, many of the employees could not afford the available housing Population patterns grew more and more segregated by race and by income. Civil rights organizations such as NAACP Branches,

League of Women Voters, and the Economic Opportunity Council, together with religious bodies and community groups worked to address this alarming situation by demonstrating and petitioning local governments to pass laws prohibiting housing discrimination based on race and to amend land use regulations to encourage lower-cost housing for families with low incomes. These activist groups collectively formed the Brookhaven Housing Coalition.

When a large regional shopping center, the Smith Haven Mall opened in 1969, Father Paul Ryan, a Roman Catholic priest, and Rev. David Bos, a Presbyterian minister, planned an interdenominational non-profit 'ministry in the marketplace' to be located in the Mall. Smith Haven Ministries enabled churches of all denominations on Long Island to pool their resources to offer help, primarily counseling, to people with low incomes. One major problem identified was the lack of safe, suitable housing for families with low incomes, so one portion of the Ministries was a housing office, called 'Suffolk Housing Services (SHS),' which was separately incorporated as such in 1977. Volunteers were recruited to interview home seekers as to their needs and then help them search for low-rent housing primarily through ads in local newspapers and by calling real estate offices. These activities immediately revealed widespread routine racial discrimination in the housing market as real estate agents often asked whether the home seeker was black or white to determine whether they had any leads for the family. Thus, SHS focused on identifying evidence of housing discrimination and preparing formal legal complaints to the New York State Division of Human Rights." [14]

Suffolk Housing Services (SHS)

Suffolk Housing Services informally started in 1969 as an all-volunteer group. It became an independent, non-profit, fair housing agency. The group successfully challenged real estate agencies, management companies, landlords, and owners where investigation revealed solid evidence for discrimination. The agency doggedly brought and supported major litigation challenging restrictive zoning that effectively prohibited development and opportunity for affordable housing. These zoning challenges undertaken resulted in landmark decisions and exposure of the harmful social and economic effects of such barriers. SHS conducted tests that proved that black prospective tenants were falsely denied rental housing at the Watergate Apartments in Patchogue while contemporaneously whites were encouraged. In the mid-1980s the agency became nationally acclaimed for its investigation and testing abilities with an Eastern District landmark jury award of $565,000 in favor of two black air traffic controllers.

In 1971 as part of the Brookhaven Housing Coalition, SHS helped organize a lawsuit challenging the lack of low-income housing for employees of the IRS processing center being built in Brookhaven Town. The National Committee against Discrimination in Housing (NCDH) and Suburban Action Institute provided the highly skilled lawyers and researchers for this major Federal Court challenge, and SHS' counseling records and clients provided the testimony of housing needs. Direct local impact was construction of a 431-unit complex of federally subsidized lower-rent housing and legal precedents that supported later litigation. Critical for future SHS programs was the close working relationship developed with NCDH lawyers Richard Bellman and Lewis Steel and the Suburban Action Institute director Paul Davidoff. These resources enabled SHS' strong fair housing enforcement actions over the next forty years.

Thanks to these experienced lawyers and the provisions of the 1968 Fair Housing Act, SHS had the resources to bring individual cases of racial discrimination directly to the Federal Courts. When an African American counseling client was refused housing, SHS staff sent carefully trained white volunteers to "test" whether the housing was available to them. When these investigations showed solid evidence of discrimination, the lawyers filed the lawsuits, and SHS staff and volunteers testified in the proceedings. Many of these individual cases were successfully litigated between 1975 and 1985, including a racial steering case against two real estate firms that were shown to be showing houses to white homebuyers only in all-white neighborhoods and houses to black homebuyers only in black or integrated neighborhoods.

Every individual lawsuit is extremely time-consuming. First the detailed testing and detailed affidavits and documentation, days of depositions, pre-trial motions from both sides, and many meetings, interviews and settlement discussions, as well as days of trial for those that do not settle. For example, SHS' most famous case (where a jury award of $565,000 damages was the highest award in the country at the time) was investigated over several months in 1982, filed in March, 1983 and the trial wasn't held until late June, 1984. As important as it is to uphold the civil rights of individual plaintiffs, these intensive efforts do not end segregation. That requires large challenges to government policies of systemic discrimination.

Funding the agency has always required major time and effort in writing proposals and securing grants from a variety of foundations and government sources as well as making public appeals for donations from people in the community. The need for litigation to challenge systemic discrimination was understood by the North Shore Unitarian Universalist Veatch Program which funded an SHS' Litigation Fund from 1975-1989. This enabled SHS to launch major challenges to exclusionary zoning, Suffolk Housing Services et al. v. Brookhaven and Housing Help, Inc. *et al. v.* Huntington, and abuses of the federal Housing and Community Development Act Community Development Block Grant program, Rodriguez v. HUD & Suffolk County. These cases not only set important legal precedents with impact throughout the U.S., but indirectly made it possible for private developers and nonprofit developers to gain local government approvals to build assisted complexes and homes affordable to families with lower incomes. From the beginning SHS was in active coordination with private fair housing enforcement agencies throughout the country. Working together, these agencies convinced HUD to set up a system for funding private agencies directly for fair housing enforcement work, which is still in place as a competitive contract program.

Suffolk Housing Services has grown and prospered, expanded its services into Nassau County and is now incorporated as Long Island Housing Services (LIHS). On April 30, 2013, LIHS sponsored a gala celebration in honor of the 45th year of the Fair Housing Act, at which Janet Hanson, Executive Director of SHS from 1973-1987 was asked to share some of her reminiscences from those 45 years.

> I shall begin with an admonition. KEEP A DIARY!! I cannot believe all the things that I have forgotten! When I was living them, they were so all-consuming I was sure I would never forget a single detail. So, all of you involved in fair housing and equal justice work--KEEP A DIARY!!

> And now I shall follow that admonition with a disclaimer. In this talk I will not try to play lawyer and explain the legal intricacies of the constitutional and legislative issues that the staff of Long Island Housing Services wrestles with day in and day out. Nor will I attempt to emulate Robert Schwemm with a clear scholarly history of fair housing in our country. Instead, I just want to tell you a few stories from the past 45 years.

> Forty-five years ago on, April 4, 1968. I was at choir practice in the Port Jefferson Presbyterian Church. One of my fellow choir members was Kenneth Anderson, a prominent African American civil rights community leader. Those of you who know Ken know that he has a deep, powerful, Paul Robeson-like bass voice. When Ken was at choir practice, you could hear the bass section strong and powerful. When he occasionally wasn't at practice, the bass section was hard to hear. That evening the bass section was very weak sounding, but Ken was there--I saw him. Finally our director said, "Ken. Sing out. I do not hear you." and Ken mumbled something and then said "I cannot do this. I have to leave,' and walked out with a tortured, stricken look on his face. I asked the person next to me "What is wrong with Ken?" and he said "Martin Luther King" was shot today. To me, Martin Luther King was a famous person whom I admired greatly, but I thought, "That cannot be the problem. Ken looks personally devastated!" As I got more involved in racial justice, I quickly learned what it is like to take it personally. Similar to what President Obama expressed after the

recent bombings in Boston when he said, "For millions of us, what happened on Monday is personal. It is personal!"

So one week after Martin Luther King was shot, Congress passed the Fair Housing Act--technically Title VIII of the Civil Rights Act of 1968. There are a few key facts and phrases that are important or significant to those of us for whom Fair Housing is personal. First is that efforts were made to pass fair housing legislation in 1966--but the efforts were defeated. Another attempt in 1967 also failed. But, much as it hurts to realize, Martin Luther King's assassination was what brought swift passage in one week's time.

Second, the goal of the Act was integration. When Senator Mondale proposed the Fair Housing Act, he stated the purpose is to replace the ghettos 'by truly integrated and balanced living patterns.' The Report of the National Advisory Commission on Civil Disorders commonly referred as the Kerner Commission Report--released on February 29th, 1968, had warned that 'our nation is moving toward two societies, one black, and one white— separate and unequal.' The legislative history in the Congressional Record speaks of the need to eliminate the 'blight of segregated housing and the pale of the ghetto' and that Title VIII is a way to help 'achieve the aim of an integrated society. Thus, the Act was to benefit not only blacks and other minority groups, but, 'the whole community.' Accordingly, Suffolk Housing Services' earliest stated mission was to offer a multi-faceted program dedicated to equal housing opportunity, service to the community, and the creation of racially and economically integrated housing on Long Island.

Third, lest we forget, racial segregation was strenuously enforced by the federal government and carried out openly by all facets of housing programs from 1865 when the 13th amendment abolished slavery through at least 1950 and one might argue, through 1964 when the Civil Rights Act of 1964 prohibited discrimination in federal-assisted housing programs. Zoning laws provided legally enforced zones for whites and zones for people of color. In 1917 when the court declared racial zoning to be unconstitutional, the practice of racially restrictive covenants declaring that properties could only be sold to people of the Caucasian race were widely used and even required for mortgage loans to be ensured by FHA and VA. Public housing was built in areas with concentrations of minorities and/or public housing projects were designated only for whites or only for African Americans.

So little by little racial discrimination by a government was declared unconstitutional or illegal by statute, but private discrimination- housing denials by private owners or landlords--was not prohibited until 1968- but not only by the Fair Housing Act! 1968 was a real watershed year! A case called Jones v. Mayer brought a ruling that the 1866 Civil Rights Act prohibits discrimination by private parties as well as by government. All citizens of the United States shall have the same right as is enjoyed by white citizens thereof to inherit, purchase, lease, sell, hold and convey real and personal property. These early laws were designed to 'remove the badges and incidents of slavery.' That 'peculiar institution' haunts us still today.

Suffolk Housing's first major involvement was in working for housing for families with low incomes who did not have safe, sanitary housing suitable for their needs at rents that they could afford. SHS joined a group of organizations banded together as the Brookhaven Housing Coalition with administrative support from the housing director of the Economic Opportunity Council--a man named Robert Ralph. The "cause" of housing for families with low-incomes was and, I am afraid, continues to be, an extremely unpopular cause. I have been known to acknowledge this phenomenon by simply reviewing the terms through which society has tried to somehow address the public's hostility to this desperately needed housing by progressively changing its name,-- from public housing, to subsidized housing, to low-income housing, to lower-income housing, to low-moderate income housing, to workforce housing, to affordable housing, which absent any "affordable for whom" identity is suitably meaningless for now. But I digress...

It came to pass that the Federal General Services Administration sought a site in Brookhaven Town for a large IRS processing center. However, there was a federal requirement that there be adequate low-income housing in the area to meet the needs of the IRS workers. With the expertise and legal resources of the National Committee Against Discrimination in Housing, the Brookhaven Housing Coalition sued GSA and Brookhaven seeking to enforce this requirement. Those three sentences attempt to portray an extremely complicated action lasting from 1971 to 1978 which resulted in construction of a 431-unit subsidized complex and provided significant factual and legal information and rulings that we used in subsequent major litigation for housing for lower-income families. The NCDH lawyer, Richard Bellman, remained an excellent lawyer for SHS and Long Island Housing Services from when we met him in 1971 until last year when he finally succumbed to Parkinson's Disease.

There was such hope in 1975 that we could actually be successful in eliminating exclusionary zoning. Municipalities have the power to zone land providing for what kind of development can be allowed on it. This power is subject to the state constitution and is to be used for the "general welfare,"--not just the welfare of the affluent. Both New

York and New Jersey have this "general welfare" standard in their constitutions. In 1975 the highest court in New Jersey handed down a far-reaching standard for constitutional zoning called the "Mount Laurel Doctrine." And that same year the highest court in New York handed down what is called the "Berenson Doctrine." Both doctrines in simplest of layperson terms say that municipalities must use the zoning powers that affect housing in such a manner as to enable housing that will meet the needs both for their residents and to take into consideration housing needs in their region. And with this hope, Suffolk Housing Services v. Brookhaven was filed. Fifteen years later, the Court of Appeals ruled that they could not or would not take on the task of overseeing the zoning of Brookhaven Town to ensure the 'general welfare.' Exclusionary zoning maintains segregated living patterns, and the efforts to eliminate such policies run into very powerful barriers. We did have significant success in challenging a blatant and egregious zoning ordinance in the Town of Huntington in the case of Huntington Branch NAACP and Housing Help v Huntington which critically established that the Fair Housing Act is violated by discriminatory impact as well as by intent. It took eight years to establish that precious precedent, but another 15 years battling very powerful barriers to achieve the housing development that is at the center of that case.

We brought the first private individual Federal Court case under Title VIII in Suffolk County in 1975 on behalf of Gwendolyn Edwards, an African American single mother on public assistance who was refused an apartment in Centereach. Testing evidence and a temporary restraining order enabled Ms. Edwards to secure the apartment. The defendant paid damages to Ms. Edwards and attorney fees and court costs. An interesting aspect of this case was that damages had to be carefully limited to money for 'essential household items' because Ms. Edwards was receiving public assistance.

Such limitations were not a problem in our most famous case, that of Jacqueline Grayson and Alethia Futtrell v. S. Rotundi and Sons Realty which we fondly call our Watergate Case, for those of you old enough to remember Watergate and the movie 'All the Presidents Men.' These two African American women did not know each other until them each at different times tried to rent an apartment at Watergate Gardens in Patchogue. When each was told nothing was available, we sent white testers, and when the white testers were offered apartments, we prepared the evidence for Richard Bellman to file the case. The trial was held before a jury, and the jury found violation of Title VIII and awarded $65,000 in compensatory damages and $500,000 in punitive damages to the two women. This was the largest total damage award for a fair housing case in the country at that time.

To say that the Fair Housing "industry" was ecstatic is an understatement. The next morning I received calls from Fair Housing centers across the country rejoicing and telling me, "'Please, Janet, settle this case." Settle it, why? Because we all wanted that large award to remain as a precedent that other fair housing litigators could refer to as an accepted standard--and all the fair housing professionals knew that the Rotundi defendant would seek to appeal the award, and none of us wanted the Appellate Court to rule such an amount as excessive. The defendants did have to first ask the trial judge to reduce the judgment, and we are glad that motion was made, because Judge Mishler's ruling is beautifully written. (If they had just accepted the jury verdict, we would not have a written opinion on the case.)

Needless to say, I cannot regale you with summaries of the hundreds of Fair Housing cases we have enforced in this agency. And LIHS enforcement actions have increased greatly since 1989 when the Fair Housing Act as Amended added familial status and handicapped persons to the protected classes. But I did say I wanted to tell you a personal story or two that may give a sense of how this kind of work can affect you. One defendant's lawyer was deposing--examination before trial--one of our testers, a lovely middle-aged African American woman. Defendant attorneys will often try to find out if a minority witness just sees discrimination everywhere. So he asked her "Have you ever felt discriminated against before?" Dorothy thought a minute and then replied, "Yes, when was young I once was traveling in the South, and I had to ride in a Jim Crow car. I felt discriminated against then." The lawyer said "Ride in a what?' Dorothy said 'a Jim Crow car' and the lawyer said "What is that?' That was too much for Lewis Steel, our attorney. He almost lost it. "You do not know what Jim Crow is? How can you be in this country and not know what that means!" The lawyer said, "I know what segregation is but I have never heard of Jim Crow" and the court reporter joined in that she had never heard of Jim Crow either. As I recall, that pretty much brought the deposition to an end.

And sometimes plaintiffs are a challenge. One couple had been refused housing--we tested it--gained evidence of discrimination--met with a lawyer (a different lawyer this time) and he filed a case in Brooklyn Federal Court. But then they felt a little overwhelmed, I think. They were actually homeless--it was summertime and they were camped in Wildwood State Park. We had to report to the court in Brooklyn for a negotiation session with the defendant, and my client did not want to go. 'You do not need me' he kept saying. 'The lawyers can take care of it.' I told him he had to be there and had to show up so I drove out to Wildwood early that morning and told him to get in the car. 'We' are going to Brooklyn.' In court we met our lawyer and the judge told us to try to settle it. Our lawyer came back after talking to the other lawyer and said they want to know 'What' is your go-away price?' We accepted a check for $5,000. On the way back, my client said, "It really was necessary for me to be there, wasn't it.' Yeah--it was." [15]

News Story

Newsday's article **"Village Vote Backs LI's 1ˢᵗ Negro Trustee," (March 20, 1968)** by Bill Kaufman reports on Russell N. Service's election as the first black person to serve on a village board on Long Island.

Leadership Training Institute (LTI)

"Mel Jackson recognized the need for a structured program to develop and nurture leadership skills in the black community. Initially, LTI worked with groups of promising blacks to develop commitments responsibility and community leadership. Jackson feels that LTI's initial success was significantly due to the non-governmental, corporate support provided by the private business sector, the State University at Farmingdale, and Hofstra University. Among the corporate supporters were LILCO, Fairchild Space and Defense Systems, Franklin National Bank, A & S, New York Telephone Company, Sperry Rand Corporation, and Kollsman Instrument Corporation." [16]

For further information, visit Part III, profile of Mel Jackson.

The Jewish Association Serving the Aging (JASA)

"JASA was created as a multi-service, autonomous agency affiliated with the Federation of Jewish Philanthropies (now UJA-Federation of New York). The agency's development began with a decision by the Federation's Committee on Communal Planning, which recognized that an escalating number of elderly New Yorkers required coordinated programs and services to meet their needs. The goal was to attract lay and professional leadership with imagination and courage, and to mobilize the financial resources to address all unfilled needs of the Jewish aged in New York." [17]

Self Help

"The organization's Kissena Apartments opened as the first state-aided building developed by a nonprofit organization with partial funding by the Jewish Restitution Successor Organization featuring on-site supportive services for the elderly." [18]

1969

Suffolk Community Council (SCC)

"SCC began an annual program of analyzing the county's budget, preparing and presenting testimony to the legislature, and advocacy in behalf the service agencies and the people they served. During this period and into the 1970s, SCC played major roles in the development of health planning institutions including the Regional Medical Program, the Community Health Plan, and the Long Island Hospital Planning Council. When these organizations merged into the Nassau-Suffolk Health Systems Agency (HAS), SCC played major roles with its executive director serving as chairperson of the Suffolk County Council of the HSA.

"Furthermore, during this period, SCC provided technical assistance and support that resulted in the creation of many new organizations and SCC-sponsored programs including: the Day Care Council of Suffolk; RSVP; Voluntary Action Center; Nassau-Suffolk Center for Health Education; Community Health Plan of Suffolk; Suffolk Action Coalition; Bay Shore Resource Network; Suffolk Network on Adolescent Pregnancy; and South Fork Community Health Center. SCC also published a *Directory for Senior Citizens* as well as a *Directory of Preschool and Child Care Services.*" [19]

News Story

A *Newsday* article **"Family Planning Clinics Form Council"** by Barbara Shea **(January 3, 1969)** announced the establishment of a central phone number that Nassau residents can call to find out where to turn with questions regarding family planning. The council was formed in the offices in the Planned Parenthood office located in Mineola. The central phone number developed as a result of the work of representatives public and private health and family planning agencies. Mrs. Irving Weil, council coordinator and executive director of Planned Parenthood of Nassau County said: "People have been unaware these clinic services exist or they do not know where to go." Weil indicated that the clinics provide birth control and premarital counseling along with as well as educational programs.

PRONTO of Long Island

"PRONTO started out in the basement of St. Anne's Church in Brentwood serving people in need. As the demand for its services grew so did the organization. Over the years thanks to the work of Frank Sinisi and other dedicated volunteers, the organization grew and expanded its services. Jerry

Wolkoff of the nearby Heartland Industrial Park built the 10,000 square foot facility for PRONTO. *(see Sinisi's profile in Part III).*

"Pronto is a nonprofit community outreach center which provides basic human services for the homeless, unemployed, immigrants, uninsured and anyone in need of basic human services. Food is provided through a food pantry, used clothing and household goods through a thrift center and warehouse. Also provided are other necessary services including immunizations in cooperation with the Suffolk County Department of Health and three levels of ESL and GED classes. Additionally, Pronto's intake staff assists clients with many other services where to facilitate care provided by partnering agencies." [20]

Alternatives Counseling Center (ACS)

"ACS started as a group of Southampton residents united to form a community council to reach out to young people in difficulty with drugs and to offer them aid. Their first project was a community effort to construct a pre-cut wooden dormitory building, to be donated to and erected for a rehab center for drug addicts in Hillsdale, N.Y. This would provide a place for local youth in need of treatment. This effort was followed by offering alternatives to prevent drug abuse. Over the years ACS evolved into a non-profit, NY State Office of Alcohol and Substance Abuse Services (OASAS) licensed agency providing medically supervised outpatient treatment in addition to prevention programs for our schools and community in the East End Towns. Now in our 43rd year we hope to continue providing affordable, caring, and professional services to our East End community for many years to come." [21]

North Shore Child Guidance Center (NSCGC) (Later to be Renamed North Shore Child and Family Guidance Center)

"NSCGS opened other clinics in Port Washington and Roslyn." [22]

News Story

In a *Newsday* story, **"Anti-Poverty staff in Welfare Protest,"** by Ray Larsen **(May 10, 1969)** Suffolk welfare commissioner James Kirby said that paid staff members of the county's anti-poverty program helped to organize a demonstration at his department's offices to protest state welfare cuts. Anti-poverty workers felt that they were authorized under federal poverty guidelines to assist the poor to express themselves just like any other Americans.

"Reliefers Living on Streets of Despair" by Bill Richards (December 3, 1969) a *Newsday* story reports welfare recipients were being "dumped" in such places the Carleton Park section of Central Islip, a description that welfare commissioner sounded challenged. "We do not dump anyone. But we do need to find some shelter for these people or them in motels," said the commissioner. "With less than 1% of the housing stock for rentals, there is a desperate need for low-income housing in the county," Kirby continued.

The Community Development Corporation of Long Island (CDCLI)

CDCLI was founded in 1969 as Long Island's first non-profit housing assistance and development organization. It was formed by civil rights and religious group activists and government representatives, including Bob Ralph (who is associated with Housing Help in Huntington), Andy Hull, of Brookhaven Laboratories and Arthur Kunz, Suffolk County Planning (add data from early corporate papers/annual reports). The advocates wanted to address two issues: Racial discrimination in housing and the need for affordable housing for low and moderate-income families.

The advocates decided to form two organizations, Suffolk Housing Services (SHS) (which is now Long Island Housing Services) to be the fair housing advocate working on discrimination in housing including the pursuit of legal remedies while Suffolk Community Development Corporation (SCDC) became the organization focused on development of new housing opportunities. Actually, according to the original incorporation papers, the organization's original name was the Suffolk Citizens' Development Corporation. SCDC remained Suffolk-focused until 1995when it expanded into Nassau County. [23]

For further information, visit Part III, profile of Bill Klatsky.

The Suffolk Youth Services Coordinating Committee (SYSCC),

SYSCC, an ad hoc group, was established to bring together representatives of youth serving agencies on a monthly basis at Mary Haven in Port Jefferson. The organization sought to promote exchange among participants and to expand youth services throughout Suffolk County. The establishment of a county youth board was a SYSCC top priority. Represented were: Mildred Kuntz, Joanne Fogg, Barbara Strongin, and Tina Hamilton; Father Richard Dina of the Catholic Youth Organization; Anthony Tramontano of Cooperative Extension; Walter Stockton of Mary Haven; Tom Williams and Martin Timin of the School of Social Welfare at Stony Brook; Carol Tweedy of the Smithaven Ministries, Arfin and Symonds of the YMCA of Long Island, Andy Casazza and Ed King of the Town of Huntington Youth Board; and others." [24]

YMCA of Long Island

The YMCA's change from being primarily a recreational programs provider for middle-class families to one that also offered child care and counseling traces to when the corporate board of directors made a major decision, to conduct a long range planning process involving the entire organization, lay and staff. The board approved the submission of a grant request to the Pratt family of Glen Cove that awarded a three-year grant of $100,000 to assist the YMCA to conduct the long range planning process to guide the organization into the future. Senior YMCA executive Sy Symonds was assigned by YMCA executive director Bob Schmidt to work on the project. Symonds conducted his work while securing a Masters in Social Welfare at the new School of Social Welfare at Stony Brook. Symonds was a career YMCA executive and strongly believed that the organization had a social responsibility to serve the entire Long Island community. He felt that the YMCA's "apple pie and motherhood" image could be applied to services to marginalized people. He was passionate about his feelings while diplomatic in his approach to the board of directors knowing that it consisted of many conservative members. He felt that through consciousness raising and education, common ground could be found among liberals and conservatives on which to build the progressive YMCA that he envisioned.

The YMCA board of directors created a long range planning committee consisting of board members as well as representatives of a number of nonprofit organizations, elected officials, a Superintendent of Schools, Senior vice presidents of Long Island business corporations, union officials, attorneys, CPAs, small business owners, executive directors of other nonprofit organizations, and lay members of local YMCA branch boards of directors. Among its members were Henry Bang, a leader in the Salvation Army and other charities and a key player in the development of the Fire Island National Seashore; Lionel Goldberg, a senior executive for the international insurance firm, Alexander and Alexander; Ralph Hayden, a senior executive at King Kullen; Anne Mead, a former Suffolk County deputy county executive; Frank Mac Kay, a Long Island Lighting executive (LILCO); Elston Swanston, a successful business executive; Peter Mastaglio of Cullen & Dykman, Jean Esquerre, a member Tuskegee Airmen; and Audrey Jones, an African American personnel official at LILCO, and many other senior executives of Long Island businesses. The committee met regularly over a two-year period.

It was clear from the start that some committee members felt ambivalent, if not outright critical, about what the effort was all about including some who feared that the tradition YMCAs might be forced to incorporate social work programs. They feared that their middle class, predominantly White clientele would object to these new circumstances and not enroll in the YMCA's swimming, camping, and other programs. These attitudes were evident at monthly meetings of YMCA directors were most branch directors said or implied that the new programs would destroy the organization. Other laymen and staff were quite excited by the prospect of the YMCA serving the poor, disabled, elderly, and minorities in response to the changing face of the suburbs. Executive director Bob Schmidt appointed Paul Arfin and Ken

Stevenson, two young staffers to the committee knowing full well that they would support efforts to reform the YMCA of Long Island.

The committee's work resulted in various recommendations that were brought to the corporate board of directors and included significant changes to the YMCA of Long Island's incorporation papers and mission statement that would broaden the YMCA's mission to meet the needs of the Long Island community. The proposed changes met with mixed reactions in the YMCA both among senior staff and the board of directors but were ultimately approved by the board of directors. New people were invited to join the board to provide representation from the programs that Arfin and Stevenson had brought into the organization from their work in what was called the outreach services division.

Symonds continued to educate the board of directors about the importance of the new programs and how effective they were, emphasizing how they were consistent with the YMCA's history serving in urban and rural centers throughout the world. He also conducted a number of consciousness raising events for YMCA staff to assist them to prepare for the organizational changes to take place. This included a three-day "white racism retreat" held at the Immaculate Conception Seminary in Lloyd Harbor. Symonds engaged the full staff, from secretaries and custodians to branch directors and the Executive Director in sensitivity training exercises to elicit feelings about their racial attitudes and behaviors in the hopes that awareness would lead towards positive changes on the job. Under the new organizational structure, two divisions were established, a branch division that provided the traditional programs and an outreach services division that provided day care, family counseling, and youth services to at-risk youth. These programs were launched while the long range planning committee conducted its work with funding secured from county and state government agencies.

Government contracts were secured by Arfin and Stevenson during the 1970s that placed the YMCA as one of the Island's largest providers of children's day care, youth services, and family counseling services. The first contract was a $21,000 grant secured in 1971 from the newly-formed Suffolk County youth board, one of the first two issued by the agency. Under the grant, Arfin was hired to establish a youth center in the former Parish Hall on the grounds of St. Patrick's Church in Bay Shore at the corner of Main Street and 5th Avenue, a busy Bay Shore intersection. The building, provided by the church on a rent-free basis, had been a haven for young people to "hang out" in with supervision provided by church volunteers, especially Perry Craven, Kay name, and Lon Fricano. At the time, Bay Shore was in a depressed state, often called the 'waiting room' for the nearby Pilgrim State Hospital that discharged thousands of former patients using psychotropic medications. Former patients wandered the streets, many living in Okonee Hotel located a few blocks from the new youth center. Besides attendance by these mentally ill people, the youth center attracted disaffected youth who often used drugs and whose families evidenced emotional and social problems.

The youth center became a program of The Great South Bay YMCA that was in its infancy offering traditional programming in rented quarters throughout the area. Arfin reported directly to the branch manager who was supportive of the effort to integrate non-traditional programming into the branch. Together, they worked to build the branch board with people who supported the "new YMCA." The group included the manager of JC Penny's department store in the South Shore Mall and Marie Greene, a member of the Bay Shore board of education

Resistance to the youth center emerged as its attendees evidenced their psychological and social. Greene became an active advocate for expanded youth services. The young peoples' 'hippie' dress, their language and behavior offended church parishioners and shoppers on Main Street. They were perceived as, and often were, hostile towards society and its institutions. Efforts were made to collaborate with school district officials, probation and police department workers, local clergy, and others to work to provide services to the at-risk youth that attended the youth center on a regular basis where they found unconditional acceptance despite their often acting-out behavior. Window glass was broken, items were stolen, fights broke out, and drugs were used on the grounds outside the center.

The end result of the youth center-based program was neighborhood complaints especially from church leadership who contacted the county youth board. The youth board informed the YMCA that it needed to leave the church location. Arfin proposed a radical answer to the crisis: That the youth program relocated to inexpensive office space in a commercial area from which outreach would be conducted to the targeted youth. The idea was revolutionary at the time since it did not provide the much needed volume of "youth served" expected by the new youth board's contracted agencies. The youth board was trying to demonstrate to the county legislature that its efforts were producing measurable results. The other funded youth programs served thousands of youth. Arfin proposed serving dozens. Reluctantly, the youth board agreed to the proposal.

Arfin felt that the key to youth work was in the formation of relationships which could be formed without the labor intensiveness of managing a youth center. The focus, he felt, was to meet the young people on their turf and help them cope with systems that did not understand them and often treated them unfairly. When the center closed and an office was established, he trained, and supervised a small group of part-time staff and deployed two VISTA volunteers to serve as outreach workers who met youth afterschool, on weekends, and during evenings at the bowling alley, in the pizza joints, on Main Street, and on the playgrounds. Each person had a caseload assigned to him/her. They often went to Family and Criminal courts with the young people to provide emotional support when they got in trouble. They met with school officials to seek patience and understanding of their clients' family circumstances. They arranged for tutoring and psychological counseling where needed. They helped young people and their families to find and sustain employment. They served as 'big brothers and big sisters' to youth living in what was termed 'dysfunctional' families.

The other outcome of closing down the youth center was a decision that other funding was required to sustain the youth services program. Without the time demands of running a youth center opened five nights a week, Arfin wrote grants to the county's new Criminal Justice Coordinating Council (SCCJCC) and Suffolk County Drug Control Authority (SCDCA). The effort to the SCCJCC failed after a presentation was made at a meeting of the SCCJCC, by Arfin and a member of the YMCA's corporate board of directors, where they proposed the funding of a youth and family counseling service directed to at-risk youth in the Bay Shore/Brentwood area. It was apparent from the quiet response to council members (members included the police commissioner, the head of the probation department, two judges, and the sheriff) that our request was seen as wasteful of public dollars and unrealistic. After the presentation, as the YMCA board member and Arfin approached their cars in the parking lot, the county sheriff drove past them, slowed down, and appeared to be writing down their license plate numbers. A week later, Arfin was told that the board member, a high-level employee of the Long Island Lighting Company (LILCO) decided not to be involved in the outreach programs efforts any longer. Arfin began to understand how far corporate board members might go as youth advocates.

Arfin directed part of his attention to developing a movement of individuals and organizations to reform Suffolk's juvenile and criminal justice system. Working with member organizations of the Suffolk Youth Services Coordinating Committee (YSCC), the League of Women Voters, the American Association of University Women, and attorneys at Hofstra Law School, a conference was held at Stony Brook University that was attended by over 400 people. The most practical result of the conference was the organization of efforts to establish a community-based mediation center, the first one in a suburban American community. The center trained community volunteers to settle interpersonal disputes out of court. In order to secure grant support to establish a mediation center, Arfin along with Jonathan Gradess and Bob Saperstein, the attorneys from Hofstra's Law School and other members of the YSCC, met with the Suffolk's District Attorney Harry O'Brien, Angelo Mauceri, Suffolk County's Chief Administrative Judge, and representatives of the police commissioner, to seek their support of a grant submitted to federal Law Enforcement Assistance Administration. They also met with many county legislators who had to approve the grant application. The county probation department objected to the mediation center being sponsored by a non-governmental agency so efforts were made to neutralize their objections. It took two years to secure support from all parties. For its first two years, the center was sponsored by the YMCA after which the center became an independent entity.

During this period, the YMCA entered Long Island's child care scene developing afterschool day care programs in various Nassau and Suffolk counties under contracts with the departments of social services in both counties. A day care division was established.

The outreach services division was able to secure a small grant from the Suffolk County Drug Control Authority (SCDCA) to support a youth and family counseling program, an extension of the program funded by the youth board. The authority was established in response to the growing use of drugs in the county and public outcries that something is done to deal with it. The authority, under the leadership of Larry Kennedy and later Brian Trent, funded a number of agencies throughout the county. Within a year, the authority invited the YMCA to take over the town of Brookhaven's youthful drug abuse program. An office in Coram was established with part-time satellites established in Shoreham, North Bellport, and Mastic. Later, a program was established in East Hampton.

YMCA's outreach services division also obtained a grant to hire a family advocate from the Veatch Program to conduct a telephone survey of town of Brookhaven residents to determine how they viewed their quality of life. 450 homeowners were interviewed by a staff employed through the county department of labor's CETA program to hire the unemployed. The study, supervised by Martin Timin, a Sociologist, produced a number of important findings that were made public and were the subject of a Newsday story. The study results became the basis for the Family Advocate to work with other organizations to seek reforms for low and moderate income people in the town. The youth advocate that was employed, Richard Sass, a social worker, became the chairman of the Suffolk Action Coalition that went on to become the spokesman for welfare reform in Suffolk County engaging public assistance recipients in its work. An information and referral service was also established guiding residents to public and private services that they needed.

"The YMCA board agreed in principle to the work that Arfin was doing but resistance continued from some board members and directors of YMCA branch executives. Significantly the YMCA's corporate bylaws were changed to permit board representation from the outreach division. While the YMCA board supported its outreach services division in principle, the YMCA was bleeding financially with the outcome that someone had to be held accountable. The result of these circumstances was the firing of Schmidt for not raising enough private dollars and Arfin, due to a white paper he wrote to the YMCA board of directors about how the YMCA was using its United Way funding ($175,000 annually) primarily to support its branch programs not its outreach services division as the United Way was led to believe." [25]

News Story

Newsday reported in **"Help for the Handicapped" (August 27, 1975)** that the Suffolk County Legislature created a 15-seat Handicap Advisory Board after Norman Minard, an official of the Committee to Reach All Suffolk's Handicapped (CRASH), advocated before the legislature and County Executive John V.N. Klein.

School of Social Welfare at Stony Brook University (SSW/SB)

The following story about the development of the Health Sciences Center at Stony Brook University was provided in an interview with Karl Grossman, Professor, Media Studies, SUNY/Old Westbury and Columnist. Grossman was a reporter for the Long Island Press during the period in which the center was established. Dr. Edmund Pellegrino was hired by John Toll, President of Stony Brook University to establish the health science center at Stony Brook University. In 2007, Grossman describes Dr. Pellegrino impact on the health science center at Stony Brook University.

"Forty years ago, I covered the creation of what was to be a new kind of patient-centered health complex at Stony Brook University. It was to be innovative and integrate medical sciences with social sciences and the humanities, but, most of all; it was to be about caring and accessibility at an extraordinary level.

I interviewed Dr. Edmund Pellegrino, who had this vision of a different kind of hospital and new types of schools for teaching medicine, dentistry and other aspects of health care. His specialty was and is what is called 'bioethics.'

It was fascinating to listen to Dr. Pellegrino, recruited in 1966 to be vice president of the yet-to-be-built Stony Brook University Health Sciences Center and dean of its proposed school of medicine, speak of his vision. He maintained that medicine is a moral enterprise with a doctor having a "covenant" with his or her patient. Well before the rise of "managed care" and its bean counters, he was dissatisfied with the direction medicine was taking, turning health care into a commodity, a business. He spoke passionately about a patient's needs being the commitment of a doctor. Brooklyn-born of Italian immigrants, he was refused admission to medical schools despite having graduated summa cum laude from St. John's University. A letter from one Ivy League school complimented him on his grades but said he would be "happier" with his "own kind." Italian-Americans, he was told by his academic advisor, were not welcome at major medical schools, and it was suggested he change his name. He refused.

His father, in the wholesale food business, approached a restaurateur who introduced him to a regular customer, the dean of NYU Medical School, where young Pellegrino then was able to enroll.

The University Medical Center at Stony Brook and its affiliated schools of health education are monuments to the dream of Dr. Pellegrino, who went on to become chairman of the President's Council on Bioethics and president of Catholic University of America. The author of twenty-four books, he is professor emeritus at Georgetown University and, as one journal puts it, 'recognized throughout the world as one of the most prolific and passionate spokesmen on ethics and the medical profession.'

In recent weeks, an extremely difficult family experience allowed me to observe the reality of Dr. Pellegrino's dream at Stony Brook decades later. A family member was diagnosed with a serious medical condition and treated there. From admission through the operation through the compassionate and personable care that has been provided since, I have seen the walking of the visionary talk I wrote about years back. A culture was created by Dr. Pellegrino and his colleagues. It is amazing to see how, when an institutional culture is put in place, it often survives even when those who created it are gone. The scene in the surgical waiting room had Biblical overtones. Sitting next to me was a woman who spoke of her mother losing sight in one eye and then, a year ago, starting to go blind in her other eye and no longer wanting to live. She said she desperately had taken her mother to doctors who said the situation was hopeless. Then she found a surgeon at Stony Brook. The operation was over. The surgeon, in operating room scrubs, came to the room, as is the practice at Stony Brook. The woman leaped up to speak to him and then returned. 'She can see! She can see! My mother can see, in both eyes!' she exclaimed. A veritable miracle.

Eastern Suffolk County hospitals are now in the process of affiliating with Stony Brook. Eastern Long Island Hospital in Greenport and Peconic Bay Medical Center in Riverhead have already partnered. Southampton Hospital and Brookhaven Memorial Hospital are expected to be next. Of course, in life and health, there is always bad news and in the case of Stony Brook there is the "dumb" move now underway to 'privatize' it and other SUNY hospitals.

"If this happens," says William Scheuerman, president of United University Professions,"the mission of Stony Brook and other SUNY hospitals to provide quality health care regardless of people's income, to perform research and operate teaching facilities would all be undermined. This stupid push must be stopped to save a wonderful vision turned reality."

The 400 acre parcel of land on which the university was established was donated by Ward Melville. Melville joined his father's company, the Melville Company, and created the Tom McAn shoe line, a very popular shoe line of the time. He served as CEO. Melville was involved with many local charities in the Stony Brook area. Melville settled in the Stony Brook area where he owned much land. He served as a member of the school board in Setauket, where he donated the land for the high school.

Melville was interested in having a small town New England-scale college as an adjunct to his Stony Brook village restoration project. According to Grossman, Melville never envisioned the kind of giant university that arrived. Among his philanthropic activities, Melville supported the restoration and preservation of historic buildings and supported conservation of natural areas. He also developed land for the high school in Setauket, which was named for him. His larger contribution was the donation of 400 acres of land and money to New York State to establish what is now the State University of New York at Stony Brook, which was founded in 1957. Initially, the university operated with classes in Oyster Bay. Its current campus opened in 1962, emphasizing teacher education in mathematics and sciences. The university has developed as a major public research institution in medicine and science."

The following account of the development of the Health Sciences Center at Stony Brook University was provided in a 2014 interview with Dr. Peter Rogatz, director of the University Hospital and Patient Care Services of the Health Sciences Center in its formative years.

In 1966, Rogatz learned of the plan to establish a Health Sciences Center (HSC) at Stony Brook and reached out to Dr. Edmund Pellegrino, founding director of the HSC, to explore ways to establish an affiliation between LIJ and the HSC. A year later, Pellegrino offered him the position as director of the University Hospital and Patient Care Services, which Rogatz accepted. His major responsibility was to oversee the planning for the University Hospital, but he made the time to become very actively involved in Long Island community affairs, including serving as vice president of the Health and Welfare Council (1968 to 1972), Vice-Chair of the Nassau-Suffolk Comprehensive Health Planning Council and a board member of the Nassau-Suffolk Regional Medical Program. When the two latter groups (CHP and RMP) completed their work, many of their activities were absorbed by the Nassau-Suffolk Health Systems Agency.

Pellegrino's leadership group at Stony Brook HSC included, in addition to Rogatz, the deans of five schools: Alfred Knudson (Basic Sciences), Sanford Kravitz (Social Welfare), Ellen Fahy (Nursing), Howard Oaks (Dental Medicine) and Edward McTernan (Allied Health Professions). Other key people were Malcolm Skolnik (director of media and communications) and Emil Frey (director of library services). Over time, Pellegrino and his group became very concerned about budget cutbacks planned by the state, which would involve significant reductions in the HSC facilities. Pellegrino and his top staff met with Stony Brook President John Toll and SUNY Chancellor Sam Gould, outlining the serious impact that the reductions would have. Rogatz was particularly outspoken about his concerns over the potential impact on patient services.

Rogatz attended Columbia College and Cornell Medical School. His medical training was in internal medicine but, after conducting an extensive, two-year study of home care in New York City (published by the Harvard Press), he received a fellowship enabling him to return to Columbia and earn a Master's Degree in Public Health. This led him to pursue a somewhat unconventional medical career. He became Associate Medical Director at the Health Insurance Plan of Greater New York (HIP) and Medical Administrator of the East Nassau Medical Group in Hicksville. This was followed by an 18-month study of the ten hospitals affiliated with the Federation of Jewish Philanthropies of New York, co-authored with Dr. Eli Ginzberg, Professor of Economics at Columbia University School of Business. Subsequently, after several years as Deputy Director of Montefiore Medical Center, he was appointed Director of Long Island Jewish Medical Center. There, he pursued concepts he had learned at Montefiore, reaching out into the community to engage its stakeholders and to strengthen the ambulatory services of the hospital.

Uneasy about the HSC situation, Rogatz considered and then declined a new challenge: to serve as the first president of the New York City Health and Hospital Corporation. A year later, he left Stony Brook to become Senior Vice President of Blue Cross/Blue Shield. After five years, he founded RMR Health and Hospital Management Consultants, Inc., where his wife, Marge, became a key member of the staff. Some years later (1984) he was appointed Vice President for Medical Affairs at the Visiting Nurse Service of New York, from which he retired in 1991.

During his retirement, Rogatz involved himself more deeply in medical ethics, a primary interest throughout his career. In 1998, he co-founded Compassion and Choices of New York, counseling patients and families regarding end of life decisions and advocating for legislation to improve pain control, to strengthen patient autonomy, and to legalize physician aid-in-dying. He was the first chair of the ethics committee of Family and Children's Association and serves on the ethics committees of North Shore-LIJ Health System, the Hospice Care Network, and the Medical Society of the State of New York.

Peter Rogatz comes from a family background of liberal secular humanism. Of the many defects of society against which he has struggled, he sees xenophobia and widespread selfishness as the most serious.

Among Dr. Pelegrino's appointments was Sanford (Sandy) Kravitz, the founding dean of the School of Social Welfare. Kravitz had been trained at the Heller School of Social Welfare at Brandeis University and was the former deputy director of the Office of Economic Opportunity (OEO.) in the administration of President Lyndon Baines Johnson. Kravitz brought the spirit of the war on poverty to the school and recruited others who shared his orientation including Robert Lefferts, Steven Rose, Tom Williams, Neil Friedman, Steven Holloway, Steven Antler, John Haynes, Howard Winant, and Michael Reich among others. The School of Social Welfare, (which began its planning year in 1971 in Dutchess Hall on Stony Brook's South Campus) in its very name, signaled to the wider world that its vision, mission, goals, objectives, strategies, and tactics was to be much broader than that of traditional social work. Whereas social work focused on the development of therapeutic coping mechanisms that might improve the emotional and psychological well-being of individuals, families, and small groups, and trained students to become clinicians adept at implementing interventions for clients, social welfare focused on the development of institutional change that might bring about social and economic justice, especially for those who had been historically oppressed and marginalized and trained students to become social change agents. The thrust of social work was to mitigate and adjust individuals to their life circumstances, where the thrust of social welfare was to transform the structures of society and empower citizens. The transition from social work to social welfare was well discussed among core faculty and resistance both from the local political establishment and local professional practitioners was expected."

The following description of the School of Social Welfare at Stony Brook University was written by Ruth Brandwein, Ph.D., Professor Emerati, School of Social Welfare at Stony Brook University and former dean of the school and former Commissioner, Suffolk County Department of Social Services.

In 1993, after returning from her leave of absence as commissioner of the county department of social services, together with Dean Francis Brisbane and Professor Robert Lefferts, Brandwein created a social justice center. She served as its director until her retirement in 2010. The center sponsored annual conferences, co-sponsored by Suffolk and Nassau NASW units, examined social justice related bills before the State legislature and workshops on legislative advocacy were held. Students in the social policy classes were all required to visit a legislator and advocate for an issue of their choice.

Through the years there have been students at the school interested in learning clinical skills, the school was unique in the community for enunciating and maintaining its social justice mission. Its admission criteria included social action experiences, and the curriculum was revised in the 1990s so that all students were required to take an advance macro practice course, including community organization as well as planning and administration. All students were required to have a year of social policy, whose framework was oppression and marginalization.

Brandwein feels that the Stony Brook School of Social Welfare, since its inception, has changed the face of human services on Long Island with its emphasis on threading social justice concerns into social work practice."

The following story of the School of Social Welfare at Stony Brook University was provided in an interview with the current dean, Frances L. Brisbane, Ph.D.

The school's first dean, Sandy Kravitz, was one of the top designers and administrators of the federal War on Poverty program. 'He did not want the school to seek accreditation feeling that accreditation was inconsistent with the School's mission.' He traveled around the country recruiting and hiring some of the top people involved in anti-poverty programs and found that most of them were not social workers. The reality, however, was that Dr. Edmund Pellegrino, head of the HSC refused to permit the school to operate without accreditation. Based on Pellegrino's position, Kravitz also recruited graduate social workers like Drs. Brisbane, Reginald Wells, Esther Marcus, Robert Lefferts, Shirley Jones, Karie Nabinet, Steve Antler, and Steve Holloway to provide more balance to the group that Kravitz had assembled earlier.

Before the school opened, Kravitz, focusing on empowerment, instituted a controversial policy having to do with the selection of the School's first student class, one that was extremely unique from other schools of social work. Students were given significant roles in key decisions including in faculty hiring and student admissions. In particular, was a group of fourteen older black students recruited from Mississippi. These students were hand-selected by Kravitz due to their years of successful community organizing work and leadership skills during the turbulent civil rights struggles of the 1960s and Mississippi's development of health and human services in what was one of the most racist states in the nation. They were assigned to serve on every school committee. Most of these individuals had Bachelor Degrees. Kravitz knew that the Council on Social Work Education permitted admissions directly into graduate programs in schools of social work of older, seasoned, exceptional individuals who did not possess educational degrees. Many of these students later went on to earn Doctoral Degrees at prestigious universities

Another controversial policy had to do with field placement. Students were assigned to interview prospective field work agencies, a policy that agencies 'did not like at all,' being accustomed to students being assigned to agencies by schools of social work. The school made no secret of its focus on social change and social justice causing agencies to be concerned that students would not acquire what were regarded as foundational social work skills and, instead, would try to reform the agencies. To address this issue, Ester Marcus, a member of the school faculty and a skilled clinician, was assigned to serve as the school's spokesperson to arrange for student placements. Marcus was well-respected in Long Island's social work community through her board memberships in a number of agencies and through her private clinical practice. Ester helped to convince agencies that the school's curriculum was consistent with good social work practice."

The following story about the School of Social Welfare at Stony Brook University was written by Tom Williams who served as the school's first director of admissions.

I was the first director of Admissions for the newly established School of Social Welfare at SUNY Stony Brook. So I jumped at the chance to work in Suffolk County and to work at addressing the causes of social problems.

"Sanford Kravitz was selected to be the dean of the new School of Social Welfare. Kravitz had a lengthy and influential career as a social worker, working under Attorney General Robert Kennedy and playing a leading role in the design of the Community Action Program in the federal Anti-Poverty Program. In January 1964 he was the only social worker asked to join President Johnson's task force on poverty. In this role he was one of two persons responsible for the design of the Community Action Program portion in the Economic Opportunity Act. In the spring and summer of 1964 he visited scores of cities to interpret the poverty legislation and to enlist political support. He came with high ideals and ideas that would hopefully radicalize social work education. Social workers would no longer be just visiting families with their 'little black book' and trying to ameliorate their lives. They would be working to end homelessness, hunger and poverty.

The school's mission was often in conflict with traditional social service agencies that were devoted to serving individuals and not engaged in social change. Sometimes it was difficult to place students who were champing at the bit to engage in community organizing and confronting the establishment. But slowly the school did engage the social work community on Long Island and has been a strong advocate for the provision of social work services."

By the late 1960s, New York legislators were concerned about a rising problem of illegal drug use. The number of drug arrests had skyrocketed. In response, Governor Nelson established a Narcotic Addiction and Control Commission primarily aimed at reducing addiction among addicts and, later, a methadone maintenance program. When little reduction in drug abuse was evident, stricter penalties were enacted mainly mandatory minimum sentences of fifteen years to life imprisonment for possession of four ounces of narcotics about the same as a sentence for second-degree murder. The statutes enacted in 1973 began to be known as The Rockefeller Drug Laws. The laws produced an increase in convictions but no increase in overall crime and prevented judges from using discretion in sentencing. These laws were replicated in other states. New York's drug laws were reformed after over 30 years by Governor David Paterson." [26]

Notes: Chapter V

1. Lee E. Koppelman, interview of March 7, 2014, Stony Brook, NY.
2. Information obtained from film's website: www.kingsparkmovie.com.
3. Information obtained from organization's website: www.nsls.org.
4. Gail Horton, interview of June 10, 2014, Greenport, NY.
5. Rick Van Dyke, interview of March 26, 2014, Port Washington, NY as well as author's personal familiarity with FSL history.
6. Andy Casazza, interview of January 14, 2014, Vero Beach FL as well as author's personal familiarity as CDY's center director.
7. Alan Gartner, email correspondence of December, 2014.
8. Information obtained from agency's website: www.longislandhome.org.
9. Information obtained from agency's website: www.adelantesc.org
10. Information obtained from agency's website: www.vclc.org.
11. "Collection of the Suffolk Community Council" (Special Collections and University Archives at Stony Brook University).
12. "Collection of the Suffolk Community Council" (Special Collections and University Archives at Stony Brook University).
13. Information obtained from agency's website: www.literacynassau.com
14. Father T. Peter Ryan, telephone interview of June 1, 2014.
15. Janet Hanson, "Speech presented on April 30, 2013 and oral interview of May 20, 2014).
16. Information obtained from agency's website: www.lti.org.
17. Information obtained from agency's website: www.jasa.org.
18. Information obtained from agency's website: www.selfhelp.org.
19. "Collection of the Suffolk Community Council" (Special Collections and University Archives at Stony Brook University).
20. Information obtained from agency's website: www.prontoli.org.
21. Information obtained from agency's website: www.acs.org.
22. Information obtained from agency's website: nscgc.org.
23. Information obtained from agency's website: www.cdcli.org.
24. Tom Williams, interview of February 26, 2014, Bellport NY.
25. Information provided by author.
26. "New York's Rockefeller Drug Laws," Madison Gray (TIME, April 2, 2009).

Chapter VI: 1970-1974

Overview

Richard Nixon Presidency. The "Me Decade." Earth Day. Kent State Killings. Constitutional Amendment Lowering Voting Age to 18. Pentagon Papers. Normalization of Relations with China. Watergate. Roe vs. Wade. Paris Peace Accords. Arab Oil Embargo. Rockefeller Drug Laws. Resignation of President Nixon. The Oil Crisis. America's Withdrawal from Vietnam. Stagflation. Coup in Chile. Supplemental Security Insurance. Block Grants. Comprehensive Employment Training Act. Revenue Sharing. Title XX. Child Abuse Prevention Act. Rehabilitation Act. Juvenile Justice and Delinquency Prevention Act.

Demographic Factoid

During the 1960-1970 decade, both of Long Island's counties continued to grow, particularly in Suffolk County which had a 1970 population of 1,124,950 as compared to 670,213 in 1960. The county had grown by 454,737 residents, a 67.8 growth rate. Nassau's 1960 population of 1,300,171 had grown to 1,428,838. The county had grown by 128,667 residents, by a much more moderate 9.9 growth rate. [1]

In Suffolk County, a county legislature replaced the board of supervisors. In Nassau County, the board of supervisors remained the governing body. In both counties, the party bosses dominated local government.

"In the late 1960s and early 1970s, criminal and juvenile justice issues in America were very much in public view. This was partly because of President Lyndon Baines Johnson's efforts to address crime in America. In 1965, President Johnson launched the most comprehensive study of crime in U.S. history speaking frequent about his concerns and desire to reduce crime. The President's Commission on Law Enforcement and Administration of Justice was launched in 1965. It recommended reorganization plans for local police departments and many reforms both in the criminal and juvenile justice system. The Commission led to the establishment of the Law Enforcement Assistance Administration (LEAA), a U.S. federal agency within the U.S. Department of Justice. It administered federal funding to state and local law enforcement agencies, and funded educational programs, research, state planning agencies, and local crime initiatives. LEAA was established by the Omnibus Crime Control and Safe Streets Act of 1968. Its predecessor agency was the Office of Law Enforcement Assistance (1965–1968)." [2]

"In the mid-1970s, there was growing concern about crime control in America particularly in urban areas. This concern spread to the suburbs as crime statistics showed greater incidences of criminal behavior. The federal government offered localities opportunities to apply for grant funding under the Law Enforcement Assistance Administration (LEAA). Both Nassau and Suffolk counties established departments to apply for funding and coordinate efforts among its police, district attorney, courts, probation, sheriff and other departments. A good deal of attention was given on Long Island to jails in both counties and their children's shelters. Activists often protested living conditions and urged the counties to establish alternatives to incarceration for minor offenses. Cases of police brutality especially among the black population also occurred with regularity with little done to address it.

"Social agency leaders applied for grant funding from the CJCCs to develop treatment and prevention programs that might reduce anti-social behavior particularly in high crime areas. Many of their requests were denied as too soft on crime. The vast majority of new funding went to the police department and the sheriff's office for technology and hardware items with some approved for court reform and probation department programs. But there were exceptions made if applicants effectively presented their cases that social interventions will reduce crime. Some of the programs funded with LEAA grants during this period include EACINC, the Victims Information Bureau and the Community Mediation Center operated by the YMCA of Long Island. Probation departments received most of the social work-oriented projects which many advocates objected to feeling that more interventions should be made before entry into the juvenile and criminal justice system and probation department. The issue was the subject of much debate.

"In Suffolk County, a Criminal Justice Coordinating Council (CJCC) was established in the county executive's office in the late 1970s that brought together heads of different county departments. The agency gathered data from the various criminal and juvenile justice agencies both demographically and by incidences and developed proposals for funding. The CJCC's purposes are to improve criminal justice policy and program decision-making by providing agencies and government with a better understanding of crime and criminal justice problems; fostering cooperation among agencies and local government; improving the allocation of resources; and provide comprehensive system wide planning toward understanding crime and criminal justice problems within the county. Its goals are to stimulate and direct the allocation of new funding and technological advances and other innovations for preventing crime; increase the efficiency of the law enforcement and criminal justice systems through improved productivity, training, organization and equipment; to encourage coordination in planning by law enforcement and criminal justice agencies in Suffolk County, all for the basic purpose of reducing the incidence of crime which threatens the peace, security, and general welfare of all; and provide a continuing systems overview resulting in improved coordination and cooperation among local criminal justice agencies.

"Social agency leaders applied for grant funding from the CJCCs to develop treatment and prevention programs that might reduce criminal behavior particularly in high crime areas. Many of their requests were denied. The vast majority of new funding went to the police department and the sheriff's office for technology and hardware items with some approved to the probation department. But there were exceptions made if applicants effectively presented their cases that social interventions will reduce crime.

"Throughout the 1970s and into the 1980s, social agencies sought funding support from not only newly-formed county criminal justice coordinating councils but other county agencies as well including drug control authorities, departments of mental health, departments of social services, and youth boards. In addition, as funding opportunities were developed at town levels, some agencies sought funding there as well. While many nonprofits secured funding support to create new programs, many town and county governments chose to operate social programs themselves which was often criticized by nonprofit agency providers who felt that they could provide services more effectively and less expensively than public agencies. They also made the case that public agencies often made hiring decisions based on political party affiliations not on professional competence." [3]

———————

"In the early 1970s, Long Island had three psychiatric hospitals housing over 30,000 patients. These hospitals employed thousands of Long Islanders in professional and nonprofessional roles many who lived in the lower middle class neighborhoods near the hospitals. The patients came from the boroughs of New York City and Nassau County. When deinstitutionalization occurred, its impact was significant both for the patients, their families, and the communities where they lived as people with mental illnesses that had lived in the state hospitals – often for many years - tried to adjust to non-institutional life. Some had been treated with aggressive treatments, such as lobotomy and electro-convulsive therapy. The advent of pharmaceutical alternatives to institutionalization led to decisions to release patients with these psychotropic medicines. Dr. Henry Brill served as the director of Pilgrim from 1958 to 1974 and presided over both the introduction of the new anti-psychotic medications and the large numbers of discharges. Discharged patients were often placed in former hotels and adult homes located in Long Beach, Bay Shore, and Sayville." [4]

Most recently, Journalist and Professor of Journalism, Karl Grossman, wrote about another public figure that significantly affected Long Island history, former U.S. Congressman Otis Pike. Pike's story says a lot about corruption and political courage during the 1970s and beyond. It provides wisdom to elected officials.

Otis G. Pike was the greatest member of Congress from Long Island I have known in 52 years as a journalist here. Pike, who just died, was simply extraordinary. He was able to win, over and over again as a Democrat in a district far more Republican than it is now. His communications to constituents were a wonder - a constant flow of personal letters. As a speaker he was magnificent - eloquent and what a sense of humor! Indeed, each campaign he would write and sing a funny song, accompanying himself on a ukulele or banjo, about his opponent. He worked tirelessly and creatively for his eastern Long Island district. And he was a man of complete integrity. That, indeed, was why, after eighteen years, Pike decided to close his career in the House of Representatives.

In 1975, as issues about global U.S. intelligence activities began to surface — similar in matters of arrogance and deception to the disclosures in recent times of widespread U.S. surveillance — Pike became chair of the House Special Select Committee on Intelligence.

A U.S. Marine dive bomber and night fighter pilot in the Pacific during World War II, who with the war's end went to Princeton and became a lawyer, he embarked with his committee, Donner its chief counsel, into an investigation of the assassinations and coups in which the Central Intelligence Agency was involved. His panel found systematic, unchecked and huge financial pay-offs by the CIA to figures around the world. And, yes, it found illegal surveillance.

On the Central Intelligence Agency's website today is an essay by a CIA historian, Gerald K. Haines, which at its top asserts how "the Pike Committee set about examining the CIA's effectiveness and costs to taxpayers. Unfortunately, Pike, the committee, and its staff never developed a cooperative working relationship with the Agency"

A "cooperative working relationship" with the CIA? Pike's committee was engaged in a hard-hitting investigation, a probe by the legislative branch of government, into wrongdoing by the executive branch. It was not, in examining the activities of the CIA and the rest of what historian Haines terms the "Intelligence Community," interested in allying with and being bamboozled by them.

To make matters worse, leading components of the media turned away from what the Pike Committee was doing. Pike told me how James "Scotty" Reston, the powerful columnist and former executive editor of *The New York Times*, telephoned him to complain: "What are you guys doing down there!" The Times and other major media began focusing on the counterpart less-aggressive Senate committee on intelligence chaired by Senator Frank Church of Idaho.

Then, in 1976, even though a majority of representatives on the Pike Committee voted to release its report, the full House balloted 246-to-124 not to release it.

What an attempted cover-up! Fortunately, the report was leaked to CBS reporter Daniel Schorr who provided it to *The Village Voice* which ran it in full.

I still vividly recall sitting with Pike and talking, over drinks in a tavern in his hometown of Riverhead, about the situation. He had done what needed to be done — and then came the suppression. He thought, considering what he experienced, that he might be more effective as a journalist rather than a congressman in getting truth out." [5]

The following recollections of Otis Pike were written by David Starr, who was a reporter and columnist for the daily Long Island Press. Starr, the editor of The Press and national editor of the Newhouse newspaper chain, always thought the world of Pike. Starr made an arrangement under which Pike would write a column distributed by the Newhouse News Service. Pike did not run for re-election for the House of Representatives - and starting in 1979, for the next 20 years, he was a nationally syndicated columnist.

Pike's columns were as brilliant as the speeches he gave as a congressman. They were full of honesty, humor and wisdom - as was the man.

Starr, still with Newhouse Newspapers, commented on Pike's death on January 20th; "the country has lost a great thinker, a mover and shaker, and a patriot." [6]

Thomas J. Downey and Suffolk County Politics

Downey's election to the Suffolk County Legislature in 1972 at age 21 was a model of a grassroots community organizing effort significantly involving young people in a political campaign. Downey's election as a Democrat to the 94th United States Congress at age 25 were statements on the new politics emerging on Long Island in the 1960s and 1970s where Democrats could win elections in traditionally Republican districts. Downey's defeat of James R. Grover, a six-term member of Congress, was the first such evidence. The continued arrival of democratic city dwellers during the period accounted for the change in election results. It was also evidence that a young person could get elected if he ran a well-organized grassroots campaign. .The growing number of young people living on Long Island that protested the war in Vietnam and worked in the women's movement provided Downey with a cadre of workers. Downey's elections also demonstrated that a liberal politician could win in a traditionally conservative area of Suffolk County.

Downey graduated from West Islip High School, West Islip, New York, 1966. His interest in politics was encouraged at home. He got involved in politics during high school and continued in college when he earned a B.S. from Cornell University in 1970. He later attended St. John's University Law School from 1972 to 1974 and earned a J.D. from American University, Washington College of Law in 1980. He was elected as a Democrat to the 94th United States Congress at 25 as the youngest member of that Congress." [7]

The following discussion with Evelyn Roth. Roth describes her experiences in the early 1970s. Roth is former Suffolk Deputy County Executive in the Patrick Halpin administration and director, Federation Employment Guidance Services (FEGS)/Long Island Division.

Evelyn Roth was shocked at vehement opposition to a five-unit low income senior housing complex, learning that the opposition was based on fear that a black person might move into one of the apartments. She got involved in support of the housing and through it met Assemblyman Stanley Harwood and volunteered to work in his campaign. Through this involvement, Roth met Karen Burstein in 1971 who was elected in 1972 to the New York State as the first woman and the first Democrat elected to the Senate. In that same year, Carol Bellamy and Mary Ann Krupsak were also elected to the Senate. Roth helped run Burstein's campaign and became a member of her senate staff at a time when much was accomplished to promote women's rights and issues. Roth recalls those years in Albany as a time of struggle but a "transformative time, when a lot got done."

The next step in Roth's political career occurred when she helped in Irwin Landes' campaign to become Nassau County executive. There, she met Michael Del Juidice who was working for Stanley Steingut, the Assembly Speaker. Steingut offered her a position in his office. When Steingut lost his re-election bid, Roth began to work for Governor Hugh Carey. During the Carey administration, Roth recalls that there was a growing realization that government could not provide the needed services on its own, that it needed to build an infrastructure of agencies to deliver health, mental health, and housing programs. When Burstein left the Public Service Commission to become head of the Consumer Protection Board, she arranged for Roth to become her executive deputy. The Board became the statutory convenor for the Shoreham Nuclear Power Plant case to make the consumer's case against the Shoreham plant. Later, Roth joined Burstein at the Civil Service Commission where she helped to open up government employment to women, minorities, veterans and people with disabilities. [8]

Human rights' concerns grew in the early 1970s. In 1970, the Suffolk County Human Rights Commission joined a law suit against the town of Brookhaven and the federal government over the lack of low-income housing in the town. During the upcoming years, incidents of police brutality were brought to the attention of county legislators. They called for the establishment of a civilian review board. In 1971, James Rice, executive director of the county human rights commission said 'housing on Long Island is difficult for anyone but for members of minorities, their problem is doubled."

Blockbusting had prompted complaints in both counties. When residents request that attention being given to the matter, the state ordered real estate agents to stay out of a neighborhood. Some 15,000 such requests were on file for Brooklyn, Nassau and Suffolk. In 1972, the Nassau Human Rights Commission reported on a study showing black and Puerto Rican welfare recipients are housed in hotels and motels in much greater percentages than white recipients.

The Nassau's Human Rights Commission took a stand against the abortion ban at the Nassau Medical Center. Larry Smith, head of the commission's abortion committee said "the hospital exists for the benefit of residents of all races, all classes and sexes. Middle, and upper-income women have recourse to private hospitals and clinics. The poor are forced to seek abortions by abortionists operating illegally.

In 1973, the Suffolk Human Rights Commission adopted a 10-point health bill of rights in response to complaints by a Brentwood community group that its health rights were violated at the Brentwood Health Center. Commission chairman Daniel DePonte called the health center controversy "one of the most important issues that has come before the commission within the last year." The bill of rights calls for quality health care regardless of ability to pay, equitable health services, and an end to race and sex discrimination in health institutions." [9]

Lawrence Levy, director of the National Center for Suburban Studies at Hofstra University, Levy discussed the emergence of Long Island as a suburb and the evolution of social service and social action programs since the end of World War II.

Levy sees the existence of myths and stereotypes that describe suburbs as conservative, prosperous, homogeneous places. He feels that it is not true that

Long Island has no problems and it is not true that nobody wants to do anything about them. He says that, "for generations, there has been a core of people not only personally committed to confronting the ills of the community, but possessing real professional skills to address them."

In the late1950s and into 1970s, it was a time when people were affected by the changes occurring around the country pursuing new ideas, new ways of living, and greater sensitivity to different kinds of people. You had a lot of educated people moving to Long Island who grew up in working class households and poorer homes who did not forget their roots.

Levy reports that after World War II, relatively few of the people who left the city for Long Island were social progressives but those who were, were very intense, educated and talented. They knew how to get things done and kept the pressure on local governments to do things. And, once the federal government opened the spigots with funding, there was no reason for county governments, regardless of their political ideology, to reject the federal money so they could provide services for the electorate while spending very little in local tax dollars. In addition, when the federal government began the War on Poverty program in the 1960s, it opened up viable career opportunities for socially-liberal suburbanites who might have just volunteered their time on weekends at a soup kitchen but, instead, could follow their passions and earn a living to do well by doing well.

In the early days, Levy describes the politics of human services in both counties as very much wrapped up in the politics of race. Some of the push-back and the ghettoization of blacks and other minorities into a relatively handful of communities had to do with white people who did not want poor people or black people in particular living in their communities. In some cases, white politicians supported government aid to minority groups because they understood that everyone needs a helping hand at one point or another. In other cases, their support may have been because they did not want the problems to spill over into white areas. Sometimes their support may have been to reduce the likelihood of protests by minority groups.

At the time, Suffolk was growing tremendously in the 1950s into the early 1970s so government had lots of tax money. For centuries, the county was led by a board of supervisors consisting of ten men representing the county's ten towns. There was no county executive or legislature. A legislature and county executive office were formed in 1970 composed of lawmakers from eighteen individual districts to reflect the views of each distinct population area. Some areas like Wyandanch, Amityville, Brentwood, Riverhead, and North Bellport had large black and Hispanic populations but very few residents ran for elected office. This began to change in the 1980s and continues today. Today, the presiding officer of the county legislature, DuWayne Gregory, is black. He is one of three legislators who are either black or Hispanic.

Meanwhile, in Nassau, until a legislature was established in the 1990s, citizens could only elect two councilmembers from all of each of the county's three towns, with the result that most often white Republicans were elected. Like Suffolk had been, Nassau County government was managed by a board of supervisor representing the three towns. Thus, at the time, if you wanted to get something done or you had a problem or your child needed a summer job in Nassau, you went to your Republican block captain or political leader if you lived in a Republican area and your Democratic leader if you lived in a Democratic area. Since Nassau was predominantly a Republican-controlled county, most power was in Republican hands. Most issues never rose above the neighborhood level, handled by residents' appeals to their local political leaders and civic associations. Where a local leader had a lot of political clout, he could get a lot done. Otherwise, not as much could be done. Today, the nineteen-member, Nassau legislature consists of four minority group members, three black and one Hispanic, a woman, Norma Gonsalves, serves as Minority Presiding Officer.

Nassau's black clergy played an important role in securing government support to establish community services in communities with heavily black populations. This was accomplished through relationships developed with local, town, and county Republican leaders. Clergy like Reverend Reginald Tuggle built close ties to local, state, and national Republican leaders. They developed many programs especially in Roosevelt, Hempstead, Glen Cove, Elmont, and Uniondale. Levy believes that there was the belief among white Republican politicians that there were not a lot of black people who were going to vote for Republicans in black communities but if their leaders were treated well they also were not going to come out in droves to vote against their candidates.

With respect to John Kearse, the head of the Economic Opportunity Council of Nassau, Levy sees him as getting a lot done but as a controversial figure because of his strong personality. "Many white politicians were afraid of Kearse which helped him since they did not want a lot of trouble from him. It hurt him since they did not want to associate with him and they knew that they could not control him. At times, politicians went after him with allegations of improprieties but never found any problems of substance," says Levy.

With respect to the development of social programs, many started because they had people on their boards of directors with the financial means to help get them started or had connections to political leaders or foundations. This often resulted in stronger, more established organizations receiving support rather than new organizations without such connections. Thus, according to Levy these factors sometimes were more important than whose needs were being serving, the merits of proposals, or the skills and talents of the organizations.[10]

For further information about Lawrence Levy, visit Part VII, Influence of the Media

Social Agencies by Year

1970

Suffolk Rehabilitation Center (later renamed: United Cerebral Palsy of Suffolk)

The 1970s dawned with full day children's programs filling the space at the Suffolk Rehabilitation Center on Indian Head Road. Portable activity rooms were added at the rear of the property and a vocational exploration and rehabilitation program began. Ladies Auxiliaries and participation in a new nationwide Telethon became the core of volunteer fund raising efforts. In 1979, the organization joined an affiliate network, becoming known as United Cerebral Palsy Association of New York State, Suffolk County Committee. It was also at this time, that the concurrent growth of the child and aged population and the need for more rooms for adult programs necessitating the relocation of children to the Smith's Lane School, known today as the UCP Children's Center. [11]

Suffolk Youth Services Coordinating Committee (YSCC)

The SYSCC was instrumental in convincing the Suffolk County legislature to establish a Suffolk County youth board. Members found a friend in legislator Lou Howard of Amityville, a retired football coach in Amityville. Howard was able to counter the strong objections of legislator Jane Stanley who viewed the youth board infringing into family matters. The next key question to be addressed was who would become the youth board director. At a retreat held at Minden House in Bridgehampton in May 1970, town of Islip councilman Jack Finnerty (who went on to be Suffolk's sheriff), predicted the outcome. "It will probably go to some political hack from the probation department," Finnerty told the attendees. As Finnerty, predicted, the youth board position was filled by a resident of the town of Islip, following the longstanding Suffolk tradition that county department heads were appointed by town political leaders. So, a career probation department employee, Charles Merwin, a resident of the town of Islip, was selected rather that the youth services' community selection, Andy Casazza, who was highly regarded due to his success as the founder and director of the town of Huntington's youth board. Not only was Casazza not from the town of Islip, he was a Democrat. [12]

News Story

Newsday followed the trial and tribulations of establishing a Suffolk County Youth Board. **"Suffolk to End Youth Board" by Maurice Swift (March 25, 1970); "Suffolk Youth Board Still Struggling"** by Jim Toedtman **(April 24, 1970); "Time Running Out on a Youth Plan" (June 5, 1970); "Suffolk Youth Board Sticks to Its Choice" (June 12,1970); and "Youth Unit Elated at Search's End."** (December 11, 1970)

Day Care Council of Nassau

The Health and Welfare Council of Nassau (later renamed the Health and Welfare Council) established a day care steering committee due to its concerns regarding the need for increased day care services. The committee consisted of representatives of a variety of agencies, organizations, parent groups, and individuals. After several months, the group decided that an autonomous membership organization should be established and took steps to establish the Day Care Council of Nassau as an independent, nonprofit organization. By 1973, thanks to a $30,000 grant from the Veatch Program, Eleanor Kirk was hired as the council's executive director. In subsequent years, grants were also received from The Long Island Community Foundation. [13]

Smithaven Ministries

The Smithaven Ministries evolved through the commitment and collaboration of four individuals concerned with the widespread changes occurring in American society in the late 1960s. They were especially concerned about the alienation of young people and the racial divide that existed on Long Island.

Reverend David Bos, working for the Presbytery of Long Island, was hired to explore and identify how Presbyterian churches might develop new ministries to serve current and new congregants. Bos came to the position with misgivings about the relevance of traditionally structured congregations. While at Union Theological Seminary, he developed a student discussion group between the seminary and the Jewish Theological Seminary. He was also a founding member of the Olean, New York NAACP chapter. Upon his arrival on Long Island, Bos met with other clergy and found common interests in working together to establish what was considered an "experimental ministry" to address emerging social conditions.

One of the people, Bos contacted was Kenneth Anderson *(see Anderson's profile in Part III),* an African American elder in the Presbyterian Church in Port Jefferson and member of the Suffolk County Human Rights Commission. Bos and Anderson assembled others to join them. Key was the Reverend T. Peter Ryan, a priest of the Roman Catholic Diocese of Rockville Centre, associate pastor of St. Peter the Apostle's parish in Islip Terrace and also a member of the human rights commission. The three men were exponents of post-Vatican II Catholic-Protestant and interfaith cooperation. They proceeded to develop their vision and plans for an experimental ecumenical ministry called initially, "The Ministry to the Nesconset Area." They decided to explore the possibility of establishing the ministry at the planned regional shopping mall being planned to be called the Smithaven Mall.

The 'Ministry in the Marketplace, later to be named the Smithaven Ministries, was the first ecumenical ministry to be located in a New York State shopping mall. It was originally located on the main floor of the shopping mall and then moved to the second floor where it was less visible. But problems persisted and, years later, was forced to leave the mall entirely due to management's concern about the image of the mall. It was an innovative approach to reaching youth and people with difficulties where they congregated; the concept being that suburban Long Island did not have a 'downtown' area and the mall was the closest to that idea. But the community opposition was too great and they were forced to leave.

The group made contact with Gary Katica, head of a real estate agency who was an active layperson in his Greek Orthodox parish. Katica offered the use of property he owned adjacent to the new mall to house the ministry. Soon, the fourth key player in the experimental ministry came on the scene, Dorothy Ryder, an active member of the Smithtown Presbyterian Church. Ryder brought a deep belief in the importance of mobilizing volunteers to serve in the new ministry. She had organizational skills and many contacts on Long Island. Ryder became the first chairperson of the steering committee of Smithaven Ministries when it began operations in the mall in 1970. The other key player in the story was William T. Rambo of the Long Island Presbytery. Rambo leadership produced substantial ecumenical support from regional and national ecumenical organizations.

When arrangements were made to lease property in the mall, Father Ryan served as executive director facing political and practical issues that had to be dealt with. Indeed, the ministries welcomed young people who rejected traditional values and whose dress and behavior angered mall customers causing complaints and efforts to remove the project from shoppers' views. Bos recalls two situations in particular. In one instance, a student theatrical group in whiteface portraying horrors of the Vietnam War demonstrated in the mall corridors. In another instance, a young man, feeling excluded from the ministries' youth program, set a fire to a pile of card board at the mall's rear entrance. Besides the youth program, the ministries housed Suffolk Housing Services, a fair housing organization. Lead by Janet Hanson, Suffolk Housing Services played a very important role documenting housing discrimination *(see the organization's story earlier in this chapter)*. A child care program for shoppers, a program to assist runaway youth, a consumer advocacy project, pastoral counseling services, an emergency food pantry, and a community information and referral service were also established. What is now known as Theater Three located in Port Jefferson began at the ministries. The organization broadened its funding base by securing contracts with the Suffolk County's Youth Board, Drug Control Authority, Criminal Justice Coordinating Council, and Department of Social Services.

The Smithaven Ministries grew over the years despite many challenges under the leadership of Father Peter Ryan. One key program developed in 1976 was Seabury Barn located in Stony Brook. Carol Tweedy, a seasoned social worker, served as the project director. The program provided short-term, emergency housing and counseling and support services for young people who had fled families in conflict. The program provided family court, police, social service, and probation officials an alternative to placing at-risk youth into the county shelter. In 1983, SHM changed its name to the Ministries and left the mall to locate in Coram where it continues to operate in the new century primarily serving poor and vulnerable Long Islanders with food, clothing, school supplies, an adopt-a-family program, and holiday gifts. An information and referral service is offered as well as a summer camp and counseling and case advocacy programs. Seabury Barn continues to shelter homeless and runaway youth.[14]

Suffolk County Girl Scout Council

The council, under the leadership of Mildred Kuntz, began to reach out to bring girl scouting programs to minority communities. Staff members Joanne Fog, Barbara Strong in, and Tina Hamilton provided human relations training and support to these efforts. The council was also one of the early agencies to join the youth service coordinating committee and its work to establish a county youth board. [15]

Independent Group Homes for Living (IGHL)

In the early 1970s, a series of televised reports graphically exposed to a shocked public the inhumane treatment of people with developmental disabilities at Staten Island's Willowbrook State Hospital. The images and the disturbing testimony caused an outcry for reform. In an historic ruling, the U.S. District Court demanded immediate changes designed to provide improved care.

Walter Stockton played a major role in the development of services for developmentally disabled individuals in Suffolk County. From his work at The Mary Haven School in Port Jefferson as a Recreation Supervisor and faculty member in therapeutic recreation at Suffolk Community College, Stockton moved on to establish IGHL to establish a new agency dedicated to offer non-institutional services to people with developmental disabilities.

Stockton brought together a group of concerned members of the Eastern Long Island community to establish the Independent Group Home Living Program (IGHL), a nonprofit agency dedicated to the enrichment of the lives of people with developmental disabilities. Stockton was named IGHL's first chief executive officer, a position which he continues to hold. IGHL's board of trustees is comprised of a group of dedicated members of the community some who are parents of children and adults receiving IGHL's services. The mission of IGHL is to provide programs, services and support for people with developmental disabilities so they can realize their full potential as human beings and contributing members of their community.

IGHL opened its first group home in Mt. Sinai, New York in 1978. The purpose of the project was to provide a community-based, homelike environment that encouraged personal growth and a genuine sense of belonging to a community. To Stockton, opening the first group home did not meet with community opposition since it was housed in a former adult home and, thus, did not change the character of the neighborhood. The situation was different with many of the other homes. In one instance, Stockton recalls noticing dozens of yellow buses parked in the school parking lot when he arrived for a public hearing regarding the proposed group home. Upon entering the auditorium, he learned that hundreds of local residents were there to object to the project.

Residents could not accept that they had no say in whether to accept a group home in their community after the 1978 adoption of what became known as The Padavan Law, named after New York State Senator Frank Padavan. It allowed group homes to bypass local zoning, as long they met state codes. It allowed community protests, but on limited grounds - if an area was oversaturated with group homes or if a better site could be found. The law set timetables. A community had 40 days to file a protest. A commissioner ruled in 90 days. A community could go to the courts, but in the meantime the home opened. [16]

South Oaks Hospital

"The hospital established Hope House as a specialized inpatient unit for young men and women who were addicted to drugs. In 1971, new programs and services followed in quick succession. The first was the opening of Bailey House, an alcoholism detoxification unit that followed the precepts of Alcoholics Anonymous. In 1971, recognizing the special needs of adolescents with emotional problems; the hospital opened an adolescent pavilion for young people between the ages of 13 and 20. Knowing that education was an essential part of active therapy; classes and one-to-one tutoring were held five days per week. In addition, South Oaks was approved by the New York State Education Department as a testing center for the high school equivalency examination. The All Faiths chapel-auditorium was completed in 1971 as part of a two-level building that also housed the boiler plant and a fully equipped laundry.

As South Oaks entered its tenth decade, the construction programs continued and both inpatient and community outreach programs were expanded to meet the changing needs of society. In 1972, South Oaks set up a training program for alcoholism counseling. The training program, one of only a few in the country, graduated many trained counselors. The Institute of Alcohol Studies at South Oaks was formed in 1972 and was chartered by the Board of Regents of the New York State Education Department. During this decade, demographic studies showed the "graying of America." Subsequently, in 1973 construction began on a new 200-bed facility on the grounds and in 1974, the new Broadlawn Manor Nursing Home and Health Related Facility opened." [17]

The Suffolk Community Council (SCC)

SCC conducted a luncheon at Felice's restaurant in Patchogue with world-renowned_anthropologist Margaret Mead. Council also received a $10,000 grant from Suffolk County in support of its partnership with county government to produce a directory of community services. [18]

1971

News Story

As reported by Bob Keeler and Tom Demoretcky in *Newsday* **"Mental Health Agency Waste Denied" (July 27, 1971),** a State Assembly sub-committee, chaired by Assemblyman Robert C. Wertz of Commack, began investigations about alleged abuses in the State Department of Mental Hygiene's state hospitals and state training schools including Pilgrim State Hospital, Central Islip State Hospital, Kings Park State Hospital, and Suffolk Psychiatric Hospital. An important issue being considered was that patients were being discharged prematurely often wandering the streets of Bay Shore, Long Beach, and Sayville and other communities. Other issues concerned which government agency should pay the welfare costs for the needed community care, the Suffolk County where the former patient lived or Nassau County, where the patient was from.

Middle Earth Switchboard (later renamed the Long Island Crisis Center)

According to a James A. Goodman article in *Newsday*, **"Help! I've Got Trouble," (December 9, 1973)**, the organization evolved from a drug crisis program at Adelphi University. A $7,000 grant from the New York State Department of Education's College Volunteers to Combat Drug Abuse program permitted the rental of a storefront. Later, a 24-hour suicide prevention and crisis intervention hotline was established primarily funded by the Nassau County Youth Board.

News Story

In 1970, *Newsday* in a three-part series, reporter Rhoda Amon, followed the child day care story speaking of "a growing need with more than four mothers in ten now working outside the home, the need for day-care centers is burgeoning, but facilities fall far short of the mark." **"Day Care: The Growing Need, 1970." (September 24, 1968)** In 1973, Amon wrote another *Newsday* feature story **"The Threat to Day Care: A Threat to Working Mothers."(May 21, 1973)**

Suffolk Community Council (SCC)

A council day care committee decided that an independent day care organization should be established. With the legal assistance of attorney Anne Mead, the group was incorporated as the Day Care Council of Suffolk. The council proceeded to serve as a coalition representing the interests of consumers and providers of day care services, urging elected officials to support the expansion of quality, affordable day care. [19]

News Story

"Drug Agency Bill Given Good Chance," (February 4, 1971) a *Newsday* article chronicles the work of Perry Duryea, Jr., an Assemblyman from Montauk's efforts to establish county narcotic control authorities with state funding. The funding supported coordination of local narcotics guidance councils and comprehensive narcotics plans.

1972

Family Service Association (later to be named Family and Children's Association)

In 1972, FSA executive director Sal Ambrosino hired Rick Van Dyke as Director of Family Advocacy without a job description. According to Van Dyke, Ambrosino just said, I want "advocacy" so go do it. At first, Van Dyke contemplated how advocacy fit into the community organization framework of social planning, community development and social action. He finally determined that he would move on two fronts:

One of the key changes that Van Dyke implemented had to do with implementing the "case-to-cause" model throughout the agency. Van Dyke went to each FSA office (mental health centers, aging, child development, etc.) and trained the staff in the concept. He developed a form for the staff of each program to submit on a monthly basis with cases that might become causes, as well as to identify trends such as the number of evictions reported and when they increased and when the number of requests for emergency food went down. Two advocacy efforts that were particularly successful were convincing the department of social services to stop calling out client names into their waiting room; instead they changed to numbers. The other had to do with grandparents who could not get foster care payments if they were taking care of grandchildren. Van Dyke wrote and proposed legislation and simultaneously initiated a class action lawsuit against DSS. The legislation passed and was signed into law by Governor Hugh Carey.

The other front for Van Dyke was creating large, community-based coalitions including the Nassau Action Coalition (NAC), the Nassau Coalition for Safety and Justice, and the Coalition for a National Health Care Plan. NAC, which initially focused on Supplemental Security Income, later spread its actions to poverty, welfare, housing, food stamps and domestic violence issues.

In 1974, Ambrosino promoted Van Dyke to assistant director of FSA. He told Van Dyke that he had done more in two years to get FSA on the map and knew than he had been able to do in twenty years. In addition to Family Advocacy Van Dyke was authorized to hire an Assistant Director of Family Advocacy, a secretary and took over responsibility for managing the county-wide counseling program, drug counseling, debt counseling and the bereavement center. Van Dyke was also commissioned to conceive and develop a model family center. Van Dyke worked on these projects until 1980 when he resigned to accept the position as executive director of the West Nassau Mental Health Center. Six years later, Van Dyke went on to become CEO of Family Service League in Suffolk County. Upon retiring, Ambrosino served as a board member for Hempstead Boys & Girls Club. *Newsday* covered a wide range of social issues during this period as evidenced in the following three news stories about legal services for the poor, the need for youth services, and emergency housing. [20]

News Stories

"The Poor Lose in Fight on Legal Aid" (January 5, 1972) is the headline of a *Newsday* story written by Sidney C. Schaer that describes how Suffolk's population of poor people was shortchanged when it came to protecting their legal rights.

"In Middle Earth: A Warm Shoulder of LI's Hobbits," (February 8, 1972) *Newsday* reporter Kevin Lahart reported on the creation of a new Levittown-based nonprofit organization that serves as a hotline, walk-in crisis center, and information disseminator. Over the upcoming years, such programs proliferated throughout Long Island towns facing youthful drug abuse and mental illness.

"Motels House Mostly Blacks, Study Reveals" (February 8, 1972) is a *Newsday* article written by Edward G. Smith that describes the results of a study of emergency housing in Nassau County.

In the spring and summer, *Newsday* followed other social issues including mental health, disability services, and law services for the poor.

News Stories

In a *Newsday* article, **"Caso Under Fire on Mental Health,"(April 1, 1972)** Joan Saltzman as executive director of Community Advocates "called on the county board of supervisors to ensure that the mental health board's $12M budget be subjected to the same kind of budget review that other departments undergo."

"Facilities Lacking for Retarded" (June 2, 1972) was a *Newsday* story reporting that the Nassau County Medical Center admitted that it could not give adequate treatment to a youth and a woman who there as "mental defectives." The article indicated that there were more than 2,000 patients waiting to be accepted by the state's schools for the retarded.

In the late 1960s into the 1970s and beyond, the women's movement took root nationally and on Long Island. **"Women on Long Island: Leaning Toward Liberation"** by Deborah Leavy **(July 5, 1972)** was a *Newsday* story describing the evolution of women exercising their rights. According to the article, a National Organization for Women chapter in Nassau County was established in 1969 when ten students at Old Westbury College organized a class called "Women's Oppression" with ten women who focused their attention and advocacy on political action regarding abortion, the Equal Rights Amendment, and equal employment educational opportunities. According to the article, Women's Centers were soon established Port Washington, Woodmere, and Northport. In the Hamptons, a group called the "South Fork Women's Liberation Coalition" was formed. NOW chapters were later established in Huntington, the south shore of Suffolk County and the east end of Suffolk County. NOW was an important force in the coalition that began the Suffolk Coalition Against Domestic Violence.

"Citizen Advocates for the Poor," (August 8, 1972) a *Newsday* article written by reporter Rita Amon, described the work of Nassau County Law Services Committee to recruit and train volunteers to help the poor negotiate government agencies' bureaucratic maze. Leonard S. Clark the committee's director indicated that they were looking not only volunteer attorneys but people with compassion and a high level of tolerance since the bureaucracy is often difficult and frustrating to deal with.

<u>Nassau County Mental Health Association</u>

In her capacity as executive director of the association, Sadie Hofstein was extremely active as an advocate for community-based services for people with mental illnesses. No group homes existed in Nassau County despite the law that said that group homes were permissible as long as they did not "over-saturate" a neighborhood. They required no changes to existing zoning requirements. Residents could object by their show of anger but there was no government jurisdiction that could stop their development. Nevertheless, residents and elected officials opposed them. Under the auspices of the Association, Hofstein organized family members of people with mental illness into a political force. They attended public meetings to make the case for group homes. She recalls the effort in Westbury to establish a group home there. Supported by a contingent of family advocates, Hofstein spoke before a crowded room of mostly-angry local residents, elected officials, and the press.

Residents envisioned mentally ill people wandering their streets, endangering their children, and lowering their property values. Hofstein recalls that at a meeting in Westbury, a village trustee expressed concern to Hofstein about what would happen if they approved one group home. 'It would open the door to approval of a group home in every neighborhood in the county,' said the trustee. Hofstein, quick on her feet and staring straight at the trustee, said: "Your nightmare is my goal. That is exactly what we hope will happen." The pioneering work that Hofstein initiated with the Nassau Mental Health Association lead to the development of three adult homes one children's home, and a home for autistic children.

These homes were the forerunners of efforts of numerous other nonprofit organizations to develop additional group homes. But, according to Hofstein, community resistance continued in every community. It wasn't until New York State Senator Frank Padavan successfully secured legislation that no community could object to a group home unless it could be proven that it was being saturated. It allowed group homes to bypass local zoning, as long they met state codes. It allowed community protests, but on limited grounds - if an area was oversaturated with group homes or if a better site could be found.

Hofstein went on to lead the Mental Health Association to build the first apartment house for mentally ill adults that exists today. The association also operated work projects and college projects. Reflecting on the period in which she pioneered the development of group homes, she says: "There was money available from the federal and state governments, even from the county. If I were in a position to start up an organization today, I would be very leery. Money simply is not available. [21]

Concern for Independent Living and the National Association for the Mentally Ill (Concern)

The development of Concern and a Suffolk Chapter of the National Association for the Mentally Ill significantly trace to the volunteer work of Davis Pollack, D.D.S., a dentist for over 35 years on Long Island. During this period he has been a staunch advocate for eliminating the stigma against mental illness and providing quality care for people with mental illnesses. His interest and concern about mental illness stem from the personal experiences of close family members including his wife's brother who had a diagnosis. According to Pollack 'he lived and died in Brooklyn State Hospital.' Pollack describes the hospital as a 'snake pit' with no services. 'People were put there to die. Because of the stigma placed on mental illness relatives and friends would not visit. They were afraid and did not want to witness the horrendous conditions facing patients. Mental illness was seen as a 'shanda,' a disgrace by family members.' Pollack recalls well the public's attitude towards those diagnosed with mental illness.

Concern was originally founded as an advocacy organization. For over forty years, the organization has provided supportive services to individuals their families. Concern began operating housing over twenty-five years ago and was among the first operators of licensed community residences in Suffolk County and has been used as a model for the development of similar programs. Concern is the largest nonprofit provider of supportive housing for individuals and families on Long Island." [22]

For further information, visit Part III, the profiles of Davis Pollack and Max Schneier.

Response of Suffolk County (Response)

The organization was established following a series of Stony Brook University student suicide attempts. Two local clergymen and university faculty members came together to consider what could be done. It was clear that a crisis hotline with local referral information was needed, and it needed to be open day and night. They gathered professional staff and volunteers, and created a training program for them. From these humble roots, the agency grew to serve all of Suffolk County and is now a nationally accredited program. Response's mission was to provide callers in crisis or in need of support with unconditional acceptance, compassion and respect in order to lower anxiety and facilitate the coping skills they already have; help callers capitalize on their strengths in the prevention of self-destructive behaviors or suicide; provide referrals and information about community programs and resources; and to heighten public awareness of suicide prevention through community education, outreach and training. In the next two years, Long Island had over

40 hotline and crisis counseling center both in the community and on college campuses." [23]

<u>Suffolk Community Development Corporation (SCDC and later named Community Development Corporation of Long Island (CDCLI)</u>

L. Von Kuhen, a senior vice president of Community Development Corporation of Long Island (CDCLI), reports that the first SCDC housing project was development of 431 units of low and moderate income housing in Homestead Village in Coram in the early 1970s. This set the path for SCDC's future pattern to seek and obtain funding support for new housing developments and housing improvements through federally-funded programs of the U.S. Dept. of Housing and Urban Development (HUD) and Farmers Home Administration (FmHA) as well as to offer comprehensive services to the residents and communities. Other programs were launched over the next two decades, particularly on the East End. In 1978, SCDC began to administer the Section 8 program in Suffolk County that has grown to over 4,000 housing units. In the mid-1980s, when New York State established its Affordable Home Ownership Program, SCDC began to build affordable homes and home improvements under this program. In the late 1990s, the organization became chartered as a NeighborWorks® Organization, and received funding to establish two NeighborWorks® Home Ownership Centers, in Centereach and Freeport. The Home Ownership Centers provide comprehensive pre-purchasing education and counseling. [24]

News Story

In a *Newsday* article **"The Illegal Apartment Boom: A Growing Long Island Trend, (May 28, 1972)"** Wilbur Klatsky, a housing expert that would become president of the Community Development Corporation of Long Island said: "It is happening in the best of neighborhoods. Many substantial neighborhoods are showing signs of this, and it is beginning to affect property values" In Nassau County, Norman Blankman, a civic activist, said: "…the Nassau County treasury is being affected because those houses being taxed on the basis of single-family occupancy are undertaxed." Local officials and housing experts agree with a highly-reputable real estate agent that there are over 50,000 Long Islanders living in multiple-family dwellings in violation of town codes. Illegal apartments do not pay their fair share of property taxes thus placing a burden on municipal services and school districts.

<u>UCP of Suffolk</u>

"The 1970s dawned with full day children's programs filling the space at the Suffolk Rehabilitation Center in Commack. Portable activity rooms were added at the rear of the property, and a vocational exploration and rehabilitation program began. Ladies Auxiliaries and participation in a new nationwide Telethon became the core of volunteer fund raising efforts. In 1979 the organization joined an affiliate network, becoming known as United Cerebral Palsy Association of New York State, Suffolk County Committee. It was also at this time, that the concurrent growth of the child aged population and the need for more rooms for adult programs necessitated relocating our youngsters to the Smith's Lane School, known today as the UCP Children's Center. [25]

Federation of Parent Organizations for the New York State Mental Health Institutions (later to be named Federation of Organizations)

The federation was organized during the era of hospital-based care, and has remained a leader in the development of community-based social model mental health services for people living with mental illness. The organization was incorporated as an alliance of mental health advocacy groups. These groups were comprised of relatives of individuals who were patients in psychiatric centers in New York State. At that time, each center had a "concerned citizens' group" or "hospital guild" that worked to improve conditions for patients through direct services and advocacy. Usually, these groups were made up of family members who were advocating for good treatment and safe environments for their loved ones. During this period, the standard treatment for mental illness was indefinite hospitalization.

With the advent of psychotropic medication, impelled by financial considerations and the civil rights movement, the early 1970s saw the return of many people to the community, rather than enduring long-term hospitalization. Two-thirds of the patients released from hospitals in the first wave of deinstitutionalization went back to their families of origin. There were, unfortunately, very few support services in the community, and the responsibility of supporting these individuals was placed on the family.

Family members were prominent among those who advocated for resources to be developed in the community. It was a long fight, but now it is clearly recognized that community treatment is the best path to recovery from mental illness. The struggle for resources continues and there are many challenges especially the pressure for cost containment.

Morton Posner was the organization's executive director and a founder and past president of Voice for the Handicapped a coalition of mental health organizations. He was the parent of five children, one of whom was a 22 year old daughter, a resident of a New York State institution for the mentally retarded. It was as an active member of the parent organization that he initiated a voter registration drive after many years of frustrating attempts. Later, Posner was a co-founder of the Illinois Association for Retarded Children and an officer of Voice of the Retarded, an Illinois coalition. [26]

<u>Middle County Public Library (MCPL)</u>

A new main building was opened in Centereach. With the vision of a creative and entrepreneurial director, Paul Cirino, MCPL quickly assumed a leadership role within the library profession focusing on customer service when this term was unheard of in the library industry. Breaking images of the traditional library, staff focused on listening to patrons to learn what they wanted and needed. The collections and programs were driven by patron requests and positive responses to services.

Children's services began when the new building opened in 1972 and Sandy Feinberg (re-located from Michigan) was hired to be the children's librarian. After becoming a parent, she personally experienced a need for companionship with other parents and a place to go for information about her baby. A speech therapist and friend who worked at St Charles Hospital (Port Jefferson) told her about a new mothers' support group to which Sandy immediately turned. In this program, resource professionals met with the moms and their babies to discuss a variety of topics while moms formed friendships and a sense of community – a necessary respite in the early months of new parenthood.

When she went back to work, Sandy realized that it would behoove children's librarians to consider this new audience and, in fact, create 'something' that would welcome caregivers, infants and toddlers into the library setting. This required a new way of looking at programs and collections and a determination to reach moms and children at a much earlier age than those who traditionally visited the library. What those services could be and how they would be offered began to take shape but not without help from the early childhood and family service communities.

The initial program was the Parent Child Workshop (PC Workshop), a five-session early childhood and parenting program that focuses on the information and social needs of parents/caregivers and the social, emotional and literacy needs of children, birth through three years. Based on family-centered principles, the PC Workshop helps caregivers to build relationships with other families, gain information on child development and early literacy, and connect families with local services. Unlike traditional story time programs, the PC Workshop emphasizes unstructured play with a variety of developmentally appropriate learning materials. While the families are playing, a resource professional from a local agency (who specializes in speech, nutrition, child development or movement) casually peruses the room and interacts with the caregivers. Cornell Cooperative Extension, St. Charles Hospital and Family Service League provided the first resource professionals. The librarian serves as a facilitator and information specialist.

A major upshot of the PC Workshop was the formation of the Suffolk Coalition for Parents and Children (Suffolk Coalition) which held networking and information sharing meetings among librarians and agency professionals and created resource listings on a multitude of youth-related topics. During this same time period, the library's adult services department was asked to participate in a grant to offer career counseling services in partnership with Stony Brook University. The library decided, because of popular demand, to continue and develop this service even when the grant ended.

The PC Workshop, the Career Counseling Services and the resource directories developed in partnership with members of the Suffolk Coalition were initial forays into the subsequent evolution of the regional and national Family Place Libraries™ initiative and the creation of the Computerized Community Information Database for Suffolk County which evolved into the Community Resource Database of Long Island (CRD) and the 2-1-1 Long Island Database (Database). [27]

1973

News Stories

In a Jack Altshul column **"Helping Troubled Kids and Their Families,"** **(June 8, 1973)** it is reported by a director of North Shore Child Guidance Association that "it costs the state as much as $15,000 a year to institutionalize a disturbed kid. We keep about 800 kids a year out of institutions."

"Helping Mothers Get off Welfare" (July 23, 1973) was a *Newsday* story written by reporter Ahmed Chett about a Wyandanch children's day care center where parents receiving public assistance and are looking for employment or are enrolled in job training programs bring their children to be cared for. The need for quality, affordable, accessible child day care was to become a major family issue in the coming years as more-and-more women entered the work force often for the first time.

Harbor Child Care

Jill Rooney started a play group for nine children in her Sea Cliff home. Within two months, there were 25 children in the renovated basement causing Rooney to look for a larger space. Rooney's passion for quality child care motivated her to establish Harbor Child Care as a nonprofit organization. 41 years later, as the founder and executive director of Harbor Child Care, Rooney oversees seven separate child care centers for 1,000 children, employing 280 full time teachers and staff in Nassau County. The organization provides early care and learning to children 12 weeks old to 12 years old. There is a before and after school program, holiday care, and a summer program. The education curriculum is based on the High Scope Cognitive Development Program which is a 40 year research based curriculum generally regard as a leading early childhood educational approach.

Over the years, Rooney was also an effective advocate for county, state, and federal funding of child day care as well as for corporate sponsorship of child care programs where she assisted the Community Programs Center of Long Island to establish its first center near Melville and, later, to establish a Harbor workplace center at Cablevision in Woodbury

In 1973, Harbor Child Care was faced with an unacceptable Nassau County Department of Social Services rule. The rule said that 80% of the children in care had to be from the poverty level with the remaining 20% coming from parents who could pay the entire fee. This was a non-regulated, discretionary decision which Harbor vigorously objected to. Harbor proposed a class action suit against Nassau County Department of Social Services. The threatened suit led the County to revise its 80/20 rule and open child care to the entire community.

In 1975, Fran Purcell, then county executive, planned to approve the purchase of a new fleet of executive cars for the Supervisors. At that time a child care center received $50 a week for child care. Rooney organized a protest at the next board meeting where a large number of children marched carrying signs that said "kids not cars." As a result, Mr. Purcell authorized an increase from $50 a week to $55 a week for 11 hours of care." [28]

News Story

Joan Saltzman of Community Advocates was also concerned about the quality of care afforded patients at the Nassau County Medical Center. In a *Newsday* story **(June 26, 1973)** written by Kevin Lahart, **"Patients Voice Med Center Gripes,"** along with Alonzo Merritt of Community Organization Services. Saltzman was active with consumers to address grievances including job discrimination against blacks, the lack of translators for non-English speaking patients; a lack of women or minority group members on the hospital's five-member board of managers; and a need for 24-hour emergency room coverage by social service workers to help with social problems related to patient care.

1974

Nassau Action Coalition (NAC)

During the mid-1970s on Long Island, there was a push to move ahead some important social policy agendas. Among these were the Nassau Action Coalition (NAC) and the Coalition for a National Health Plan. The coalition focused the attention of its 43-member agencies on the needs of people receiving Supplemental Security Insurance (SSI). The coalition was aware that SSI recipients were going hungry because they were not eligible for food stamps and because SSI did not increase its payments when landlords raise monthly rental fees.

Early NAC activists were Barry Rock of LIJ Hillside social worker; Mary Wiley Smith, a strong-voiced consumer; Henry Doliner a social activist and president of Nassau Senior Forum; Joan Saltzman and Evelyn Weinstein of Community Advocates; and Elaine Haymes, Joan Wachtler, Ellen Beldock, Sandy Oliva - graduate students in Social Work from Adelphi; and Elaine Schulman of the League of Women Voters. & Jay Connelly, a senior citizen who was involved in a nursing home reform coalition and Ombudsman program's coalition.

NAC began because of a crisis encountered by Nassau's aged. A meeting was convened by Family Service Association of other nonprofit service organizations in the spring of 1974. Following much discussion, the group decided to call itself the Nassau Action Coalition (NAC) of beneficiaries of Supplemental Security Income and advocates. Established, this body quickly moved into action to secure emergency benefits from the board of supervisors and the New York State legislature. Learning what Nassau was doing, the Suffolk Action Coalition (SAC) was organized through the Suffolk Community Council.

With temporary emergency assistance secured, the NAC moved forward and organized around proposed cutbacks to welfare housing allowances, basic welfare grants, and day care for children. In addition to NAC and SAC, coalitions arose in nearby counties to support a larger effort. Large mobilizations with protesters carrying signs and banners descended on Albany, the governor's office in Manhattan, Nassau's Department of Social Services, the New York State office building in Hauppauge on the same day, and major concessions from government were won. NAC and SAC continued for several years, working to bring attention to various conditions of the poor and disenfranchised, and mobilizing for action.

During the same period, Family Service Association and Community Advocates initiated meetings to discuss the possibility of a LI grassroots mobilization for national health care program. As a result, the informal group learned more about three different proposals from Washington for a national health plan and decided to mobilize the broader community. Thus, the Nassau Coalition for a National Health Care Plan was organized in late 1974. The coalition held a major conference at Adelphi University with approximately 450 in attendance. The coalition continued to meet for a few more years after which more Suffolk residents became interested and it became the Long Island Coalition for a National Health Care Plan. [29]

News Story

Hugh A. Wilson, a former social worker, assistant professor of political science at Adelphi University and founder of Adelphi's Institute for Suburban Studies wrote an article in *Newsday* **"The Nation of Suburbia,"** (September

29, 1974). In the article, Wilson says: It is hypocritical to blame suburbia for the sins that have characterized all American growth." The institute, supported for two years by The Veatch Program, was formed in recognition of the enormous population shift that was occurring at the time and the absence of understanding of the psychological, social, political, educational and political ramifications of the shift.

The Puerto Rican Legal Defense Fund

Newsday reporter Robert Fresco reported that the fund filed a law suit against the Patchogue-Medford School District that result in a ruling that the district's teaching English to Hispanic children wasn't an acceptable substitute for bilingual education. The judge mandated that the district develop a bilingual program. [30]

Cornell Cooperative Extension of Suffolk County (CCE)

CCE developed a wide variety of youth development programs throughout Suffolk County initially under the leadership of Tony Tramantano and later Kermit Graf and Tom Williams. Under CCE leadership, faculty and staff, the Suffolk County Farm and Education Center developed with a three-part mission to provide educational programs for youth and families which would increase understanding of agriculture, food and environmental issues, provide vocational experiences for jail inmates in areas related to agriculture and the mechanical sciences, continue to produce and process food for county institutions using the latest research based information and techniques from Cornell University and other land grant universities. [31]

News Story

Newsday reporter Michael Unger wrote **"Issues of Suburbia Entering Academia," (January 28, 1974)** describes the plans of Hugh A. Wilson's plans for Adelphi's new Institute for Suburban Studies. Wilson indicates that the institute will study problems such as suburban crime, health care, pollution, population and employment, housing, transportation and zoning.

The Urban League of Long Island (UL)

The league was founded and incorporated as one of nearly 100 affiliates of the National Urban League. The National Urban League is the nation's oldest and largest community-based movement devoted to empowering African Americans to enter the economic and social mainstream. [32]

Economic Opportunity Council of Nassau (EOC Nassau)

The Office of Economic Opportunity (OEO) in Washington decided to develop a pilot project that addressed a growing concern faced by people throughout the country, the rising costs of fuel oil. The project entailed training homeowners to weatherize their homes through caulking and weather stripping their windows and doors and installing insulation where necessary. OEO needed a competent organization to field test the project. EOC Nassau was selected to pilot the project as the first in the nation.

An essential project element was the employment of the chronically unemployed. EOC Nassau recruited and employed hundreds of people who were provided with job training and supervision as well as supportive services. The training included learning skills in carpentry, painting, and good work habits. Many of the participants started their own businesses. [33]

EAC Network

In the late 1970s, many social activists launched campaigns for prison reform and alternatives to incarceration both nationally and locally including on Long Island principally supported by the Veatch Program of the North Shore Unitarian Fellowship (now named the Unitarian Universalist Veatch Program at Shelter Rock). EAC was very much a part of these actions coalescing with groups such as The New York State Council of Churches, the Community Service Society, the Vera Institute for Justice, Prison Families Anonymous, and Long Island groups such as the Veatch Program-supported Nassau Coalition for Safety and Justice and the Suffolk County Conference on Juvenile and Criminal Justice.

Rene Fiechter was hired for a summer to help with a bail program and possibly raise some funding at The Port Washington EAC, EAC (now named EACINC) when it first started in 1974 fresh out of law school. He later went on to become the agency's Senior Associate Executive Director. Today, he is a Nassau County Assistant District Attorney and Director of Community Affairs.

Fiechter describes himself as a native long Islander raised in Queens, who moved to Nassau and now lives in Suffolk. His parents were French/Swiss survivors of World War II, who met on the boat in 1946, fell in love, married, and had a son, Rene. Fiechter attended New York City public schools and then finished off at St. Paul's in Garden City. His father advised him to always study that which he did not like. After all, he said "you already are good at the other matters." Based on his dislike for business and his distrust of lawyers Fiechter went to the University of Pennsylvania's Wharton School for four years to study finance and then pickup Law Degrees from Hofstra and New York University (NYU).

In 1974, Fiechter turned down job offers in finance and law as he realized that what he liked most was teaching at a school for troubled youth and working with Professor David Kadane at Hofstra's first law clinic over a fish store in Hempstead. As a clinic student, he could represent indigent clients and go nervously into court where the judges looked at the students quizzically and said "so you are Kadane's kids!" "Yes we were…and still are," continued Fiechter.

While at Hofstra, prison riots at upstate Attica Prison exploded. At that time, to help defray Fiechter's expenses, the school arranged for a number of students to work in the county probation department as well as the Queens Legal Aid Society. Already heavily in debt with student loans, Fiechter decided to add another year's expenses to attend NYU to study criminal law while waiting to see if he passed the Bar.

At NYU, Fiechter found himself studying with leading judges, prosecutors, and policy makers. Most of them were working full time with no time to prepare for class while he, the fulltime student and, as he puts it, probably least gifted, read the assignments and was able to truly enjoy the discussions. Upon graduation, Fiechter applied to work for the county Legal Aid Society and District Attorney's office but, although getting offers, saw an ad for a lawyer for a small nonprofit in Port Washington to help with a bail program for kids in trouble with the law. The nonprofit was formed by four women including Joan Boden, Diane Freed, Nadine Heyman, and Barbara Gross.

It is there that Fiechter met Boden, a woman who Fiechter describes as "remarkably feisty," who like Kadane, smoked cigars. She explained that the job was just for a few weeks as they may be going out of business but the four founders and she were looking for ways to keep it afloat. She asked if Fiechter could write grants. He told her that he knew zero about grants but Boden dismissed it saying that soon enough he would be winning million dollar grants. Fiechter signed on for a summer to work with this small group of educators and ex-offenders for what he thought would be a short and curious adventure in the world of social work and the law and maybe find some funds.

One day, Boden casually suggested Fiechter visit Edward Lawrence, director of the brand new Veatch Program at the North Shore Unitarian Fellowship. With nothing to lose, he called Lawrence and was invited to come on over. He met Lawrence in his office, congenial in summer attire, glasses atop his head, looking up and asking: Do you sail?" Fiechter did sail so for the next few days they drifted around Manhasset Bay on Lawrence's C and C sloop. Lawrence explained his desire to be a progressive force of change over a spectrum of areas starting on Long Island. One of those areas was criminal justice. He asked if Fiechter had any ideas. Fiechter had just written ten papers at NYU so he prepped a short reform plan covering juvenile justice, police, courts, corrections, probation and parole. Fiechter thought he was dreaming.

Lawrence explained the principles of Unitarian Universalism, 'to strive through our grant-making to encourage a free and responsible search for truth and meaning; justice, equity, and compassion in human relations; and the use of the democratic process.' He drew a picture of wanting to enable the Veatch Program's projects to effect change and be able to speak out without fear of retaliation or fear of being defunded. This was the very thing that David Kadane had concern about. A few days later, Lawrence called Fiechter to say that the Veatch committee would grant $100,000 to put the plans in to place. The summer project became a twenty three year adventure. Boden passed away shortly afterwards but she inspired Fiechter and started EAC as a small but passionate counseling center that went on to become a significant agency on Long Island and New York State.

That year EAC could have folded. Its main funding, through Nassau County's Vocational Educational Extension Board (VEEB) and the Department of Drug and Alcohol, were dropping EAC funding but the Veatch Program support changed Commissioner Harold Adams' mind. He then collaborated with EAC to launch a major new initiative, Treatment Alternatives to Street Crime.

The Veatch Program also funded the Long Island Bail Commission, Long Island Friends of Fortune, Prison Families Anonymous and many more groups including the New York State Defender's Association which today is a nationally acclaimed state center for all New York's defense attorneys.

To harness the work of all these groups, the Veatch Program funded the Nassau County Coalition for Safety and Justice and the Suffolk County Conference on Criminal and Juvenile Justice as well as the New York State Coalition for Criminal Justice. For the next ten years, Lawrence's leadership made it possible for EAC to launch dozens of projects including Treatment Alternatives to Street Crime, police councils, women's programs, and family court programs. The Veatch Program supported EAC's Developmental Learning Program that saved many young people. Eventually, EAC was running projects and alternatives to incarceration programs throughout NYC and Long Island.

Fiechter is fairly sure that today's EAC staff has little idea how, but for Lawrence and the Unitarians, there would most likely not be an EAC at all. He believes that "those early efforts had profound impact on the criminal justice landscape of Long Island and New York State. In looking back, today, because of these efforts, Fiechter feels that a whole generation of people was schooled in nonprofit management, reform and advocacy, coalition building and making change. [34]

100 Black Men of Long Island (OHBMLI)

"The organization was established as a nonprofit organization with the purpose to improve the quality of life in Nassau-Suffolk counties. The organization supports various programs: For the Future; Mentoring, Education, Health & Wellness and Economic Development. The membership of OHBMLI is composed of men who demonstrate excellence in a broad range of professional endeavors. [35]

Notes: Chapter VI

1. United States Census Bureau. www.census.gov.
2. "The Challenge of Crime in a Free Society" (President's Commission on Law Enforcement and Administration of Justice, 1967).
3. Tom Williams, interview with author, July 22, 2014, Bellport NY and recollections of the author.
4. Davis Pollack, interview with author, April 1, 2014, Islip NY.
5. "Before There Was a Snowden There Were Representatives Like Long Island's Otis G. Pike," Karl Grossman (lipolitics.com 2014).
6. David Starr, email correspondence to author July 3, 2014.
7. Information obtained on website: www.futurecivicleaders.org.
8. Evelyn Roth, interview with author, August 21, 2014, Farmingdale, NY.
9. Vera Parisi, telephone interview of April 25, 2014.
10. Lawrence Levy, interview with author, October 1, 2014, Garden City NY.
11. Information obtained from agency's website: www.ucp-suffolk.org
12. Tom Williams, interview with author, July 22, 2014, Bellport NY and recollections of the author.
13. "Child Care Council of Nassau, Chronology," (A Report Prepared by Jan Barbieri, 2014).
14. Father T. Peter Ryan, telephone interview with author, June 1, 2014.
15. Tom Williams, interview with author, July 22, 2014, Bellport NY and recollections of the author.
16. Walter Stockton, interview with author, June 30, 2014 and information on agency's website: www.ighl.org.
17. Robert Detor, interview with author, Amityville, NY, April 3, 2014.
18. "Collection of the Suffolk Community Council" (Special Collections and University Archives at Stony Brook University).
19. Ibid.
20. Rick Van Dyke, interview with author, Port Washington, July 22, 2014.
21. Sadie Hofstein, email correspondence of April 21, 2014.
22. Davis Pollack, interview with author, Islip, NY, April 1, 2014.
23. "Help Is at the End of Their Line," A.J. Carter (Newsday, May 17, 1973).
24. L. Von Kuhen, interview with author, Centereach, NY, August 28, 2014.
25. Information obtained from agency's website: www.ucp-suffolk.org.
26. Information obtained from agency's website: www.fedoforg.org.

27. Sandra Feinberg. email correspondence of November 15, 2014.
28. Jill Rooney, email correspondence of July 21, 2014.
29. Joan Saltzman, interview with author, Great Neck, NY, June 7, 2014 and Rick Van Dyke interview with author, Port Washington, NY, August 6, 2014.
30. "Brutality Suit Names Suffolk Police, Klein," Robert Fresco, Newsday. Dec 18, 1973).
31. Tom Williams, interview with author, Bellport, NY, July 22, 2014.
32. Information obtained from agency's website: www.urbanleaguelongisland.org.
33. Leone Baum, interview with author, Hempstead, NY, January 29, 2014.
34. Rene Fiechter, interview with author, Mineola, NY, March 5, 2014.
35. Information obtained from agency's website: www.100blackmenofli.org.

Chapter VII: 1975-1979

Overview

Presidencies of Gerald Ford and Jimmy Carter. Communist Takeover of Saigon. Helsinki Accords. Cambodian Genocide. Israeli Egyptian Peace Treaty. Supplemental Security Insurance. John Paul II. Jonestown Massacre. Camp David Peace Accord. Three Mile Island Nuclear Accident. Iranian Revolution with Ayatolla Khomeneini. Soviet Invasion of Afghanistan. Chrysler Bailout. Iranian Hostage Crisis.

Beginning in the late 1970s, an HIV/AIDS epidemic affected Long Island and continued through the last half of the 20th century. Through Christine Hunter's groundbreaking efforts on behalf of the Nassau County Department of Drug and Alcohol Addiction, the department secured the first HIV/AIDS testing grant in 1985 for the Long Island region from the New York State Department of Health. This initiative offered early testing, identification, prevention and referral to Long Island residents and their families impacted by HIV disease and substance abuse. Twenty consecutive years of HIV/AIDS testing grant re-funding were secured that brought over $5 million in HIV/AIDS testing and prevention funds to Long Island. [1]

The following interviews describe social welfare issues of the late 1970s from three different perspectives.

Steve Englebright has been a New York State Assemblyman since 1993. Englebright discussed his involvement in environmental issues during the 1970s and his legislative record both as a state assemblyman as well as a Suffolk County Legislator from 1984-1992. His work protecting the environment is included due to its impact on the health of Long Islanders.

In 1971, Englebright came to Stony Brook University to assume the position of Curator of Geological Collections, teach a Geology of Long Island course and teaching methods courses in the Graduate Studies Program, and set up the

Museum of Long Island Natural Sciences. Englebright, to portray a dramatic destruction of pine barren land, made the museum's first exhibit depict the plight of the pine barren land that had been transformed into the Hauppauge Industrial Park. Through his coursework preparation it became clear to Englebright that Long Island was facing a crisis with regard to the safety of its drinking water. He helped to introduce the concept of a ground watershed, a catchment area for drinking water a radical idea for the time. Englebright developed a traveling slide show presentation about the importance of these environment issues and their implications.

Until Englebright took an interest in Long Island's interior forest or Pine Barrens, their wholesale leveling continued with little attention to protecting the forests. He visited many of these areas and growing became concerned about how land use patterns were harming Long Island's drinking water. It also struck him how little public attention was given to the linkage between the fate of the forests and the quality of drinking water, certainly a public health issue. Most attention by environmental advocates had focused on protecting Long Island's tidal wetlands which had been severely damaged and filled in over the years. Englebright recalls frequent *Newsday* articles often featuring about contaminated wells, industrial accidents, tanker trucks spillage but no one was putting the pieces together to consider the policy implications of these circumstances.

At the same time, New York State Assemblywoman May Newburger established a state Water Resources Commission and hired Englebright as a consulting geologist. Working with both legislative branches, Englebright found common ground among Democrats and Republicans. To protect the Pine Barrens, The Long Island chapter of the Nature Conservancy, founded by Robert Cushman Murphy, along with businessman T. Decker Orr, a strong conservationist and chapter chair, wished to acquire a 5,000 acre parcel of land called Maple Swamp in Southampton adjacent publicly-owned land. Murphy was Curator Emeritus of Oceanic Birds at the Museum of Natural History and a member of the National Academy of Sciences. Murphy was a major figure in the story of land and wildlife preservation on Long Island, and thus, the health of humans who live on the island. Murphy, with his impressive scientific credentials, was able to convince previously- resistant and skeptical members of the county board of supervisors that conservation measures were needed to assure the safety of Long Island's drinking water.

In order to make the acquisition, the county legislature had to match a $1.5M pledged by the Nature Conservancy. At the meeting of the legislature's parks committee in the Riverhead legislative auditorium, 25 students in Englebright's college class joined him in speaking in favor of the acquisition. It became apparent that some legislators, particularly John Rosso and Anthony Noto opposed the county purchase of land for preservation. Another of the opposing legislators was Ferdinand Giese, the legislator for the district where

Englebright lived and worked. Giese was also the chairman of the parks committee. Geist was the last to voice his vote. He stared moved his microphone close to him, stared at Englebright, and in a snarling voice said: "Noooo!" Despite the opposition, the land purchase was approved."Geist's attitude motivated me to seek political office," says Englebright. Two years later, Englebright defeated Giese and entered the county legislature. [2]

Gregory Blass paints a picture of his 34-year history of a Long Islander with a commitment to public service who became an important figure in Suffolk County during the county legislature's formative years. Blass went on to serve as a Family Court Judge helping to reform the county's Family Court, and later, bringing important changes to the county's social services department as commissioner of social services.

Gregory Blass was born in Freeport in 1949 and grew up there with six brothers and sisters. His father was a podiatrist while his mother carefully raised seven children while involved with PTA, church drives, a bridge group, and musical societies. His father engendered a tremendous work ethic in his children. His father was dedicated to his family and professional career. He describes his home life as "always in motion." In thinking about this, Blass recalls years later when Suffolk County Legislator Michael Donohue told him "you create chaos! You thrive in it."

Blass lived in an integrated area in Freeport during his formative years, the1950s and 1960s where single breadwinners, with families of four-five children each with a car, nice lawns, and television sets. He looks back at this period of his life witnessing a bucolic area getting developed. "I enjoyed seeing beautiful woods that we camped in and hiked through. It was a wonderful, safe time," says Blass. To see bulldozers were a harsh reality that bothered him. This influenced him as he got older. Throughout his youth, Blass held various jobs including a newspaper route with the *Long Island Press* and a small landscaping business that he organized with some friends. He was taught the value of a dollar and how to work with customers.

He attended Brooklyn Prep commuting on the Long Island Railroad where he received a Jesuit education that encouraged the taking apart of ideas and analyzing them. Blass was heavily influenced by the Jesuit humanistic and social responsibility view of life. "From your freshman year on during high school, you were taught that 'whatever you do for the least of mine you do for me' said Blass. He was impressed by how Jesuits seemed to always have the right person in place in each of the school's departments and the teaching of the basic classical curriculum. He enjoyed tutoring disadvantaged students from Crown Heights and Bedford Stuyvesant during this time.

Blass attended college in the tumultuous late 1960s, attending Fordham University, also a Jesuit school, where he majored in both accounting and

English. He helped form *Focus,* an underground newspaper featuring parodies and political opinions that the regular school newspaper would not print. To this day, Blass cannot figure how they allowed students to publish the articles they did. Blass recalls this period of his life as one in which he opened his eyes to the world. "Everything was on the table to evaluate and reconsider our opinions," he recalls. He began to take up unpopular causes when views were polarized; perceived in black and white. He served as president of student government and as floor leader of the student senate.

When the Kent State massacre occurred in 1970 and Fordham University was closed down for exams, Blass wondered with deep concern how a governor could send National Guard troops onto a college campus. He began to view things differently from how he had before. He got involved in politics as president of Fordham's Young Republican Club. He worked in the John Lindsay mayoral and Nelson Rockefeller gubernatorial campaigns even though it was fashionable to be democratic. He did not agree with many Republican positions even though his parents were Republicans. Abraham Lincoln, Teddy Roosevelt, and Fiorello LaGuardia were, and continue to be, his political role models. In college, he particularly appreciated Rockefeller's environmental record especially cleaning up the Hudson River and Roosevelt's environmental record in the Adirondacks and many other parts of the country. Years later, Roosevelt's portrait was displayed on Blass' office wall irking some fellow Republicans to no end.

In 1970, with the military draft lottery looming over him, Blass decided to join the Navy instead of being drafted. He had always loved the beach, surfing, boating, and water skiing. He was concerned about the dumping of sewage in the ocean. He filled out what was called a "dream sheet" stating what his dream for a naval career would be like. It was to get his commission at Officer Candidate School, go law school and graduate, and then become a naval attorney in the Judge Advocate General Corps (JAG). In the navy during 1971, he was assigned to a swift boat like John Kerry but did not go to Vietnam as most ensigns had before President Nixon had arranged for the South Vietnamese military to be trained for these roles with the result that Blass did not go to Vietnam. At age 22, Blass attended Fordham Law School graduating in 1974. He then passed the bars in New York and Florida and went into navy as a JAG.

In 1978, Blass bought property on the water in Jamesport became a Republican committeeman and got involved with local groups such as the Lions and the NJROTC Booster Club. During this time, he worked for a small Riverhead law firm. One year later, County Executive John Klein, who was running for re-election as county executive wanted the Conservative Party's endorsement. To get the endorsement, Klein made a deal to "give away" Dennis Hurley's County First District Legislative seat when he decided not to run again. The plan was to run what was considered to be a weak Conservative Party candidate, a retired correction officer, who would run with Republican endorsement. This would pay back Conservative endorsement of Klein. You Blass decided to run for the seat as a protest against the deal. He was annoyed with the western Suffolk/Smithtown bosses selling out the East End. He met with local politicians to persuade them that the East End would suffer with a weak legislator and got their support. While he felt sorry for the weak candidate, he won both the primary and general elections. His platform was to support the establishment of a separate Peconic County; oppose the Shoreham and Jamesport nuclear power plants; a strong environmental agenda; and address the prevalence of domestic violence." [3]

Betty Schlein, a feminist and former Long Island Representative for Governor Hugh Carey provides the following views regarding women's issues during the 1970s.

"The ERA failure in New York State in 1975 was where we met the real opposition. To encourage women to run for office we worked with the Women's Political Caucus. It was the time of the pill, the sexual revolution, Roe v. Wade and battles for enforcement at local hospitals. Demonstrations were held frequently. The effort to end sexual violence, rape and misogyny goes on to this day as does the fight to end discrimination and for economic equality." [4]

News Story

"The Homosexual Life-Style: Out of the Shadows," a 1976, *Newsday* two-part series discusses the experiences of Long Island homosexuals in what was defined as the "normal" world. David Behrens, the staff writer spent three months preparing the article and chronicles the existence of "nearly two dozen gay bars not counting the Fire Island bistros; the Gay Student Union at Stony Brook University, an officially-recognized student organization; weekly rap sessions for male bisexuals and homosexuals at the Middle Earth Switchboard; a Nassau-Suffolk Task Force on Lesbianism offering workshops on social problems and legal rights; Womankind, a Nassau feminist organization providing seminars on sexuality and the women's movement; Gayphone, a Suffolk telephone hotline; the Women's Liberation Center in Hempstead; community youth agencies such as Port Alert in Port Washington and SCAN in Syosset who offer counseling; a Gay Caucus at Adelphi University and an officially-recognized Gay Student Union at Nassau Community College.

Social Agencies by Year

1975

News Story

In 1975, *Newsday* reporter Amanda Harris wrote **"Bias Suit Filed for Hispanic Students" (February 27, 1975)** on a law suit against the school district was filed by The Puerto Rican Legal and Educational Defense Fund. Two years later, the suit was settled in favor of LUH and The Puerto Rican Legal and Educational Defense Fund with the district mandated by U.S. District Court Judge Jacob Mishler, to develop a bilingual education program.

1976

Coalition Against Domestic Violence Nassau County (CADVNC)

At a meeting of the Levittown Inter-agency Coordinating Council in 1976 a momentous coming together of the right people at the right time occurred. Dr. Sherry Radowitz, who was chairperson of Nassau NOW's new Task Force on Household Violence/Battered Women and Associate Director of the Action Council of Central Nassau had just recently moved back to New York from Colorado where she was involved in the Fort Collins NOW chapter. She entered into a conversation with Beverly Merkinger, mental health worker, and Arlene Siegelwaks, assistant director of Consultation and Education, both employed in the Community Mental Health Center at Nassau County Medical Center (now NUMC), about battered women on Long Island. They concurred that not much was known about the issue. A social worker began going into the community to talk about violence against women. This small effort fueled a survey to Nassau County agencies and organizations to determine if battered women were asking for services and what was being offered.

An initial planning session was held in September of 1976 with organizational representatives to determine a strategy for making services available to victims. Members of this planning session formed the nucleus of the coalition that was named at the first meeting, the Coalition for Abused Women. Beverly and Sherry shared the administrative responsibilities in the initial phases and co-chaired the coalition with goals of improving communication and increasing membership to strengthen the organizational structure. Radowitz then became the first president.

As it was determined that no agency could provide the direct services needed, the coalition initiated steps toward incorporation to obtain grants to provide services. Through the efforts of Arlene, Nassau County Medical Center provided donated space and Comprehensive Employment & Training Act

(CETA) workers, supervised by Siegalwaks, for the initial staffing. Sherry took hotline calls at her home until the coalition in 1977 started its hotline staffed by volunteers. The coalition's first grant was from the Veatch Program for a phone device to enable the hotline to be available 24 hours a day and volunteers could have the calls diverted from the emergency room at the hospital to their home throughout the night.

Radowitz, Merkinger and Siegalwaks served many years on the coalition's board of directors, shouldering the responsibility for organizational direction and fiscal oversight. The dedication, hard work, contributions of time and energy and their combined wisdom assured the creation of a stable organization that sets a benchmark in quality services for victims and is a standard for the community." Later, Sandy Oliva served as the organization's executive director for many years. [5]

Peconic Community Council (PCC)

PCC was established to promote social justice through the identification of gaps in health and human services, advocating for solutions and acting as a catalyst to effect social change. It is a nonprofit coalition of organizations and individuals dedicated to the promotion and preservation of a comprehensive system of health and human services for the East End of Long Island in Suffolk County. The organization started as a program of The Suffolk Community Council as part of its efforts to provide services on the East End. The Harnisch Family contributed to PCC since its inception. Louise Stalzer served as the organization for many years.

Together, representatives of local businesses and government, concerned citizens, health and human service agencies actively serving the needs of the East End s residents, make up the membership of more than 250 organizations.

PCC provided the leadership to identify problems and resources in the five East End towns of East Hampton, Southampton, Shelter Island, Southold, and Riverhead and sets up collaborative programs to meet pressing needs; acts as a catalyst to creatively effect social change; gathers and disseminates material relative to quality of life issues on the East End; and networks among the members to utilize existing services efficiently. The PCC mobilized people and resources to meet human needs. PCC believes that through the collaboration of agencies, businesses, government and caring individuals the quality of life for Eastern Suffolk communities can be improved.

Local issues PCC addressed over the years include: Homelessness on the East End, with the creation of the Peconic Housing Initiative and HOPELINE; Adult literacy improvements in cooperation with the North Fork Hispanic Apostolate, St. John's School and the Patchogue-Medford Adult Literacy Program to teach English as a second language; Concerned Communities for

Alternatives to Incarceration, educating and publishing the inefficiency of the current system, including the lack of mental health and substance abuse pre-courts to assist those accused of non-violent crimes.

Maureen's Haven, a PCC program, continues to provide safe, warm temporary housing to those who are homeless from November to April. Transportation to and from the many houses of worship is included in the services provided. Volunteers provide dinner, breakfast, and encouraging support. A toll free phone line provides information, referrals and financial assistance to the homeless and those at risk of homelessness, assisting individuals and families with security deposits, rental arrears and utilities in an effort to prevent eviction and eventual homelessness. An achievement center empowers individuals who are homeless or at risk of homelessness. The center offers ongoing workshops, such as a men's support group, a life skills group, creative art classes, and health care workshops. [6]

<u>Glen Cove Boys & Girls Club at Lincoln House</u>

Lincoln House Settlement moved into its new 30,000 square foot facility and opened its doors in 1976, officially as Glen Cove Boys Club at Lincoln House. To recognize the participation of girls, the organization officially changed its name to what it is known as today, Glen Cove Boys & Girls Club at Lincoln House. [7]

News Stories

In **"Final Touches for Bi-county Health Unit," (February 2, 1976),** *Newsday* reporter Bruce Lambert Jr. describes the Nassau-Suffolk Health Systems Agency whose purpose was to design and improve health care on Long Island. According the article, the new agency will replace the Nassau-Suffolk Regional Medical Program; the Nassau-Suffolk Comprehensive Health Planning Committee; and the Long Island Health and Hospital Planning Council.

Newsday reporter Bob Master wrote in **"Prepaid Health Plan Set for Suffolk," (July 25, 1976)** about the establishment of Suffolk County first health maintenance organization, the Health Systems Planning Group of Suffolk Inc. The group was formed to establish a health center serving 25,000 subscribers in western Brookhaven town. It was funded with federal funds under the Health Maintenance Organization Act of 1973 to provide complete medical and hospitalization coverage. The organization was shepherded by Priscilla Redfield Roe who serves as board chairperson. Dr. Marvin Leeds, a professor of community medicine at Stony Brook University served as project director. The only other health maintenance organization operating on Long Island is the Community Health Program of Queens-Nassau which was sponsored by Blue Cross in conjunction with Long Island Jewish Hospital.

Junior League of the North Shore of Long Island

The league opened a community youth services center in Oyster Bay and placed an emphasis on advocacy against violence on children's television. It soon initiated CAP, a child abuse prevention, parenting education program for high school students. The organization also established YES, Youth Environmental Services, a crisis intervention counseling program in the Massapequa area and Mad Hatters, a reading encouragement program for elementary school children. [8]

Habitat for Humanity International (HFHI)

Habitat for Humanity International (HFHI) was founded in 1976 by Linda and Millard Fuller. HFHI is an ecumenical Christian partnership of concerned people working together on principles of fellowship, charity, and a firm belief that everyone deserves a decent place to live. Habitat affiliates around the world invite people of all backgrounds, races and religions to build houses together in partnership with families in need. Originally working out of a garage in Rocky Point before moving into a church office, the Habitat Suffolk founders began developing relationships with municipalities, corporations, churches, schools, private groups, and individuals to form the organization as it is known today. [9]

The Suffolk County Coalition Against Domestic Violence (SCCADV)

The Suffolk County Coalition Against Domestic Violence (SCCADV) developed as the result of the work of a number of women's organizations. It was incorporated in 1976 as a nonprofit organization to provide services to victims of domestic violence in Suffolk County. From the beginning, SCCADV recognized that the most important need for victims is safety. With a program of shelter, supportive services and prevention, SCCADV began to offer victims options as they took the first steps in reclaiming their lives. In its early days, SCCADV set up a 24-hour hotline and volunteers opened their homes and their hearts by providing "safe houses." A network of safe homes was established, and the crisis hotline and supportive services were all provided by volunteers.

During the next few years, funding was secured and in 1983 the Safe Harbor shelter opened, enabling SCCADV to provide safety and shelter for victims of domestic violence. The shelter provides clients the core services necessary to help flee abuse, develop a plan of action and find permanent housing all in a supportive environment. Safe Harbor was the first shelter in Suffolk County specifically for victims of domestic violence.

Continuing as a pioneer in the field, SCCADV launched the Domestic Violence Precinct Outreach Project in 1989. This program was the first of its kind in the nation. The project placed a domestic violence advocate in each Suffolk County Police Department Precinct. Advocates act as a resource and provide direct client services.

Over the years, SCCADV and the Coalition Against Child Abuse and Neglect (CCAN) worked closely together. They discovered that the two agencies experienced a great deal of overlap with their clients. In fact, they often shared clients. Typically, family members of the children seen at CCAN had current or prior trauma histories which had not been addressed. Additionally, SCCADV often uncovered child abuse within the families they were working with around issues of domestic violence. [10]

The Victims Information Bureau of Suffolk (VIBS)

VIBS was established as a pioneer in the domestic violence and rape crisis movements. In 1974, when VIBS was just an idea, no one imagined that there was so much abuse in suburban Long Island. In 1976, when VIBS held a press conference to announce the grand opening of the center, few people understood the scope and complexity of intimate violence. What the founders did understand was that abused women were calling the new hotline in droves, and that the program needed to grow. Compelled by mission and guided by experience, VIBS has pioneered innovative and effective programs to address domestic violence and sexual assault. [11]

News Stories

In 1977, *Newsday* reporter Sylvia Moreno reported in *"LI's 'Other' Minority,"* **(February 28, 1977)** that the stereotypical image of "lazy" men was unfair. Hispanics had worked to make LUH a successful agency with a board of directors that represents the Hispanic communities and organizations, serving over 17,500 people last year. According to Anthony Cotto, Executive Director of La Unión Hispánica: "Our programs have expanded to include mental health, adult education, nutrition of which many are self-sustaining by community volunteer labor." Cotto was confident that LUH had taken the right steps to build a united organization and deserves greater public support despite the dissension among different Hispanic nationality groups about how services should be provided and administered.

La Unión Hispánica continued to provide its services continuously while experiencing financial problems a common reality of small, nonprofit agencies principally funded by the county. In 1981, *Newsday* reporter Sylvia Moreno wrote in **"Troubled Social Agency Fires Chief,"** **(January20, 1981)** that LUH's board fired Cotto amid allegations that he had mismanaged the agency.

In response, Cotto said that he had told the board that the agency needed to borrow money from a bank and hold fund raising events or arrange for an advance from the county until the county paid what was due from prior months. In the early 1990s, La Unión Hispánica's services were absorbed by Federation Employment Guidance Services (FEGS).

1977

Long Island Pine Barrens Society

The Long Island Pine Barrens Society is a non-partisan, nonprofit organization dedicated to the study, appreciation and protection of these unique woodlands. Founded in 1977, the Society has become one of Long Island's most effective champions of preserving natural resources through sound land use. Through our scientific research and programs of public education and advocacy, we have shaped public debate on the subject." [12]

Hispanic Counseling Center (HCC)

HCC was established by the Nassau County Department of Drug and Alcohol Addiction to provide substance abuse treatment services to the county's growing Latino population. The agency grew over the years, adding programs to respond to the community's most urgent needs.

Youth programs, funded by the Nassau County Youth Board, were added in 1979 to provide prevention, education, and counseling for young people and their families with limited fluency in English [13]

News Story

Newsday, in **"Study Is Critical of Juvenile Court,"** reported that: "Judges who inadequately explain to juvenile offenders their rights in court, and court-appointed attorneys who are unfamiliar with court procedure are two major shortcomings of the Nassau Family Court" according to a six-month study conducted by the Fund for Modern Court.

Big Brothers Big Sisters of America Long Island (BBBSLI)

Big Brothers Big Sisters of America (BBBSA) is the oldest and largest youth mentoring organization in the United States. BBBSA operates under the belief that inherent in every child is the ability to realize their endless potential. BBBSA makes meaningful, professionally supported matches between adult volunteers ('Bigs') and children ('Littles'). Its Vision is that all children achieve success in life. BBBA's mission is to provide children facing adversity with strong and enduring, professionally supported one-on-one relationships that change their lives for the better, forever.

Unique to BBBSA, is a system of ongoing evaluation and support which is proven by independent studies to help families by improving the odds that 'Littles will perform better in school, avoid violence and illegal activities, and have stronger relationships with their parents and peers. Children are matched between the ages of 7 and 14. Volunteers are ages 18 and over. BBBSLI is a full member agency member of BBBSA. Both are private, non-sectarian, nonprofit organizations. It operates in 12 countries and is headquartered in Philadelphia, PA.

Bill Tymann, the retired CEO of the organization, was born in 1948 in Flushing, the oldest of five children. The family moved in 1952 to Hicksville and lived an uneventful childhood except for the fact that his father died of cancer when he was 18. As the oldest child, Tymann took on new family responsibilities. He commuted daily on the Long Island Railroad to attend catholic, all-boys Archbishop Molloy High School in Queens. He obtained an academic scholarship at Fordham University initially as a pre-med student and later changing to earn a Bachelor's Degree in Social Work in 1970. In his senior year, he married Celeste, the girl next door who he knew since age 5. Tymann has two children. Lisa is a corporate attorney in New York City and Brian owns his renewable energy company and lives in Westhampton. Tymann is looking forward to his first granddaughter's birth this summer.

"After college, Tymann did a stint in the Air National Guard and then took a job as a caseworker under Monsignor John Fagan at Little Flower Children's Services in Wading River, a foster care agency, serving children and youth from the city. Tymann worked for Little Flower for nine years establishing group homes throughout Long Island. He became its assistant director. This experience provided him with experience in real estate, local and state regulations concerning group homes, and laws regarding legal guardianship. Tymann recalls communities' negative attitudes towards group homes. Residents did not want the children, mostly black, in their neighborhoods and viewed the children as "bad seeds" that would lower their property values.

He recalls one experience trying to open a group home in Patchogue in 1973 where local officials claimed that group homes violated zoning regulations. Little Flower went to court and won the suit setting an important legal precedent that a group home be treated as a single-family home.

At another group home, in West Hempstead, the house parents were Fred and Una Dodsworth, a wealthy, retired military couple from England and Ireland. The Dodsworths decided that they wanted to bring the ten boys to spend a month in England as an educational and cultural experience. They would make the arrangements and pay for the trip. This involved arranging for the purchase of a bus for the month, securing permission from the department of social services and obtaining passports. The Dodsworths and Tymann did what was necessary over a several month period to overcome bureaucratic resistance and obtain the required authorizations for the trip. The boys had a wonderful experience visiting castles and meeting with royalty. The trip serves as testimony to the love and commitment of many families to children at-risk.

Tymann came to feel frustrated by the day-to-day hardships faced by the children in the foster care system. He searched for an opportunity to help children in a preventive way by identifying needs at their early stages where assistance was possible. He heard about BBBSLI which Jim Boyle had started in 1976 and applied for a position. At the time, BBBSLI was operated by Catholic Charities with separate programs in Nassau and Suffolk counties. In 1979, Boyle, who was director of the Nassau program, left the agency and Tymann became its Executive Director. Tymann, Catholic Charities, and Nassau Youth Board director Ann Irvin decided that it would be best for the Nassau program to become independent from Catholic Charities to remove the perception that BBBSLI was a sectarian agency which it never was. At the same time, the newly-formed Suffolk County Youth Board funded a BB/BS program. Under Tymann's leadership, the Nassau and Suffolk groups took the necessary steps to merge into Big Brothers/Big Sisters of Long Island, thus reducing overhead and combining boards.

After the merger, the agency grew establishing unique fund raising programs including "duck races" and 'bowling for kid's sake' eventually raising $150,000 each annually, large sums at the time. These fund raising programs were part of Tymann's belief that if he was going to serve many more young people, it would not be due to government funding. The Nassau Youth Board grant, at the time of the merger, was $165,000. Tymann was convinced that this sum would never grow substantially and that it would only be through private fund raising efforts with a stronger board, a business board familiar with marketing, finances, public relations, and fund development, that growth was possible. Tymann was also convinced that government was inefficient in the spending of tax dollars and wanted to extricate BBBSLI from government.

An important program innovation that Tymann launched in 1980, started in the East Meadow School District, was the High School Program, a program to identify students at early ages through the participation of school administrators, teachers, and guidance counselors. The program also matched high school students with younger students. Part of the program's benefit was that you could directly reach the student without depending on the parents who sometimes were not very good at parenting and, thus, did not see the program's benefit. Ultimately, the high school program was replicated throughout Long Island and throughout the country as he served for three years as a consultant for the federal ACTION program. Tymann's creativity, vision and hard work had been taken to another level.

Tymann emphasizes the important of networking and describes successful networking among people who were big brothers in the past like Jed Morey, owner of the *Long Island Press* and Bill O'Reilly, nationally-syndicated radio and television personality. "It is also about how and when to ask and how to 'schmooze,'" says Tymann.

At the same time, Tymann decided to further diversify BBBSLI's funding base. Specials events were extremely labor intensive and had limited time spans of popularity. Networking was pursued to individuals with the capacity to influence others and had access to resources were important. They included Tom DiNapoli, Glen Cove's Mayor; John Tillota, president of Long Island Savings Bank; Dave Woycik, an attorney and Hofstra University trustee; and Jim Metzga, a successful businessman and Hofstra's president Stuart Rabinowitz. Woycik donated a building to the agency that houses BBBSLI's Nassau County offices.

Through his travels, Tymann knew of the Savers, a 50-year old thrift store company that was doing business with BBBS in Phoenix, Arizona. Tymann did his homework and learned that the company only did business west of the Mississippi and was planning to come to the east coast, he got in touch with them to discuss doing business on Long Island. Savers usually selects nonprofits with nationally-recognized names to do business with. Tymann convinced Sabers to try out Long Island as a location for clothing collections to be distributed to their outlets throughout the U.S. The BBBSLI board was initially tentative about the idea concerned by liability issues even though Savers offered to guarantee $25K in the first year. "They had a 60s 'mentality," says Tymann.

Tymann responded by suggesting the establishment of a separate corporation with members possessing the needed business expertise. To assure the interests of BBBSLI in the new venture and the board's expressed liability concerns he proposed a five-member board with at least one of them being on both boards of directors. Tymann was so convinced that this was the way to go, that he would resign if the board did not give him one year in which to demonstrate that the business would succeed. The board agreed to move forward. Over the years, the clothing business grew to gross sales of $4.2M in gross sales which produces about 40% of BBBSLI's $1.3M program operations. BBBSLI currently receives no county funding one of Tymann's objectives. The balance of the budget is covered through fund raising and contributions.[14]

Transitional Services of New York for Long Island (TSLI) and Haven House/Bridges, Inc. (HHB)

The two charitable organizations have provided housing and support services for over thirty years to people in need. TSLI, a Community Residence Program, has been helping the mentally ill gain their independence, enjoy caring guidance, and most importantly, achieve and maintain a sense of usefulness and personal dignity. TSLI's programs include Pathways, Special Employment Program (SEP) and Summit. [15]

The Rauch Foundation

The foundation was established.

(For an in-depth view of the foundation, see Nancy Rauch Douzinas' profile in Part III). [16]

The Suffolk Y Jewish Community Center

The center was established by a group of visionary, community oriented people who had a dream to fill a void in the Jewish community of Suffolk County – a place concerned with individual growth through meaningful group experiences. The Suffolk Y Jewish Community Center is a social service agency concerned with individual growth through meaningful group experiences. The JCC's comprehensive program of guided leisure-time activities is both educational and recreational and is directed toward strengthening Jewish cultural identity and the Jewish family unit. [17]

<u>1978</u>

The Long Island Community Foundation (LICF)

Information regarding LICF's history dates back thirty-six years. According to the Foundation's 1981 annual report, the foundation became a division of The New York Community Trust in 1978 in order to make the Trust's resources more accessible to Long Island donors and grant-seekers. Frederick Arthur Ross served as chairman of the foundation's board of advisors and Ed Lawrence served as staff associate. In 1978, the foundation issued grants totaling $22,740. Its Annual Report indicates that the organization had grown substantially since its origins. The report states that the foundation fund raised $1.6M for 44 beneficiaries in 1958 to $7.9M for 129 agencies and hospitals in 1978.

The 1981 annual report lists examples of grants awarded by the advisory committee including: Suffolk County Conference on Juvenile and Criminal Justice, Prison Families Anonymous; the Nassau Day Care Council; the New York State Defenders Association, the Long Island Chapter of the Nature Conservancy; and the Suffolk Community Development Corporation. Grant awards ranged in size from $2,500 - $5,000 for a total of $110,000 awarded."[18]

Literacy Suffolk

Literacy Suffolk was established to provide a variety of literacy services to adults, thereby enabling them to achieve their personal goals. Literacy Suffolk recruits volunteers and trains them to tutor fellow adults in basic language skills: reading, writing, listening, speaking. [19]

Attention to the issue of child day care took on greater importance in the late 1970s as more-and-more women and advocacy groups focused media attention on the subject.

News Stories

In 1978, *Newsday* covered the children's day care story in **"Working Mothers Plead for Aid on Day Care" (January 31, 1978)** telling the story of 200 working mothers pleas for greater support for day care subsidies. A *Newsday* story **"A Children's Crusade for Day Care," March 14, 1978)** written by Patrick Brasley describes a demonstration by over 100 working mothers, children, and day care providers pleading for more funding for county day care centers. Later in the year, in **"Nassau Plans to Shift Aid to Help Day Care" (May 29, 1978)** it is reported that Nassau County officials would raise the income eligibility for children of working mothers. This action came directly as a result of the advocacy of scores of working mothers and their children before the county board of supervisors organized by the Child Care Council.

1979

The Long Island Progressive Coalition (LIPC)

The Coalition emerged from the work of the Democratic Socialist Organizing Committee that had a chapter in the 1970s in Nassau County. From their discussions, the idea evolved to establish a new nonprofit Long Island organization for the purpose of developing 'a progressive movement to counter the 'right-wing revolution' sweeping through the nation that led to the election of Ronald Reagan as President in 1980." [20]

For a further discussion of LIPC, see Part III for Marge Harrison and David Sprintzen.

Coalition Against Child Abuse and Neglect (CANNC) (renamed The Safe Center of Long Island)

The Coalition Against Child Abuse and Neglect of Nassau County was established as a coalition of organizations addressing issues around child welfare following the establishment of New York State Child Protective Services' says executive director Cindy Scott. Founding organizations included the Nassau County Department of Social Services, Nassau County Department of Drug and Alcohol, and the Junior League of the North Shore of Long Island.

Scott continues: 'We had an advocacy focus, looking at how different systems were working and what needed to be changed to keep kids from falling through the cracks." One of CANNC's first contracts was through the Nassau County Department of Social Services to provide education and consultation with Nassau County Child Protective Services to coordinate cases that involved child sexual abuse. It involved pulling together all the entities involved and establishing a multi-disciplinary team and has experience with collaboration - and co-locating services with other providers. As the convening agency for Nassau County's Child Advocacy Center, CANNC hosts teams of police detectives, child protective services workers, district attorneys, and medical staff who jointly investigate cases of child sexual abuse or extreme physical abuse - while simultaneously offering its own advocacy, counseling and support for victims and their families. [21]

News Story

Newsday reporter Sylvia Moreno wrote the article **"Youth Services Termed Inadequate" (January 4, 1979)** that a bi-county government survey revealed that Long Island's young people are not receiving adequate services and the counties were risking the loss of half of their state aid unless they developed long-range plans. In response, Nassau County Youth Board director Ann Irvin said "our biggest problem is the out-migration of youth from Nassau because of the lack of employment opportunities, transportation, and the high cost of housing. We have a community that has begun to age rather rapidly and that is of grave concern to us."

Author's Reflection

From 1970 to 2002, I directed youth service and child care programs in Suffolk County. This was a period when most county legislators did not feel that the county should provide financial assistance to nonprofit service organizations for children, youth, and family services. Nonprofits were seen as simply "contract agencies" lumped with other county vendors and suppliers of goods and services who wanted county funding. As a result, nonprofits had to conduct annual appeals for support from their county and state representatives, thus reducing the time that could be dedicated to service delivery to their clients. This absence of dedicated funding made long range planning impossible and caused constant stress and uncertainty among staff and board members. You were made to feel like you were always begging for charity rather than presenting facts and figures on how best to meet the needs of the county's growing population. We were viewed as the "budget-busting" idealists who did not understand the county's financial situation.

News Story

Newsday ran a series written by Aileen Jacobson **"No Cure-All Solutions in Sight" April 11, 1979)** dealing with how government, schools, and counselors were dealing with children drinking earlier and in larger numbers. According to the article, Colin Campbell, director of the Suffolk Chapter of the Long Island Council on Alcoholism feels that "It is time for us to look at our society and our habits, and not blame everything on the kids." Joseph Kern, director of Nassau County's alcohol addiction services said "there is a lack of services for these kids."

In the late 1970s, many news stories appeared concerning the patients discharged from Long Island's three state hospitals for the mentally ill. Family members organized new advocacy and direct service organizations.

News Story

"Suit Says Aged Are 'Warehoused'" (was an article published in *Newsday* reporting that "hospital wards hold 10,000 patients who should be in nursing homes. A class-action lawsuit, prepared by plaintiffs the Long Island Regional

Council of the Federation of Parents Organizations for the New York State Mental Institutions; the Coalition of Institutionalized Aged and Disabled; and the Friends and Relatives of Institutionalized Aged was filed in U.S. District Court.

Suffolk Network on Adolescent Pregnancy (SNAP)

On the day before her retirement in June, 2013, Marcia Spector, SNAP's founder and executive director, was interviewed by a staff member about her long and industrious career as a leader in the field of adolescent pregnancy prevention. Here is a summary of that interview tracing SNAP's development:

"I moved to Suffolk County in 1978 from Brooklyn to accept a position with Brookhaven Hospital as the director of Community Health Education and Outreach. My Master's Degree was in community health and health care administration and I had always been interested in maternity and child health programs, especially those involving adolescents. I had a rough adolescence myself and I think I always wanted to make it a smoother ride for young people.

"In the late seventies there was a growing awareness of the rising incidence of adolescent pregnancies, and at the urging of the Suffolk County Youth Bureau director, Jim Leigh, and the youth board chair, Martin Richmond, The Suffolk County Executive, John Klein, formed a 'blue ribbon' task force to study the problem, with membership from county departments, educational and civic organizations, and both Catholic Charities and Planned Parenthood. I represented Brookhaven Hospital. The task force was chaired initially by Ann Coates, a dynamic community advocate, who left a short time after her appointment to go to law school. Although I had been in Suffolk County for a short time, I was selected to replace her. Under the joint auspices of the Suffolk County Youth Bureau and the Suffolk Community Council, the task force met monthly from 1979 to 1985, sponsoring conferences, workshops, providing technical assistance, facilitating collaborations, and conducting research. It was a full time job, on top of the one I already had, but I loved it. I remember one of my friends saying to me that this was going to be a big issue, and I should stick with it. And she was right!

"In 1985, SNAP became a funded agency of the Suffolk County Youth Bureau. I was hired as the executive director, and Helen McIntyre, the chair of the Suffolk County Youth Board's Comprehensive Planning Committee, was appointed as the board chairperson of SNAP. With initial county funding of $52,000, quietly slipped in to the budget by the youth bureau, we had no money for rent, furniture, or equipment, and everything had to be donated. The town of Islip gave us surplus furniture and provided our initial office space. Southside Hospital gave us permanent donated space (that the agency still enjoys, twenty five years later). For the first few years we did not have money for a computer, copier or a fax machine, so several times I day I was down in the administration suite making copies, faxing documents, or borrowing supplies. Without Southside, there would have been no SNAP.

"We started off without nonprofit or charitable status or a tax exempt number, all of which required much time and effort. Schools and organizations were calling for speaking engagements or technical assistance, frantic parents were requesting help, teenagers were asking for information. I was working 80 hours a week, and loving every moment of it.

"Our first part time secretary was a twenty-one year old former teen parent with a five year old daughter and an abusive former boyfriend/ father of her child. A few times we had to close down the office because he was threatening her. So it was like living through teen parenthood firsthand. She became our first success story, ditching the boyfriend and returning to school and becoming a physical therapy assistant.

"In our second year, we were awarded a $365,000 competitive collaborative state grant, for which we served as the lead agency. We also got a $75,000 increase from the county legislature, championed largely by our supporter, Sondra Bachety. So we went from almost nothing to a sizeable budget in less than a year. Those were the wonderful, heady years, when there was money available for worthwhile projects. Even though teen pregnancy was a very controversial issue, the county legislature was largely supportive, and I quickly made friends on both sides of the aisle. I would invite legislators to my house for dinner as a way of making alliances. There were only one or two Indian restaurants at that time in all of Suffolk County, most people had never had it, and I enjoyed making Indian food, so I invited people to my home for Indian food, and it became a joke: "Have you been invited yet to Marcia's house for Indian food?' I even invited former County Executive Steve Levy once, before he married his wife Colleen, because I wanted to fix him up with my secretary. I do not think he even noticed she was at the table. He was too busy talking politics.

"But there were bumps in the road. In those days if you had a small budget you only had to pay your payroll taxes once a month. If you went over a certain amount you had to pay your payroll taxes every ten days. We had no money for a payroll service, so we had no idea of the change. After our funding went up we were slapped with a huge penalty fine from the I.R.S. and we had to ask for congressional help from Tom Downey to get it waived. When we applied for charitable status from the IRS, we asked for his help again, as was the practice at the time. However, our I.R.S. contact informed us that since we had requested a "congressional investigation" he was going to make our lives miserable, and he did! (These were the Reagan years, and programs like ours were not looked upon with favor by the administration)

"I really liked the political part of my job, and it was always one of my favorite activities. For some reason, I was particularly successful with the conservative Republicans. I guess they thought I was "motherhood and apple pie" and they trusted me. They were often uncomfortable with some of the more controversial issues, but they understood that teen pregnancy and childbearing were social problems that they had to address, and we gave them the opportunity to do so.

"In a way, the more things change, the more they stay the same, as the French expression goes. When I first became involved in teen pregnancy, schools were routinely counseling girls to drop out, until pregnancy was deemed a medical condition and that practice was made illegal. Now they do not tell them they cannot come to school, they just do not provide the support systems they need to make it possible for them to continue attending. They basically said there is a seat in the classroom for you. Figure it out on your own.

"What has really changed today is that the resources are not there. We all know the numbers are down significantly, 50% in Suffolk County from the early 90's until now, but the teens' stories are more compelling and the cases harder and more complex. The girls seem younger; many more are undocumented and/or victims of rape or incest. The BOCES programs for pregnant and parenting teens and the school social workers assigned to work with them have disappeared.

"We had opposition from the beginning, and it has not really gone away. When we had monthly network meetings, opposition folks would appear. There was one little old man, Ray, who came to our meetings faithfully. He had a hearing aid that would make loud buzzing noises in the middle of our meetings. We never knew if he heard or understood anything that was said, but he was obviously sent to spy on us. We also had Right to Life demonstrators who would appear at the county legislature meetings to demand that we be de-funded.

"There were always wonderful, dedicated and talented people working in this field. Nobody goes into this work for the money; they do it because they really want to make a difference. These days more men are working in the field of adolescent sexual development, and that is a welcome change.

"One of the hardest challenges for me was dealing with racism. I was surprised by how much racism there was in the African American community, and we definitely were on the receiving end of it, particularly in Wyandanch and Riverhead. I think racial attitudes have changed a lot since the late seventies. Race has taken on much less significance with the young people with whom we work today; interracial dating is much more common, young people have multiple racial identities and do not want to be pigeon-holed into a particular racial category. I think that is a good thing; I would like to see the day when race is no more relevant than ethnicity, like being Italian, or Irish. I would like to think that we are moving in that direction.

"My biggest accomplishment, I believe, is in nurturing and developing my staff and in finding my personal fulfillment in their growth. I have always felt that I wanted to develop staff to the point where if they want to stay, that is great, but if they are ready to move up the career ladder, then I have done my job. To me, that is the mark of a good leader. I am also very proud of the internship program that we developed through the years. It is a way of giving back to the field, helping future graduates. It is fun being part of a learning environment and having young, idealistic students who question the status quo.

"I was fortunate to have had incredibly dedicated and generous mentors in my work, too numerous to mention, but a few stand out. In its early years, SNAP would not have continued without the invaluable help given by Linda Devin Sheehan, then principal planner of the Suffolk County Youth Bureau. Others include, SNAP board presidents Ralph Etchepare, Barbara Jordan, Allen Breslow, and board members Tom Williams, Cindy Pierce Lee, Marilyn Proios, and Martha Mobley.

"Jesus Garcia was another important mentor, board member and friend I met early on. He was a Cuban refugee who struggled to make a life for himself after leaving Cuba, becoming the de facto head of the Latino community in Patchogue. He was an amazing human being. Although he was highly educated, when I first met him, as an immigrant with a strong Spanish accent, he was still working as a night supervisor in a factory. In those days, people thought nothing of poking fun of his English or of his ethnicity. But he was such a likeable, good natured guy that he developed a huge following. As a Cuban, he was drawn to the Republican Party, which at that time was very powerful in Suffolk County. In those days, the Republicans would host lavish fundraisers, and Jesus would always invite me as his guest, enabling me to hob-knob and network with the power brokers.

"He was probably the most influential and helpful person to me, certainly at the beginning, because he was the one who opened many doors politically. And really, some people have trouble admitting this, but I learned from him…you go after the power. The Republican party on a national level today is a disaster, but in those days in Suffolk County, on a local level, whether you were a Republican or a Democrat often did not really matter that much; it really depended on who was in power, and for many years it was the Republicans. So much of our support came from them. Certainly the Democrats were more likely to support our issues, but the Republicans supported us because Jesus asked them to. Jesus had only one biological child, Jesse, but he and his wife Miriam opened their doors to dozens of foster children, some of whom they adopted. He had a heart of gold. Jesus also gave me an appreciation for Latino culture; opening my eyes to the richness, warmth and vibrancy of Latinos. He was a very special man, who died much too young, and I shall always be grateful to him.

"My most honored moment was when the Islip town NAACP gave me an award. I felt very touched, understanding the depth of despair and anger in the African American community. Learning how to handle it has been, I think, the hardest thing I have had to deal with. Sometimes I felt I got the brunt of that anger when I tried to do what I thought was right. So getting the award from the NAACP was very meaningful. I was also very touched by the award from the Long Island Volunteer Center. But honestly, my biggest reward has been enjoying my relationship with my wonderful staff.

"As far as embarrassing moments, there was the time during the Halpin administration, when we were viewed as more of a Republican organization. During the annual budget battle, our funding was eliminated and given instead to the Office for Women. After intense lobbying, the Legislature restored our funding, but there was a technical flaw in the legislation, and they had to do it all over again. I think it was when I got the news that we got defunded that I laid down on the floor of our office suite, kicked my feet and screamed. But we had good political contacts, and the Legislature voted 18 to 0, twice, to restore us. That was nice.

"When all else is said and done, I think in this profession one needs to be kind, above all. I think to be kind really trumps all other attributes. We are here to help people and to help each other and kindness is an underappreciated virtue. I think I have learned to be a kinder, better, more humane person in this job. I am grateful to have had wonderful opportunities and mentors who have taught me the importance of kindness. [22]

News Story

In a 1979 article, "**Suffolk Snubs Hispanics, Study Says**" *Newsday* reports that LUH had conducted a year-long study, funded by the Unitarian Universalist Veatch Program at Shelter Rock, revealing that 1.77% of the county's workforce was Hispanic while its Hispanic population represented 6.75% of the population. The study also indicated that the Hispanic unemployment rate was 15% and the median income of a family of four was $7,000. The study also showed that very few Hispanic youth receive county services. The study said that a major deterrent to providing county services to Hispanics is the language barrier.

The Bellport Area Community Action Committee (BACAC) and the Bellport, Hagerman, East Patchogue Alliance (BHEP)

News Story

"**North Bellport: The South Bronx of Long Island,**" *(1979)* *Newsday's* shocking headline greeted residents of the neighborhood commonly known as North Bellport one day in 1979. It called out for action - a community meeting convened by Howard Jennings, Director of the Bellport Local Action Center, and Nancy Marr, Director of the Bellport Area Community Action Committee, brought out residents of the Bellport and East Patchogue area. It was no surprise that the community had problems, largely seen as the falling sales value of their homes and the reluctance of purchasers to buy homes in the area. The people who came to the meeting acknowledged that it was time to do something about it.

The following information was provided by Nancy Marr. Marr is a longtime community activist in the Bellport area, the former director of the Bellport Area Community Action Community (BACAC), as well as a member of the League of Women Voters.

The three square mile North Bellport and East Patchogue area had been developed in the early 1950's by contractors who marketed their houses to the post-World War II population who were eager for housing and able to obtain V.A. and F.H.A. mortgages with low down payments. It was just north of Montauk Highway and the Long Island Railroad tracks, which separated it from Bellport village, a community with a diversity of housing and population including very affluent homes along the Great South Bay. From its beginning the community had problems. Many families had come from New York City and never owned a home; many husbands commuted back to the city for jobs leaving their families alone, often without transportation. Reports came from new residents that local stores would not grant them credit, that they were made to feel unwelcome in the churches and schools, that their children had no place to go after school. Families who had invested little in their new homes tried to sell them, and often just walked away, leaving the property to real estate developers. They often turned to another group of people eager for housing and often unable to acquire it - minorities from New York City and Queens.

Once the realtors had made a few sales they were able to spread rumors that more homes would be sold or rented to minorities and white people would be unable to sell their homes. The block-busting was eventually heard in court and the realtor most guilty lost his license, but by then the neighborhood had begun to tip - not only racially but toward rentals rather than homeownership. For people who were searching for affordable housing, this was attractive. And for Suffolk County, whose department of social services was faced with the task of finding housing for people displaced by the County's urban renewal efforts it was especially attractive.

During the 1960s, the community began to lose its original white homeowners, and by the end of the seventies its population was primarily black or Hispanic, and at least half of the homes were rented. Other problems followed: landlords who rented to clients of social services were able to find renters even though their homes were substandard. The department provided security deposits for their clients when they moved to another, maybe better, home, and the landlords developed a pattern of forcing their tenants to move in order to obtain another security deposit. As landlords churned the tenants from house to house many of them became dilapidated and were left to decay.

When the churning was identified and the department changed its policy of repetitive security deposits, tenants were faced with the struggle to get their landlords to repair problems in their current homes. The proportion of residents who had low or very low incomes, or no income, grew as more homes were rented to families on public assistance, affecting the care they gave their homes and sometimes affecting the care they were able to give their families. One of the worst results of the housing problems was the transiency that resulted; families moving within the community or moving out of the community and then back in, moving their children from school to school and feeling no roots in any community. The landlords were able to charge exorbitant rents for poorly maintained properties and seldom objected if tenants took in others to help them pay the rent.

The groups that had gathered to combat the community's problems met regularly to create an alliance of the organizations that were concerned in order to find solutions. Choosing to be as inclusive as possible, they called the organization the Bellport, Hagerman, East Patchogue Alliance (BHEP). They wrote by-laws and elected a board of directors, applied for incorporation and then for charitable status with the IRS. They tackled various community issues, gaining the support of organizations in the surrounding community. To help new homeowners with their property taxes, they had a training program by New York Public Interest Group on grieving taxes.

They applied for a grant and got funds from Catholic Charities and hired Paul Arfin as a consultant to train community volunteers to be block captains who would be available to help their neighbors. It was thought that the emphasis on helping neighbors would be more successful than a Neighborhood Watch, which would pit neighbors against one another. With the help of Joop van der Grinten, we got funds for a Tenant Effectiveness program from the Capuchin Friars of White Plains. It made it possible for Nina Stewart, later the Housing and Community Development Director of Easthampton Town, to work with the block captains to develop a guide for renters to help them get better service from their landlords. The guide they wrote was adopted by the Department of Social Services for distribution to their clients. Plans to help landlords understand the needs of their tenants, although planned, did not take place. The Alliance worked closely with the Town of Brookhaven Community Development Department on code enforcement and its grants to homeowners to fix up their homes.

As a volunteer organization, it relied on many community volunteers who had ideas about how to improve the community through better housing alternatives. Because so many of the homes had been built with little insulation, volunteers came to show people how to make their homes more energy efficient at a low cost. Joop van der Grinten organized volunteers from local churches and the community to actually repair homes for homeowners, and renters, who could not do it themselves. The program, called SWAP (Summer Work Action Program) enlisted wiling volunteers each summer, many of whom described the transformative experience of meeting people in need and realizing they could help them.

Help from Sister Joan Spencer at St. Joseph the Worker Roman Catholic Church in East Patchogue helped Nina Stewart and myself write a successful grant proposal to the National Catholic Conference, and the Alliance hired its first full time staff person, Helen Martin, and opened an office in the community. Although many members of the board of directors were inexperienced, their enthusiasm and concern for the community made them take their responsibilities seriously, and they supported Mrs. Martin whenever she needed advice or help.

Despite the many efforts of the board and the volunteers, however, it was clear that there was no way they could effectively deal with the housing problems without more drastic action; they could not adequately protect renters from their landlords and could not help homeowners who were finding it impossible to sell their homes. The Board decided the next step was to actually get into the housing business. Martin began to explore the possibility of obtaining funds that could be used to rehabilitate some of the homes that were falling apart and affecting property values. The commissioner of the Town of Brookhaven Department of Community Development, Ed Romaine, was challenged by the community's problems, looking for new ways to help, perhaps on a block by block basis. He offered to transfer three properties to the Alliance that would need rehabilitation. Once fixed up, they would be rented by the Alliance to Section 8 tenants who could pay as rent only one-third of their income. The Alliance would carry a debt to the town but would not have to pay it as long as the property remained in the hands of the Alliance and was rented to a low income family.

Thus, began the creation of a housing agency that has contributed to the stability of the community by providing sound rentals for as long as tenants need them with the long-term goal of home ownership. The day the Alliance welcomed the first family into one of the homes, *Newsday* carried the story of the event with an interview with the mother of the family. When asked how we knew that the program would work when tenants cannot care for their homes, I responded with Martin the belief that well-maintained rentals would create responsible tenants. She was convinced that that tenants who knew they could remain in their house as long as they paid the rent would see it as their own and take care of it.

The funds that had been received from the National Catholic Conference over a three-year period helped the Alliance establish itself, but it was obvious that a longer stream of money was needed if more was to be done - funds were needed to acquire homes, rehab them, manage the rentals, assist tenants with their problems, and participate in the upgrading of the community. Martin and I met with many funders to request funding that would sustain a program of housing, but even in the days when government and funders acknowledged the need for more affordable housing, we met with little success, largely because funders did not think our program would be sustainable. The programs that did succeed in attracting funding, moreover, were dedicated to homeownership, with few funds for renters.

Finally, with the help of Ernest Langhorne, a staff member at the New York State Division of Housing and Community Renewal (NYSDHCR), Martin applied for funding as a rural development project which could fund the Alliance operations as a housing rehabilitation agency. After many conferences and changes, the Alliance was designated a rural development project, which would entitle it to ongoing funding to create housing for low and moderate income families. After many years, it was transferred within DHCR to the Urban Development section since it was within the boundaries of the more urbanized section of Long Island.

Since 1979, when it was established, the Alliance has rehabbed over sixty homes, which have been rented to low income tenants, many with Section 8 subsidies. Ten of the families have managed their finances and purchased the homes they were living in, and other homes have been sold to first-time homebuyers who were not tenants. In cases where Section 8 subsidies were not an option, tenants paid reasonable rents, made possible by the low overhead of the Alliance and tax abatement by the town and school district. If it were to pay the property taxes, and rent without the subsidies, it would be impossible to charge rents that would be within the means of many of the families.

From 1983, when Martin became director to 2006 when she retired, her leadership of the Alliance and her relationships within the community, played important roles in maintaining stability. She always viewed her role as community participant rather than as an executive director. She found ways to meet the needs of families living in Alliance homes. The board's hope that good rental housing management would make good renters proved to be true in most cases. The Alliance became a spokesman for the rights of renters in the community along with those of homeowners. Through budget and job counseling, Martin helped many residents to accomplish their goals. Some were not so fortunate so Martin had to be flexible as they struggled to rental money. Her ability to remain friendly but firm did not always work so some residents had to move.

Martin was a co-founder and board member of INN Friendship, a soup kitchen that has been in the community for many years. Her staff collects toys at Christmas and turkeys at Thanksgiving. Many people in the community attend an annual Christmas party that includes tenants, staff, funders, and supporters from the wider community. Martin also developed a senior citizens' support program that holds annual commemorative events on Martin Luther King's birthday and during Black History Month.[23]

News Story

A *Newsday* editorial **"Patronage Won't Train the Hard-Core Unemployed" (April 5, 1979)** reports that Suffolk County Labor Commissioner Lou Tempera warned Republican leaders that "it would be against the law for him to place people in federally-funded CETA jobs because of political referrals. The editorial indicates that such political influence is used in Nassau County and upstate Erie County. County officials are urged to train people who are hard to employ and make them self-sufficient, the intent of the CETA program.

Special Acknowledgement

The organizations described in these pages are all nonprofits with one exception. Because Just Kids Early Childhood Learning Center is an outlier, a wonderful example of a trail-blazing service organization, its for-profit status does not seem important. Its founders Steve Held and Steve Gordon established a replicable model of services for children of working families as well as children with special needs.

Just Kids' philosophy and mission statement was developed on the notion of "whole child" development in an inclusionary environment. The mission of the program is based on developmentally appropriate early childhood philosophy that supports the importance of early childhood learning experiences including play and a planned program that supports the needs of young children and their families. Just Kids believes that all children can learn and that learning occurs in all areas of development – social, emotional, cognitive, linguistic, and physical. Just Kids believes that all areas of development are interrelated and interdependent and that learning occurs at different rates for different children and that the child's early learning environment and experiences significantly impact on their lifelong development. Just Kids believes that the best outcomes for children occur when families and professionals work together in partnership to meet the unique needs of the child and family.

Just Kids Early Childhood Learning Center is a comprehensive preschool program providing a full range of services to children and families. The organization has several center based special education programs throughout

Suffolk County. Just Kids also is a Universal PreK provider for both the Longwood and William Floyd School districts. [24]

Notes: Chapter VII

1. Christine Hunter, email correspondence of October 21, 2014.
2. Steve Englebright, interview with author, East Setauket, NY, August 14, 2014.
3. Gregory Blass, interview with author, Jamesport, NY, July 23, 2014.
4. Betty Schlein, email correspondence of July 7, 2014.
5. "Collection of the Suffolk Community Council" (Special Collections and University Archives at Stony Brook University) and July 22, 2014 interview with Tom Williams.
6. Sherry Radowitz, written correspondence of January 11, 2015.
7. Information obtained from agency website: www.glencovebgc.
8. Information obtained from agency's website: www.jlli.org.
9. Information obtained from agency's website: www.habitatsuffolk.org.
10. Information obtained from agency's website: www.sccadv.org.
11. Information obtained from agency's website: www.vibs.org.
12. Information obtained from agency's website: pinebarrens.org.
13. Information obtained from agency's website: hcc.org.
14. Information obtained from agency's website: www.bbbsli.org.
15. Information obtained from agency's website: www.tsli-hhb.org.
16. Information obtained from agency's website: rauchfoundation.org.
17. Information obtained from agency's website: suffolkyjcc.org.
18. Information obtained from agency's website: licf.org.
19. Information obtained from agency's website: literacysuffolk.org.
20. Information obtained from agency's website: www.lipc.org.
21. Information obtained from agency's website: thesafecenterli.org.
22. Marcia Spector, written correspondence of August 20, 2014.
23. Nancy Marr, written correspondence of September 21, 2014.
24. Steve Held and Steve Gordon, interview with author, June 15, 2014.

Chapter VIII: 1980-1985

Overview

Jimmy Carter and Ronald Reagan Presidencies. Recession. Multinational Corporations. New Industrialized Economies. Laissez-faire Economics. Debt Crises. Mt. St. Helen's Volcano Eruption. John Lennon Murder. Vietnam Memorial Dedicated. First Woman Astronaut. Beirut Embassy Bombing. Star Wars. Colombian Narco-Trafficking. Intifada. Ethiopian Famine. Terrorists Hijack TWA Flight 847. First Famine Relief Concert.

Demographic Factoid

In 1980, Nassau County's population was 1,321,582 slightly greater that Suffolk County's population of 1,284,231. However, Nassau County's population had decreased by 107,256 residents, a 7.5 percent decrease. Suffolk's population continued to increase growing by 159,281 residents, a 14.2 growth rate. [1]

In the late 1970s and early 1980s, *Newsday* frequently reported on waste, mismanagement, administrative problems as well as criminal activity regarding the Southwest Sewer District. Newsday also followed accounts of developments that resulted in the decommissioning of the Shoreham Nuclear Power Plant.

For further discuss of the impact that the Shoreham plant had on Long Island see the Gregory Blass interview in this chapter.

News Story

In **"Suffolk Sewer Work Criticized in Report," September 20, 1978)**, *Newsday* reporter Fred Tuccillo writes that "the legislative committee investigating Suffolk's Southwest Sewer District is recommending that the county establish an 'Office of Public Works Inspector General' to guard future construction projects from the problems that have plagued the $832-million sewer program."

AIDS arrived on Long Island in the early 1980s as can be seen in this *Newsday* article:

News Story

In **"The Plague Years AIDS Has Been Here since 1980, No Cure is in Sight, Uncaring, Incompetent Government is a Reason" (May 31, 1987),** *Newsday* reporter Larry Kramer writes about the Reagan administration and the AIDS epidemic: "As a (Ronald Reagan) AIDS bureaucrat told me recently: "God help us with the AIDS epidemic, because the U.S. government won't. Washington, D.C., is not interested in AIDS."

John Gallagher, former Chief Deputy Suffolk County Executive and Police Commissioner, represented the county executive's office as a board member for the EOC of Suffolk. The following are his reflections on his board tenure:

"In the early 1980s as Suffolk's chief deputy county executive, I noticed that the public health and human service portions of the budget were created in a vacuum; none of Suffolk's anti-poverty program network or its mental/public health agencies was given a chance to see their part of the proposed budget. I directed that the agencies affected be given the opportunity to meet with us, go over the proposed budget and offer suggestions. An unhappy budget director set up conferences with representatives from umbrella councils of the agencies involved. While often their pleas for more funding were unsuccessful, at least they had a day in court." [2]

Jane Devine was a Suffolk County legislator from 1978-1987. The following are her reflections on her term in office and her other public service work.

Before entering politics, Devine did church work at St. Patrick's Church in Huntington particularly doing publicity work and writing press releases. She began her political career when a call arrived one evening at her Huntington house from a friend who asked her if she had a camera and a long dress. Devine had both and followed instructions to get over to the Huntington Town House by 7:30pm. Upon her arrival wearing an evening dress and with camera in hand, Devine was approached by town councilman Tom Casey and town supervisor Jerry Ambro. They said: "Let us make Jane our Bess Meyerson." (Note: Bess Meyerson was a TV and movie celebrity and head of New York City's Department of Consumer Affairs) Jane responded by saying: "I do not know what you are talking about. I will not be your Bess Meyerson but I will be your Jane Devine."

She soon joined the town's consumer protection board and later worked for New York State's consumer protection board, followed by a stint as a consumer educator for the town. While in this position, she heard that Claire Sauer wasn't going to run for re-election as a county legislator. Devine decided to run for the vacant seat and won. This was a period in the county legislature when Democrats were in the legislative majority but lost seats in this election. Devine recalls her first day in the legislative auditorium in Riverhead. "*Newsday* ran a front page story featuring a photo of me, the only woman in the horseshoe, with my white suit among seventeen men in blue suits," she recalls. "I remained the only woman in the legislature for four years." Being a legislator, Devine feels, was the "best job I ever had and I have had lots of jobs," she continued. She describes her tenure as free of political interference on substantial issues from Dominic Baranello, the county's Democratic leader. His main focus was electing Democrats at all levels of government.

Devine sees the controversy about the operation of the Shoreham Nuclear Power Plant as having had a major influence on the legislature. She decided to tour the plant and remembers her reaction, looking down into the pool of spent rods. "It was the scariest thing," she recalls. Devine became an opponent to the plant. She recalls Shoreham as an extremely important political issue, as shown when county executive Peter Cohalan did a sudden about-face to support Long Island Lighting's evacuation plan after the accident at the Three Mile Island plant in Pennsylvania amid growing public opposition to the Shoreham plant led by county legislator Wayne Prospect and others who emphasized the issues associated with evacuating people off Long Island.

A particularly troubling recollection that Devine has of the social service scene was her relationship with Alice Amrhein, Suffolk County Executive Peter Cohalan's appointee as commissioner of social services. Devine recalls her as a 'bean counter' lacking the understanding and empathy to understand the poor. Amrhein opposed Devine's appeals for a social service center in Huntington Station because, according to Devine, Amrhein said "you do not have enough zip codes." According to Devine, at every meeting of the legislature's human services committee, the commissioner referred to county residents as "zip codes." Devine found this reference to people to be sterile and uncompassionate and not an attitude she wanted to see in a commissioner of social services. It also suggested to Devine that the commissioner was "doing someone else's bidding."

Devine recalls that her office developed a reputation among residents living outside her district who needed help from the department of social services, including people who had suddenly lost jobs and their homes due to economic conditions. The calls often came in on Friday afternoons with people seeking food to get through weekends. She recalls a visit to an elderly couple's depressing apartment. The couple had not married because they could not afford to lose their benefits. In another case, a formerly wealthy woman, divorced from her husband, was working in MacDonald's and needed further financial assistance. She recalls her visits to middle-class housing developments in Brookhaven town that included dozens of boarded-up, not-too-old, split level homes. These calls and face-to-face experiences affected

Devine and increased her understanding of the changing face of poverty on Long Island. Presiding Officer Gregory Blass appointed Devine to serve on the legislature's public safety committee knowing that she did not plan to run again. According to Devine, Blass figured I wasn't afraid to investigate the police department and the district attorney's office, and which he was right.

As a legislator, Devine came to see how diverse Suffolk County was socio-economically from the East End with its wealth in the Hamptons, poverty in Riverhead, and New England villages on the North Fork. She came to appreciate with the help of Sondra Bachety cultural differences between residents of the south shore compared to the north shore.

Where social agencies are concerned, Devine feels that if a legislator visits a social program to see how it helps individuals and families they are likely to support it. She always felt that nonprofits should be required to raise the equivalent of 10% of what the county provided in a grant through contributions and events. She still feels it was a good starting point to expect each organization to build local financial support for its program. She has always felt that the county should not just limit its support of needed social programs to what federal and state agencies funded.

She was mindful that all decisions on funding non-mandated services always came back to the use of the tax base to support community programs so legislators had to be careful not to go too far in spending county dollars. "The budget is where policy and priorities are set," says Devine. She recalls legislator Giese saying on one occasion: "Watch, you give them $30K one year and the next year they will want desks and chairs and cars. It'll never stop." Speaking about how nonprofits came to the legislature every year to make their cases for support, she recalls how unfair it was since some organizations did not have access while others did." [3]

Gregory Blass discusses the political climate of the 1980s and his role as a county legislator.

Gregory Blass did not expect to win a county legislative seat but was sworn in and remained in office until 1989. Blass, in reflecting on something he learned as a politician, commented, "your friends come and go but your enemies accumulate." Klein had lost the Republican primary to Cohalan in 1979, whose first budget cut child care dramatically, something that Blass could not accept. He saw that most legislators knew little about child care and other social programs for the poor. "Day care was being decimated," recalls Blass, who understood how important child care was to working families. "They were simply viewed as budget items to be cut. Politically-appointed department heads were not about to risk their jobs as forceful advocates," Blass continued.

Public hearings on County Executive Peter Cohalan's 1981 budget, with its draconian cuts to county services, met with widespread public concern and budget scrutiny and criticism not only by legislators but also the public. Blass raised the child care issue and other social issues in Republican caucus meetings and in the Legislature's committees and was able to help rally the first wide spread public opposition to Cohalan's budget. He proposed and cosponsored many amendments to Cohalan's budget which upset Cohalan and his deputies, both Frank Jones and Howard De Martini.

The ten town party leaders were aghast at the political fallout with the assemblies of people, both recipients of social, health, youth, and aging services and the nonprofit providers of these services, who were attending meetings of the Legislature and speaking out and getting the attention of the media. They were uncomfortable with legislators voting out of line. Town leaders had controlled county government since its inception. They viewed the Legislature as a growing nuisance. It was during this period that Blass developed the reputation as a maverick.

Blass sees the development of public policy as "a combination of half personality and half the merits of the issue requiring interpersonal skills." As a legislator, Blass worked both sides of the aisle to make deals to get votes and to raise consciousness of social issues and how they impacted economic conditions. He wasn't alone in this regard. John Foley, Jane Devine, Steve Englebright, Jim Morgo, Sondra Bachety, and others were very supportive of the need to expand social programs at a reasonable rate and to make them work better and more effectively.

Blass, like legislator Jane Devine and assemblyman Steve Englebright, feels that the Shoreham Nuclear Power Plant proposal significantly affected the social and health services. It was front page news for years and polarized the legislature in debate and decisions about taking legal action against Long Island Lighting Company. During 1984-86, Lou Howard was the presiding officer and an ardent Shoreham supporter. Blass was chairman of the legislature's health committee and then chairman of the human services committee, as punishment by the political powers then in control. He brought health concerns into the Shoreham debate resulting in a period of heated debate. In fact, at one heavily-attended public hearing on the subject of 'Tough Love,' the public address system was suddenly disabled by someone in the presiding officer's office.

Newsday was also very pro-Shoreham and, thus, against the legislature opposition and law suits. The paper called the legislature 'a group of self-serving wackos.' County Executive Klein described the legislature as the 'wild west of politics.' Then, County Executive Peter Cohalan also a mild opponent of Shoreham, switched his position to be in favor of the plant's opening.

Fusion government developed due to the public pressure that was a mix of the nonprofits as well as citizen groups and legislative aides sympathetic to their causes who gave off-the-record information and advice to these groups. The days when all decisions were made behind closed doors were being challenged. The public began to be able to speak for more than three minutes at the podium. Committees began to hold hearings. In 1986, when Blass became presiding officer, he led the drive and helped rally the legislators and soon reformed legislative rules to enable greater public scrutiny. He noted that there were no stenographers so they were then assigned routinely at meetings of the full legislature, its committees, and hearings. Budget proposals from county executives had not been made public until the last minute but Blass pushed for a rule to vote on the budget before Election Day and succeeded. The public portion of hearings was very limited, discouraging attendance. This completely changed and the public involvement rose to record levels. [4]

In the late 1970s and early 1980s, Long Island social pioneers, aware of funding opportunities and wishing to avoid premature nursing home placements and non-medical care for the frail elderly, began to develop social adult day care centers. Many of them were modeled on existing programs operating as the Syosset Senior Day Care Center and the Peninsula Counseling Center in Woodmere, the former lead by Dorothy Weiss and the latter by Ellen Tolle. The Nassau County Department of Senior Citizen Affairs partially funded both programs. [5]

In 1980, the New York State Division for Human Rights empowered both the Nassau and Suffolk human rights commissions to conduct investigations on behalf of the state division and thus have direct access to the state's powers to subpoena witness and records, make rulings in disputes and set compensation for damages. Vera Parisi, regional director of the State Division for Human Rights, indicated that the counties would be able to handle many more cases. [6]

James Couch, director of the Long Island Sickle Cell Project delivered a number of "black state of Long Island" speeches at community organizations and colleges in which he said that "the plight of black people today is worse than when I was a kid." He urged people to work together in electoral politics to effect change. [7]

For further information, visit Mr. Couch's profile in Part III.

Social Agencies by Year

1980

In 1980, the Suffolk County Office for the Aging started to issue grants for social adult day care, awarding grants to programs at the Senior Day Care Center at St. James, the Community Programs Center of Long Island in Dix Hills, the Huntington Senior Day Care Center, and the Senior Day Care Center in Centereach. Over the years, these programs, and others, struggled without dedicated public funding streams. Because the programs served small numbers of elders when compared to large senior centers, they were not able to demonstrate what was increasingly the only measurement of their worth, their cost effectiveness. They tried to convince policy makers that they provided important health related services which were not only supportive to the frail elderly but were invaluable to caregiving sons, daughters, and spouses. Efforts were also made to document that, in the long run, community based care reduced the costs of medical and residential care. [8]

Círculo de la Hispanidad (Círculo)

The Círculo story is rooted in the experience of its founder and executive director, Gil Bernardino. When Bernardino, a teacher from Spain, first arrived as an immigrant in 1974 he began working at the Long Beach Youth Board, serving as an active member of the Long Beach Spanish Brotherhood, and teaching in the Long Beach Adult Education Program. It was there that he first recognized the many diverse needs of his Hispanic community.

To give form to the Círculo of his imagination, Mr. Bernardino joined together in the 1970s with two dedicated and talented allies: Barbara Dubow, a bilingual community organizer and successful grant writer and Pat McCormack, Director of Long Beach Youth Services, who generously offered crucial advice and direction. Both helped transform Círculo, 'the Idea,' into Círculo, the viable, enduring organization it is today.

Bernardino and Dubow remain leaders of the organization which stands today, more than ever, as a testament to the power of dedication, productive idealism, and enormously hard work. Since 1980, they have dedicated their lives to building a strong, progressive organization that would help this family-centered hard working community of new arrivals fulfill their promise to grow stronger together as productive members and citizens in their new country of choice, the United States of America.

Círculo was awarded its very first grant in 1980 by New York State, which was matched by another grant from the Nassau County Youth Board. The dream of Círculo then became a reality as the organization was incorporated as an independent, nonprofit organization dedicated to community service. [9]

Junior League of Long Island

 The Junior League established the Discovery Room, a hands-on museum in conjunction with the William Cullen Bryant library exhibit at the Museum of Fine Arts and established a community service fund. [10]

Independent Group Homes for Living (IGHL)

 Throughout the early 1980's, agency CEO Walter Stockton worked with state officials who sought group homes to house children and adults from Suffolk State School in Melville and other state facilities. IGHL continued to develop mid-sized, seven-to-nine bed residential homes on Suffolk's north shore and in the Moriches area. By the mid 1980's, the need to develop homes became so acute that it prompted IGHL to develop seven twelve-bed and two ten-bed homes by the end of the decade. This expansion, during a short four-year period, more than tripled the service network, not only by the number of residential opportunities available, but by the geographical area being served by the agency. In 1982, the first IGHL day treatment program was opened in East Moriches, New York, which also contained the administrative offices that had, to that point, been located in Riverhead, New York. Its original capacity of 120 was expanded to accommodate 155 participants as an additional programming wing was built in early 1985.

The day treatment building was later called upon to accommodate nearly 100 additional participants during a rare evening day treatment program that was in operation from December 1985 through the spring of 1987. Additional administrative space was temporarily added in 1984 and removed in lieu of a more accommodating administrative office wing that was completed in 1987. Right next door, the IGHL day care center opened its doors in the spring of 1988.

The mid-1980's also brought the advent of IGHL's efforts to provide services directly to the consumer and their family in their home or in their immediate community. The spring of 1985 saw the initial offering of in-home respite services as well as the first sessions of our Saturday recreation program. In 1986, IGHL opened its first of two free-standing respite homes, in Shirley with the Holbrook respite program opening in 1988.

The day treatment building was later called upon to accommodate nearly 100 additional participants during a rare evening day treatment program that was in operation from December 1985 through the spring of 1987. Additional administrative space was temporarily added in 1984 and removed in lieu of a more accommodating administrative office wing that was completed in 1987.

Right next door, the IGHL day care center opened its doors in the spring of 1988.

Throughout the early 1980's, IGHL continued to develop mid-sized, seven-to-nine bed residential homes on the north shore and in the Moriches area. By the mid 1980's, the need to develop homes became so acute that it prompted IGHL to develop seven 12-bed and two 10-bed homes by the end of the decade. This expansion, during a short four-year period, more than tripled the agency's service network; not only by the number of residential opportunities available, but by the geographical area now being served by the agency.

The mid-1980's also brought the advent of IGHL's efforts to provide services directly to the consumer and their family in their home or in their immediate community. The spring of 1985 saw the initial offering of in-home respite services as well as the first sessions of the Saturday recreation program. In 1986, IGHL opened our first of two free-standing respite homes, in Shirley, New York, with the Holbrook respite program opening in 1988. [11]

<u>Long Island Cares</u>

Long Island Cares is one of the region's most comprehensive hunger assistance organizations, serving thousands of individuals and families in need. Its mission is to bring together all available resources for the benefit of the hungry on Long Island providing food when and where it is needed, sponsoring programs that promote self-sufficiency and educating the public about the causes and consequences of hunger on Long Island. Its vision is a hunger-free Long Island.

Founded as the first food bank on Long Island, New York, in 1980 by the late singer, Grammy Award-winning songwriter and social activist Harry Chapin, the organization now provides nutritional food and support services for a network of more than 580 community-based member agencies, including food pantries, soup kitchens, emergency shelters, child care programs, disability organizations, veterans' services programs and more.

Sandy Chapin, Harry's widow, is chair of the board of The Harry Chapin Foundation, which is dedicated to bringing together diverse community resources to promote human dignity and human rights. She served on the board of WHY Hunger, founded by her late husband to address national hunger and poverty issues and has, in the past, been actively involved with the Huntington Arts Council. She has served on the New York State Nutrition Watch Committee, the New York State Food Council and the New York State and Suffolk County Martin Luther King Jr. Commissions. A writer, teacher and advocate, she is the mother of five children and grandmother of seven. She and her late husband wrote the gold record "Cats in the Cradle" and the ABC TV film "Mother and Daughter: The Loving War." Sandy is also president of

Chapin Productions LLC, a license administrating and music service company that handles Harry Chapin's music. [12]

News Story

"A Deadly Birthright for Kids with AIDS: Since 1982, there have been 191 reported cases of AIDS in children under 13. Of those, 120 died. Eighty-two of those cases and 56 of the deaths were reported in New York State," a Newsday story **(October 4, 1985)** written by Marilyn Goldstein reports on the growing prevalence of AIDs. The article indicates that all but five of the New York State reported cases were in New York City but notes that suburban children treated in city hospitals were counted as city cases.

United Cerebral Palsy of Greater Suffolk (UCP Suffolk)

The 1980s were a time of major growth and milestones with United Cerebral Palsy of Greater Suffolk becoming an autonomous affiliate of the national association in 1983. A new adult day treatment program and vocational rehabilitation spread to several locations, introducing supported employment services in addition to evaluation and an on-site workshop. The children's center added an eight week summer component and expanded briefly into schools in Commack and Kings Park. Seven family-sized intermediate care facilities (ICFs) were acquired from New York State and UCP Suffolk now had a residential program, soon complemented by the transformation of the original Indian Head Road building into a community residence for 31 adults. This was the first non-nursing home on Long Island to offer residential care to adults with physical disabilities. UCP Suffolk's competitive sports team, the Suffolk Seagulls, was born in the 1980s with two cyclists with money raised through bike-a-thons, galas and golf outings. [13]

1981

South Oaks Hospital

South Oaks Hospital conducted an extensive study and three-part program on compulsive gambling. With the advent of this program, South Oaks became one of the first hospitals in the country to offer services for compulsive gamblers and their families. A key feature of this program was South Oaks Gambling Screening (SOGS), a valuable tool for the detection of compulsive gambling problems. Developed by South Oaks staff members, SOGS is copyrighted and has been translated into several foreign languages. This effective diagnostic tool is still made available to other healthcare institutions throughout the world at no charge.

During the 1980s, South Oaks increased the capacity of Broadlawn Manor to 320 beds and developed specialized units to provide care for individuals suffering from Alzheimer's related dementias. This was one of the earliest efforts to care for Alzheimer's patients. [14]

News Story

In **"Service Agencies Battle Hard Times," (May 31, 1981)** a *Newsday* reporter Noel Rubinton wrote that dozens of nonprofit human service agencies were losing their federal support under the Comprehensive Employment and Training Act (CETA) because President Reagan decided to phase out the program. The agencies reported that they will have to discontinue services and close programs. Adrian Cabral, executive director of the Health and Welfare Council said "a basic restructuring of human service programs has begun." He warned "of dire consequences for many programs as further cuts are made."

The Viscardi Center

When Henry Viscardi retired as the center's president, his successor, Dr. Edwin W. Martin, introduced many new ideas to help people with disabilities achieve independence. Among the innovations the Center experienced in the 1980s was the introduction of an adult education program which integrated physically challenged adults with non-disabled adults. This program was the first of its kind in the United States. [15]

The Suffolk Action Coalition (SAC)

SAC was formed and served as the advocacy arm of the Suffolk Community Council until 1988. Council continued its roles of gathering and maintaining serving as a major forum for analysis and advocacy on the county, state, and federal budgets; coordinating individuals and organizations and sustaining dialogue with government officials. Leadership was provided through the issue of publications, sponsorship of organizing meetings and rallies, and training to help nonprofit agencies achieve economies and find other sources of income to supplement the loss of federal funds. Among SAC' early leaders were Luke Smith, Father Ron Richardson, and Richard Sass who served as executive director. [16]

The Community Programs Center of Long Island (CPC)

The following story about CPC is written by the author who served as the organization's founder and executive director for twenty-two years from 1980-2002.

CPC was incorporated as a charitable, nonprofit organization. Its story provides a vivid illustration of the nonprofit world of the early 1980s on Long Island.

In the late 1970s and early 1980s, national news stories abounded about corporations around the country establishing child care centers and documenting lower employee absenteeism, greater loyalty, and reduced recruitment costs. In 1981, President Ronald Reagan encouraged "public-private partnerships" to address social problems as an alternative to government operations.

CPC was established with a mission to develop affordable, quality child care programs for working families of all income levels in collaboration with businesses. No other Long Island nonprofit or for-profit company had made the effort. Existing services were geographically scattered and inconsistent in quality. Most did not accommodate early morning/late afternoon schedules of working families and only a handful provided care for children under age 2. Government provided subsidies for a handful of centers but no support for moderate or middle-income families. Head Start funding was available only to extremely low-income families. Corporate support was limited to one afterschool day care center at CMP Publications in Manhasset.

CPC's founders, Jill Rooney and Paul Arfin, assembled a board of directors. Rooney was executive director of Harbor Child Care. Arfin was the former executive director of the YMCA of Long Island's Outreach Services Division and youth center director. The board decided on a co-Executive Director administration with Rooney as director of child care programs and Arfin as administrative director. While the arrangement tapped the expertise of both parties it led to irreconcilable issues of leadership style and control. The situation created internal tension that could have destroyed the organization if the board had not intervened. Board members mediated an agreement in which Rooney left the organization with Harbor Child Care assuming ownership of a CPC center that had been established in New Hyde Park.

CPC's strategy was encouraged by interest expressed by the *Newsday* corporation that had recently established a new plant and offices in Melville. A group of female employees had filed a sexual discrimination law suit partly based on the lack of affordable child care services. In 1981, the company sought assistance to conduct an employee needs assessment survey to assess the degree of employee interest in child care and demonstrate concern for its female employees. CPC was selected to conduct the survey. It revealed a need for a child care program in close proximity to the company's Melville offices. CPC proceeded to market the center at *Newsday*, other companies, and the community-at-large. It soon became apparent that the level of *Newsday* employee interest wasn't sufficient to sustain a *Newsday*-only center. In addition, company management made it clear that it wasn't interested in providing direct financial assistance to its employees. Instead, *Newsday* gave CPC a $10,000 charitable contribution to help operate the center in its infancy. These circumstances portended what obstacles were to come with regard to support from other corporations.

When the center opened in Fall 1980, it was featured as a half-page story by *Newsday* reporter Patrick Brasley "A Business Boost for Day Care." (October 25, 1981). On opening day, only twenty-one fulltime and part-time children were enrolled with the result that expenses exceeded income which continued through the first year of operations with center enrollment growing monthly. Nevertheless, the deficit of $75,000 that was incurred caused delayed payments to vendors and suppliers. Payrolls were met because Chemical Bank did not covered bi-weekly overdrafts. The pressure was tremendous yet it was necessary to project confident optimism to staff and families, for if the organization's true financial condition was revealed, trust in the organization would deteriorate.

CPC met with officials of other large area corporations to seek additional corporate support. A child care committee was established consisting of personnel directors in the Melville corporate hub. However, the companies contributed little financially towards the new center. Meanwhile a suitable, nearby building was found, an excessed public school building close to the Long Island Expressway in Dix Hills. A lease was signed with the school district on a year-to-year basis since the district intended to eventually sell the property. The lease terms were so attractive that CPC felt it should go ahead despite the financial risk.

A marketing campaign was undertaken with paid print advertising, signage on heavily-trafficked Deer Park Avenue, and directly to the employees of local corporations by arranging for worksite presentations and presentations to business groups. Classroom and office staff was hired and equipment, furniture and supplies purchased. Both Rooney and Arfin drew no salaries during the first year and drew part-time salaries in the second year.

An early effort was also made to secure a contract with the Suffolk County Department of Social Services to enable low income workers to qualify for the center's services. The department refused to issue new contracts outside of high-poverty areas despite an acknowledged need for new providers and the documented fact that low income workers lived and worked near the new center.

At the same time, CPC secured grant requests to the Veatch Program of the North Shore Unitarian Church and the Long Island Community Foundation to support CPC's efforts to stimulate corporate child care investments. In later years, both the foundation and the Veatch Program awarded additional small grants to CPC for program enrichments and expansions. They made it clear, however, that their grants would not continue indefinitely. Another threat to organizational survival resulted due to the low salaries that the organization paid its child care staff. Several staff members contacted a local union that was interested in unionizing CPC's workers. Fortunately, few employees left the organization, a statement about child care workers' need for employment and their love for the children in their care. The union discontinued its It is unionizing efforts.

A further assumption that did not work out was that CPC would provide afterschool child care for the local school district. Because the district refused to provide transportation from their schools to CPC, the center was unable to generate income for this service. Fee-paying, school-age children would have generated net income for the organization. A partial solution was to operate a summer day camp and a holiday child care program. These programs were launched and produced much-needed income. In fact, for two summers, CPC operated one of the largest computer day camps on Long Island, 'Compu-Day Camp.' But soon camp enrollment declined since most children in middle-income families had their own computers and did not need to attend camp to learn how to use computers. To generate additional income, center space was rented during off-hours and on weekends. A series of pre-Christmas flea markets and bazaars were also held that generated income and helped to market the center's services.

In 1983, Arfin learned about the opportunity to secure federal funding from the U.S. Department of Health and Human Services (HHS) to establish a Head Start Program in an unserved area of Brookhaven Township. With the assistance of Glen Winters, a recently-retired HHS employee, an application was submitted. By 1984, a grant was approved, covering a share of CPC's overhead expenses.

Another effort, to diversify CPC's services was launched to explore the feasibility of establishing an adult day program in conjunction with the child care program. Assistance from Dorothy Weiss, founder of the Syosset Senior Day Care Center, was obtained while applying for a grant from the Suffolk County Office for the Aging (SCOA) which enthusiastically awarded a grant to CPC confident of the need for adult day care as a result of the growing aging population. The program was launched thus creating Long Island's first intergenerational day care center. A grant was also secured through N.Y.S. Senator Owen Johnson's office to hire a public relations firm to market the intergenerational program. The result was substantial media coverage including many stories on national and local television and radio stations.

Steps to strengthen CPC's board of directors were taken with the assistance of the publicist. New board members came on board to lend their names to the organization and set policy direction. They joined long-standing board members like Dan Panessa, Mary O'Hagan, Charles Schneck, Gil Schwab,

Larry Maltin, Pat Feder, and Richard Turan. Other cultivation efforts did not bear fruit especially with Larry Cohen, CEO of LUMEX/CYBEX, Chris Ahrens of Aetna, Gil Picart, a prominent real estate broker, and Joseph Gundermann of Gundermann Insurance. However, these individuals and CPC board members were unwilling to use their connections or influences to attract contributors or political support. Sometimes, their reluctance was political in nature since child care was viewed as a 'liberal' program, some did not want to be viewed as too liberal so their association with CPC was cautious. Others enjoyed the friendly camaraderie of attending meetings as part of a good cause.

Meanwhile, Arfin continued to do what he could to avoid an organizational shutdown. In 1985, wrote a business plan and enrolled in a course at New York University to help him establish a business providing leisure time programs to middle-class older adults, a growing population on Long Island. New board members were recruited who were familiar with business operations and finances. His idea was to create a new source of revenue for the nonprofit operation. They conducted focus group meetings with older adults to guage their interest in the business model. Thanks to a grant from the Veatch Program, CPC secured the assistance of Richard Dundore, a retired investment banker with a market study and presentations to investment bankers, the Avon Corporation and individual investors with no positive results.

CPC moved into late 1980s with a large debt and struggled to survive. It continued to rent space in excessed school buildings on a year-by-year basis, thus never having long-term security. With respect to corporate support for child care, Arfin continued to pursue opportunities to gain support of local businesses. In the early 1990s, CPC was selected over stiff competition to design and operate a new child care center at Computer Associates' International new facility in Islandia. But one year later, the company discontinued the contract because it decided to operate the center itself.

It is apparent that the decision to move forward without sufficient start-up funds was unwise financially. However, when weighed against the social and economic benefits of the services provided to working families, children and the elderly, the decision to move forward was a resoundingly sound one. Today, Arfin feels that he might have been more effective if he had been bolder in his requests for support from corporations and foundations. Presenting a larger vision of the organization and its potential to meet Long Island's child and elder care needs might have resulted in larger grants from groups like the Veatch Program and the Long Island Community Foundation. The reasons that CPC survived were the loyalty of its board members and the strong relationships that Arfin developed and his creative marketing. He also recognizes the help he received in areas where he was not familiar, as in the Head Start program, the adult day care program, and combining them into an intergenerational program. [17]

Rainbow Chimes International Child Development Center

Registered nurse Kathleen Roche, soon to give birth to her first child, began researching local child care facilities. To her surprise, she was unable to locate a single program licensed to care for infants in her entire township of over 100,000 residents. With only $1,500 in borrowed funds, Roche and her husband founded Rainbow Chimes. The nonprofit's mission was to provide children with early educational skills and the ability to challenge assumptions so that they can make thoughtful decisions and develop into positive and productive adult leaders. Children were encouraged to actively use creative representation, language and logic to achieve decision-making, negotiation, and problem-solving skills.

Back when Roche started she could only call her services a "preschool" or a "day school" if she hoped to have any credibility. "The words 'day care' or 'child care' connoted something negative to private pay parents, said Roche. Over time, due to increasing amounts of press and employer support, the terminology "early education and care" came to mean a quality learning environment that was licensed and reputable. Because of this, child care became a big-business industry, and for-profits finally dominated the child care scene on the one hand, with unregulated and registered homes dominating the other end of the spectrum. Independent nonprofit programs mostly disappeared from Long Island especially in Suffolk County, continued Roche.

Roche recalls that anyone who wasn't poor did not want to be associated with those who *were* poor, as if poverty was contagious. Her early education program started in the more "hip" 1980s, but she remembers being struck that parents who were enrolling their children wanted to make certain that the center did not have any poor children enrolled unless it was just one or two on a special scholarship - the implication being that scholarships were for the more deserving, meritorious people who just happened to be poor due to some unfortunate circumstance.

Roche provided services to anyone who could access them within the system, regardless of the reason. "The organization never had much money for scholarships, but accepted as many low-income working poor families that the County was willing to pay for - at one point 60% of the enrolled families met the working poor criteria of the day, recalls Roche.

Roche recalls that there was very little congruence among regulatory agencies and governments as to supporting our agency's purpose. She cites the need for fire doors and where they specifically had to be placed. It was an issue at two of her sites, and while the State and local officials as well as insurance companies and donors battled it out, children languished for lack of licensed care.

Roche also recalls that welfare reform forced many, many more women into the workforce, and child care needs skyrocketed. Grandmothers and other relatives could not quit their own jobs to care for a family member's child. The greater realization grew by everyone that quality matters when it comes to early education...now if there were only funding to back up this growing sentiment. *Newsday* did a week-long series on the state of child care affordability, accessibility, and quality on Long Island. This had a huge impact in getting the New York State Office of Children and Family Services to look at quality concerns. [18]

Federation of Organizations

In 1981, Federation developed a program to employ individuals with psychiatric illness to assist in the provision of services, and has been a pioneer in this field ever since. The organization's first group home was opened in the North Bellmore community using a live-in staffing model. This home accepted seven boys from Northeast Nassau Psychiatric Hospital and Sagamore Children's Center.

Under the leadership of Barbara Faron since 1986, the organization has substantially expanded its services to become a multi-service, community-based social welfare agency operating programs that utilize peer support within a self-help model. It has developed programs that are designed to meet the needs of special populations, such as people recovering from mental illness, the homeless, low-income seniors and at-risk children. [19]

1982

Options for Community Living (Options)

Options was incorporated as state psychiatric centers were closing, leaving many people with mental illness homeless and without treatment services in the community. By 1984, Options had opened two community residences certified by the New York State Office of Mental Health. Two years later, Options initiated its Mental Health Supportive Apartment Program. [20]

Suffolk Community Council (SCC)

SCC began publication of a widely-distributed pocket-size handbook, *Where to Secure Help: A Guide to Social and Health Services in Suffolk*. The agency continued throughout the decade to provide support and technical assistance, which produced additional new SCC services including: the Retired Senior Volunteer Program (RSVP); Clearinghouse for Community Residences; Developmental Disability Advocacy Program; Suffolk County Interagency Coordinating Council; Human Service Action Coalition; a Computer User

Group, and the Homeless/Hunger/Health Advocacy Committee to address mutual concerns of shelters and agencies serving these populations. SCC also published its first *Human Service Directory* and sold it to public and private organizations and the public-at-large. Tom Chawner played an important role at the council from 1974 to 1986 as director of research and planning, planning director, assistant director and acting executive director. He served under executive directors Helen Gould, Edmond Ross, Frank Freda and Ruth Kleinfeld. After Kleinfeld's tenure, council leadership was assumed by Tom Williams, Paul Lowery and Judy Pannullo. [21]

Family Service League (FSL)

FSL secured its first New York State license to operate an alcohol and substance abuse treatment clinic, the Family Recovery Center, as well as new mental health programs. These developments took place under the leadership of Rick Van Dyke who became FSL executive director in 1986. Van Dyke served in this capacity until 2009. FSL grew substantially during Van Dyke's tenure developing programs located throughout Suffolk County. During this period, FSL's budget grew from $1K serving 2,300 people to a budget of $23K serving 42,000 people. In 2005, FSL began providing preschool services in Nassau County. In addition, during Van Dyke's tenure, FSL achieved national accreditation with the Council on Accreditation for Children and Family Services. [22]

Children's House

The sale of the agency's square block campus in Mineola provided the impetus and the funding to begin developing community-based, non-residential services in addition to a series of group homes as it became abundantly clear that government was increasing in these areas. [23]

La Fuerza Unida

Pascual Blanco founded La Fuerza Unida as a community service and advocacy agency to meet the needs of the area's Hispanic community. His community organizing in the Glen Cove community created alliances with the NAACP and other community organizations. [24]

Self Help

Self Help's first Naturally Occurring Retirement Community (NORC) was created in partnership with the Town of North Hempstead. With congruent missions, the organizations moved together to expand housing opportunities for seniors and other vulnerable populations, integrating social services and health care into affordable housing complexes, and in particular providing the elderly the support they need to age with independence and dignity. [25]

South Oaks Hospital

The hospital established Sage House; a rehabilitative program for young men aged 13 to 20 who had a history of abusing more than one drug, in combination with alcohol. Sage House, like Hope House, was a separate cottage which combined the therapeutic community environment with the complete treatment facilities of the hospital.[26]

Further information is available in Part II, Chapter IV in an interview with Robert Detor.

The National Coalition of 100 Black Women, Long Island Chapter Inc. (NCBW, LI)

As the 1970's came to an end *Newsday,* began publishing a series called *"Long Island at the Crossroads"* outlining the problems facing Long Island. The series noted the fragmentation of Nassau and Suffolk counties and concluded that a plan was needed to address these problems and identify solutions. Active leaders in local women's organizations raised their voices to urge the inclusion of both women and people of color in the ongoing deliberations. While their efforts opened up a new dialog, it became apparent that there remained a void that needed to be filled for the greater good of the community.

In 1982, sixteen women took a stand to ensure a role for women of African descent in the mainstream of Long Island, and incorporated 100 Black Women of Long Island, Inc. The organization worked to tackle several local issues and later joined forces to become an affiliate chapter of the emerging National Coalition of 100 Black Women. Sheila Johnson Page served as president during the organization's infancy providing important leadership.

Charter members are: Gwendolyn Carroll, Thelma Drew, Jean Gillis, Gladys Harrington, Flo Holland, Louise Hughes, Aileen James, Sheila Johnson Page, Audrey Jones, Patricia Hill Williams, Mary McKight-Taylor, Edna Peterson-Boothe, Angela Shaw, Phyllis Simmons, Nancy Washington, and Evelyn Wells.[27]

1983

Child Care Council of Suffolk (CCC/SC)

Due to the strong commitment and leadership of Janet Walerstein and technical assistance of the Suffolk Community Council, the child care council was established as the nonprofit planning and coordinating agency dedicated to making child care work for all of Suffolk County's diverse communities.

Walerstein was an effective advocate, securing state member items as well as county grants. Of course, this meant "begging" before the legislature every fall to assure that grants would be renewed for another year. Walerstein, along with other child care providers, board members, and parents were also able to secure support for salary enhancement funding, a significant achievement that resulted in much-improved salaries for the county's child care workers. Unfortunately, this funding was discontinued.

Walerstein had earned a Master's Degree in 1979 in early childhood education. While employed as director of the Bay Shore Day Care Center, she worked with other child care center directors, especially Jean Heacock, Ronnie Strum, Audrey Van Dussen, Johanna Greene and Katie Roche to develop the council as an independent nonprofit organization. The Suffolk Community Council provided a great deal of support and advice to the emerging council during this period and served as its fiscal agent for a grant from the Long Island Community Foundation. With this grant support, Barbara Jordan was hired as the council's first director. Walerstein worked closely with Gloria Wallick of Nassau County and the directors in Westchester and Rockland counties as child care advocates frequently traveling to Albany together to hammer out annual child care legislative agendas. Wallick served as a valuable mentor to Walerstein. [28]

Nassau Child Care Council *(see the following News Story)*

News Story

In a *Newsday* article titled **"Day-Care 'Trick' Draws Treat From Purcell,"** **(November 1, 1983)**, reporter Lawrence C. Levy wrote that Jill Rooney, the child care council's president pleaded: "We would like to stop having weekly bake sales and be able to operate with a little dignity." From its inception, the council had a vision in which every family could access the child care that is needed and that best prepares every child for success in school and life. The council provides child care counseling and referrals to families, professional development and technical assistance to active and potential providers, and offers services to employers interested in the child care needs of employees' families. Through research and support of child care friendly public policy and development, Council serves as an informational resource and public voice for issues facing Nassau County's diverse communities.

Central American Refugee Center (CARECEN)

The Central American Refugee Center (CARECEN) is a nonprofit immigration and human rights organization serving the refugee community on Long Island and throughout southern New York State. Since its founding, CARECEN has worked to protect the civil rights of immigrants, increase understanding between the native born and newcomer communities, and raise awareness of the interaction of human rights disasters and immigration. Legal services are provided in a variety of areas including: Permanent residency (Green Card); asylee and refugee assistance; and immigrant employment. [29]

National Association of Puerto Rican Hispanic Social Workers (NAPRHSW)

NAPRHSW was founded by graduates of the School of Social Welfare at Stony Brook's Title XX program for the education of Hispanic social workers, a grant obtained by Professor Angel Campos. Through the grant, dozens of Hispanic social workers graduated and became leaders in Long Island's professional social welfare community. NAPRHSW is and was dedicated to the enhancement and general welfare of Puerto Rican and other Hispanic families. Its members are social workers, other human service professionals, and students interested in issues that affect and impact the Puerto Rican/Hispanic communities. The organization seeks to organize social workers and other human service professionals to strengthen, develop and improve the resources and services that meet the needs of Puerto Rican/Hispanic families.[30]

For further information, visit Pauline Velazques' profile in Part III.

The Interfaith Nutrition Network (INN)

The INN was founded in Hempstead by Michael Moran and Pat O'Connor and a small group of thirty, concerned citizens who became aware of the need for food on Long Island, and established a soup kitchen, which became the first one in Nassau County. During its first three years, The INN's original kitchen was located in three different local churches, operated by volunteers and supported by surrounding churches in the community. After three years of operation, no church or community facility would offer space, and The INN was forced to leave Hempstead. The INN was invited to Freeport to offer a free meal in their local church. It continued feeding people in Freeport, using the volunteers and donations from Hempstead.

Local Garden City resident, John Brennan learned of The INN's plight of leaving Hempstead. He stepped forward and offered major funds to make it possible to purchase the building at 146-148 Front Street. This building became the Mary Brennan INN, named after his mother. Thanks to this donation The INN was able to finally relocate back to Hempstead. While The INN opened the first kitchen in Nassau County, other communities across Long Island recognized the same need and asked to join its effort as part of The INN's network. Freeport continued operations on its own and joined the network. At this point in time, four similar efforts in other communities were already launched by The INN Long Beach, Hicksville, Central Islip and Patchogue. Freeport became number five in 1986.

In September of 1984, a new effort was established by The INN – Emergency Shelter. This was in response to the death of two male guests from The INN's first soup kitchen. They were found frozen to death in an abandoned car in Hempstead, in the winter of 1983. This original shelter, named Hospitality INN, was located in a private house which was rented by The INN from The Diocese of Rockville Centre (Roman Catholic Church). This building was used as the first emergency shelter for families and individuals from 1984 until 1990, when it was destroyed by a fire. Fortunately, no one was injured and everyone escaped unharmed.

Jean Kelly, the INN's executive director, reflects that "the 1980s was an unusual time in that there appeared to be more and more people in need of food and shelter making them seen and heard for the first time on Long Island. Individuals and groups, many with a maverick philosophy, sought to answer their need. In many ways their quick response met with successful results and fulfilled both the needs of those facing hunger and homelessness as well as their own need to be of service [31]

Middle Country Public Library (MCPL)

Throughout the 1980s, MCPL's PC Workshop programs met with some opposition from both the library and the social service professional communities. Children's librarians often lacked the skills for working with very young children, parents and caregivers; serving as an information and referral specialists; and/or working with community partners. Some library administrators and boards felt the PC Workshop was out-of-bounds for the library setting. On the other hand, professionals in the early education and social service fields were also skeptical. Remembering their own experiences with libraries, they questioned why librarians might be "sitting at the table" in a networking meeting or involved in early childhood and/or parent education.

It soon became apparent that the PC Workshop was not just another program to implement but rather a model for transforming children's services in public libraries. Within several years of its initiation, five Suffolk County libraries replicated the program. The resource professionals and other providers met through the Suffolk Coalition encouraged MCPL to help other libraries make this transition. In 1985, Sandy Feinberg and Kathy Deerr published the *Parent Child Workshop Handbook* through the Suffolk Cooperative Library System, designed a course for LIU's Palmer School of Library and Information Management and began to present at professional conferences.

During the same time period, the Suffolk Coalition continued to evolve as a multi-disciplinary networking group of librarians, social service and health professionals, family support providers, and educators, meeting five times per year in the library's community room. Soon after being organized, the group broadened its scope to include issues impacting children and youth, birth through 18 years and their families. Bi-annually, topics for discussion, suggested by local professionals, include a range of health and social issues such as bereavement and children, the autism spectrum, gay and lesbian youth, immigrant families, the importance of play, etc. The professional who suggests the topic is responsible for organizing a panel of local providers to present on the topic. The coalition has served as an ongoing source of continuing education and interdisciplinary networking for more than thirty years. From the beginning, MCPL hosted the meetings, maintained the mailing list and created flyers for each program; the Suffolk County Youth Bureau mailed them. Currently, over 1000 professionals belong to the Coalition and the meetings are publicized via email.

Other spin-offs from the PC Workshop and the Coalition include the Parent Educators' Network co-founded by Barbara Jordan of MCPL and Nancy Olsen-Harbich of Cornell Cooperative Extension to serve as a training and support network for professionals providing parent education in Suffolk County; the Librarians Alliance for Parents and Children organized as a sharing network of Suffolk County librarians who conduct the PC Workshop; and the Suffolk Family Education Clearinghouse which includes a collection of specialized materials for parent educators and family support professionals housed at MCPL.

During the 1980s, MCPL expanded and became the largest library on Long Island and a leader in the development of youth spaces in public libraries. In 1984, the local school district gave the library its oldest elementary school and converted it into the Selden branch with a separate early childhood room staffed by early childhood teachers. In 1986, the Centereach building was expanded to include a 10,000 square foot children's room, one of the largest in the country. In subsequent years, the library developed the Museum Corner, the Teen Resource Center, the Underground and the Nature Explorium, all of which are spaces for youth.

It was during this decade that computers were making headway into the library world while many nonprofit partners were still without access to computers and the skills needed to use them. In addition to putting their librarian research skills to work, the library was one of the few organizations that had computers and trained staff with the ability to create directories in-house. Working collaboratively with the Child Care Council of Suffolk County, MCPL produced the Child Care Directory (1986, 1989). In 1988, MCPL staff worked with the Family Services Branch of the YMCA of Long Island and the Suffolk County Executive's Task Force on Family Violence to create the *Sexual Abuse Treatment Services Directory*. In 1991, MCPL staff partnered with the Suffolk County Youth Bureau to create *Services for Families Affected by Agent Orange and Families of Vietnam Veterans: A Directory of Community Services.* During this same time period, the library's adult services and career information staff created the *Vocational Sourcebook,* an extensive handbook that included resources for employment, workforce development, vocational services and other education and training opportunities that existed on Long Island.

In 1984, Feinberg was appointed to the New York State Task Force on Child Abuse and Neglect and worked with Matilda Cuomo, New York State's first lady and the NYS Council on Children and Families. In addition to bringing the PC Workshop model to the attention of state leaders, this work lead to the publication of several resource listings for parents. MCPL along with other Suffolk County children's librarians were instrumental in the development and publication of The *Family Resource Book* which was distributed throughout the state. In 1988, the library garnered the involvement of several librarian coordinators around New York State to help create and publish *Welcome to Parenthood: A Family Guide*. These countywide publications were distributed statewide through libraries, hospitals and community centers. MCPL staff was responsible for the Suffolk County publication. [32]

Women on the Job

To address sexual harassment in the workplace, the organization's director Lillian McCormick and Charlotte Shapiro urged Nassau County to adopt guidelines to define and prevent sexual harassment in the workplace. In 1983, County Executive Francis Purcell and the board of supervisors adopted such policies and procedures. [33]

For further information, visit Part III for the profile of Lillian McCormick.

1984

Hempstead Hispanic Civic Association

The Hempstead Hispanic Civic Association is a community-based, nonprofit organization whose mission is to serve the minority population in the incorporated village of Hempstead and surrounding communities by providing low-income housing, youth programs and after school educational initiatives. The organization provides English as a Second Language (ESL) classes, an after school tutoring program, and a summer camp, Affordable housing and tenant advocacy are also provided. Prior to this position, George Siberón is the executive director. Previously, Siberón was the executive director of the Nassau County Youth Board developing and implementing policies and providing funding to over forty community based organizations. Siberón has also worked as district manager for U.S. Congresswoman Nydia Velazques, deputy director at Aspira of New York; and the Puerto Rican Family Institute. Academically, Siberón earned a Master of Social Work Degree from Fordham University and a Master of Public Administration Degree from Baruch College, where he graduated with honors. Siberón is a graduate of the prestigious National Urban Fellows Program and is a member of Phi Alpha Alpha, the national honor society for public affairs and administration.[34]

Health and Welfare Council

With the help of graduate nurses from Adelphi University, the Health and Welfare Council interviewed 200 low income families about hunger and released the second hunger study in the nation.[35]

News Story

"Equitable Health Care" was a *Newsday* Opinion article **(October 3, 1984)** written by John T. O'Connell, Deputy Director of the Health and Welfare Council of Nassau. The article, printed during election season, discusses rising health care costs and the burden that is placed on older people to pay higher shares of these costs. In the article, O'Connell says: "The issue is a complex one: Certainly, the availability of health care is a public policy issue in need of thorough discussion. However, if there is true equity and fairness, then cuts in service should not be made at the expense of the elderly. Health benefits are health benefits, whether or not they are achieved through direct expenditures or tax write-offs. If Medicare and Social Security affecting millions of working and retired Americans can be revised, so also the tax structure favoring the wealthy can be changed."

Notes: Chapter VIII

1. U.S. Census Bureau: www.census gov
2. John Gallagher, *interview with author, March 19, 2014.*
3. Jane Devine, *interview with author, August 15, 2014.*
4. Gregory Blass, *interview with author, July 23, 2014.*
5. *Author's reflections as a founder of adult day centers during the period.*
6. Vera Parisi, , *telephone interview with author, April 25, 2014*
7. Jamir Couch, *email correspondence with Couch's daughter, Jamir Couch, August 20, 2014.*
8. *Author's reflections as a founder of adult day centers during the period.*
9. Gil Bernardino, *email correspondence of August 27, 2014.*
10. Information obtained from agency's website: www.jlli.org
11. Walter Stockton, *interview with author, April 5, 2014.*
12. Information obtained from agency's website: licares.org
13. Information obtained from agency's website: ucp-suffolk.org
14. Information obtained from agency's website: www.south-oaks.org
15. Information obtained from agency's website: www.viscardicenter.org
16. *"Collection of the Suffolk Community Council"* (Special Collections and University Archives at Stony Brook University)

17. *Author's reflections as the organization's founder during the period.*
18. Information obtained from agency's website: www.rainbowchimes.org
19. Information obtained from agency's website:
20. Ralph Fasano, *email correspondence of September 20, 2014.*
21. *"Collection of the Suffolk Community Council"* (Special Collections and University Archives at Stony Brook University)
22. Information obtained from agency's website: www.fsl-li.org
23. Richard Dina , *interview with author, January 15, 2014*
24. Information obtained from agency's website: www.lafuerzaunidacdc.org
25. Information obtained from agency's website: www.selfhelp.org
26. Information obtained from agency's website: www.south-oaks.org
27. Information obtained from agency's website: www.li100bw.com
28. Information obtained from agency's website: www.childcaresuffolk.org
29. Information obtained from agency's website: www.carecen.org
30. Information obtained from agency's website: www.naprhsw.org
31. Jean Kelly, *email correspondence of November 1, 2014.*
32. Sandra Feinberg, *email correspondence of November 15, 2014.*
33. Lillian McCormick, *interview with author, July 23, 2014.*
34. Information obtained from agency's website: www. hempsteadhispanic.org
35. Information obtained from agency's website: www.hwcli.com

Part III

PHOTOGRAPHS OF EXEMPLARY COMMUNITY

LEADERS AND GRASSROOTS ORGANIZERS

Nilda Alvarez

Kenneth Anderson

José Avila

Murray Barbash

Leone Baum

Ruth Corcoran

James Couch (l)

Nancy Rauch Douzinas

Hazel Dukes

Marge Harrison

Roberta Hunter

Mel Jackson

David Kadane

Wilber "Bill" Klatsky

Richard Koubek

Lilo and Gerard Leeds

Peter Levy

Lincoln Lynch

Lillian McCormick

Helen Mc Intyre

Ann Mead

Robert C. Murphy

Elsie Owens

Sonia Palacio-Grottola

Davis Pollack

Dennis Puleston

Leroy Ramsey

Priscilla Redfield Roe

Marge Rogatz　　　　**Charles Russo**

David Salten　　　　**Joan Saltzman**

Janet Walsh Schaberg

Betty Schlein

Marilyn Shellabarger

Frank Sinisi

Joyce Spencer Insolia

David Sprintzen

Leon "Jake" Swirbul

Paul Townsend

W. Burghardt Turner

Joyce Moore Turner

Pauline Velazques

Ralph Watkins

Profiles of Exemplary Community Leaders and Grassroots Organizers

At the risk of omitting other deserving people, I put forth the profiles of a number of what I consider exceptional Long Islanders for the period 1945-2014 who contributed substantially to the development of a more just and caring society through their advocacy for social service programs and social action for progressive social change. I knew many of them personally. Others, I have gotten to know through this writing. What they have in common is an uncompromising commitment to a cause, a vision for what needed to be done, passion, will power, and the ability to earn the trust and involvement of others.

These lay leaders dedicated their time, energy, and sometimes, their financial resources to their voluntary work. Their fields of interests varied from civil rights, to health care, mental health, child care, aging services, housing, homelessness and hunger, disabilities, and youth services. Their altruism, perseverance, and commitment to good government and a just society should be a call to action to others.

Nilda Alvarez (1923-2013)

At age 11, after her mother died of tuberculosis, Nilda Alvarez found herself living in a Brooklyn group home. Scarred by a difficult childhood Alvarez went on to devote her adult life to help others.

As a longtime leader of Pronto of Long Island, a Suffolk-based charity, she helped feed, clothe, train, tutor and counsel needy Hispanics and others. After years of volunteer work, she was named Pronto's executive director after retiring from Entenmann's. During her nearly fifteen years in charge, Pronto opened a $1.5 million outreach center in 2005. Alvarez raised funds, obtained grants and hawked donated items to help more people. Her work earned plaudits, among them the Hispanic Heritage Award presented in 2006 by New York State Owen H. Johnson. Before her volunteer and paid work with Pronto, Alvarez was a union representative at Entenmann's for Local 3 of the Bakery, Confectionery and Tobacco Workers International Union. After retiring, Alvarez returned to volunteering at Pronto.

Among her many community activities, Alvarez served on many boards of directors including the National Conference of Puerto Rican Women, LI Chapter; the Town of Islip Counseling Center; former Congressman Rick

Lazio's Hispanic Advisory Board; the Breast Cancer Coalition; the Brentwood Health Clinic and Southside Hospital's Advisory Board; and the Puerto Rican/Hispanic Parade Committee.

Alvarez was born Nilda Salicroup in Brooklyn, the only child of Frances Miranda and Augustin Salicroup, a longshoreman. Alvarez grew up in the borough's Carroll Gardens section and graduated, in 1950 from Girls Commercial High School, now Prospect Heights High. Alvarez moved to Brentwood in 1968, part of a wave of Puerto Rican migration from the city. "An acre was cheap, and it reminded us of our hometowns," she told *Newsday* in 2002. She attended St. John's University's human resource program, worked at a phone company and finished Entenmann's baking school. She worked first as a baker, then an assembly-line boss. [1]

Kenneth Anderson (1928

Ken Anderson was born in 1928 and raised on the east side of Wilmington, Delaware where he attended all-black schools facing the problems of segregation. His grandfather was a coachman for the Dupont family. His grandmother's brothers were sharecroppers in Delaware with forty acres and a "jenny mule." He recalls that Delaware was called "the first southern state." Anderson recalls that there was one movie theater in Wilmington for blacks. He also recalls that he could buy notions at the Woolworth 5 and 10 cent store but you could not sit at the lunch counter. He recalls the hand-me-down books and band instruments in his school that came from the all-white Dupont family schools. At home, he remembers his mother getting food and clothing from white families and from the dry goods store. His mother worked "in service," doing housekeeping for white families. Anderson recalls learning quickly as a child that there were physical boundaries in Wilmington where you either felt safe or unsafe and that you had to learn to fight or run fast because white boys were hostile and went out of their way to fight black boys.

"We could not sit at a lunch counter in the five-and-dime. We could not try on clothes…The black section's grocery, liquor, pharmacy, and dry cleaning stores were owned by whites. Wilmington was one of those cities challenged on school segregation by the NAACP. We could not play against the white schools in sports," recounted Anderson in a 1981six-page *Newsday* interview by reporter Sid Cassese.

His singing career began as a boy soprano where he sang in a high school production of Bizet's *Carmen.* Anderson's mother played the violin and sang in the church choir, as did an aunt, Vashti. He began to learn the old Negro spirituals, the church rituals, and patriotic songs. In high school, Anderson sang as a soprano.

During World War II, Anderson was too young to be inducted into the Army so he worked at a variety of jobs in Delaware and Pennsylvania. It is here that he believes he developed his social consciousness working as a laborer, pushing a wheel barrel and hauling material. Anderson became a member of an all-white, principally Italian union in a large plant manufacturing landing craft for the Navy. Later, Anderson worked on a track team for the Reading Railroad and then moved to Syracuse, New York, to work in a steel mill on a project that was the first span of the Delaware Memorial Bridge.

In the early 1950s, in his early 20s, Anderson was working as a bookie and had not reported to his draft board. He was later caught and drafted into the Army. He was sent to Camp Breckenridge in rural Kentucky where the majority of inductees were young, white southerners from Appalachia and Mississippi, Alabama, Georgia, Ohio, and upstate New York. This was a period just after President Harry S. Truman integrated the armed forces. During basic training, his two white sergeants assigned Anderson to be squad leader. They saw that, being older than most of the other draftees, he would be able to handle himself well even with young white men. The sergeants had fought alongside blacks in Korea where they credited black soldiers for saving their lives. Anderson was struck by their openness to look beyond the color of a person's skin.

After basic training, Anderson was assigned to Germany as part of a Special Services entertainment group that was made up of a "hillbilly" band that entertained soldiers in the service clubs singing Grand Old- Opry-type music. The group Anderson played with had been an opening act for Vic Damone and had contacts back in the states, so Anderson hoped to get bookings for the group when they returned stateside. Interpersonal problems erupted, so the group dissolved and Anderson returned to Wilmington where he took a job as an orderly at the Delaware State Hospital. Soon afterward, a girlfriend informed Anderson of a supervisory job at Delaware General Hospital. Anderson was hired, and within a short period of time had demonstrated his competence and reliability. The Chief of Anesthesia offered him the opportunity to attend medical school. Anderson thought about the offer and declined to accept it feeling that he had too many family obligations to go through with the tremendous undergraduate, graduate, and residency requirements. Instead, using connections he had made in New York City, Anderson applied to Manhattan State Hospital's School of Nursing.

Anderson's formal education between 1956 and 1962 includes a Registered Nurse Diploma from the Manhattan State Hospital; from an Anesthesia Residency at Harlem Hospital he was awarded a Certificate. Later, Anderson earned a B.S. in Nursing at the State University of New York at Stony Brook and a M.S.W. in Social Work also at SUNY/Stony Brook's School of Social Welfare. In 1999, Anderson was inducted into Phi Beta Kappa as an alumnus of Stony Brook. From 1961-1987, he worked as a Nurse Anesthetist at Mather Hospital in Port Jefferson.

In the interview with Casesse, Anderson was asked about his motivation to move from Harlem to Long Island.

"My motivation to move out here was the same as that of many black people; there was a job opportunity and my wife and I had a sense of wanting our kids to have the best kind of education. It was not a case of wanting to get away from New York City's underclass. ...I used to go down to 125th Street to check out Malcolm X, and I certainly had my consciousness raised," Anderson said.

Anderson was involved in other community activities which impressively stand alone. He served as a founding member of the Suffolk County Civil Liberties Union; a board member of: The Suffolk County Boy Scouts and Girl Scouts Councils; the Long Island Council of Churches; and was one of the first two male members of the League of Women Voters of Long Island. He was also a member of the National Presbyterian Commission on Religion and Race.

Besides his distinguished educational and social justice accomplishments, Anderson is an accomplished musical performer who is well-known for his repertoire renditions of singer, actor, and social activist Paul Robeson. He sang in a special quartet touring Europe while serving in the U.S. Army Special Services during the mid-1950s; sang in New York's Riverside Church Choir in the late 1950s and early 1960s; sang at the 100th anniversary of Paul Robeson's birth on a number of occasions; and sang with folk singer Pete Seeger at the 50th anniversary of the 1949 Peekskill Riots (anti-communist riots with anti-black and anti-Semitic undertones that took place at Cortlandt Manor, Westchester County, New York).

Anderson has also sung with Long Island University's Chorus and was a frequent soloist for the North Shore Choral Society where he sang the solos in Latouche performances and Robinson's *Ballad for Americans.* He has appeared on stage in *Aida* with Opera Delaware and *The Magic Flute* with the Kimberton Light Opera Company, and soloed in numerous performances of Handel's *Messiah.*

Anderson's career as a social activist features significant activism on Long Island. In 1963, Anderson, while living with his wife and children in Port Jefferson, founded the North Brookhaven Council on Human Relations and became the President of the town branch of the NAACP. He went on to serve as Suffolk County Coordinator and Long Island Regional Director of the NAACP's 18 Long Island branches. Ken also joined CORE (the Congress of Racial Equality) working closely with Lincoln Lynch. On a number of occasions, he was arrested in Hempstead while protesting discriminatory practices in housing. Also in 1963, Anderson purchased a home in Port Jefferson. By 1964, Anderson integrated previous all-white housing development in the Village of Port Jefferson. In 1965, Anderson along with four other members of the Long Island Congress of Racial Equality was arrested during a sit-in demonstration protesting housing discrimination in Hempstead. In 1973, a 10-point Health Bill of Rights was adopted by the Suffolk County Human Rights Commission amid numerous complaints by a Brentwood community group that its health rights were being violated. The bill was crafted by Anderson and Elsie Owens, a civil rights and health care advocate from Coram. The bill called for "quality health care regardless of the ability to pay, equitable distribution of health services throughout the county, and an end to race and sex discrimination in the county's health institutions."

In the Cassese interview, the reporter asked Anderson why he was attracted to the NAACP during the 1960s. "It was the NAACP's endurance," said Anderson. " I was impressed that the organization had 1,800 chapters around the country, the kind of network that no other civil rights group had, although I was impressed with CORE's focus on grassroots organization, challenging the system in innovative and provocative ways, developing a sense of self-pride in community and self-awareness. But I felt that the NAACP was doing that and more, legally challenging obstacles to black progress," continued Anderson.

Cassese asked Anderson if blacks have to deal with something special on Long Island, in suburban America. Anderson responded.

> ...Long Island was built on the premise of creating a white enclave, a haven for whites fleeing the city. And it is in housing that this becomes apparent. Back in the 1960s, I hooked up with a network out here called Open Island, that along with the NAACP, tried to help blacks purchase housing because Joe Realtor wasn't going to give them a fair shake - and a lot of them have bad head (social awareness) and were coming out here for the same reasons as white folks.... But they quickly found out what the real deal was.... Very often I would get a phone call asking me to come to a neighborhood where black folks had purchased a house and it had been broken into. There would be feces on the wall, kitchen cabinets torn out and all kinds of hate acts. Those kinds of things do not appear to be happening out here these days, and the economy is such that anybody, generally speaking, with the money can purchase housing out here.

But Anderson also recognized that the majority of black people could not afford to buy a house, so he focused a great deal of his attention on affordable multiple-family housing, which affects blacks' ability to work and survive on Long Island. To do this, Anderson organized voter education and registration campaigns. He told Cassese:

> ...our primary mission is to insure, to the degree possible, that goods, and services and resources are directed to those communities so that they remain vital. Because as long as we do not control the power

structure, the power structure will tend to direct resources away from those communities and make it a self-fulfilling prophecy that where there is a black community, there is a problem.

Cassese asked Anderson to comment on why blacks seem to be unified when violent incidents occur in America's large cities.

...For one thing, it is like when there was talk during the Nixon administration about concentration camps for blacks – it brought a sense of common fear...one thing that it did was bring a sense of solidarity among black folks that I had never seen before. It was a sense of common destiny and knowing that we needed to get together. And if anything positive comes out of Reagan's election it is the possibility that I sense, which I see as strengthening us as an organization. That is why I think that a lot of folks are sending us their memberships and calling us, saying, 'How can I join the NAACP?'

In the Cassese article, Anderson expresses the fact that he missed the 1963 March on Washington D.C., one of the most significant events of that decade. "I had the money and the time but not the appreciation. I felt my Mississippi was here on Long Island. So I missed an historical event," Anderson said.

In 1968, Anderson was shocked to hear that parents of children at Port Jefferson's Scraggy Hill Elementary School were raising funds to send the school's white children on a field trip to the nation's capital and the black children to tour Harlem in New York City. The visit confirmed what Anderson heard. --that the trips were part of an annual fundraising drive. Shocked, Anderson expressed his concern about this situation. The school principal responded by denying the situation.

In 1969, Anderson was appointed by County Executive H. Lee Dennison, to the newly-established Suffolk County Human Rights Commission. For several years in the 1970s and 1980s, Anderson served as the Suffolk County government's first community organizer. Today, Anderson jokingly reflects that he was a community organizer before President Barack Obama.

In the mid-1970s, Anderson joined the National Low Income Housing Coalition and became a board member of the Suburban Action Institute when Paul Davidoff was its Executive Director. Anderson sued the Department of Housing and Urban Development (H.U.D.) and local towns and villages on Long Island for misuse of community development block grant funds. During this period, Ken attended Tri-State Regional Planning Committee meetings with Davidoff so that he could have an impact on the lack of affordable housing on Long Island. In 1976, four years after President Richard Nixon's dialogue with Mao Tse Tung, he represented the NAACP as a member of a 20-

person delegation to China with the U.S./China Peoples' Friendship Association.

Anderson also initiated an effort to bring together members of the black and Jewish communities by forming the "Black/Jewish Long Island Dialogue" after Louis Farrakhan was accused of referring to Judaism as a "gutter religion."

When asked what he considers his greatest legacy, Anderson refers to the Health Bill of Rights that he and community activist Elsie Owens wrote and shepherded through the Suffolk County Legislature in the 1970s.

In 1979, while sleeping in their Port Jefferson home, Anderson, his wife Arlene, and their son Michael, experienced the trauma of facing a cross-burning on the lawn of their home.

On April 4th, 2014, forty-six years to the day after the assassination of Dr. Martin Luther King, Casesse spoke to Anderson by phone. He reflected on where he was when he heard about Dr. King's death.

I was in an operating room at Mather Hospital in the midst of a complicated operation on a seven-year old boy who was under deep anesthesia. A nurse came into the operating room shouting. 'They shot him!' Someone asked who was shot. When she said Dr. King, I nearly fainted but could not react due to the circumstances. After completing my duties, I went to an adjacent room, sat in a rocker and cried.

Weeks later, Anderson arranged for a memorial service to be held at Infant Jesus Church. The event was sponsored by the Brookhaven Human Relations Committee and was attended by hundreds of mourners including Brookhaven Town Supervisor Charles Barraud who shared with the assemblage his childhood experiences with blacks and how everyone got along during his school years. He later told Anderson how upset he was at the current racism that was evident on Long Island. [2]

José Avila (1969-)

Since he arrived in America in 2000 with his wife and baby daughter from Colombia, José Avila has served his adopted-country as an exemplary citizen. Avila is a community-minded advocate for human rights with substantial knowledge of immigration issues. He has experienced many of the anti-immigrant attitudes that face new immigrants on Long Island while learning a new language and culture, finding affordable housing, and securing permanent legal status in the United States. When Ecuadorian teenager Marcelo Lucero was brutally killed by a group of local Patchogue teenagers in 2008, Avila quickly joined other new immigrants from Central and South America to protest the racial incident and seek justice from the court system.

He is a skilled marketing and public relations professional who has contributed substantially to the quality of life of Long Island's new immigrants especially those from Central and South America.

His leadership skills as a director, coordinator, fund raiser, and supervisor have benefited many Long Island nonprofit organizations. His credits include serving as co-founder of the Long Island Hispanic Roundtable, a business networking organization that brought together representatives of established and emerging Latino businesses. Avila, proud of his Colombian heritage, is also a founding member of the Colombian-American Chamber of Commerce of Long Island promoting Colombia-United States relations, Colombia culture, and assisting the Hispanic community to adjust to life in the United States.

Avila's public service includes considerable volunteering at Pronto Long Island where he developed "The Personal Training Center," training more than 600 people in computer skills since 2006 and preparing 200 people to complete the United States citizenship test. Using his professional marketing skills, has donated countless hours to produce nonprofit websites, plan fund raising events, repair computer systems, and design public relations strategies for nonprofit organizations. For two years, he was responsible for coordinating the annual Colombian Independence Day festival in Brentwood. Avila has been an active member of the Brentwood Chamber of Commerce having served as secretary, corresponding secretary, and currently, as first vice president. He is also the president of the Crossroads Counseling Center and a board member of the Latino Health Initiative.and SEPA MUJER.

Avila was awarded public recognition by the Town of Islip in 2006 and from New York Senator Owen Johnson in 2008 in celebration of Hispanic Heritage Month. In 2011, he was recognized by Nassau County Executive Edward Mangano and the National Association of Hispanic Social Workers as Advocate of the Year. In 2014, Avila received the Visionary Leadership Award from Crossroads Counseling Center. Most recently, the Town of Islip NAACP awarded its 2015 Legacy Award to Avila.

José Avila is married to Carolina Franklin. Their two daughters, Maria and Sari, are exceptional students and athletes at Catholic schools on Long Island. [3]

Murray Barbash (1925-2013)

Karl Grossman, a syndicated columnist and author wrote the following obituary about Murray Barbash:

> A giant in modern environmental and energy history on Long Island, Maurice 'Murray' Barbash, has passed away. He was a key in creation of the Fire Island National Seashore and, in so doing, stopping Robert Moses' plan to build a four-lane highway on top of that extraordinary

barrier beach and, flipping the Fire Island strategy, stopping the Shoreham nuclear power plant.

He had this instinct for getting the big things right,' said his son, writer Shep Barbash, in his eulogy at the memorial service for Murray.

My first big story as a reporter on Long Island was back in 1962 on my first week at the *Babylon Town Leader.* Mr. Moses had just announced his highway plan and the newspaper—which had long challenged the schemes of Mr. Moses, a Babylon resident—sent me to Fire Island to do an article about the impacts of the highway. The consequences were obvious: it would pave over such natural treasures as the Sunken Forest and destroy many of the unique, indeed magical communities on the road-less beach.

The day my article appeared, I got a telephone call from Murray who said he was preparing to fight the Moses road. And did he!

With his brother-in-law, attorney Irving Like, who a few years later would co-author the Environmental Bill of Rights of the New York State Constitution, Murray create the Citizens Committee for a Fire Island National Seashore?

Saying no to the Moses road wasn't enough, Murray and Irv felt. There needed to be a focus on the positive and, also, there was no way to stop Moses on the state level. Moses failed dismally in a run for governor, so instead amassed huge power, not through democracy, but with his state commissions and authorities.

As chairman of the Citizens Committee, working with Irv, renowned Long Island naturalist Robert Cushman Murphy and others, Murray succeeded in saving beautiful Fire Island.

Meanwhile, I was writing article after article about the Moses' highway plan and the initiative for a Fire Island National Seashore, federal involvement neutralizing Moses' state power.

Two decades later, the great threat to Long Island was the cluster of nuclear power plants—seven to eleven-the Long Island Lighting Company sought to build. The first would be Shoreham Nuclear Power Station 1. There would be two more nuclear plants at Shoreham, four at Jamesport and more in between, and possibly on the South Shore in Bridgehampton, too.

For this, Murray and Irv flipped the Fire Island strategy.

There was no way to stop the federal government from approving these nuclear plants. By 1980 it had given a construction license and was getting set to give an operating license to LILCO for Shoreham and had given a construction OK of the first two nuclear plants at Jamesport. The federal nuclear agencies - the Atomic Energy Commission and its successor, the Nuclear Regulatory Commission (NRC) - never (to this day) denied a construction or operating license for a nuclear plant.

"So, here, the strategy would be to use the power of the state to blunt this federal nuclear rubber stamp.

"Citizens to Replace LILCO were created by Murray and Irv with also a focus on the positive—establishment of a Long Island Power Authority with, under the state's power of eminent domain, the clout to eliminate LILCO if it persisted with its nuclear scheme. Also, the law which founded LIPA committed it to emphasize safe, clean, renewable energy.

"Suffolk County government's argument before the NRC that evacuation would be impossible on dead-ended Long Island in the event of a major Shoreham accident held back the opening of the plant for a time. Mass protests, political organizing, legal action and other moves were also very important. But in the end it was this strategy that stopped Shoreham and LILCO's plans to build many other nuclear plants on Long Island.

"Murray and his wife of 65 years, Lillian (Irv's sister) have also been great contributors to arts and culture on Long Island including the founding of the Long Island Philharmonic.

Murray, of Brightwaters, died on March 13 at 88 of complications from heart bypass surgery—after a great run." [4]

Leone Baum (1929-

"It is challenging to try to make sense out of a lifetime of work in a way that explains to my own satisfaction the 'hows' and whys' of this lifetime. I wondered about and tried to understand what it means to be a woman and a community activist, a warrior in the never ending War on Poverty in the second decade of the 21st century, and about how I got to this point in my personal odyssey.

"The first decade of my life was spent in Freeport where I started school, and where I lived in an extended family, immigrant grandparents, American born parents, young aunt and uncle, and my baby sister until the depression caused us to move to Brooklyn for better access to the jobs which would be held by all the adults except grandma who stayed home to cook and clean and raise the children. I think that this situation taught me to prefer the life of a man, and to try to avoid the role of my grandmother and my mother.

"I learned about politics at home where there were animated discussions. We were Democrats as opposed to our neighbors who were Republicans for the most part and I remember having my first political battle at the age of seven with the little girl next door, actually rolling around on the lawn, biting and scratching over whether Alf Landon or Franklin Roosevelt should be president. I encountered my second political problem when I was seventeen and could not vote but was actively supporting Henry Wallace who was opposing Harry Truman, and thus earning the title of Communist from my Socialist grandfather. Simultaneously, I learned about racism, and anti-Semitism. I attended Pratt Institute in Brooklyn as part of the three percent of Jews allowed to enroll. I found that the sororities were, all but one, closed to me, so I pledged for the remaining one. After being accepted I learned that my sorority did not accept blacks, and worked successfully on changing the charter to correct this, and before I graduated, we had an integrated sorority.

"After graduation I worked at various jobs in Manhattan where I began to understand the inequities of the workplace. Although I had a nice title and real responsibilities, one of the tasks I had in one of my first good jobs was to walk the standard poodle of my boss. Max was the size of a small horse and our office was on the forty-first floor of the Empire State Building, so the walk began in the office, continued down the corridor, into the elevator and onto Fifth Avenue with Max barking and finally doing his business on the curb. Another real and seriously demeaning problem was being ordered to attend fancy business meetings in private dining rooms in hotels such as the Astor or the Waldorf, with the job responsibility of 'decorating the table.' There was little opportunity for advancement as that was reserved for my male colleagues. I resigned and never again allowed myself to be used as a female and not for my abilities. Thanks to some marvelous women, we have come a long way baby, but as we know, the price we have paid is too high, and we have still got a long way to go. I have never espoused the cause of women, but have tried to live my life with equality and dignity.

"In the 1950s, I became a wife and a stay-at-home mother. This is when I learned about activism and volunteerism. I worked to build the Herricks' High School, and to start a newsletter for the newly built Center Street School that is still being published today. I also became the Chairman of the Anti-Defamation League Chapter in New Hyde

Park, and won a National prize for the newsletter I put together for that organization. That experience taught me about the condition of segregation that was growing in Nassau County and I learned to tell the difference between words and deeds. Chairing a meeting about housing segregation, at which the speakers were Don Schafer, founder of the Working Families Party and Lincoln Lynch, civil rights activist, I heard to my embarrassment a prominent member of the New Hyde Park community ask Lynch if he was 'threatening' integration. Lynch responded, 'No, I am promising you.' The dialogue educated me to the goings on in Nassau County, which is now the third most segregated county in the United States.

"In the 1960s, we moved to a larger house in East Meadow and I took a class at Hofstra University that changed the course of my life. The professor who gave the course, Dr. Richard Block, was the head of the Psychology department with a grant to establish a class of what he called 'middle-age coeds' to be trained in Social Science research. The year was 1967 and the federal Anti-Poverty program was just falling into place. I, and four others from the class, were immediately hired to become the research department for the Economic Opportunity Commission of Nassau County. I was to remain on staff for the next thirty-five years, moving from a part-time data collector to the executive assistant to the chief executive officer, John L. Kearse. In short, when I returned to the world of work, I left the profit-motivated fashion business, embraced social action and activism which was to engage me for the rest of my life.

"In the 1970s, I divorced my husband of twenty-one years, moved out of my comfortable suburban life, into an apartment house in the ethnically, racially, and economically diverse Village of Hempstead, and became an advocate for and organizer of the poor, which I have continued to be for the second half of my life. Politically, as part of my job, I became a committeeman (Democrat), ran for delegate when Jesse Jackson ran for vice president, attended the anti-Vietnam War peace rally that Congressman Al Lowenstein organized in Mineola along with Senator John Kerry, and learned from Nassau County Democratic Chairman Stanley Harwood about the way political districts were organized. The latter was in preparation for obtaining the ability for representation in government for the poor and minority residents of Nassau County which they had been denied until that point.

"President Barack Obama's work in Chicago as an organizer is reflective of my own experience. The mission was to organize poor and minorities around the issues that affect their lives. I participated in reorganizing the local community action programs so that they were controlled by the community boards and employed community people. Head Start programs were upgraded to full day year round programs offering the opportunity to parents to go to school and become credentialed staff in those programs.

"In the 1970s, I learned to enjoy jazz, spending time in New York City with many of the greats. I also began to escape the limitations of being a woman in what was still the male dominated workplace. I became involved in community development at the EOC, sought and won a grant for a Community Economic Development Corporation and began the process of land purchases in the target communities, the struggle for a real piece of the pie began here. It is okay to feed people and do other paternalistic activities but do not touch money or jobs.

"In the 1980s, the di-centennial census showed that an Assembly district could be formed which would permit minority representation to be sent to Albany for the first time in the history of Nassau County. The time I had put in with Stanley Harwood placed me in the position of being sent to Albany to work out of Assemblyman Arthur Eve's office and designing what was to become the 18th Assembly District.

"Baum is the immediate past president on the Hempstead Chamber of Commerce where she represents the Wendell Terrace Owners Corporation, a 239-unit cooperative in the village where she made her home since 1973. She is a member of the Village of Hempstead Community Benefits Corporation and served as vice president of its Traffic and Safety Committee. She is also co-chairman of the diversity committee for the National Center for Suburban Studies at Hofstra University, a member of the Hempstead for Hofstra Board of Directors, and is participating in the development of "Oral History of Hempstead" and in a series of films about the history of Manhasset." [5]

Ruth F. Corcoran (1910-1991)

Ruth F. Corcoran was a woman ahead of her time. She was the first woman to be elected to a Suffolk County town board. She won a seat as a councilwoman in Huntington town in 1961 and served until 1965. During this period, Corcoran took a special interest in the needs of the growing youth population. She played an instrumental role in the founding of the Huntington Youth Bureau and the development of youth development corporations throughout the town.

Always a believer in the importance of youth being heard, Corcoran took steps to include young people in government. In 1962, *Newsday* reported in *"Teens Get a Voice in Government"* on the formation of youth advisory councils in Huntington town, the first of its kind in Suffolk County. As the mother of five children, I have always been aware of this desire of youth to be heard. Many times they talk and we do not hear them – we just do not listen," said Corcoran. The youth councils, as designed by Corcoran, will be asked to share their ideas and solutions which will be brought to the town board by a youth representative of the council. This idea was revolutionary for its time. Youth should be seen, not heard was the norm of the time.

In 1969, Corcoran advocated at the Suffolk County legislature for the establishment of a county youth board. She was appointed by County Executive H. Lee Dennison to serve as chairlady of the newly-formed Youth Board. The *Long Islander* reported that Corcoran, in her capacity as chairlady, formed a youth advisory committee. She assembled youth from recreational, educational, religious, and social programs to contribute to the thinking of the new county department, again a radical idea at the time.

Author's Reflection

As director of Community Development for Youth's (CDY) Huntington center, I recall Corcoranas an enthusiastic person who did more than talk-the-talk. On one occasion, she invited the predominantly black young people from CDY's Huntington Station center to her home to enjoy an afternoon swimming at her Huntington village home. Neighbors must have wondered what was going on when thirty black teenagers enthusiastically disembarked from a bus and entered her backyard.

Corcoran's daughter Lucille Buergers recalls that her mother hated being referred to as "councilwoman" or "chairlady...she always referred to herself as councilman and chairman, not wanting to be seen as something different or less than what she actually was."Buergers thinks that, at the time, her mother felt it would minimize her role (women should still be at home, etc.) "She was a feminist without flaunting it...just believed women were capable and that there should be no question about it," Buergers continues:

"Mom got her start as a community activist when the sand and gravel pit at the corner of Southdown Road, and Wall Street (now condos) began to encroach on the area and its trucks would come barreling down Southdown Avenue past our house. This was a threat to the neighborhood and dangerous for anyone who got in the way. More and more of the hill was being carved out and getting closer to homes. She advocated for a stop to be put on the excavating and actually confronted a bulldozer one day by standing in front of it as it was about to dig too close to homes. She got the name "Gravel Gertie." This was the beginning of Citizens Efforts Against Sandpit Encroachment. Eventually, they successfully got the pit to be controlled and after a number of years it closed down completely. There was talk of some mob connection and possible connections to the leadership in the town. This was all an eye opener for her that eventually led her to run for the town board.

"Prior to that her first dip into the pool of activism, mom got involved in the Mother's March Against Polio. Triggered by the impact that polio had on our family, she lead local efforts to raise money and awareness of this awful epidemic. I still remember the preparation and planning that seemed to take endless hours. When I was about seven or eight, we used to go to the firehouse to work on mailings, plans, and other tasks in order to make it a successful event.

"Once there were enough folks from both parties who were fed up with the local government (she was always an Independent), the Fusion Economy Party was formed (modeled after Fiorello LaGaurdia's NYC effort). They had a ticket made up of people who wanted to turn the town board around. Despite party affiliation the ticket won. I remember campaigning and the motto was "Sweep Clean Town Hall". One event that was particularly memorable was the purchase of a large quantity of brooms that were wrapped at the bottom with the slogan and then going to the old town hall and posing with a group sweeping off the front entrance. The ticket that year included Bob Flynn, Norman Olsen, Bob Caputi, Grace Ragle (for town clerk), and my mom. There was quite a celebration when they swept the election!

"During her stint on the Board through the formation of the Junior Advisory Council (JAC), she advocated for a youth bureau and was successful. Once she was out of office she became Chairman of the youth board and was involved for many years and helped develop the system of youth development agencies (YDA) that evolved out of the JAC (representation from every school district) Ultimately, there were seven YDA's located in the seven school districts.

"She also was president of the Huntington Historical Society and started the Huntington Arts Council. Her passion for the arts and appreciation for local history drove her to stay committed and involved.

"My mother got most of her gumption from my grandfather, Richard Finnegan who was editor of the *Chicago Sun Times*. At one point, he made a run for Congress in Illinois. He was a champion for the downtrodden and always spoke out against injustice. When mom was 27 and pregnant with her second child, her husband died suddenly of a brain aneurysm. At the time they were living with my grandparents in Chicago at a house that they were building for their growing family. My grandfather told her 'You are going to make sure that house gets finished and you will take over your husband's life insurance agency and you will be able to survive on your own.' With his encouragement, support, and guidance she did all those things. I cannot imagine what that was like....especially back in 1939! She learned the insurance business and eventually met my father, Charles who worked for Manhattan Life at the time and who coincidentally lost his wife to tuberculosis when she was 27. Many years later, mom went back into the insurance business and became a registered representative for New York Life. She had the instinct to survive and not to have to rely on anyone...a gutsy broad!

"Her first love was the restoration of our home which, when they moved into it in 1947 had an outhouse! You probably remember it and over the years it became a beautiful, antique-filled home where the family gathered for many memorable events. She lovingly collected antiques in need of restoration and did the painstaking work herself and got so much satisfaction from it. She got the greatest kick from being able to spot something that had seven coats of paint and knowing that it was mahogany underneath and then turning it into a showpiece.

"As a kid, I remember the endless telephone calls to the house and the hours spent on the phone that tied her up. That was exasperating and annoying even though I knew it was all for a good cause...one of the necessary evils of public service. But, she did not neglect our needs. As a young adult she was my mentor as I went into the field of social work. While I was in grad school I moved back home and we enjoyed each other's company. We even bowled together on a local league. We were fortunate to have her as a Mom and role model. She was a force to be reckoned with!

"I imagine that she would feel that her greatest accomplishment was raising five kids and seeing them with their kids (10 grandchildren). After that I think it would be all the good she did for the youth of Huntington through all the things she was involved in. She drove around with a bumper sticker that said 'Invest in Youth' which I think she coined as an outreach/PR tool for the youth bureau and the YDAs. She was also proud of her efforts to keep Huntington a nice place for families to live through certain zoning regulations that she influenced in her time on the town board. I think she would be pleased with how Huntington has maintained its village and hometown appeal. Her portrait (which was an old campaign photo) hangs in Town Hall in the board meeting room." [6]

James W. Couch: (1935-2009) (written by his Daughter Jamir R. Couch, Esq.)

James W. Couch, a teacher by training, had an extensive career in nonprofit and governmental positions in both Nassau and Suffolk counties. He originally moved with his wife, Miriam D. Couch and young daughter, Jamir to Long Island in 1966 to teach history as the first African-American teacher at Locust Valley High School having been recruited by the principal, Mrs. Elliot a few years after his graduation from Cheyney University outside of Philadelphia, PA.

In 1969, Couch headed to the Economic Opportunity Commission office in Glen Cove. There he was a staunch advocate for the city's low income residents especially when local officials cut the commission's budget forcing him to layoff many local workers. In 1971, Couch moved on to become deputy director and director of field operations of the Nassau County Economic Opportunity Commission (EOC) working closely with John Kearse, the commission's executive director. During this period, Couch also served as chairman of the state Alliance for Community Action Programs as well as coordinator of the Mobilization for Domestic Unity.

In 1973, Couch joined the newly-formed Long Island Sickle Project as its executive director. Sickle Cell is a hereditary disease. [Sickle cell disease is an inherited blood disorder. It is not a virus and is not contagious. An individual acquires sickle cell disease from genes by both parents, much in the same way as blood type; hair color and texture, eye color and other physical traits are inherited.] The project was funded under the National Sickle Cell Anemia Control Act of 1972. The Act formed the sickle disease branch in the Heart, Lung and Blood Institute of the National Institute of Health. It also established ten comprehensive sickle cell centers throughout the United States to develop programs for research, education, screening, counseling and improved care of individual with sickle cell. Since its inception, the project's fourteen staff members had distributed information to 75,000 people and tested 29,000. The project estimated that 1,700 Long Islanders were carriers with 300 or more families having one or more members who suffer from the disease.

Couch traveled to fourteen countries to set up sickle cell clinics. He also worked closely with the National Institute on Health and legislators in Washington, D.C. as well including participating in President Ford's White House public forum on domestic policy on November 18, 1975 in Philadelphia, PA as the co-chairman for the National Association of Sickle Cell Clinics. Locally, he worked incessantly to educate elected and appointed officials about Sickle Cell and dispel myths and assumptions surrounding the disease. He battled against mandatory screenings and the lack of distinction between a carrier of the sickle cell trait and the anemia itself. Couch spoke forcefully of the legal, ethical, and psychological issues involved and the need for comprehensive health care facilities. He cautioned against race being the primary determinant for policy and program decisions.

Speaking before the Nassau County Medical Center's task force on priorities for the future he said: "In no appreciable case have minorities had a key role in planning and operational guidelines in health delivery on Long Island." Couch worked with other consumer advocates towards the establishment of an ombudsman position in the hospital. He brought a similar message to the newly-formed Nassau-Health Care Systems Agency. Couch was also a health care advocate on other issues including infant and maternal morbidity.

Couch also served as chairman of the Black Parents Council in Huntington town where he urged the town to stop discrimination in housing and establish a department of minority affairs. In this capacity, he also battled a Suffolk county plan to reduce services and staffing at the six existing social service centers.

In 1980, Couch along with other Long Island civil rights leaders delivered a 'black state of Long Island address.' According to *Newsday*, (January 16, 1980) Couch said: 'The plight of black people today is worse than it was when I was a kid." He urged audiences to work together in electoral politics. Having grown up in the rural south in the late 1930s and 1940s, Couch's statement was quite an indictment of the state of affairs on Long Island.

In 1983, Couch became coordinator for the Long Island Minority Coalition advocating for a national holiday in commemoration of Dr. Martin Luther King, Jr. During the same year, he served as interim director of the Economic Opportunity Council of Suffolk. In this position, he criticized state policies and procedures in their administration of anti-poverty program funding through their federal block grants.

In 1988, Couch was appointed by Suffolk County Executive Patrick Halpin as a county executive assistant to supervise affirmative action, the criminal justice coordinating council, veterans' affairs and youth programs. One of his first efforts was to change screening procedures used by Suffolk's volunteer ambulance companies who refused to respond to calls in minority communities until police dispatchers verified that medical emergencies existed. Since he was the most senior African-American in Halpin's Administration and the first African-American assistant county executive, he assisted the county executive to fill senior positions in his administration with other minorities.

As a member of the Mandela Welcome Committee Couch was involved in the rally the group organized in 1990 held in Hempstead to welcome Nelson Mandela to New York. He also served as the chair of the Suffolk County Black Democrats and in 1991, welcomed then Democratic National Chairman to Long Island to speak on behalf of then presidential candidate, Bill Clinton.

In 1993, continuing as a county executive assistant, Couch joined three other top administration staffers to file a federal lawsuit against then-county executive Robert Gaffney in response to what was commonly felt to be a political move to undermine the social service department.

According to one article, Couch worked for Addiction Research Treatment Corporation and as executive director of the National Alliance of Black Organizations against Alcohol and Drug Abuse. He later served as Vice President of Research & Development, Addiction Research & Treatment Corporation (ARTC), in Brooklyn an agency providing services for drug abusers in six clinic sites in the New York metro area. He then served as Vice President of Operations for AMRON Management Consultants as an Administrator, Health Watch Information and Promotion Services, special AMRON initiative.

"During his career, Couch received over 40 awards, citations and proclamations for his outstanding community service. He presented over 25 papers on minority health. Appeared on numerous television programs and was a speaker for over 100 events regarding human rights, civil rights & race relations."

In the words of Jamir Couch, Esq., Couch's daughter:

> "I am proud of all of my father's accomplishments, as a teacher (first black teacher/coach at Locust Valley High School), community activist/advocate/organizer, and college professor, as a public health administrator…and as my dad. I was happy/proud for him when he became the President of the National Association of Community Health Centers (NACHC) in 1996, perhaps the first African-American in the position, and we (my sister, her husband, and me) all went to his installation in San Francisco. My father's dedication to others prompted the NACHC executive director to drive several hours to his funeral to express his appreciation for my father's commitment to helping others gain access to health care during his time as president/member of the organization. Since his passing in 2009, I have heard from many of his colleagues about his dedication and others.

> "I think he was an intelligent, informed advocate for the underserved Long Island community. He was proud of his community and not afraid to speak up on their behalf or on behalf of others; no matter what the consequences were. He did what he thought was right; and, working with other like-minded people, was able to provide a 'seat' at the table for the Long Island minority community. He also advocated for the underserved throughout the U.S. His advocacy impacted millions -- in his role as a sickle cell advocate (testifying in DC for the Sickle Cell Anemia Control Act, 1971) and as the President of the National Association of Community Health Centers.

> "He definitely had an impact on us, me. Growing up in the 1960s on Long Island as an African-American woman was not easy. It made me aware of my surroundings and determined to help others, especially in my community. Also, to speak up, even if it is not popular (and generally it wasn't in the schools I attended.) We were taught by my parents to be proud and believe in yourself and believe that all people are equal and there is fairness and justice in society.

"He would take me to museums around Long Island and the country and took the time to educate me about history and other issues. I also went with him to his offices/jobs and events. For, even as a small child I went with him to Locust Valley school and sports events. One summer I even served as a camp counselor at a New Hampshire camp for children affected by sickle cell when he was the executive director for the sickle cell project.

"As an adult, it continued - we even had the opportunity to attend a few Congressional Black Caucus legislative weekends together where we were both speakers. My dad was my best friend/teacher/advisor (along with my mom). It had a tremendous impact on me and my interest in the law & politics. I was a science/math student who ended up in law & politics. We talked/debated all the time about so many political issues; up to the day he died. I believed in justice, fairness and giving back to others. I thought I could make a difference. I believed in speaking my mind. I still believe in being fair, giving back and speaking up for what I believe in; I have some doubts about the justice system.

"There are so many issues that need to be addressed on Long Island and throughout the U.S. Is there a cohesive approach/strategy to addressing these issues on Long Island? I think my biggest concern is the lack of intelligent informed advocates, elected or otherwise, who can speak on behalf of those in need and are willing to challenge the system if they have to. My question is: What is the quality of our leadership on Long Island and in NYS? Is it inclusive? During the last few years I have spent more time on Long Island and I still see it as a segregated community. LI has never elected a minority/woman county executive in either county and there still is not a lot of diversity in Albany either.

"Economic inequality, to me, is one of the major issues that still exist today. All of the issues (poverty, social justice, social action and access to health) all revolve around an individual/family's economic status/financial stability.

"Since I have been in both the public and private sector, I believe there is definitely a role for public/private partnerships in addressing some of these issues. Of course, as with any partnership, it depends on how clearly the goals are outlined between the parties in order for it to be successful. All parties have to be open to new ideas and be able to communicate in order to determine options that will help the entire community." [7]

Nancy Rauch Douzinas (1948-

Douzinas' impact on the quality of life on Long Island over the past 45 years cannot be underestimated. As a philanthropist and articulate spokesperson for improving the quality of life for all Long Islanders, she has made an indelible mark.

Douzinas assumed the leadership role of the Rauch Foundation in 1990 after a 20-year career as a psychologist and family therapist. She became president, and under her leadership, the Rauch Foundation became a high-profile change agent on Long Island and in Maryland. During her tenure, the foundation has focused its priorities and expanded its professional staff.

The Rauch Foundation is a Long Island–based family foundation that invests in ideas and organizations that spark and sustain systemic change in our communities. The foundation focuses on areas where it can have the greatest impact: children and families, the environment, and regional leadership. The foundation believes in taking a comprehensive approach to problem solving. Its activities extend beyond traditional grant making to include significant research and communications efforts.

In all of its work the foundation is guided by its entrepreneurial roots. Philip Rauch Sr. was an automotive engineer and the inventor of the hose clamp, a small part that played a big role in the growth of the auto industry. His two sons, Philip Rauch Jr. and Louis Rauch, created the foundation in 1961 to support a wide range of educational and social causes.

Historically, in 1977, the Rauch Foundation was established to give back to the community where the family lived and has lived. In 1985, the foundation began to consider a priority to award grants in early childhood education. In 1989, the foundation developed a strategic program focus for greater impact. First priority area identified as children and families. Louis and Ruth Rauch soon spearheaded foundation support for YMCA leadership development and the Huntington YMCA Family Center. Louis Rauch believed in what the YMCA stood for and that it offered in opportunities for skill development and fun for the average person as its fees were reasonable. Having grown up in East New York and attended YMCA's, he knew what they could give a person. He was on the YMCA of Long Island board for many years and worked to develop a strong board and strengthen management. He then recruited a cousin, John Treiber, to take over his place on the board where John remains to this day.

In 1993, the Rauch Foundation starts formal operations by hiring staff and building its board of directors. In the following year, the foundation formally establishes its environmental program and in 1998 awarded grants to bring the Parent-Child Home Program to four communities. Also, in 1998, support was given for replication of the Family Place Library model, bringing innovative family-centered services to public libraries.

In 2004, the foundation began development of the Long Island Index and published its first index on Long Island's quality of life. The Energeia Partnership was created in 1998 to build regional leadership. In 2007, an important article '*What Every Long Islander Should Know*' article written by Nancy Rauch Douzinas was published in *Newsday*.

Over the next several years, two new initiatives were developed including the Early Years Institute and the Sustainability Institute at Molloy College. In 2010, the Foundation launched the 'Build a Better Burb' project to focus attention on the issue of affordable housing.

In 2012, Douzinas was named to the *Long Island Press* Power List Hall of Fame, which noted, 'The Rauch Foundation had become a true agent of change for our region. Douzinas knows she does not have all the answers but she is fearless when it comes to championing the search - and doing what she can to make Long Island a better place.'

Douzinas believes that the lessons learned for foundations are to 'become long term investors in their goals and key organizations but at the same time develop means of tracking progress; to work with other foundations and with others from different sectors like government, business, labor, civic because since that is where the power for real change comes in; and to build capacity in the organizations you support, develop management, communication skills and finally to remain open to new and creative ideas."

In keeping with her broad range of community concerns and personal interests, Douzinas serves on the boards of Teachers College, Columbia University; the Society for the Preservation of Long Island Antiquities; the Energeia Partnership; the North Shore Land Alliance; the Stony Brook Foundation; and the newly-created Accelerate Long Island.

A lifelong resident of the New York area, Douzinas graduated from Smith College and received a Master's Degree and Doctorate from New York University in Community Psychology. She and her husband reside in Lloyd Harbor and have two married daughters and five grandchildren. [8]

Hazel N. Dukes (1932-

An important civil rights activist of the 1960s and 1970s and a campaigner for over 30 years, Hazel Nell Dukes is a leading figure in the National Association for the Advancement of Colored People (NAACP) and served as the organization's national president between 1989 and 1992. Dukes built a career in various social service agencies, but she was most successful working for the New York City Off-Track Betting Corporation (NYCOTB). She worked for the corporation for 25 years before being made its president by New York City Mayor David Dinkins in 1990.

Hazel Nell Dukes was born in1932, in Montgomery, Alabama, the daughter and only child of Edward and Alice Dukes. Dukes was raised in Montgomery and, intending to become a teacher, attended Alabama State Teachers College (now Alabama State University) beginning in 1949. But in 1955 she moved with her parents to New York City and began studying at Nassau Community College while she worked at Macy's department store. Her studies in business administration soon led her into working for governmental organizations. In 1966 she became the first black American to work for the Nassau County attorney's office and later worked for the Nassau County Economic Opportunity Commission (EOC) as a community organizer. There she was responsible for organizing day care and schooling for poor children, as well as for coordinating transportation for people unable to attend college or find work because they were unable to travel. Throughout her life Dukes has shown a deep commitment to the importance of education and worked hard in the 1960s to improve the educational chances of many people in deprived areas.

Dukes' career saw her work in many government agencies concerned with helping low-income families. She became known in the 1960s as an outspoken campaigner on behalf of minority groups, especially through her work with the Nassau County Consumer Division, and as a board member of the State of New York Mortgage Agency. Most significantly Dukes worked for the New York City Off-Track Betting Corporation (NYCOTB) and was appointed its president in 1990 by mayor David Dinkins. While she found success in business, Dukes was also working for the NAACP, participating in many marches and having six arrests to her credit as a protester. She was president of the Great Neck, Manhasset, Port Washington, Roslyn chapter and national president of the organization from 1989 to 1992. She was ousted from office during a period of in-fighting that threatened to destroy the organization.

Dukes' political activism extends also to campaigning for the Democratic Party. She worked for President Lyndon Johnson's "Head Start" program in the 1960s and was the first black vice-chair of the Nassau County Democratic Committee. She served on the party's national committee from 1976 to 1982. During the years of the Reagan and Bush presidencies in the 1980s and early 1990s Dukes was an outspoken opponent of policies that she felt undermined the achievements of the civil rights movements of the 1960s.

Dukes spearheaded several important campaigns, especially efforts to persuade a new generation to take over leadership of the NAACP. She has also pushed for education reforms and views the civil rights movements of the 1960s as unfinished business. In a speech made in the fall of 2004 Dukes linked the NAACP campaign to reduce class sizes in New York City Schools with important earlier battles in the civil rights movement. She declared that "Only if your deliberations end in smaller classes, for all children in all grades, will they be provided with their constitutional rights to a sound basic education. Only then will the promise of Brown vs. Board of Education be achieved."

Dukes is president of the NAACP New York State Conference and a member of the NAACP National board of directors, a member of the NAACP Executive Committee and well as an\ active member of various NAACP board sub-committees. Dukes is a woman of great strength and courage. Her dedication to human rights and equality is exemplified by her role linking business, government and social causes. She is an active and dynamic leader who is known for her unselfish and devoted track record for improving the quality of life in New York State.

A harsh system of civil and human injustice persists; intimidation, violence, and the recent rash of "nooses," speak to the widespread de facto absence of a civil and human rights agenda in America says Dukes, and the fires of frustration continue to burn.

Dukes is president of the Hazel N. Dukes & Associates Consultant Firm, specializing in the areas of public policy, health and diversity and a member of the Assembly of Prayer Baptist Church where she served as executive assistant to the pastor, is a member of the board of trustees and teaches in the church's adult Sunday school.

Dukes received a Bachelor Degree in Business Administration from Adelphi University and completed post-graduate work at Queens College. In 1990 she was awarded an Honorary Doctor of Laws Degree from the City University of New York Law School at Queens College and in 2009 was conferred the Honorary Doctor of Humane Letters, at Medgar Evers College. Dukes is former president of the Metro-Manhattan Links Chapter, in 2010 was appointed the National Links NGO Representative and is a former trustee of the State University of New York and Stillman College. She is a member of the National Council of Negro Women, Inc., and National Black Leadership Commission on AIDS, and a member of the executive committee of the American Baptist Churches, USA.

Dukes is the recipient of numerous awards for her outstanding leadership activities, Ellis Island Medal of Honor, YWCA City of New York John La Farge Memorial Award for Interracial Justice, Guy R. Brewer Humanitarian Award, and the 2007 The Network Journal's 25 Most Influential Black Women in Business Award, member Ford Motor Company Funds Committee of Honor for Freedom's Sisters, was honored and received a proclamation at the New York City Council's third annual Martin Luther King, Jr., awards ceremony at City Hall in New York. Dukes is an active member of the Delta Sigma Theta Sorority Rockland County alumnae chapter and has been selected to receive the sorority's Althea T.L. Simmons Social Action Award in August 2010. In 2007, Dukes was incorporated as a Pi Eta Kappa Fellow and her biography has been selected for publication in many journals and directories including: Fisk University Library, Minority Women Contribution, American Biographical Institute Personalities of Northeast, Who's Who Among American Women and Who's Who Among Black Women." [9]

Marge Harrison (1952-

Marge Harrison grew up in Freeport, on the south shore of Nassau County, where her parents were active in the local Democratic Party and in the 1956 Adlai Stevenson presidential campaign. She feels that Freeport was a good place to grow up in part because it was one of the few integrated villages in Nassau and also because Jones Beach, a monument to public endeavors, was close by. Her earliest memory of political action, as an elementary student, was of her brother and her doing door-to-door literature drops for Democratic candidates. As a teenager, Harrison was very much influenced by Martin Luther King Jr.; in particular, his emphasis on the essential dignity of each person shaped her thinking about what kind of person she wanted to be, how she wanted to approach working alongside others.

Her first political meeting took place on her lawn in 1968 or 1969 when an organizer for Cesar Chavez's grape boycott campaign contacted her. Her task was to go into the local supermarket and ask the manager to honor the boycott. During her last two years in high school, she attended a lot of antiwar demonstrations and went to amazing youth congresses in Manhattan where the banners and posters opened her eyes to political viewpoints that she did not normally encounter in her suburban life. In 1968, she got involved in the Eugene McCarthy presidential primary race and spent hours at the headquarters near the Baldwin LIRR station. The college student volunteers who had come to Nassau from colleges all over the east coast awed her. She wanted to be like them, and when she went off to college, she got involved in student antiwar politics and the last remnants of Students for a Democratic Society (SDS) at the University of Rochester. There she attended huge antiwar meetings attended by key leftist historians on campus including Herbert Gutman, Eugene Genovese, and Christopher Lasch. This made a deep impression on her: the application of scholarly insight in developing political strategy and organization. This was in the early seventies when the New Left student movement was gravitating to community activism as compared to a campus-based approach. It was at Rochester that Harrison met her future husband, Fred Harrison, who had also grown up in Freeport, and who remains her constant political collaborator forty years later.

Finishing up her undergraduate years at Barnard College in 1974, Harrison became involved in the New American Movement (NAM), which was formed by former student leaders and young community organizers. NAM was launched with the specific goal of finding a way to bring a New Left orientation into organizing in the neighborhoods, towns, and cities where she had landed post-college. The focus on organizing was critical.

Harrison had done research in college on the Progressive-era movement for nonprofit ownership and control utilities, the public power movement. Moving back to Freeport after college, she got active with PeaceSmith House in Massapequa, a place that brought together activists involved in a lot of issues and that blended the politics of the baby-boom generation with that of the civil rights movement/Old Left/Depression generation. There was an emphasis on grassroots organizing. The lead organizers there, Susan Blake and Karl Bernhard, among others, had launched a campaign against the Long Island Lighting Company (LILCO), its high rates and its nuclear plant at Shoreham, which was under construction. Many such efforts were springing up all over Long Island, starting in 1973 with the first energy/oil crisis. When the Three Mile Island plant in Pennsylvania started to melt down, the pace of this LILCO work accelerated. Harrison found herself driving all around Long Island giving talks about why rates were so high, why Shoreham would only guarantee high rates (and danger) and what could be done about it: organize for a public takeover of LILCO, which was doable under existing state laws. Harrison met Dave Sprintzen when a call went out for the formation of what became the Long Island Progressive Coalition (LIPC).

LIPC came together around the idea of bringing the various strands of left-oriented activists together with labor and community groups. A key person in those early crucial meetings in 1979 and 1980 was Adelphi social work professor Sylvia Aron, who had an enormous network of labor and community contacts, and brought great wisdom and organizing experience going back to the 1930s.

After the formation of LIPC, the public power/anti-nuclear campaign became a major focus of the LIPC as the Long Island Public Power Project. In this effort, Harrison placed particular emphasis on doing educational work, in living rooms, church basements, with groups large and small, that aimed to equip people with the analysis and information they needed so that they could become active leaders in the movement themselves. Harrison and others produced numerous fact sheets and white papers, distributing thousands of pieces of literature, and helping to ignite a real grassroots outpouring of support for the platform. She saw that a clear, common-sense populist proposal could rally support across the partisan and ideological spectrum.

For example, Harrison was invited to speak at a Uniondale, Nassau County community meeting, held in a junior high cafeteria. She had been 'warned' that this group was very conservative and might not go for what was essentially a proposal to turn one of the largest segments of LI's economy, the electricity infrastructure, into a publicly-owned and democratically-controlled nonprofit industrial sector; referred to in the academic literature as 'municipal socialism.' But happily, these admonitions proved totally unnecessary. The audience responded very enthusiastically to hearing the LILCO reality being decoded in a way that explained things clearly and made sense. This work was tremendously exciting and inspiring as public opinion and politicians moved. The work deployed its labor connections gained through the LIPC and their involvement in the labor-led Mario Cuomo Democratic primary and gubernatorial campaigns in 1982 to meet with the officials of the IBEW local representing LILCO workers. This led to the inclusion in our public takeover plan of a 'successor' clause to ensure that LILCO workers would be protected if municipalization took place. Sprintzen and Harrison had organized Mario Cuomo's first meeting with anti-LILCO/Shoreham advocates in July of 1982 during the primary campaign.

From 1982 to 1994, Harrison served as a vice-chair of the New York State Democratic party, an elected, volunteer position, representing the Reform Caucus, a group of progressive Democratic state committee members, led by Esther Smith, a Manhattan and Fire Island resident who an impressive organizer and from whom she learned a lot. Her party work and Shoreham work on the county and state levels led her to being asked to serve on Gov. Cuomo's Shoreham Fact-finding Commission including specific information about the negative economic impact of high LILCO/Shoreham rates. Harrison agreed to join with the proviso that Sprintzen serve as her alternate as she was a high school teacher at that point and could not always attend daytime commission sessions. They worked hard to push public power and safe energy viewpoints into the Commission's report and submitted minority reports on specific points.

By the late 1980s, LIPC was evolving from a volunteer-based group to one with a paid staff with specific grant-funded projects. There was an earnest and lively debate at LIPC board meetings about these new strategies for organizational growth and development. Organizing on Long Island is difficult and these were honest disagreements about future trajectories and organizational identity, with the group entering a new phase in its evolution. The opportunity to affiliate with Citizen Action New York (CANY) and thereby establish more institutional stability was very attractive. Harrison served for a time as the LIPC's representative on the CANY's executive board.

By this time, Harrison was a library research teacher at Lawrence High School and deeply involved in union work and related community politics in the Five Towns and decided to step down as co-chair of the LIPC in 1988. The anti-LILCO/Shoreham campaign was nearing its end with the closure of the plant and the bailout of LILCO as accomplished through the public takeover of the company and the establishment of the Long Island Power Authority. The LI Public Power Project has been calling for a closure of Shoreham with LILCO being taken over through an eminent domain process with the creation of a nonprofit municipally-owned utility governed by an elected board. Shoreham was decommissioned but LIPC's prescriptions for a democratic public utility obviously did not come to pass as we had hoped.

Harrison's work for the Lawrence Teachers' Association, as a member and officer, proved to be just as challenging and compelling as her work with the LIPC and the Democratic Party. In collaboration with LTA president Steve Clements (1985-2006) and others, Harrison enjoyed the union work in part because it was very concrete, with a defined membership and targeted strategies related to school budgets, the school board, and organizing pro-public education efforts. Unlike the open-ended nature of general community organizing undertaken by groups like the LIPC, in union work the constituency and the work were very nitty-gritty and direct. This experience made Harrison even more aware of how difficult it is to do general political organizing on Long Island.

Throughout the 1980s, Harrison was doing a lot of reading in political science and political theory, which helped her enormously in her own work. She decided to pursue an MA in American history at Columbia, which she was able to do part-time while continuing her day job. She continued on and earned a Ph.D. in 2006 at Columbia, writing her dissertation on the midcentury Nassau Republican party with Kenneth Jackson and Herbert Gans as advisors. Her general interest was middle-class political identity in suburbia. She wanted to try to find out why so many people who moved to Nassau in the 1940s and 1950s gravitated to the local GOP even though they had identified with the Democratic Party in their former city neighborhoods. What she found was that the Nassau GOP had undertaken innovative and successful organizing strategies to attract both young people and the large number of newly-arrived ethnic-group voters, such as Jews and Catholics. For example, the county GOP ran social clubs for "twenty-somethings" which blended party work with parties, and by prominently including "ethnics" on the ballot.

Harrison feels that she has been fortunate in being able to blend her interest in and reading about organizational and political questions with on-the-scene organizing; She undertook two Ph.Ds. in a way: one at Columbia and one in the nuts-and-bolts work of community political organizing, working with the LIPC, in the public power/anti-nuclear campaign, in election campaigns and union work, among other efforts. Fortunate also in that she have gotten to know a lot of interesting, engaged people from a broad spectrum of life in her political work and career and benefited from the deep friendships formed in the thrust and parry of politics. [10]

Roberta Hunter (1952-

Most Long Islanders probably are not familiar with the lives and culture of the 1,400 people living on the 5,000 acres on Long Island's south fork owned by the Shinnecock Nation. Roberta Hunter's role in behalf of her community has had lasting impact. She has committed her life to assure that Shinnecock Nation achieves its rights as a Native American tribe with the rights and opportunities to which it is entitled. She has worked passionately to preserve Shinnecock traditions and culture and strengthen the tribe's economic future.

Shinnecock history dates back centuries and is recorded in oral history. Shinnecock are Algonquin people. Today, due in good part to the work of Roberta Hunter and other tribal members, the Shinnecock Nation is a federally-recognized Indian Nation. This recognition was achieved in 2010 after thirty-two years of struggle with the Bureau of Indian Affairs making the Shinnecock Nation the 565th federal tribe.

Hunter's family owned land in Shinnecock but lived and was educated in Queens while spending many weekends and vacations on the family's land. Her father, now age 97, is a Shinnecock and was a navigator and pilot in World War II serving in the Pacific arena. He could have chosen to serve in a black troop but chose a white one instead. Hunter's mother was Jamaican. Her parents experienced racism when they tried to buy a home in Levittown in the late 1940s. Her parents were active politically in the community and encouraged Hunter to have a voice. Among their many organizing activities was to organize veterans of color. Hunter lived in a home where there were always petitions being written, signs being made, and events being organized. Her parents wanted their children to attend white schools so Hunter assimilated with people of diverse backgrounds at an early age. Hunter was a very good student, involved in school government. In junior high school, she organized a campaign to get girls to be able to wear pants.

Hunter attended Bennington College where she was an activist concerned with the many social issues of the early 1970s. She was selected to serve on the progressive college's board of trustees majoring in Anthropology and Photography. During college, Hunter increasingly saw herself as an "outsider," committed to social justice issues. For her master's thesis, Hunter completed a photo essay on the Shinnecock Nation which was displayed in the college library.

After college, Hunter furthered her education earning a Master's Degree in Public Administration at C.W. Post Her thesis at C.W. Post addressed the status of Indian nations and, particularly, the treatment of the Shinnecock Nation by the Bureau of Indian Affairs (BIA). At C.W. Post, Hunter was selected to participate in a Presidential Management Internship Program which she viewed as an opportunity to enter federal government service with the Bureau of Indian Affairs, her career goal at the time. She was the only Native American among the other fifty-two interns. After completing the internship program, Hunter applied for a position at BIA but was denied since the Nation was regarded as a legitimate tribe. This action further propelled Hunter to seek legal redress in behalf of the Nation.

Needing employment, Hunter accepted a position as director of AARP's Senior Community Service Employment Program in Suffolk County. During this period, she earned a Law Degree at Queens College and helped to file a land claim in behalf of the Shinnecock Nation for the 5,000 acres under the 'Non-Intercourse Act.' This act did not permit transfers of real property between any party and an Indian tribe without congress' consent. Hunter worked with a group of Native American attorneys to file the suit which sought to recognize the Nation as a legitimately-recognized Indian tribe by the Bureau of Indian Affairs. Hunter knew that winning the suit could lead to the Nation being able to file a law suit against the town of Southampton to recognize the Nation's status.

Hunter worked for years to organize tribal support for the law suit dealing with a male-controlled board of trustees. She understood that it was critical to convince tribal members that the law suit should be pursued. Hunter decided that women's voting was a key to this effort and began to organize women after a child was seriously injured on a piece of old playground equipment. Hunter viewed this event as an opportunity to help women to see that they could organize themselves and move on to influence other tribal issues. [11]

Mel Jackson (1932-

Mel Jackson's activism began when he was raising funds for the Freedom Riders in 1961. The Freedom Riders was a movement to challenge segregation in interstate travel by having integrated groups riding from north to south. He saw his activism and career choices as directly related to the constraints of the times. Even though he would have preferred an academic career this was not an option for him. The fears of the Sputnik period right after the McCarthy era were more intense because of the suspicion of people of color and in his field of engineering necessary security clearances were not possible. He was drawn instead to the civil rights movement as a way to take a stand since things did not appear to be getting any better even with new federal laws and lip service to racial equality.

 Growing up in Texas where he encountered apartheid like conditions, he saw how the poor and disenfranchised were used by politicians and it appeared to him that the situation was not improving. Even in the scientific community racism was prominent. Therefore, even though experiencing real fear, participating in the movement seemed necessary given the evils of the time and threat of even greater evils in the future. He realized that even with his education and profession, the situation was dire. Everything came to a head as several forces for change came together.

He worked with the NAACP and CORE where programs and issues were dealt with from New York to Montauk. Efforts included helping migrant workers who were almost in a slave situation (brought in and not able to leave, having to buy everything from the crew chief of farmer and more). He helped organized the duck farms and improved the conditions of migrant workers and helped to close down some of the worst farms. He dealt with the difficult lessons of de-facto segregation realizing that even though there were no segregated facilities as such there were ways that housing and schools were totally segregated and access was denied to people of color. You could not get into the better school districts because you could not get a home there. He worked to help these segregated districts but these districts are still failing today. That is why he feels that it is so important now to merge all the Long Island school districts.

Over his extensive career of public service, Jackson has been chairman of: The Employment Opportunity Corporation and the Black Caucus. He served as a board member of the Economic Opportunity Council, Nassau County's anti-poverty program and served as an area district commissioner and Nassau County representative to the Boy Scouts of America. He served as a regional advisor for the NAACP's youth and college division and as a Roman Catholic Diocesan member of the tri-faith committee.

Jackson, a black man born in the South, an electrical engineer by profession and an active participant in community affairs is a good way of describing Mel Jackson. He is founder and president of the Leadership Training Institute (LTI). He has lived with his wife and three children in Hempstead since 1958. Jackson was born in San Antonio, Texas and attended schools in Texas and California, attending City College of Los Angeles and then Howard University in Washington, D.C. where he graduated Cum Laude in 1957 with a Degree in Electrical Engineering. He then went on to graduate work at Northwestern University with a Technological Institute Fellowship. After graduating, Jackson held a position as Program Manager for Sperry Gyroscope, the second-largest employer on Long Island."[12]

David Kadane (1914-1991)

The contributions made by David Kadane to Hofstra were part of an unusually diverse career that continued almost to the moment he died," said Stuart Rabinowitz, Dean and Alexander M. Bickel Distinguished Professor of Law at Hofstra University School of Law in 1991. In the Summer Issue of Hofstra's Law Review, Rabinowitz shared the following account (edited for brevity) of Kadane's career:

Kadane was born in New York City in 1914, the son of a lawyer. He attended public schools and graduated from the City College of New York in 1933 after which he received his LL.B. Degree from Harvard Law School. After law school, Kadane did law work with the U.S. Senate Committee on Interstate Commerce, the Security and Exchange Commission. Following this government service, Kadane was employed by the Long Island Lighting Company (LILCO) where he developed a national reputation for his work involving government regulation of utility rates. While on leave from LILCO, Kadane and his wife Helene left their Rockville Centre home to serve in Tanzania as a member of the Peace Corps, serving as a legal advisor to the government and its president, Julius K. Nyerere.

In 1970, Kadane joined Hofstra's School of Law as one of its founding faculty members, especially interested in creating new programs in clinical legal education while making his own local contribution to the war on poverty. Just prior to his appointment as the first director of the Hofstra Law School's Neighborhood Law Office in Hempstead that continues today as the Community Legal Assistance Corporation. The Law School Dean Mahon asked Kadane to explain his intended LILCO retirement at age fifty-six. In a note to Mahon, Kadane noted that his children were grown and he no longer had the financial need. He offered the following terse explanation of his interest in opening a law office in one of Long Island's poorest neighborhoods: 'Surely a professional man has a duty to apply his capacities, if he can, where they would seem to be most needed. As a lawyer, I am in the business of helping people get justice. I think this a good way to do it.'"

Rabinowitz went on to describe Kadane's "spirited commitment to a new and exciting experiment in legal education," "serving as a gadfly, the inquisitor, never letting anyone relax or become complacent, constantly questioning our basic assumptions."

In 1964, Kadane, then serving as LILCO general counsel, was instrumental in the establishment of the United Fund for Long Island, telling a group of 100 business and community leaders at a dinner meeting in Salisbury Park that the new fund could" raise from $12M - $17M a year, compared with the $7.5M raised at the time through individual agency drives. In 1968, he was appointed by Nassau County Executive Eugene Nickerson as chairman of the Nassau County Youth Board. In 1969, Kadane served as chairman of the newly-formed Nassau-Suffolk Comprehensive Health Planning Council and was also chairman of the Health and Welfare Council.

David Kadane was honored by many community and professional organizations. In 1987, in a memorial appreciation of his career, Kadane reflected on his beliefs:

"All in all, I have deduced one principle of personal ethics and one in social ethics. The former is that pain is the evil, psychic or physical. What is bad is the infliction of pain, what is sinfully bad is the deliberate infliction of pain. What is good is the removal of pain, what is gloriously good is the removal of pain for which one is not responsible but which one may be fortunate enough to be able to remove. The social ethical principle I draw is that no people-serving institution can be trusted, after it has been in business for a while. It will gradually forget its original objective, and start to serve itself; and I mean all institutions: clubs, schools, corporations, human rights organizations, government units, chamber music groups and bowling leagues. They all begin to behave as though they were created for the providers." [13]

Wilbur "Bill" Klatsky (1931-2011)

Wilbur "Bill" Klatsky was a devoted public servant who made countless lives easier through his work in community development. For his family, friends, and those who benefited from his service, to know him was to love him.

Klatsky, who lost his father when only twelve, grew up in Tottenville on Staten Island the youngest of five children, and the family's only boy. Klatsky served in the Air Force and graduated from Columbia University in 1960. In 1964, he moved to Connecticut where he became the planning coordinator for new development in New London and taught at Rutgers University and Connecticut College. After spearheading urban renewal projects in New London, Klatsky came to Long Island in 1969 where he and a committed group of activists founded the Suffolk Community Development Corporation (SCDC). Klatsky served as the organization's first staff member. SCDC later changed its name to the Community Development Corporation of Long Island (CDC).

The mission of CDC was Klatsky's life passion and he served various roles within the organization until his retirement in 2009: CEO, President, and long-time board member. While at the helm of CDC, Bill focused on affordable housing and lending for underserved individuals. In 1995-96, CDC purchased and rehabilitated sixteen empty homes at the abandoned NIKE site in Wading River. CDC facilitated a lottery that allowed disadvantaged families to move in as renters and later purchase their homes. Klatsky's passion for providing affordable housing continued throughout the years and in 2005-06 CDC purchased a 7.4 acre parcel in Mattituck and broke ground on 22 affordable two-bedroom houses. A lottery afforded 22 qualifying applicants the opportunity to purchase new homes. Furthermore, he created a commercial lending department at CDC, one of whose programs helped home-based childcare providers improve their programs with low interest rate loans.

Klatsky selflessly gave years of time, effort, love, and expertise to SCDC, CDC, and the countless board and agencies through which he was able to help the less fortunate. However, Klatsky's passion for helping others extended beyond his career. He was known to fix flat tires for anonymous strangers (a local bookmobile once relied on his kindness) and then drive off into the distance like the Lone Ranger. One time, when he heard that a CDC staff member had been involved in an accident while driving her mother to chemotherapy, Klatsky went out and purchased her a used car. If this was all Klatsky had done in his lifetime, he would have been considered a very special man, but there was more to Bill than his commitment to social welfare.

Klatsky served on the boards of the radio station WSHU, the Kimmel Foundation, the Child Care Council of Nassau, and the Shoreham Library. His involvement with WSHU stemmed from his love of classical music, which could always be heard in his home and office. He would have to save his beloved Louis Prima music for the office since he was the only fan in his family! Governor David Patterson appointed Klatsky to serve as one of the eight community members on the prestigious New York State Banking Department in 2010. He has been honored by numerous nonprofit organizations including the Kimmel Foundation and the Child Care Council of Suffolk. In addition, Klatsky served as the honorable mayor of the Village of Shoreham for many years until his passing in 2010.

Klatsky was well known to have a hearty laugh and is remembered by friends and family as a sports enthusiast, animal lover, woodworker, and host nonpareil of the annual "Thanksgiving in August" gathering. He was known for his frank statements of affection for friends and family. He lived in a home that resembled a treehouse and most always said "goodbye" by making the peace sign with his fingers.

His many talents ensured Klatsky's success not only in business, but also in his personal pursuits. He tried out for his beloved New York Giants baseball team at the Polo Ground as third basemen, and while at Columbia, he personified style as a sweater model. It was at Columbia that he met his future wife, Adelaide Corhus. After inviting her on only a handful of dates, Klatsky married the love of his life and had their official wedding photo taken on the Staten Island Ferry.

Always prepared with a quip to defuse a tense situation, Klatsky was a loving jester to the last. Before his final operation, clad in hospital robes, he turned to his attending nurse and scolded, "No peeking!" It is in this spirit of jest and care for others that Bill is remembered as a kind friend, loving family man, and dedicated public servant. [14]

Richard Koubek (1942-

Richard Koubek, Ph.D., has played a critically-important role as a volunteer as an affordable housing educator and advocate in the Town of Huntington, where he resides, as a member of the Huntington Township Housing Coalition (HTHC) since 2000. He is currently serving as the coalition's president. In addition, he has volunteered as chair of the Huntington Interfaith Coalition for Affordable Housing Now (ICAHN) since 2004 and helped to create the

Huntington Interfaith Homeless Initiative (HIHI,) an interfaith program that houses homeless people in Huntington congregations, November through March of each year.

The Huntington Township Housing Coalition consists of twenty agencies and congregations that educates and advocates to expand the stock of affordable housing. ICAHN is a coalition of fifteen Huntington congregations that approaches the lack of affordable housing from a faith perspective. Koubek participated in, initiated or organized as a volunteer leader of both HTHC and ICAHN. His volunteerism produced many results including the adoption of the Huntington Homes Law requiring a 20% set aside for affordable housing for people earning less than 80% of the Area Median Income in all developments that seek a density bonus. The Huntington Homes Law was used as a model for the New York State Workforce Housing Incentive Act which HTHC and ICAHN advocated for, and which was adopted in 2008. The Huntington Homes Law was recently applied to an Avalon Bay complex in Huntington Station that created 132 affordable units in a complex of 540 units. Most of the affordable units will be rental apartments available to people earning under 80% of Area Median Income; 10% of the rentals will be for people earning 50% of Area Median Income. HTHC and ICAHN turned out citizens at the Town zoning on behalf of the affordable housing units at the Avalon Bay development.

Koubek's leadership resulted in the creation of a town requirement that 200 units at The Greens development in Dix Hills be set aside for affordable housing for senior citizens. The HTHC released a report in 2007, *Broken Promises at The Greens,* criticizing the Town's failure to construct the remaining 100 units of senior affordable homes. Since then, these units have been completed. A year-long, 2004-2005, ICAHN reflection on racial prejudice in Huntington and its negative effects on affordable housing were produced and included the publication of weekly educational inserts in Huntington congregational bulletins that profiled the extent of racial discrimination on Long Island. In this year-long program, ICAHN also hosted several educational forums on racial prejudice in Huntington that utilized a discussion guide, "Overcoming Prejudice in Our Neighborhoods," developed by Dr. Koubek.

Koubek's volunteerism also produced many other results including and a town-wide education campaign about the need for affordable housing in Huntington on the eve of the town's visioning process to draft a new master plan. Partly as a result of this campaign, the 500 Huntington residents who attended the visioning sessions selected affordable housing as one of five top priorities for the master plan. The master plan was adopted with an excellent section on affordable housing that includes most of the policy priorities advocated by HTHC and ICAHN. Among the activities in this education campaign were placing full-page ads in Huntington newspapers, just before the visioning sessions began, which showed the need for affordable housing. As chair of the Long Island Campaign for Affordable Rental Housing (LICARH) Education Committee, Koubek helped create these ads; Hosting an interfaith prayer service for affordable housing on the eve of the visioning sessions; training residents to speak on behalf of affordable housing at the master plan visioning sessions; testifying for the adoption of the affordable housing section of the master plan at a public hearing; and helping to create an *Affordable Housing Roadmap Task Force* to expedite implementation of the master plan's affordable housing proposals.

Currently, Koubek serves as an HTHC representative on the Huntington Affordable Housing Trust Fund Advisory Board that oversees the use of the Town's $2.8 million fund for the creation of affordable housing that will be used to implement some of the master plan's recommendations. He has also developed policy recommendations to expand the stock of affordable housing in Huntington which have shaped the HTHC agenda. Seventeen of these recommendations have been implemented or are under serious consideration by town officials. Koubek's leadership has also produced many public educational forums on the need for affordable housing, Martin Luther King Jr. interfaith prayer services; and a planned a town-wide education campaign on the need for affordable rental housing in Huntington.

Koubek grew up in Bayside and attended St. John's University, Fordham U for a Master's Degree. He attended, Queens College for a second masters and CUNY Graduate Center for a Ph.D. in Political Science. He was first drawn to this work by his mother who was very motivated toward justice and fairness. This was reinforced when he was a young teacher in Plainview during the turbulent 1960s when his extraordinary colleagues came together, often with the students, to envision and work for a more just society. Jeffrey Miller, the young man killed at Kent State whose photo has become an icon of the19 60s, was a Plainview student. His mother worked with Koubek. Also, at Plainview, he served as an officer in the teacher's union which was very much shaped by the thinking of the great community organizer, Saul Alinsky. Koubek recall that Plainview was the only Long Island school district to have had three strikes.

The other great motivator for Koubek was his membership in a very progressive Catholic parish, Our Lady of the Miraculous Medal in Wyandanch. The church sponsored a series of "worker priests" very committed to preaching and living Catholic social teaching. It was from here that he was hired by Catholic Charities. Charities' CEO, Fr. John Gilmartin, was a priest residing in the parish at the time. Gilmartin's vision for Charities was to be cutting edge, community organizing, working with parishes to identify issues of concern to the poor, then organizing, educating and advocating for those issues. Hence, Koubek was given the leeway to get involved in the affordable housing issue since parish outreach coordinators identified this as one of the main reasons people sought heir help. With rents too high, they had to get food and clothing at the parish outreach center.

While at Catholic Charities, Koubek deepened his understanding of Catholic social teaching and liberation theology, which have motivated much of his justice work and shaped his outreach to the faith community. Some of the core principles within these teachings are recognizing the dignity of all people; living in solidarity with one another; offering a preferential option for the poor; valuing work as much as property; valuing community interests as much as personal interests; working to liberate people from the systems that oppress them. [15]

Gerry Leeds (1922-2014) and Lilo Leeds (1928-

Lilo and Gerry Leeds present an inspiring story of refugees committed to social change on Long Island whose efforts have produced admirable legacies to be emulated.

They met in a ski lodge in the Adirondack Mountains in 1950, were married in 1951, and have a family of five children and 13 grandchildren. They are both refugees from Nazi Germany. They arrived in the U.S. in 1939 with virtually no money. Gerry was 16 years of age from Germany and Lilo was 11 years of age from France. They both had had the rudiments of a good primary education and supportive families when they arrived and were hopeful about the future. They lived in Manhattan, Flushing, and Forest Hills before moving to Great Neck. At one point, the Leeds tried to purchase a home in Bronxville but the seller refused to sell the house to Jews, a reality of the times in many New York's growing suburbs. Lilo recalls that Great Neck had a good public education system and had a large Jewish population.

Eventually, the Leeds became successful business entrepreneurs, and continued as social entrepreneurs, with a primary focus on improving the public school education of children in poor communities. In 1971, they launched the highly successful publishing company, CMP Media, Inc., which became a leading publisher of business newspapers, magazines and Internet services for the high-tech industries-electronics, communication and computers. They established a set of principles for the company that became a guide for all their future business and management activities. The company became known for its excellent socially responsible policies, its great products, its great services and, especially, for its pioneering on-site infant and child day care center established by Lilo Leeds. Fortune and Working Mother magazine repeatedly cited CMP as one of the '100 Best Companies to Work For.'

In 1988, Lilo and Gerry transferred the management of the company to two of their sons, Michael and Daniel, who accelerated the growth and profitability of the company while expanding its socially responsible management. Moving away from the day-to-day management of the company gave Lilo and Gerry the opportunity to focus their efforts on helping students in poor, underserved school districts get a better education. In 1990, they founded and chaired the Institute for Student Achievement, now a major force in school reform for children in poor communities with approximately 20,000 high school students in 60 high schools. The goal of the Institute is to improve the education of students in low performing school districts who grow up in poverty to succeed-first by completing their high school education, and then by going on to college or other post-secondary education and become educated, productive, contributing adults.

Together, Lilo and Gerry have served on the Institute's board of directors, and are on the boards of several other organizations working on education issues, including the Alliance for Excellent Education, the Caroline and Sigmund Schott Foundation and Schott Center for Public and Early Education, and the Lipmanson Foundation.

Gerry Leeds was instrumental in the founding of a new organization, Alliance for Excellent Education, Inc., based in Washington, D.C., which is committed to making an excellent education the right of every child a national policy and a reality within the decade. He was also the co-founder of the National Academy for Excellent Teaching (NAfET) at Teachers College, Columbia University, and was a member of the board of Community Organization for Parents and Youth, Inc. (COPAY). Lilo Leeds has made the improvement of education for students in less affluent communities, universal early education and the advancement of women the focus of her work. Lilo is co-founder and member of the board of the Schott Center for Public and Early Education, the Great Neck/Manhasset Community Child Care Partnership and was a member of the board of the North Shore Child & Family Guidance.

Gerry and Lilo are recipients of a large number of civic awards, including Socially Responsible Entrepreneurs of the Year, LIA Humanitarian Award, and Outstanding Philanthropists of the Year for NSFRE/L.I. They were honored by the Urban League of L.I., the NYS Chapter of NAACP, the NYS United Teachers Association, and the American Jewish Committee. They were cited by *Newsday* in its report on "100 Who Shaped a Century," and were also among the 10 honorees selected by WCBS-TV for recognition in its annual "Fulfilling the Dream" celebration of the birthday of Dr. Martin Luther King, Jr.

Lilo earned her Bachelor's Degree in mathematics from Queens College and her Master's Degree from the State University of New York at Stony Brook. Both institutions have since awarded her honorary doctorates, and she was also honored at Adelphi and Hofstra Universities. Gerry pursued an education in engineering and business management and spent three years as an electronics specialist in the U.S. Army. He holds a Bachelor of Arts and Science and an honorary doctorate from Adelphi University and a Masters of Arts and an honorary doctorate from the State University of New York at Stony Brook. He has taught management at Long Island University and Hofstra University, and at Hofstra, lectured annually to MBA students on socially-responsible business management.

Earlier in her career, Lilo worked at Bell Labs where she became aware that women earned half what men earned. Along with two other women employees, Lilo met with the company president and asked 'do you think it is fair that women earn so much less than men?' Within a year, women's salaries were the same as men's. 'You have to speak up,' says Lilo. 'Women still work for free until March every year," Lilo continues, "to get equal pay with men the rest of the year.'

In the early 1980s, some of CMP's female editors spoke to Lilo about the fact that they could only work part-time because their children came home from school at 3PM. The Leeds decided to set up an afterschool day care program at the workplace to accommodate these employees. A summer program soon followed for these school-aged children. Lilo also became aware that some of CMP's employees were pregnant and had to leave to raise their children. Then, two years later, the company's personnel manager announced her pregnancy. Lilo and Gerry then offered an onsite day care program at CMP for infants, toddlers, and preschoolers, making CMP the first company on Long island to offer onsite child care services. Lilo also encouraged other companies to develop onsite and near site day care centers but other Long Island companies were unconvinced that family issues should be addressed through company sponsorships. Others feared liability issues and objections from employees with no children.

Lilo believed that these programs were important, both for humanistic reasons as well as because she wanted women to become managers, to have upward mobility in their careers. This understanding and concern resulted in the opening of the *Lilo and Gerry Leeds Child Development Center*, not just to CMP employees, but also to employees of nearby North Shore University Hospital, as well as to children with disabilities referred by the Association for Retarded Children. The center started with just two babies and now has 115. Lilo reported that the town is now refusing to renew the license forcing the center to move to a new nearby location.

The Leeds have four sons and a daughter who was a very good baseball player. She wanted to join Little League but because she was a girl, was denied team membership. The Leeds asked the Civil Liberties Union to challenge the decision and won the case. Her daughter made the All Star team. All of the Leeds' children are involved in social change in the fields of education, animal rights, conservation, and legal rights. Her son Greg is writing a book titled: "When We Fight, We Win; and Other Lessons on Transformation."

In reflecting back on her life, Lilo feels she wants to "help make the world a little better." [16]

Peter Levy (1960-

Peter Levy has been an advocate for community services in Nassau County for over 25 years beginning with his 1989 board membership at the Five Towns Community Center. In 1988, he ran for a seat on the Lawrence Board of Education with a platform that encouraged voters to understand youth needs and perceptions. He served two terms as Five Towns Community Center's president from1993-1995 and from 1996-2002. Prior to that he served on the board of directors from 1989 and chaired numerous board committees. Since his 'retirement' from the board, he has continued to serve as special legal counsel on a number of matters. Levy recalls his interest in public service beginning when he attended meetings of the Lawrence board of education.

Perhaps his role is as the unpaid president of the Coalition of Nassau County Youth Service Agencies, Inc. since 1996 is Levy's signature effort, battling in behalf of Nassau's youth service agencies and the young people that they serve. His interest in youth services evolved from his volunteerism at the Five Towns Community Center where he became familiar with the lack of youth services and the problems facing nonprofit organizations under contract with the county. He reached out to other nonprofit youth and family service organizations to see if there was interest in forming a coalition for the purposes of unifying advocacy and collaborative fund raising. The organizations were receptive and met regularly to face the new county legislature as a unified body. Levy believes that the coalition may be the only youth advocacy entity in New York State with a membership of youth service agency providers.

Membership in the coalition, ranges between 32-45 members, is diverse both in organizational size and ethnic and racial diversity. Membership has decreased since 2012 when the legislature reduced youth service funding by 50% with the result that smaller agencies were forced to shut down or dramatically reduce their services. In a September 6, 2012 Newsday letter to the editor titled "Nassau youth have lost services," Levy indicates that services were lost to 35,000 young people due to the cuts. On October 29, 2012, *Newsday* published an Opinion column written by Rabbi Judy Cohen-Rosenberg of the Community Reformed Temple in Westbury and the Reverend Stephanie Pope, Pastor of St. Stephen's Lutheran Church in Hicksville that says: 'Our shared faith demands that our most vulnerable children must be a priority, not a bargaining chip. Our social safety net should be made as efficient as possible, but it should not be cut completely. The county's dire fiscal situation is all the more important reason to invest in prevention – by supporting, not slashing human services – rather than hiring an additional dozen correction officers, as legislators voted to do last month.'

Coalition members pay annual dues ranging from $100 to $200 depending on size although, according to Levy, they often go unpaid. The coalition's small budget pays for the incidental expenses of the coalition including annual legislative breakfasts and rallies.

Levy says that coalition members run the gamut regarding their attitudes towards advocacy, some being uncomfortable about involving young people in legislative appeals while others see this strategy as part of youth development. Some legislators complained that the coalition was 'using' young people during legislative meetings. In its appeals to maintain current funding levels, they point to the county's $2.8B budget with just $6.8M spending on youth services.

Under Levy's leadership and political savvy, the coalition is now focusing on Albany on seeking to convince the Governor and state legislature to establish a large dedicated funding stream for youth services. 'Doing the 'dog and pony show' in Mineola every year will continue to be a battle for survival. Uncertainties about changes in the county's budget do not stop when the annual budget is adopted. We need to increase state aid and make it dedicated," says Levy When asked if the coalition might be open to seeking Hagedorn support to help the coalition form a separate lobbying arm, Levy believes that many members may feel conflicted about this strategy since they often face legislators as paid agency directors.

When asked about coalition member interest in social enterprise, he says that the subject has been discussed but nothing done to date. It is on the agenda but there is a general feeling that members feel that 'they are the organizations of last resort in their communities.' When Hurricane Sandy hit, the youth agencies actively helped with food, clothing, and counseling. Thus, they're very reluctant to spend too much time and energy in developing business enterprises even though they may, in the long run, provide them with a much-needed funding stream. The other concern is that government would reduce its funding with any profits generated by the nonprofit business.

Levy feels that the coalition has successfully reduced further drastic cuts in youth services in the county and established itself as a force to be dealt with. He also points to a number of administrative reforms that the county has instituted due to the coalition's unified advocacy.

Levy's other community work has been with the Hagedorn Fund-support 'Fight for Families Coalition,' the Health and Welfare Council of Long Island, Temple Beth El of Cedarhurst, Five Towns Democratic Club, and Nassau County Democratic Committee.

Levy has been an attorney in private practice for over 25 years. The practice is concentrated in the areas of commercial litigation, personal injury, real estate, elder law, criminal law, wills and estates. Levy is a graduate of the Tulane University School of Law and the Wharton School of Business of the University of Pennsylvania. Within the legal profession, Peter served three terms in the House of Delegates of the New York State Bar Association (NYSBA). As part of that organization, he chaired the state wide Committee on Lawyers and the Community. He currently serves on the NYSBA nominating committee.

From 2008 – 2009, he served as president of the Nassau County Bar Association (NCBA), the largest suburban bar association in the United States with close to 6000 members. Within the NCBA, in addition to his terms as an officer and member of the board of directors, Levy was development chair of the We Care Fund from 2003-2006 and is currently co-chair. He has chaired the organization's District Court Committee, Community Relations Committee, County Clerk's Committee, General Practice Committee, Awards Committee and Nominating Committee. He has served as a mentor, Academy of Law lecturer, Grievance committee member, mock trial coach and has authored numerous task force reports for the NCBA.

Levy has served also on the Board of Directors of Nassau Suffolk Law Services since 1994 and is currently that organization's Treasurer. He is a former trustee of Temple Beth El of Cedarhurst and was a recipient of the Ann M. Irvin Youth Advocate Award, the Thomas Maligno Pro Bono Attorney of the Year, the New York State Bar Association President's Pro Bono Service Award, the Stephen Gassman We Care Award, the Nassau County Bar Association's President's Award and the Five Town's Community Center's Centennial Award.

Levy attended The Wharton School at the University of Pennsylvania with a dual concentration in Marketing and Political Science and a B.S. in Economics 1982.

Since 1988, Levy has maintained a general law practice in commercial litigation, personal injury, criminal defense, elder law, wills and estate administration, corporate and real estate transactions. [17]

Lincoln Lynch (1920-2011)

In the fall of 1962, as America's gaze turned south to black student James Meredith's struggle to attend the all-white University of Mississippi, a similar struggle simmered in Long Island's Malverne school district.

Confronted by rules that prevented his children from attending the district's mostly white elementary school, Lincoln Lynch pursued a lawsuit to end the district's de facto racial separation. Lynch lost his court challenge on a legal ruling. But the loss only seemed to spur him to become one of Long Island's most ardent and audacious civil rights activists.

Lincoln Lynch, born in the West Indies, fought in England's Royal Air Force as a machine gunner in World War II and came back from the war forged by his experiences there and by the segregation he faced in the United States after he settled on Long Island. There, as head of the local chapter of the Congress of Racial Equality, he worked ardently to bring to light the racial bias on Long Island.

For example, he sent testers to show racial bias in housing using picketing and sit-ins to bring the situation to the public's attention. He was frequently derided for his methods but was fearless in both minority and white communities where he pointed out the problems and the problem of minorities who were trying to be middle class and therefore not acting to redress grievances.

He became vice president for the New York Urban Coalition and a Professor of Social Work at Stony Brook University where he taught community activism. He remained committed to this activism and remained passionate and vocal about injustice and about the racial bias on Long Island that led to economic and educational inequalities. He fought within the courts, in school districts, with housing authorities and anywhere else he saw these inequities that needed publicity and correction.

 Lynch eventually became a vice president with the New York Urban Coalition and taught community activism at Stony Brook University. In 1999, when he was almost 79, he was one of more than 1,000 people arrested near police headquarters in Manhattan for protesting the police killing of unarmed immigrant Amadou Diallo. [18]

Lillian McCormick (1930-

Lillian McCormick, a resident of Port Washington since 1953, embodies the best of civic activism. Her life began in Florida where her grandmother established one of the state's first orphanages. McCormick feels that her grandmother served as a role model – "to see a wrong and try to correct it." McCormick recalls her childhood sensitivity to the plight of white people's domestic help who lived on the other side of the tracks and were called "colored" or "blacks." She could never understand why they were treated so differently. Her favorite friends were the colored housekeepers' children who came with their mothers to clean the white folks' homes. Those were the only times that she could play with them because she was not allowed to go on the other side of the tracks. These childhood memories had a powerful effect upon her. Fighting for civil rights and stamping out Jim Crow racism became her battle.

In the 1940s, McCormick attended a small college for white girls in Missouri. There she conducted the first sit-in where she brought Negro girls into the college tea room for sodas. The staff refused to serve them so McCormick bought the sodas and they all sat down together. McCormick was certainly not popular but determined saying "It is their right to be served".

After graduating from the University of North Carolina, McCormick earned a Master's Degree in Social Work at the University of Pittsburgh in 1951 with a concentration in Community Organization. Upon graduation, she became a Board member of the Pittsburgh YWCA, moved on to Washington, DC and became Program Director at an all-white settlement house. Her first job was to develop an inter-racial program to serve the neighborhood and so she did.

 In 1953, McCormick moved to Port Washington, NY with her family. She became director of the United Neighborhood Activity Center in Great Neck. Here she addressed the educational, social and recreational needs of North Shore domestic workers who had been brought up from the South to work in white people's homes. Again, she heard stories of how some were mistreated; i.e. sleeping in basements without proper ventilation. Her Board was not ready or in a position to address these problems. McCormick moved on!

McCormick's first volunteer job in Port Washington was with the Community Chest to help raise dollars for local nonprofit agencies. She represented the Chest in an effort that resulted in receiving a building known as Publishers Clearing House from Harold Mertz. The building was gifted to the Community Chest for the purpose of housing nonprofit organizations and was named the Mertz Community Center. The first tenants were EAC, Community Chest, North Shore Child Guidance and the local Community Action Council. The building still serves the community.

In the sixties, President Lyndon B. Johnson developed the Anti-Poverty Program to help the poor in our country. Port Washington was designated as a poverty area to be served. McCormick became the social worker employed by the local school district to identify thirty children who would meet the federal guidelines for the Head Start Program in Port Washington. McCormick remembers talking to one of the top school administrators about the need to have classrooms available for the program. His response was 'I guess they will be taking babies out of their cribs next.' The Head Start program continues today. In the 1970s, McCormick became aware of the plight of homeless children being placed in institutions in New York State. She heard judges and social service officials complain that they had no options for placements. There were no group homes for run-aways found in railroad stations or wandering the streets at night. McCormick said: "I know of a home in Port for sale but zoning became a problem with neighbors complaining 'not in my backyard.'" Legally, zoning in residential areas did not permit two or more unrelated by blood to live in a one family residence. McCormick sought the advice of David Kadane at Hofstra Law School. "How are we going to do this?" McCormick asked. Kadane replied "Just change the law." McCormick retained the services of Leonard Weintraub, an attorney, who filed a law suit against the town known as Group House of Port Washington.

The case was won in the NYS Court of Appeals and is being used around the nation to benefit a wide variety of other at-risk populations. The result of this decision in 1973 led to the establishment of Group House of Port Washington, a home for seven children who could not live at home. Group House was financed exclusively through stipends paid by the State for each child on a per diem basis and private fund-raising was frowned upon. Thus, McCormick could see that the Group House could not survive and that another organization had to be found in order to assure proper care.

Under her guidance, Group House merged with Nassau House (now a part of Family & Children's Association) that had been operating the county's only orphanage since 1883. She donated the house and $17,300 to Nassau House with the stipulation that the dollars would be set aside for scholarships for children who wanted to go to college and had no resources. McCormick is especially proud of this effort which continues today and has awarded $1.4 million dollars since its inception to young adults wanting to pursue college or educational training programs.

In 1979, McCormick went to The Unitarian Veatch Program at Shelter Rock and asked David DeRienzis, assistant director, for a feasibility grant to establish a local shelter for abused women. Through DeRienzis' advocacy, a feasibility grant was approved by the Veatch Program that led to the development of a Manhasset-based shelter in1981, the first on Long Island. As associate director of the Coalition for Abused Women, McCormick opened and supervised Long Island's first shelter. McCormick and community leaders took on the giant task of mustering millions of dollars. The feasibility study funded by The Veatch Program concluded that the project was possible but not probable. It was a challenge and it took ten years to put it together. McCormick never gave up on her dream!

Then, always wanting new challenges to address issues of concern to her, McCormick decided to take on the plight of working women. The problems such as sexual harassment, unequal pay, lack of women in the trades, on corporate boards and in top government positions. She and her associate, Charlotte Shapiro, founded Women on the Job (WOJ), an education and advocacy organization in 1982. As part of their work, they met with Nassau County Executive Fran Purcell to ask him to establish a sexual harassment policy for county employees. Purcell laughed and said: 'We do not need one. Also, that would give the appearance that there is sexual harassment." McCormick informed him that New York City Mayor Koch had just established such a policy in New York City. Due to McCormick's advocacy, Purcell agreed to establish such a policy and later posted it in every county office, as McCormick recommended.

McCormick acknowledges that progress had been made during her 25 years as executive director of Women on the Job. She pays tribute to her task force, a coalition representing community organizations, unions, government, and religious groups standing up for women's workplace equality. McCormick emphasizes that there is much more to be done. She adds 'at least now in social gatherings, I do not hear men joking about sexual harassment not being a problem because women like to be sexually harassed.'

In 1985, the Board of Education in Port Washington decided to close the Main Street Elementary School and put the building up for sale to the highest bidder. She realized that the property would probably be sold for high-risers. She also knew that many older, local people were leaving the town because of the rising costs of living. McCormick understood that Port Washington needed affordable senior housing for these folks who wanted to remain in town. Another group of Port residents wanted a community center.

McCormick, again using her community organization skills, played a key role in organizing the Port Washington community to work together to convince the board to sell the building and property to Landmark on Main Street, the newly formed nonprofit organization. The town voted yes to the referendum, which McCormick referred to as a "major coup." After the referendum was passed, she took on the giant task of mustering the millions of dollars of financial support needed to purchase and renovate the building and purchase the land. It took ten years. When McCormick was asked today how the current Landmark stacks up against the original vision of the small group who came together in her living room almost thirty years ago, she responded: 'It far exceeds our original expectation. It shows what a group of committed people working together can achieve. If enough people believe in it, you can move a mountain.'

Lillian McCormick was indeed fortunate not to be the family's breadwinner during those times allowing her to dedicate herself to the community work that she loved to do. She pays tribute to her three sons who have followed her lead in doing for others and to her good friends Claire Kramer, Winifred Freund, and Alfred Devendorf who were a major part of her journey. She provides an inspirational story to those who want to improve the quality of life in Long Island's communities. Her passion, determination, intellect, and training have served her community well. Future leaders can learn from her. [19]

Helen McIntyre (1927-2002)

Helen McIntyre was heavily involved in the 1970s in the development of the Huntington Youth Board into a model youth service program serving the entire township. After the county established a youth board, she served as chairman of the Suffolk County Youth Bureau's Comprehensive Planning Committee where her considerable enthusiasm, intelligence and skills were evident to the many agencies and organizations involved in the youth board's development. Her leadership role lead to the creation of youth bureaus in other Suffolk towns. Her focus then turned to the issue of adolescent pregnancy.

Between 1984 and 1990, McIntyre served as the first president of Suffolk Network on Adolescent Pregnancy which seeks to prevent premature sexual activity and pregnancy particularly in high-risk Suffolk communities. In 1985, SNAP's first year of operations, there were 4,179 pregnancies to young women ages 10-19. In 2000, there were 1, 911. She and her husband moved to Oyster Bay Cove in 1997. McIntyre worked closely with Marcia Spector, SNAP's executive director to build the organization into a respected, strong organization.

Between 1984 and 1998, McIntyre served as chairman of the Long Island Community Foundation. During that period, she transformed the Community Foundation, once an outpost of the New York Community Trust, into a major philanthropic force of its own. 'She was the leader of this foundation and this board,' recalled Suzy Sonenberg, the foundation's director. 'I came in 1988 and we took this little foundation from making grants of $25,000 and with assets of $800,000 and we built it into a foundation with assets of $50 million that gives away $10 million each year.[20]

Anne F. Mead (1924-2010)

Mead, a native of Sayville, was a trail-blazing lawyer who inspired many women to enter public service. Her entry into politics was motivated by her belief that women should be involved in grassroots government. Her first effort was to run for justice of the peace in Islip town 1955.

As Suffolk County's first deputy county executive, Suffolk County's first woman to be appointed or elected judge in a court of record, and later the first woman to chair the state Public Service Commission, Mead was the embodiment of active citizenship. She is reported to have been a forceful consumer advocate in her role on the commission opposing rate hikes to consumers instead of only thinking about the needs of the utilities.

Her public career spanned four decades in which she worked as the top aide to Suffolk's first county executive, H. Lee Dennison for eight years beginning in 1960. By many reported accounts, Mead was Dennison's 'go-to' person when he wanted legislation written and when he needed something else done and done well. Mead was a highly-respected person who spoke softly but forcefully on the issues that motivated her. Former county executive John V.N. Klein called Mead a 'voice of reason' when things got contentious between Dennison and the then-county board of supervisors.

Mead had her political losses, losing bids to become county welfare commissioner, a Family Court judgeship, and a District Court judgeship. Her career went beyond partisan politics and included being the first woman executive director and Board Member Emerita of the Suffolk Community Council where she fought for the poor and underserved. Mead was also first president of the Suffolk County Human Rights Commission, the Suffolk County Mental Health Association, director of the county's Tuberculosis and Public Health Association, a member of the New York State Welfare Conference, and the Nassau-Suffolk Committee on Alcoholism. [21]

Robert Cushman Murphy (1888-1973)

Robert Cushman Murphy, a resident of Stony Brook, was one of America's foremost naturalists and environmentalists as well as one of its premier ornithologists. At age 72, he was awarded the Antarctic Service Medal for his exploration of the Antarctic's Bellingshausen Sea.

After growing up on Long Island, Murphy graduated from Brown and Columbia Universities and joined the American Museum of Natural History where he traveled extensively on many expeditions to study birdlife. He returned from his travels to work at the museum and publishing many books about birds many that were believed to be extinct. Murphy became a curator emeritus of Ocean Birds at the museum and member of the National Academy of Science.

Robert Moses is said to have regarded Murphy as an 'uncompromising ecologist' when no one knew the word. In 1933, Murphy urged that Fire Island be set aside as a park area and nature preserve. He actively opposed DDT spraying and offshore dredging in order to conserve the Island's water resources, convinced that Long Island could not maintain a rising population and maintain its natural ecology intact. Murphy campaigned extensively against these and many other plans to over-develop Long Island. He is significantly responsible for Suffolk County's extensive system of parklands one of which was named in his honor. Before Murphy's efforts, politicians viewed public parks as just recreational in nature but he was able, with his extensive knowledge of the environment and wildlife to convince legislators of the dangers of over-development.

When Murphy became concerned about a potential danger to the Island's environment, he brought his concerns, his substantial knowledge and world-renowned reputation to H. Lee Dennison, Suffolk's county executive as well as the county board of supervisors. This advocacy included concern about Flax Pond in Old Field. When the pond was threatened, Murphy spoke to his neighbor Ward Melville of his concerns. Melville, who later donated the acres of property to New York State on which to build a university, understood Murphy's concerns for the environment and went on to assure that the new university purchased the Flax Pond property as well as establish a marine sciences center at the university. Today, the center is a major regional center.

Suffolk County's first park was names after Robert Cushman Wakefield as was a junior high school in Setauket. [22]

Elsie Owens (1929-2006)

Elsie Owens and her husband, Robert Owens, moved to Gordon Heights in 1959. She became a community activist almost at once, starting with a campaign to get the roads of Gordon Heights paved and fighting for the installation of street lights and public water. When Elsie Owens moved her family from the Bronx to Gordon Heights in the Town of Brookhaven in 1959, she had such high hopes of giving her children a chance at a better life that she was not put off by the lack of streetlights, the unpaved roads or the absence of public water.

Owens walked down every block in her neighborhood to organize the people who lived there, started petitions and got the town of Brookhaven to pay attention to our needs," said her daughter Roberta Owens of Coram, the third of her five children. "We got those streetlights pretty quickly." In her quest for better neighborhood services, Ms. Owens pressed police and town officials to treat members of the predominantly black community fairly.

Owens took a job as a maintenance worker on the night shift at the State University at Stony Brook where she noticed that blacks had a hard time getting jobs outside the maintenance department. That led her to join the Brookhaven NAACP and serving as its president for twenty years.

In the late 1960's, Owens began to focus a great deal of her efforts on the establishment of a health center to serve those in the greater Coram community who were unable to afford private health care. After a nearly 10-year fight, the North/Central Brookhaven Health Center offers comprehensive health services to community members, with fees based on income. Owens never gave up representing her community to county officials and successful negotiated a contract with Stony Brook University Hospital. She was also a leader in the successful efforts of the time to establish a Head Start program in Gordon Heights where she lives.

Despite her community activism and time spent raising her family, Owens still managed to find time to return to school, earning her Master's Degree in social work from Stony Brook University in 1978.

Owens was nominated for the 7–Eleven Beacon of Light Volunteer Award by the Suffolk County Police Department's Chief Inspector Joseph L. Monreith and the head of the Department's Bias Crimes Bureau, Joseph C. Zito. Other accomplishments include an appointment by Governor Mario Cuomo to serve of the Board of Visitors for Sagamore Children's Center; appointments by Suffolk County Executive to the Mental Health, Mental Retardation and Alcohol Planning boards; member of the Advisory Board of SUNY at Stony Brook; member of the Greater Gordon Heights Civic Association; founder of the Gordon Heights Community Watch and a charter member of Brookhaven Town Black History Night Commission.

Owens has been the past recipient of numerous awards, including the National Association of Social Workers "Social Worker of the Year" award, the President's Affirmative Action Award from Stony Brook University and the Sojourner Truth Meritorious Service Club Award from the National Association of Negro Business and Professional Women Club, Inc. She was also named Woman of the Year in 1991 for community service by the Brookhaven town Women's Services.[23]

Sonia Palacio-Grottola (1934-

Sonia Palacio-Grottola was born Sonia Torruella Aleman to Puerto Rican parents in Washington Heights. She has lived in Commack, New York for over fifty years. After relocating to Commack, she first attended Suffolk Community College and continued to complete her education as a licensed clinical social worker to make a difference in the lives of individuals and families. This was accomplished at Stony Brook University's School of Social Welfare where she earned a Master's in Social Work and, subsequently, a post-graduate certificate from Adelphi University which prepared her to be a social activist for the betterment of the underserved and for all families.

Palacio-Grottola feels that she was gifted with two languages and that she should use this gift to help Latino immigrant families improve their quality of life. She feels it is extremely rewarding to help families with limited English proficiency to navigate through the systems of health, education and public assistance.

Her education and volunteer work for the National Association of Social Workers prepared her to work on local, statewide and national levels. She is proud of her work especially proud of her work as the president of the National Association of Social Workers, New York State Chapter. Palacio-Grottola maintains a private practice and serves as a consultant for the Suffolk County Department of Health as a social worker in its early intervention program. Her role for early intervention is to visit immigrant families with handicapped children (0 to 3 population) helping families through parent training, counseling, support, and advocacy. She feels only through training and education, that immigrant parents will be better able to advocate for their children. She continues her work with Long Island's immigrant population.

Palacio-Grottola is co-founder of the National Association of Puerto Rican Hispanic Social Workers, Inc. (NAPRHSW) and to see it grow and become a force in the local, state and national communities wherein its advocacy and lobbying work ultimately improves the lives of Latino families in. She was past-president and continues in other roles and has mentored students in the Brentwood School District. She continues to mentor social work students in the Association (NAPRHSW) with the hope that they will carry on the torch of advocacy, social justice and social responsibility to improve the lives of Latino families. She has supported the NAPRHSW who has dedicated itself to offering workshops for students for over seventeen years entitled "La Vision Youth Conference" also offering national conferences on 'The Diversity and Strengths of the Latino Family.' Palacio Grottola is the editor of the website of the National Association of Puerto Rican Hispanic Social Workers and continuously encourages clients and social work students to get out the vote and work in voter registration drives. She has worked on many voter registration drives in cooperation with many agencies.

Palacio-Grottola views her proudest accomplishment being part of the grass roots efforts that defeated the "English Only" bill three times on Long Island and the response of the coalition that joined together to lobby against this bill. She chaired the Long Island Coalition for English Plus during these successful fights in 1988, 1996 and 1998.

Palacio-Grottola is a board member of the Suffolk Center on the Holocaust, Diversity and Human Understanding and a member of the Long Island Language Advocates Coalition. She is proud to be the first woman in her family to complete graduate school. This accomplishment was completed late in life as a widow with two children. She serves as a role model for older, single mothers who may have a desire to return to school "against all odds." She has won many awards and citation but is most proud of her two children Paul and Sabrina and their accomplishments, her son-in-law, Joseph Grottola and her four grandchildren, Deanna Marie, Joseph Anthony, Cristal Marie and Joseph James." [24]

Davis Pollack (1924-

Pollack points to the public response to former Missouri Senator Thomas Eagleton as an indicator of public attitudes towards mental illness. When it became public knowledge that Eagleton had been hospitalized for depression and had undergone electroshock treatment, Eagleton withdrew his candidacy for the vice presidency. The Democrats wanted badly to beat Richard Nixon in the 1972 election and felt that the Republicans would press Eagleton's mental health record during the campaign questioning his ability to have his 'finger on the button' amidst the 'Cold War' that existed with Russia.

"Eagleton had a strong record as a U.S. Senator and was well-regarded by his colleagues. 'On three occasions in my life, I have voluntarily gone into hospitals as a result of nervous exhaustion and fatigue,' Eagleton told reporters at the time. 'As a younger man, I must say that I drove myself too far, and I pushed myself terribly, terribly hard, long hours, day and night," he said. Despite his best efforts to address what happened in an honest way, the pressure began to mount. Democratic Party stalwarts called on Eagleton to step down. Locally, Pollack recalls a conversation at this time with a School Psychologist friend who said he would not vote for Eagleton. Upset at this attitude towards a distinguished U.S. Senator, Pollack told his friend that, if he served on the board of education, he would have fired him.

Pollack's first organizational involvement was with Fountain House in Manhattan one of the leading organizations in the mental health field at the time. Pollack served as first Vice President of NAMI. He established Suffolk County affiliates of the National Alliance for Mental Illness (NAMI) and Clubhouse of Suffolk in Ronkonkoma, modeled on Fountain House's program. He served as founder and chairman of Clubhouse until recently. Pollack also worked with consumers and the State Office of Mental Health Regional Office to establish a bi-county mental health consumer group. In all of his efforts, Pollack worked closely with Suffolk County Legislator John Foley and former Suffolk Deputy County Executive Anne F. Mead. Pollack credits them as significantly responsible for the reforms that have been put in place over the years.

When asked whether things have changed in the past forty years, Pollack says that "there is now more public acceptance of mental illness if measured by the degree of resistance to the presence of group homes in the community and it is easier to convince employers to hire people with mental illnesses." He points to the impact of what is known as the 'Padavan Law' shepherded by New York State Frank Padavan during the late 1970s.

It was through the efforts of people like Davis Pollack, working at the federal, state, and local level that the Padavan Law became a reality opening the door for thousands of people to remain in the community rather than facing state hospitalization. "The stigma is worse that the illness itself," says Pollack, "to have mental illness is to be ostracized, ignored, and downgraded."

One of Pollack's passionate appeals at the state level has been to convince legislators to replicate a Maine-based program to fund billboards around the state to heighten awareness of mental health and guide people to where help can be found. [25]

Dennis Puleston (1905-2001)

According to the New York Times obituary of June 16, 2001, Dennis Puleston, was "a naturalist, boat designer and yachtsman and who was founding chairman of the Environmental Defense Fund played a leading role in getting the insecte DDT banned in the United States and many other countries." According to the obituary, Puleston grew up in the fishing village of Leigh-on-Sea acquiring a love of boats and a taste for adventure. He became a naturalist and painter of birds.

Puleston studied biology and naval architecture in England. In 1931, he sailed with a friend in a small sailing boat on a six-year odyssey down the eastern seaboard of the United States, around the Caribbean and across the South Pacific.

During World War II, Puleston worked for a group of naval architects he helped design the Duck-like two-and-a-half-ton DUKW amphibious landing craft adopted by the Allies training American forces on the craft who used it. He took part in amphibious operations in the Solomon Islands, New Guinea and Burma, where he was wounded. After a period in the hospital, he went to Britain to train allied forces in preparation for the Normandy landings. He then returned to the Pacific to take part in the invasions of Iwo Jima and Okinawa. Puleston was awarded the Medal of Freedom by President Harry S. Truman in 1948 for his work during the World War II in designing the DUKW amphibious landing craft.

According to information gathered from the Post Morrow Foundation Dennis Puleston Osprey Fund, where Puleston grew up in England, the osprey was never a common bird. When he moved to the Hamlet of Brookhaven on Long Island after World War II, he was impressed that ospreys nested high in old trees along the Carmans River. Little did he know then that his beloved ospreys would seriously decline in his lifetime only to be restored by his commitment to their well-being.

After joining the Brookhaven National Laboratory in 1948, Puleston studied a large breeding colony of ospreys -- birds of prey that live off fish and are sometimes called fish hawks -- on the privately owned Gardiners Island, off eastern Long Island. At the request of the Gardiner family, Puleston studied ospreys each year on their island in Gardiners Bay. He discovered that the rate of successfully fledged osprey chicks was dropping dramatically. He brought unhatched eggs for analysis by new scientific techniques conducted by Dr. Charles Wurster at Stony Brook University. High levels of DDT confirmed the warnings of Rachel Carson in her 1962 book, Silent Spring and prompted action to ban DDT.

By the early 1960's he had concluded that these ospreys were dying out as a result of the dichloro-diphenyl-trichlorethane, or DDT, being sprayed in the area to keep down mosquitoes; it weakened the shells of the birds' eggs so much that they could not protect the live chicks inside.

As an expert naturalist testifying in a Suffolk County courtroom in 1966, Puleston along with others presented the scientific evidence showing that DDT thinned eggshells. This trial spurred the creation of the Environmental Defense Fund in 1967 with Puleston as its first chairman. By the time he passed the leadership baton of the board five years later, William Ruckelshaus, the first administrator of EPA, had banned DDT in the United States. Today the Environmental Defense Fund is one of the leading environmental lobbying groups in the United States, with about 300,000 members and an annual budget of about $40 million.

Puleston retired from Brookhaven National Laboratory in 1970. He subsequently made more than 200 trips around the world as a lecturer, and acted as senior naturalist on two scientific expeditions to the Siberian Arctic. In his later years, Puleston concentrated on painting and writing about Long Island wildlife. In 1993, he published a month by month guide called *A Nature Journal*, which became a best seller.

Because the osprey is so much a symbol of the environmental health of Long Island and is so intimately connected with Puleston, friends and his family formed the Dennis Puleston Osprey Fund. The purpose of the fund is to encourage research on ospreys on Long Island, to improving the nesting opportunities and educate the public about them. His family still lives along the Carmans River where they remain good stewards of the Osprey families that nest there." [26]

Irwin Quintyne (1927-2004)

The following recollections of Irwin Quintyne are written by Delores Quintyne, Irwin's wife.

A World War II Navy veteran, he and his wife, Delores, originally moved from the projects in Harlem to North Amityville, Long Island in 1961. She was the first chairman of Suffolk County CORE in 1963. He became chair in 1967 and remained chair all the way into the 1980's when he was made a member of CORE's board of directors. He was also vice president of 100 Black Men of Nassau-Suffolk, Inc. and the head of Nassau-Suffolk Minority Coalition. He ran unsuccessfully for the New York State Assembly and for positions on the Amityville school board and the Babylon Town Board. Quintyne worked as a field representative for the Equal Opportunity Office and the Suffolk Human Rights Commission.

"Irwin was dedicated, committed, and compassionate to his family and community. He kept a self – balance. He worked hard to raise his family and worked harder for the people in his community urging them to take leadership for themselves.

Irwin was a field representative for Stony Brook University. He also taught community analysis at Wyandanch Community College. He had other positions including Deputy Director of the Long Island Affirmative Action Program and as a Commissioner of the Suffolk County Human Rights Commission.

Irwin was a great leader when he joined The Congress of Racial Equality (C.O.R.E.). He was born in New York City where his experience with racially-motivated incidents were few, however, after moving to Long Island reality set in when we started looking for housing. We went to Levittown where they told us 'we do not sell to n------ .' We left in a hurry. That was Irwin's first real encounter with racism.

We continued to look for housing finally purchasing a home in Amityville. Irwin joined forces with CORE Chairman Lincoln Lynch. Together, they fought for equal rights for all people. The first project he encountered in Suffolk was a housing discrimination case in which two persons of color were denied housing of an apartment in Amityville. Irwin worked with the negotiating team to resolve the issue. We picketed and demonstrated along with a 'sit-in.' Needless to say, we won. Irwin took on the school board of education for racial imbalance in the Amityville School District's Northeast School located on Albany Avenue in North Amityville which was 96% black. The Northwest school located on County Line Road was 96% white. The NAACP and CORE worked together on this plan of action. Irwin saw this as a plan for social justice. I am proud of Irwin, because he had vision and knowledge of issues that directly affected the community and families who suffered from poverty, housing needs, health concerns and a lack of economic security.

Irwin had many challenges in his attempt to find work in Suffolk County. He was too outspoken for some and too black for others. As a field Representative for Stony Brook University, he envisioned that job as a stepping stone for all people who were socially discriminated against because they were the last hired and the first to be fired. He challenged the system and its hiring practices.

One of Irwin's projects was, to help young people who suffered with drug problems. In the 70s, parents were up in arms their children were hooked on drugs. We had funerals almost every week. It was devastating. Irwin went to court with parents whose sons and daughters were arrested for drugs and attended funerals for the same reason. One day, he said 'enough.' He helped to co- found Alba-Neck Halfway House an outpatient drug clinic in Amityville. Irwin had a problem securing space for the program because we still had community residents who were in denial that the community had serious social and economic problems. Irwin met with some of the ministers in our community to seek approval to utilize one of our local churches to house the program temporarily. He was turned away. They did not want to get involved. Irwin demonstrated daily to shed light on his attempt to secure a building and protest the drugs being shipped into the area. Finally, a community leader agreed to share his building. Irwin hired a staff of young men and women some of whom were past drug users. They were successful identifying the young people abusing drugs. The program grew into an inpatient as well as outpatient program.

The major poverty problem today is homelessness, people losing their homes with no place to go. We have a lack of affordable housing in Suffolk County. Housing prices are out of control our living wages are different in order to have economic success we must maintain decent employment. We still suffer with small patterns of segregation this is also a problem with education, health, criminal justice and political representation we need someone to speak for the people most town boards are not diverse. We need to address the issue that directly involves our families who are suffering while the powers to be fight among themselves. We have so many Health Problems due to high cost of food families cannot afford nutritional food. Often families eat food that are not healthy this can cause problems with High blood pressure, diabetes, obesity, heart problems and other underlying health problems. food banks are depleted because of a lack of funds and the states have cut back on food stamps all this has created more poverty. Years ago we were able to receive funding for various programs funding now is not accessible to the grass root organization. They fund through the towns and pet projects that have an affiliation with organizations that are already collecting funds.

Irwin supported me when I went back to college to complete my Master Degree in Human Services. He was my 'rock,' my inspiration. We had some trying times however. Without his strong family values and support, I would not have completed my education and graduated. Irwin was my friend, my soul mate, my knight in shining armor. He is truly missed. I try to keep his legacy alive. Irwin's last project was to incorporate North Amityville. He stated: 'If we want to control what comes into our community we have to take our destiny in our own hands.' Not unlike the words of Frederick Douglas who said: "There is no progress without a struggle.zzz' Irwin's famous words were: "Keep the Faith!"

The following recollections of Irwin Quintyne are written by Madeline Quintyne, Irwin's daughter. She is currently commissioner of human services for the town of Babylon.

"I want to say that, as his daughter, that I was extremely proud of my father. He gave me insight as to which battles to fight. He taught me how to become a community-minded person and to always give back. My father involved me into the various community organizations early as a young adult. He taught me how to work with the community, giving information so people stay informed with what was happening around them. He introduced me to political figures so I would understand the process. We demonstrated for social justice and made sure it was peaceful.

I miss this giant of a man who gave everything in his power to move our community to the level in which we all can be proud of. I watch him struggle with the Community Development Corporation in North Amityville. He begged me before he passed to stay the course. My father stated that times will be hard but you can do it, encouraging me all the way. He always carried himself like a gentleman and had much respect from all who knew him.

I watched my father for many nights get out of bed 2:00AM - 3:00AM in the morning responding to a knock on the door. The many men and woman now tell me how they loved my father because he took time to go and fight for them no matter what the situation was. My father gave his life for the North Amityville community and his mission as my mother stated was to incorporate North Amityville. I have, like my mom, continued to keep my father's dream alive. There has been tremendous movement but there is so much more to go. He tried so hard to cure everything and the men and women who worked right alongside my dad have been important leaders as well. I know I took on a heavy plight.

It is for the community and our families. I know he is smiling down on me because he always wanted me to work for the Town of Babylon and his dream and mine came true. When you have strong parents who give you all the love, energy, commitment, education, strength, and empowerment, how can you not succeed?

My sisters and brothers have all been very successful in their respective lives. That tells you what kind of man my father was. I say this because he still has an impact on this North Amityville community. I Love You Dad and I truly miss you. May God's Peace continue to move this community into a working uplifting community. It takes all of us to realize this and that' is what my father Irwin S. Quintyne stood for: 'Excellence.'

Finally after all these years I have gone back to school to obtain my Master's Degree in Social Work because he told me to arm myself with education. He found the good in everything we did and made it into positive action." [27]

Leroy Ramsey (1923-2013)

Ramsey grew up in poverty in racially troubled Meridian, Miss., the son of a railroad laborer and a fourth-grade-educated mother who taught him to read. The strapping southerner helped shape Long Island, championing school desegregation efforts here in the 1960s and 1970s, and founding the African American Museum in Hempstead in 1970. 'He knew the struggle because he came through it himself in Mississippi, and never forgot it,' said Reneer Reed, a Lakeview resident who worked with Ramsey to integrate the Malvene school district in the 1970s. 'He tried to do what was right.'

A by-product of segregated schools, Ramsey left Mississippi in 1960 to take a job at then virtually all-white Plainview-Old Bethpage High School, in an era when the southern civil rights movement was forcing a re-examination of race relations in northern communities. With young children of his own, he soon found himself a leader among black Long Islanders pressuring local and state officials to end the practice of steering black children from schools white students attended.

In a *Newsday* article, *"A Tortoise Pace for Civil Rights on LI,"* (May 29, 1978), Ramsey concludes by saying: "Most important, black activists of the now moribund struggle must somehow persuade the younger generation of blacks to commit their energies, skills, resources and finances to the struggle that seems to have no end, the search for equal justice and equality in America."

"He was named to Nassau County's Human Rights Commission. Hired by several area colleges, including Hofstra University, he introduced black history courses. A black history exhibit he organized at Hofstra drew such support that he founded the museum in Hempstead to house the material. He was hired by the New York State Education Department in 1972 to direct its efforts to integrate school systems across the state. He left state employment in 1982.

"In Mississippi, Ramsey did not begin attending school until he was eleven years of age but managed to graduate high school when he was nineteen. Offered a scholarship by Lincoln University in Pennsylvania, a school founded by black Civil War veterans, he could not raise $40 to get there.

"He married Velma Alexander in 1942, the same year he joined the Army. He served in the Pacific, and was injured when a Japanese plane attacked his anti-aircraft gun. He returned to Mississippi in 1946 and attended Jackson State. After graduating in 1952, he taught in Mississippi, then, starting in 1960, on Long Island. In 1972, he earned a doctorate at New York University, for studies on government discrimination.

A prolific author, he wrote dozens of articles and essays about black military history in the last decades of his life.

"In the late 1960s, Ramsey set up a Black History exhibit at Nassau Community College, in celebration of Black History Month. Due to popular demand, the exhibit was left in place and Ramsey used his personal collection of artifacts to change the exhibit from time to time. Before long the exhibit outgrew its space so he established the Black History Exhibit Center in a Hempstead store front later purchased by Nassau County. Professor Ramsey's Black History Exhibit Center became the African American Museum of Nassau County in 1985." [28]

Priscilla Redfield Roe (1921-2011)

Priscilla Alden Redfield Roe was born in Philadelphia. She attended the Baldwin School and Radcliffe College where she earned a Bachelor's Degree in 1943. She married Nathaniel W. Roe in 1942. During WW II, she worked as an analyst for the Office of Strategic Services in Washington, D.C., while her husband served in the Navy. After the war, Roe continued her studies in history at Radcliffe (1946-1948) and Oxford University (1948-1949). She then taught Latin, English, and History at Tenacre Country Day School in Wellesley, MA. This was the second of only three paid positions she ever held.

During her life, Roe was caught up in one absorbing enterprise after another, which drew her into the world of organizing people working for institutional or political change. She was always an active member of the local League of Women Voters because it provided a platform to work for change through the persuasion of sound research, clear presentation of fact, and cogent argument. She began more than a decade of land and water resources conservation campaigns in Massachusetts when she chaired a League of Women Voters' committee that successfully advocated for the establishment of a Sudbury Town Conservation Commission.

When the family moved to New York Roe continued to focus on the protection of coastal shores and wetlands, farmlands, and natural lands from the Hudson Highlands to the great barrier beach off Long Island, miles of which are now within the Fire Island National Seashore.

Priscilla Redfield Roe's legacy of public service on Long Island is substantial. Roe's life was altered in 1965 when she was asked by Joyce Turner to join the EOC of Suffolk's health committee. It changed the focus of her life for the following twenty-six years. Her first assignment was to agree to the request of Phyllis Vineyard, a family planning expert, to write a federal family planning grant application to be submitted to OEO. Not familiar with the subject, Roe did her customary diligent research with reasons and statistics. She could foresee that Dr. George Leone, the county health commissioner's support in order to advance the proposal was essential so she and Vineyard met with him where they found him to be much in favor of the project. Rowe recalled that she regarded Leone as a mentor for many years.

Roe went on to work closely with EOC's executive director Alan Gartner to apply for federal support to develop community health centers. She did her research and identified a program at Tufts Medical School that became the model on which the first Suffolk County community health center was based.

Roe's focus changed in 1967 to problems related to what she called "our wonderful/terrible health care system" when she was asked to serve on the Suffolk County Economic Opportunity Council (EOC) and chair its health committee. Three items on this committee's agenda were among the several important innovations EOC was instrumental in bringing to the County: family planning, Head Start, and neighborhood health centers. Roe's proudest accomplishment was providing the blueprint for Suffolk County that resulted in the opening of the first of the neighborhood health centers in 1968.

In 1971, Roe took her third and last paid position for one year as coordinator for the watch-dog council overseeing a grant to HIP of Greater NY to provide prepaid health care in Suffolk County. But the next major project was planning and establishing an institution designed to increase access to comprehensive and preventative health care for everyone in the County. Enabled by the federal Health Maintenance Organization (HMO) legislation of 1973 and using models that showed promise or were successful like Kaiser-Permanente, the Community Health Plan of Suffolk (CHPS) opened its doors in its own building in Hauppauge in 1978.

Roe received many awards and acknowledgements for her accomplishments in environmental conservation and in healthcare system reforms. Although Roe retired to Big Boulder Farm in 1982, she continued to be the 'great communicator' by maintaining close relationships with an extraordinary number of colleagues, friends, classmates, and family. Her daughter, Cynthia R. Barnes, president of the board of trustees of The Three Village Community Trust, recalls that her mother was extremely proud of her role in getting the Fire Island National Seashore established despite the powerful opposition of Robert Moses. To quote my mother: "Meetings were held by the group working on this right under Moses' nose," says Barnes.

And always the historian, she recorded the recollections of those with whom she had worked on Suffolk County Community Health Centers and, also, on a more personal note, researched the life, occupations, and discoveries of her distinguished ancestor, William C. Redfield. To keep the history alive, she wanted to keep all those connections no matter how far away the people may have been.

Roe had the ability to work with people with exceptional educational backgrounds as well as grassroots people who had little formal education. Everyone could feel her trustworthiness and commitment to the cause.[29]

Marge Rogatz (1928-

Marge Rogatz's story embodies nearly a fifty-year period as a consultant, organizational leader, community organizer and activist/volunteer. It is a story of a substantial lifetime commitment to social justice.

Rogatz's parents had an apartment in the multi-racial, mixed income Lewis Mumford Sunnyside development that housed many families who were involved in progressive organizations, including the Spanish Anti-Fascist League. She attended one of the most progressive schools of the time, Little Red School House in Manhattan, with other children from the development. When she was nine years old, her parents bought a house in Lawrence where Rogatz attended the Lawrence/Cedarhurst/Inwood school system and graduated from Lawrence High School in 1946. At that time, the schools were integrated in terms of economic, ethnic, racial and religious background, drawing primarily white children from Lawrence and Cedarhurst and children of both Italian and African American heritage from Inwood.

Russell Sprague was head of the Nassau Republican Party and a prominent figure in the National Republican Party. Sprague knew that Rogatz's parents were among the few registered Democrats in their election district and that they were very active in the community. Her father was chairman of the Five Towns Community Chest while her mother was president of the PTA and the local Red Cross. Sprague asked Rogatz's father, an attorney, if he had run on the Republican ticket. Her father, who was proudly progressive, refused the offer.

In high school, Rogatz was active in student government, serving as an officer and also as a leader in establishing a weekend afterschool program. Her home was a central meeting place for community activists and her parents, her brother's and her friends. Rogatz' mother described their home as having 'elastic walls' in order to accommodate everyone. During the summers while in high school, Rogatz worked as a summer day-camp counselor.

In 1947, close family friends introduced Rogatz to her future husband, Peter, who was attending Cornell Medical School in New York City. She was attending Smith College at the time and transferred to Barnard College where she earned a B.A., Phi Beta Kappa. She and Peter got married in 1949. During her husband's internship, Rogatz worked first as a model in the garment industry and then at the New School helping to connect foreign students to NYC host families and social activities. Through acquaintances at the New School, she was invited to join the national board of directors of the Urban League, where she was its youngest (and she recalls, its "only non-distinguished member").

During the 1952 presidential campaign, she worked at Adlai Stevenson's NYC headquarters where, at the age of 24, she met and mingled with numerous well-known New York social and political leaders. This led to her working for Mayor Robert Wagner during his campaign and serving as an aide to his wife. She also met Governor Averell Harriman who once invited her to join him on the drive back from Albany.

Among Rogatz's most exciting and memorable experiences from these years was the evening she and her husband spent with Eleanor Roosevelt, who had accepted an invitation from Rogatz's father (as chair of the Five Towns Community Chest) to speak at a huge dinner held in Lawrence High School. They picked her up at 5:00 PM at her Washington Square apartment and drove her to Rogatz's parents' home in Lawrence, took her to the dinner, and then delivered her back to her apartment at 11:00 PM. Mrs. Roosevelt was the US Representative to the United Nations at that time; she was not young but she seemed indefatigable. She asked her young driver and his wife questions about their lives (his internship, her job, their educations, their aspirations, etc.) all the way to Long Island and, despite having greeted hundreds of admirers and delivered a fairly lengthy speech, she asked more questions all the way back to the city.

In 1956, the Rogatzes moved to Roslyn Heights with their almost two-year old daughter and infant son. She immediately joined and became an officer of the Roslyn Democratic Club and was very active in local, county and national political campaigns. She became personal friends with future Nassau County Executive Eugene Nickerson and future federal court Judge Jack Weinstein. She was a leader of Lester Wolff's successful 1972 Congressional campaign (he was the first Democrat Congressman elected from a Nassau district, served from 1973 to 1980, and was succeeded by Democrats Gary Ackerman and current Congressman Steve Israel).

Rogatz was president of the Roslyn Cooperative Nursery School for three of her children's four pre-school years. In 1958, with her friend, Hazel Dukes, she co-founded the Roslyn Committee for Civil Rights and the Long Island Coordinating Committee for Civil Rights. She became very involved in Long Island CORE (the Congress of Racial Equality), working closely with its brilliant leader, Lincoln Lynch, and serving on LI CORE's executive committee during the anti-discrimination struggle concerning the Malverne school district, a number of housing and health care battles, and the fight to help migrant farmers in Riverhead. She was a leader of the local campaign on behalf of Mississippi Freedom Summer and the March on Washington for Freedom and Jobs, in which she and her husband, Peter, and hundreds of other Roslyn residents participated. She and her husband tested homes and apartments throughout Roslyn and neighboring areas for African Americans, starting in 1958 when she successfully tested an apartment for Hazel Dukes.

During1965-1966, Rogatz served as special assistant to James Farmer, the national director of CORE and, subsequently, for a short time for his successor, Floyd McKissick. Her responsibilities included public relations, research and speech writing; fundraising; and providing support for CORE's education, health, welfare, housing, voter registration and leadership training projects across the country. During this time, she was a participant herself in community organization and leadership training by Sol Alinsky and has repeated and advocated for similar training ever since. Rogatz left the national CORE office after helping to secure a large Ford Foundation grant. She then served as a consultant to the New York City Head Start In-service Training Program at NYU where she helped design and carry out training for personnel in NYC Head Start centers. Her work focused on parent involvement, development of paraprofessional/professional teamwork, community organization, and the inclusion of Afro-American curriculum and history.

In 1968-1969, she served on a consulting assignment funded by the federal Office of Economic Opportunity (OEO) for Nassau County Executive Eugene Nickerson that examined the accessibility and responsiveness of community action programs in designated poverty areas, analyzing housing, employment, social services, health care, child care, education and transportation services in those communities. The same problems, resulting from historic structural racism and continuing discriminatory policies and practices, can still be found on Long Island 45 years later.

In 1969-1970, Rogatz conducted a user-needs study of public libraries for New York City Mayor John Lindsay and his Parks, Recreation and Cultural Affairs Administration. In late 1970, Rogatz founded the Nassau-Suffolk Day Care Consultation Service, a nonprofit community-based agency which she headed for six years. The Service provided consultation, technical assistance and training to various public and voluntary agencies and community groups, regarding the funding, establishment, licensing and operation of quality comprehensive child care programs. Between 1971 and 1976, Rogatz carried out several assignments for the Office of the County Executive in Suffolk County. She headed consultant teams which designed and developed county-wide training programs for child care staffs, parents and boards and provided technical assistance to establish, strengthen and expand child care. She also profiled and evaluated the organization and programs of the Suffolk Economic Opportunity Council and the Suffolk Cooperative Library System.

In addition, as a consultant for the Comprehensive Human Services Planning and Delivery Demonstration Project, one of five such demonstration projects in the nation funded by the Department of Health Education and Welfare, Rogatz examined the administrative structure, service delivery system, and constraints and gaps in services of the Suffolk County Health Services Administration; the Departments of Social Services, Labor, Probation, Consumer Affairs, and Veterans Affairs; the Office of the Aging, and the

Youth Bureau. Concurrently, in 1972-1973, Rogatz headed a consultant team for the State University of New York at Stony Brook, carrying out the first assessment of child care needs, services, training and resources in the bi-county area and producing the Comprehensive Report of Child Care Needs: Nassau and Suffolk Counties. Following these consulting assignments, from 1976 through 1985, Rogatz worked as a staff member of RMR Health and Hospital Management Consultants with responsibility for major consultations in East Harlem, the Bronx and other underserved areas.

In January 1986, Rogatz committed herself henceforth to undertake only volunteer, unpaid work and positions. Joan Saltzman, a longtime friend and colleague who had served as the president of Community Advocates, Inc. since founding CA in 1972 and the CA board asked Rogatz to join the board and succeed Saltzman as CA president. Between 1972 and 1986, CA had earned a significant reputation (see Joan Saltzman's profile in this part and Community Advocates' story in Chapter VII and Part IV) establishing rental apartments for persons being discharged from mental hospitals on LI; developing patients' rights statements for patients in Nassau hospitals and residents in its nursing homes; creating what became the model for ombudservice programs in nursing home not only in Nassau County but across NYS and many other states; bringing thousands of eligible people into the food stamp program; and publishing and disseminating throughout Nassau County 200,000 copies of a monthly newsletter in English and Spanish.

While Rogatz has been serving as the full-time, unpaid president and CEO of Community Advocates since 1986, she has simultaneously been an active member, leader and co-founder of nonprofit organizations on Long Island, in some cases going as far back as 1956 when she and her husband relocated from an apartment in Manhattan to a house in Roslyn Heights. In the 1950s and 1960s, Rogatz was a co-founding board member of the Roslyn Neighborhood Corporation an advisory body responsible for overseeing the development of low and middle income housing and a community center in Roslyn Heights; a founder and leader of the Roslyn Committee for Civil Rights and the Long Island Coordinating Committee on Human Rights, and a member of the Executive Committee of Long Island CORE. For many decades, she was a board member and, often, an officer of the Health & Welfare Council where some fifty years ago, she was a co-founder of the Day Care Council of Nassau County. She was a co-founder and officer of the Nassau-Suffolk Coalition for the Homeless, Sustainable Long Island, the Long Island Campaign for Affordable Rental Housing, and ERASE Racism, the organization to which, along with Community Advocates, Rogatz has devoted most of her energy and skills during the last dozen years. She also served for many years on the Long Island Community Foundation board and still is an active member of its grants committee which, since LICF's establishment, has been a significant source of funding, technical assistance and encouragement for the growth and development of nonprofits across LI.

Rogatz has been appointed to a number of public committees and boards. Nassau County Executive Thomas Suozzi appointed her to the Nassau County Homeless Task Force, the Nassau County Panel on Next Generation Housing, the Nassau County Executive's Common Sense for the Common Good Task Force and, as the appointed chair, to the Nassau County 10-Year Plan to End Homelessness. In 2007, New York State Comptroller Thomas DiNapoli appointed Rogatz to be his representative on the nine-member board of the State of New York Mortgage Agency (SONYMA). As a SONYMA board member, she also serves on the New York State Homes and Community Renewal (HCR) Mortgage Insurance Fund Committee and the HCR Governance Committee. In these capacities, she participates in decision-making that affects affordable housing finance and development across New York State.

As Rogatz looks back at her work with human service organizations over the years, she feels that among the most important things she accomplished were bringing together groups that had not worked together before and bringing minority-led organizations and smaller agencies into collaborations with larger, more traditional agencies.

When asked what has changed since 1985 in the social service and social action scene on Long Island, Marge Rogatz points to the tremendous cuts in governmental services and change in funding priorities; President Bill Clinton's revisions of federal welfare policies; less progressive attitudes and policies everywhere, including on Long Island; a less level playing field with less chance for upward mobility; more poverty; and the weakening of the middle class with greater inequality overall. She notes that there are also different and fewer people 'marching.'

Marge, at age 86 and Peter, at age 88, reflect that if they had been younger, they would have joined the Occupy Wall Street protesters. Their hope is that young people, growing up in a more multi-racial, multi-ethnic, multi-cultural society and world, will approach change differently than prior generations did. Speaking about racism, both Marge and Peter Rogatz see racism as "pervasive, stubborn, difficult to eradicate and not well understood by many otherwise sophisticated people in the human services." [30]

Charles Russo (1950-

Charles Russo has dedicated his life to public service. Russo grew up in the East New York/Crown Heights section of Brooklyn, New York. Educationally, Russo was a marginal student. He was awarded a grant-in-aid in football to the University of Vermont. There, he became interested in volunteering to work with 'tough' kids like the ones he grew up with. Upon graduation, Russo went to C.W. Post College on Long Island where he earned a Master's Degree in Criminology.

After completing these studies, he took a job in a New Jersey Probation Department. To his dismay, the job did not provide the direct contact with young people that he had expected so he quickly left and took a position in the Nassau County Children's Shelter. He was powerfully struck by the agency's physical and emotional mistreatments of the children under its custody. This experience was an eye-opener for him, one that re-affirmed his career path to serve young people in trouble. Russo left the children's shelter and moved to Suffolk County to take a youth worker position in a recently-formed agency called Melville House located in Melville in Huntington Town where he worked for almost seven years.

In 1972, Melville House was formed by Ken Goldman and Jack DeSantis, experienced social workers to provide a home, supportive, and mental health services, to homeless, troubled young men who often were members of low-income families. Previously, Goldman had been director of social services at Sagamore Children's Center in Dix Hills while DeSantis was a social work supervisor also at Sagamore. They assembled a group of others, including friends and relatives, to offer the business and therapeutic skills needed to move forward. Goldman and his professional team were frustrated with the state structure and red tape in which they functioned at Sagamore. They sought a way to have a more professionally-rewarding career with more autonomy to design programs and services and assist young people to remain in their communities.

Before Melville House was established, when these young people faced judges to be adjudicated in family court, they were often sent to upstate New York State Division for Youth training schools, hours from their Long Island homes or were placed in Long Island mental hospitals. Melville House provided family court judges with an alternative placement where the presenting problems did not necessitate psychiatric hospitalization or incarceration due to criminal behavior. According to Goldman: "One good year in Melville House - costing $14,000 per child per annum - might prevent dozens of bad years later. Most of these kids might very easily have ended in jail, in mental institutions, on welfare or into drugs if something like Melville House wasn't available."

While working at Melville House, Russo married and had his first child. He also attended Hofstra's Law School from 1975-1978. Russo and the other youth workers gave their all to the young people in Melville House's care, treating each resident as a unique family member to whom they would do anything to assist in putting his or her life on a positive tract. Russo feels that the close relationships he and the other in-house staff fostered with the young people were the keys to the program's success, more important than the psychotherapeutic services provided by the trained social workers and psychologists who did not physically live in the residence. Russo counseled young people; he went to court with them where he witnessed politically-appointed Family Court judges often ill-suited to considering complex cases involving psychological and social issues, try to deal with young people and their families. Russo also found jobs for residents and provided advice to their parents and teachers. Today, many years later, Russo is able to recount dozens - if not hundreds of stories of individual growth and achievement among former Melville House residents.

After leaving Melville House, in 1980, Russo turned his attention to the work of Father Frank Pizzarelli at Hope House. A major part of his involvement was a continual direct engagement with the people who the organization served. Recently, the organization held a gala dinner to raise funds to establish an endowment fund, the purpose being to assure Hope House's future after Russo and Father Frank Pizzarelli are no longer there. Using his extensive network of contacts, Russo was able to connect with an extremely-wealthy local entrepreneur who agreed to attend the event. After the event, the entrepreneur asked Russo for Hope House's financials which Russo provided. After reviewing them, the entrepreneur, looking skeptically, noted Hope House's extremely low overhead costs. Russo explained that "Father Frank earns no salary and I have donated all of my legal services every year. In addition, I am able to obtain tons of donated goods and services from the people I know. That is why the overhead is so low." A week later, a check for $2M was received at Hope House's offices with a note from the entrepreneur saying that his gift was towards the new endowment fund; that he wanted to assure that Hope House continued into perpetuity.

In another instance, a truck driver who had read about Russo and Hope House came to Hope House just before Christmas to ask what he could do to help. Russo thanked the fellow and said that he was certain that he could help in a variety of ways using his truck, delivering goods between the residences. While there, the truck driver noticed a hallway bulletin board and read of residents' Christmas wishes. This included one wish by a boy who wanted a tuba, an expensive musical instrument. On Christmas day, Russo, who attends all Hope House events, noticed a tuba near the Christmas tree. To his surprise, the note attached to the tuba revealed that the truck driver had donated the tuba. Listening and cultivation had paid off again thanks to Russo.

Russo feels that: "It is important to engage people in "quality time, doing stuff together. It makes you feel like a million dollars.' An example of this lesson is given when Russo asks prospective wealthy donors to dress up like Santa Claus. 'It triggers something in them. They cannot do enough after their experience," Russo says. He gives people as much positive experiences as possible so that 'it sticks' and generates good feelings, urging them to do more. Russo speaks passionately of the satisfaction that he personally gets by being with the network of people he has developed over the years. He often arranges weekend field trips upstate to be with them and Hope House residents.

A good number of Hope House residents have gone on to successful employment and professional careers. Nine residents became interns in Russo's law firm and later became attorneys. Russo feels that his greatest legacy is his ability 'to witness program graduates who are now married with families and engaged in successful careers, and, to get up every morning and try to get a judge to give a kid another chance. "My legacy is that the kids become self-actualized. Some Hope House residents are now legislators, teachers, social workers, police officers, union members, and bank presidents.' Some work for Russo's law firm as attorneys and paralegals," Russo says.

In reflecting over his 40-plus years of community service, Russo feels that little has changed. Long Island continues to resist the integration of minority groups, the homeless and mentally-ill and fight their entry into our communities. Russo refers to facts in a recent *Newsday* article reporting that the number of homeless families has grown much faster than the shelters and resources that are available to them. The article also reveals that Suffolk has the highest homeless children school enrollment in New York State outside of New York City with 5,000 homeless students as of the 2012-13 school year, which is up from 1,956 in 2007-08. Nassau County was next with 3,200 up from 663 during the same time period.

With respect to mental health, Russo says: "We are very good at diagnosing personal problems but continue to ignore treatment alternatives to those problems." If Russo were given the power to reform the mental health system, he would take the legislative steps necessary to recognize trained former alcoholics and drug addicted people as legitimate service providers. "These individuals have valuable roles to play because they have been in the shoes of those that need help. They should be working hand-in-hand with the professionals in treatment programs. We also need educational reform to be more effective working with specialized populations such as these" says Russo.

Russo remains committed as ever to his work with and behalf of young people and their families. In recent years, this commitment has broadened to include board membership on the board of directors of the Long Island Coalition for the Homeless. Currently, Russo serves as chairman of the board of directors. His legal services continue to be provided on a pro bono basis. His network of contacts enables him to seek political support of elected officials when there is a new residence to establish. 'If it is in Babylon Town, I call Rich Schaffer, head of the Democratic Party to assign town staff to expedite the permit process. If it is in Brookhaven Town, I contact Republican Tim Mazzei, a Town Councilman. I have been careful over the years to make friends on both sides of the aisle,' says Russo.

The coalition operates an Amityville-based Community Resource Center, the former home of the Armed Forces Recruitment and Training Center. The 40,000 square foot building and the nine acres on which it sits were part of an operational military base and facility until its closure in 2011. At that time, the process began to transfer the property for its newly intended purposes: serving homeless persons and veterans. A local selection committee, comprised of representatives from veteran agencies, the Departments of Social Services and Veterans Services, housing agencies and public housing authorities, reviewed proposals for the development of housing on the property. The committee selected Concern for Independent Living, which is in the process of developing 60 units of permanent, affordable housing for 60 veterans and their families on 4.5 acres of the property.

The Community Resource Center, which is located on a parcel in front of the residential units, was transferred to a subsidiary of the Long Island Coalition for the Homeless. The center in Amityville is a major project, which allows the Coalition to house ten organizations serving LI's homeless and veteran folks in one location. The cost-sharing helps all agencies involved reduce overhead and free up funds for direct services. It also allows a more cohesive, comprehensive, 'one stop' method through which homeless folks and veterans can access housing and services.

The goal is to provide a location where persons in need can make an appointment and get housing assistance, case management, employment training, counseling and other necessary services all in one visit through various agencies. The building includes a distribution center where organizations working with persons in need can obtain food, clothing, personal care and other essential items.

Each January, the Long Island Coalition for the Homeless coordinates point-in-time counts of sheltered and unsheltered persons in Nassau and Suffolk counties. Sheltered count numbers include individuals and families who were in emergency shelters and transitional housing for homeless persons on the night of the count. Unsheltered count numbers include 'unsheltered' individuals and families who volunteer enumerators interviewed on the night of the count. Unsheltered numbers do not include those who were doubled- or tripled-up, living in substandard conditions, or facing eviction.

When asked to reflect on the problems facing nonprofit organizations today, Russo feels that: "Nonprofits have been placed in an extremely competitive game fighting for funding. Instead of working together, they often work apart."
31

David G. Salten (1913-2006)

David Salten, Superintendent of Long Beach Schools from 1950 to 1962, was a passionate educator whose work had national impact and a tireless advocate for educational innovation and school desegregation. He also fought against pressure from political bosses and against what he saw as poor decisions that would have negative effects on the education and well-being of Long Island communities.

Dr. Salten had a doctorate in educational research and helped spearhead the formation of the School of Performing Arts and the Maritime High School in New York City. However, he felt that his work promoting civil rights in schools was his most important accomplishment.

Salten's views had national impact when he was asked by civil rights attorney Thurgood Marshall, later the first black U.S. Supreme Court justice, to testify as an expert witness in the landmark school desegregation case in Little Rock, Ark. He testified that the presence of eight African-American students in Little Rock High School had not lowered the quality of education. He also would testify in desegregation cases in Baltimore and New Orleans. 'From the historical perspective, my work in promoting civil rights in American public school systems is the best thing I have done' he was quoted as saying in a 2002 magazine article. Salten also made a mark as an economic developer on Long Island, directing the Nassau County Economic Development Agency for 20 years.

Born in New York City, Salten attended Washington Square College from which he graduated when he was 19. He then attended Columbia University and New York University, where he earned a doctorate in educational research in 1944. He received four honorary doctorates and citations from government, community and business groups for his achievements in school integration and curriculum reform.

Later in his career, Salten played an important role in the economic development of Long Island where he directed the Nassau County Economic Development Agency for twenty years. He served as consultant to the president of Hofstra University and later as the executive vice president and provost of New York Institute of Technology.[32]

Joan Saltzman (1919-

Joan R. Saltzman is the embodiment of personal dedication, civic responsibility and inspiring leadership. As an advocate and activist, she has worked to protect Long Island's and New York State's most vulnerable children and adults, combating discriminatory practices and strengthening and expanding health and human services to include African American and Latino residents and underserved communities.

A graduate of Barnard College, Saltzman has had a significant impact on health and mental health services, laying the foundation for citizen involvement and equal access by persons of differing ages, races, backgrounds and abilities to improved resources, including safe, supportive and affordable housing.

On the state level, Saltzman served as a member of key state policy and planning bodies, including the NYS Health Coordinating Council; the NYS Office of Mental Hygiene Planning Council and its Advisory Council on Alcohol (appointed to both by Governor Carey); as chairperson of the Special Housing Task Force of the Office of Mental Hygiene Council on Citizen Participation; and as co-chair of the NYS Special Mental Health Committee of the Task Force for the Development of Community Residential and Rehabilitation Programs. On the local level, she served as planning chair of the Nassau County Mental Health Board.

In 1960, Saltzman helped found the North Shore Child & Family Guidance Association, serving as a board member and as its president. In 1972, she co-founded Community Advocates, a nonprofit organization that has been a major catalyst for social and racial justice, affordable housing and housing for homeless individuals and families on Long Island. She served as president of Community Advocates for 14 years and still serves on its board and executive committee. She was a founder of the Long Island Community Foundation in 1978, serving on its board and grants committee for more than 30 years, and also a founder of the Long Island Fund for Women and Girls (recently renamed the Long Island Women's Fund). The Family Service Association, the Community Mainstream Associates and the New York State Communities Aid Association are just three of the many agencies on whose boards she served as an active member and leader.

Through her special interest, involvement and leadership, Saltzman became known as an expert in the development of apartments and group homes within the community for persons leaving psychiatric institutions and persons with emotional and developmental disabilities. Starting in the early 1980s, she founded Long Island's first residence for children with autism and related disabilities, and then founded residences for teen-agers and for adults with similar special needs.

Saltzman and her husband, Ambassador Arnold A. Saltzman, shared a lifelong dedication to helping people in need. In 1991, through their vision and generosity, a new facility was built on the Hofstra University campus to house child development and outreach programs for families and children from Hempstead and surrounding communities. In recognition of their support of Hofstra and their commitment to human services, the University named the facility the Joan and Arnold Saltzman Community Services Center. Saltzman is chair of the Center's board.

Saltzman has been the recipient of numerous awards for her social justice advocacy, community activism and humanitarian service. [33]

Janet B. Schaberg (previously Walsh) (1956-

Schaberg was born as Janet B. Walsh in Brooklyn and was raised in Jackson Heights, Queens. She attended Mater Christi High School (now St. John's Prep), and John Jay College of Criminal Justice. In 1975, she ventured down to Wall Street, and fell in love with the fast paced action of trading options. As a market maker on the American Stock Exchange, she earned the respect of the 'Good Ol' Boy's Club,' and successfully participated in stock option trading.

In 1969 at age 58, Walsh's father had started to experience difficulties with performing his job as a mechanical engineer, and exhibited some confusion. At first, he would argue with his boss and wife, claiming they were incorrect when noticing his inability to perform certain tasks. For years, doctors would listen, and offer a medication for sleep, or depression. As a union member, his union representatives would find him new jobs each time he was let go from a position. Pleading with his union reps, he would tell them he could not work, but their response was always the same, without a diagnosis, he could not be considered disabled. His family had to remove his car, his hunting guns, and basically keep him under house arrest. Finally in 1973, he was diagnosed as having Alzheimer's disease, a rare brain disorder. At that time, Alzheimer's was considered a disease of the young (people under 65), and senility was considered a natural process of aging. This diagnosis was delivered as Walsh's father lay restrained in a straight jacket for several weeks in their local community hospital. The neurologist making the diagnosis, while sympathetic, could offer no suggestions for care other than sedating medications. He was admitted to the Northport VA Hospital, where he would remain until his death in 1981.

The VA Hospital had only one solution for Walsh's dad's care, and that was the Psychiatric Unit, where he was gently removed from the highly sedating drugs prescribed to control him at the community hospital. He spent his first years at the VA surrounded by young men returning from the Vietnam War, no longer able to function in society. The staff had no experience with Alzheimer's disease, and would allow him the same privileges as other patients, cooperate and you would get certain freedoms, such as outings to the Commissary. Her dad would be given a pass to leave the locked unit, as he made his bed every day, followed instructions, and was cooperative. Unbeknownst to the staff, Walsh's dad had drawn a schematic map of the pipes leading to outside the building; he escaped, got on the VA bus and headed to the town of Northport. He was going home. In Northport, he found a car running outside a food market; dad got in, and drove off. As he had not driven in years, his driving was erratic, and he was pulled over by the police. Explaining that he had left his wallet at home, able to give the police his address in Queens, and with no warrants for him, they were about to let him go, then they saw his hospital bracelet. Thank goodness, as there was a young child asleep in the back in a car seat. Sid Resnick taught the Northport VA hospital what it meant to have Alzheimer's disease. After spending his final four years bedridden at the VA hospital, Walsh's dad passed away in 1981.

In 1986, while fund raising for the Alzheimer's Association, Walsh testified before a U.S. Congressional Field Hearing on the hardship of having a family member with Alzheimer's disease, and how this disease affected the person afflicted, and those who gave care. Her story was printed in the U.S. Congressional Record. In 1987, Janet joined the board of the Stony Brook Foundation and helped establish the "Center for the Study of Aging," a research facility focused on finding the cause, and hopefully, cure for Alzheimer's disease. To this day, this laboratory led by Dr. Dmitry Goldgabor, recipient of a Nobel Prize Nominee, continues to collaborate with others around the world to find the answer to ending Alzheimer's and related diseases.

In 1988, along with four other women, Walsh founded the Long Island Alzheimer's Foundation (LIAF), in her kitchen. LIAF has grown to become a leading social service resource center model focused on Alzheimer's disease and related memory disorders. While leading LIAF, she played a vital role in the development of numerous successful programs for the Alzheimer's community, including a day services program (The Memory Lane Club), early stage Alzheimer's disease and caregiver support groups, and a weekly lecture program to stimulate the minds of those with early stage Alzheimer's disease, known as 'Al'z Club.' In addition, Walsh produced a trio of videos entitled *'Living with Alzheimer's,'* which received the 1994 Telly Award and appeared on PBS. Walsh was the day-to-day hands on supervisor of LIAF for the first sixteen years, which included administration, fiscal oversight, fund raising and housekeeping.

Walsh created the *Long Island Directory of Services for Alzheimer's disease* in 1989. She was responsible for initiating and executing LIAF's annual Coping and Caring Conferences for Alzheimer's caregivers in 1989, and has organized four International Symposia on Alzheimer's disease and other related disorders.

In 1995, Walsh served as the chair of the Health Care Committee, NYS Delegation to the White House Conference on Aging, as well as serving as the Nassau County Delegate to the NYS Governor's Conference on Aging. She was a member of the National Task Force on Alzheimer's disease for the National Council on Aging in 1998, and was a member of the NYS Task Force on Alzheimer's disease and Related Dementia from 1993-1996. Walsh went to Denmark in 2007 as a U.S. Ambassador for Aricept (Alzheimer's medication) on behalf of Pfizer, and presented LIAF's programs and services to health representatives of 18 countries, representing Europe, the Middle East, and New Zealand.

A sought-after expert on the topic of memory enhancement techniques, Walsh has lectured throughout the United States on a variety of memory-related topics. She has appeared often on radio, TV and in print as a spokesperson for Alzheimer's disease. In addition, her experience in undergoing genetic testing for the Alzheimer-risk gene Ape was featured in a 1997 PBS documentary, '*A Question of Genes: Inherited Risk.*' The testing process confirmed that Walsh carries the risk gene for late onset Alzheimer's disease from both her mother and father. For the past 18 years, Walsh has participated as a volunteer in research studies at NYU's Center for Brain Health, undergoing multiple PET scans, MRIs, psychological, neurological and physical exams, medical testing such as spinal taps and recently, a sleep study program. She completed her latest round of these tests in August, 2012, and will once again begin the testing process in 2015.

Walsh will be the first to tell you that the road to establishing a social service agency serving the Alzheimer community on Long Island in the 1980s was an uphill climb. She found one of the greatest obstacles to moving forward quickly with her work in memory loss was the stigma attached to Alzheimer's disease. Overcoming the mindset that Alzheimer's was an old person's disease, and that those with Alzheimer's had little expectation for leading a productive life, had to be dispelled through education. Through social programs, supportive philosophies and ongoing therapeutic programs, the Long Island Alzheimer's Foundation has enabled thousands of families to face a progressive disease with an open mind, a support system, an educated approach, and programs to help our brains maintain good health longer.

In the 1980s and 1990s, diagnosing Alzheimer's was difficult until the disease had become well advanced. The need to develop and train geriatric medical specialists was another hurdle for Long Island, and elsewhere in the U.S. Today, the diagnosis of Alzheimer's disease remains a process of exclusion but may also include detailed symptoms, imaging of the brain, genetics, and other testing including written, oral and physical tests. All of this testing is quite expensive. Therefore, we are still awaiting a simpler diagnostic process. The silver bullet for treating Alzheimer's is still at-large.

The same road blocks were present in the fundraising process for Alzheimer's disease. Once again the stigma that the disease affects only old people was the perception. It took years to help the public understand that when a person has memory loss, at least one to two other family members are also removed from society due to the custodial and longtime care required. Competing for community, county, and state dollars for programs was difficult when Alzheimer grants were placed alongside requests for aiding children, cancer, and heart disease. It took Alzheimer's reaching epidemic proportions worldwide, draining the health system, reaching astronomical costs for caregiving, and taking away our loved ones to get the attention needed. But it is still not enough.

The recipient of the Congressional Achievement Award in 1988 and a New York State Senate "Woman of Distinction" Award in 1998, Walsh has also served as an associate trustee at North Shore-LIJ Health System, a trustee for the Fashion Institute of Technology, and remains as chairman emeritus of the Long Island Alzheimer's Foundation.

Walsh lives with her husband, Buzz Schaberg and their dog Max, on Longboat Key, Florida, and Shelter Island, New York. She presently participates as a pet therapy team with her dog Max. Together, they visit memory loss programs, nursing homes, and rehabilitation centers. [34]

Betty Schlein (1931-

Betty Schlein exemplifies a person who has focused her attention on positive social change through the political process thus affecting thousands of women, men, and families not only on Long Island but throughout New York State.

Schlein was born in Brooklyn where she lived with her extended family during the harsh years of the 1930's Depression. Her mother encouraged her to get a college education and sacrificed to enable her to do so. Schlein matriculated at Smith College and later transferred to Cornell University in 1952. Cornell's Liberal Arts College accepted only one woman in five. Today, of course, this policy is called 'discrimination.' After graduation, Schlein went to Washington DC to seek employment and found that they only jobs available for women were as secretaries. Disappointed, she returned to New York and earned a Master's Degree in Early Childhood Education at Columbia's Teacher's College after which she married and had three children before she was 30 years of age.

Schlein soon got involved with the anti-Vietnam War movement on Long Island and worked for Allard K. Lowenstein in his congressional office. After attending a talk at her Merrick synagogue by a panel of feminists, she began to attend meetings of a new chapter of the National Organization for Women. Schlein's consciousness grew and she committed herself to get more deeply involved with others as a change agent. Schlein was soon elected president of the NOW chapter, an event that she feels changed her life. Under Schlein's leadership, the chapter grew from 70 to over 500 members and became the third largest in the country. The chapter helped organize New York State NOW and the Women's Political Caucus. At the same time, Schlein worked with others to form the Coalition Against Domestic Violence, Nassau Divorce Information Center, and many other issue-oriented organizations.

These actions lead to dramatic change in Schlein's life. She was elected as a member of the New York State Democratic Committee and elected vice-chairwoman. She nominated Mary Ann Krupsack the first woman to run for and win the office of Lieutenant Governor. She then headed the Women's Division of the New York State Democratic Committee which had been founded by Eleanor Roosevelt in the 1920s. Schlein worked to make the Women's Division a training ground for women to learn to organize, prepare and deliver speeches, and lobby for women's issues. She also became a member of the group working to restore Eleanor Roosevelt's home at Val-Kill.

In 1978, Schlein was appointed assistant to the New York State Governor Hugh L. Carey. In this capacity, she worked closely with the Governor's Appointment Secretary Judith Hope to identify talented women to assume leadership positions in state government. Schlein went on to organize the Long Island Women's Network, the Women's Fund of Long Island, helped develop Emily's List, and the Eleanor Roosevelt Legacy Committee. Schlein also served on the board of directors of the Long Island Community Foundation and many other nonprofit boards.

"One of Schlein's greatest pleasures is to continue to provide support and encouragement to young activists and the causes that are dear to her. She looks back at a rich, long, and fortunate life and is enormously grateful to been born and lived her life as a suburban Jewish woman in America in the second half of the twentieth century. She can think of no better time or place in history." [35]

Max Schneier (1917-2002)

Max Schneier, J.D., 85, a founding member of NAMI, died this week at his home in Florida after a brief illness. Mr. Schneier was well-known nationally and internationally as a leading advocate for persons with mental illnesses. A keynote speaker at the first NAMI Convention in Madison, Wisconsin in 1979, he made the motion from the floor to form the national NAMI organization.

When Max Schneier's adolescent daughter was first diagnosed with mental illness in New York City more than 30 years ago, an eminent psychiatrist told Max that she was a "hopeless schizophrenic." The physician advised Max and his wife, Jody, to go home to their apartment and institutionalize their daughter and forget about her. He did not realize that Max Schneier was a man who thought nothing was impossible, who never took "no" for an answer, and who had the tenacity to shake up any bureaucratic system to make it better. Schneier traveled across the country and eventually found Harvey's House, a psychosocial rehabilitation program in northern California to help his daughter.

Soon after, Schneier retired from a successful career as a businessman and devoted the rest of his life to becoming an unpaid mental health advocate. He was driven by an agenda that only he defined, and he was frequently brusque and unyielding with organizations and advocates who did not agree with him. Yet, he also frequently pulled together coalitions of advocates to successfully work on issues of great importance to people with mental illnesses and their families.

In 1972, Schneier asked the television reporter Geraldo Rivera to investigate the Willowbrook State School for the Mentally Retarded. The way Mr. Schneier told it to his son Jeffrey, he had been alerted by workers and patients to abuse and neglect at the vast institution, which had 4,000 residents. After someone slipped him a key, he led Mr. Rivera and a TV crew into a building there, scuffled with a guard and confronted the director, all on camera. Mr. Rivera's reports on the conditions led to the closing of Willowbrook and a precedent-setting promise by the state to provide supervised housing for needy retarded people in the community, not in institutions.

Schneier also established a nonprofit corporation called Transitional Services for New York, which in 1975 opened a halfway house in Queens for patients discharged from mental institutions. In 1979, he helped found the National Alliance for the Mentally Ill, still a powerful lobbying group.

He served on federal advisory committees on health and mental health, and in recent years he concentrated on lobbying a wide circle of policy makers and program directors for improving treatment of people with both mental illness and drug addiction. He argued that treatment was hindered by the government's insistence on separate financing for the conditions.

Schneier devoted much of the last decade of his life to championing the policy of integrated care for persons with co-occurring mental illness and substance abuse. Ironically, his death occurred on the eve of a meeting to finalize a major national report that will be issued shortly by the Substance Abuse and Mental Health Services Administration (SAMHSA) on the treatment of people with co-occurring disorders.

No one worked harder than Max Schneier on the issues he cared about. In 1990, Schneier convinced NAMI to draft a friend of the court brief in a Florida case, Sanbourne v. Chiles, because he objected to a proposed settlement that would have guaranteed services to people released from South Florida State Hospital for only 30 days after discharge. According to Ron Honberg, NAMI's legal director, "Max appointed himself as my personal law clerk and spent several days in a law library reading cases and finding obscure citations and precedents. He would call me at home at midnight, reading me quotes from these cases and insisting that I insert them into the brief. Of course, he was right on point!"

E. Clarke Ross, D.P.A., NAMI's former deputy executive director for Policy and recalls Schneier's significant role in promoting reforms in the use of mechanical and physical restraints. "Max was outraged when he read a series in the *Hartford Courant* describing scores of deaths of children and adults in restraints. As always, he translated his outrage into action. Max was an integral part of the advocacy that led to significant reforms in the way restraints are used today." [36]

Marilyn Shellabarger (1927-

Marilyn Shellabarger presents social activists with a wonderful illustration of health care advocacy during a period of dramatic population growth and social change. She demonstrated the capacity to work effectively with both elected and appointed officials as well as people living in poverty who suffered without adequate health care.

Starting as a volunteer in 1977 on both of the South Brookhaven Advisory Boards, Shellabarger carried the baton for the survival and growth of Suffolk County's nine community health care centers for more than twenty-years. She was passionate in her belief in the importance of her mission, displaying extraordinary fidelity and staying power as well as intelligence and effectiveness defending the interests of the centers and those that needed them. I recall her articulate, frequent presentations before the county legislature and its health and budget committees during periods when county executives reported financial crises and that there had to be cuts in health and human service funding.

Standing in front of the podium, before the horseshoe of nineteen legislators, Shellabarger, a small, smiling Caucasian woman, was a force to be listened to and respected. A contingent of community health care consumers joined her in making presentations. You always knew she had done her homework, had lined up her ducks, leaving no details to chance despite the economic situation or forecasts of doom.

In 1982, Shellabarger chaired the newly-formed central coordinating committee representing all of the health center advisory boards. The committee brought the power of solidarity to bear particularly in reviewing budgets when they were endangered by cutbacks in aid. Later, she served as a member of the twenty-four member Blue Ribbon Health Panel established in 1996 when County Executive Robert Gaffney charged the panel to conduct a thorough study and evaluation of the entire health center network and the role that the county should play in supporting it.

It was a grateful community in 2000 that acknowledged her long years of dedicated advocacy by naming the South Brookhaven Center East in her honor." [37]

Joyce Louise Spencer (1927–

Joyce Louise Spencer was born in 1927 in New Rochelle, NY, the daughter of Charles L. and Dorothy Schmidt Spencer. Joyce grew up in nearby Port Chester, NY, where as a girl she was strongly influenced by her father, a WWI veteran who was a leader in the local American Legion Post, who taught her to be concerned about her community. She remembers selling poppies on the street to raise money for the care of veterans and visiting disabled veterans at the Castle Point Hospital, assembling toys and holiday food baskets for the poor and rolling bandages for cancer patients.

Her mother and aunt, Emma Schmidt, the first policewoman in Westchester County, urged the Joyce, a good student and avid reader, to go to college, an uncommon aspiration for a middle class teenage girl in the early 1940s. She did and went on to graduate from NYU and took a job t as a social worker in the Westchester County Department of Family and Child Welfare. These traits, her concern for her community, and her daring to take on challenges that others avoided, shaped her adult life.

In 1950, she married Anthony E. Insolia, whom she met as a Journalism student at NYU. In the mid-1950s, Insolia was hired by *Newsday*, Long Island's daily newspaper, which took the couple and their young family to Huntington, NY, where they bought their first home. Before long Spencer became involve in her first community cause, joining a group that successfully advocated for the establishment of a public library in their Greenlawn/Harborfields neighborhood. She then joined the Huntington Township Committee on Human Relations, one of the first such groups in the United States, whose primarily interest was fighting substandard and racial discrimination in housing.

Joyce Spencer Insolia helped rally citizens of conscience against housing discrimination and helped organize a march on Huntington town hall led by Bayard Rustin that highlighted unsanitary conditions and the plight of black families who were blocked from securing better rentals. The Committee on Human Relations pressured Huntington to establish a housing authority and to prosecute landlords who failed to provide safe and sanitary conditions to renters.

In order to address racial discrimination, Spencer Insolia organized a Housing Committee sponsored listing service of available houses and apartments. In November 1963, as co-chair of the Housing Committee with local Huntington attorney Sam Raskin, she led a group that sent pairs of "test" renters, some black and some white, into the offices of local real estate brokers many of whom steered the couples based on race. The results were presented to the Secretary of State, resulting in the suspension and revocation of licenses of the offending brokers.

In collaboration with the local office of the National Conference of Christians and Jews, she initiated an in-service training course on racial discrimination for teachers in Huntington's eight school districts, enrolling 160 in the first session taught by Charles Raebeck, the Director of Education at Adelphi College. This course found a wide audience was repeated many times in schools across Long Island.

Spencer Insolia testified at the Metcalf Baker hearings in Albany documenting the patterns of racial discrimination she had found in Huntington. The ultimate outcome of the hearings was a law enacted by the New York State Legislature that banned discrimination in housing on the basis of race, creed or national origin.

Spencer Insolia led the first sit-in in Suffolk County when a local landlord refused to rent an apartment to a black nurse whose husband was serving in Vietnam and was arrested along with five other members of the Human Relations Committee.

She also joined the Long Island Chapter of the Congress on Racial Equality (CORE) led by activist Lincoln Lynch. CORE staged a major protest in Riverhead following the fatal fire on the Hollis Warner Duck Farm that claimed the life of several migrant workers. When two of CORE's leaders, John Moscow and Dave Thompson, were arrested, she organized the effort to raise bail for her two colleagues. Spencer Insolia herself was arrested twice at fair housing sit-ins, once in Amityville and again in Hempstead, where landlords refused to rent to black apartment seekers. Her final arrested took place at the Schaefer Beer Café in the New York World's Fair in 1964, where she joined picketers protesting the company's refusal to hire black delivery truck drivers.

As a volunteer for the State Committee Against Discrimination headed by Fran Levinson, Spencer Insolia organized a national conference of leaders in the field of human relations whose goal was to mobilize support for President Kennedy's "Stroke of the Pen" Legislation that sought to outlaw discrimination on a national level.

In 1972 Spencer Insolia earned an MSW from Stony Brook University, and in 1977 she completed the doctoral course in social policy toward a DSW Degree from Columbia School of Social Work.

Joyce and Anthony Insolia divorced in 1979 after twenty-nine years of marriage. She reclaimed her maiden name of Spencer and turned her attention to a new generation of challenges. She became an organizing member of the Suffolk County Women's Political Caucus, which set as its goal increasing the direct participation of women in the political process and urging qualified female candidates to run for public office. She went on to serve as president of the Suffolk County Caucus and as a board member on the New York State Women's Political Caucus.

Spencer Insolia joined the board of directors of the Victims Information Bureau of Suffolk (VIBS), a spouse abuse and domestic violence prevention agency where she served for twelve years, first as secretary and then as chairwoman for four years. During her tenure, VIBS became recognized as one of the most effective domestic violence prevention and women's service provider and advocacy agencies in New York State, raising the plight of abused women and helping to craft new laws, policies and new prevention programs.

She has also served on other boards and committees, including the Suffolk Chapter of NYCLU, where she was board secretary, AARP, Literacy Volunteers of America and United Way of Long Island.

At present she is a committeewoman and member of the Suffolk County Democratic Committee from the Town of Huntington and volunteers with the Suffolk Child Care Council as an evaluator of their Parent Leadership Training Program. [38]

Frank Sinisi (1934-

Every year, in the weeks before Thanksgiving Day, Frank Sinisi is one busy retiree. He is standing in front of the walk-in freezer of Pronto, the North Bay Shore nonprofit community organization, for which he served as unpaid president for many years.

A retired business executive from West Islip is Italian-American with a French-Canadian background, and speaks only a few words of Spanish. Nevertheless, Sinisi has become a hero to one of the largest Hispanic population areas in New York through his work with Pronto, which serves Central Islip, Bay Shore, Brentwood and surrounding communities. His fundraising skills and business connections have helped build the agency into a charitable powerhouse. 'He is a premier fundraiser,' says Jim Marcos, a Bay Shore attorney who does pro bono work for Pronto clients and serves on Pronto's board of directors. He describes Sinisi as 'persistent, unwilling to accept 'no' for an answer, and he is very good at getting people to empathize with the struggles of the Suffolk County Hispanic community.' 'He is made Pronto what it is today,' says Santiago Reyes, who also serves on the agency's fourteen-member board.

Sinisi became involved with Pronto after successful careers. He owned a restaurant in Forest Hills from 1959 to 1965, then worked as a marketing executive in New York and Chicago through the mid- 1980s. He was accustomed to earning a six-figure salary most of his adult life, during which he also ran an executive headhunter firm on Long Island.

A heart attack at age 62 motivated him to retire from the corporate world, but Sinisi thought his skills as an executive were still valuable. In recalling that time, Sinisi says he "felt that I was still young enough to give my time back to the community and back to my faith. I always wanted to get into working with the poor and the needy."

In 1998, when he started volunteering at Pronto's small building in North Bay Shore, he had already served as director of a religious education program at St. Luke's Church in Brentwood. He became vice president of Pronto in 2001, and president in 2002, volunteering his time to the agency. During Sinisi's tenure, the number of clients served by Pronto has increased from 3,000 to 50,000.

With Sinisi's help, Pronto has raised more than $2 million. Under his leadership, the agency built a modern building for its headquarters. Pronto, which began in 1969 in the basement at St. Anne's Roman Catholic Church in Brentwood, had been located inside a small house for years. Sinisi obtained an $800,000 mortgage to construct the $1-million, 10,500-square-foot facility on a one-acre parcel, which Pronto owns. The building houses a food pantry, a thrift shop, a warehouse and three classrooms for English as a second language courses and computer training. So far, $300,000 of the mortgage has been paid, Sinisi says.

One of Sinisi's last official acts as president was to participate in distributing Christmas toys to about 2,500 local children. Sinisi is an unpaid consultant and fundraiser. He has advice for other people his age: 'Stop watching television, get up and contribute your time and talent to your community.'

In recognition of his community service, the Latin American Chamber of Commerce of New York gave Sinisi its Man of the Year award. [39]

David Sprintzen (1939-

Sprintzen grew up in an apolitical family. At Bryant High School in Brooklyn, Sprintzen played the role of Joe McCarthy in a high school presentation where he won an American Legion Medal. As a student at Queens College from 1957-1961, he was active in "Students-for-Kennedy." He met Jerry Rubin in 1964 who had just returned from a trip to Cuba, and argued with him, defending U.S. policies. Concerned with U.S. social policies, Sprintzen got involved in JFK's political campaign. He considered joining Volunteers in Service to America but withdrew his application when he learned that service in VISTA (Volunteers in Service to America) did not provide a draft deferment. He enrolled at Penn State University, secured a three-year fellowship and studied to obtain a Doctorate in Philosophy.

Sprintzen and Marge Harrison who is profiled in this chapter, formed the Long Island Progressive Coalition. Together, they assembled a group of activists that were supported by a nominal coalition of some sixty progressive organizations. The coalition supported a range of progressive causes, lacking staff, money, or resources. The primary focus of its activities was determined by the interests, commitment, and efforts of the activists. Organizing tended to focus on one to two issues, most particularly, the promotion of a democratically-elected public utility to replace the Long Island Lighting Company (LILCO) in connection to the campaign against the Shoreham nuclear power plant.

LIPC was incorporated as a nonprofit organization totally operated by dedicated volunteers. In its early years, LIPC operated with an annual budget of less than $5,000. During the first years, the organization searched for funding sources that would support its advocacy and community organizing work. Efforts to meet with officials at the Unitarian Universalist Veatch Program at Shelter Rock were unsuccessful until contact was made with a member of the Program's board. Sprintzen suspected that LIPC was viewed as a "radical, left-wing organization," not a serious group worthy of grant funding. A meeting was scheduled in 1984 with Ed Lawrence, the Veatch Program's director. The meeting resulted in the awarding of a $20,000 grant and the beginning of what turned out to be a 30-year relationship that has featured number grants for a variety of progressive actions.

Over the years, LIPC's scope has broadened, its funding expanded, and it has moved away from the coalition structure to becoming a grassroots, membership organization with a staff, a series of projects generally directed by citizen activists. Efforts were made in this direction but it did not work as planned. Most recently, a network of neighborhood-based chapters has emerged. In 1988, LIPC affiliated with Citizen Action of New York (CANY), becoming an autonomous regional affiliate. In 1994, a Massapequa house was donated to the organization to serve as its headquarters by Katherine Smith, a long-time socialist and human rights activist who hosted Norman Thomas and James Farmer, among others.

Sprintzen describes work that LIPC did with the Building Trades Council many years later, after preparing a detailed report on constructive development. They were able to work together even though LIPC and the Council were on opposite sides when it came to the widening of highways. "You have to know how to respect people; treat them respectfully even though you differ."

Sprintzen describes a progressive view of social welfare as one "that views a decent society as one that provides a basic social wage and no individual is destitute. Social welfare programs require adequate funding which can only be provided federally since it is the only source large enough to provide sufficient funding." [40]

Leon A. (Jake) Swirbul (1898-1960)

During World War II, when the United States was furiously striving to turn the tide of battle in the Pacific, Swirbul focused his considerable energy on developing the Grumman Hellcat, the fighter plane that helped the Navy to gain the upper hand.

Swirbul was a sensitive man who looked to solve broad problem-solving issues at Grumman. During the war, he established nurseries for the children of Grumman's female employees thus providing them with peace of mind knowing their children were nearby and being well-taken care of. He also sent an average of 200 employees a year for check-ups at the Mayo Clinic, free of charge and set up a welfare department to help employees with personal problems. Swirbul was famous at Grumman for always having his door open to any employee and never turning them away. His employees called him 'Jake.'

In 1950, Swirbul was asked by radio show host Tex McCrary to contribute to his efforts to raise funds for the new North Shore Hospital. Swirbul, a big thinker, said he would get involved but only if the effort was to raise funds for all Long Island hospitals. His idea and leadership led to the creation of the Long Island Fund which conducted annual corporate and employee gifts to meet the needs for expansion of nonprofit Long Island hospitals and agencies.

According to *Newsday*, ("Jake Swirbul: He Had the Human Touch," June 29, 1960), Swirbul's charity work 'wasn't limited to the successful, large-scale impersonal drives he sparked, backed or conducted for organizations such as the Long Island Fund, the American Cancer Society and the City of Hope.' Swirbul recognized the need to support smaller organizations to get established. He also was very much involved in the development of Long Island's educational facilities. At Adelphi College, Swirbul worked toward the establishment of an Adelphi branch in Suffolk County.

Swirbul anticipated that that Long Island could no longer look to a few families to donate most of the charitable funds needed as Long Island grew. He encouraged others to maintain the tradition of nonprofit community hospitals, built by voluntary contributions, directed by local citizens serving without pay and meeting the health needs of our communities without regard to the individual's national origin, religion, or ability to pay. [41]

Paul Townsend (1919-2005)

In her 2005 *Newsday* obituary about Paul Townsend, staff writer Denise M. Bonilla wisely said: "The life of Paul Townsend in many ways reflects the history of Long Island development itself. His 45 year career as an advocate for Long Island cannot be matched. He was concerned that Long Island develop itself economically and not remain in the shadows of New York City. He used his professional skills and personal passion in these efforts through the establishment in 1953 of the *Long Island Commercial Review* (which was later renamed the *Long Island Business News*)." The "Townsend Letter" became his vehicle in which advocate the causes he believed in.

Townsend was born in Port Washington and grew up in Centerport. After receiving a Bachelor's Degree from Hobart College and a Law Degree from Columbia University, Townsend joined the Army, serving in the Philippines with an intelligence unit. Afterwards, he joined a Manhattan public relations firm and went to work for William Levitt, developer of Levittown in the late 1940s.

Townsend's involvement in Long Island social welfare causes began with his work as a public relations consultant to North Shore University Hospital. This post led to his appointment as chairman of the hospital's board of directors. During this time, Townsend was instrumental in the establishment of The Long Island Fund, the region's first coordinated fund raising effort, assembling the leaders of the Island's substantial industrial, commercial, and labor leaders. Townsend enjoyed relationships people such as Leon A. (Jake) Swirbul, president of Grumman Aircraft, Joseph Gramer, business manager of Local 25 of the International Brotherhood of Electrical Workers (AFL-CIO), George A. Heaney of Security National Bank, Roy Carlton of Sperry Gyroscope, and many others.

From 1951 to 1959, Townsend worked on a part-time basis for the Fund, raising millions of dollars for Long Island hospitals an effort that he was passionate about. This work featured the annual sponsorship of 'Star Nite' celebrity shows held at Roosevelt Raceway and Belmont Racetrack. The events gathered the involvement of nationally-known radio and television, sports, and movie celebrities including Tex and Jinx McCrary, Perry Como, Buddy Hackett, Ester Williams, and Henny Youngman. Later, proceeds of the Fund were not only awarded to hospitals to the growing number of health and welfare organizations being developed to address the needs of Long Island's rapidly-growing population. In 1958, The Fund began the Island's first effort to solicit employee and corporate contributions among retail, commercial, financial, industrial and utility companies, associations and unions.

In 1959, Townsend was asked to become the Fund's director but turned the offer down in order to continue work as president of Townsend Associates with his wife Terry and their numerous other business and community interests. Ultimately, it was Townsend's charitable work that led to the establishment of the United Way of Long Island. Over the years, Townsend's imprint on Long Island grew. He coordinated campaigns to save Republic Airport and to designate Nassau and Suffolk counties as a separate Standard Metropolitan Area from New York City. He and his newspaper actively joined the fight with Fire Island residents and conservationists to establish the Fire Island National Seashore seeking federal authority to oppose Robert Moses' plan to build a four-lane highway through Fire Island. He was also instrumental in the establishment of the nonsectarian golf clubs at Mill River and Old Westbury. [42]

Joyce Moore Turner (1920-

Joyce Moore Turner is a native New Yorker who was born and attended public schools in Harlem. She was the wife of W. Burghardt Turner (1915 - 2009) for sixty-six years, and mother of three children: Mitchell, Sylvia and Richard. Preparation for her professional career and volunteer services included a BA in Chemistry from Hunter College; and both a MA in Nutrition in Public Health, and a Professional Diploma in Supervision and Administration from Columbia University.

Turner worked as a nutritionist for the American Red Cross in Queens, and the New York Tuberculosis and Health Association in Harlem; and as a teacher and assistant principal for Curriculum at the Brentwood Union Free School District in Suffolk County for twenty years. During that time she served as a consultant to the New York State Department of Education and in leadership roles on committees of the Patchogue-Medford Union Free School District and BOCES II. She also taught occasional courses for New York University and Brooklyn College.

When Turner and her husband moved from Jamaica, New York, to Patchogue in 1954 primary health care was provided only by private physicians and there were no institutions of higher learning. They both became active participants in the establishment of health and education institutions in Suffolk County. "She was appointed by County Executive H. Lee Dennison to the initial Suffolk County Economic Opportunity Council in 1964. The Council became the Suffolk County Economic Opportunity Commission and Turner became the first elected chairperson.

Subsequently she also chaired the Nassau-Suffolk Health Systems Agency (1976-1978), the Consortium of Health Systems Agencies of New York State, the Suffolk County Perinatal Coalition, and the South Brookhaven Health Council (1972-1973). She was also involved in the Nassau-Suffolk Comprehensive Health Planning Council, the New York State Governor's Health Advisory Council, the New York State Special Advisory Commission on Minority Enrollment in Medical Schools, the Suffolk County Task Force on Hospitals and Related Services, as well as on the boards of the Brookhaven Memorial Hospital Medical Center, the American Health Planning Association, and the Stony Brook Foundation.

Turner appeared many times before the Suffolk County Legislature on behalf of the concept of community centers which would sponsor Head Start programs along with addressing other local needs, and for neighborhood health centers as sites for comprehensive health care in place of the prevailing inappropriate use of emergency rooms in local hospitals. Despite the opposition of some of the members of the medical profession and government officials she was instrumental, along with other advocates, in helping establish a network of Head Start programs and neighborhood health centers which are still in operation.

In addition Turner was a delegate to the White House Conference on Nutrition, and the White House Conference on Families (1980). She also served on the Board of Directors of the Action Committee for Long Island, the Suffolk County Council, and was a charter member of the Unitarian Fellowship of Brookhaven (now Unitarian Universalist Congregation of the Great South Bay). Her community activities also extended to the Civil Rights Movement, particularly with the executive committee of the Brookhaven Branch of the NAACP in a variety of leadership roles. She initiated a job counseling program which became the model for the Suffolk County Human Rights Commission program.

Her awards include: the Adelphi University "Fellow of the School of Social Work" (1966); the C. W. Post 'Outstanding Leadership in Health Care Planning' (1978); the Suffolk County American Red Cross 'Clara Barton Humanitarian Award' (1981); and the University Hospital and Medical Center of Stony Brook 'Women Pioneers of Suffolk County Health Care. In 2014 Stony Brook University announced the new Joyce Moore Turner Dissertation Fellowship Award that was named in her honor.

Turner and her husband, who was an assistant professor of history at Stony Brook University, collaborated on several works on history including Richard B. Moore, *Caribbean Militant in Harlem,* published by Indiana University Press. She authored *Caribbean Crusaders in the Harlem Renaissance* published by University of Illinois Press which was selected by the Association of College and Research Libraries as one of their Outstanding Academic Titles for 2006. The book is a study of the emergence of African American radicalism in Harlem, a crossroads of the African Diaspora in the early twentieth century. Turner reveals that the Harlem Renaissance was more than just an artistic fluorescence; it was also a political movement to counter racism and colonialism. To explore the roots of the Caribbean emigres' radical ideology and the strategies used to extend agitation from Harlem to national and international platforms, the study draws on the papers and writings of Hermina Huiswoud, Cyril Briggs, the Reverend E. Ethelred Brown, Langston Hughes, and Richard B. Moore. In 2012 her article, "Richard B. Moore and the Caribbean 'Awaymen' Network" was published in The Journal of Caribbean History.

Joyce Moore Turner moved to Tucson, Arizona in 1995, and then to Silver Spring, Maryland in 2006. She continues to be active in community affairs at Riderwood Village where she resides, and has maintained her interest in Suffolk County affairs.

Joyce Moore Turner's career is an example of a community activist whose leadership skills were sought in a variety of community service arenas ranging from poverty, human rights, and health care.

In 1964, when the federal Economic Opportunity Commission of Suffolk was launched with its need for a strong, person to serve as its chair, County Executive H. Lee Dennison called upon Turner to assume this important position. Turner organized efforts against congressional efforts to reduce antipoverty program funding. Dennison also appointed Turner to join his Task Force on Hospitals & Related Services to assure consumer participation in the development of a health care plan.

Turner assumed many important roles in EOC's early development besides chairmanship. As chair of the personnel committee, she maintained high standards in the selection process. She would not yield to attempts to use racism rather than qualifications and logic in the hiring process to select executive directors. This was an especially sensitive matter in the late 1960s when EOC encouraged and facilitated low income adults with little organizational experience to be involved in its community action programs. It took people like Turner to often balance the best interest of the organization with the wishes of some of its outspoken constituency.

In another instance, when a program member was accused of inciting welfare recipients at an OEO center to demonstrate against the county social welfare department, Turner supported the staff member because she felt that she what she had done was consistent with the program's objectives to educate people about their rights and entitlements and encourage people to fight for their rights.

For seventeen years, Turner served as a member of the Nassau-Suffolk Comprehensive Health Planning during that time she served as chairperson of the committee on minority enrollment, chairperson of the planning committee vice-president and president 1986-1988. She also represented the local councils of the Nassau-Suffolk region on the New York State body referred to as TALCOVE (The Association of Local Councils on Vocational Education).

In 1979 U.S. President Jimmy Carter set in motion a series of regional, state and national conferences focusing on families. Turner served on the nominating committee for the Long Island region and as a delegate to the regional meeting of the White House Conference on Families.

When the health systems agency was established in the mid-1970s and required exceptional leadership to mediate competing interests among physicians, hospitals, mental health organizations, and consumers, it was Turner who was asked to lead the organization. She used her personal qualities and organization skills to move the organization forward.

As an educator and community activist, Turner was involved with the Patchogue NAACP chapter's task force on equal employment opportunity joining her husband W. Burghardt Turner. Turner was also a member of the Long Island Action Committee, the Island's leading business association. [43]

W. Burghardt Turner (1915-2009)

The following description of the life of W. Burghardt Turner was written by his wife Joyce Moore Turner.

Wyatt Burghardt Turner was born in Jamaica, New York, the third of eight boys. His parents, Frosty and Frank M. Turner grew up in the small town of Richmond, Kentucky and attended Wilberforce University in Ohio. His father worked as a secretary for Dr. W. E. Burghardt DuBois, who was a professor at Atlanta University, and when DuBois accepted a position with the newly organized National Association for the Advancement of Colored People (NAACP) as editor of the *Crisis* magazine he invited Turner to join him. The two men launched the office of the NAACP in 1910 and Frank Turner was to serve as the accountant for the organization until his death in 1941. When Burghardt was born in 1915 he was named for DuBois.

W. Burghardt Turner, as he identified himself, attended public school in Jamaica, then switched to the segregated high school in Richmond KY, in order to help care for his grandmother. He attended Kentucky State College and graduated cum laude with majors in history and sociology. He returned to New York in order to attend the graduate history program at Columbia University. He married Joyce Webster Moore who was also a graduate student at Columbia. The World War II military draft interrupted his education and he was assigned to the 92nd Division headquartered first at Fort McCellan, Alabama, and later at Fort Huachuca in Arizona. He passed tests offered by the army for officers' training school but was denied the opportunity to attend advance training by his commanding officer whose policy was that no white service man should ever be commanded by an African American officer. As a result of a back injury he was reassigned to an engineer truck company with which he served in Italy for one year. Following his discharge in 1946 he resumed graduate study and earned a Master's Degree with the assistance of the GI Bill, but did not have sufficient funds to complete his Ph.D. dissertation. He obtained a job teaching social studies at a girls' junior high school in Harlem, then worked as an archivist for the Navy Department in Pennsylvania.

Turner was eager to return to New York and took a job in Suffolk County as a claims examiner for the Social Security Administration in Patchogue. The house he and his wife chose to purchase disappeared off the market when the neighbors noticed the buyer's complexion. They had to resort to having a close white friend buy the house and then turn it over to them. Later when Turner decided to return to teaching, he submitted applications to twenty-five school districts on Long Island and was rejected. A Columbia University MA, courses toward a Ph. D. in history, New York State teaching certificates, and teaching experience in New York City were not sufficient credentials for an African American male despite the pressing need for teachers at the time. He eventually obtained a job as a sixth grade teacher in Bay Shore in 1956, and the following year as a social studies teacher at Patchogue-Medford High School.

Turner took leave in 1965 to be the director of the National Education Association's Project on Civil Rights and Continuing Education, where he was responsible for developing a nationwide program to effect the merger of segregated NEA teachers' associations. The task of integrating the organization was challenging because of the resistance of white teachers and the reluctance of African American teachers to relinquish the power they had gained in their own organizations.

Turner's move to Suffolk County in 1954 coincided with the area's growing interest in higher education and he continuously supported various plans for the development of colleges. Suffolk Community College started with classes in a high school in 1959 and moved in 1962 into the building which had been the county sanatorium for tuberculosis patients. Also in 1959 Adelphi University established a four year Adelphi Suffolk College in an old public school building in Sayville, and then relocated in 1963 to the Vanderbilt estate in Oakdale as Dowling College. C.W. Post College established Southampton College in 1963. Turner taught some history and sociology courses there and was associate director of the Institute on School Integration conducted in the summer of 1966 to prepare teachers to deal with problems ensuing from the integration of schools. The establishment of the State University of New York at Stony Brook in 1962, following its start in an Oyster Bay mansion in 1957, was the grandest and most significant gift advancing higher education that the State of New York could grant the people of Suffolk and Nassau Counties. With no vested interests to block the establishment of colleges, Suffolk County was transformed within four short years by the development of a two year state college, a state university, and two private four year colleges.

"n *From the Ground Up: A History of the State University of New York at Stony Brook*, professor Joel Rosenthal, reminds us that restrictive housing covenants were still shaping the Long Island social and economic scene at the time the university was established. He described the neighborhood climate as 'conservative, heavily white, slow to accept Blacks.' It was not simply the denials of housing and employment, and other racist attacks Turner suffered personally that led to his decision to establish a branch of the NAACP. His family background and his study of history had established an understanding of racism in the nation, and colonialism around the world.

The Patchogue Branch of the NAACP, which later became the Brookhaven NAACP, was founded by Turner in 1962 to address hate crimes and discrimination in the education and health care systems. The welcome sign of a cross, burning on the lawn of a home purchased by Augustus and Willa Prince in Port Jefferson when he joined the staff of physicists at Brookhaven National Laboratory in 1966 was one of the typical cases referred to the local NAACP.

It was Turner's leadership as president of the local NAACP that led to his affiliation with Stony Brook University. When the chairman of the history department, Hugh Cleland, got to know Turner he questioned why he was teaching in a high school with credentials almost equivalent to a Ph.D. At that time Professor Cleland was in need of a history professor who would conduct classes on the teaching of history. He recognized the wealth of experience Turner had gained while teaching at all levels of education. The invitation to teach at Stony Brook was very attractive but paid considerably less than the salary Turner had helped his Patchogue colleagues negotiate with the Board of Education. After much deliberation, the decision was made in 1968 to take a year's leave of absence and accept the offer. Thus, he became the first African American to teach in the History Department at Stony Brook University. He taught 'Materials and Methods of Teaching Social Studies' and introduced new courses on African American History and Native American History. He attained tenure as an assistant professor but had to accept the title 'Professor Emeritus' in 1979 because of his loss of vision due to Graves Disease.

Throughout his years at Stony Brook University, Turner continued his involvement with the local, regional and New York State organizations of the NAACP, served as chairperson of the Suffolk County Human Relations Commission, was a charter member of the Unitarian Fellowship of Brookhaven, served as an officer of the Legal Aid Society of Suffolk County and the United Fund of Long Island. He also served a term as chairperson of the Suffolk County Economic Council. In 1969, Stony Brook's President, John Toll, established the University Equal Employment Opportunity Committee and appointed him chairman. The twenty-one members appointed initially represented administration, faculty, students, service departments, and the community. At the first meeting, Dr. Toll explained that while contending with the State University Construction Fund to increase employment of African

Americans in the building program, he realized the university had undertaken no systematic effort to insure equal opportunity in the positions it controlled. He charged the committee to survey all jobs on campus and develop a program to increase the employment of disadvantaged persons and minority groups.

The minutes of the meeting reveal that after considerable discussion on the mission, Turner pointed out that it was no longer enough merely to hire African Americans and Puerto Ricans who presented themselves for employment; it was necessary to seek members of such groups, train them for available jobs, and encourage them to move forward once employed. He had distributed a statement in which he made a distinction between the terms 'equal opportunity' and 'affirmative action.' He pointed out that in order to provide true equal opportunity it might be necessary to discriminate in the same way that handicappers do at the race track. He considered that to try to treat everyone equally would be to accept the disparity that currently existed and that the committee would have to devise a program that 'gives a push forward and a lift upward to the person that the American society has for so long pushed down and held back; who has been made to even see himself as powerless, hopeless and worthless.' His concept of affirmative action was of a program designed to eliminate the hobbling disparity that existed in order for equal opportunity to be achieved. The committee adopted a motion to expand the mandate to cover construction problems, campus employment, and training program.

> The Underrepresented Graduate Fellowship Program established in 1987 by the New York State Legislature was named for W. Burghardt Turner at Stony Brook. He considered the program the best model to assure contributions to society that in the past had remained unrealized. The second honor was bestowed in 2007 when Stony Brook granted him an Honorary Degree, Doctor of Humane Letters. He considered that those two honors represented an appreciation of his joint efforts as an academic and as a community activist. Not only did he revel in the act of teaching, he believed that academia has a responsibility to contribute to the making of history, and thereby move society closer to a realization of democracy. His concept of 'town and gown' considered the university a resource for the community, a promoter of equality rather than elitism, a model of responsible citizenship, as well as a reservoir of intellectual pursuits and understandings of the real world, organized to prepare future leaders of society. He often counseled the TurnerFellows that their responsibility was not solely to master their fields but to serve as resources and leaders in their communities.

Among Turner's publications are articles on Joel A Rogers in *'Negro History Bulletin';* and *'Black Scholar';* on Richard B. Moore in *'Caribbean Studies Journal';* introductions to new Black Classic Press editions of *'The Name*

"Negro' Its Origin and Evil Use' by Richard B. Moore, and *'The Negro'* by W E. Burghardt DuBois; a chapter on *'The Polemecists'* in *Black American Writers'*; and as co-editor with Joyce Moore Turner for the book, *'Richard B. Moore - Caribbean Militant in Harlem.'*

While Turner would be the first to suggest that the institutional changes which occurred in Suffolk County might have happened without his efforts, the point is that he was an active participant, and a leader who involved others in many organizations and institutions in order to improve the lives of residents. A multitude of contributions and coalitions were needed to create the changes that took over a half century to be implemented.

It is important to take into account the success of the Civil Rights Movement at the national level that removed laws, regulations and practices that had re-enforced denial of voting rights and segregation for two centuries. Efforts at the local level, however, also played a role. Change occurred in Suffolk County due to the impact of the wisdom shared by the university that was combined with the voices released by the Great Society programs. Most importantly, the governments of Suffolk County, New York State, and the nation all invested in and supported innovative programs in education and health, and provided jobs.

We must not forget that Stony Brook served as an important economic stimulus for Long Island; the university became the largest employer in Suffolk County. Its growth also supported the expansion and success of local businesses, as well as raised the level of job opportunities for minority residents. The process of building education and health systems through investments by community members and three levels of government was a model of leadership and democracy at work.[44]

Pauline Velazques (1931-2014)

Pauline Velazques was born in Santurce Puerto Rico. When she was 13, she moved to New York City with her sister Petra when she was 13. n 1951 she married Roberto Velazquez and they had three children: Roberto, Ana Delia and Evelyn. In 1967 she also became the caregiver/mother to her nephew and two nieces: Diana, Joseph and Mercedes.

In 1965, she and Roberto moved to Brentwood where she has resided ever since. Her employment history is as varied and colorful as Velazques herself. Initially, she trained and worked as a beautician for several years. She also worked as a seamstress in the local factory. Later, she became a teaching assistant and school attendance officer. In that capacity, she became well known by the students in Brentwood's schools, becoming both 'sheriff' and mother to many.

Velazques always recognized the value of education and over the years became an example herself, earning her Masters of Social Work from New York University in 1983. She worked as a senior advocate for Suffolk County until she retired from that position. But retirement for Pauline only meant finding another outlet to utilize her knowledge and compassion. She continued to work for Pronto of Suffolk County as a social worker.

Over her years as a social worker, Velazques dealt with many aspects of the aging process and the services needed to support the elderly. She was instrumental in securing New York State legislation to assist low income senior citizens with property tax relief. In fact, the bill was named the Velazquez Bill in honor of her contribution to the process. She held membership on many civic, educational and community organization and distinguished herself as a leader within Long Island's Hispanic community and beyond.

One of her passions was the Nassau/Suffolk Hispanic Task Force which she chaired for many years implementing conferences to develop legislative agendas for the Long Island Hispanic community that still serve today as a guide for statewide lobbying efforts. Velazques was a founder and active member of this organization for years. She became the president of the organization. She was also a founder and active member of Adelante of Suffolk County, a referral agency for the Hispanic community. The organization is responsible for the annual Suffolk County Puerto Rican Day parade of which she was named Grand Marshall.

Some of the many honors Velazques received in her lifetime are reflective of both her compassion and spirit of activism including: Hispanic Social Worker of the Year; Governor's Community Service Award; Lifetime Achievement Award by National Organization of Puerto Rican Women; Inductee to the Latina Women's Society Hall of Fame; a *Newsday* "An Everyday Hero"; an outstanding role model for the Latino Community by Diocese of Rockville Centre and Fleet Bank; and Lifetime Achievement Award from the National Association of Puerto Rican/Hispanic Social Workers. [45]

Phyllis Vineyard (1924-1996)

Throughout the 1970s and 1980s, Phyllis Vineyard of Bellport was an extremely active member of Long Island's social welfare community. She was the founding president of Planned Parenthood of Suffolk and the first woman elected to the Long Island Lighting Company's board of directors. Born in Ridgefield Connecticut, Vineyard and her husband George, the director of Brookhaven National Laboratories, moved to Long Island to become very active citizens.

For many years, Vineyard served as president of the Suffolk Community Council guiding the organization as the county's clearinghouse for information about social issues and spokesman for the voluntary sector. She also served as chair to several community organizations including the Women's Health and Counseling Center in Farmingdale, the State University Council of Old Westbury, the Corporate Initiative for Child and Elder Care. Her concern regarding maternal and child health caused her to play an active role as a board member of the South Brookhaven Health Council.

She was especially passionate regarding population issues and was a member and former chair of the Board of Population Institute while also chair of the New York State Health Coordinating Council and a founding member of the Long Island Community Foundation, an affiliate of the New York Community Trust.'

In a 1983, *Newsday* article, *"Helping Women Enter the Boardroom,"* Vineyard urged women in leadership not to be 'corporate pawns' saying it is dangerous to be on the outside, because you do not have access to information…women must avoid being perceived as favoring one person or another on the board over another, or one executive over another. You must demonstrate total fairness,' she said. She also encouraged women to sit on unpaid nonprofit boards where they can effect social change. [46]

Ralph Watkins (1927-2002)

(In 2002, Newsday reporter Martin C. Evans wrote an obituary about Ralph Watkins. The following is excerpted from this obituary).

In 1963, Ralph Watkins was an Air Force veteran who worked with an elite group of aviation specialists - air traffic controllers - helping to make the skies safe for commercial flight. A well-read man, he loved books, listened to opera, and soon developed a fondness for sailing on the Sound.

But when he moved to Kings Park, someone burned a cross on his lawn just the same. "We woke up one night, and there it was," his former wife, Frances Watkins. "But there was always vandalism the first year we were here. We would have to go out and rake the garbage off the lawn every morning."

Watkins, a black man who grew up in segregated Baltimore and became a champion for civil rights on segregated Long Island. Many who knew the Port Jefferson resident said he was a determined but steadying influence during Long Island's passage through the racially turbulent 1960s and 1970s. "Until you got to know him, which fortunately for me wasn't long, he could be intimidating, but you got the feeling he was right about the stuff he cared about," said Aaron Godfrey, a lecturer at Stony Brook University. 'He did not care if you were black or white, if you were a friend, he would walk a mile for you.'

In 1963, fresh from his battle to buy his Kings Park home, Watkins was named one of the Suffolk Human Rights Commission's original members. During his 12-year tenure, the commission developed a swashbuckling style - bold, anti-establishment, confrontational style that contrasted with the conservatism of its Nassau County counterpart.

On September 21, 1967, when a *Newsday* reporter asked him if he intended to "make waves," as the chairman of the Suffolk Human Relations Commission, he replied, "If making changes is making waves, we will make waves." And make waves he did.

In 1968, he asked Sen. Robert F. Kennedy (D-N.Y.) to check allegations of job discrimination at Grumman. Soon, Grumman hired 28 black workers. In 1969, after he staged a one-man sit-in, the Central Islip school board agreed to teach black history and expand minority hiring. But many of his ideas - including a countywide housing plan and integrating classrooms by consolidating school districts - fell on deaf ears. He resigned from the commission in 1975, after it declined to back a United Farm Workers boycott of grapes.

Instead, he directed his activism toward his work at Stony Brook University, where he directed programs for disadvantaged students and Vietnam War veterans from 1968 to 1979. His own career began in 1945, when he enlisted in the Army Air Forces, and eventually was promoted to Air Force lieutenant. "After his honorable discharge, Watkins studied at Morgan State College in Baltimore. He then married his former wife in 1955. They had one son, Ralph, who died in a 1991 workplace accident. He moved his family to Long Island in the early '60s, eventually settling in Kings Park.

Friends said the hostility he faced persuaded him to fight so people could live where they wanted to live. "He stood for right and fought for right," said fellow commissioner Fred H. Morris Jr. of Stony Brook." [47]

Notes to Part III

1. Information obtained from organization's website: www.prontoli.org.
2. Kenneth Anderson, telephone interviews and written material provided to author during Spring 2014.
3. José Avila, interview with author, Hauppauge, NY, August 10, 1014.
4. Karl Grossman, written material provided to author.
5. Leone Baum, interview with author, Hempstead, NY, March 2, 2014.
6. Lucille Buerghers, email correspondence with author, June 5, 2014.
7. Jamir Couch, email correspondence with author, August 28, 2014.
8. Nancy Rauch Douzinas, email correspondence with author, July 15, 2014.

9. Information obtained from NAACP website: www.nysnaacp.org/officers.html.
10. Marge Harrison, email correspondence with author, June 7, 2014.
11. Roberta Hunter, interview with author, Riverhead, NY, July 11, 2014.
12. Mel Jackson, email correspondence with author and information on organization's website: www.lti.org.
13. Rene Fiechter and Lillian McCormick, interviews with author and Hofstra Law School's website: www.hofstra.edu.
14. L. Von Kuhen and Adelaide Klatsky, author interviews September 15, 2014.
15. Richard Koubek, email correspondence with author, September, 2014.
16. Lilo Leeds, interview with author, Great Neck, NY, July 15, 2014.
17. Peter Levy, interview with author, Hicksville, NY, August 1, 2014.
18. Joyce Spencer Insolia and Kenneth Anderson, email correspondence with author, Spring 2014.
19. Lillian McCormick, email correspondence with author, Spring 2014.
20. Marcia Spector and Andy Casazza, email correspondence and telephonic interviews with author,
21. Lee Koppelman and Tom Williams, interviews with author, Spring, 2014 and author's personal remembrances of Anne Mead.
22. Steve Englebright and Tom Williams, interviews with author, Summer, 2014.
23. Information obtained from Stony Brook University's School of Social Welfare website: http://socialwelfare.stonybrookmedicine.edu/.
24. Sonia Palacio Grotolla, email correspondence with author, Fall, 2014.
25. Davis Pollack, interview with author,
26. Steve Englebright and Tom Williams, interviews with author, Spring
27. Delores and Madeline Quintyne, email correspondence of Spring, 2014.
28. Newsday article "A Tortoise Pace for Civil Rights on LI" (May 29, 1978) and Collection of the Suffolk Community Council (Special Collections and University Archives at Stony Brook University).
29. Cynthia Barnes, email correspondence and written material provided to author, Summer, 2014.
30. Marge Rogatz, interview with author, Manhasset, NY, July 20, 2014.
31. Charles Russo, interview with author, Hauppauge, NY, April 3, 2014.
32. Lillian McCormick, email correspondence with author and author's personal recollections.
33. Joan Saltzman, interview with author, Great Neck, NY, July 14, 2014.
34. Janet Schaberg Walsh, email correspondence with author, September, 2014.
35. Betty Schlein, email correspondence with author, June, 2014.
36. Information obtained on organization's website: www.nami.org.
37. Marilyn Shellabarger, email correspondence with author, November, 2014.
38. Joyce Spencer Insolia, interview with author, Northport, NY, April 22, 2014.

39. Information obtained on organization's website: www.prontoli.org.
40. David Sprintzen, interview with author, Hicksville, NY, April 7, 2014.
41. Information obtained from Newsday articles cited in Part II, Chapter II.
42. Information obtained from Newsday articles cited in Part II, Chapter II.
43. Information obtained in written form from Joyce Turner.
44. Information obtained in written form from Joyce Turner.
45. Information obtained from organization's website: www.naprhsw.org.
46. Collection of the Suffolk Community Council (Special Collections and University Archives at Stony Brook University).
47. Information obtained from Office of Diversity and Affirmative Action at Stony Brook University and Collection of the Suffolk Community Council (Special Collections and University Archives at Stony Brook University).

Part IV

Significant Changes Since 1985

Overview

George H. W. Bush and Bill Clinton Presidencies. Rise of Multiculturalism and Alternative Media. Thawing of Cold War. Increased Skepticism towards Government. The dissolution of the Soviet Union. Rodney King Beating. Rwandan and Bosnian genocides. Oklahoma City Bombing. Million Man March. World Trade Center bombing and the Oklahoma City Bombing. Million Man March in Washington DC. AIDS Crisis. Tiananmen Square. Nelson Mandela Freed and Elected President of South Africa. Fall of Berlin Wall. Global Warming Awareness. AIDS Crisis. Black Monday on Stock Exchange. Pan Am Flight 103 Bombed. Exxon Valdez Oil Spill. Tiananmen Square Uprising.

George W. Bush Presidency. CHADS in Florida. September 11th Attacks. Japanese Tsunami. War in Afghanistan. Second Intifida. Earthquakes in El Salvador. The Great Recession. Iraq War. Al-Qaeda Terrorism. Hurricane Katrina. Second Intifada in Israel. Marcelo Lucero Murder. Mexican Drug Wars. War in Darfur. Civil Wars in Somali and Angola. Earthquakes in El Salvador.

Barack Obama Presidency. Haitian Earthquakes. Emergency Economic Stabilization Act. BP Deepwater Horizon Oil Spill. Chilean Earthquake. Sendai Japan Tsunami. Hurricane Irene. Mexican Drug Wars. Arab Spring. Tea Party. Occupy Wall Street. WikiLeaks. U.S. Troops to Afghanistan. War on Terrorism. Boston Marathon Bombing. Pope Francis. Malaysian Airlines Flight 370. Superstorm Sandy. Greater Acceptance of GLBT People. Edward Snowden Leaks. Congressional Impasse. Michael Brown Death in Ferguson Missouri. North Charleston Police Murder of Michael Thomas Slager.

Politically, the national scene became extremely polarized between liberal and conservative philosophies of government with ongoing impasses among the legislative and executive branches of government with the result that little aid flowed to localities to address their infrastructure problems and the other socio-economic problems they faced. Meanwhile, the tremendous growth of the state's Medicaid program placed financial pressure on the state as well.

Demographic Factoid

By 2013, Long Island's population had grown to 2,851,929 residents with the majority living, for the first time, living in Suffolk County. Suffolk County had 1,499,783 residents while Nassau County had 1,352,146. Suffolk's growth rate since 1980 was 16.8 percent while Nassau experienced a much more modest growth rate of 2.0 percent.

A more detailed review of Long Island population growth rate since 1945, reveals that the total population grew by 267 percent since 1945 with Suffolk County's rate of 485 percent far-surpassing Nassau's rate of 154 percent by more than three times. [1]

In 2013, Long Island's white population represented 67% of the total population as compared to 77% in 2000 representing significant growth among racial and ethnic minorities in just thirteen years. The Hispanic population grew by 56 percent from 2000 and 2010 representing 15.5 percent of the population. Hispanics organized themselves and successfully gained elected political offices in both counties. In addition, substantial growth occurred in the over age-65 population especially in Nassau County as the result of the baby boomer population entering traditional retirement age. Meanwhile, many older adults unable to afford to retire on Long Island with its high taxes and energy costs, fled to warmer climates taking their savings, purchasing power, and social capital with them. [2]

The Hispanic population also grew substantially since 1985 especially among people who arrived after fleeing political and economic turmoil in their native countries of Central and South America. In some communities, their arrival has resulted in tensions and conflicts that have plagued Long Island as these newly-arrived black and brown people assimilated while facing racism and discrimination. [3]

(For further discussion of immigration issues, see The Hagedorn Foundation profile in this chapter).

During the period, Long Island's population of military veterans grew as men and women returned from tours of duty in the Middle East. According to the Department of Veterans Affairs, there are 5,000 Iraq and Afghanistan veterans living on Long Island and one in two has a mental health issue. 5,500 Long Island veterans are homeless. Veterans often brought with them serious health and mental health conditions requiring services that did not exist such as post-traumatic stress disorder, traumatic brain disorder. According to the department, eighteen veterans commit suicide daily. Many need employment opportunities and affordable housing. [4]

In addition, part of Long Island's demographic change has been the rise of the population of gay, lesbian, bisexual, and transgendered people. They often faced discrimination and a lack of access to services such as counseling, mental health and support groups as well as advocacy for victims of violence, sexual assault, hate or bias crimes or pick-up crimes. The population sometimes also needs opportunities for specialized social and supportive discussions for young people, seniors, women and parents. [5]

For additional demographic information, visit the Appendix.

A major Long Island problem that has grown in dimension is a lack of affordable housing perhaps especially for young people who want to work on Long Island near their families and friends. This lack of affordable housing stock has forced many to leave Long Island, taking their knowledge and skills with them. In *"The Future of Fair Housing in a Diverse Suburbia,"* a chapter in *Social Justice in Diverse Suburbs,* Powell and Reece report that "recent statistics from suburban Long Island exemplify national trends. Despite being one of the nation's wealthiest suburban areas, Long Island has not been immune to the economic crisis. Not only has Long Island led New York State in its rate of distressed mortgages; the population that receives public assistance has increased by 20 percent between 2009 and 20101, far greater than the 3 percent increase in New York City during the same period." The authors also inform us that the nation's suburbs, including Long Island are growing more diverse. They further remind us that "although some people of color have gained access to premier communities of opportunity by moving to the suburbs, far too many are moving to suburban communities that are experiencing economic, fiscal, and social challenges.[6]

Martin R. Cantor, CPA, director of the Long Island Center for Socio-Economic Policy at Dowling College has conducted a number of studies regarding Long Island that help to portray key economic changes that impact Long Island today. In one of these studies Cantor says:

"Long Island once had prime military contractors such as Fairchild-Republic, Eaton, Sperry, Hazeltine and Grumman Corporation. Today, it has none. This contraction has led to manufacturing workforce reductions, which continue today, impacting much of the regions less skilled and less educated workers. At the same time, influenced largely by the globalization of economic events, the demand for more skilled and more educated workers has been growing in Long Island's high technology industries and in the growing financial and banking sector." So, according to Cantor, "the mystery of what Long Island is to become is yet before us. To be sure, the requirements to succeed in the global economy are much more complex than what was required for success in the economy and society during the heady days after the end of World War II, when returning veterans found their way here and built America's first suburb. How Long Island succeeds, and what it will look like, will be very dependent on how Long Islanders adapt to the constant changes in the global economy; how we accept our newest residents; and how we understand the economic potential of communities of color and the importance of economic equality and opportunity." [7]

Economists suggest that Long Island's economic challenge today is to reduce heavy reliance on service industries and expand opportunities in small business innovations and technology and increase investments in infrastructure, especially in affordable rental housing located near transportation hubs. They also urge steps be taken to provide educational and training opportunities that produce a workforce whose skills match the needs of the changing environment.

Millennials who became unemployed after the Great Recession and cannot find affordable housing to enable them to leave their parents' homes may also be a group for social welfare advocates to target to support reform measures. Cantor provides insights into the importance of Millennials to Long Island's future:

Having the Millennials remain is critical because they are Long Island's future middle class, with much of this new middle class creating a demand for housing. Over 90 percent of responding Millennials live with their parents or relatives, or rent apartments, with nearly the same percent of Millennials planning to purchase their own home. This future market for housing will sustain local housing values and cannot be allowed to leave. Something young people through their responses predict they will.[8]

It has been well-documented that the suburbs are changing. The suburban stereotype of uniformly prosperous, financially stable, politically-conservative voters is no longer the case. A 2012 survey conducted by the National Center for Suburban Studies at Hofstra University, suggests that continued progressive reform in the suburbs may be possible. The survey indicates that "a majority of suburban voters support higher taxes on the wealthy and government action to 'substantially reduce' income disparity." The poll showed suburbanites supportive of social spending, especially for the elderly, than of tax cuts. "Forty-four (44%) percent of survey respondents reported living paycheck to paycheck; 73 percent said they had lost a job or knew someone who had; and 43 percent said they or someone they knew had lost a home. Two in five suburbanites, 40 percent, say they live paycheck to paycheck always or most of the time. More than half of suburbanites, 51 percent, now fear they will not have enough money to live on when they retire. That is an increase of eight percentage points since 2008. [9]

In a 2014 interview with Lawrence Levy, director of the National Center for Suburban Studies at Hofstra University, Levy provided the following description of the emergence of Long Island as a suburb and the evolution of social service and social action programs since the end of World War II.

He sees the nonprofit sector changing as the field's founding professional leaders are aging and retiring, causing a need for a new generation of leaders. He also sees some philanthropic sources ceasing to support the causes they did in the past or likely not to exist in the future. The founding professionals may have been very good at what they did fifty years ago but the demands of operating nonprofits today have changed dramatically creating a need for a different type of leadership. "There is more segmentation and specialization in the delivery of services, a greater level of sophistication and red tape required by government funders, and less certainty about funding. There is also a much greater need for understanding of diverse cultures and the impact of language barriers," says Levy. In addition, Levy sees the fact that the population has aged as another contributing factor that challenges nonprofit service providers to think and act differently.

Levy feels that the old guard of professional leaders dedicated their lives to the organizations that they lead and, in many instances, have resisted change, the consolidation or merger of their operations and are now entrenched in their personal needs to hold onto the power and prestige that they earned over many years.

Levy reports that Long Island has spent more on discretionary budget items relative to its population than New York City. He feels that Long Island politicians have worked across party lines without substantial ideological battles to support public funding for social welfare programs and believes that they will continue to do so.

He says that there has also been a big change in the corporate landscape. The aerospace industry, a major supporter of nonprofits in the past, shrunk in size substantially. Many other large corporations merged with other institutions with the result that the larger did not give as much as the total companies that were absorbed.

Levy feels that Long Islanders, are more moderate and tolerant than they are often given credit for and have been willing to tax themselves to near the breaking point to fund programs they feel are important and that includes social services. He points to a national suburban poll that the center conducted as indicative that Long Islanders are willing to spend tax dollars on the young, poor, sick and aged and are reluctant to lay off public workers to balance the budget. For all the discrimination and segregation that persists today, Levy feels there is still "a good strong heart that bleeds on Long Island. Levy views suburbanites as evolutionary in their conservatism. "They are open to new ideas and change but change takes time. It is as if they need to get used to it and will accept change as long as they do not feel it will affect their overall quality of life. They're also sensitive to the needs of the sandwich generation to care for dependent elders. In projecting into the future, Levy believes that nonprofits need to cultivate new relationships with wealthy, younger Long Islanders who have accumulated substantial wealth such as hedge fund managers.

Levy is, therefore, optimistic that suburbanites will continue to evolve. As more and more of them experience the need to house their children and parents on Long Island, they will change and begin to accept the need to change zoning regulations that limit the amount of higher density housing. They will do so out of their own self- interest. Levy points to Paul Pontieri, the village's mayor, as an example of what can be accomplished by a skillful politician who worked over many years to transform the village into a diverse, vibrant community.

In a 2014 interview with Rene Fiechter, Esq., Director, Community Affairs, Nassau District Attorney's Office and former Deputy Executive Director of EACINC Fiechter provided background on Nassau's development of a county legislature and drug treatment court system.

According to Fiechter, Nassau established its county legislature in 1996 after 100 years of operating under the control of a board of supervisors. This significant change began in 1993 when United States District Court Judge Arthur D. Spatt ruled the county board of supervisors' form of government unconstitutional based on the fact that it did not represent one person, one vote. A Commission on Government Revision was established redefining the role of the County Executive; creating an independent budget review office; changed the fiscal year and budget review process; and strengthened the code of ethics. The commission also proposed a map consisting of 19 legislative districts and adopted it in 1994. The formation of the legislature changed the system of government in Nassau County, increasing representation and mandating two minority districts. The first election for the legislature took place in November 1995 and the historic first session began on January 1, 1996.

Fiechter also reports that drug treatment courts were developed in the 1990s as a way to divert many convicted drug offenders into substance abuse residential programs as an alternative to incarceration. Christine Hunter was a driving force in fostering the operation and development of drug treatment courts in both Nassau County district and family court and, in 1992 spearheaded the drive to have the drug treatment court licensed and accredited by the New York State Office of Alcoholism and Substance Abuse Services (OASAS), the first such drug treatment court program of its kind in New York State. As a result of those innovative criminal justice courts, additional special courts have since been formed for DWI offenders, veterans and mental health patient offenders. Today, Hunter is supervisor of Drug and Alcohol Treatment Services at the Nassau County Correctional Facility and in 2014 was appointed by the Nassau County executive as the chairperson of the Ryan White Nassau Suffolk HIV Health Services Planning Council.

The following description of the Nassau County Legislature is written by Peter Levy, Esq., the unpaid president of the Coalition of Nassau County Youth Service Agencies, Inc.

"A unique and at times fascinating feature of Nassau's legislature, since its inception, has been the public comment period held usually at the beginning of each Legislative meeting. These public comments from a cross-section of Nassau's citizens who have found these periods to be an excellent opportunity to directly address government on matters of personal concern or global implication. All speakers are allotted three minutes in the spotlight and for the most part the legislators listen and react.

"Although often months go by in a year without any significant news from the legislature, Nassau County's legislature has taken an active role in the budget process. Currently, the county executive submits the next calendar year's budget to the legislature on September 15th of each year. The legislature spends the next six weeks holding hearings, making additions and subtractions and finally approving the budget by its deadline of October 31st.

"From almost the beginning, the community-based nonprofit organizations that serve the public in Nassau County have appeared before the legislature. On a regular basis the executive directors, board members and clients of these organizations have stood before the legislators to update them on their work, educate them as to the needs of the community and seek the financial resources necessary to sustain their existence. These include times when funding has been severely slashed and other times completely eliminated, depending open the county's then-current financial outlook.

"Unfortunately for these nonprofits, the financial standing of the county has never been bright in the years since the legislature's inception. The concept of 'light at the end of the tunnel' has yet to reach Nassau County's books and, therefore, nonprofits' funding struggles continue."

In Suffolk County, the county legislature matured into a deliberative entity with both Republicans and Democrats holding majorities at different times since the legislature was established in 1970. With legislatures now operating in both counties, nonprofit organizations focused their attention on educating legislators about their constituents' needs and the worthiness of their organizations while both counties dealt with one budget crisis after another. County funding of non-mandated services to nonprofit organizations was reduced. Virtually no new programs were established while some were eliminated altogether.

According to Vera Parisi, former New York State Division for Human Rights Regional Director for Suffolk County and executive director from the American Civil Liberties' Suffolk chapter, charges of discrimination in housing, employment, sexual harassment, and police brutality especially of the poor a and disabled continued to be filed with her office. [10]

In a 2014 interview with New York State Assemblyman Steve Englebright, he described his work at the state level since 1992.

In 1992, Englebright was elected to the state assembly seat vacated when Robert Gaffney was elected Suffolk County executive. Englebright felt that his desire to continue to protect the Pine Barrens needed to now focus at the state level. His initial focus was to advocate for passage of the Pine Barrens Protection Act whose prime sponsor was Tom DiNapoli, now the state's controller. Englebright also became the prime author of numerous other environmental initiatives.

Later, for five years, Englebright served as chairman of the Assembly Committee on Aging. Paul Harenberg of Bay Port had served in this capacity for many years instituting many progressive projects. His initial focus was to seek the dismissal of the then-director of the State Office for the Aging. His policy concern was primarily the need to establish policy to address the needs of the tremendous population of baby boomers. He worked closely with New York State Senator George Maziarz of Rochester to shepherd passage of legislation to license assisted living facilities. This involved Englebright visiting many assisted living facilities and gaining the support of assisted living organizations. He helped them to see that their good names were being harmed by unscrupulous operators and that they should voluntarily develop licensing regulations to be passed into law rather than waiting for legislators to do so.

Currently, Englebright serves as senior member of the Long Island Assembly Delegation and chairman of the State Committee on Government Operations overseeing over 30 agencies. He has three priorities at this time: Greater environmental protection for Long Island; the development of some form of 'floodgates' to protect New York City from Sandy-like storms; and reinforcement of residential and community-based programs for older adults including an insurance program for long term care in a manner similar to the Social Security payroll deduction system.

Englebright points to the rising costs of Medicaid as the 'Achilles Heel' of the state budget due to the aging of the sizable baby boomer population and their eligibility for coverage of long term care under Medicaid. Unfortunately, he says, the federal government appears unwilling to develop a national long term care program so it is left to each state to decide whether to address the issue. He also notes a limited array of advocates on this issue at this time. He says that they tend to be focused on one issue at a particular time or their personal agendas not on the big picture. Englebright feels that long term care of the elderly should be one of the highest priorities on the state's agenda. He is hopeful that, as state legislators begin to experience their own long term issues they will begin to act. He wishes he was still chairman of the Aging Committee so he could more forcefully push on the issues. The other important issue that he feels requires greater attention to the needs of suburbia and, in particular, the need for affordable intergenerational housing on Long Island that, he believes, should be constructed above shopping centers and in downtown villages particularly ones where railroad access is present.

Englebright describes state government as very different from the 'intimacy' of county government. He says state government is big, tough environment but a forum in which you can occasionally get important things done. It takes a decade to learn who is on first base and who is on second base. He says that there are moments of elation and despair. He points to Long Island as a place that pioneered many significant environmental advances of national significance including the first environmental impact statement at JFK airport, the Fire Island National Seashore, and the Farmland Preservation Program.

The following discussion is the result of a 2014 interview with Gregory Blass about his service as a Suffolk County Legislator, Family Court Judge, and Commissioner of Social Services.

In Suffolk County, in 1989, Democrat Patrick Halpin defeated Michael Lo Grande for the county executive position making Halpin the first Democrat to be elected county executive since H. Lee Dennison's election in 1960. Republican Gregory Blass from the East End served in an important position during this period as the loyal opposition holding onto the Republican caucus while getting things done working with Democrats and also being re-elected repeatedly as presiding officer and minority leader. Former *Newsday* columnist Lawrence Levy wrote a February 1989 article about how some of his fellow Republicans did not like Blass: "But the saving grace for taxpayers is that he is a serious legislator. Even a Democrat like Halpin's deputy executive for human services, Evelyn Roth, says Blass is strong on social issues, citing his efforts in affordable housing."

In 1989, Blass left the legislature after losing a primary to Michael Caracchiolo, who showed little interest in social programs but whose staff, once Blass's staff, worked well on social service issues for constituents. From

1989 – 1993: Blass was in private practice/family law then returned to legislature for two years 93-95. He also served as attorney for the Village of Greenport.

During Blass's term as a Family Court Judge, from 1996-2005, he helped effect a number of reforms. The period saw the County Attorney's office assume a stronger advocacy role. Child protective workers became more pro-active roles in their case studies and reporting while case workers became more dependent on judges to help them gain greater respect from those they were serving. Probation officers began to provide more help petitioners more effectively with guidance and advice. Criminal courts began to notice family dysfunctions as significantly contributing to cases within the criminal domestic violence cases brought before them. Blass also saw that the Sheriff's department served papers for petitioners who often would not follow through with serving the necessary papers. And, significantly, custody and visitation rights' decisions were increasingly were based on what is best for children. He also settled many cases that would have gone to a divisive trial, leaving a family scarred.

In 2005, Blass ran again for Family Court Judge but party leaders reneged on their agreement for cross endorsement so he became a Court Appointed Referee in Family Court where he presided over trials and case conferences.

In 2006, County Executive Steve Levy asked Blass to become chief deputy commissioner of the Department of Social Services under Commissioner Janet Demarzo whose five- year term ended in 2006. From 2007-2013, Blass served as commissioner of Social Services. He points to the following as a way to describe the social service commissioner job as "begathons" where he had to plead with county executives to maintain current staff positions so that clients did not suffer as caseloads grew and caseworkers did not burn-out. It was a period when caseloads increased as the economy nose-dived. The commissioner's job involved a tremendous amount of creative budgeting to maintain services at tolerable levels and boosting the morals of the department's workers.

To get a first-hand view of working conditions, on occasion, Blass dressed in ragged clothes to observe how clients were being treated when they applied for assistance. He also sat in client for client interviews indicating that he was an intern. He noticed the heavy presence of mental problems among the lobby crowd and also how some clients felt they were "brushed off" by staff to discourage their applications for services which was the clients' frequent misinterpretation of the rigid application standards set by State regulations which county social service workers had to enforce. His conclusion was that morale was low. Statistical reports showed that there were low personnel retention rates. He established an open door policy as commissioner and instituted civil workplace training for all staff.

These changes to generate greater respect and recognition for the work that staff did resulted in better morale and retention rates. Client services also improved. Blass feels that these issues did not receive the attention they deserved in previous administrations.

Blass points to important improvements in the area of housing of the department's clients. He credits CHI, a contract housing agency for finding housing placements that resulted in the department being able to move 30-40 families into decent permanent housing on a monthly basis. Homelessness was increasing due to deepening job losses so people of all economic backgrounds were becoming homeless.

Another inroad Blass instituted was making arrangements for food stamps eligible school children to be eligible for the federal lunch program, and where available, breakfast programs. In addition, arrangements were made for homeless sex offenders to live in trailer homes to be moved every 90 days so that community residents' burden was being shared by all communities. However, the county decided against the rotation of sites of trailers for sex offenders. Steps were also taken to increase Medicaid eligibility by eliminating means test applications which still had to be done within 90 days an unrealistic period of time.

The following description of the late 1980s to the early 2000s is based on a 2014 interview with Evelyn Roth, a former Suffolk deputy county executive in the Patrick Halpin administration and director, Federation Employment Guidance Services (FEGS)/Long Island Division.

In 1987, Roth was asked to assist on Patrick Halpin's campaign for Suffolk County Executive. After his election, Roth was assigned, with co-chair Thomas MacAteer, to assemble and lead a large transition team. They brought together a diverse group of people with a wide variety of skills and backgrounds to look at every aspect of county government. Halpin, upon taking office, appointed Roth as the County's first Deputy County Executive for Human Services.

Roth recalls that one of the major issues in Suffolk County, and indeed the nation, during this period was AIDS. Halpin and Roth worked to open up people's eyes to the epidemic and to fight the stigma associated with the disease. They visited support groups sponsored by the Long Island Association for AIDS Care (LIAAC) and spoke with clients and family members. Roth's older son was diagnosed with AIDS during this time so this was an especially important effort for her. She worked with advocates to secure the first person with AIDS admittance to the county nursing home. Her son Marc died of AIDS in 2003 after "a long and valiant struggle."

Homelessness was another major issue of the time and Roth recalls the many tours she took throughout Suffolk County with Andrew Cuomo in his Bronco, promoting his program, HELP, a cutting-edge, multi-service shelter program for homeless families, which was built and still operates in North Bellport.

Roth was active in bringing people together from outside government to talk with county department officials. Ruth Brandwein who was appointed as Halpin's Commissioner of Social Services worked closely with Roth during this period on many initiatives including a Domestic Violence Task Force. When three Suffolk women lost their lives at the hands of their abusers early in Halpin's administration, Roth helped prepare Halpin's first executive order which instituted a pro-arrest policy in domestic violence cases, the first of its kind in any major municipality in the State. The task force was established with representatives of the sheriff, District Attorney, probation, Family Court, social services, police, health who sat around the table with service providers, advocates and survivors. The task force also became a model for the state.

To accommodate the needs of the county's workforce for child care, a center was established at Suffolk County Community College in Brentwood and at the Dennison Building in Hauppauge, pursuant to recommendations made by another task force appointed by Halpin - this one on child care.

Speaking of political opposition to Halpin's social agenda - indeed to anything he tried to accomplish - Roth describes it as "difficult", especially in the light of the serious budget constraints facing the County. Roth recalls that the more conservative members of the Legislature tried to stamp her with the label "too liberal for Suffolk County." And yet much was accomplished with the help of Deputy County Executive and Legislative Liaison Larry Schwartz and many supportive members of the Legislature. "After all," she says, "our health and human service reforms were a drop in the bucket compared with the entire County budget." She points to the domestic violence initiatives, the homeless services and modernization of DSS under Brandwein, expanded day care services and growth in accessibility and transparency of County government.

After leaving the Halpin administration in 1991 to be closer to her son Marc, Roth worked for the State Department of Substance Abuse Services (DSAS), which was later merged with the alcoholism services office to become OASAS - Office of Alcoholism and Substance Abuse Services. The agency was in the midst of capping and even cutting funding to many of its contract agencies while drug addiction remained a serious and growing concern. So when she was asked to come back to Long Island in 1993 to become the first executive director of FEGS-Long Island Division, she accepted. The parent organization, Federation Employment and Guidance Services (FEGS) is a member agency of the UJA/Federation Network. Today, the agency is called FEGS Health and Human Services System, but it remains the State's largest multi-service, nonprofit provider. "This was a big departure for me," Roth says. "Politics was always a means to an end for me. It wasn't the battles I relished; it was getting the right people into the right positions so you could accomplish things. But here was a chance to work directly in the field." Roth substantially expanded FEGS programs on Long Island during her tenure. With the help of the development staff at UJA/Federation, she was able to initiate a range of Jewish family services, as well as programs to serve the entire community. In addition to establishing services for those coping with family violence and with AIDS, she worked with the New York City operation to grow mental health, developmental disabilities and employment programs across Long Island, both clinic and residence-based. These included the first residential program for women with AIDS. "This was the beginning of a decade's commitment, the longest job of my career," she said.

In the early 2000's, UJA/Federation was a major force in the effort to provide services for the metro region's growing senior population, and was very involved in the NORC (Naturally Occurring Retirement Community) movement to establish services in small NORC areas (criteria defined in State Law) for seniors who wanted to "age in place." Roth, then a retiree and working as a consultant to FEGS, brought the idea of starting the first suburban NORC with local government sponsorship to John Kaiman, then Supervisor of the Town of North Hempstead. FEGS-Long Island would be the social services partner. The Town agreed and the agency won a New York State NORC grant and began its program in an unincorporated area of New Hyde Park in 2005. The NORC program was so successful that Kaiman decided to expand the services for all seniors in the town, regardless of whether they lived in a NORC or not. During this period, Madge Kaplan, a long-time advocate who was then in charge of the town's senior services became ill and passed away. Kaiman asked Roth to lead the non-NORC expansion effort as the town's first commissioner of the newly established Department of Services for the Aging (DOSA).

With funding from the federal Administration on Aging, the Town established Project Independence, a non-NORC aging in place initiative for which any of the 50,000 town residents aged 60 or older was eligible. Project Independence (PI) began its expansion of services in 2009, community by community. The first such effort in the state and probably the nation to be sponsored by a local municipality, (PI) connected seniors to services and groups that provide transportation, medical and mental health care, educational and social programming, and other services like home repair. Working with consultant Mary Curtis who had been Nassau County Executive Tom Suozzi's Deputy for Human Services, Roth helped the town win an $854,000 New Freedom grant for its senior transportation services.

Since its inception, the PI program has expanded substantially. Two of its main features are the provision of transportation services provided by local taxi companies, via contracts with the town, and a contract with The Rehabilitation

Institute in Westbury under the terms of which young adults with disabilities, as part of their job training, provide home-based services for the elderly, doing such things as cleaning gutters, moving furniture, touch-up painting, changing light bulbs and smoke detector batteries and other minor repairs. Other towns from throughout Long Island have visited Project Independence to learn how to start and operate the program but during this period of severe funding constraints, they have chosen, instead, to borrow only parts of the idea. Speaking of the growing need for community-based aging services, Roth says: "They did not realize what was coming down the pike." Roth wishes that other municipalities were doing more to address the growing need for such programs which can dramatically reduce the rising costs of Medicare, Medicaid and the frequency of hospitalizations and emergency room visits - all of which will only grow while baby boomers age and enter the years when their need for services grows.

The following remarks are the result of a 2014 interview with Richard Schaffer, Suffolk Democratic Leader, former Babylon town supervisor, and Suffolk County Legislator.

Schaffer grew up in West Islip. His mother was an alcoholic and killed someone in a driving accident when he was 14 years of age. His father had walked out of the family when Schaffer was 11 years old. Our house was foreclosed on by the bank. An aunt and uncle living in North Babylon provided a home for him. Schaffer feels that he learned to be compassionate and considerate of every person's special situation. "It made me grow up much quicker than my age," he says. Through his childhood friend Jeff Downey, Schaffer got involved while in elementary school with Jeff's brother Tom's congressional campaign in 1974.

Schaffer recalls that "Mr. Downey would take us on "lit drops" and then buy pizza and soda for us. We distributed thousands of pieces of literature throughout the congressional district. I kind of got the political bug during this time." Schaffer worked on Richard Lambert's legislative campaign in 1975 and Downey's 1976 campaign against Peter Cohalan.

At SUNY Albany, Schaffer earned a B.A. in Political Science with a minor in History in 1985. He was president of the student association for two years. Soon after his graduation from college, he entered Brooklyn College Law School and began to work part-time for as a legislative aide for Sondra Bachety, a Suffolk County legislator. He also did volunteer work for Assemblyman Patrick Halpin.

In 1987, Schaffer ran for a county legislative seat and took the seat in 1988. He recalls that there was an economic crash that placed the county budget in "free-fall' with the result that the county's nonprofit contract agencies were placed on the "chopping block." The legislature was split politically 9-9 and taxes were increased with the result that legislators were very cautious and unsympathetic to pleas for assistance from charitable organizations. They did not want to spend funds on any non-mandated projects. In fact, there was a rallying cry that "even if it is mandated, it should not be mandated on us," says Schaffer. Schaffer recalls Legislators Rose Caracappa, Michael O'Donohue, Joe Rizzo, and Paul Sabatino II leading the conservative positions.

It was a tough time to be a legislator, Schaffer recalls, "you were balancing the political realities of a tough economy, laying off county workers and not being able to support needed social spending. It was also at the end of the Reagan years of "trickle down economic theories." Schaffer feels that the controversy about the law suit against Long Island Lighting Company's Shoreham Nuclear Power Plant also had an impact on the legislature's willing to support social spending.

In the late mid- and late 1980s, Schaffer remembers a big issue being what to do about young people with physical and mental disabilities that were becoming age 21 and "aging out" of state institutional care. Their parents came to the legislature pleading for understanding and county assistance. Meanwhile, the state imposed rules and regulations on the county regarding community-based services but did not provide the funding to implement them.

This period was also a time when reforms were instituted in the legislature opening it up to more public input and scrutiny. Contract agencies during this time also became more politically sophisticated involving their clients in appeals to the legislature. "They learned to work the process in order to protect their agencies," says Schaffer. "It was also a time when relationships developed between legislators and their aides with the leaders of contract agencies. Today, things are very different than they were in the 1980s. Suffolk County does not fund new social programs. "A maintenance of effort attitude prevails in the legislature," say Schaffer.

Schaffer feels that "nonprofits should not become identified with any particular political party just like any business. You need to support those who support your causes. You would be failing your organization if you did not support those who support you and their re-election. You need to work both sides because that is how it benefits your organization."

Schaffer is concerned about the future of human services from the perspective of what types of people are going to enter the field. He also feels that the extreme cuts in funding imposed by government on nonprofits over the past several years have placed tremendous burdens on them with no reciprocal funding increases.

In thinking about social welfare "takeaways," Schaffer says that "the more things change the more they remain the same. We are still trying to educate about what the best ways to treat people with addictions and mental illness are and why it is best to deal with these issues early rather than later at considerably higher social and economic costs. Take heroin, for instance a very serious problem. It costs $5 a packet and you are addicted after one try. It destroys that person's life and everyone around him. It produces crime. We need to do a better job convincing people to take their heads out of the sand on such issues."

The following recollections of the late 1980s are written by James Gaughran, a former Suffolk County Legislator and current chairman of the Suffolk County Water Authority.

"One of the issues I recall from the late 1980's was the increase in drug-related violence in Huntington Station and the difficulty the police were having with communication within the growing Spanish-speaking community. Many community residents wanted to speak out but were fearful of immigration policies and possibly being deported. All the Suffolk County police were concerned with was getting credible information to make arrests and have them stick in court. The clergy at St. Hugh of Lincoln Church arranged for me to speak after the Spanish-speaking mass in the basement of the church. The place was packed. I spoke to the community along with representatives of the Suffolk County Police Department who assured the group that they were only interested in getting information to help make the community safe and that they had nothing to do with immigration. We spent hours taking down information which led to numerous arrests and at least temporarily wiped out the drug activities in the immediate area. I was then able to set up a police trailer in the area which helped further. It also began a dialogue about other community issues such as drug rehabilitation and day care needs which really did improve the quality of life."

Leone Baum is the former executive assistant to the CEO of the Economic Opportunity Commission of Nassau County. Since that time, she has continued as a civic activist. In the following story, Baum describes her activism in Nassau County during the 1990s and beyond in the following essay.

"In the 1990s, I worked on drawing the lines for not one but two legislative districts which could elect minority representation to a Nassau County legislature. I then participated in organizing a lawsuit against the county which found the government, a board of supervisors, to be unconstitutional by federal judge Arthur Spatt, and resulted in a nineteen-member legislature and in 2013, a third minority legislator was elected in district 3.

As the century ended and a new one began, my world changed forever as the twin towers came down and the scourge of terrorism began. I retired and am satisfied with the role I have been able to play as an activist and organizer. I am glad to have been asked to share what I have done and hope that my work is exemplary and can help the poor and minorities to become more equal in the home, workplace and politics, all of which leave the place we live in a better and more fulfilling place for our sons and daughters."

The Nonprofit Sector since 1985

This chapter section highlights a number of the more-significant developments that have taken place in the past 25 years in Long Island's nonprofit sector. The following discussion has been excerpted from the 2011 "Doing More with Less During a Period of Economic Change," report. The report assembled approximately 1,500 nonprofit, mostly small, organizations and agencies into the study. It includes museums, religious and grant-making organizations, environmental, political, human rights and social advocacy organizations, and civic, social, business, professional, labor and arts organizations.

The report shows a 9.3% increase in the number of providers between 2000 and 2006. The report indicates that nonprofit enterprises continued to grow at a faster rate than all Long Island enterprises, 12.6% versus 8.4%. However, the growth of nonprofit health care providers, 29.6% was particularly dramatic reflecting the proliferation of new medical technologies and treatments and the fact that Long Island's aging population utilizes health care facilities more extensively.

Speaking of challenges facing Long Island's nonprofit sector, the report says: "Whereas private, for-profit enterprises are subject to the discipline of the marketplace, nonprofits are able to proliferate without market discipline as long as they can obtain the funding they need. This often results in the creation of many smaller nonprofit organizations that lack the capacity to grow and function efficiently." The report also notes that "a recent wave of mergers, acquisitions and consolidations within Long Island's private sector economy has reduced the number of potential private sector donors and narrowed the funding stream available to local nonprofits." Some of these organizations are discussed earlier in this chapter.

The report points to common themes among the nonprofits respondents as to the most significant human service needs. They were: few housing and emergency shelter options; a lack of constructive activities for young people; the presence of child abuse and family violence that leads to mental health issues; a lack of services for older adult services and the disabled population; a lack of health care, and child care particularly for low and moderate income families; and a need for an emphasis on advocacy, information, referrals and legal assistance to enable people to navigate bureaucracies.

Long Island's nonprofit sector accounts for a significant share of the bi-county economy. There were 132,000 nonprofit jobs in 2010 which represented 11 percent of all Long Island jobs and impacted Long Island's quality of life as well. These institutions bring major amount of federal aid to the region and generate income, sales, and FICA taxes. The report discusses some of the support mechanisms that have been implemented. Continued dialog, coordination and cooperation between the business community, government at all levels and local nonprofits can go a long way toward ensuring that available resources are put to their best use.

Since the 1980s, Long Island nonprofit organizations have faced many new challenges. Some have called it "the new normal," created by a combination of resource-scarcity and the need to do more with less. Changed conditions were obviously affected by recessionary periods and, significantly, the depression of 2008 with its dramatic impact on personal wealth and government spending. As the number of nonprofit organizations increased so did competition for grants and charitable giving through fund raising events and personal appeals."

Lastly, the report shows individual responses that are worth noting and includes the fact that the nonprofit sector is: "traditionally weak in marketing"; "the inability to properly remunerate very experienced and dedicated staff is causing a serious lack of candidates for the nonprofit field"; "the need to do better development work is increasingly critical"; "computers and computer systems are often outdated and need to be upgraded and keeping up with technology is expensive"; "administrative support is limited by funding"; and "legal and financial expertise is often lacking."

The Long Island nonprofit sector is dominated by health care providers, social service agencies and miscellaneous civic associations and religious organizations. Collectively, these industry segments generated annual payrolls of $6.4 billion in 2010, double their level of a decade ago. Employment and earnings supported by the sector in 20120 produced $10.8 billion. The health care sector accounted for more than 82 percent of this payroll spending." [11]

The United Way of Long Island continued to make efforts to expand corporate and individual giving through workplace campaigns and public campaigns. Unfortunately, charitable giving on Long Island never reached its potential with per capita giving remaining at about $3.00 per resident, far below regions with comparable population sizes (Houston: $36.00; Chicago: $19.00; Denver: 13.56; or nearby Westchester County: $11.00. Some regions, much smaller in size than Long Island have achieved much greater success such as: St. Louis: $72.00; Rochester NY: $71.00; and Forsyth County VA: $47.00). [12]

As can be seen in prior chapters, Long Island has progressed in the number of social programs and social justice organizations. It also launched significant social legislative measures that were enacted into state law. In fact, Long Island nonprofit leaders, elected officials, and governmental units initiated many new policy and program initiatives.

For further information about these initiatives, visit Part V, "Suburban Trail-blazing."

Important Changes in the Regulatory Environment for Nonprofits

The following discussion of changes in the nonprofit regulatory environment was written by Michael E. Nawrocki, CPA, Managing Partner of Nawrocki Smith LLP, one of the leading providers of professional accounting services to nonprofit organizations on Long Island since 1986.

The past 25 years have also seen significant changes in regulatory requirements. Implementation of the Single Audit Act of 1984 required nonprofit organizations to provide not only an accounting for federal award programs, but assurance that laws, regulations and grant provisions were being complied with, and an adequate system of internal control was prevalent throughout an organization and over the federal award program. In 1996, for the first time in twenty years, the Financial Accounting Standards Board (which oversees U. S. generally accepted accounting principles) issued new guidelines on accounting and financial reporting for nonprofit organization.

Changes in revenue recognition principles and new requirements to track donor restricted funds were introduced. Notwithstanding the initial difficulties in implementation, these new guidelines brought more uniformity to nonprofit financial statements. In response to numerous corporate scandals (such as Enron), Congress enacted the Sarbanes-Oxley Act to provide more accountability and transparency on Wall Street. Proposed legislation by states throughout the country sought to impose Sarbanes-Oxley type requirements on nonprofit organizations, although, such legislation never came to fruition. However, numerous "charitable watchdogs" such as the Better Business Bureau's Philanthropic Advisory Service began evaluating the "charitable worthiness" of nonprofit organizations based on information found in organizations' Form 990 and annual reports.

In 2008, the Internal Revenue Service revamped its information return requirements (which had remained relatively unchanged since 1979) for nonprofit organizations, including extensive disclosures on mission, programs and activities, corporate governance and oversight. As part of a 13 state initiative, in 2012 New York State proposed legislation to limit nonprofit salaries and impose administrative expenditure caps on nonprofit organizations receiving funding from the State. Finally, the New York State Nonprofit Revitalization Act of 2013 resulted in extensive changes in nonprofit law in New York for the first time in over 40 years, making many of the Internal Revenue Service guidelines such as conflict-of-interest and whistleblower policies, as well as compensation setting procedures into statutory requirements.

Nonprofit organizations in New York State are now grappling with the mandatory establishment of audit committees to oversee fiscal accountability. All of the aforementioned regulations and statutes have come at a price, and nonprofit organizations continually face the same conundrum; that is complying with ever-increasing laws and provisions, while keeping administrative expenditures to a minimum."

The interviews with organizational leaders reveal a significantly different funding environment existing today featuring a decline in government's role in the funding of youth, family, mental health, drug and alcohol, aging, and human rights programs. On the other hand, there has been increased attention in the areas of: Health care; disabilities, hunger and homelessness; disaster relief; military veterans; and gay, lesbian, bisexual and transgendered people. There has also been a substantial increase in the funding of prisons to incarcerate those found guilty of criminal offenses especially for drug-related charges.

"According to the 2011 Long Island Association report *"Doing More with Less During a Period of Economic Change"* Long Island nonprofit enterprises account for a significant share of Long Island's jobs and payrolls. They are also one of the fastest-growing segments of the Long Island economy. Employment and payroll data compiled by the New York State Labor Department illustrate this point. Nassau-Suffolk employment covered by unemployment insurance, which accounts for the preponderance of jobs on Long Island, increased 1.3 percent. Employment in industries dominated by nonprofits increased by more than 32 percent. As a result, the nonprofit sector accounted for 8.4 percent of bi-county jobs in 2000 but for 11.0 percent of the total in 2010. The nonprofit sector is dominated by health care providers, social service agencies and miscellaneous civic associations and religious organizations. Collectively, these industry segments generated annual payrolls of $6.4 billion in 2010, double their level of a decade ago. The health care sector accounted for more than 82 percent of this payroll spending. [13]

Nonprofits have also faced changing demographics especially in the growth of the Latino and other minority populations as well as growth among new immigrant groups. Nonprofits have had to adjust their services in order to meet these new population groups with their cultural and language differences. Long Island nonprofits working with and behalf of new immigrant groups are often supported by The Hagedorn Fund that is discussed later in this chapter.

According to Cerini & Associates' Nonprofit Survey of 2010, 4 percent of organizations were in the process of merging with another and 8 percent were considering it. As the economy stalled, mergers and acquisitions trended up with more organizations realizing they cannot make it alone. Abilities (now named The Viscardi Center) engaged in merger talks with another nonprofit with a complimentary mission and business objective. SNAP Long Island, an organization focused on adolescent pregnancy prevention and services for pregnant adolescents and their families was acquired by the Economic Opportunity Council of Suffolk, a multi-service organization.

In addition, Family Residences and Essential Enterprises entered into affiliations with the Stephanie Joyce Kahn Foundation and the Child Development Center of the Hamptons. This allowed FREE to efficiently broaden the services it provides to certain populations among its clients with disabilities. The Nassau and Suffolk chapters of the American Red Cross will cut costs when they complete their merger to form the American Red Cross on Long Island." [14]

Other examples of organizational consolidations, collaborative projects, and mergers including:

- The Coalition Against Child Abuse and Neglect with the Coalition Against Domestic Violence formed "The Safe Center LI."
- Family Counseling in Westhampton Beach established collaborative relationships with school districts and other nonprofit agencies to develop mental health services.
- The Long Island Fund for Women and Girls co-located with the Association of Mothers' Centers for both programmatic and economic reasons. As part of the arrangement, the Fund acquired Women on the Job.
- A partnership formed between Long Beach Reach and the Lynbrook Counseling Center enabled the expansion of services with local school districts.
- Children's House and Family and Children's Association built their capacity through a merger.
- Clubhouse of Suffolk, a non-profit provider of psychiatric rehabilitation and support services, the Mental Health Association of Suffolk County, a local chapter of a national and statewide network of associations dedicated to improving the mental health of local communities through education, workforce training, information and referral services, and advocacy, and Suffolk County United Veterans.
- The Long Island Association for AIDS Care in Hauppauge has long collaborated with EOC of Suffolk and Seafield Inc., which provides

substance abuse services, to expand the services it can offer to its
clients.

- Suffolk Community Council, which provided community and
advocacy services since 1933, dissolved with the United Way of Long
Island managing the oversight of the dissolution. It took over the
contracts of SCC's programs in the short term while the Health and
Welfare Council, which also provides advocacy services, will fill that
role for the region.

Cerini and Associates' Tenth Annual Long Island Nonprofit Survey in 2013 of
125 responding organizations provided a profile of key challenges facing
nonprofit organizations:

- Organizations are not effectively utilizing technology to build their
networks and donors.
- Organizations expressed that their largest concern are cutbacks in
funding.
- Government audits continue to be prevalent with most government
funded organizations reporting some level of audit activity.
- Average staff raises are anticipated at around 2 percent for the sector
inclusive of almost fifty percent of respondents reporting that they do
not anticipate providing raises to their staff.
- Organizations are feeling the cash crunch with approximately 29
percent of agencies with two months or less of cash on hand.
- 82 percent of respondents have served more clients in the current year
than they had in the prior year, a trend that has been occurring every
year of the survey.
- The sector is experiencing a certain level of contractions, as 4 percent
of agencies are considering ceasing of operations, with 13 percent in
the process of undergoing mergers and 12 percent considering merging
with another organization. [15]

Another important change has been the establishment of new technical
assistance services for nonprofit organizations described below. These services
are principally provided by the Nonprofit Leadership Center at Adelphi
University and the United Way's Capacity and Optimization Tank. In addition,
during the 1980s, new opportunities were established to finance capital
construction for affordable housing, housing and centers for people with
disabilities, housing for the homeless and for children's day care centers. The
period was one in which many nonprofit organizations changed the
composition of their boards of directors by expanding the number of
representatives of business organizations especially from banks and larger
corporations with histories of charitable giving. A number of banks increased

their services to their nonprofit clients with bridge loans, lines of credit, and financial expertise.

The question of whether Suffolk County government should operate a nursing home has been around for over twenty years in Suffolk County. It is a story about county government's ambivalent and inconsistent attitude towards its vulnerable people. In 2012, Karl Grossman chronicled this story of the John J. Foley Skilled Nursing Facility in the *Sag Harbor Express, the Southampton Press, the East Hampton Press, South Shore Press, and Shelter Island Reporter.*

> "The late Suffolk County Legislator John J. Foley was a model for compassion in government. He was dedicated to the care of the ill. And thus it was fitting that the historic Suffolk County Infirmary was renamed the John J. Foley Skilled Nursing Facility. It was Mr. Foley of Blue Point - a county legislator for 18 years - who, in 1990, fought the plan of fellow Democrat, then County Executive Patrick Halpin, to close the infirmary and won bipartisan support to build a replacement $34 million facility.
>
> The Foley facility is important for being the nursing home in Suffolk that will accept those that other nursing homes will not- notably poor people with serious illnesses requiring long-term care that private nursing homes shy away from because of financial issues. In recent years, there has again been a call for the county to no longer run it. Former County Executive Steve Levy conducted a major campaign to close or sell the facility.
>
> In 2008, a year before he died at 90, Mr. Foley wrote a letter to *Newsday* noting that its "masthead says: 'Where there is no vision the people perish,'" yet 'the paper's editorial board says, 'Suffolk should get out of the nursing home business.' But that is the point here—we are not in a business. The poor will perish if we do not keep our commitment to deliver quality of care via the John J. Foley Skilled Nursing Facility at Yaphank; not a business, but a commitment to deliver quality of care to the poor.'
>
> "Let us preserve our vision, our commitment to the poor,' wrote Mr. Foley. 'Let us also realize that the county executive's (Mr. Levy's) game plan is to take Suffolk out of health services, and by so doing, penalize the poor.' The future of the Foley facility is at a crossroads again. Under the budget for county government for 2012, its 250-person staff faces lay-off on June 30 - causing a closure of the nursing home - unless that is changed. Legislators Kate Browning of Shirley, a

Working Families Party member who runs with Democratic cross-endorsement, and John Kennedy of Hauppauge, the Republican leader of the legislature, has been in the forefront in seeking to save Foley.

'I do not think Steve Bellone is of the same mindset as Steve Levy,' says Ms. Browning. 'I think he has a heart.' The new county executive, she acknowledges, 'is dealing with a tough financial situation.' Still, the county's nursing home 'has been there for 100 years. It survived the Depression.' And it is critically needed. It is the nursing home in Suffolk that 'accepts those others will not.' She and Mr. Kennedy want to work with Democrat Bellone in developing a 'public-private partnership' for the 264-bed facility. Ms. Browning speaks of the 'compassionate side of me... We are not commodities but human beings. It takes only one health-related emergency to put you at the bottom - and with no place to go.'

After reimbursements from federal and state governments, Foley has been costing the county $6 million a year. Ms. Browning says 'I am not going to say Foley will be a profit-maker, but we can get it to operate as close to the black as possible and have it sustain itself — if we have the opportunity to do that.' She does not want to see it closed 'to fill a budget hole.'

Foley provides excellent care. "It is the jewel of Suffolk County and should remain a facility that is under the control of Suffolk County government," testified Cheryl Felice, then president of the Suffolk County Association of Municipal Employees, before the legislature in 2010. She also asked: "Does the Suffolk County jail make a profit? Do the Departments of] Social Services or Health Services make a profit? Why is it that Foley is being held to a different standard of having to make a profit?"

The Foley facility, like the man it is named after, is about compassion and helping those who desperately need it. This is a vital mission of local government. It is beyond partisan politics. We must continue the legacy of John J. Foley.

As Legislator Kennedy said as the legislature voted 11-to-6 in 2010 against a Levy resolution to close Foley: 'I have always been impressed with the resourcefulness of my colleagues and of this body....That resourcefulness has been the impetus for some great legislation that has impacted not just this county, but this nation. I refuse to accept that we have only a choice to sell or a choice to close. Neither can we accept that.'

Volunteerism: An Important Element in the History of Community Activism
on Long Island

*Diana O'Neill joined the Long Island Volunteer Center (LIVC) in early 1997
and became executive director in June 2001. She co-founded the Long Island
Volunteer Hall of Fame and has chaired the steering committee for ten years.
O'Neill is a past president of the Junior League of Long Island and was the
inaugural chair of the LIVOAD and convener of the LIVOAD Volunteer
Planning Group. She has served as vice president for Programs of the
Association of Professional Volunteer Administrators and on the LIVE
steering committee. O'Neill is currently on the Long Term Recovery Group
Executive Committee and a board member of the Health & Welfare Council of
Long Island. The following essay was written by O'Neill to provide an
overview of volunteerism and civic engagement as well as the emergence of
the Long Island Volunteer Center.*

"Long Island is a convergence of unique circumstances - a bucolic
suburbia where life became more complicated as its population
swelled. Long Islanders are resilient, smart and compassionate - and
more than capable of tackling community issues head-on.
Volunteerism, especially through effective community organization,
has an important part to play in strengthening the civic fabric of the
region. Human kindness, truly the essence of volunteering, takes on
many forms and its impact can be felt exponentially. This is an
overview of the growth of volunteerism as an industry on Long Island
as individuals rose up to address serious societal issues and through
passion, drive, and determination created opportunities to build
community. Volunteers most assuredly are the backbone of many
Long Island organizations that serve the common good.

As individuals began to concern themselves about community issues,
it was done through a volunteer lens well before the mechanisms were
in place to create infrastructure. One or more people shared a vision,
galvanized a team, sought out skilled leadership and board
governance, secured federal and state approvals, began fundraising,
and created an organization that in order to sustain it, needed more
volunteers as well as funding for sustainability. This was the pattern
for the origins for most nonprofit organizations that developed across
Long Island since the mid-1900's and continues today. Recruiting
volunteers takes many formal and informal methods from word of
mouth to advertising to headhunting through volunteer portals.
Management of volunteers has also become a priority human resources
objective. As the number of volunteer needs escalated, the number of
people willing to give back increased, and the necessity to manage that
asset well became evident; an industry began to take shape.

The first local "response" for a central clearinghouse began with local government in the late 1980's funded by New York State. Nassau and Suffolk Counties created directors of volunteer services that referred residents to nonprofit organizations seeking volunteer support. Joan Imhof led the Nassau County efforts. Simultaneously at the national level, the Points of Light Foundation (established in 1990 and inspired by President George H.W. Bush's inaugural speech invoking a thousand points of light) merged with the National Volunteer Center Network in 1991. The County volunteer offices were both defunded in 1992 due to state cutbacks. While handling calls at home from nonprofits still seeking support,

Imhoff applied for and secured funding from the Points of Light Foundation and the Mott and Kellogg Foundations, to establish the Long Island Volunteer Center (LIVC) to serve as a hub organization for matching individuals and groups to nonprofit organizations throughout Nassau and Suffolk counties and as a regional resource center for volunteer programming. American Red Cross of Nassau County donated office space in Mineola and with help from Anna Lyons and Paul Salerno, LIVC secured its independent nonprofit status from the IRS in 1993 and incorporated in 1994. The Long Island Volunteer Center remains a legacy Points of Light affiliate. In response to President Bush's call to action, Points of Light Foundation was created in 1990 as an independent, nonpartisan, nonprofit organization to encourage and empower the spirit of service and extends President Bush's vision, understanding that "what government alone can do is limited, but the potential of the American people knows no limits.

In 2007, Points of Light Foundation and HandsOn Network merged to become Points of Light, creating the largest volunteer management and civic engagement organization in the nation. People have always been at the center of change. People today have more power to drive change than ever before. At the same time, society is demanding much more from the world of volunteerism in the 21st century as a rapidly globalizing economy puts increasing pressure on governments, businesses, nonprofits and other institutions to do more with less. To meet that need, volunteer organizations must be able to help people make the greatest impact possible with not only their time, but also their talent, voice and money. As the world's leading volunteer organization with more than 20 years of history and a bipartisan legacy, Points of Light connects people to their power to create positive change and address the critical needs of our communities."

Recognizing the advent of a corporate social responsibility movement across the country, a committee of for-profit and nonprofit representatives formed and in 1993 created LIVE, Long Island Volunteer Enterprise, a corporate community service initiative. Representatives from Deloitte, IBM, Long Island Volunteer Center, and PricewaterhouseCoopers were among the early leaders in the start-up. Estee Lauder, Fleet Bank, Keyspan, United Way of Long Island, and many others took up the gauntlet soon after. Original founding members, Sandy Viola and Rosemary Mascali (with support from Bob Purcell and Joan Connor) continue to lead the program today.

Founded in 1993, LIVE - Long Island Volunteer Enterprise - mobilizes volunteer teams from the corporate, academic and nonprofit sectors to complete a one day project that will significantly improve the quality of life for many who live and work on Long Island. Now in our 22nd year, LIVE has matched volunteer teams with nonprofit agencies looking for assistance with varied projects. Visit our honor roll to see the over 400 companies and organizations that have adopted a LIVE project over the years. In cooperation with the United Way of Long Island and the Long Island Volunteer Center, LIVE promotes corporate volunteerism on Long Island for the betterment of our community and helps renew Long Island's spirit, beauty and quality of life. Studies show that corporate volunteering is a Win-Win situation for all involved. It benefits the companies by enhancing their image in the community; it benefits volunteers by promoting teamwork, building morale, and presenting opportunities to develop valuable workplace skills; and it benefits community organizations by providing much needed manpower."

As volunteer coordinators were being established to manage the influx of volunteers, a Long Island coalition formed and established the Association of Professional Volunteer Administrators in 1996. Led by Maida Cherry, the founding committee included representatives of AHRC, Coe Hall Planting Fields Arboretum, Epilepsy Foundation of Long Island, Long Island State Veterans Home, and United Cerebral Palsy of Nassau County. LIVC representatives helped augment board positions soon thereafter.

Our mission is to promote professionalism and strengthen leadership in the field of volunteer administration from a wide variety of settings on Long Island. The vision is to be a resource for volunteerism and volunteer administrators, to provide educational workshops promoting excellence in the field of volunteer program management three times a year, to continue to bring professionalism to the field, to offer resources and networking opportunities for those who manage volunteer programs, and to be a member-driven organization."

In 1997, after a fortuitous conversation with Imhof in the parking lot of *Newsday*, where both had served as judges for *Newsday's* volunteer of the year program, Diana O'Neill came on board as the vice president of Special Projects. Patricia Sands next joined the LIVC as outreach coordinator. In 1999, the American Red Cross notified LIVC that they were no longer able to donate office space for LIVC due to reorganization. After a frustrating and disappointing search, Diana happened to discuss the space problem with Mary Ellen Cirrito after a chance meeting in a local store. Mary Ellen told her that her husband Mike just happened to have a space in a house converted to law offices in Hempstead that could be donated for the agency. Due to their generosity, LIVC became the recipient of that donated space where they still reside. O'Neill moved on to become the executive director in 2001 so that Anna Lyons could concentrate on special projects including the directory update and developing and maintaining a website. Prior to serving the LIVC, O'Neill had been volunteering at the Junior League of Long Island where she helped established the prom boutique in 1995. The prom boutique, which provides prom gowns to girls of families unable to afford the expense, has now become a beloved yearly event that it is run by LIVC."

In 2000, Imhof was recruited to *Newsday's* community affairs and for ten years helped direct FutureCorps, a student-driven community service initiative. Liz Dysart took over and has coordinated the program to date. Over the course of its fifteen year history, over 930,000 students have volunteered to assist local causes ranging from hunger and homelessness, veterans and military families, cultural arts, health and special needs, and at risk children. In the early years, LIVC provided its complete directory of volunteer opportunities and community resources for use in project identification and served on panels to judge grant applications from schools seeking resources to fund projects. A few LIVC collaborative efforts with schools have been featured, namely the Nassau Community College prom boutique service learning program and the NYIT Carleton Group corporate activation initiative and Next Generation Award for the Long Island Volunteer Hall of Fame.

The 1995 Kobi earthquake was the impetus for worldwide volunteer response and in gratitude, the Ambassador of Japan asked the United Nations to officially designate 2001 as the International Year of Volunteers (IYV). The idea for IYV emerged from deliberations among several major international NGOs in the early 1990s. The formal proposal to proclaim 2001 as the International Year of Volunteers was made by the Japanese government, co-sponsored by 123 countries, and was approved by the UN General Assembly. Aimed at increased recognition, facilitation, networking and promotion of volunteering, the International Year of Volunteers 2001 (IYV) provided a unique opportunity to highlight the achievements of the millions of volunteers worldwide who devote some time of their lives to serving others, and to encourage more people globally to engage in volunteer activity. Volunteering is a fundamental building block of civil society. It brings to life the noblest aspirations of humankind - the pursuit of peace, freedom, opportunity, safety, and justice for all people." IYV generated an outpouring of international interest in the power and impact of volunteerism as a change agent. Led by Susi Wood of AHRC Nassau, a Long Island delegation was formed with members representing American Red Cross of Suffolk, The EGC Group, Federation of Organizations Foster Grandparents Program, Fire Island National Preserve, Girl Scouts of Nassau County, Junior League of Long Island, Long Island Cares, Long Island State Veterans Home, Long Island Volunteer Center, Nassau County Retired Senior Volunteer Program, The Nature Conservancy, SCO Family of Services, Stony Brook University, Suffolk Community Council, United Way of Long Island, and Urban League of Long Island. Year-long events and activities were planned to bring about greater awareness of IYV including participation in two National Assemblies at the United Nations, a volunteer conference at Stony Brook University, a volunteer merit awards luncheon hosted by the Junior League of Long Island, media promotion by *Newsday* and *Anton Publications*, a calendar contest through the Girl Scouts of Nassau County, a volunteer survey of Long Island nonprofits, and a close-out ceremony at the Fire Island Lighthouse.

The most significant and lasting outgrowth of the Long Island response to IYV was the creation of the Long Island Volunteer Hall of Fame which had its inaugural induction ceremony and reception at Stony Brook University in 2002. The hall of fame recognizes and honors volunteer founders, whose vision and humanitarian spirit provided the impetus to create non-profit agencies on Long Island. In addition, individual volunteers are also honored as "lifetime achievers" for their lifelong work in community service, inspiring volunteers are recognized for exemplary contributions, and outstanding youth are bestowed The Next Generation Award (created by the New York Institute for Technology Carleton Group student communications/marketing internship). 133 individuals have been inducted since inception representing twelve different categories of volunteer activity. *(See Appendix for listing of inductees)*

Working closely with New York State Office of Parks, Recreation and Historic Preservation, the Long Island Volunteer Hall of Fame has a permanent home at Bethpage State Park in Farmingdale. To commemorate inductees, benches with inscribed plaques have been installed at the Carlyle on the Green clubhouse grounds and golf course tees on the blue, green, yellow and red courses. The first bench dedication (sponsored by an anonymous donor) was in 2006 to honor Harry Chapin, founder of Long Island Cares - The Harry Chapin Food Bank. Twelve additional benches have been dedicated over the years.

After working together as a coalition on IYV, the organizing agencies decided to establish the Volunteer Hall of Fame to honor individuals who founded the many nonprofit organizations found on Long Island. These organizations continue to advance the vision and causes advocated by their founders. We celebrate their humanitarian spirit and promote volunteerism on Long Island. With the help of our independent panel of volunteer judges new honorees have been inducted annually since 2002.

September 11, 2001 is a date that forever changed the national psyche. Patriotism led to greater volunteerism; everyone wanted to "do something" in response. The Health and Welfare Council of Long Island adopted a FEMA strategy to create the Long Island VOAD (Voluntary Organizations Active in Disaster). In the days and months after 9/11, governmental and health and human service organizations worked painstakingly to respond to the needs of those affected. The unprecedented scale of that disaster meant there was no appropriate paradigm to guide all levels of emergency response. No systems were in existence that could provide clear, reliable information to the thousands of traumatized victims or to equip the nonprofit and governmental organizations working to manage the crises. Within a short time, it became clear that more formalized coordination would be crucial, and so the LIVOAD was formed. The Health & Welfare Council of Long Island has been intimately involved in the planning and coordination of disaster response activities in Nassau and Suffolk counties since the creation of the Long Island Voluntary Organizations Active in Disaster (LIVOAD) coalition, which is made up of regional nonprofit, for-profit and governmental agencies. LIVOAD works to foster a coordinated approach to disaster recovery, identify what services are needed and develop efficient ways to deliver them.

The Long Island Volunteer Center organized the inaugural LIVOAD Volunteer Planning Group, followed up by leadership from St. Vincent de Paul, and United Way of Long Island. Early members of that group included representatives from AHRC, American Red Cross of Nassau and Suffolk Counties, FEGS, Island Harvest, Long Island Cares, Nassau County Medical Reserve Corps, Nassau County OEM,

Salvation Army, Suffolk County FRES, St. Vincent de Paul, and United Way of Long Island.

The purpose of the group is to create a plan for managing spontaneous unaffiliated volunteers that respond to disaster. A preliminary plan was drafted in 2008. To coordinate relief and recovery efforts supporting Super Storm Sandy, the Long Island Volunteer Center (in partnership with the AmeriCorps St. Louis Emergency Response Team) ramped up the LIVOAD Volunteer Recovery Center in donated space from Sleepy's from December 12, 2012 through August 15, 2013. This facility became the hub for all LIVOAD member agencies meetings, trainings, and collaborative efforts.

During this period, HWCLI convened the LIVOAD's Long Term Recovery Group to organize the assistance efforts of health and human agencies for storm-affected families months and possibly years into the future. The Long Term Recovery Group expands agencies' opportunities to help storm survivors, makes possible the best and most extensive use of agencies' services and resources, and allows agencies to share information and therefore avoid duplication of services and efforts. Through subcommittees made up of participating organizations, the Long Term Recovery Group is helping manage key areas related to disaster response, including case work, home cleanup and other housing issues, volunteering, donations, and the special needs of the undocumented population. With secured funding from American Red Cross of Long Island and in partnership with the Southern Baptists (a disaster response group), HWCLI opened a Disaster Recovery Center on the campus of New York Institute for Technology in Central Islip in January 2014 to house volunteers and maintain offices of the Long Term Recovery Group (including the Long Island Volunteer which supports recruitment and referral of disaster volunteers). Response to recent historic flooding in Suffolk County was also coordinated through this Disaster Recovery Center by Long Term Recovery Group AmeriCorps VISTAs.

In 1993, President Bill Clinton signed the National and Community Service Trust Act, which initiates the founding of AmeriCorps, a national service program that engages Americans in voluntary action to address the country's most critical issues. In 1994, the Corporation for National and Community Service (CNCS) officially begins operation. CNCS is a federal agency that engages millions of Americans in service through Senior Corps, AmeriCorps and Learn and Serve America." In response, New York State created a Commission on National and Community Service, Stony Brook University was selected as an AmeriCorps site serving volunteer needs of Long Island organizations, and NYS Senator Ken LaValle from

Long Island was nominated as a Commission member. From newyorkersvolunteer.org: "The New York State Commission on National and Community Service was established in 1994 by an Executive Order of the Governor, and administers programs funded by the National Community Service Trust Act of 1993, including AmeriCorps State and AmeriCorps Education Awards programs. Commission members are diverse and bi-partisan and are appointed by the Governor. The Commission seeks to improve lives, strengthen communities, and foster civic engagement through service and volunteering in New York State. In 2008, New Yorkers Volunteer website was launched as a statewide initiative to engage more New Yorkers in volunteering and community service. It provides information and training opportunities for local volunteer organizations. It provides a marketing and media campaign to promote volunteering. And, it educates New Yorkers about state and federal funding opportunities for national service and volunteer programs.

In 2009, President Barack Obama signed the historic Edward M. Kennedy Serve America Act which authorizes creation of the Volunteer Generation Fund as a national call to service. The Serve America Act reauthorizes and expands national service programs administered by the Corporation for National and Community Service (CNCS) by amending the National and Community Service Act of 1990 and the Domestic Volunteer Service Act of 1973. Since the Act's signing, volunteering is up, momentum is strong, and a new vision for service is taking effect. This landmark law is making America stronger by focusing service on key national issues; by expanding opportunities to serve; by building the capacity of individuals, nonprofits, and communities; and by encouraging innovative approaches to solving problems."

New York State was one of 14 states awarded a Volunteer Generation Grant by the Corporation for National and Community Service to establish and enhance a regional volunteer infrastructure throughout New York State. The New York State Commission on National & Community Service through the New Yorkers Volunteer Initiative announced the establishment of ten regional volunteer centers across the State, whose goal is to foster the recruitment of one million new volunteers state-wide through partnerships with thousands of non-profit organizations. The regional volunteer center websites, as well as social media such as Twitter and Facebook, are invaluable in connecting with all those who want to volunteer, but may not have found the right match. The state commission and its partners leverage the impact of AmeriCorps, VISTA, and Senior Corps programs to address the needs identified in the State's service and civic engagement agenda in the core areas of education, environmental stewardship, healthy futures, disaster services, veterans and military families, and economic opportunity. Engaging volunteers to solve community issues is a primary focus.

A year-one initiative undertaken by the Long Island Volunteer Center as a newly designated Regional Volunteer Center was launched in February 2012 when Dr. Don Levy, Director, Siena College Research Institute gave two presentations of the just-published New York State Civic Health Index which measured the level of civic engagement of New Yorkers according to established metrics. One was hosted by the Health & Welfare Council of Long Island for heads of member agencies and the other was held at United Way of Long Island for volunteer coordinators and community leaders. Over 100 Long Island organizations were represented. *FIOS News* and *Newsday* covered the events and published excerpts from the findings reporting that the Long Island region leads the state both in rates of volunteerism and in making charitable donations but that some challenges continue to exist in satisfactory volunteer experiences, recruiting volunteers for effective placement, and volunteer management capacity. In addition to organizing the events, the Long Island Volunteer Center secured panelists representing different sectors of community including academia, business, government, service organization, seniors, and youth to talk about their experiences in advancing the cause of volunteerism and to react to the findings of the study. With Dr. Levy were two members of the New York State Office of National & Community Service, Beth Tailleur and Eric Czupil, who sponsored the research. Since then, the Long Island Volunteer Center has sponsored September 11 and Martin Luther King, Jr., National Days of Service,- coordinated Make a Difference Day and National Volunteer Week community based projects, sponsored annual Long Island Volunteer Fairs and the Tenth Annual Long Island Volunteer Hall of Fame Induction Ceremony and Reception, supported corporate activation projects through LIVE and Points of Light, partnered with all five SUNY campuses on emergency preparedness projects, and led volunteer disaster response to Hurricane Irene and Super Storm Sandy.

LIVC also converted to a new website platform HandsOn Connect, a web-based, searchable volunteer matching software application that allows individuals and organizations to access and promote volunteer opportunities. It publishes seasonal lists of volunteer opportunities and holiday volunteer needs as well as an on-line directory of volunteer opportunities and community resources. Facebook, Twitter, Blog and LinkedIn accounts have been established to promote access to volunteer information and increase use of technology in volunteer recruitment. In addition, The EGC Group selected the Long Island Volunteer Center for its annual CreateAthon in 2011 and developed a pro-bono marketing and advertising campaign. For the past three years, the LIVC has also conducted two focus groups and six trainings in volunteer management and surveyed nonprofit organizations twice a year tracking volunteer numbers and hours, analyzing reported obstacles to volunteer recruitment, and seeking recommendations for increasing volunteer engagement.

In addition, since January 2012, *Newsday* has published a monthly Volunteer Nation series featuring volunteer activity at nonprofit organizations and counts with a thermometer gauge the number of volunteers giving back to Long Island causes. The LIVC regularly has over 40,000 unique visitors to the website each year and over 330 partner nonprofit agencies and 4000 volunteers are registered users of the on-line posting capabilities. It links to an additional 150 agencies that seek volunteers. Annually, over 2000 individuals and groups contact the agency with volunteer inquiries via phone or email. Looking to the future, LIVC is creating a youth advisory council and doing more programming in veterans and military families, special needs, and corporate activation."

See Appendix for a listing of LIVC's annual award recipients.

Health and Human Services in Nassau County

In 2005, Nassau County Executive Thomas R. Suozzi implemented "No Wrong Door" a major, innovative transformation of public sector health and human services described in Chapter V by Dr. Louise Skolnik. This unique service delivery system illustrated how capable leadership and good government can make a positive difference in peoples' lives without sacrificing efficiencies and taxpayer dollars. "No Wrong Door" replaced decades of service delivery that was fragmented, difficult to access and for some services-specifically those which served the economically challenged-reflective of an anti-client/ blaming the victim ethos.

Suozzi and his Deputy County Executive Dr. Mary Curtis created the No Wrong Door program with input from a large team. Commissioners and program directors, department supervisory and line staff, non-profit agency leaders, and even clients participated in designing this model program. In 2004, Suozzi asked Skolnik, Deputy Commissioner of the Department of Social Services and on leave from Adelphi University, to become the county's first director of human services so she could use her social work education and program development expertise to help guide the development of and prepare staff for the new system.

No Wrong Door was established with a view that people who apply for public services are deserving of caring and respectful treatment .A major objective of the new system was to ensure that all needs of a client and his or her family were met. All eight of the health and human service departments were relocated in to one welcoming state-of the-art facility. Clients walked through one door to access any and all needed services. The Departments of Health , Social Services; Aging, Youth, Veteran's Affairs, Physically Challenged, Drug and Alcohol, Mental Health worked collaboratively, met weekly to discuss challenging practice situations(known as Case of the Week) with interdepartmental consolidation where appropriate(e.g. staff development, grant and program development, fiscal management, information technology). The waiting room became a welcome center with a children's center, a client library, daily program activities, comfortable seating, smart security, and volunteers trained to guide clients through the application process.

In a 2006 *Newsday* article, columnist Lawrence C. Levy wrote "Doors Open to a better way to help those in need" "The idea was not just to save money, as conservatives espoused, or to assist more people as liberals demanded. The idea was to save money *and* deliver more help." "By bringing all the agencies under one roof, by linking them electronically and getting clients relatively less expensive health care, for instance, to head off huge bills down the road, the county expects to save beleaguered taxpayers...and by treating clients not like prisoners or freeloaders but people in real need, by determining their eligibility and getting them help faster, the county better serves its neediest elderly, kids, and disabled, ill, and poor," Levy continued.

In 2010, after County Executive Suozzi lost a bid for a third term, "No Wrong Door" as concept and program ceased to be although the building housing the Health and Human Services is still in operation and vestiges of the program endure including Case of the Week. [16]

New and Changing Funding Opportunities

Over the past twenty-five years, a number of important new funding streams have emerged on Long Island. They include The Hagedorn Fund and The Women's Fund of Long Island. A description of the United Way of Long Island's new initiative is also described. Note is also made that many new and older funders mentioned in earlier chapters collaborated with one another through the formation of the Long Island Funders Group.

The Long Island Community Foundation (LICF)

In the 1980s the giving trend at LICF was focused mainly on Arts, Education, self-help community groups, and social services to help disadvantaged people. Arts seemed to be a huge area that was funded and included, historical societies, bringing art education into the schools, and helping increase audience-bases.

From 1995-2009, the priority areas had become more general and broad – serving "Critical Communities, Critical Needs, Critical Organizations. The "great recession" saw a slowing down of new funds coming in and the number of people willing to bequeath funds. Then in 2010, shortly after the change in leadership from Suzy Sonnenberg to David Okorn, the LICF board and staff had reviewed the grant-making priorities in order to achieve more measureable results and greater impact for the Long Island region. As part of this review, LICF conducted an online survey of community, business, and government leaders to help identify the most pressing needs across our region. The survey, as well as other recently published reports and studies, was used as the basis of discussion for a staff and board retreat. Eight new priority areas for competitive grant-making were decided upon:

- Arts and Culture - to support and promote projects that emphasize the potential of the arts in regional economic and community development;
- Community Development - to build and sustain strong communities by building and preserving affordable rental housing;
- Environment - to protect and preserve Long Island's natural resources, ecosystems and public health;
- Equal Access to Education - to support and promote access to quality education for all;
- Health - to support hospital programs that provide health care to the underserved and to meet the mental health care needs of military veterans;
- Hunger to alleviate hunger and increase food access for poor people;
- Technical Assistance - to strengthen the nonprofit operations to achieve greater impact in our communities;
- Youth Violence Prevention to support and strengthen programs that prevent and deal with bullying and gang involvement and to promote juvenile justice reform.

In recent years, LICF asked members of its communities what they feel are the most critical needs. This resulted in revisions to the foundation's funding guidelines. "The list of critical needs was substantial, consisting of over 100 issues. The foundation pared the list down to what was felt to be the most important investments of the approximately $1.5M available annually. This wasn't an easy job," says Okorn.

Today, LICF's average grant size is $20-$25,000. Grant decisions are made three times per year. Okorn reports that the foundation continues its long standing tradition of funding startup grants for new organizations focusing on the foundation's areas of interest. There are no limits on how long LICF may continue to fund a particular organization. It used to be that grant awards were given for no longer than two or three year periods. Now, according to Okorn, the focus is on which organizations are doing the best work and able to address the priority issues.

LICF also continues to work collaboratively with other funders through the Long Island Funders Collaborative. It continually looks for ways to bring groups, to share resources, to learn from one another, and sometimes fund projects together to achieve greater impacts. Okorn points to the establishment of the Long Island Sound Funders Collaborative consisting of funders not only from Long Island but New York City and Connecticut as well, as an example of such collaborations. In the areas of housing, LICF brought together not only funders but builders, nonprofits, and governmental agencies to address the tremendous need for affordable housing.

The other foundation focus area is publicity to get the word out throughout Long Island that the foundation exists. Okorn feels that LICF's potential donors are people of all means since it only requires $5,000 to establish a fund. There are two other areas of LICF interest. One is technical assistance to conduct feasibility studies to assist organizations that would like to consolidate, affiliate, or merger with one another in order to more effectively deliver their services. The other is assisting organizations to form social enterprises to produce new revenue streams for their organizations. To date, no organizations have approached LICF for support of such social enterprise purposes.

Knowing that the foundation's current ability to address pressing needs is limited, Okorn reports that a very important priority area is to build a substantial endowment fund to have more permanent assets that enable the foundation to be able to address an even wider array of community needs into the future. This will enable the foundation to address the foundation to award sizable grants among a broad array of issues. "Our board is working diligently on this priority," says Okorn. "We are also working with donors and donor advisors to listen to them to find out where their interests and passions lie. We sometimes take them on site visits to see programs themselves. We sometimes provide them with short summaries or extensive write-ups of organizations we are familiar with that meet their areas of interest," Okorn continues. Donor advised funds represent 80%-90% of total LICF giving.

When discussing the increasing demands on nonprofit leaders to have business skills, he feels that "we need not only people with skills in finance, real estate, human resources, and accounting but also people who understand individual, family, and group dynamics. You need both."

In 2013, annual grant giving had risen substantially to nearly $4.9M reflecting the work of the foundation in heightening awareness of the foundation's existence and identifying donors to support the foundation's work in one or more of a variety of ways whether through donor advised funds where the donor selects the organization to receive support, or, through contributions to organizations selected by the advisory committee as the issues to be addressed. Donor advised funds represent a large majority of the foundation's grant giving through approximately 200 funds.

David Okorn has a B.A. in Business Administration and Master's Degree in Energy Management at New York Institute of Technology. He worked as an accountant for Grumman. Afterwards, he moved to LILCO doing budgeting and strategic planning work. He later was selected to be on the transition team handling the merger between Brooklyn Union Gas and LILCO for about two and a half years. At the newly-formed business, Key Span Okorn helped establish the company's charitable foundation and serving as its first executive director. Afterwards, his work at Key Span, Okorn was invited to assume a position at the National Center for Disability Services (aka The Viscardi Center). In a visit to the center, he was "blown away" by the quality of the services offered and the organization's programs to assure a future for the children. He felt that this experience stimulated a sense of a "calling" in him to leave his corporate career and work in the nonprofit world. Volunteerism had always been a part of Okorn's early years and encouraged by his parents.

Okorn was employed by LICF as director of development in 2009 working for Suzy Sonenberg, the foundation's executive director for 22 years. Sonenberg had invited Okorn to join LICF and indicated that she would retire in the next few years. In 2011, Okorn assumed the position of executive director. An extensive survey was conducted to assess community needs to help the foundation develop new priority areas. He also organized a board retreat featuring Pearl Kamer, director of planning for the Long Island Association to hear her views on Long Island's current and future needs that LICF should address. In the Fall, LICF will conduct another board retreat to review the priority areas and the foundation's guidelines. Okorn anticipates that the issues of homelessness, hunger, and nutrition may be areas that warrant greater foundation support. He stresses the importance of distributing more nutritious, fresh, healthy food into the food pantries because of its impact on health outcomes and reducing the distribution of high-sodium canned food. In this regard, LICF is working closely smaller grassroots in these efforts. [17]

The Hagedorn Foundation

The Hagedorn Foundation was founded in 2005 with $58-million. Hagedorn's executive director Darren Sandow's local and national leadership on immigration issues has greatly benefited Nassau and Suffolk Counties. While little-known and destined to be short-lived, Hagedorn revenue is now down to

$31-million and plans to close its doors in 2017. Under Sandow's leadership, Hagedorn has evolved into a major player in defusing the bitter immigration tensions that have plagued Long Island since Latino immigrants began flocking to the suburban area for work in the late 1990s.

The foundation jumped into the fray locally by founding nonprofits to improve perceptions about immigrants and another that seeks to engage voters and community leaders in immigrant-rights issues. Sandow has also taken a prominent role nationally, joining foundation collaboratives like the Four Freedoms Fund. Sandow traveled to Washington for a White House briefing for philanthropists on the immigration-reform debate.

Sandow met Horace and Amy Hagedorn at the Long Island Community Foundation, a branch of the New York Community Trust. Sandow became a program officer at the community foundation in 1996, after earning a Bachelor's Degree at the University of Michigan and serving as a Peace Corps Volunteer in rural, northern Costa Rica in what was billed as a Farm Management Program. On Long Island, Sandow also worked at the Nassau Health and Welfare Council for two years where he directed the Supplemental Security Insurance (SSI) Outreach Project with executive director Jack O'Connell and board members Richard Dina and Robert Pierce.

Horace Hagedorn, a former advertising executive who co-founded Miracle-Gro, had opened a donor-advised fund at the community foundation in 1995 after selling Miracle-Gro to another company. For most of his life, Mr. Hagedorn was a "checkbook philanthropist" who responded primarily to appeals from large and well-known charities, like the Red Cross and local nonprofit hospitals, says Amy, his second wife. Hagedorn, however, did more than that. He personally got involved. He participated in rallies protesting the treatment of new immigrants. He attended meetings with nonprofit executives and organized a marketing campaign he named "Fight for Families" when he became aware of proposed budget cuts to nonprofit service organizations.

But after joining the board of the Long Island Community Foundation, the couple began to learn about smaller local groups that were doing cutting-edge work. When Mr. Hagedorn became frail, Amy Hagedorn asked the community fund for help with grant making. Sandow was put on the case.

Mr. Hagedorn died in 2005 and left $58-million to philanthropy. Amy Hagedorn, who is in her 70s, used those funds to establish the Hagedorn Foundation, with Sandow as its executive director, She decided to spend all the assets by 2021, in the hope that she would live to see all the money distributed. (The date has since been moved to 2017 because the recession clobbered Hagedorn's assets.) Amy Hagedorn and Sandow plan to close the foundation's doors in 2017, allowing it to give more away than similar-size groups can. Ms. Hagedorn was a pre-kindergarten teacher before meeting Horace, so a program focused on families, children, and youths was among the first choices for the Hagedorn Foundation.

The foundation's other main program area was simply too big to ignore: Long Island had become a national focal point for suburban strife over immigration. As Latino immigrants moved to the counties for jobs, some longtime residents began to take a negative view of the newcomers. The negative atmosphere was fed by local political leaders, including Steve Levy, then Suffolk County executive and a co-founder of Mayors and Executives for Immigration Reform, a national group that wants to tighten the rules on immigrants in the United States.

In 2007, Hagedorn made a $230,000 grant to set up Long Island WINS, a communications campaign designed to highlight the positive contributions that immigrants were making in the community. By getting involved in national immigration organizations, Sandow learned about strategies he could try at home, and also steered the attention of much bigger national foundations toward Long Island. Rather than spending on direct assistance to the immigrants, Hagedorn gives more than $400,000 per year to a civic-engagement group that is focused on getting the newcomers to vote and take leadership positions in their communities.

In 2008, when, Marcelo Lucero, an Ecuadorian immigrant in Suffolk County was beaten to death by a group of white students out "beaner hopping"—a derogatory euphemism for attacking Hispanics—Long Island Wins had a blogger at the trial each day. In 2010, Hagedorn created the Long Island Civic Engagement Table, bringing together local advocacy groups. Hagedorn provides most of the group's operating budget, with a grant of more than $400,000 per year. The civic-engagement table helped focus attention on the school board in Brentwood, Long Island, which had faced allegations of racism. Ninety percent of the school district's students are black or Latino, but those minorities had never made up a majority of the school board. The civic group held a candidates' forum and encouraged local residents to vote. In 2012, voters elected new members to the board, putting black and Latino representatives in the majority for the first time.

The Civic Engagement Table also pushes to get issues that matter to immigrants on the radar of local politicians. Late last year, the new Suffolk County executive, who replaced Mr. Levy signed an executive order guaranteeing translation and interpretation services to all residents with limited English skills in their interactions with county government.

Immigration is not the only issue on which Hagedorn has been willing to agitate. When Nassau County tried to fold its youth board into a broader county department, the foundation tried to rally a group of local grant makers to protest. But only two of fifteen foundations he approached were willing to sign a petition he circulated asking for a meeting with the county. The pushed on, largely alone, and won the respect of the two county executives when the foundation offered to pay for half the salary of a youth-board staff member. The foundation's discussions with Nassau County officials led to the creation of a committee focused on improving the contracting and claims reimbursement process for nonprofits.

Hagedorn is now working to make sure its grantees, including the organizations it started, begin to diversify their sources of support before the foundation closes in 2017. It continues to address causative factors to social ills not only at the local level but at state and national levels. [18]

The Rauch Foundation

For a description of the foundation's substantial work since 1985, see the profile of Nancy Rauch Douzinas in Part III. [19]

Unitarian Universalist (UU) Veatch Program at Shelter Rock

1984 marked the 25th anniversary of the establishment of the original Veatch Committee. In 1986, Ed Lawrence retired as executive director. In his final years of tenure, he and the Veatch board successfully implemented a strategy of reducing direct building loans from the program to local congregations and fellowships. Instead, the Veatch allocation to the Unitarian Universalist Association began to earmark funds for such loans, but gave the association the authority to execute the transactions and to control it as a revolving loan fund.

In 1987 the Veatch board welcomed Josh Reichert as the new executive director and Barbara Dudley as program officer who had replaced David DiRienzis who had worked with Lawrence for many years. In hiring Reichert, the governors brought in a proven administrator from the Pew Foundation who was familiar with national issues and networks. Dudley came from the National Lawyers Guild with legal expertise that informed grant-making in the Constitutional rights sector and was an activist who brought that perspective when seeking out new grantees. The confluence of new professional leadership of the program and increased funding offered the opportunity for the program to reconsider its practices. The annual report for that year stated that the "Veatch board of governors undertook a review of priorities and goals...significantly increased funding...principally environmental protection and economic justice... and helped to promote wider political participation by the poor."

Dudley left the program mid-year in 1992 when the program's allocations totaled over $8.9 million. One of the final projects she undertook was the initiation of discussions with the Long Island Foundation and other Long

Island philanthropies. This resulted in the formation of the Long Island Unitarian Universalist Fund in 1993. By the time Dudley left the program in 1993, the Veatch board had reviewed the work of the program under Lawrence's leadership, assessed the environment in which the program was currently trying to effectuate change, examined and adjusted a number of policies, and utilized that information to amend funding strategies. Tracking the grants made in that era shows that, whether nondenominational funding was local or national in scope, the emphasis continued the shift from advocacy to funding groups for which the emphasis was on systemic change. This was all by trial and error as the political environment changed, national and state policy agendas shifted, and the radical right was increasingly recognized for the powerful force it

Marjorie (Margie) Fine began her service as executive director in June of 1993. In the annual report written by the board chair one-year later it was said that, "The Veatch Program not only landed on its feet running despite the challenges of changing staff, changing locations and even changing computer systems, but had a very productive year as well!" The congregation was informed that the staff and board began to move in new directions and that it "deepened support of ordinary people in the creation of a true democracy." Among the new directions referred to were "new ways of organizing workers...health care...economic renewal...and a southern initiative." New innovations continued and by 1996 it was reported that the program had added the New York Metro Initiative.

Regarding Veatch's leadership role in progressive philanthropy, an evaluation of the program published in 2000 reported:

"Not only has Veatch staff influenced individual grant-makers and institutions, but they have helped create and build strong networks, affinity groups, and funding collaborations. They are recognized for their leadership in calling attention to emerging movements and vibrant community efforts. Time and time again, interviewees remarked not only on their persistence and influence but on the great wisdom and knowledge that they bring to the table. Advice is grounded in careful analysis and deep understanding of the history and issues involved. As a resource and as a lively participant, Veatch staff clearly contributes much to everyone's understanding of complex and controversial issues and events in the social justice movement."

This evaluation was undertaken at the direction of the Veatch board in 1999. Published in 2000, the report, entitled *"A View of Veatch: policies, practices, and perspectives from fourteen peer grant-makers."* The report gave the board the opportunity to hear suggestions from other progressive funders as to how it might improve its focus and grant-making practices, and it collected comparative data on board governance, staff responsibilities, funding priorities, and financial information, including annual grant-making and administrative budgets and average grant size.

After attaining grant-making budget levels of $10 million and $10.314 million respectively in 2001 and 2002, Veatch's grants budget reached $10.5 million in 2003. In 2004, the Veatch budget declined to $9.5 million, in 2005 to $8.7 million, and in 2006 $8.3 million. Allocations increased modestly in the years 2007-2014.

Over the years, the congregation--through both Veatch and its own general funds--has provided operational, special program or endowment support to the UUSC, the UUA and affiliated programs, as well as millions of dollars in church building loan funds. As the program matured and its allocations increased, Veatch, first as a committee and then as a board, was able to fund nondenominational organizations. Since the beginning of non-denominational funding, priorities expanded and strategies evolved from social services to advocacy, to support for systemic change through grassroots organizing. The program continuously reflected and was influenced by congregational interests.

Following the departure of Margie Fine as executive director in 2005, senior program officer Victor Quintana stepped as interim director until July 2006, when the Reverend Ned Wight, selected by the search committee and the board of trustees as Fine's successor, began his service. Since then the UU Veatch Program has continued to focus on support for grassroots organizations working for long-term social change. With a robust economy and royalty income stream, the allocation for Veatch grants increased each year beginning in 2006. In 2009-10, the Veatch Program celebrated its 50th anniversary with a weekend of activities and the publication of a 50-year timeline in its annual report.

Throughout these years, the Veatch Program continued to sponsor a congregational bus trip to one or more Veatch grantees in greater New York, as well as an annual site visit for members of the board of governors and board of trustees to grantees throughout the country.

Beginning in 2007-08, the congregation launched its large grants program, which set aside $17.5 million from which interest income and up to 20 percent of the corpus could be allocated to a make grants no smaller than $100,000. Over the next several years, a large grants advisory group was convened to oversee the annual decision-making process, in which the congregation as a whole plays the central role. Veatch staff and consultants provided professional oversight for the program, and grants have been made to a wide range of non-profit organizations on Long Island and elsewhere. Funding areas included peace/anti-War, housing and homelessness on Long Island, UU camps and conference centers, UU theological education, immigrant rights, religious liberty, UU youth, UUCSR partner church, women's empowerment and justice, mental health on Long Island, campaign finance reform, women's health, and sex trafficking. Grants totaled $915,000 in 2007-08, $900,000 in each of the next three years, and $600,000 in 2011-12. In addition, the congregation voted $600,000 to four hunger relief organizations on Long Island in 2009-10 and $500,000 to the joint UUSC/UUA Haiti Earthquake Relief Fund in 2010. Recommendations about the future of this 7-year trial program will be made in 2015.

With over 60 percent of the congregation's annual budget being allocated to philanthropic purposes, philanthropy continues to occupy a central role in the overall mission of the Unitarian Universalist Congregation at Shelter Rock. [20]

<u>United Way of Long Island (UWLI)</u>

Over the years since 1985, UWLI has benefited by a good deal of executive leadership including Patrick Foye and Theresa Regnante. In 2010, UWLI created the Long Island Capacity Optimization and Optimization Tank (LICOT) to help nonprofits with the business side of their operations such as: Fiscal and accounting services, grant writing, graphic design, green practices, human resources, information technology, legal matters, and leadership and organizational development.

In addition, UWLI established a partnership with Adelphi's Nonprofit Leadership Center to help nonprofits lead and manage people, preparing corporate volunteers to become nonprofit board members. LICOT has also conducted workshops and seminars to help nonprofits use technology more effectively as well as to help them foster partnerships and new organizational structures to enable nonprofits to maximize their resources. This has included sponsorship of forums with state funding agencies to explore ways in which nonprofits can gain greater support from state government, minimize contracting problems, and take advantage of operational cost-saving options.

United Way of Long Island has evolved from its roots as a broad-based fund raising organization to a critical community convener mobilizing diverse people, organizations and networks to create long-term change. In the past, United Way raised funds to support local nonprofit agencies that provided assistance to Long Islanders in a wide range of service areas. Funded agencies were reviewed and monitored for accountability, but the larger picture of measurably improving the community well-being was not stressed.

As United Way moved into the 21st century, the organization established *LIVE UNITED* as its working agenda to bring about measurable change in the community. United Way's work focused on the building blocks for a good life in three key areas: Health, Education and Income Stability. The organizational goal is directed at helping Long Islanders succeed by supporting programs and initiatives that help children and youth achieve their educational potential; help people lead healthy lives; and help families improve their financial stability and independence.

To meet these goals, United Way expanded its collaborations not only with traditional nonprofit community-based organizations, but also with local, state and federal governments in both policy and direct service capacities. UWLI have developed capacity building services, such as the 2-1-1 Long Island information and referral system; built programs to serve new populations, such as returning military personnel; and addressed emerging fields, such as green job training and weatherization. And as a community partner, United Way increased its role in long-term disaster recovery services for both the Long Island region and for disaster-affected families.

Other UWLI programs include the DREAMS for Youth Scholarship Fund is a program that awards grants in the areas of Academics, Community Service, & Enrichment. These grants are awarded to students by students as the DREAMS for Youth Advisory Board, is comprised of grade 7-12 students that work under the guidance of United Way of Long Island staff.

YouthBuild Long Island is a free program that provides low-income young adults ages 18 to 24 with hands on training for housing, education, job readiness/construction pre-apprenticeship training, career development, leadership development, counseling and graduate services. Students have hands on training with the latest equipment and technology at our E3 Career Training Center in Deer Park.

Project Warmth is Long Island's only non-governmental emergency fuel fund which provides one-time grants to oil and utility companies on behalf of residents facing heating emergencies. Through a network of partner agencies, struggling Long Island families can apply to Project Warmth and receive information on other local resources to help them address greater financial stability.

Military & Veterans Initiatives: New York has the most consecutive National Guard activations in the country. Military personnel are forced to leave their families behind, overwhelmed by fewer resources and myriad other personal stresses. When discharged, they return home faced with physical, emotional and financial struggles as they transition back into civilian employment.

The federally-funded Emergency Food and Shelter Program (EFSP) provides assistance for food, utilities and shelter to individuals and families in emergency situations who meet the federal eligibility guidelines. United Way of Long Island administers the program for the Long Island region.

Today, UWLI's work is accomplished by developing programs a variety of community programs and fundraising for over 120 community partners. In 2013, over $11.8M was allocated to these community partners. According to UWLI, allocations of $5.0M were awarded in 1983 over thirty years ago. Investments are made in education to ensure children succeed in school and achieve their potential. Families are helped to become financially stable and independent. And, communities are assured that they have access to healthcare, food, and positive lifestyle choices. A staff, supported by a high profile board of directors, brings together partners and volunteers from across Long Island to discuss issues, raise funds, and develop programs. [21]

See Appendix for a listing of UWLI's annual award recipients.

<u>The Women's Fund of Long Island (WFLI) (formerly Long Island Fund for Women & Girls)</u>

The Women's Fund was founded in 1991 by Barbara Strongin, Suzy Sonenberg and Betty Schlein. Their motto was "empowerment through philanthropy." In the organization's infancy, women from all over Nassau County and Suffolk County met at home gatherings, at bi-county general meetings and in work-based focus groups to identify the most pressing issues affecting women and girls in the local communities.

In 2011, The Women's Fund changed its name to the Women's Fund of Long Island ("WFLI"). By 1993, WFLI had an active Steering Council and had disbursed $20,000 in grants to local nonprofit organizations whose programs benefited women and girls. Originally a part of the Long Island Community Foundation, WFLI became a nonprofit, charitable organization with an independent board of directors in 1995.

Each year since 1995, WFLI expanded its philanthropy through an annual "Women Achievers" breakfast. Held each October, this is the organization's major fundraising event. Exceptional women and young women leaders are honored and WFLI's annual grants are announced. Over the past twenty years, WFLI has made 465 grants to 265 organizations impacting the lives of 120,000 Long Island women and girls. WFLI connects grassroots organizations with resources, information and training to achieve sustainability and better serve their communities. Improving the lives of women creates benefits and opportunity for their families, future generations and the Long Island community.

The fund has worked together to empower women and girls on Long Island through impact grant-making, a leadership program, and education and awareness. The fund focuses on: Impactful grant-making; young women's leadership; and education and awareness. [22]

Other Funders

It should also be acknowledged that support for social programs from business corporations during the past twenty-five years continued, and in some cases expanded. According to interviewees, much of this new support came from larger business corporations and banks that had merged or consolidated. Corporate support was also evident through their executives' increased participation on nonprofit boards of directors and after Hurricane Sandy. Noteworthy firms are National Grid (Key Span), JP Morgan Chase Foundation, TD Bank (Commerce Bank), Bank of America (Fleet), Citi (Citi Group), Symbol (Motorola), Farrell Fritz, *Newsday,* Cablevison, Computer Associates, NY Community Bank Foundation (Roslyn Savings Foundation), and Bethpage Federal Credit Union.

The Association of Fundraising Professionals of Long Island (AFPLI)

Founded in 1986, AFPLI is the recognized voice of fundraising and philanthropy on Long Island. AFPLI is Long Island's affiliation for professional fundraisers, those whose positions require fundraising expertise on a professional or volunteer basis, and individuals considering a career in fundraising. Throughout the year, AFPLI offers a wide array of programs and services that include monthly educational seminars, accredited certification programs, scholarships, mentoring, career opportunities and a speaker's bureau. AFPLI is a three-time winner of the 10 Star Chapter Award, presented by AFP to chapters that have accomplished significant membership growth and chapter success. AFPLI has also won the Charles R. Stephens Excellence in Diversity Chapter Award, which honors the chapter's efforts in building diversity.

For the past 25 years, AFPLI has presented Philanthropy Day on Long Island. Fundraising professionals, board members, volunteers, business leaders, community activists and individuals gather for a day focused on improving their fundraising skills and celebrating individuals and organizations committed to making a difference. [23]

See Appendix for a listing of APFLI's annual award recipients.

Health Care

According to the 2006 findings of the New York State Health Care Commission report *"Findings of the Long Island Regional Advisory Committee"* in recent years Long Island hospitals have diversified away from medical/surgical bed capacity and expanded into behavioral health and rehabilitation, and created specialized inpatient programs and services which focus on short-stay minimally-invasive surgical procedures. In addition, many hospitals have successfully participated in area-wide health planning by joining regional health care systems which have consolidated obstetrical and pediatric bed capacity or relocated specialized services, such as cardiac catheterization from tertiary care centers to community hospitals. Over half of the 23 Long Island hospitals operating in 2005 have merged or consolidated into health systems. [24]

The health care sector is composed of family planning, outpatient medical facilities, hospitals, and nursing care facilities, and residential health care facilities. The report shows a 29.6% increase in the number of providers between 2000 and 2006. The report indicates a growth in competition for scarcer health care workers, especially registered nurses, thus limiting job growth in this sector.

Suffolk County's Health Centers

Some of Suffolk's community-based health centers underwent a number of changes since 1985. Some remained county-operated while others are now operated by independent operators. They are:

County-Operated Health Centers

Brentwood - The Suffolk County Brentwood Family Health Center

Patchogue - The South Brookhaven Family Health Center at Patchogue

Riverhead - The Suffolk County Health Center at Riverhead

Shirley - The Marilyn Shellabarger South Brookhaven Family Health Center East at Shirley

Wyandanch - The Martin Luther King, Jr. Community Health Center at Wyandanch

Affiliated Health Centers

Amityville - HRHCare Maxine S. Postal Tri-Community Health Center
Operated by Hudson River HealthCare, Inc.

Greenlawn - The Dolan Family Health Center at Greenlawn
Operated by Huntington Hospital

Coram - The Elsie Owens Health Center at Coram
Operated by Hudson River HealthCare

Southampton - HRHCare Kraus Family Health Center of the Hamptons

Operated by Hudson River HealthCare, Inc.

In 2014, the county withdrew from the health system, transferring all the health centers, except one, to the Hudson River Corporation, a nonprofit organization that is a Federally Qualified Health Center and eligible to obtain federal funding to expand services. It is governed by a board half of whom are patients of the health centers, but report to the federal government. On the East End, the three centers have merger into one. The county expects to save about half of what they were spending. [25]

For further information, visit Robert Detor's analysis of changes in the health and mental health system in Part VI.

Juvenile and Criminal Justice Services

Over the past twenty-five years, great strides have been made in expanding alternatives for adult and juvenile incarceration. New diversion programs in both counties have been created for various targeted populations including offenders with mental illnesses, drug problems, veterans, and those who committed crimes involving domestic violence. In some cases, the programs involve more intensive supervision, correctional interventions or case management by the probation department or community-based treatment provided by credentialed counselors while other cases are adjudicated in special courts that consider alternatives to incarceration services.

The movement to provide greater assistance to juveniles and teenagers has strengthened generating the creation of the Adolescent Diversion Program for 16 and 17 year olds in Nassau County with the hope that ultimately New York will catch up to the rest of the country by raising the age of criminal responsibility to 18 years old.

Much still has to be done and it is not always success right out of the gate, when one considers that in 1973, when the efforts began, the New York State prison population was 13,400 rising to a historic peak in 1999 to 71,538 inmates. Recently, efforts have taken hold with both crime and incarceration steadily declining. At the time of this writing, inmate population was down to 54,000. [26]

Child Care

Child day care services have dramatically expanded on Long Island over the past 25 years most significantly through the substantial presence of for-profit national providers such as Tutor Time, Kiddie Academy, and KinderCare. Many smaller centers have ceased to operate unable to compete successfully with the expanding national chains. According to a 2014 Rauch Foundation -

United Way of Long Island report, the child care industry is a $800M industry on Long Island with over 1,800 full and part-time programs and a workforce of almost 9,000 people.

The availability of family day care homes has grown substantially mainly through the educational and training efforts of the two child care councils. In addition, government has expanded day care subsidies for low income and working families as well. Nevertheless, the availability of affordable, quality child care has not kept pace with the need for these services. Child care program operators have continued to struggle to garner state and local political support regardless of all the substantial benefits that child care affords to children and working parents.

What has not happened is the expansion of employer-sponsored child care centers or subsidy programs despite initiatives established in the 1980s and 1990s. Computer Associates' continues to operate its large center which was managed for the company from 1991-1992 by The Community Programs Center of Long Island (CPC). In 1992, the company decided to operate the center itself while Symbol Technologies, Cablevision, and CMP Publications closed their child care centers for a variety of economic reasons. In like manner, centers supported by multiple companies such as CPC's center in Deer Park and First Class in Melville ceased to operate years ago partly for lack of corporate financial support or employee subsidies. Corporations generally viewed child care programs as too costly. In the late1990s, an onsite program was established at Belmont Racetrack for the children of the backstretch workers. The Child Care Council of Nassau provided consultation to the center's founders. The center is operated by a private operator and is partially funded by a nonprofit entity of racetrack supporters.

Other child care center development occurred through state and county government initiatives with the establishment of centers at the State University at Stony Brook, the State Office Building in Hauppauge, and Suffolk County Community College campuses, Nassau Community College, Adelphi University, Hofstra University, the IRS center in Holtsville, and Brookhaven National Laboratories.

The other important development in corporate child care is the substantial growth of resource and referral programs sponsored by the two child care councils. These programs help company employees find center-based and family day care alternatives. The councils also established a large network of family day care homes and provided training and support to family day care providers. [27]

Youth Services

According to Peter Levy, president of the Nassau youth agencies have always been the 'low-hanging fruit" for county legislators under pressure to cut the county discretionary spending and to fund only mandated services. They are often used as 'pawns' because legislators know that youth services is an issue that people care about, so youth services, for instance, was used as a pawn when the sewer system was privatized and when red light camera spending became a legislative priority. It is not just getting into the annual adopted budget every year that is at issue. It is also making sure that the county executive does not refuse to spend the money allocated in the approved budget when shortfalls arise during the year. Legislators feel compelled to cut discretionary budgets regardless of their party affiliations when they're forced by budget constraints to cut, they cut social spending. Unlike in the 1970s and 1980s, the youth board does not fund any new program initiative regardless of convincing evidence of the need for such funding. Over the past few years, the Hagedorn Fund has supported many of the coalition's member agencies. In this regard, these agencies are concerned about the loss of this funding as the Hagedorn Foundation spends down over the next few years. [28]

Funding for youth service agencies in Suffolk County paralleled Nassau County's experience where agencies worried from year-to-year about their funding levels from county and town youth bureaus. Agencies expanded their funding with state and county legislative grants which were also granted on a year-by-year basis. They sponsored fund raising events and sought charitable contributions but remained heavily dependent on government aid. Funding for expansion of existing programs occurred infrequently. Some smaller organizations discontinued their services despite efforts to convince legislators of community needs. Despite the pressures brought upon by the constant fear of funding cuts, community-based youth service organizations continue to do exceptional work in youth development and throughout all their preventive programs. They bolster the economy by providing much needed services to families, thus allowing the now common two working parent households to continue with their jobs. The parents feel safe knowing their children are involved in meaningful and productive after school programs. These agencies also are involved in mentoring, counseling and similar efforts all designed to help children. [29]

Aging Services

Over the past twenty-five years, Long Island's population of older adults has grown significantly. With this growth, services for the elderly have grown as well. Residential facilities, including assisted living centers, nursing homes, adult homes, and rehabilitation centers, operated by for-profit companies and nonprofit entities, are situated from the Queens border to the East End. Dozens of nonprofit and for-profit home health care agencies provide medical and non-medical services and a handful of medical and social model adult day services programs serve those whose needs can be accommodated while living in the community.

In addition, towns and counties and nonprofit organizations, heavily-supported by state and local grants, sponsor a variety of non-medical services and programs for older adults such as nutrition centers, meals on wheels programs, a home sharing program, respite and chore programs, employment programs, and case management services. The Town of North Hempstead launched Project Independence in contract with Federation Employment Guidance Services (FEGS) as an aging-in-place, neighborhood naturally occurring retirement community (NNORC), providing older adults that enable them to remain in their homes as long as possible. The NNORC model has also been established in the town of Huntington by FEGS and in Plainview by the Mid Island Y Jewish Community Center.

The volunteerism and civic engagement of older adults were expanded through RSVP of Suffolk and the RSVP program sponsored by the Nassau County Department of Senior Citizens Affairs the Long Island Volunteer Center.

Universities launched lifelong learning programs at Hofstra University's Project PEER, the Older Adult Learning Institute (OLLI) at Stony Brook University and the Farmingdale State's Institute for Learning in Retirement. Family Service League operates SeniorNet, a computer learning center and the federally-funded program Senior Community Service Employment Program is operated by the Urban League.

There have been several new educational programs established on Long Island since the 1980s that prepare people for social service and social action work. In 2005, the Suffolk Commission on Creative Retirement, established by then-County Executive Steve Levy, spent a year studying the needs of older adults and produced a 27-page report. The report urged the county to see older adults as tremendous social capital. The ten-person commission developed a highly-regarded series of recommendations regarding the future needs of the burgeoning population of aging adults. Unfortunately, the county executive chose to virtually disregard the recommendations despite the fact that most of them did not entail additions to the budget.

Other efforts, principally promulgated by Intergenerational Strategies urged public and private agencies to develop and implement intergenerational policies and programs. The nonprofit sponsored numerous conferences and seminars and consulted with many organizations. It discontinued its programs in 2010 due to a lack of funding. [30]

Higher Education

The following represent social work education programs established since 1985.

Adelphi University School of Social Work

The following information describes Adelphi's various social work programs launched since 1985.

Continuing Education and Professional Development

In the human services field, learning is a lifelong process. Let us make Adelphi University School of Social Work your academic center for advanced professional development and continuing education in the field of behavioral health. Whether you wish to join us for an in-depth postgraduate certificate program in trauma, addictions, school services or military trauma, or you prefer to stay abreast of current trends in one of our workshops featuring theory, practice or policy, we offer convenient and local solutions to all of your interdisciplinary needs. Come and network with your colleagues. We welcome alumni and graduates from all accredited educational institutions. Students of all ages and levels are welcome to join our community.

Certificate Programs

Certificate Programs are offered in the following areas: Advanced Trauma Studies and Treatment; Addictions; Bilingual School Social Work; Human Resource Management; Summer Institute; and Hudson Valley Certificates.

Online Course: Reporting Child Abuse

Effective September 1, 2004, licensed social workers in New York State have become mandated reporters of child maltreatment. Adelphi University has been designated as an approved provider of this course by the New York State Education Department for the training of mandated reporters of child abuse and maltreatment. Under this law, all licensed social workers must complete two hours of coursework. This online course contains the curriculum you need to meet the new requirements. [31]

Long Island Center for Nonprofit Leadership

In 2005, The Center for Nonprofit Leadership began as a grassroots effort to address leadership transition and development in nonprofit organizations on Long Island. A group of concerned nonprofit leaders met monthly for a year to seek solutions to these leadership challenges. This group included representatives from the Long Island Community Foundation, the Rauch Foundation, United Way of Long Island, and the dean and associate dean of Adelphi's School of Social Work, as well as executive directors of nonprofit organizations. Richard Dina played a critical role in launching the center.

With their support, a Long Island Nonprofit Leadership Summit was held at Adelphi as a first step in responding to the needs of the nonprofit community. This full-day event attracted nearly 300 nonprofit professionals and board members. The creation of the Center for Nonprofit Leadership grew out of their resounding consensus in favor of a Long Island-based resource that would provide help and guidance in dealing with leadership transitions, board leadership and leadership development.

The center is housed within Adelphi's School of Social Work and receives financial support from JP Morgan Chase, the Long Island Community Foundation, the New York Community Bank Foundation, and the Hagedorn Foundation. The center seeks to provide excellence in leadership within Long Island's nonprofit sector. This goal is particularly timely because of the potential void among nonprofit leaders and executives as large numbers of baby boomers retire during the next decade. There is also a dearth of nonprofit leaders from under-represented communities, which can impair the effectiveness of nonprofit organizations.

Since its inception, the center has provided customized consulting services at board meetings and retreats and assistance to new and emerging nonprofit leaders and support for existing executive directors. The center offers a nine-month leadership development certificate program for both new and emerging leaders. The center also offers a full executive transition management service for organizations currently experiencing or likely to experience a management transition. In addition, training is provided for individuals to work as consultants to nonprofit boards. The center works with nonprofit organizations to explore opportunities for potential partnerships, including opportunities for co-location, consolidation, and merger. A new leadership program will be launched in September 2014, called "Leading in Community" will focus on building leadership in communities of color.

The center's website provides useful resources such as assessment templates for board members, fundraising resources, job postings for executive directors and current research and reports pertaining to the nonprofit community. [32]

C.W. Post School of Social Work

Master of Social Work (M.S.W)

The 60-credit Master of Social Work (M.S.W.) offers Degree candidates five different concentrations –gerontology, nonprofit management, alcohol and substance abuse, child and family welfare or forensic social work. The program is a collaboration of the University's LIU Brooklyn Campus and its LIU Post Campus (Brookville), and courses are available at both locations.

The program is integrated to provide a step-wise progression in student understanding of generalist and specialized practice. The first-year curriculum includes content in the eight foundation areas of policy, practice, human behavior, field, diversity, populations at risk, and promotion of social justice and values. It introduces the student to the components of generalist practice with systems of all sizes and provides an understanding of generalist practice that distinguishes between generalist and advanced content while supporting the integration of specialized knowledge and technologies into a generalist perspective. It also introduces the student to the principles of interdisciplinary collaboration, preparing them for work in interdisciplinary fields of practice.

The second-year curriculum builds upon the first year by deepening students' understanding and demonstrated mastery of psychosocial assessment, administrative theory and practice, and diversity sensitive practice. Students select a specific area of concentration - non-profit management, substance abuse, gerontology, child and family welfare or forensic social work – for more specialized education in a particular area of practice. The research curriculum in the second year supports the concentrated study by demonstrating application of research methodology to the student's specialized area of concentration. Field experience in the second year provides an opportunity for the student to apply generalist and specialized knowledge in the selected area of concentration. The curriculum is consistent with program goals insofar as the student receives a generalist background that includes a conception of generalist practice, an eclectic knowledge base and an understanding of the relationship of values, diversity, populations at risk and promotion of social justice to the social work professional role with systems of all sizes.

Bachelor of Science in Social Work

The 129-credit Bachelor of Science in Social Work, accredited by the Council on Social Work Education, will prepares students for a career as a generalist professional helping individuals, families, groups, communities and organizations. As a social work major at LIU Post, students start on a journey toward a career in an important "helping profession," to provide guidance, counseling, referrals and practical human services to people in need.

In the context of a liberal arts education, students will study in small classes with faculty members who are both scholars and leading practitioners in the social work field. Emphasis is on gaining the knowledge, values and skills needed to promote both individual well-being and a more just society. In addition to academic courses, students will have an opportunity to make a direct impact on client populations through field work in such diverse settings as schools, homeless shelters, child and family counseling centers, charitable organizations, senior citizen facilities, and social service agencies. A very active student club provides students with opportunities for numerous and exciting community service activities.

Minor in Social Work Program

The minor in Social Work provides students with understanding of the profession's emphasis on human relationships and social justice. Students learn the bio-psycho-social-spiritual aspects of human behavior and development, the dynamics of social systems including family, group, community and organizations as well as social policy analysis and advocacy. The minor is designed for students in related disciplines such as psychology, sociology, health sciences, health care and public administration, art therapy and education. Completion of this minor will help students to broaden their skills in counseling as well as delivery of health and social services, and allow the determination if pursuing graduate study in social work is the right career path for them. [33]

Farmingdale State College

The following information was obtained on the center's website: www.farmingdale.edu

The college offers instructor-led online courses on nonprofit management, marketing and fundraising. [34]

Hofstra University Continuing Education

The following information was obtained on the center's website: www.hofstra.edu/ACADEMICS/CE

In partnership with the Association of Fundraising Professionals-Long Island Chapter, Hofstra offers an 80-hour certificate in Nonprofit Management in a Changing World. The program is designed for nonprofit administrators and staff, board members and volunteers, and individuals who may be interested in changing careers. Courses may be taken on an individual basis without participating in the certificate program. [35]

National Center for Suburban Studies at Hofstra University

The following information was obtained on the center's website: http://www.hofstra.edu/ACADEMICS/CSS/index.html

The center is a non-partisan research institution dedicated to promoting the study of suburbia's problems, as well as its promise. Rooted in the laboratory of Long Island's diverse and aging suburbs and in the shadows of the iconic Levittown, the National Center researches a broad range of issues at local, national, and international scales. The suburbs have emerged at the nexus of dynamic demographic, social, economic and environmental change in New York and throughout the world. We seek to understand the suburbs via academically rigorous research that encompasses the natural and social sciences and the humanities. The goal of the center is to identify, analyze, and solve the problems of suburbia, especially in areas of sustainability, social equity, and economic development. [36]

Fordham University Graduate School of Social Service at Molloy College

Molloy partnered with the Long Island Chapter of the Association of Fundraising Professionals to offer two certificate programs in development, philanthropy, and fundraising management for individuals who market and raise funds for nonprofit organizations. Students can earn a Certificate or Advanced Certificate in Development and Fundraising Management.

An undergraduate program or a collaborative M.S.W. program through Fordham University prepares students to work in a variety of fields and in a wide array of settings. Program features are: Flexible full and part-time plans of study with day and evening classes; Small classes with a low student/faculty ratio; Experiential learning in a variety of settings - active classrooms, hospitals, agencies focusing on mental health and family/children, homeless shelters, meetings with legislators and many other exciting opportunities; Gerontology (GRN) minor providing the most current information on older adults and issues related to aging; Extensive internship opportunities; Professional Encounter Courses provide an opportunity for students to spend a semester in the field with the on-site mentoring of a faculty member, prior to their actual field internship.

Students may also choose to enroll in a collaborative Master of Social Work (M.S.W.) program with Fordham University Graduate School of Social Service. The program enables students to earn a Fordham University M.S.W. Degree while taking some of the courses at Molloy College. This graduate program also offers flexible full or part-time plans of study that includes day, evening and weekend classes.

There are two options that offer flexibility and convenience to Long Island students. The traditional Fordham/Molloy face-to-face class option affords you the opportunity to be part of an urban university at Fordham's Lincoln Center Campus coupled with the convenience and sense of community at Molloy College. The Long Island Hybrid Option offers the flexibility of online classes along with traditional face-to-face classes held at Molloy College. Through this collaborative MSW program, students receive an education rooted in the mission and values unique to the social work profession.

The program is comprehensive, the study options flexible and the learning experience is one of excellence. Students learn and apply knowledge through a combination of classes focused on Social Work theory and practice in well-respected Long Island social service settings. Upon completion, students emerge as competent, value-based professionals. [37]

Certificate or Advanced Certificate in Development and Fundraising Management

Molloy has also partnered with the Long Island Chapter of the Association of Fundraising Professionals (AFPLI) to offer two certificate programs in development, philanthropy, and fundraising management for individuals who market and raise funds for nonprofit organizations. Students can earn a Certificate or Advanced Certificate in Development and Fundraising Management. [38]

Energeia Partnership at Molloy College

The following information was obtained from the organization's website: *www.energeiali.com*

The partnership brings together a diverse group of ethical leaders from Long Island's public, private and nonprofit sectors to help address the region's most complex issues: education, institutional racism, poverty and the working poor, land use, energy, transportation, healthcare and media/social networking. Also known as the Academy for Regional Stewardship at Molloy College, Energeia is committed to educating leaders for the benefit of all people who live and work on Long Island. Each year, the program assembles a "class" of no more than 50 ethical, proven leaders that participates in a dynamic, two-year academy featuring a series of one-day programs, each focusing on a particular issue. [39]

State University at Stony Brook/School of Social Welfare

Dual Degree Program in Social Work and Law

The MSW/JD program offers the opportunity to earn an MSW (Master of Social Work) from the School of Social Welfare and a JD (Juris Doctor) from the Touro Law Center in four years, rather than the five which would be required if the Degrees were earned separately. Applicants may apply for the dual Degree program prior to matriculation or during their enrollment in the first year at either school. Applicants must apply to and be accepted by both schools. If accepted by both schools, the student is automatically eligible for the Dual Degree program. The first year may be spent at either school, with the choice being up to the student. The second year is spent at the other school, the third year is divided between the two schools and the fourth year is spent primarily at the law school.

The Ph.D. Program in the School of Social Welfare

The Ph.D. Program in the School of Social Welfare is a Policy Research Degree that focuses on social problem/social welfare issues such as poverty, health, violence, and aging. It operates under the auspices of the Stony Brook University Graduate School and is committed to the School of Social Welfare's mission of social justice. Taking full advantage of the resources of both the Graduate School and the multidisciplinary Health Sciences Center as well as affiliated faculty throughout the University, the program features small classes, a supportive environment for doctoral students, and a rigorous course of study. Upon receipt of this Ph.D., graduates will be well prepared to teach, direct research projects in government and social agencies, and carry out policy analyses in the field of social welfare.

Graduate Program

The program provides students with the needed theoretical and practice expertise to function with maximum competence at different administrative or policy levels in social welfare fields and/or in the provision of direct services to individuals, families, groups, and communities. The school provides opportunities for study and practice that utilize the wealth of interdisciplinary resources available in the Health Sciences Center, the University, and community agencies throughout the New York metropolitan area.

The School has developed community and training programs to build specialized knowledge with the broad local, regional and global community including a Child Welfare Training Program to build an agency's strengths while providing assistance and overcome challenges to help youth in care. The *Sudden Infant and Child Death (SICD) Resource Center* improves infant and child health and safety throughout New York State. The Sayville Project is a nonprofit community based service Community Support Services agency providing services and support to adults with psychiatric disabilities. [40]

Stony Brook University's School of Professional Development offers a 300-hour online certificate program in nonprofit management. [41]

The Arts

Friends of the Arts (FOTA)

FOTA is a nonprofit organization with mission is to enrich cultural life on Long Island through the presentation of world-class performances and through stimulating educational programs for children. FOTA presents performances of classical, jazz and popular music at its outdoor Long Island Summer Festival and Long Island Jazz Festival. ArtReach, arts-in-education programs were created in school districts in Nassau and Suffolk counties. [42]

Landmark on Main Street

Landmark on Main Street is the product of more than ten years of visionary planning and dedicated work by the citizens of Port Washington. It developed out a commitment to preserve an historic landmark, the Main Street School, and to enhance community life. A unique model of community development, Landmark is a collaboration of civic-minded individuals, government, business, and nonprofit organizations all sharing the belief that a community's commitment to a richer cultural, recreational, civic, educational and social life and the celebration of diversity benefits the quality of life for all. Lillian McCormick, Reverend Charles Vogeley and Barbara Goldstein, were key leaders of the effort.

Landmark on Main Street opened in November 1995. The 87-year-old former school was converted into 59 units of affordable senior housing, a two-acre town park and a 25,000 square foot community center. A complex mix of government and corporate funds augmented by private contributions financed the $11.5 million acquisition/renovation. The area's limited rental market and high cost of construction jeopardized the existence of essential local service organizations and inhibited their expansion. The community center provides affordable space for nonprofit organizations for both long-term and per diem usage. Landmark's centralized location and proximity to public transportation (on a major bus route and within walking distance of the railroad station) makes it accessible to teens, non-driving adults, seniors and visitors.

The 1984 announcement that the board of education would close the Main Street School resulted in the formation of two independent citizen groups. One sought to expand recreational and cultural opportunities for children and create an indoor playground, pool and teen center. By surveying the community they learned that many shared their sentiments. The other group was formed for the purpose of creating affordable housing for seniors who could no longer afford to live in Port Washington. Both groups identified how to acquire public funds to accomplish their goals. They saw the Main Street School building, already designated an historic landmark and a beloved part of Port's history, as the place where these goals could be achieved. In 1986 the two groups merged and incorporated.

Landmark's founders clearly and frequently informed the community of their goals and asked for its help in realizing them. They also researched ways they could acquire the property and hired a consultant (funded by a planning grant) to explore the feasibility of their plan. They lobbied members of the school board on a regular basis both publicly and privately reminding them of their commitment to preserve open space. Leaders explored all strategies for accomplishing their goals and concluded that acquisition of the property could best be achieved if the local municipality agreed to participate. Discussion and collaboration with the Town of North Hempstead ensued and spanned two different administrations. In 1990, the Town agreed to enter into a contingency offer to purchase the property to develop the Landmark project pending a report from their own consultants. One year later, the school district and town entered into a conditional contract pending approval by district voters and Landmark's acquisition of requisite funding. In December 1991, after an exhaustive referendum campaign, voters overwhelmingly approved the Landmark plan.

Landmark entered into a relationship with a team of professionals consisting of an experienced housing developer, a builder, an architectural firm and a local property management company. Planning funds were secured from a local foundation. Leaders continued to mobilize community support for Landmark's goals. They embraced local non-profit organizations seeking to make their home at Landmark. Once it became clear that available funding would not be sufficient for the community center portion of the building Landmark launched a capital campaign to raise the needed $2 million. Local philanthropists and governments were solicited. Within several months, a $1.1 million block grant and $250,000 in private contributions were secured. In December 1992, a plan and funding package were identified. The next two years were spent completing the capital campaign and developing plans that would best suit the interest of all parties. Construction began in 1994 and was completed in 17 months.

Landmark on Main Street, a nonprofit organization, is the coordinating agency that makes the collaboration of tenant organizations possible and holds the project together. Without the benefit of any direct tax-based revenue, the organization is responsible for 40% of the total cost of operating and maintaining the Landmark building. Its full-time Executive Director, in addition to working as a liaison to the tenant organizations, oversees and coordinates rentals of common building space including a 425-seat theater, gymnasium and meeting room to tenants and community groups, plans community-wide programs and centralizes outreach and communication to the people of Port Washington and beyond. The core group that planned and created Landmark is rich in expertise in fiscal planning and development.

It is estimated that, on any given weekday, over 600 members of our community (children, teens and adults) come through Landmark's doors to attend programs in the theater, run by our tenant organizations or to participate in activities held in the rentable spaces. The Jeanne Rimsky Theater at Landmark on Main Street is vibrant with concerts, speaker-engagements, shows, body-building competitions, dance performances, meetings and birthday parties. As our marketing campaign grows and word spreads, more and more local organizations, businesses and families are utilizing this wonderfully versatile space. [43]

Long Island Arts Alliance (LIAA)

The seeds for LIAA were planted in 2002 when the Long Island Association, the region's largest business and civic organization, asked prominent community leaders to examine Long Island's assets, growth opportunities and challenges. Its arts and culture committee, made up of heads of local arts institutions, found that no measure had yet been taken of the arts' regional economic impact. As a study was planned, the committee created an island-wide alliance of nonprofit arts organizations to actively address the challenges facing the art community. The result was the formation of Long Island Arts Alliance. The study, conducted by noted economist Dr. Pearl Kamer, found that the nonprofit art community contributes nearly $200 million to Long Island's economy each year. The LIAA began a campaign to enhance media coverage of art activities on Long Island. Teaming with public television station WLIW21, LIAA encouraged the development of a new weekly arts magazine, show, Ticket, which aired for more than five years, giving Long Island audiences a weekly program celebrating the best in Long Island arts and culture. LIAA has since developed other programs designed to recognize new talent, support arts education, and boost the visibility of Long Island's thriving art community. [44]

Long Island Music Hall of Fame

The hall of fame was formed in 2004 by a group of music lovers, music educators and industry professionals with a mission to recognize, celebrate and preserve Long Island's music heritage. It has catalogued items of memorabilia and prepared information exhibits that describe the accomplishments of Long Island performers and music industry inductees. Its archives include video clips, music and interview recordings, biographical material, and other display material. The organization sponsors bi-annual induction ceremonies and provides K-12 programs at Long Island schools offering master class workshops and seminars, scholarships to deserving young physicians. It also seeks to establish a permanent space in which to establish a museum. [45]

Selected Nonprofit Organizations

Adelante of Suffolk County

The following organizational information was obtained on the organization's website: www.adelantesc.org

The agency has expanded its services dramatically over the past twenty-five years including programs offering the following services: Supported housing & case management; housing & tenant counseling; a nutrition program for the elderly; educational, family and youth, career counseling & youth leadership; an after school program; and a Medicaid service coordination program. [46]

Bellport Area Community Action Committee (BACAC) and the Bellport, Hagerman, East Patchogue Alliance (BHEP)

From 1983, when Helen Martin became BHEP's director, to 2006, when she retired, her leadership and relationships within the community played an important role in maintaining its stability. She always saw her role as a community participant, rather than as an "executive director," and found ways to meet the needs of the families in the Alliance homes. The board's hope that good rental housing management would make good tenants proved to be true in most cases, and the Alliance has been a spokesman for the rights of renters in the community along with those of the homeowners. Through budget counseling and job counseling, she helped many of them accomplish their goals. Some were not so fortunate and she had to find ways to be flexible as long as possible as they struggled to find the money for rent. Her ability to remain friendly but firm did not always work, and some tenants had to move on.

In a community that is seen as a problem area, the Alliance has played an important role advocating for tenants as important residents of the community, and finding services to assist them with needs other than housing. Martin was a co-founder and board member of INN Friendship, a soup kitchen that has been in existence for many years. Her staff collects toys at Christmas and turkeys at Thanksgiving. Many people in the community attend an annual community Christmas party each year that includes tenants, staff, funders, and supporters from the wider community. A group of senior citizens have maintained a senior support program each week, and plan events for Martin Luther King and Black History.

Fred Combs, who succeeded Martin as director, has maintained the organization as a support for tenants and is continuing programs to help tenants reach the point where they can become homeowners. He, too, sees his role as an advocate for the community and its residents in town and county planning and is part of the current revitalization of the community. BHEP has been able to arrange for a number of improvements to be made in the community including more sidewalks and street lighting, decorative trees, and better crime control measures.

While Martin was developing housing in North Bellport, Nancy Marr served as director of BACAC providing a youth service agency in small rented quarters. Marr worked incessantly in a variety of local organizations in behalf of the community always building alliances and relationships. Her longstanding reputation as a caring and trusted person helped to lead to the development of the Boys & Girls Club of the Bellport Area. The club is now an established community organization with a new $4M clubhouse that further enhances the community's services, its sense of accomplishment, and view of itself.

The work done by Helen Martin, Nancy Marr and other local leaders to bring affordable housing and community services continued after 1985. Their efforts lead to a "community visioning" experience conducted by Sustainable Long Island which resulted in the participation of hundreds of community residents including many younger residents who were not previously engaged in community affairs. As a result of the Sustainable Long Island event and the active involvement of John Rogers, chairman of the Greater Bellport Coalition and Jason Neal, Program Coordinator of the Boys & Girls Club, $1M of renovations was secured to renovate Robert Rowley Park. They continue to work together with town of Brookhaven officials, especially councilwoman Connie Keppert, to establish an affordable housing development to attract young residents and retirees. [47]

100 Black Women, Long Island Chapter (NCBW, LI)

NCBW, LI works in concert with more than 7,500 members representing sixty-four chapters in 26 states, and the District of Columbia. After more than twenty-five years, its founding vision to ensure a role for women of African descent in the mainstream of Long Island remains the principal focus of the organization. Through these events, attendees share their experiences and inspire others to inform, engage, and act.

Today, NCBW, LI advocates on behalf of women of African descent through local and national actions that promote equity in economic development, health care and education by:

- Building strategic alliances with like-minded individuals and organizations to achieve mutual goals.
- Empowering members to achieve business/professional opportunities and serve as effective leaders.
- Influencing public policy that impacts women of African descent and their communities.
- Celebrating the culture and achievements of people of African descent. [48]

Catholic Charities

The following discussion of Catholic Charities was written by Laura Cassell, CEO of Catholic Charities.

"I came aboard at Catholic Charities as the Director of Finance in 1988 and held that position until I was first appointed chief operating officer in 1995, then chief Executive Officer in 1999. Having spent those first seven years immersed in the finances of the organization I was afforded an inside look at what made us tick and it was abundantly clear to me that our agency held a leadership role in social services on Long Island. As an agency under the umbrella of the larger Diocese of Rockville Centre we are blessed with what can be considered numerous, strategic partnerships. We work hand-in-hand with more than 100 Long Island parishes as well as the Catholic Healthcare and Education systems. In reality, there is virtually no other homegrown organization in the region that can offer the kind of outreach the Catholic Church does. Bishop McGann and Bishop McHugh, coadjutor bishop at that time, knew this and conveyed to me that they felt it was the Church's responsibility to lead the way in tackling some of Long Island' unanswered problems.

Foremost among these was the shortage of affordable housing and how that impacted vulnerable populations like our senior citizens. We had already successfully worked with Housing and Urban Development (HUD) on the federal level and with various state agencies in creating affordable housing opportunities. So we decided to more creatively address the issue by developing idle diocesan properties. We opened Bishop McGann Village in Central Islip in 1998 followed by Thea Bowman Residence in Farmingdale in 1999 which was one of the first affordable housing options for people with physical disabilities on Long Island. Then we added St. Anne's Gardens, Msgr. Reel Village, Bishop Daly Gardens and Cabrini Gardens. Today we have a total of 1,329 units at 16 sites in Nassau and Suffolk, making us one of the largest providers of affordable senior housing on Long Island. To be sure, building on Long Island is always a complicated undertaking but our network of relationships and track record make us good partners. More than that, Catholic Charities' ability to identify problems and design timely and effective responses is most notable.

A perfect example would be our Immigrant Services and Refugees Resettlement Program. We have long provided legal and support services for immigrants on Long island. In fact, we handle over 11,000 cases a year and we are the only Long Island agency accredited by the U.S. government to bring cases before the Executive Office for Immigration Review (EOIR) Court. But changing times brought new sets of immigration issues. In 2001 we cared for and helped resettle nearly 100 Kosovar refugees fleeing civil war in their home country and as more and more people fled war and persecution we increasingly became the federal government's local go-to agency for support services. The same was true as human trafficking became a hot-button issue. Since 2004, we have been on the front lines and have worked with more than 200 survivors of both labor and sex trafficking and their families. Most notable was our role in assisting the victims of one of the largest human trafficking cases in the United States: the 59 Peruvian men, women and children who were being held in captivity on Long Island. We were a comprehensive partner, providing housing, medical attention, counseling and help in applying for legal status. Today, we are core members of the Long Island Anti-Human Trafficking Task Force and we serve as the regional service provider for New York State and the U.S. Department of Justice.

We played a similar role during the HIV/AIDS epidemic of the late 1980's. Unfortunately, Long Island led the nation in suburban cases so Catholic Charities again took the lead with not only day treatment programs, but special needs housing for victims and their families. We even offered a specialized dental clinic with a sliding pay scale because so many dentists were reluctant to treat victim of this new, unknown disease. One could also look at our Women, Infant, and Children (WIC) program. When the federal government sought out an agency that could provide food assistance, nutrition and health education but also offer health screenings as well, Catholic Charities was the natural choice. With access to the Catholic healthcare system of Long Island and our outreach at 133 parishes, we were first ever bi-county WIC program in Nassau and Suffolk

Time and again, our capacity to quickly target an emerging problem, pool resources, and mobilize staff is what sets us apart. Arguably it is those very qualities that help us lead the way in disaster response. In times of true crisis, people instinctively turn to the church. In the aftermath of 9/11 we distributed over $3 million in assistance, offered employment services, counseling and comfort to hundreds of grieving families for years after. We responded to Hurricane Irene, establishing a Disaster Case Management Program which soon went into overdrive when Super Storm Sandy battered our shores. Almost overnight, hundreds of people came to our doorstep, rolling up their sleeves and asking, "How can we help?" Our parking lot was immediately transformed into a voluntarily-manned distribution center for the truckloads of emergency supplies that poured in from around the country. And we were at the heart of tremendous financial support, distributing all of the nearly $2.3 million dollars we collected to hundreds of hard-hit families throughout Long Island. Today our Disaster Case Management team continues to work with the New York State Office of Emergency Management and the U.S.

Department of Homeland Security to help Long Island hurricane victims navigate and access the labyrinth of government and private resources.

For a $37 million dollar agency, with more than 60 sites and 650 employees, we are really quite nimble. It is our ability to respond quickly and effectively to Long island's changing needs which is our greatest accomplishment. When the chips are down, people know they can turn to us." [49]

Child Care Council of Nassau

In the mid-late 1980s to the new century, the child care field continued to face the serious problem of low salaries for child care workers and period of low unemployment. The council dramatically expanded its influences and services during this period including the development of a Job Bank to address staffing problems in day care centers; the expansion of its employer services and dependent care assistance plans to other employers; the publication of a Directory of Parenting Programs; the development of community partnerships with representatives from different sectors; school districts, employers, community organizations, government agencies; school-age child care training offered through partnership between the council and Cornell Cooperative Extension; and an Emergency Child Care Program was initiated for employees of CMP and Grumman. The program was assisted by a planning grant from the L.I. Corporate Initiative for Child Care and Elder Care. The program provided home health aides from Self Help Community Services at the child's home when regular arrangements break down

The council was also extremely active changing policies and practices at the local, state, and national levels including: Winning a landmark zoning decision that clarified legal status of family day care as appropriate in residential settings; its advocacy resulted in salary enhancement funds for day care centers included in the state and county budgets; and start-up demonstration grants provided for Employer-supported child care. The council also provided consultation services to school districts and corporations, and led many efforts to assist child care providers and promote public support of child care programs.

In the late 1990s, executive director Gloria Wallick and associate director Jan Barbieri were appointed to the newly-formed Commission on Child Care of the Nassau County Legislature. Founded and chaired by the legislature's Presiding Officer Bruce Blakeman, the commission held hearings across the county to identify child care needs. Council was also selected as a pilot site for its Infant/Toddler Certificate Program by New York State through Empire State College, enabling participants to enhance their professional competency and improve the quality of care and education for children less than three years of age. And, in response to Welfare to Work legislation, Council increased staff and hours and began working collaboratively with various agencies to better serve additional TANF (Temporary Assistance to Needy Families) clients.

According to Jan Barbieri, the council's executive director, "what is needed is a federal commitment to universal child care. It is not going to come from the state or county." [50]

Child Care Council of Suffolk

Over the years, the council has remained a very active advocate for the expansion of quality, accessible, affordable child care often working closely with the Child Care Council of Nassau and state and county legislators. The council also expanded its technical assistance to business corporations interested in addressing their employees' child care needs.

According to Walerstein, the need for affordable, quality child care continues today with an increase in the number of low-income families needing services since the recession. The need is present at a higher level in Suffolk County since its population of young families continues to grow. [51]

Clubhouse of Suffolk (name changed in 2014 to the Association for Mental Health and Wellness)

Clubhouse of Suffolk is a private, nonprofit psychiatric rehabilitation and support agency that was founded in 1990 by members of Suffolk chapters of the National Alliance for the Mentally Ill. Under the leadership of a national advocate, Dr. Davis Pollack, this group sought to expand the range of opportunities available to people with mental illness who desired to participate in working, learning, housing, and social environments in their community.

To guide their quest, the group turned to Fountain House in New York City which, since 1948, has been a pioneer in the international development of "the clubhouse model", a community-based center for facilitating vocational and social integration. The success of this model has been evidenced by hundreds of replications of this model in this country and around the world. The fruits of the founding group's labor were borne with the opening of the doors of its Ronkonkoma clubhouse in January 1991, an event that brought huge response among Suffolk County residents whose lives were affected by serious mental illnesses. In 1993, following a visit to Clubhouse by then-NYSOMH Commissioner Dr. Richard Surles, Clubhouse was awarded an outpatient license, Intensive Psychiatric Rehabilitation Treatment (IPRT), a license that allowed Clubhouse's program to couple with the psychiatric rehabilitation approach - as it was developed, tested, and advanced by Boston University.

In 1995, a second clubhouse, the Synergy Center in Riverhead, was opened as a result of advocacy by a united group of families and consumers on the East End who wanted to bring a clubhouse to their area. The organization's success with implementing clubhouses was called upon again in 1997 as a collaborator with two other agencies in the development and early operation of a third clubhouse in Suffolk, Journey House. These clubhouses grew to a large extent through the support of funds made possible by the passage of the Community Mental Health Reinvestment Act, an act which also led to the closure of three major State psychiatric centers in Suffolk County. Funds from this Act allowed for Clubhouse and Synergy's development of supported employment, supported education, transportation, peer support and recovery education programs and services - and Clubhouse of Suffolk and Synergy Center became well-known across New York State for our success in advancing the lives of so many people through the rehabilitation-and-recovery-focused clubhouse-based services.

In 2001, concurrent with the passage of Kendra's Law and a resultant statewide enhancement of case management services, the agency was awarded responsibility for providing supportive case management services to people with mental illnesses who reside in eastern Brookhaven and the five east end townships. In mid-decade, media and public advocacy attention to conditions and rights of people in licensed adult homes led to the award to Clubhouse of a case management and peer specialist team to assist residents of "impacted" homes. In 2007, with the advent of public policies that emphasized the importance of reaching out to people who were marginalized through the inadequate commitments of prior de-institutionalization policies, Clubhouse's case management program added a specialty teams to assist people who are homeless.

In 2005, responding to debilitating diseases that led to premature deaths of members and clients, Clubhouse successfully obtained and used grant funds from New York State Department of Health to develop smoking cessation protocols for people with mental illnesses. The agency developed and distributed nationally two training videos - the first increased awareness about the disparate public response to tobacco addiction among people with a mental illness; the second provided an evidence-based practice approach, based upon research that Clubhouse conducted, to reducing the tobacco use in community mental health programs.

In the early part of the 2000 decade, following the demise of an initiative to utilize broad managed care strategies in the early 2000s, NYSOMH conceived a new licensed program, Personalized Recovery-Oriented Services (PROS). This program moved rehabilitation and recovery-based services, driven from person-centered processes, into the center of a community service system. Bolstered by the successes of its clubhouse and case management programs, several of Clubhouse of Suffolk's leaders assumed statewide leadership roles to advocate for this transformation of the community mental health system. In April, 2007, two clubhouses transitioned its State Aid funding source and its IPRT license into two PROS licenses that allowed our clubhouses to offer an enhanced range of services. Included in this were mental health clinic services, cognitive remediation (for which Clubhouse also provided public support for the inclusion of such services in the license), and a focus upon co-occurring substance abuse and physical health of our clubhouse members. With an eye toward the critical importance of technology and information systems in health care, both programs also made use of a fully integrated electronic medical record as a platform for service delivery and documentation.

Clubhouse's supportive case management program has also grown tremendously in terms of numbers of people served and staff skills in engaging more complex and multiply-challenged individuals. In 2009, the program expanded its use of electronic record by equipping the case management staff with laptops and remote access. This allowed staff the ability to engage and collaborate with their clients with the benefit of concurrent electronic assessment and documentation tools as well as with internet connectivity that enhanced the ability to access community information and resources.

The 2008 economic downturn also led us to recognize organizational responsibilities to address the needs of its surrounding communities. Responding to a call to action by Long Island CARES to address local hunger, Clubhouse opened food pantries in our Ronkonkoma and Riverhead staffed extensively by clubhouse member and volunteers. The Riverhead food pantry is a collaboration with Suffolk County United Veterans that also reaches out to homeless and at-risk veterans.

As its programs grew and evolved so too has its core mission. At the foundation of its work has been an emphasis on the power of helping and healing relationships and a hardened belief in the potential and productivity of all people in recovery. Clubhouse of Suffolk's mission statement was revisited in 2005 and again in 2009 by stakeholder discussions of members, staff, and board of directors. The resultant statement reflects our ongoing commitment to a broad and individualized vision of recovery from the impact of mental illnesses and psychiatric disabilities. [52]

For further information about mental health services, visit Part III for the profiles of several pioneers in the field, Davis Pollack, Joan Saltzman and Max Schneier.

Community Action for Southold Township (CAST)

CAST has expanded its services since its origins in the 1960s and recently celebrated its 50th anniversary. It sponsors the North Fork Parent-Child

Program providing reading, writing and other skills to children and their parents and continues a food program for low income families. It also assists new immigrants to learning English and apply for legal documents, and manages a food stand in partnership with Southold town government to bring local produce to senior citizens. [53]

Community Advocates

Shortly after Marge Rogatz assumed the Community Advocates presidency in 1986, in response to a sharp increase in the number of homeless individuals and families across the region, CA began to concentrate its resources and energies on efforts to address homelessness on Long Island. In 1987, CA developed and distributed the first *Directory of Resources and Services for the Homeless in Nassau County* and with Nassau-Suffolk law services, conducted the first countywide training for service providers and advocates for the homeless.

In 1988, Rogatz and Michael Moran, founder of The INN, Helen Martin, founder of BHEP, and Peter Barnett, founder of the Wyandanch Homes and Development Corporation established the Nassau-Suffolk Coalition for the Homeless (NSCH). Rogatz, with the help of CA Executive Director, Miriam Salmanson (a public interest attorney who worked for CA as an independent contractor for 14 years), played a crucial role in organizing and leading the Nassau part of NSCH, including bringing minority-led agencies into the Nassau Continuum of Care Group and assisting a total of 20 housing and service agencies to obtain more than $70 million in HUD grants between 1995 and 2004. CA not only paid Salmanson to carry out this work for NSCH, but also provided other direct assistance through the efforts of a number of devoted CA board members. Roberta Schroder, for example, undertook the onerous task of producing the first region-wide *Directory/Data Base of Basic and Emergency Services for the Homeless in Nassau and Suffolk Counties* which was published under the NSCH name, with appropriate credit given to CA and Schroder.

In 1989, CA established the Community Advocates Housing Development Fund Corporation and, with a NYS $750,000 Homeless Housing Assistance Program grant and renovation grants from Nassau County, CA purchased and rehabilitated a small apartment building in Roslyn Heights. The property at 201 Roslyn Road became Nassau County's first permanent rental apartments for homeless families. This breakthrough project was accomplished with key support from NYS State Social Services Commissioner Caesar Perales and from Town of North Hempstead Supervisor John Kiernan, a Republican who identified the property for CA and staunchly supported the project despite the rise of serious NIMBYism. Rogatz and the CA Board wanted to demonstrate that there were suburbanites, including Nassau Republican officials, who favored the placement of such projects in their neighborhoods and were willing to step up to the plate despite community opposition. However, Ben Zwirn, the Democratic candidate for Supervisor, took the side of the "nimbies" and ran against and defeated John Kiernan. CA initiated a broad-based campaign, mobilized a large coalition of supporters and, after a lengthy NIMBY struggle that attracted national media attention and put homelessness on Nassau's public agenda, the precedent-setting initiative finally (nine long months after CA's acquisition of the property) won the required approval of the Town of North Hempstead, including the vote of Supervisor Zwirn.

CA played a pivotal role in organizing and helping to lead the Long Island Campaign for Affordable Rental Housing (LICARH), the first major collaborative effort to address the region's critical need for affordable rental housing. CA provided leadership and raised financial support to enable LICARH to sponsor the development of model inclusionary zoning proposals and the creation of an innovative public education and multi-media campaign which promoted affordable rental housing specifically planned for persons of all races and backgrounds in integrated mixed-income and mixed-use developments.

Noting sky-rocketing housing costs, in addition to ever-rising homelessness, CA pointed to a proliferation of illegal accessory apartments in single homes across Long Island. These illegal, often unsafe units provided desperately needed housing and were increasing in number and thriving in an underground economy. In 2006, as part of its effort to encourage the adoption of new accessory housing codes, CA gathered information from across the country regarding successful "best practice" accessory housing programs and produced *Accessory Housing: Report and Guide to Successful Programs.* The report was disseminated in hard cover and disk to municipalities, developers and housing organizations across the region in the hope that it would assist public officials in their consideration of new codes. It did result in several towns reviewing their codes and adopting more thoughtfully crafted zoning proposals.

For some forty years, CA maintained a revolving loan fund that provided no-interest loans to local nonprofit agencies to assist them in developing and operating housing for homeless individuals and families. In 2004, CA added a first-time home buyers fund, which provided $5,000 grants to help eligible low-income families pay closing costs, thereby enabling them to become first-time homeowners. In 2007, CA established an employers' assisted housing fund to provide grants to non-profit employers to help them enable their lower paid staff members to participate in the New York State and Nassau County employer assisted housing program. CA provided the outreach and grants to non-profit agencies, working in association with the Long Island Housing Partnership, which administers the Program. In 2008, CA set up the Sylvia Grossman Fund for homeless families in crisis to give grants to Nassau nonprofit agencies that requested emergency funds on behalf of families in crisis.

Although CA has always been a very small organization with a very small budget, these funds became an important vehicle for CA to intervene and help in situations where such help might otherwise not be forthcoming. CA loans and grants made a critical difference to several agencies that provide housing and services for LI's most vulnerable persons and enabled more than 70 low-income households in Nassau to obtain safe, decent homes and apartments for themselves and their children.

Rogatz was an indefatigable fundraiser who was often helped by generous and equally committed CA board members. CA's work was made possible by grants from Long Island Community Foundation, Hagedorn Fund, Saltzman Foundation, Jane and Martin Schwartz Foundation, Shore Family Fund, Washington Mutual, JP Morgan Chase, and other institutions and funders.

In 2012, Rogatz recommended the replacement of its succession plan with a new and unique plan that the Community Advocates board, after careful consideration, unanimously adopted. In accordance with this plan, in 2013, 2014, and 2015, under caveats and conditions accepted by both organizations, CA will contribute most of its financial assets to ERASE Racism (approximately $50,000 annually) leaving CA with enough funds to continue functioning until 2021. The result will be a stronger ERASE Racism and CA's continuing operation at a reduced level until it goes out of existence or decides to raise whatever funds are required for continued operation. This decision reflects Rogatz's commitment to racial equity and justice on Long Island and her awareness of the need for smaller organizations with similar missions to find a way to maximize their effectiveness and assure their sustainability. [54]

For further information, visit Part III for profiles of Marge Rogatz and Joan Saltzman.

Community Development Corporation of Long Island (CDCLI)

Von Kuhen says that the challenge for families attempting to find affordable housing on Long Island still persists and believes that there simply are not enough resources available. He feels that community resistance is often a factor but far less so today than years ago. In fact, he says that, due to Long Island's economic growth, affordable housing may be even more elusive today than in the 1960s. CDCLI, therefore, continues to address a continuum of housing needs from homelessness to rental housing to home ownership and does so through a variety of programs, with particular emphasis on the provision of rental vouchers, weatherization and rehabilitation assistance, and homeownership and rental development.

Von Kuhen points to increased willingness of some local municipalities to address housing issues as more young people leave Long Island due to the high cost of housing, taxes, and transportation. They are also concerned about the housing needs of the growing population of aging baby boomers who want to remain on Long Island and seek affordable housing options. "People of all ages cannot survive here. We have to do something without relying on federal subsidies," says Von Kuhen. He expects that solutions will evolve through public/private partnerships with towns relaxing zoning codes and other disincentives to housing developments. Towns are also seeing that there is always some level of opposition to development but that through sensible planning and community organizing, opposition can be neutralized by mobilizing project supporters. Von Kuhen points to CDCLI's successful "WinCoram" project as an example of this type of community mobilization, in this case to create a village center with both housing and retail uses on the site of a former multiplex movie theater.

Over time, under the leadership of Marianne Garvin, CDCLI's CEO, the organization has established its reputation as an effective provider of housing and related social services and has achieved special national recognition for its innovations, such as the Voucher Home Ownership Program. In 2005, with the operation of two NeighborWorks® HomeOwnership Centers serving Nassau and Suffolk counties and providing a wide range of pre-purchase and post-purchase services, CDCLI employs over 80 people, serves both Nassau and Suffolk counties, and provides a variety of programs that address the dynamic challenges faced by those who live and work on Long Island. [55]

For further information, visit Part III for profile of Bill Klatsky.

Community Programs Center of Long Island (CPC)

From the mid-1980s into the new century CPC expanded its child care and adult day service programs not only in Deer Park but by establishing centers in Ronkonkoma and Port Jefferson. Its Head Start Program also grew and was housed in the Ronkonkoma and Port Jefferson centers. For several years an adult day service program was also operated in North Babylon. During this period Arfin got involved with Generations United and the New York State Adult Day Services Association where he served as president. During his tenure, he was able to help to establish a new $1M grant program for new adult day service programs.

Financial pressure in the organization persisted despite growth and program expansion. CPC moved into the late 1980s with a large debt, struggling to survive. Unable to find affordable housing and with a poor balance sheet, the organization continued to rent space in excessed school buildings on a year-to-year basis, thus never having long term security.

In the 1990s, CPC further expanded its board of directors and raised thousands of dollars. Former Suffolk County Executive Patrick Halpin, Martin Cantor, former Suffolk County Commissioner of Economic Development, Vincent Polimeni, a real estate developer, and Don Hoffman, a CPA at Computer Associates, John Westerman, an attorney were especially helpful in raising these funds. With the assistance of Dave Boone, a retired banker and Denis Feldman, a commercial real estate broker, CPC obtained bond financing through the Suffolk County Industrial Development Agency that enabled the construction of a center in a Deer Park industrial park and a Port Jefferson center and the expansion of the Ronkonkoma Center. While the organization grew in services, its debt also grew as the organization was unable to earn enough fee income to cover its core services. Because of this, in the 1990s, CPC launched a bold effort to raise charitable funds to help offset its annual operational deficits in its child care and adult day care programs. Its board was expanded with people of means. For the first time, board members contributed to annual campaigns. Bond financing, through the Suffolk County Industrial Development Agency, was secured that enabled the construction of two new buildings and the expansion of another. The organization sponsored annual galas in which corporate leaders were honored. Over a five year period, several hundred thousand dollars were raised through the galas.

Meanwhile, Arfin continued to pursue opportunities to develop on and offsite child care center with local businesses. Automated Data Processing agreed to begin an employee-subsidy program that was utilized by many of its employees. In the early 1990s, CPC was selected to design and operate the child care center at Computer Associates International's new facility in Islandia. The center management fee provided CPC with some financial relief. However, one year later, the company discontinued the contract to operate the center itself. At the same time, LUMEX, a Ronkonkoma-based manufacturer of hospital and health care equipment, provided CPC with start-up support to open a center near its offices.

Nevertheless, the organization continued to incur annual losses. CPC was also able to secure a number of public and private grants but it could not pay current obligations as well as reduce past debt. Management and the board could see the handwriting on the wall: CPC would have to cease operations or find another organization to take it over. In 2001, efforts were taken to identify another organization to merge with or to actually take over CPC's operation.

United Cerebral Palsy of Suffolk (UCP), a growing and well-funded and managed agency, took an interest in CPC with the result that, in 2002, arrangements were made for CPC to become a separate corporation of UCP of Suffolk. The arrangement enabled CPC to benefit from UCP's talents and resources without any interruption to services or losses of employment for CPC employees. [56]

Concern for Independent Living (CONCERN)

Over the past twenty-five years, under the leadership of Ralph Fasano, CONCERN developed a job training thrift shop; established the first client run thrift shop in Suffolk County; started the first supported housing program in Suffolk County; opened the first newly constructed community residence on Long Island; opened the first scattered site, permanent housing on Long Island using Housing and Urban Development (H.U.D.) 202 funds; and is one of the first agencies to use low-income housing tax credits to develop housing for people with disabilities.

It has successfully developed and administered a wide array of housing options. Residents are currently housed in single-site supervised residences, scattered-site shared apartments, and permanent housing for individuals and families in studios, condominiums, and houses in the community. [57]

Economic Opportunity Council of Nassau (EOC of Nassau)

EOC of Nassau has remained committed to many of its early initiatives. For the program year 2013-2014, it served 531 children and families through eight Head Start programs; managed three programs which emphasize employment and employability (Youth Empowerment and Career Training Initiative - YECTI— a program for at-risk youth; the Displaced Homemakers Program— DHP a program specifically for women transitioning back into the workforce and the Temporary Assistance for Needy Families -TANF Career Paths Program– for individuals moving from welfare to work). EOC of Nassau continues to serve pregnant and parenting women through the Downstate Healthy Start Program and youth through afterschool academic and recreational programming.

Newer initiatives include services to new Americans seeking assistance with immigration and American citizenship status. Looking back over the past year, the EOC has won several battles; successfully negotiated and received a $7 million dollar commitment from the federal Agency for Children and Families to rebuild a state-of-art, Head Start program in the Long Beach community and successfully obtained a contract through the Office of New Americans - Sandy Block Grant to identify and recruit new Americans as volunteers to assist individuals and communities in the event of disasters and emergencies. The organization also received a $50,000 increase in funding for the Youth Empowerment and Career Training Initiative (YECTI) - for at-risk youth and provided 32 scholarships to youth pursuing a higher education. [58]

Even with budget cuts and a barrage of attacks on the agency, EOC of Nassau has survived and maintained programs. Fifty years later, we are still at our post, still on the frontline of the battle, still in the fight to win the war against poverty.

For further information, visit Leone Baum profile in Part III.

Economic Opportunity Council of Suffolk (EOC of Suffolk)

The agency expanded its services substantially over the years and now include programs in family development; housing; a Suffolk County Family Court Children's Nursery; and Veteran's Services. HIV/AIDS assistance; a Weed and Seed program in Wyandanch; a child care program in Montauk; Services for people with developmental disabilities; a Tutor Time Child Care in East Patchogue; youth & adolescent services (formerly operated as the Suffolk Network on Adolescent Pregnancy); and a chronic health care coordination program. Adrian Bassett serves as the agency's executive director. [59]

For further information, visit Part III for profiles of Priscilla Redfield Roe, Marilyn Shellabarger, Joyce Turner, Burghardt Turner, and Ralph Watkins.

Family and Children's Association (FCA)

In 1997, FCA executive director Sal Ambrosino and Children's House executive Richard Dina engaged the organizations in a year-long study of the viability of merging the two organizations into one continuum of care that could serve Long Islanders from early childhood to seniors in need. The end result of that study, assisted by Elliot Pagliaccio, a skilled consultant, was the recommendation to create a merger. Two reasons formed the rationale:

- The merged agencies could be more competent for the increasing numbers of clients needing multiple human services in order to gain maximum health and stability in their lives. The 50 plus services of both agencies, it was concluded, would offer a unique array of interventions under one roof.
- The merged agencies could better survive the quickly changing landscape of human service delivery. It was believed that a larger organization with more visibility and business acumen and greater impact could not only survive but also thrive.

In 1998, the merger of FSA and Children's House was consummated and a new entity, including the assets and liabilities of both parties, was created: Family and Children's Association. In hindsight, that was a more significant decision than even imagined at the time. It created a $20 million nonprofit human service agency – unusually large for Long Island - with more than 400 staff and an initial board of 85 trustees. The board's number shrunk gracefully in the first two years to the more manageable (but necessary) 40 or so trustees of today.

Adaptation to this new reality was a longer and more difficult process for staff than for members of the combined boards. It became apparent that turf and territory issues are as real in the nonprofit world as in any other sector. Also learned was that signing a merger document is but the beginning of actually merging! After many "joint" projects involving staff from both former entities, and the passage of time, all parties were on the same page by the end of the third year. Fortuitously, the decision to go for agency accreditation two years after the merger (through the Council on Accreditation for Service to Children and Families) was most helpful in engaging all parties to form and mold this new organization.

The other reality that tested the merger's mettle as a new organization was the pressure of continuing to find the resources to maintain a $20 million operation with more than 50 distinct service programs. Two realities converged into a huge challenge: government funding for human services continued to contract; and competition for fund raised dollars increased in intensity (particularly post-9/11). In addition, the "silo" reality of funding sources, both private and public, with their time honored, separate reporting mechanisms, policies and procedures, added to the complexity of managing the new organization.

Retrenchment and internal consolidations, therefore, became a necessity throughout the brief history of FCA due to naturally rising expenses that were not offset by new or increased revenue. Government contracts basically did not increase from the mid-1990s on, especially at the county level and, in fact, they underwent a massive reduction in 2000 because of Nassau County's fiscal crisis. Indeed, FCA lost $1 million in service dollars that year. Internal contractions have been necessary each year in order to provide the board with a budget that was balanced, but still capable of retaining dedicated staff to provide high quality services to the community.

At the time of the merger, there were 55 service programs in the new agency. Today, there are 35, and a dozen of these have been developed since 1998.

To assist in finding new ways to ameliorate the agency's financial pressures, significant attention and exploration has been given recently to increasing the agency's entrepreneurial skills by developing "earned income" programs - services that pay for themselves through client fees rather through government contracts or fund raising assistance. Such a transition from almost total reliance on government funding is, for sure, easier said than done. There is not only a question of gaining new business-like skills but also changing the traditional nonprofit culture that considers it government's responsibility to pay for services for society's troubled and disabled populations. Some progress has been made in this regard at FCA, mainly in services to the elderly. But more experimentation and prototyping needs to be done in the future in order to build entrepreneurial capacity.

During his retirement, Dina has served as special assistant to the president of Adelphi University and as a consultant at the Center for Nonprofit Leadership at Adelphi that he helped to establish. [60]

Family Service League (FSL)

According to Karen Boorshtein, FSL's long-standing agency commitment to advocacy continued into the 1990s and into the turn of the century both at the town, county, and state levels. Board members are viewed as "ambassadors" of the agency on behalf of FSL's constituents' needs and changing community needs. Boorshtein feels that board involvement in social issues and advocacy keeps board members engaged with the agency and understanding of the circumstances faced by FSL's clients and why FSL's services are important. FSL has frequently joined with other organizations advocating for workforce housing and senior citizen housing. At the same time, on a daily basis, agency social workers help clients with employment issues, child welfare issues, to negotiate bureaucracies, and familiarize them with their rights and entitlements.

Thinking back to her early days with FSL, Boorshtein recalls that every summer, she, her staff, board members, and clients would spend a great deal of time visiting county elected officials in their local offices to make their case for continued and expanded funding. With dozens of county funded programs under the FSL umbrella, these efforts required attendance at dozens of meetings of the legislature's budget, human service, health and mental health, and aging services committees. Then, in October and early November, they would regularly attend meetings of the full legislature to present budget testimony by documenting FSL's work and the importance of continued funding. Boorshtein feels that enabling clients to speak in their own behalf is a powerful way of helping them grow and deal with the challenges they face.

Another area where FSL has been very active was in disaster relief including trauma relief assistance with the 9-11 tragedy, a passenger airline crash, and, most recently, with Hurricane Sandy. Through their disaster relief efforts, FSL has assisted thousands of people to put their lives back together.

Agency services have especially grown in the areas of universal pre-kindergarten, mental health services, the development of housing, a group home for men, and a family shelter. Their funding streams are a lot more complicated. In particular, the changing landscape of behavioral health services. Over the years, we have seen a change in how we work with people who have serious mental illness. Gone are the days of Continuing Day Treatment Programs (CDT) to what is called Personalized Recovery Oriented Services (PROS). PROS is a different model from CDT as the consumers are more involved in program groups, and when possible, employment. Managed care, Medicaid's redesign, and the Affordable Care Act are very much part of today's scene. Boorshtein feels that "program funding may change and there is ebb and flow over the years, but the commitment to help those in need our help remains constant."

Today, FSL continues to grow. In 1993, its budget was approximately $8-$10M with 40 distinct programs. Today, the agency's budget is $30M with 52 distinct programs in 21 different sites throughout Suffolk County. Private philanthropy represents $2M of about $30M budget. Competition continually exists among nonprofits for scarcer charitable dollars.

There was no sea change in government funding of FSL until 2012 as well as private funding support. State government funding for supportive housing is available as well as for some mental health programs to reduce hospitalizations especially emergency room visitations.

By way of background, Boorshtein feels that her interest in a social work career developed through her early experiences with her mother who had a severe case of multiple sclerosis. "Always fighting for the underdog seemed to be where I was heading," says Boorshtein who earned a Masters in Social Work at Fordham University School of Social Service. Afterwards, she worked at Spence Chapin Services in New York City and then worked at Children's House in Nassau County, VIBS, and ultimately Family Service League where she has been since 1993. She began as an assistant director, later the chief operating officer and in 2009 assumed the helm as president and CEO.

In describing FSL's board, today, Boorshtein says it is a blend of community volunteers and corporate individuals. The combination makes for a good mix of ideas and discussion and strong governance.

During recent years, FSL brought on two small organizations as affiliates: Family Counseling Services of Westhampton Beach, a $2.5M East End behavioral health agency which felt they would be better positioned to align with a larger organization, as well as with the Suffolk Coalition to Prevent Alcohol and Drug Dependencies (SCPADD). Both affiliates have strengthened the organization's position as a human service provider throughout Long Island. [61]

Federation Employment Guidance Services (FEGS)

In 2008, John Kaiman, Supervisor of the Town of North Hempstead and his staff, developed the idea of creating an aging-in-place program to connect seniors to services and groups that provide transportation, medical and mental health care, educational and social programming, and other services such as home repair. Kaiman recognized the growing need of his growing older population. He contacted Roth at FEGS to see if FEGS would be interested in operating the project. Together, FEGS and the town applied for a state grant to start the project in New Hyde Park. Roth soon contacted Mary Curtis, Nassau County Executive Tom Suozzi's Deputy for Human Services. Curtis worked with Roth primarily to write a $1M federal grant to support the critical transportation component of the project. The project was approved and became the first aging-in-place program sponsored by a municipality in New York State. Since its inception, the program has expanded substantially.

Two of Project Independence's main features are the provision of transportation services provided by a taxi company and a contract with The Rehabilitation Institute wherein young adults with disabilities, as part of their job training, provide home-based services for the elderly, doing such things as cleaning gutters, moving furniture, touch-up painting, changing light bulbs and batteries, and completing minor repairs. Other towns from throughout Long Island have visited Project Independence to learn how to start and operate the program but none have chosen to follow through. They have chosen, instead, to only sponsor small pieces of the project. Speaking of the growing need for community-based aging services, Roth says: "They did not realize what is coming down the pike." Roth wishes that other municipalities were doing more to address the growing need for such programs which can dramatically reduce the rising costs of Medicaid which will only grow while baby boomers age and enter the years when their need for services occur. [62]

Note: FEGS recently announced that it is ceasing operations and transferring sponsorship of its programs to other organizations.

Harbor Child Care

Rooney recalls that, in 1988, there was a huge outpouring of providers, clients, and supporters that asked for a child care task force. A task force convened and served to promote our issues. In 1989, the task force concluded that child care staff was woefully underpaid. John Kiernan formerly Supervisor of the Town of North Hempstead, County Executive Tom Gulotta, Jill Rooney of Harbor Child Care, Vicki Mannes of Hi Hello Child Care, and Elaine McKay from the Department of Social Services worked to develop the Salary Enhancement Program which lasted for 20 years and subsidized child care teacher salaries.

Salary enhancement raised teacher salaries by $6,500, assistant teachers by $3,500 above their base salary. During the 20 years of its existence, there were three times that the program was threatened by cancellation. Each time a large group of teachers and parents protested and held off the elimination. Finally when County Executive Tom Suozzi left office, salary enhancement which cost Nassau County $3M dollars was eliminated.

Rooney looks back at her experiences as a child care provider and concludes that marshalling people who are committed to change is an effective socially action strategy. As an advocate to politicians, she advises "never make a request unless you know you are going to win, do your homework, and work the halls. It can affect change." She feels that the child care community as a whole did not exert as much pressure on legislators as it could. "Child care is a strong economic force in Nassau County as parents go to work, purchase goods and pay taxes. It is not a drain on society," she says. "In addition, child care workers are employed, also purchase goods, pay taxes and contribute to community growth," Rooney continued. [63]

Haven House/Bridges, Inc. (HHB)

HHB was formed in 1995 by the merger of two separate homeless housing programs; Haven House which was established by the Huntington Coalition for the Homeless and Bridges, which was initiated by Transitional Services of New York for Long Island, Inc. (TSLI) in 1977. Bruno LaSpina serves as CEO/House Counsel and has worked for the agency since 1978. [64]

Health and Welfare Council of Long Island (HWCLI)

Throughout 2013 and 2014, collaboration has been the highest priority for HWCLI as it worked to effect change. HWCLI has been partnering with member to provide education about the launch of New York State's Health Insurance Marketplace providing insurance plan enrollment assistance to member agencies' clients.

HWCLI is conducting a study of access and barriers to health care on Long Island partnering with faculty and students from Hofstra's Master of Public Health program, which combines the resources of the School of Health Sciences and Human Services, School of Law, Hofstra North Shore-LIJ School of Medicine and Health System. It also continues to access its health care work by collaborating with Touro Law Center on research projects related to the Affordable Care Act, including analyzing federal and state regulations to help HWCLI's Access to Health Care team better advocate on behalf of clients experiencing issues with marketplace enrollment.

Since October 2012, when Superstorm Sandy devastated parts of Long Island and left most of its residents powerless for days, HWCLI, in its role as a coordinator of LIVOAD, has facilitated communication between nonprofit agencies providing assistance to storm survivors and emergency management officials from the local, state, and federal governments. It has also convened the Long Island Long Term Recovery Group (LTRG), a partnership of health and human service agencies, corporations, foundations and universities to organize the assistance efforts for storm-affected families years into the future. Together, 150 LTRG agencies have operationalized to:

- Expand agencies' opportunities to help storm survivors.

- Make possible the best and most extensive use of agencies' services and resources.
- Allow agencies to share information and therefore avoid duplication of services and efforts.
- Ensure that those more vulnerable and at-risk are connected to vital resources necessary for recovery.

HWCLI coordinates the Long Island Unmet Needs Roundtable to help community members hardest hit by Sandy, those most vulnerable and at-risk who would often otherwise fall through the cracks without these critical resources.

HWCLI continues its partnership with community-based organizations to provide education and enrollment assistance related to the Supplemental Nutrition Assistance Program (SNAP), the largest in the domestic hunger safety net. SNAP provides nutrition assistance to eligible low-income individuals and families and provides economic benefits to communities.

Low-income, at-risk communities send a disproportionately lower percentage of students to college than their moderate to high income neighbors. Through its Financial Aid U Initiative, HWCLI partners with community-based organizations and Roosevelt, Brentwood, Copiague and Westbury High Schools to help their students complete the federal application for financial aid (FAFSA) and connect with financial aid resources that can help them fund their college education. HWCLI also aims to provide additional resource information that can enhance the quality of life for those completing the application process.

Through Building Individual Assets, HWCLI works with clients and member agencies throughout the year and during tax season to ensure they are aware of the Earned Income Tax Credit (EITC) and Volunteer Income Tax Assistance (VITA) sites. HWCLI is grateful to the Long Island Lead VITA partner, Bethpage Federal Credit Union, for making this service available in over 20 Long Island locations, making it possible for individuals to access professional tax assistance and their EITC—allowing many to receive financial education and start building a financial home.

Advocacy, research and policy analysis are important tools that HWCLI uses to serve the vulnerable and at-risk on Long Island. Along with many valuable partners, HWCLI engages in advocacy in relation to each of its programs and issues areas. The following are some highlights from the past year:

HWCLI worked with its membership, the Long Island Anti-Hunger Task Force, and national and state partners to advocate against proposed cuts to SNAP in the 2014 farm bill. Those advocacy efforts included educating HWCLI members, Long Island's representatives in Congress, and the public about the potential impact that cuts would have on the nation, the state and Long Island. Although the final version of the farm bill was not ideal, most of the draconian proposals related to SNAP were defeated. HWCLI is grateful to Long Island's elected officials who stood up for this critical support.

In addition to communicating frequently with state officials managing Long Island's recovery from Superstorm Sandy, HWCLI submitted oral and written testimony to the state about proposed changes to its Community Development Block Grant Disaster Recovery Action Plan, focusing on a new program to help vulnerable populations locate and remain in suitable housing.

In addition to participating in several coalitions advocating for high-quality, affordable health care for the most vulnerable, HWCLI submitted written testimony for a New York State Senate public hearing on the implementation of New York State of Health, the state's online health insurance marketplace. HWCLI is also participating in a coalition of Long Island agencies advocating for comprehensive immigration reform that includes a path to citizenship and keeps families together.

HWCLI works with the Long Island Language Advocates Coalition to help ensure that Long Islanders with limited English proficiency have equal access to services and programs such as health care and social services. This past year, members of HWCLI, in conjunction with a consortium of Suffolk County officials and additional community leaders, engaged the Center for Governmental Research (CGR) to conduct a community needs assessment for Suffolk County. The need for an updated community assessment was a consistent theme of a membership survey conducted by HWCLI in early 2012. In the survey, HWCLI members, consisting primarily of health and human service agencies, spoke of significant increases in demand for services, which were exacerbated in the fall of 2012 after Superstorm Sandy devastated parts of Long Island. As the members worked together closely to assist Long Islanders impacted by the storm, they recognized that the needs of the region's most vulnerable residents and the demands for services were changing and that the traditional approaches to addressing those needs also needed to change.

HWCLI members and its partners coalesced around the idea that a community needs assessment could help articulate how the needs in Suffolk County have changed, what the driving factors might be, and how county and private sector services might come together to respond to potentially new service and funding paradigms. In carrying out the needs assessment, CGR worked closely with HWCLI and a project steering committee of dedicated, engaged community leaders, including representatives from government, nonprofit service providers, the business community, funders/philanthropic organizations, and other community stakeholders. [65]

See Appendix for a listing of the HWCLI's annual award recipients.

Hispanic Counseling Center (HCC)

In response to dramatic growth in Nassau's Hispanic community and need for its services, HCC substantially expanded its services in the past twenty-five years. In the late 1980s, it opened an after-school homework help and tutoring program for school-age children and a six-week summer camp program opened. ESL classes for adults were added followed by Spanish literacy classes and vocational and computer classes. Gladys Serrano served as HCC's founding executive director until her retirement in 2014 when. Dr. Maria Munoz Kantha assumed the position.

HCC received a license from New York State to become Nassau County's first bilingual, bicultural alcohol/drug rehabilitation clinic. Having achieved this goal, and deeply aware of the tremendous need for Mental Health services in the clients' native language, the agency persuaded the Nassau County Commissioner of Mental Health to grant HCC a mental health license in 1992. HCC became and remains the first and only agency to provide mental health services in a completely bilingual/bicultural environment. A supported housing program for mentally ill clients was begun in 1993. Mental Health services for people with HIV/AIDS have been offered since 2001. In 1995 a domestic violence program was created in response to overwhelming demand by the legal system.

A respite program, the children and family support services program, was begun in 1994 to offer help to families who have children with serious emotional problems. A Medicaid service coordination program was opened in 1996 to serve individuals with developmental disabilities who waive the right to live in an institution and choose to live at home with their families. HCC began to provide supervised visitation for non-custodial parents in 1999, at the request of Family Court. In 2005, the agency received a license to operate a school-age child care program and also opened its teen drop-in center.

In 2007, HCC began two new programs for adolescents, children, and their families. The adolescent outpatient pilot program, funded by Office of Alcoholism and Substance Abuse Services serves youth ages 12-18 that are using drugs and alcohol and are at-risk of placement in the child welfare or juvenile justice systems. Through the Office of Children & Family Services, HCC provides the safe alternatives for family enrichment (SAFE) Program, to serve children who are at risk of placement in the child welfare system and their families, and to expedite the family reunification process for youth and their families that are already involved.

In 2008, to meet the demand for services in Suffolk County, a satellite clinic was opened in Bay Shore, offering chemical dependency services. The shelter plus care program was opened to provide housing for people in recovery from alcohol and substance addiction. More HCC services will be offered in Suffolk

County in the near future. The Hempstead site expanded by purchasing an adjacent building to provide bilingual mental health services and services for seniors and primary health care integration. HCC now serves over 1,400 clients a month through 18 programs, with a staff of 60, including two bilingual, bicultural psychiatrists. [66]

<u>The INN</u>

The following description of The Inn was written by Jean Kelly, the organization's executive director.

"As one of the original volunteers who helped open the first soup kitchen in Nassau County in 1983, I was fortunate to become the second executive director in 1993. I have seen the initial grassroots efforts blossom into a community-wide organization which attempts each day to provide the basics of food, shelter, clothing, toiletries and support to all who find themselves in need, all within an envelope of emotional strength and unconditional love. In understanding the evolution of The INN and what has made it so unique, is that it began with a simple mission, to feed neighbors in need, within an atmosphere of dignity and respect. No questions were asked and no judgment was made. Communities were organized using churches, temples and mosques as the base because that is where most people in need were already showing up asking for help. We allowed everyone to help from those faith-based homes and also welcomed individuals who were not faith-based in their practice of spirituality. We always say we shared an overall faith in humanity that together we could solve the problem of hunger by first making it visible and then making it go away, by feeding those who were hungry. We called everyone who entered a "guest" because that is who they were….a "guest" in whatever house of worship offered us hospitality.

We went on to open emergency shelters and also started a long term housing program with comprehensive support services, all in response to the needs of the guests. What was always critical in every response was that the services would be provided with dignity, respect and love for everyone who found themselves in need of the services. What was also unique was that everyone involved who was volunteering to help was showing up and providing the services without regard to their own ego or need for recognition. This continues to be a struggle but one that is met with sensitivity and humor as we all recognize our human tendencies and limitations.

My other observation is that to do this work, either as a volunteer or a paid staff member, you need to recognize and understand that to interact and meet those who are in need, in many cases in dire and difficult circumstances, you are going to share in their experience and actually face vicarious trauma which causes burn-out and leads to compassion fatigue. This is why we have instituted spiritual retreat days for the staff (annually) and for the volunteers of The INN (when possible) to help them address their own spiritual needs to recharge, recognizing everyone's unique personal spiritual journey.

Finally, my other observation about the entire human services area of nonprofit organizations is that the structure that exists is very fragmented (i.e. one organization deals with food, another with rehab, another with furniture, etc.) and the needs of the individuals are varied and many faceted. Those who need help are often feeling broken and fragmented by their experience of living in poverty and they are asked to seek assistance from a system of very limited and fragmented, not-for profit, human service agencies....all on an island without an adequate public transportation system nor the funds to utilize that which exists.

We strive each day to continue to offer the basic necessities of food and shelter along with all the missing pieces of support and inspiration within a holistic model of meeting as many needs as possible under one roof. Our ultimate goal is to go out of existence and not be needed anymore. (When we are told this is not possible because it says in the Bible that "the poor will always be with you" we reply we know it says that but we also know they forgot to notice the asterisk after that saying which said:

Over the years, The INN established shelters and permanent housing and other services to address a wide variety of needs and people including: those escaping the war in El Salvador; the interest of religious women to live in an emergency shelter to provide assistance to undocumented women and children; soup kitchens for homeless and hungry people; emergency shelter for families; emergency night shelter for single men as well as emergency shelters and long-term residences for people with AIDS and military veterans.

Since 1984, The INN became aware of the needs of the guests in its emergency shelters, there were a number of families who were in need of more than housing. They needed intensive supports and basic living skills in order to recover from their chronic homelessness. This brought about the formation of the Long Term Housing Program. In 1990, New York State made available special funding though their Homeless Housing Assistance Program (HHAP). The INN applied for and received three grants totaling two million dollars. With that money The INN purchased thirteen single and two family homes throughout Nassau and Suffolk Counties.

In 1992, a legal boarding house was purchased and renovated in Hempstead. The Hospitality INN was re-named the Edna Moran INN in 1993, as a gift to Michael Moran on his departure from The INN. It was named after his mother. The Edna Moran INN continues to be in operation as the largest family shelter in Nassau County. It is the only handicapped accessible shelter for families in Nassau County and the only one that accepts intact families, mothers, fathers and children.

The INN was later approached by Sr. Mairead Barrett who had been one of the founding Sisters at the Angela Merici INN. She was beginning her own human service agency, called New Ground, based on her understanding of the specific supports that families who are homeless need. The INN entered into a contractual arrangement with Sr. Mairead and New Ground at the beginning of this Long Term Housing Program. Today, there is room for 20 families and there are currently 20 adults and 60 children participating in the INN's Long Term Housing Program. "Today, there are fourteen soup kitchens in operation, working in twenty-one locations throughout Nassau and Suffolk counties. Over the years there have been other housing options made possible by The INN. These include the purchase of houses, the management of sixteen single family homes which had been used for military housing, as a transitional housing program for four and a half years, providing support needed to locate independent housing and eventually gain economic independence. The INN also operates a total of three emergency shelters: The Edna Moran INN (EMI), a family shelter and the only handicap accessible shelter in Nassau County.

In thirty-one years, the INN conservatively estimates that it has served ten million meals and sheltered approximately sixty thousand people who were homeless. This has been accomplished with the support of thousands of Long Islanders who believe in how The INN provides its services with dignity, respect and love. In the process of providing these services The INN has brought people of all faiths together to address the issues of hunger and homelessness in their communities. The INN has also worked with its staff to make sure that they are mindful of the potential for burnout in this field. As an antidote to the stress, The INN offers spiritual retreats once a year to help the staff learn skills to relax and take care of their spirits.

The starting of The INN and its first ten years has been documented by its co-founder, Michael Moran, in a book called 'Give Them Shelter.' While a book has not yet been written for the last twenty years, Jean Kelly, The INN's director says that they have the title for the sequel: 'Give Them Shelter...And Then What?'" [67]

Island Harvest

Island Harvest was created in 1992 by one woman with a cooler, a station wagon, and a strong desire to help people in need. Linda Breitstone, the organization's founder who was infuriated that food from a local convenience store was being thrown away at the end of the day - with a safe house for women and children down the street. In response, she established Island Harvest and its mission, "to end hunger and reduce food waste on Long Island."

Since those early days, Island Harvest has become Long Island's largest hunger relief organization. Volunteers and staff deliver millions of pounds of good, surplus food - much of which might otherwise go to waste - to a network of Long Island-based food pantries, soup kitchens and other non-profit organization that offer feeding services for those in need. By doing this, the organization provides a vital supply of food to counter the sharply rising problem of hunger on Long Island.

With the leadership of Randi Shubin Dresner, Island Harvest recruits businesses and members of the public to donate food and pioneering innovative distribution methods. Since its inception, the organization has delivered 71 million pounds of food, supplementing close to 66 million meals. Hunger awareness and education have long been a part of the organization's programs, as they develop and strengthen key allies in our community.

In recent years, Island Harvest began to attack hunger in targeted and strategic ways. The most visible example of this is a Weekend Backpack Feeding Program. Piloted in 2006, this initiative provides 35,000+ packs of nutritious food to school children who rely on school lunches and breakfasts and may not receive solid meals on weekends. [68]

Jewish Community Centers

The centers grew a great deal over the past thirty years expanding their programs and services dramatically. Currently, there are five:
- Barry and Florence Friedberg Jewish Community Center in Merrick and Oceanside
- Five Towns Jewish Community Center in Cedarhurst
- Mid-Island Y Jewish Community Center in Plainview
- Sid Jacobson Jewish Community Center in East Hills
- Suffolk Y Jewish Community Center in Commack

These centers offer a wide range of programs and activities including: Youth groups, senior citizen services, early childhood education and nursery schools, day schools, fitness, recreation, and summer camping. [69]

Junior League of Long Island

The league continued to expand its activities by establishing Project HOME to provide goods for low-income housing residents along with a mentoring program. The organization also worked with the Long Island Children's Museum and the Parent and Child Education Center to offer parenting workshops to underserved people. In addition, Launch for Caring Kids, a school violence prevention program was established. Community service grants were awarded. [70]

Literacy Nassau

Since its inception when it was known as Literacy Volunteers of America, Literacy Nassau has had a single and unwavering mission: to promote and foster literacy in Nassau County among adult learners in need of improved skills in Basic Literacy and English for Speakers of Other Languages. Through trained volunteer tutors in one-to-one and small group learning experiences students are matched with tutors to achieve the educational, economic and social goals they and their tutors have identified as important to them. Literacy Nassau provides services each year for hundreds of Nassau adults who are functionally illiterate, assisting them, their families - and hopefully future generations - toward self-sufficiency and personal success. Students are referred to Literacy Nassau by family, friends, local libraries and other community-based organizations. Volunteers are recruited from all over Nassau County. Tutors are trained, certified and supported by Literacy Nassau throughout the year. [71]

Literacy Suffolk

Statistics show alarming rates of low literacy in Suffolk County. One in seven Suffolk County adults (14%) are functionally illiterate, 75% of unemployed adults are nonreaders and almost 45% of adults living below the poverty level do not possess the basic reading and writing skills to improve their lives and the lives of their families. They have difficulty using the basic reading, writing, speaking and computational skills necessary for functioning in everyday life. Only 10% of those needing help are getting it.

People with low literacy skills often drop out of school and, therefore, may lack the basic skills needed to adequately provide for themselves and their families. Low literacy has an economic impact on society as well. Hundreds of millions of dollars are lost to industry annually in remedial programs for employees, low productivity, errors and accidents as a result of basic skill deficiencies in workers.

Leadership of the organization during the period was provided by executive directors Maxine Jurow and Gini Booth and the board leadership of Aldustus Jordan.

Since its inception, Literacy Suffolk has helped thousands of adults to acquire the skills necessary to realize their potential and become fully participating members of society. The organization is dedicated to providing a variety of literacy services to adults, thereby enabling them to achieve their personal goals. Literacy Suffolk recruits volunteers and trains them to tutor fellow adults in basic language skills: reading, writing, listening, speaking. The waiting list of students in Suffolk County remains consistently at about 500. [72]

Long Island Association for AIDS Care (LIAAC)

LIAAC is a regional community-based nonprofit agency, established in 1986, that delivers comprehensive services to all Long Islanders infected and affected by HIV/AIDS and other infectious diseases. Additional priorities include services and supplemental support to promote health and wellness. Utilizing a field-based mobile outreach model, the organization's staff provides a continuum of client services, responsible public policy, aggressive advocacy and effective testing/prevention education. LIAAC's driving philosophy is to provide a stable and comprehensive safety net that ensures our services reach the many diverse communities of Nassau and Suffolk Counties.

The organization got started at the height of the epidemic. It got started mostly because nobody was really dealing with a lot of the HIV problems, and they were looking for different groups to deal with HIV in the community. LIAAC was selected to be the HIV agency for Nassau and Suffolk County and has been working with the state, the federal government, Suffolk County, and foundations since then.

The biggest challenge that LIAAC faces is that as the disease changes, it is necessary to change with the disease. And sometimes the interventions that are based on the funding sources may not be the best for our constituency. The problem is that most of the programs being paid from government dollars are looking for a lot more accountability. Sometimes they're asking for programs as part of their accountability that may not be as successful here as they are in the city, or may not be as successful in the city as they are here in suburban or rural areas. They try to do that one-size-fits-all approach, and that does not always work.

The hallmark of LIAAC's integrated mobile service program is: using traveling service centers proactive wheeled approach (vans/recreational vehicles and trained mobile staff) to overcome barriers and literally bring an array of core services to disadvantaged clients "on their own turf," in culturally and linguistically sensitive ways. The program builds and earns trust among distressed community members by helping them first receive services that are most needed and most important to them. LIAAC's "no wrong door" policy means that every individual encountered through the program receives access to a wide net of services: medical care, food & shelter assistance, mental health treatment, and social service advocacy, as well as help obtaining benefits.

Under the leadership of Gail Barouh, LIAAC's president and CEO, the organization has received funding from a wide variety of government sources, enabling special areas of focus and attention during service delivery including HIV rapid testing (supported especially by the multiple agencies, including Centers for Disease Control and Prevention—(CDC), the Substance Abuse and Mental Health Services Administration (SAMHSA), the Office of Minority Health, and the New York State Department of Health (NYSDOH); linkage to substance abuse treatment facilities (supported by the Substance Abuse and Mental Health Services Administration (SAMHSA); specialized attention to Hepatitis C prevention and assistance to people recently released from jail (supported by SAMHSA); specialized attention to Black and Latino individuals at-risk (supported by all, including the Office of Minority Health); and specialized attention to issues of nutrition (supported by New York State Department of Health). Each of these government agencies helps support not just these narrow focus areas but also many closely related aspects of the mobile service delivery and the integrated nature of LIAAC's service delivery.

Recently, New York State launched a new initiative to end the state's three decade AIDS epidemic with the goal of reducing the number of new HIV infections. The task force, created by Governor Andrew Cuomo seeks to develop ways to expand prevention and access to testing and treatment with a focus on at-risk groups. The group is also working with drug companies to bring down the cost of drugs that fight the infections. [73]

Long Island Child and Family Development Services

Today, the agency provides services to over 1,675 children and their families a substantial increase from the number served in1985. In addition to the twenty-two Head Start sites located across Suffolk County, the organization has four Early Head Start program sites that offer services to pregnant women and infants. These Early Head Start Programs are located in Central Brookhaven, Huntington, Islip and Patchogue. All of the Head Start and Early Head Start sites provide ongoing comprehensive training and support services to families in the following areas: Education, Disabilities Services, Health (medical &

dental), Nutrition, Mental Health, Family/Community Partnerships and Parent Involvement. [74]

<u>Long Island Coalition for the Homeless</u>

The following information was obtained from the organization's website: www.addressthehomeless.org and a 2014 oral interview with Charles Russo, the organization's chairman.

The coalition was established in 1987 to reduce and eliminate homelessness in Nassau and Suffolk Counties and alleviate the difficulties related to homelessness for homeless and at risk persons on Long Island. In 2014, Greta Guarton, the coalition's executive director indicated that the homeless population on Long Island increased between 2013 and 2014 likely due to Super Storm Sandy and the Island's lack of affordable housing. Guarton estimates the homeless population to be approximately 3,200. They're served by forty agencies receiving funding from the U.S. Department of Housing and Urban Development (HUD) that operates emergency shelters and transitional housing. Guarton reports that it is very likely that the number of homeless people is significantly undercounted due to HUD's "point-in-time" policy of counting the homeless population on a single night in January each year. [75]

For further information, visit Charles Russo's profile in Part III.

<u>Long Island GLBT Services Network (LIGALY)</u>

LIGALY is the original organization of The Network as it was founded in 1993 and is nationally known for its work with GLBT youth in the areas of education, advocacy, youth leadership and development and support. The Center and SAGE-LI along with the Network was founded in 2005 to unite these non-profits to help more GLBT people across the lifespan and create a cost efficient way of serving the Long Island GLBT Community.

Long Island GLBT Services Network is an association of non-profit organizations working to serve Long Island's GLBT community throughout the lifespan: Long Island Gay and Lesbian Youth (LIGALY), The Long Island GLBT Community Center (The Center), and Services and Advocacy for GLBT Elders – Long Island (SAGE-LI).

With shared administrative staff between all organizations, this structure eliminates duplication of administrative and executive staff thereby allowing each organization of The Network to share resources. This unique model reduces overhead costs and expenses and as a result more than 80 cents of every dollar raised are channeled directly into critical programs and services for Long Islanders of all ages and walks of life.

Together, each organization works within The Network to end homophobia and transphobia, to provide a home and safe space for the GLBT community, and to advocate for equality.

Since 2012, The Network also produces the annual Pride Parade and PrideFest celebration every June and *Living Out* magazine each month. Both Pride and *Living Out* build community and celebrate our identities while also providing visibility to our movement. [76]

Long Island Housing Partnership (LIHP)

The organization was created to address the need for and to provide affordable housing opportunities on Long Island for those who are unable to afford homes, through development, technical assistance, mortgage counseling, homebuyer education and lending programs.

Prospective homebuyers who meet maximum annual income restrictions and qualify for private mortgage financing are selected by lottery or computerized random number generating systems, and then on a first come first serve basis, if additional applicants can be accommodated.

Technical assistance is provided to private developers, municipalities and other nonprofits that are providing affordable housing on Long Island. [77]

Long Island Mentoring Partnership

The Mentoring Partnership's mission is to enable every child in need to be paired with a caring adult in a quality, structured mentoring program. This is accomplished by providing training, technical support, advocacy and resources to program providers and volunteers engaged in mentoring.

The organization was founded in 1993 by James O. Boisi, Chair, and Joan S. Brennan, founding Executive Director. The Mentoring Partnership serves as the go-to resource for research and best practices in all aspects of mentoring youth on Long Island for any youth development program. Its focus is to assist in the startup and support for quality based mentoring programs that are safe and successful for young people. No-cost technical assistance, support and training has been provided to 180 different programs that serve nearly 8,000 young people. All of this work is evidence-based to insure the best possible outcomes for youth.

Since their inception, the organization has touched the lives of over 100,000 Long Island young people. Nearly 15,000 mentors have been trained and thousands of mentoring program coordinators and youth development workers. The organization's annual, "Mentoring Matters Conference" is in its 11th year and held at LIU Post, hosting 500 + youth workers, mentors and mentees.

The organization's goals are:

- To expand mentoring on Long Island by helping start new programs, expanding existing programs and recruiting mentors
- To share the knowledge of best practices in mentoring
- To raise awareness about the importance of mentoring 78

<u>Long Island Progressive Coalition (LIPC)</u>

LIPC is a unique nonprofit organization principally because it is board-run and focused on progressive social change. Policy is set by a diverse board of directors that includes staff as voting members (with the exception of personnel decisions). The board meets regularly to set and oversee the organization's public policy priorities and strategies. The organization is not only a 501(c)(3) but a 501(c)(4) thus enabling it to legally to influence legislation in Mineola, Hauppauge, Albany, and Washington. The organization selects political candidates to endorse and actively supports the Working Families Party's (WFP) platform and campaigns. WFP is focused on tackling the political, economic, and educational inequality that deprive working and middle class families of opportunity. WFP's vision is to build a New York that is fair for all not just the wealthy and well-connected. The organization seeks to recruit, train, and elect the next generation of progressive leaders to local and state office — candidates who fight for the needs of working class, middle class and poor families. Its core issues are raising the minimum wage and guaranteeing paid sick days, fighting the influence of big money over politics, and defending quality public schools.

Lisa Tyson started as LIPC's director in 1995 at a time when the organization had a $200K budget with a handful of staff to one with a $500K-$1MK budget five years later. The funding increased due to foundation support of a handful of targeted campaigns rather than the twenty smaller campaigns sponsored earlier. Tyson helped the organization secure private support for its progressive efforts most significantly from The Unitarian Universalist Veatch Program at Shelter Rock, the Hagedorn Fund, and the Rauch Foundation. In thinking about foundation support, Tyson says "it is all about relationships." In thinking about changes that have occurred since 1995, Tyson points to a substantial decline in foundation support in the past five years and a focus by these funders on project funding rather than general support funding. Foundations also want to see their support result in little changes rather than the achievement of big lofty goals.

Tyson believes that LIPC's work to influence public policies and politicians helps traditional nonprofit service organizations. She feels that LIPC organizing is a much better social investment than funding direct service organizations since LIPC influences passage of laws that benefit social spending such as the progressive income tax that enabled government to fund social programs. Tyson feels that the state's needs are so significant that government is not going to fill in the gap nor will foundations that are negatively affected by the current economy and market conditions.

With rare exception, the organization does not seek or accept funding from government since, according to Tyson, "government funding ties your hands. You have to be willing to lose the funding," she continues. Fund raising has changed a lot over the past twenty-five years. To offset these losses of funding since 2012, LIPC has contracted with Green Jobs-Green New York, a program of the New York State Energy Research and Development Authority (NYSERDA). The $720K grant enables LIPC to assist low and moderate income Long Island homeowners through the energy efficiency process of lowering utility costs. Tyson admits this type of work is not what the organization set out to do but it does enable LIPC to fund its organizing work around some its core progressive issues.

Besides the Green Jobs-Green New York campaign, LIPC's other campaigns address:

- Long Island's affordable housing crisis, working to develop more affordable homeownership and rentals through Island-wide organizing, called *"Yimby."* (Yes in My Backyard)
- The fight for high-quality public education from pre-kindergarten to high school through the Alliance of Quality Education (AQE). AQE is a statewide nonprofit that unites parents, children's advocates, schools, teachers, clergy, and others.
- The battle for election reform focuses on the public financing of elections, lowering contributions, ending pay-to-play practices, and stronger enforcement and transparency.

LIPC has also entered into agreements to serve as an Independent Contractor to national, state, and local political organizations and political candidates and the Community Development Corporation of Long Island by conducting canvassing work for them. This has helped the organization to diversify its income.

Diana Coleman was a very important LIPC board member. For over a decade Coleman was the co-chair of the Long Island Progressive Coalition working to build the organization and to impact social, economic and racial justice. Earlier, Coleman was the lead plaintiff forcing Nassau County to redistrict due to the impact on minority communities. She has been a leader in Long Island's civil rights battle over and over. [79]

For further information, visit Part III for profiles of Marge Harrison and David Sprintzen.

Mental Health Association of Suffolk (MHAS)

In 2013, after one year of due diligence and deliberations, the board of directors of the Mental Health Association in Suffolk unanimously approved resolutions to merge with Clubhouse of Suffolk, a non-profit provider of psychiatric rehabilitation and support services. The MHAS is a local chapter of a national and statewide network of associations dedicated to improving the mental health of local communities through education, workforce training, information and referral services, and advocacy.

MHAS board president Dr. Kristie Golden explained the board's rationale for the merger: "Today's non-profit organizations are being confronted with important strategic choices in an increasingly competitive funding environment. This has driven the need to operate collaboratively with similar organizations in order to carry out an agency's mission and better ensure its sustainability. By joining Clubhouse and MHAS, we have created a stronger entity that will be more responsive to the pressing needs of our mutual constituents, including consumers, families, and professional providers." Michael Stoltz, Clubhouse's CEO was appointed CEO of the merged organization.

Clubhouse of Suffolk is a provider of psychiatric rehabilitation and support services that was founded by families of adults with psychiatric disabilities in 1990. Clubhouse serves over 1200 people each year through a range of community programs. In addition, the organization manages Suffolk County United Veterans, an organization serving homeless and at-risk Veterans, many with mental health and substance abuse problems.

In this new alignment, each organization retained its corporate identity. The board of directors and administrative functions merged. Executive Director Colleen Merlo was appointed associate executive director while Clubhouse's executive director assumed the MHAS's reins. Merlo notes, "This affiliation allows both organizations to build upon our strengths. We will have a greater capacity to address the current and emerging needs to ensure quality care for children and adults with mental health challenges."

Dr. Davis Pollack, Clubhouse's founder and board president assumed responsibilities for board oversight of the MHAS. Dr. Pollack noted, "The MHAS and Clubhouse have long been partners in eradicating stigma and promoting better understanding of mental illness and mental health in general in our communities. With recent tragic events involving people with mental health problems, there has never been a stronger need for more public information and advocacy."

One focus in the merger is to expand Long Island activities during National Mental Illness Awareness Week, during the first week of October. This includes advocacy efforts and education of our communities, schools and lawmakers.

The Mental Health Association of Suffolk County is an affiliate of Mental Health America and the Mental Health Association of New York State, Inc. Since its inception, MHAS has advocated for improved services and funding for adults and children living with mental illness. [80]

For further organizational information, visit Part III for a profile of Davis Pollack.

Middle Country Public Library (MCPL)

The following organizational profile was written and edited in 2014 by Lori Abbatepaolo, Tracy LaStella and Sandy Feinberg, the former director.

By the early 1990s, over fifteen Suffolk County libraries were conducting the PC Workshop. Sandy Feinberg and Kathy Deerr along with MCPL staff continued to write books and journal articles as well as present at library and other professional conferences. They worked with the NYS Developmental Disabilities Council to develop statewide training focusing on the role of the library could play in early intervention. During this same time period, the Rauch Foundation provided support for replication of the PC Workshop in five Nassau County libraries. Replicability along with the books, articles, presentations and courses formed the cornerstone for the national Family Place Libraries™ initiative.

During this same time period, MCPL lead the way to the creation of what was initially called the Computerized Community Information Database for Suffolk County. In 1989, a steering committee was organized under the leadership of Barbara Jordan and Sandy Feinberg of MCPL, Betty Eberhardt from United Way and Tom Williams with the Brookhaven Youth Bureau and the Suffolk Community Council. All of the major hotlines and helplines in Suffolk County were asked and participated on this committee. Many were creating their own paper files and there was general agreement that a centralized computerized system would not only save time but would provide access to a wider variety of services for their clientele.

Funding was secured through a New York State member item grant to purchase the *Community Services Locator* software, a disk distribution system that included the *Info Line Taxonomy of Human Resources*. Pilot sites were selected in a variety of settings including the Suffolk County department of health, the Islip Hotline, United Way First Call for Help, Mastics-Moriches-Shirley Community Library and BOCES I. The Suffolk County Youth Bureau and the Department of Social Services purchased subscriptions to the database and provided funding for the addition of specific resources. A contract was created outlining the responsibilities of both the pilot sites and the central manager.

MCPL was selected to be the central manager of the database, responsible for data collection and input of services. A team of clerks and librarians worked under the leadership of Barbara Jordan to design the system for collecting and entering data. Forms were designed that mirrored the way data was entered into the computer system. MCPL staff worked daily on entering original data and developing an ongoing schedule for updating the information annually.

The library continued to progress in the world of technology. They purchased a stand-alone system for patron records, circulation and technical processing. Patrons began to access their own records as well as the library's holdings online. As part of this system, the library was able to purchase an information and referral software module. In 1994, the database was converted to this online platform, accessible via modems and passwords. When the system changed from disk distribution to online access, the data was able to be converted electronically, another benefit to computerized records.

Initially the scope of the database was on services for families and children. With funds garnered from state member item grants, county government and the library, the database developed gradually from one focused on children and families to a comprehensive database including a wide range of health and human services. It grew from several hundred entries to include over 4,000 Suffolk County resources. In 1997 information on education, training and workforce preparation resources was included as a strong secondary focus, increasing the number of resource listings to over 5,000.

During the 1990s, nonprofit agencies were beginning to look towards computerization and consolidation as a way to reduce costs of operations and, at the same time, provide wider access to reliable and updated information. Suffolk and Nassau residents were beginning to see themselves with similar needs and an understanding that people who lived in one county may need services in the neighboring one. Having one information database for Long Island controlled by one entity would help to reduce costs and produce a more comprehensive, accessible and consistent product.

In 1996, private foundation funding permitted the creation of a business plan to examine the feasibility of expanding the Database to include Nassau County resources and to consider sustainability needs and options. The Steering Committee expanded to include representation from Nassau County agencies and government departments as well as significant involvement from the labor and business communities. With the plan in hand, MCPL and members of the steering committee identified and solicited funding for additional entries. The result of this collaborative work was the evolution of the *Community Resource Database of Long Island (CRD)*. Within a few years, the Database had grown to over 10,000 entries and included both Suffolk and Nassau resources. Funding was provided through multiple supporters including Suffolk and Nassau counties, private foundations, business sponsors and subscriptions.

The major enabling forces for the CRD were the many partnerships and collaborative services that were formed between MCPL and other agencies. MCPL staff was involved in projects with the early intervention community, the Island-wide family support network and the GATEWAY initiative involving BOCES, Suffolk County Community College, Suffolk County Department of Labor, the Private Industry Council and the Nassau and Suffolk Counties' departments of Social Services. Other enabling forces included the Library's ability to manage information and its technological capacity. Integrated computerized work processes and having the Internet available within MCPL at an early stage were critical to the evolution and expansion of the Database.

A primary road block was the lack of partnerships with Nassau agencies and their inability to understand why MCPL was in a position to be the central manager. Another restraining force came from agencies that already had some form of resource directory or database which generated revenue and a marketing position for the agency. MCPL was viewed as a competitor.

The United Way of Long Island (UWLI) supported the database and its development from the beginning and, along with other Long Island funders and supporters, continually supported the role of MCPL as central manager. UWLI officially endorsed its development and expansion in the late 90s and provided additional funding particularly when it expanded into the CRD. In 2007, New York State United Way began to work towards a statewide 2-1-1 system and the CRD was again converted to a new software platform - Vision Link. MCPL manages the database for Long Island and works in partnership with United Way Long Island and United Way Hudson Peconic, the manager of the 2-1-1 call center.

In tandem with the evolution of the Database, MCPL's children's services forged ahead as a leader in the development of library-based family centered services. In 1996, MCPL was approached by Libraries for the Future (LFF), a national library advocacy organization whose mission was to target innovative community oriented library programs and promote them nationally. They selected MCPL as a national model for early childhood and parent education in public libraries and together MCPL and LFF coined and trademarked the term Family Place Libraries™. The PC Workshop, the development of early childhood and parent spaces, professional training and coalition building became the cornerstone components of the national initiative.

In 2007, LFF disbanded. MCPL continues to manage the national initiative including onsite and online training, site visits, conferences and publications.

In 2012, MCPL was awarded a national grant from the Institute for Museums and Library Services to implement and evaluate the model in 27 libraries in eight states. The current network has over 400 libraries in 27 states including close to fifty libraries in Nassau and Suffolk counties. Known as Family Place Long Island, these libraries serve as an incubator for a number of collaborative services that are vetted on Long Island and promoted nationally.

Judging from the many evaluations of program impacts, Family Place has affected the development of MCPL as a Long Island institution, the libraries that have adopted the program and the roles they play within their local communities, and the many families throughout the United States who have experienced the family centered and early childhood environments and services that have been replicated. Public libraries are undergoing major transformations in who they serve, what they offer and why they exist. Family Place has been recognized as a viable way to serve the public, particularly focusing on the potential role that libraries can play in the development of very young children and their caregivers.

The fact that Family Place and the Database remain in existence is a result of the many years of work by and dedication of MCPL staff and its many supporters. While staff developed and expanded their skills, abilities and knowledge base about family centered services and technology, the projects evolved with many twists and turns. Without perseverance and consistent leadership, neither initiative could have come to fruition. Without the assistance and support from funders and multiple agency professionals and their willingness to partner with MCPL in their creation and development, Family Place and the Database would not be as inclusive or embedded in the daily lives of patrons and users.

Sandy Feinberg, head of children's services and director, MCPL, provided the impetus and leadership for both the development of the PC Workshop and the subsequent Family Place Libraries initiative and the creation and evolution of the Database. She continually thought "out of the box" in order to move the projects forward while working with staff, boards and funders to manage and develop the projects within the context of the library setting. Under her leadership, the library formed the Middle Country Public Library Foundation, principally responsible for raising money for Family Place and the Database as well as other projects. From 2001 to 2004, she oversaw the expansion of both buildings and, in 2011, the integration of a new circulation self-serve system using radio frequency and an automated conveyor system.

Barbara Jordan, children's services librarian and assistant director played a fundamental role in the development of Family Place and the development of the many partnerships that MCPL cultivated with other agencies. She was instrumental in the evolution of the Database from its inception, the establishment of the Suffolk Family Education Clearinghouse and the administration of the Middle Country Public Library Foundation including all of the major grants.

Kathy Deerr developed the PC Workshop in the Mastics Moriches Shirley Community Library, was a leader in the Suffolk Coalition, created the Library School course with Sandy Feinberg that eventually became the Family Place Training Institute and co-authored many publications and grants on family centered services in public libraries. In 2002, she became the MCPL assistant director for Family Place Libraries™ and has been instrumental in furthering the national and regional initiative.

Betty Eberhardt from UWLI was part of the initial "think tank" for the CRD and has been continually involved in the details of its development throughout her career with United Way. From the first meeting with members of the Suffolk Coalition, Betty was determined and focused on making this project happen. She served as a critical connection among the nonprofit community, the library and United Way.

The Long Island Funders Group, including the Rauch Foundation, Horace and Amy Hagedorn Foundation and the Long Island Community Foundation, were instrumental in the development of Family Place and the Database. Rauch was particularly supportive in the development of MCPL as a lead institution including the creation of the MCL Foundation. Many other public and corporate funders provided support for one or both initiatives. Some of the major collaborators for Family Place include Cornell Cooperative Extension of Suffolk County and Libraries for the Future as well as all of the Long Island Family Place libraries that have worked closely with MCPL in the evolution of the model. Some of the major collaborators for the Database include United Way of Long Island, the Suffolk County departments of social services, health, youth, women, handicapped services and labor, Suffolk Community Council, Health and Welfare Council, and Nassau County department of social services.

Ongoing funding is a constant concern. Developing a sustainable model, not too dependent on the whims of funders, is tantamount for success. The Family Place Libraries initiative, which is very solvent, is funded through a combination of grants and training/technical assistance fees. The 2-1-1 Long Island Database is still undergoing financial difficulties. In 2010, while Suffolk County maintained their support, Nassau County pulled out their funding. MCPL and United Way have been able to "piece together" some funding but it is always tenuous.

Both initiatives prove the critical importance of working in partnership to achieve a goal that would not be attainable alone. The Parent Child Workshop - the core component of Family Place - cannot be conducted without local community resource professionals. This forces the librarians to reach out to and maintain relationships with other family support providers. It gets them out of the library and places them "at the table" with other community organizations that support family centered practice. The Database would not exist without the involvement from other agency professionals with either the contributions to the basic data that underlies the database or their ongoing use and communication regarding the accuracy and timeliness of the information. [81]

North Fork Spanish Apostolate

Since 1963, Sr. Margaret Rose Smyth has been an activist and educator, working to help minority communities. Well known on eastern Long Island as an advocate for the Latino population, she began her efforts in Crown Heights, Brooklyn, where she taught high school and assisted the Hasidic community. She also ran meetings for thousands, worked in storefronts, marched with Caesar Chavez and ran numerous workshops for women.

An Irish immigrant, Sr. Margaret Rose identified with the challenges of foreign born immigrants: leaving their home country, adjusting to an unfamiliar culture and being far from family and friends. Sr. Margaret Rose was inspired to help the impoverished by empowering them to use their voice, according to an account of her career from the National Catholic Development Conference.

In 1997, Sr. Margaret Rose became the director of the North Fork Spanish Apostolate (NFSA), based in Riverhead and Greenport. It reaches low-income residents who are dependent on public transportation. As executive director, Sr. Margaret's goals have included building opportunities for education and employment and focusing on parenting and immigration issues.

She works with the Long Island Immigrant Alliance, Family Service League, New York Immigration Coalition, Peconic Community Council, Maureen's Haven, Riverhead Anti-Bias Task Force, area hospitals, and local government and school officials. She provides healthcare workshops for residents, visits the sick and works with volunteers to coordinate home visits. She created a bilingual court mediation program and English literacy and computer programs, in addition to serving as a translator. [82]

North Shore Child and Family Guidance Center (NSCFGC)

In the 1990s, NSCFGC created the intensive support program (ISP), a school-based mental health partnership with Nassau BOCES to prevent children and youth with serious emotional problems from out-of-home placements. ISP is recognized by the New York State Education Department as one of the twelve model school-based mental health collaboratives across the state. Also in the 1990s, another program for high-risk youth was established "turnabout." The program uses a foster parent model for meeting children's needs.

Other programs and services were added over the years including a wilderness program that takes emotionally-troubled teens on weekend outings to state parks as well as crisis services provided counseling and support services during times of crisis such as when the Avianca Airlines plane crashed; the Long Island Railroad Massacre; and in response to local violence.

By the turn of the century, NSCFGC had grown substantially as did its fund raising results, government contracts, foundation grants, and corporate support. Attractive buildings were purchased and an endowment fund established. The board of directors remained true to its mission in spite of extremely difficult funding streams and managed care. [83]

Long Island Pine Barren Society (LIPBS)

In the late 1980s, the LIPBS recognized that the region was threatened by encroaching development that was threatening to disrupt the ecological balance required for the survival of the Pine Barrens ecosystem. The focus of the group shifted from an educational awareness to designing an active preservation campaign.

With the leadership of Richard Amper, Executive Director, LIPBS has been active in the halls of state and local government as well as in the courts, pushing for needed action and winning an impressive list of victories. The Society is best known for leading the Pine Barrens Preservation Initiative - an ambitious, ten-year legal and legislative campaign. This initiative led to approval by the New York State Legislature of the Pine Barrens Protection Act and the Comprehensive Management Plan, which permanently preserved more than 50,000 acres of Pine Barrens while directing strictly controlled development to the least sensitive areas. The preservation of the Pine Barrens has become a national model. The Society was instrumental, for example, in:

- Securing the transfer of 7,200 acres from the RCA Corporation to New York State to establish two major Long island Pine Barrens Preserves.
- Saving thousands of acres of Suffolk County land scheduled for public auction. This land is now part of the County's park system.
- Protecting from development the 850-acre Oak Brush Plains at Edgewood State Hospital in Brentwood.
- Obtaining nearly $500 million in state, county and local funding to purchase Pine Barrens land across the Island.
- Winning public support for land preservation funding referenda in Nassau and Suffolk, including the popular and successful Suffolk County Drinking Water Protection Program and the East End Community Preservation Fund. The residents of Long Island have authorized more money to protect drinking water and preserve open

space and farmland than the residents of 45 of the 50 states in the union.

- Petitioning for referendum to ensure that money for Pine Barrens preservation cannot be used for other purposes.
- Played a major role in securing funding for open space preservation through the creation of the Community Preservation Fund, the Suffolk County Drinking Water Protection programs, and through Bond Acts in Nassau, Suffolk and many Long Island Towns.
- Led drive to ensure enforcement of Pine Barrens Protection Act through litigation and legislation. [84]

Planned Parenthood of Nassau (PPNC)

More than 13,000 people use the services at PPNC health centers in Hempstead, Glen Cove and Massapequa for cancer screenings, birth control, prevention and treatment of STDs, breast health services, pap tests, sexual health education, information and counseling. Through comprehensive sexuality education, evidence-based workshops and street outreach, 32,000 more learn how to make smart, well-informed and safe choices. More than 70 percent of patients use some form of subsidized care, and the majority of the organization's education workshops are offered free of charge. PPNC also work actively across Long Island to engage and mobilize community members in support of women's health and rights. [85]

Planned Parenthood of Suffolk (PPSC)

In 1983, PPSC opened its Riverhead center with the intent of serving the East End of Suffolk County. By 1986, services were expanded to the South Fork through the establishment of the satellite facility in Amagansett. In 1994, PPSC established its sixth location - and its first comprehensive center – with the opening of the Smithtown medical center.

The merger of Planned Parenthood Westchester, Rockland, and Putnam with Planned Parenthood Suffolk County was formalized in January 1998. The new entity that emerged was called Planned Parenthood Hudson Peconic, Inc. (PPHP), after the two main waterways that geographically define each of the regions served by the original affiliates. The merger was driven by the changing health care marketplace and was intended to position PPHP as a major provider of reproductive health care for the region and a leading public advocate in the suburban metropolitan area. Today, PPHP is in fact that provider and advocate. [86]

Rainbow Chimes International Child Development Center

When asked about her legacy, Katie Roche, Rainbow Chimes' executive director, says: "Persevere; band together with other organizations; scream, shout and advocate; engage the press; make the constituents work towards their own salvation. Just make sure you carry enough insurance and you can take more risks to survive. Be entrepreneurial, or at least enterprising. Bully your board if you have to, but endure…the mission is what you get up to carry out, every morning."

Today, Roche sees government support for child care continuing to wax and wane, subject to fiscal crises with middle-class parents not able to afford the cost of care due to the quality mandates and few public dollars invested to meet the needs of low-income families. She also feels that licensed programs are required to provide better educated staff, but there is nowhere near enough money to do this, nor will many colleges offer the curriculum when they know graduates can only hope to earn poverty-level wages. [87]

St. Christopher Ottilie (SCO)

The following agency information was obtained in a 2014 interview with Douglas O'Dell, Interim Executive Director and Chief Program Officer as well as from the agency's website.

In 1985, St. Christopher's Home merged with the Briarwood, Queens-based Ottilie Home for Children, which cares for adolescents with serious emotional needs and developmental disabilities. Originally known as the Ottilie Orphan Home, it was named after Ottilie Seibert, a young woman who died of pneumonia, leaving behind two young children. Ottilie's father, John Miller, founded the orphanage in 1892 as a memorial to his only child. The merger between St. Christopher's Home and Ottilie resulted in St. Christopher-Ottilie.

A second merger took place in 1996 with Madonna Heights Services in Dix Hills. Madonna Heights Services serves adolescent girls recovering from trauma and/or struggling with behavioral health issues, as well as women coping with domestic violence, battling addiction, and/or in need of temporary shelter.

In 1999, St. Christopher-Ottilie merged with Family Dynamics, an organization in Bedford-Stuyvesant, Brooklyn dedicated to improving the lives of children by strengthening families struggling with poverty, abuse, teen pregnancy and drug addiction.

As a reflection of the tremendous growth in the scope and range of our services, the organization changed its name from St. Christopher-Ottilie to SCO Family of Services in December, 2004. Today, SCO Family of Services provides a comprehensive array of services to children and families throughout New York City and Long Island, helping 60,000 vulnerable New Yorkers to meet critical needs and build a strong foundation for their future. [88]

Suffolk Community Council (SCC)

During the 1990s and into the new century, SCC increased its role to identify gaps in services for people who had aged out of the educational system and were in need of special services. The agency expanded its advocacy in behalf of nonprofit organizations and the people they served through HUSAC, the Human Services Action Committee as a unified voice for human services. As the assault on human services continued, SCC, with support from the Long Island Community Foundation, county and state government developed CRISS/CROSS, as an effort to reorganize service delivery in the county according to school district lines. SCC operated CRISS/CROSS operated in several school districts for several years in collaboration with county departments and nonprofit agencies. It was discontinued during a period when the Health and Welfare Council was broadening its role in both counties. According to Tom Williams, SCC's a former SCC executive director it is unclear exactly why the project was discontinued due to lack of funding both through the SCC's budget and the lack of funding and staff support from various county agencies and school districts.

In the late 1990s and into the new century, the council under the leadership of Tom Williams and Judy Pannullo developed a number of new initiatives including the Clearinghouse for Community Residences, a database of State-licensed community-based housing in Suffolk County; the Mediation Project for Consumers in Community Residences, providing mediation for residents in mental health housing; Accessible and Universal Design Long Island, promoting multigenerational housing using barrier-less designs; the Unity Project, a Brentwood community-building, education project addressing immigration issues; and the Network of Women in Disabilities, a project to increase awareness of and address issues facing women with disabilities and improve health care access.

According to Tom Williams, a former SCC executive director support for the Council's advocacy, planning and coordinating efforts on behalf of agencies was losing ground to the need for practical hands-on client oriented programs that were more palatable to funders. At the same time, the Health and Welfare Council was expanding its advocacy into Suffolk County which resulted in their filling the leadership, coordination, and advocacy gap filled by SCC. By 2010, the council ceased to operate. [89]

See Appendix for a listing of SCC's annual award recipients.

Suffolk Housing Services (now named Long Island Housing Services (LIHS)

In 1991, the agency expanded its services to investigate discrimination in Nassau County and became Long Island Housing Services. LIHS' work in challenging all kinds of discrimination, but especially race, handicap, and familial status, has received national attention. In 1994 LIHS' successful testing program was highlighted on CBS' "48 Hours" news magazine show. The story featured undercover black and white testers being given false information about availability of housing by the broker.

Today LIHS continues to challenge racial and economic discrimination and has established itself as the lead Long Island agency challenging unlawful disability discrimination. Since 2002, the agency has successfully conciliated landmark complaints against several major developers in pursuing compliance with the Fair Housing Act's requirements for accessibility in multi-family design and construction in senior and non-age restricted rental, co-op and condo settings, increasing housing opportunities for people with disabilities in well over 1,000 units.

In addition to litigation, LIHS has helped to informally resolve and obtain needed modifications and accommodations for countless others with disabilities. In the last few years, more than half of the individual claims of discrimination reported to LIHS relate to people with disabilities encountering housing denial and discrimination.

LIHS has also successfully challenged a number of housing providers that have published discriminatory advertising that particularly impacts families with children, people with disabilities and others. In many of these cases, testing has helped to establish proof of exclusionary, discriminatory practices.
90

United Cerebral Palsy of Suffolk (UCP Suffolk)

UCP Suffolk ended the 20th century with extraordinary growth and expansion strengthening its original focus, a revitalized diagnostic and treatment center re-opened in the portables at Indian Head Road. A 57,000 square foot site acquired in the Hauppauge Industrial Park was completely renovated to house adult daytime programs welcoming over 250 individuals daily, and all administrative offices. The residential program more than doubled in size, adding individual residential alternatives (IRAs) for persons needing less direct support than those in the intermediate care facilities. A HUD grant facilitated the purchase of land and construction of a 13 unit fully accessible apartment complex. Named Eaton Knolls in honor of UCP Founder, Nina Eaton, this was created for people with developmental disabilities, who could live independently. New programs and services included day habilitation focusing on personal choice and community integration, creative arts, service coordination and mobility opportunities via education - MOVE, an approach to functional movement and independence. The UCP Suffolk Children's Center became the first MOVE model site in the northeast. The "Down Under

Scramble" and "Women-in-Business Golf Outings" were added to the fund raising calendar.

As the new decade and century began, UCP Suffolk stayed true to its mission. The acquisition of the Community Programs Center (CPC) brought UCP expertise to day care services for preschoolers and the elderly affected by dementia. The children's residential program was initiated with two beautiful homes featuring 24/7 nursing and the integration of the school age education program. The agency was named Long Island's Outstanding Nonprofit organization by both the LIA (Long Island Association) and the HIA (Hauppauge Industrial Association). After many years of planning, the UCP Suffolk's health center opened, providing a compendium of medical and clinical services, delivered by experienced, caring and credentialed professionals in a spacious, accessible setting. [91]

New Initiatives Launched Since 1985

Boys and Girls Clubs

Boys and Girls Clubs were established in the areas of Bellport, Hempstead, Hicksville, Stony Brook, and Oyster Bay/East Norwich bringing character building, recreation, and youth services to thousands of young people. [92]

Community Land Trusts

The following description of the development of community land trusts on Long Island was written in 2014 by O. Andrew Collver, Ph.D., Chairman and Research Director, Community Builders Long Island.

The modern community land trust (CLT) was developed in the 1960s as a democratically controlled and mostly voluntary nonprofit institution that holds land for the common good and makes it available to eligible users through long-term leases. The land may sometimes be used for business, charitable or cultural activities or rental housing, but most often it is dedicated to home ownership at a reduced cost. Cost reduction is achieved in two ways. First, the initial buyer needs only to pay for the house and not the land, which remains in CLT ownership. Second, the resale price of the house is controlled by the CLT to ensure that it will remain affordable for future buyers.

The CLT model has been successful in many parts of the U.S. from coast to coast, but has been very slow to take hold on Long Island. In the years from 2005-2010, Community Builders Long Island, Inc., (formerly New Directions Community-Based Research Institute), with leadership from Andrew Collver and Robert Mulvey, took on the task of introducing the CLT to the region. Supported in part by grants from Citi Foundation and Ford Foundation, a team from Community Builders went to civic groups in several communities from

Long Beach to North Bellport to tell the story of this unfamiliar answer to affordable housing. The result was the incorporation of five local CLTs in Long Beach, Hempstead Village, Uniondale, Farmingdale and North Bellport. At about the same time, Burlington Associates from Vermont introduced the model in Greenport, bringing the total to six. On request, Community Builders followed through by helping the new organizations to incorporate, adopt bylaws and apply to the IRS for charitable tax exemption. They also laid the groundwork for regional coordination of the small local organizations by establishing the Federation of Long Island Community Land Trusts, Inc. Tax exemption for the Federation is pending.

The next challenge was to obtain grants of land for the several local CLTs. That effort revealed a consistent pattern of resistance to the idea of shared equity housing at all levels of government and among the established housing organizations. In view of this resistance, Ford Foundation, on the advice of a well-respected consultant, John Davis of Burlington Associates, decided not to continue funding the work.

The local units have dealt with the situation in different ways, some of them by remaining inactive. Uniondale CLT decided to broaden its bylaws to include community organizing, which could keep the organization active in other ways than originally planned. Farmingdale CLT has kept up a consistent and steady campaign to establish its first property. In 2013 they entered into a municipal agreement with Farmingdale Village to create a mixed use shared equity project near the railroad station. In July 2014 they were still waiting for a site control memo from the Village. South Country CLT (North Bellport) revised its bylaws to allow the option of selling the land with the house. They have received one vacant building, designed a house and engaged a builder, who is now waiting to begin construction once an eligible buyer has a commitment for financing. In September 2014, after operating informally for many years, the Southold CLT is raising funds to incorporate and obtain tax exemption, and goes ahead with hopes of obtaining land on which to provide housing for essential but modestly paid workers. [93]

ERASE Racism

ERASE Racism, an independent nonprofit, charitable organization since 2004. It was launched in 2001 as a special initiative of the Long Island Community Foundation to address the ways in which policies and practices of government at all levels, businesses and others, directly affect racial equity in the region-in particular the quality of life for Long Island's African American residents and other people of color. Issue areas of focus include housing and community development, public school education and the relationship between health behaviors, health status and the neighborhoods in which people live. Elaine Gross is the founding executive director and continues in this capacity.

ERASE Racism is a regional organization, funded by foundations, corporations, and individuals, leads public policy advocacy campaigns and related programmatic initiatives to promote racial equity in areas, such as housing, public school education, public health and community development. It engages in a variety of research, education and consulting activities to address institutional and structural racism. Long Island, New York was the site of ERASE Racism's initial work and continues to be the geographic home and key focus area. At present, ERASE Racism's work is expanding to encompass statewide and tri-state regional activities with related national work as needed.

ERASE Racism achieves its objectives by utilizing research, education, policy advocacy and civic engagement of Long Island leaders, community organizations and community residents. It also forms partnerships with other Long Island institutions to help make the goal of racial equity into a regional priority.

ERASE Racism's Housing Project analyzes the practices and policies of both public and private institutions whose work affects fair housing. The Equity Education Initiative catalyzes a strategic dialogue about the benefits of creating racially and ethnically diverse, high performing schools throughout Long Island. The agency works to identify racial disparities in public health and health outcomes. Lastly, ERASE Racism utilizes research and outreach programs to reveal how structural racism continues to deeply affect people of color and the region as a whole.

On April 28, 2014, ERASE Racism submitted a civil rights complaint to the U.S. Department of Housing and Urban Development (HUD), alleging that Nassau County (the County) discriminates against African-Americans and perpetuates racial segregation in the administration of its housing and community development programs. The Complaint identifies violations committed by the County itself, as well as the County's failure to enforce federal civil rights requirements on members of the Nassau Urban County Consortium.

Each year, the Nassau County Office of Community Development allocates millions of dollars of housing funds to municipalities that are part of the Consortium. In Fiscal Year 2014, the County received $15,734,513 in HUD block grant funds. Acceptance of the funds obligates the County and members of the Consortium to comply with Title VI of the Civil Rights Act of 1964, the federal Fair Housing Act and the separate obligation to affirmatively further fair housing ("AFFH"). The AFFH obligation requires the County and Consortium members to promote integrated living patterns by overcoming historic patterns of segregation.

The Complaint alleges that the County has not taken the affirmative steps required by these federal laws, and has continued to fund municipalities with restrictive zoning and housing practices. As a result, the County has reinforced segregated living patterns, rather than working toward their elimination. According to the 2010 Census, Nassau County is part of one of the most racially segregated regions in the country. While African Americans constitute 11.1% of the overall population of Nassau County, the vast majority of the municipalities in the Consortium have over time maintained disproportionately small or disproportionately large African-American populations.

ERASE Racism President Elaine Gross noted, "It has been 50 years since the passage of Civil Rights Act of 1964 that made discrimination based on race or color illegal, yet, as this complaint to HUD shows, African Americans are still being denied housing choice and, consequently, equal access to the same opportunities that white residents of Nassau County enjoy."

In the complaint, ERASE Racism asserts that the county awards funds and dedicates county-owned land for affordable housing for families, but does so predominantly in communities characterized by high rates of poverty and large concentrations of African American families. In contrast, when the county supports affordable housing for families and seniors in majority white communities, it often permits the use of residency preferences or requirements, which reinforce patterns of racial and economic segregation.

Further, the complaint alleges, the county has provided millions of dollars of HUD funds to highly segregated municipalities with predominantly white populations for purposes other than for integrative housing-such as streetscape improvements, economic development and community centers - even though such municipalities have long histories of racial segregation and very small minority populations.

While the County's most recent analysis of fair housing impediments finds that "the Nassau-Suffolk PMSA [Primary Metropolitan Statistical Area] ranks as the third most segregated suburban region" in the country and identifies local opposition to integrative, affordable multi-family housing as an impediment to fair housing choice, it proposes no appropriate actions to actually overcome such barriers. As a consequence, a number of municipalities have engaged in discriminatory land use policies and practices, such as zoning exclusions and residential preferences, which serve to limit the number of African Americans in their communities.

"ERASE Racism felt compelled to file this complaint because the county has closed its eyes to continuing problems with segregation for far too long," said Elaine Gross. "We have seen positive outcomes from HUD fair housing complaints in other parts of the country, and are confident that shining a light on Nassau County will lead to increased housing choices for people of color."

On Wednesday, September 24th, 2014, ERASE Racism joined Suffolk County residents and other community organizations to witness County Executive Steve Bellone's signing of HR 1620 into law. Elaine Gross, President of ERASE Racism called this "a win for fair housing."

Passed by a unanimous vote in the Suffolk County legislature earlier in September, the bill expands the county's Human Rights Law to provide residents meaningful protection from discrimination in areas including housing, employment, credit, and public accommodations. Strengthening housing provisions, this amendment prohibits discrimination against individuals based on their lawful source of income, including income derived from Social Security or housing assistance, such as the Housing Choice Voucher Program (also known as Section 8).

Standing alongside County Executive Bellone and other community leaders at the signing in Hauppauge, Elaine Gross remarked: "The signing of this amended Human Rights Law, offering expanded protections against discrimination, is applauded by ERASE Racism. Among its many provisions, home-seekers in Suffolk County can no longer be denied housing because of their source of income."

The changes effected by the signing of this bill will benefit many residents, including vulnerable veterans, immigrants, racial and ethnic minorities, single mothers with children, and seniors. It represents an important step forward for the promotion of residential integration and economic equality which is at the heart of ERASE's mission. There is much more work that has to be done. Statistics reflect that Long Island is one of the most racially segregated regions in the state. This is a direct by-product of the existing school district/property tax structure. This existing tax structure supports the disparity in the quality of education, public support services, affordable housing, and, again, improved access to quality health care services in many the Long Island communities. The affordable housing issue has reached a crisis stage, particularly for new immigrants and their children. This crisis will not improve without social change and social services action by all stakeholders. The Affordable Health Care Act will prove to be a significant quality of life ingredient for thousands of county residents, however, access to the health care services, due to the geographical and demography overlay of the region. [94]

For further historical information regarding racism and the civil rights struggle on Long Island, visit Part VIII.

Early Years Institute (EYILI)

EYILI began as a research project called Early Care and Education – Long Island (ECELI) in April, 2002 initiated by five funding organizations: the Long Island Community Foundation, Rauch Foundation, Hagedorn

Foundation, Sandy River Charitable Foundation, and United Way of Long Island. After a year of research, a four-year strategy was designed to improve the quality of child care. ECELI, under the leadership of Dana Friedman, worked on these goals with the help of an advisory committee comprised of 52 executive directors from a range of intermediary organizations and community institutions that support children and a quality circle, a team of 50 early childhood teachers and experts working on the "front line" from all forms of child care programs. These two groups have met quarterly since 2004 and several collaborations and innovative partnerships have emerged demonstrating the value of interdisciplinary thought and action.

The success of these efforts led the original funding organizations to recommend that ECELI incorporate, which it did in 2008 under the name The Early Years Institute. The original mission of ECELI was expanded to go beyond the regulated market of child care to informal care (e.g. parents, relatives), where over half of children under age six spend their days. EYILI finds families by going "where they pay, play and pray." This has led EYILI to work with such sites as parks, libraries, museums, pediatrician's offices, schools, and places of worship. These potential learning sites define the stakeholders with whom to partner.

The STEM nature project involves the development and implementation of a curriculum by teachers in Westbury's early childhood programs and in grades K-3. A group of local and national experts will provide education, training and experiential learning using one of our greatest scientific assets; the native wildlife and habitats of Long Island. The featured wildlife we will be using is the osprey, a locally found fish hawk with a strong conservation history and message. Given that the Osprey is a cosmopolitan species found in five continents, this focus will enable students from different cultures to readily connect with this species.

The Early Years Institute is in a unique position to develop and implement this project through its program, the Long Island Nature Collaborative for Kids (LINCK) and the generosity of the Motorola Solutions Foundation grant awarded to The Early Years Institute.

Just prior to going to press, Dana Friedman, EYILI's founder, announced the following great news about funding for early childhood education.

> Thanks to a grant from the U.S. Department of Education, New York will see 1,725 new full-day Pre-K slots created and an additional 1,350 existing slots will be expanded to meet the definition of a full-day High-Quality Preschool Program. This grant will also strengthen our infrastructure of support and data collection statewide. Community coalitions will be created to help the pilot sites improve quality and offer services that address the whole child. I am very proud that two of

the innovations that EYI brought to Long Island have been included for replication in this grant.

In a statement, Governor Cuomo said, "By expanding pre-kindergarten across the State we are giving children the chance to learn from an even earlier age and raising the bar for how this country prepares its student for the future. Our administration is fundamentally reimagining New York's schools with that in mind, and I am proud to have the federal government's support in this endeavor."

The U.S. Department of Education has committed $226,419,228 for this expansion of pre-K. NYS was one of 13 states to receive a Pre-K Expansion grant. Three-quarters of the funding has been allocated for expansion grants.

Uniondale is one of five pilot sites, which were chosen for having the state's highest percentage of unserved four-year olds. The other sites include two districts in Westchester, as well as Indian River (a rural district upstate) and a neighborhood in New York City. Districts will receive $10,000 per child served in the new or expanded pre-K programs.

The innovations that will be supported and tested in each pilot site include QualitystarsNY and a process of examining pre-K through 3rd grade alignment. All early childhood programs in the district will be asked to use the Common Metric, which makes it possible to compare findings from different assessment tools. Additionally, funds will be used to enhance the state's Longitudinal Data System that will allow children to be tracked from pre-K through 12th grade on a range of measures. There is a special focus on reaching children with special needs and those for whom English is not the language spoken at home.

The Early Development Instrument (EDI) that The Early Years Institute has used to great effect in Westbury will also occur in the pilot sites. The community coalition that comes together to review the EDI data will then create the implementation of interventions to improve school readiness. In addition, EYI's UPK School Leadership Project will be replicated in the pilot sites. This involves the creation of learning communities for principals, pre-K administrators and directors of community-based organizations (CBOs) contracting with the districts to offer pre-K, as well as professional development for teachers in both school-based and community-based pre-K programs. There will also be coaching to districts to help principals support continuous quality improvement.

What is so important is that this funding is not just about new slots. It is about creating smarter, stronger children and a smarter, stronger America. [95]

<u>First Baptist Church of Riverhead</u>

The church provides a wonderful model of a faith-based organization that goes well-beyond traditional religious services. Lead by Charles and Shirley Coverdale, First Baptist actively seeks to empower people both as individuals and as a collective community to achieve excellence in realizing their full potential to effect positive change in our world. As such, First Baptist has established several programs and agencies which provide direct services, as well as organizing efforts intended to train and develop the poor and disadvantaged.

It is one of several founding organizers of LION - Long Island Organizing Network, a nonprofit federation of faith-based and community organizations whose collective voices bring about positive change and social justice on Long Island.

For several decades, First Baptist has been an active force in initiating positive programs for the youth and families of our community including, after-school mentoring & reading programs, computer literacy programs, and summer enrichment programs targeting at-risk community youth. Additionally, First Baptist has subsidized and supervised youth travel abroad to conferences in both Scotland and Zimbabwe.

First Baptist has been active in the mission field, both in supporting local and domestic projects, as well as projects abroad. Most recently, First Baptist members have been raising funds to purchase a brick manufacturing machine for a multi-village building project in Ghana.

The church provides meals to homeless and impoverished individuals through our weekday soup kitchen, as well as our food and household goods pantry which provides emergency assistance to needy families as well as a child development and learning center and a summer arts program.

First Baptist is currently seeking town approval of a major community project that includes 125 units of much-needed rental housing, recreational facilities, a performing arts theater, a 24-hour child care facility, a senior citizen wellness and day care center, a major sports and recreational compound, and intergenerational services that will serve Riverhead and other East End communities.

Other faith based initiatives were undertaken in both counties with many establishing or expanding their food pantries and other assistance to the poor. In other cases, day care and adult day care centers were formed. [96]

Intergenerational Strategies

In 2002, Intergenerational Strategies was developed to promote the development of intergenerational policies and programs. Over the next ten years, the organization sponsored several conferences and seminars and assisted dozens of organizations. The organization assisted Dowling College to establish a campus-based intergenerational program of educational events and course offerings. Seniors4Kids, a program of Generations United, was sponsored in which older adults were engaged as advocates for early childhood education programs. The organization ceased its operations in 2010. [97]

Long Island Crisis Center

In its forty-two years, it has grown from one hotline to six. I staffed round-the-clock by volunteer counselors who undergo nine months of intensive training. Annually, the organization responds to more than 11,000 calls on telephone hotlines, on-line (interactive and live) a chat site, mobile phone texting and walk-in counseling.

The Long Island Crisis Center established Pride for Youth (PFY) in 1993 to serve Long Island's lesbian, gay, bisexual and transgender (LGBT) youth and their families. With a disproportionate number of suicide calls being received by the Crisis Center's hotlines, it became evident that this population was at a greater risk for suicide and suicide attempts (studies indicate that they are at a four time greater risk for suicide than their straight counterparts). PFY delivers free services that include: individual, family and group counseling; sexual health services to provide education on HIV (including testing), STDs and unintended pregnancies; youth leadership opportunities; Empowerment, HIV/AIDS and Hepatitis C prevention through community outreach and education to young men of color. Pride for Youth's cornerstone project is The Coffeehouse, a weekly, Friday evening drop-in center for LGBT youth and their straight allies.

The organization's community outreach program has brought educational workshops to schools. Topics addressed include: suicide awareness and prevention; self-injury; anger management; cyber bullying; suicide prevention for professionals; runaway/child abuse prevention; understanding homophobia; understanding transphobia; working with and creating a safe environment for LGBT youth. Linda Leonard serves as the organization's executive director. [98]

Long Island WINS

Long Island WINS is a nonprofit communications organization that focuses on promoting practical immigration solutions that work for everyone, rooted in respect and dignity for all Long Islanders, the organization works to shift the debate about immigrants and immigration policy on Long Island and to educate Long Islanders about sensible policies that work for and will benefit everyone. The goal is to highlight the contributions of immigrants in our community, enhance public perception of immigrants, and build support for immigration initiatives that maximize immigrants' contributions for the benefit of all Long Islanders. This includes support for comprehensive immigration reform - a bill that would make long overdue changes to an outdated immigration system. And it includes local solutions that mean a more welcoming Long Island. We know that immigration can work-if we have the right policies. Research and commentary is provided to shape public engagement and organize Long Islanders working towards a common goal. A website provides local and national immigration news, and online organizing tools to help Long Islanders create change that will respect the rights of all. Marilyn Sinclair Slutsky serves as executive director of the organization. [99]

New York Communities for Change

New York Communities for Change is a coalition of working families in low and moderate income communities fighting for social and economic justice throughout New York State. By using direct action, legislative advocacy, and community organizing, NY Communities' members work to impact the political and economic policies that directly affect us. Through neighborhood chapters and issue-based committees, we are working to ensure that every family throughout New York has access to quality schools, affordable housing, and good jobs. It is through the power-in-numbers approach that NY Communities is able to win REAL change for our towns and neighborhoods. Its campaigns are: Education equity; non-toxic Schools; affordable housing; foreclosure prevention; and workplace justice. Jon Kest served as the organization's executive director until his untimely death when Jonathan Westin was appointed Organizing Director. [100]

Parents for Megan's Law and the Crime Victims Center

Parents for Megan's Law (PFML) and the Crime Victims Center is a nonprofit organization dedicated to the prevention and treatment of child sexual abuse and rape, the provision of services to victims of violent crime, and elderly, disabled and minor victims of all crime. Violence directed against victims is an abuse of power, often directed at our most vulnerable, and must be met with unwavering resolve to hold perpetrators accountable, and provide victims with the support and services they need. Parents for Megan's Law and the Crime Victims Center is committed to informing victims of their rights, involving them in the decision making process, securing crime victim compensation to which they are entitled and treating every victim with respect and dignity.

In 1999, PFML established the first and what continues to be the only National Megan's Law Helpline. The Helpline is designed to educate callers about accessing sex offender registration information, responsible use of information, child sexual abuse and rape prevention, and crime victim support and services. Locally, in 2013, passage of the Suffolk County Community Protection Act by County Executive Steve Bellone and the Suffolk County Legislature, created a first in the nation public-private partnership between law enforcement and a nonprofit organization to assist police in their efforts to maintain an up-to-date and accurate sex offender registry. PFML retired law enforcement staff conduct in-person home address verifications of registered sex offenders and provide leads to law enforcement for registrants who may be out-of-compliance. There has been a 69.05% reduction in registered sex offender's recidivism rate in Suffolk County since the inception of the sex offender address verification program.

In 2007, working collaboratively with the Suffolk County Police Department, the agency was the first to respond to the needs of all victims of violent crime, elderly minor and disabled victims of all crime and all hate crime victims. Working with police, the agency established the first comprehensive direct crime victim referral program where police transmit crime victim support referrals to agency advocates in the immediate aftermath of the crime for victim services follow-up. The agency has ranked number one in New York State in facilitating the largest return of victim related expenses to victims compared to any other funded nonprofit in the State.[101]

Sepa Mujer

SEPA Mujer has been working to support immigrant women on Long Island since 1993, bringing together community members and advocates to push for change, speak out against injustice, provide access to opportunities and services and take a stand against domestic violence and other abuses. The organization works with individuals and in partnerships with organizations (immigrant rights, civil rights, and domestic violence based). It has educated hundreds of people about their basic legal rights in a variety of areas and has developed a leadership program, building capacity for community members to participate in business, civic and political life on LI. [102]

The Social Enterprise Alliance (SEALI)

In 2012, the Social Enterprise Alliance-Long Island Chapter (SEALI) was established to encourage and support the growth and development of nonprofit and for-profit enterprises that simultaneously pursue self-sustaining revenue and measurable social impacts. The group consists of entrepreneurs in the for-profit and nonprofit sectors, potential social enterprise investors/philanthropists, foundations, and other interested parties. Ken Cerini provides leadership for the organization.

Over the past 25 years, social enterprise initiatives have been launched on Long Island especially by agencies serving people with disabilities, training and employing their clients in various forms of assembly and service jobs. Examples of other entrepreneurial projects that have been launched include: Habitat for Humanity's ReStore that sells new and used building materials; FREE's human services management company; Goodwill's temporary staff service enterprise; IGHL's retail store The Flower Barn; Big Brothers/Big Sisters of Long Island's used clothing business; and FEGS' information systems integration consulting company.

The other arena in which new social enterprise initiatives have been launched is among faith based organizations. Abundant Communities Together (ACT) assists churches to develop social enterprise projects while the Reverend Patrick Duggan of the United Church of Christ's Church Building & Loan Fund assists new and renewing congregations with the purchase of their first building, providing technical and planning assistance, along with loans for site purchases, construction or the purchase of an existing building. The church building and loan fund also assists faith-based organizations to create revenue generating initiatives in housing, economic and community development. [103]

Suffolk County United Veterans (SCUV)

When John Lynch was out to dinner one night in 1989, his evening was disturbed when he came upon a fellow former Vietnam soldier from his squad who was homeless and eating from a garbage can. Lynch's return to civilian life had been marked by a successful career in the international shipping industry, but he could not ignore the despair of his former mate. He went about helping the Vet get into a home, only to take notice that this Vet was not alone in his adversity – there were many former soldiers who served our country whose transition to civilian life was obstructed by a range of barriers.

Lynch encountered his "moment" - despite his own comfort and success in his life, he could not ignore the stark contrast for people who had meant so much to him earlier in his life. This inspiration led Lynch to build an agency with a mission dedicated to addressing the barriers returning Vets face. SCUV's approach emphasizes veterans-helping-veterans, recognizing that the military experience often represents the period of greatest success among Vets needed help. With unique understanding, Vets who face addiction, mental health conditions, physical challenges, unemployment, and family strife all find unique understanding and guidance from fellow Vets and staff. Services include a food pantry, case management, training for employment, housing, and peer support. SCUV is now a program of the Association for Mental Health and Wellness. The program director is Wilkins Young. [104]

Sustainable Long Island

In 1996, a group of environmentalists, civil rights advocates, philanthropists, developers, business people and civic leaders came together. Despite individual efforts to make improvements, things were getting worse rather than better. As the need to protect Long Island's diverse population, this group of leaders realized they could not continue to solve problems individually – they needed a new approach. Together, they had a chance at developing a model that would bring about positive change by working side-by-side. Determined to improve the region, they formed Sustainable Long Island.

"We were helping to model a process that helped people understand the most effective ways to use their voices," notes Marge Rogatz, who took an active role from the very beginning. Participants, she points out, who represent very different goals "worked together to make something happen while being respectful of others' visions.

In listening to those voices, this group began to develop a process. At one meeting, Elaine Gross, President of ERASE Racism, helped focus on the equity issue underlying the other challenges plaguing Long Island. They realized that there are some basic needs that all Long Islanders from every community have a right to—the right to a healthy environment and thriving economy. All Long Islanders should have access to public transportation; clean land, water and air; a racially diverse population; parks, community centers and other recreational opportunities; a range of housing options; thriving downtowns; trees and grass, safe streets and neighborhoods; access to quality and affordable food; and employment opportunities.

These elements are what make up sustainability and despite different backgrounds; those who helped build the organization recognized that the sustainable movement was the solution to their respective causes. In 1998, the term "sustainability" was not on anyone's radar and "our efforts without a doubt put the issue of sustainability on the map of Long Island," notes Nancy Douzinas, a founding member. "We educated the public, politicians and leaders way before 'sustainability' became the buzzword it is today."

They pushed to build an agenda that would create positive change in communities. They developed a course of action in which business leaders, clergy, civic associations, community members sit at the table with their respective town government in order to plan for the future – much the way they did in forming Sustainable Long Island. In Roosevelt, Greater Bellport, Elmont, Wyandanch, New Cassel, Middle Country, and communities across Long Island, we see examples of the model working. This is what Sustainable Long Island does today: bringing all stakeholders to the table to create positive change for communities.

These leaders from the Long-Island based Rauch Foundation, the Horace and Amy Hagedorn Fund, the Unitarian Universalist Veatch Program at Shelter

Rock, and the Long Island Community Foundation among others, set the wheels in motion for a brand new approach to growth on Long Island. Today, Sustainable Long Island has facilitated downtown revitalization efforts in numerous communities, advised elected officials at all levels, linked tens of millions of dollars in investment with communities in need, and emerged as the regional leader for brownfield redevelopment and food access projects. More importantly, Sustainable Long Island has helped make the concept of sustainable development – a model of economic and environmental growth that will protect Long Island's diverse people and resources – a new regional paradigm.

Staff leadership of the organization was originally provided by Sarah Lansdale who was replaced by Amy Engel in 2011. Engel has lead Sustainable Long Island's ongoing recovery and revitalization efforts throughout the City of Long Beach and other hard-hit areas following Hurricane Sandy. Under Engel's direction, Sustainable Long Island has launched a new community gardens initiative with an opening project in Long Beach; expanding its youth-staffed farmers' market model to new communities in Wyandanch, Freeport, and Great Neck; releasing an extensive Food System Report Card detailing the state of Long Island's current food system; and partnering with North Shore-LIJ Health System on the Carbon Footprint Challenge – an initiative designed to increase awareness of pollution prevention.

Engel coordinates community input and public participation projects in numerous Long Island communities, recently including those in Hicksville, Riverhead, and Bethpage. In addition, she is frequently mentioned and quoted as an expert on sustainability in both local and national print and online publications. [105]

Teatro ExperimentalYerbabruja

Teatro Experimental Yerbabruja, Inc. ("Yerbabruja"), was incorporated in 2004. Yerbabruja began life in the living room of its founder, Margarita Espada, an experienced and acclaimed experimental theatre artist with teaching certification as well as an M.F.A. degree. Espada's initial focus was on the use of experimental theatre, in her Central Islip, Long Island community, as a means of encouraging understanding among her community's culturally diversified youth, including the need for such understanding among the varying Latino cultures. By 2008, Yerbabruja had expanded its geographical reach to include Brentwood, North Bay Shore and other Long Island communities, and had incorporated other performing, as well as visual, arts in its efforts to promote constructive social change among Long Island's increasingly diverse youth and other residents. Yerbabruja began developing plans to transition into an organization with the resources to impact its communities on a long-term, and even more significant, basis. Included in such plans was a permanent home where, in addition to administrative space, local performing and visual artists could create and present their work and, together with Yerbabruja, hold classes and workshops to teach and learn from each other and from others. [106]

VISION Long Island

Since 1997, Vision Long Island has advanced more livable, economically sustainable, and environmentally responsible growth on Long Island through Smart Growth. Smart Growth focuses on infill, re-development, and open space preservation. It supports mixed-use, mixed-income communities that are convenient, attractive, pedestrian-friendly, and that make affordable housing and public transportation desirable and realistic. Eric Alexander has served as the organization's executive director since its inception working with layman Ronald Stein.

Vision has counseled downtown villages and towns, and has been a resource for the county, state, and federal governments, as well as the business and civic community on downtown revitalization, planning and infrastructure. Vision has made over 1,900 presentations, performed 20 community "visionings" and advanced over 70 public and private planning projects towards implementing the goals of Smart Growth on Long Island. [107]

Notes: Part IV

1. U.S. Census Bureau website: www.census.gov.
2. IBID.
3. IBID.
4. Information obtained from agency's website: www.scuv.org.
5. Information obtained from agency's website: liglbtnetwork.org.
6. Christopher Neidt, "The Future of Fair Housing in a Diverse Suburb," (Social Justice in Diverse Suburbs, Temple University Press, 2013).
7. Martin R. Cantor, CPA, "Economic Benefits of Diversity: Untapping the Potential of Long Island's Black Community" (Long Island Institute for Socio-Economic Policy at Dowling College, 2008).
8. Martin R. Cantor, CPA, "Long Island's Young People: Why They Will Continue to Leave Long Island" (DestinationLI, June 2014).
9. "An Even Split in the Suburbs: Obama, Romney Tied as Election Nears," (Princeton Survey Research Associates International for the National Center for Suburban Studies at Hofstra University, October 2013).
10. Vera Parisi, telephone interview with author, April 1, 2014.

11. Pearl Kamer, "Long Island's Nonprofit Sector: Doing More with Less During a Period of Economic Change," (Long Island Association, 2011).

12. Author fact-checking on various United Way of America websites.

13. Pearl Kamer, "Long Island's Nonprofit Sector: Doing More with Less During a Period of Economic Change," (2011).

14. Long Island Nonprofit Survey 2010, (Cerini and Associates)

15. 2013 10th Annual Long Island Nonprofit Survey, (Cerini and Associates).

16. Louise Skolnik, email correspondence of March, 2014.

17. Information obtained from foundation's website: www.licf.org and interview with David Okorn, Melville NY, July 17, 2014.

18. Ben Gose, "Small Grant Maker, Closing Down in 4 Years, Is a Force in Immigration," (Chronicle of Philanthropy, May 5, 2013).

19. Information obtained from foundation's website: www.rauchfoundation.org and interview with Nancy Douzinas.

20. Ned Wright, written and email correspondence with author, July 2014.

21. Theresa Regnante, written and email correspondence with author, November 2014.

22. Information obtained from agency's website: www.womensfundli.org.

23. Information obtained from agency's website: www.afpli.org.

24. Findings of the Long Island Regional Advisory Committee," New York State Health Care Commission Report, 2006).

25. Information obtained from Suffolk County's website: www.suffolkcountyny.gov.

26. Rene Fiechter, interview with author, Mineola, NY, March 5, 2014.

27. Author's reflections of the time period.

28. Peter Levy, email correspondence with author, July 2014.

29. Author's reflections of the time period.

30. IBID.

31. Information obtained from school's website: www.socialwork.adelphi.edu.

32. Information obtained from center's website: www.nonprofit.adelphi.edu.

33. Information obtained from foundation's website: www.liu.edu/CWPost/Academics/Schools/SHPN/Dept/SW/Graduate-Programs/MSW.

34. Information obtained from school's website: www.farmingdale.edu.

35. Information obtained from foundation's website: www.hofstra.edu/ce.

36. Information obtained from center's website: www.hofstra.edu/Academics/NCSS.

37. Information obtained from school's website: www.molloy.edu/academics/.../graduate-social-work.

38. Information obtained from organization's website: www.afpli.org.

39. Information obtained from agency's website: www.energeiali.org.

40. Information obtained from school's website: socialwelfare.stonybrookmedicine.edu.
41. Information obtained from school's website: www.stonybrook.edu/spd.
42. Information obtained from agency's website: www.friends-arts.org.
43. Information obtained from agency's website: www.landmarkonmainstreet.org.
44. Information obtained from agency's website: www.longislandartsalliance.org.
45. Information obtained from agency's website: longislandmusichalloffame.org.
46. Information obtained from agency's website: adelantesc.org.
47. Nancy Marr, email correspondence with author, March 2014.
48. Information obtained from agency's website: li100bw.org.
49. Laura Cassell, written and email correspondence of August 2014.
50. Jan Barbieri, interview with author, Commack, NY, July 23, 2014 and written correspondence of September 2014.
51. Janet Walerstein, interview with author, Commack, NY, July 23, 2014 and written correspondence of September 2014.
52. Michael Stoltz, email correspondence of August 2014.
53. Paul Squire, "Not Just Surviving, But Thriving" (Suffolk Times, November 13, 2014).
54. Marge Rogatz, interview with author, July 24, 2014 and written correspondence of August 2014.
55. Von Kuhen, interview with author, Centereach, NY, August 28, 2014 and written correspondence of August 2014.
56. Author's reflections as organization's founder during the period.
57. Information obtained from agency's website: www.concernli.org.
58. Information obtained from agency's website: www.eoc-nasssau.org.
59. Information obtained from agency's website: www.eoc-suffolk.com.
60. Richard Dina, written and electronic correspondence with author, March 2014.
61. Karen Boorshtein, interview with author, June 8, 2014, Huntington, NY, and written correspondence.
62. Evelyn Roth, interview with author, Farmingdale, NY, August 21, 2014, August and written correspondence of August 2014.
63. Jill Rooney, email correspondence with author, July 2014
64. Information obtained from agency's website: www.tsli-hhb.org.
65. Information obtained from agency's website: www.hwcli.com.
66. Information obtained from agency's website: www.hispaniccounseling.org.
67. Jean Kelly, email correspondence with author, November 2014.
68. Information obtained from agency's website: www.islandharvest.org.
69. Information obtained from agency's website: jcca.org.
70. Information obtained from agency's website: www.jlli.org.

71. Information obtained from agency's website: www.literacynassau.org.

72. Information obtained from agency's website: www.literacysuffolk.org.

73. Information obtained from agency's website: liaac.org.

74. Information obtained from agency's website: www.liheadstart.org.

75. Charles Russo, interview with author, Hauppauge, NY, March 14, 2014 and agency's website: www.addressthehomeless.org.

76. Information obtained from agency's website: liglbtnetwork.org.

77. Information obtained from agency's website: www.lihp.org.

78. Information obtained from agency's website: www.limp.org.

79. Lisa Tyson, email correspondence with author, July 2014.

80. Michael Stoltz, email correspondence with author, September 2014.

81. Lori Abbatepaolo, Tracy LaStella, Sandra Feinberg, email correspondence with author, November 2014.

82. Grant Parpan and Carrie Miller, "Sister Margaret Smyth to be honored as Good Samaritan by national Catholic organization," (Suffolk Times, September 15, 2012).

83. "Guiding Families Through Changing Times: A History of the First Fifty Years," (North Shore Child and Family Guidance Center, 2006).

84. Information obtained from agency's website: www.pinebarrens.org.

85. Information obtained from agency's website: http://www.plannedparenthood.org.

86. Information obtained from agency's website: http://www.plannedparenthood.org.

87. Katie Roche, email correspondence with author, September 2014.

88. Douglas O'Dell, email correspondence with author, November 2014.

89. "Collection of the Suffolk Community Council" (Special Collections and University Archives at Stony Brook University) and interview with Tom Williams.

90. Information obtained from agency's website: www.lifairhousing.org.

91. Information obtained from agency's website: www.ucp-suffolk.edu.

92. Information obtained at agencies' websites: www.bgcbellport.org; www.hbgclub.com; www.hycbgc.com; www.bgcsuffolk.com; www.bgcoben.org.

93. Andrew Collver, email correspondence with author, November 2014.

94. Marge Rogatz, email correspondence with author, July 2014 and agency website: www.eraseracismny.org.

95. Information obtained from organization's website: www.eyi.org

96. Information obtained from church's website: www.firstbaptistchurchriverhead.org.

97. Author's reflections as organization's founder during the period.

98. Information obtained from organization's website: www.longislandcrisiscenter.org.

99. Information obtained from organization's website: www.longislandwins.org.

100. Information obtained from organization's website: www.nycommunities.org.
101. Information obtained from organization's website: www.parentsformeganslaw.org.
102. Informatin obtained from organization's website: www.sepamujer.org
103. Author's reflections as organization's co-founder during the period.
104. Information obtained from church's website: www.scuv.org
105. Information obtained from church's website: www.sustainableli.org.
106. Information obtained from organization's website: www.teatroyerbabruja.org
107. Information obtained from church's website: www.visionlongisland.org.

Part V

Suburban Trail-blazing

It may come as a surprise but Long Island, the place where hundreds of thousands of city dwellers fled after World War II, where the term "suburbia" began, has been the launching pad for much progressive social action. Long Island, a home of decades of one-party dominance, where racism found a welcome home and where it was believed that everyone who wanted to would get his share of the American Dream, enacted many progressive laws and social programs. Some were "firsts" in a suburban area or replicable models in New York State or the nation as a whole. The following is offered in testimony to this claim.

1. In the early 1960s, North Shore Child and Family Guidance Center became the first agency in New York State to receive a license (Outpatient Chemical Dependency for Youth) enabling the agency to provide mental health services to its substance abuse population.
   Andrew Malekoff, *email correspondence of August 21, 2014*

2. In the mid-1960s, the Carmans River played a significant role in banning the use in the U.S. of DDT and the subsequent creation of the Environmental Defense Fund, a national nonprofit organization that has had a significant role in protecting the environment. DDT was banned in Suffolk County in 1967, New York State in 1970 and nationwide in 1972.
   www.epa.gov/history

3. In 1966, Nassau Suffolk Law Services became the first legal services corporation program in New York State.
   www.nsls.org

4. In 1969, the Lynbrook Schools hired America's first fulltime drug educator.
   John Imhof, *interview with author, Uniondale, NY, August 10, 2014*

5. In 1970, the "Ministries in the Marketplace," later to be named the Smithaven Ministries, became the first ecumenical ministry located in a New York State shopping mall.
   Mon. Peter Ryan, *telephone interview of April 21, 2014*

6. In the 1970s, Congress passed The Runaway Youth Act (RYA), Title III of the Juvenile Justice and Delinquency Protection Act of 1974. The Runaway Youth Program developed by the Huntington Youth Board was funded and became a national model.
   wwnchew.org

7. In 1973, New York State Assemblyman Peter J. Costigan of Port Jefferson, chairman of the Select Committee on Child Abuse, with the assistance of many advocates, shepherded passage of the Child Protection Services Act of 1973 which established a 24/7 state central register of child abuse and maltreatment that also required school personnel, day care workers, and others to report suspected cases of abuse and neglect.
   www.ncjrs.gov

8. In 1973, Group House of Port Washington filed a law suit against the Town of North Hempstead to open a group home for seven homeless boys unrelated by blood to live in a home designated as a one-family residence. The case was won in New York State's Court of Appeals and is being used around the nation to benefit other at-risk populations. The records are archived in the Robert E. Wagner Library of New York University.
   Lillian McCormick, *interview with author, June 4, 2014*

9. In 1974, EOC of Nassau secured an Office of Economic Opportunity (OEO) grant to weatherize homes by unemployed individuals. The project was the first such program in the nation funded by OEO and enabled 100 formerly-unemployed people to start their own small businesses.
   Leone Baum, *interview with author, January 29, 2014*

10. In 1974, Suffolk County government's decentralized network of community health centers became an innovative model in New York State for the delivery of health care services.
    Priscilla Redfield Roe "The genesis of neighborhood health centers in Suffolk County: 1965-1968" (Long Island Historical Journal, Vol. 15, Nos. 1-2, pp.72-103).

11. In 1974, the Farmland Development Rights Program was inaugurated as a first in the nation in terms of the mechanism it uses to save farmland -- purchase of development rights. Through this program, open space programs, drinking water protection programs, and land preservation programs, the county has protected over 50,000 acres.
    www.suffolkcountyny.gov

12. Community Advocates (CA) developed the first ombudsmen programs in nursing homes in New York State. The model was established in Nassau County during the mid-1970s and was then implemented across New York State and in nursing homes in other states across the country.

   Leone Baum, *interview with author, July 5, 2014*

13. In 1976, The Victims Information Bureau of Suffolk (VIBS) launched New York State's first emergency motel housing program for battered wives in response to growing evidence of rape, domestic violence, and sexual abuse. The program was funded by the Veatch Program of the North Shore Unitarian Society in Plandome.

   www.vibs.org

14. Suffolk County was the first county in the nation to initiate a ban on phosphates in detergents to preserve the water supply in 1976.

   Paul Sabatino II, *interview with author, May 5, 2014*

15. The Community Mediation Center, funded by the Law Enforcement Assistance Administration (LEAA) in 1977, was originally sponsored by the YMCA of Long Island as the first interpersonal dispute settlement center in an American suburb.

   Author's *knowledge as organizational co-founder*

16. In 1978, New York State's Padavan Law (Section 41.34 of the Mental Hygiene Law), was passed under the leadership of New York State Assemblyman Robert Wertz, enabling group homes to be situated in communities if they demonstrated that they did not saturate a community.

   www.mhnews.org

17. In 1979, Suffolk County won a NACO (National Association of Counties) award for its leadership efforts in establishing a partnership with the "Blue Ribbon Task Force" consortium of agencies that led to the establishment of the Suffolk Network on Adolescent Pregnancy, Inc.

   www.naco.org

18. In 1980, the first "economic impact statement" to be included in a consumer intervention against a Long Island Lighting Company rate increase request before the New York State Public Service Commission was organized and presented by a Long Island ratepayer group, Long Island Citizens in Action.

   Paul Sabatino II, *interview with author, July 5, 2014*

19. In 1981,the Viscardi Center in Albertson established the nation's first adult education program which integrated physically challenged adults with non-disabled adults.

www.viscardicenter.org

20. In 1981, Long Island-based "Women on the Job" established New York State's first regional women's equal employment rights agency to organize women employed in school districts and counties to use collective bargaining rights for pay equity and sexual harassment prevention policies Their records are archived in the Robert E. Wagner Library of New York University.
    Lillian McCormick, *interview with author, June 4, 2014*

21. In 1983, Nassau County approved a policy on sexual harassment in county government.
    Lillian McCormick, *interview with author, June 4, 2014*

22. In 1983, due to action by the Suffolk County legislature, Long Island became the first place in the world to successfully defeat and dismantle the Shoreham Nuclear Power Plant, a completed nuclear power plant before it could be put on line.
    www.lipower.com

23. In 1984, the county adopted Resolution 940-1984 the first statutory pro-arrest policy in New York State for victims of domestic violence.
    www.suffolkcountyny.gov

24. In 1985, Suffolk County addressed equal pay in 1985 with a resolution for study and policy and in 1987 provided $2 million of county funding to address this issue.
    Lillian McCormick, *interview with author, August 21, 2014*

25. In 1985, Suffolk County passed a bill prohibiting requests for documentation by county employees in connection with applications for any county service.
    Evelyn Roth, *interview with author, August 21, 2014*

26. Suffolk County Local Law in 1988 began a program for county-funded day care at county facilities for county employees. County Executive Patrick Halpin actively supported the initiative that was a first in New York State.
    Evelyn Roth, *interview with author, August 21, 2014*

27. In 1989, Suffolk County Executive Patrick Halpin and Deputy County Executive Evelyn Roth established a Task Force on Family Violence that was the first in New York State to bring together all public and private stakeholder agencies to work on issues of child abuse, partner abuse, and elder abuse.

Evelyn Roth, *interview with author, August 21, 2014*

28. Circa 1989, the Domestic Violence Advocate Project, the first of its kind in the United States, was established by the Suffolk Coalition Against Domestic Violence, beginning to place advocates in police precincts to assist victims and police.

    Ruth Brandwein, *interview with author, September 10, 2014*

29. Long Island was a leader among suburban counties with the passage of the Pine Barrens Preservation Act and later led the effort to secure passage of the Pine Barrens Protection Act of 1993 in New York State.

    www.pinebarrens.org

30. In 1993, Suffolk County developed the first New York State program to seize vehicles used by drunken drivers.

    Paul Sabatino II, *interview with author, July 5, 2014*

31. Suffolk County adopted the first finger printing program for social service benefit eligibility in 1993. New York State adopted the program statewide in 1994

    Paul Sabatino II, *interview with author, July 5, 2014*

32. In 1996, the Middle County Public Library (MCPL) was approached by Libraries for the Future (LFF) - a national library advocacy organization – to see if the library would serve as a national model for early childhood and parenting services in public libraries. MCPL agreed and went on to assist libraries throughout the nation to establish the model.

    Sandra Feinberg, *email correspondence of November 5, 2014*

33. In 1999, Parents for Megan's Law established the first and what continues to be the only National Megan's Law Helpline. The Helpline is designed to educate callers about accessing sex offender registration information, responsible use of information, child sexual abuse and rape prevention, and crime victim support and services. Locally, in 2013, passage of the Suffolk County Community Protection Act by County Executive Steve Bellone and the Suffolk County Legislature, created a first in the nation public-private partnership between law enforcement and a nonprofit organization to assist police in their efforts to maintain an up-to-date and accurate sex offender registry.

    Laura Ahearn, *email correspondence, January, 2015*

34. Suffolk County resolutions in the early 2000s required county vendors and suppliers to report incidents of sexual abuse and to take measures to mitigate them.

    Paul Sabatino II, *interview with author of July 5, 2014*

35. ERASE Racism was established in 2001 as the first organization in an American suburb solely dedicated to fight racism.

    www.eraseracismny.org

36. The "No Wrong Door" program of the Nassau County Department of Social Services established in 2005 by County Executive Tom Suozzi was the first such program in New York State bringing under one roof the entire array of the county's health and human services agencies. The program was developed by Louise Skolnik, Nassau's Director of Human Services.

    Louise Skolnik, *interview with author, March 21, 2014*

37. In 2005, Project Independence, initiated by Town Supervisor Tom Kaiman of the town of North Hempstead, was the first aging-in-place program in New York State sponsored by local government. It has also served as a national model.

    Evelyn Roth, *interview with author, August 21, 2014*

38. In 2011, the first suburban chapter of The Social Enterprise Alliance was established to promote and facilitate social enterprise development on Long Island.

    Author's *knowledge as organizational co-founder*

39. In 2014, the tri-states' first affordable housing project for gay, lesbian, bisexual and transgender seniors was launched making it the first such project in an American suburb.

    www.liglbtnetwork.org

Part VI

Interviewees' Reflections and Recommendations

In 2014, the following nonprofit leaders, community organizers, elected officials, and academics who were interviewed offer wisdom and practical advice for consideration.

Gregory Blass, Esq. is a former Suffolk County Legislator and Presiding Officer, Family Court Judge, and Commissioner of the Suffolk County Department of Social Services.

Gregory Blass, in speaking about being an effective advocate, feels that you need to get your facts together and be a salesperson. You have to be effective both in one-on-one meetings and before large groups and combine skills of thinking from the heart as well as on your feet. As an elected official, you also need to hold public hearings to engage people in the debate. He feels strongly that it is important to heighten general awareness of a problem to generate actions. Blass also urges nonprofits to engage with politicians and their staff as well use of the media to educate the public and public officials about the conditions facing their clients.

Today, Gregory Blass feels things have gotten worse for the poor. He has hope that more young people will choose public service careers to address the very serious issues that we face. His basic belief is that most people want to take care of themselves and their families and some may need some help along the way. Few want to live without a decent home, food, and clothing for very long. Blass encourages young people to enter the helping professions despite its problems and challenges. He hopes that they share his belief that we need to leave the world a little better off than we found it.

In his post-public service career, Blass remains involved in community work. He is a member of the board of directors of Aid to Developmentally Disabled, the East End Hospice, and the Child Care Council of Suffolk. He is also a volunteer at Camp Good Grief where he is a counselor to a group of 14-six year old children. He enjoys playing the piano, reading history, tropical fish, writing, kayaking, swimming, and gardening.

Karen Boorshtein, LCSW, Chief Executive Officer, Family Service League.

Boorshtein feels that an agency needs to grow in order to survive. "You need to be larger to manage all the contractual responsibilities, and simply to maintain the infrastructure which is an absolute requirement in the times we are living now," she says.

Ruth Brandwein, Dean and Professor Emerita of the School of Social Welfare at Stony Brook; former Commissioner of the Suffolk County Department of Social Services and President of the New York State Chapter of NASW. Currently, Brandwein is PACE chair of NASW-Florida, Legislative Chair, Sarasota Unit, NASW Member, Sarasota County Human Services Advisory Council, and co-chair Jewish Family and Children's Services Advocacy Committee.

"The year was 1993. I had just returned to my tenured professor position at Stony Brook University's School of Social Welfare after spending six months at the University Of Utah School Of Social Work where I held the revolving Spafford Chair for Women and Families. While there I focused my research on the connection between domestic violence and the use of welfare. President Clinton had announced "an end to poverty as we know it" and had proposed the Personal Responsibility Act, which would replace welfare as an entitlement and replace it with Temporary Assistance to Needy Families (TANF). I became involved with a national group of feminist scholars, The Women's Committee of 100, which was advocating against the bill and publicizing the idea that 'welfare is a women's issue.'"

"I decided it was also necessary to work at the local level. I organized a 'teach in' on welfare and family violence to help social workers and the general public understand that survivors of domestic violence often needed the financial support of welfare to enable them to make a new start for themselves and their children. I spoke at a conference organized by the Health and Welfare Council of Long Island, trying to help social service professionals understand the anticipated negative consequences of TANF.

"What I discovered to my dismay was that many of the social service organizations were reluctant to advocate for this issues although it would affect their clients. Most received funding from State and County government and feared retribution. They did not dare to endanger their funding sources. Given the politics at the time, their fears were justified. The two organizations, in addition to the Health and Welfare Council who were prominent in the fight were Catholic Charities and the Long Island Progressive Coalition, neither of which was dependent on government funding.

"For the next two years, I spent a large part of my time speaking to religious groups, writing articles, organizing a 'teach-In' at Stony Brook and lobbying women senators and representatives. With other members of the Women's Committee, along with two members of the Committee, we compiled a reader on welfare and the proposed bill, received funding and published hundreds of copies that were circulated to social work and women's studies departments, not only on Long Island, but throughout the U.S.

"Eventually, our efforts failed and the TANF bill became law. Much of what we predicted came to pass. With a five year maximum, many women on Long Island now receive no financial assistance. The work provisions requiring employment or alternate training or job preparation was partially successful when the economy was strong, although the employment tended to be in low-paying jobs without benefits. One positive postscript: At the state level, the Legislature was required to pass enabling legislation. One provision would have reduced coverage for child care for working women for children up to age 12, which had been NYS law, to age 6, the minimum required by TANF.

"Determined to pursue the issue further, I made an appointment with then- new New York State Senator Carl Marcellino. When I arrived at his office, his secretary informed me that he had been called away and asked if I wanted to reschedule or speak to his legislative aide. As I had already driven to Oyster Bay and had all my materials ready, I opted to meet with the young aide who was not very informed of the issue. I spent the better part of an hour with him, explaining how the state would find itself in a Catch 22-if the mother abided by TANF regulations and participated in work activities, even if she could not find adequate care for her young children, she was in danger of being accused of child neglect by Child Protective Services. If, not finding reliable, safe and affordable care, she stayed at home with her seven or eight year old child, she would be removed from the program and have no resources to support her family. After our discussion the aide asked if I would return to speak to the Senator. I readily agreed and made a similar presentation to him. Eventually the State Legislature voted to maintain child care up until age 12 and I was subsequently pleased to learn that it had been Sen. Marcellino who pushed for that provision within the Republican caucus.

"From 1989 to 1993, as Suffolk County Commissioner of Social Services, I took a leave of absence from my position as Dean of the School of Social Welfare at Stony Brook, because a Family Support Act had recently passed Congress, which gave women on welfare the opportunity to attend college or other preparatory educational programs while receiving Medicaid and child care. I believed this was a great opportunity to make a difference and help women get off welfare and earn enough to support their families. Despite a number of bureaucratic obstacles, because it was the County Labor Department that was charged with assessing and placing the women, we were moderately successful.

"Before I left the position, we had helped 500 women enter community college programs and an equal number in GED, ESL or other vocational training programs. I personally followed some of these women who eventually went on for their Bachelor Degrees and well-paying jobs; one at Stony Brook Medical Center and another at the Suffolk Community Council. When I returned to Stony Brook, however, the program was abruptly terminated, as the federal and state policy was now "work-first." I had been writing occasional op-ed pieces for Newsday, but two days after I published an article about the end of the educational programs at the Department of Social Services, I received a letter terminating my position with the Task Force.

"Another story describes how domestic violence was viewed in the 1980s. In 1987, soon after Patrick Halpin was elected Suffolk County Executive, I was sitting in my office as Dean of the School of Social Work at Stony Brook University and got a call from someone I did not know, but who would eventually become my mentor and great friend. Evelyn Roth introduced herself as the Deputy County Executive for Human Services. When she admitted 'I cannot believe I am now in charge of the welfare department... in the '60s I used to picket outside their offices in NYC.' I immediately knew I would like this woman. She told me she was organizing a new County task force on family violence and wanted me to chair it. I protested that my area was family policy but I had not done work in domestic violence. That' is fine, she said. 'We are bringing together organizations and county departments concerned with partner abuse, child abuse and elder abuse. We had lots of experts but need someone who has no organizational bias, but has the position to lead the task force.'

"I agreed and together we organized cross-cutting committees so that people working in the three areas were no longer in their silos but working together on training, legal and systems issues, research or other areas. We brought together staff from the County Attorney, sheriff, police, family court, social services and health departments along with nonprofit social service and advocacy groups. We conducted training programs on financial abuse of the elderly, violence against the disabled, against gay youth and other vulnerable populations. We had an annual memorial service honoring victims of violence and celebrating survivors.

"When I became commissioner of Social Services in 1989 I offered to resign my chairpersonship as I feared it might be a conflict of interest as I was now in the position of funding the member agencies of the task force. Ms. Roth insisted I stay. When I finally resigned as commissioner in 1993, to return to academia, I met with County Executive Robert Gaffney who asked me to remain as chair, explaining the two positions were not connected. After studying the history of the task force, Mr. Gaffney agreed that I could continue as chair. However, after writing the *Newsday* article about the termination of the education program for women on welfare, my position as chair was summarily terminated. Eventually, I was invited to join the board of the Suffolk County Coalition on Domestic Violence and served as vice president until leaving Long Island.

"I have often been asked "How can you keep working on these difficult issues that never seem to be solved." My response was "How can I not?" I am often reminded my students of the Hillel maxim "It is not for you to complete the task, but neither may you refrain from starting it."

"The Kaballah teaches when God created the world it was evenly balanced between good and evil. Each of us, every day in all our actions, can tip the scale in one direction or the other. Therefore, it is incumbent on us to consider our deeds and how we are contributing to make this world better or worse.

"And then of course is the Eugene V. Debs great quote 'While there is a lower class I am in it, while there is a criminal element I am of it, while there is a soul in prison I am not free' and JFK who said 'If a free society cannot help the many who are poor, it cannot save the few who are rich.' or FDR who said 'The test of our progress is not whether we add more to the abundance of those who have much, it is whether we provide enough for those who have too little.'"

Frances L. Brisbane, Ph.D., MSW, MA, Dean, School of Social Welfare at Stony Brook University.

Speaking about changes in social work education over the past forty years, Brisbane believes that the school offers the foundational skills and specialized education like other schools of social welfare do while also continuing its tradition of attention to social change and social justice. Besides student field placements in more traditional settings like family, children, youth, and senior citizen agencies, student placements have increased in three areas: Public schools, governmental and political offices, thus providing students opportunities to address causative factors impinging on individuals and families.

Brisbane feels racism as much now as in the 1960s, saying: "I have felt racism more-keenly since President Obama was elected into office than I felt during the previous twenty years. I think that people feel that it is "open season" on anyone else that they do not like. People used to mask their racism but today they feel it is okay to say anything negative like they did before and in the 1960s. Many people are more hurtful today and do not give their hatefulness a second thought. It is as if they feel that blacks should be grateful for the advances over the past fifty years. White people used to give me the benefit of the doubt that I was different. They treated me according to my professional title rather than solely as a black person. That does not happen anymore." Meanwhile, Brisbane feels that "we' are better prepared and organized today to fight racism. We will not let people get away with their racist agenda. We' will fight them with everything short of bloodshed."

She continues saying that "many politicians are angry and are trying to vilify President Obama," seemingly because he had the audacity to not only win in 2008 but then again in 2012. They know that the President could not have won these elections if it were not for white votes so they're saying to whites: "Do not let this happen again. They are, thus, dedicated to oppose everything he tries to do."

When questioned whether current students continue these racist attitudes, Brisbane reports that many of the school's students are the children of former School graduates. "They're here because they want to be here and share our views," says Brisbane.

Brisbane speaks with enthusiasm about the future of social work and its place in social change and social justice. She feels that social workers have unique skills to assess individual, group, and family dynamics as well as skills to change institutional policies and she is optimistic that young people will stand up and fight reactionary forces over-and-over again. She indicates this optimism is present among schools of social work across the nation. In support of her views, Brisbane points to young peoples' activism in the Occupy Wall Street movement and, currently, the heavy participation of young white people in Ferguson, Missouri after the murder of Michael Brown, an unarmed black teenager. She feels that today's youth will not accept the racism that her generation accepted. She also sees the substantial activism of many faith-based organizations and the NAACP as reasons for optimism."

Jamir R. Couch, Esq., founder and president of Knowles Hall Consulting and an advisor to Kota Global Securities.

"With respect to social action and social justice work, she has continued in her father's James W. Couch's path having served as an advisor to the New York City chancellor and first executive director of the Wall Street Project (WSP) an initiative of the Rainbow Push Coalition where she played an instrumental role in the first WSP conference on Wall Street. During the Clinton administration, she served as a special assistant and acting deputy counsel at the U.S. Department of Housing and Urban Development.

"There are many issues that need to be addressed on Long Island and throughout the U.S. Is there a cohesive approach/strategy to addressing these issues on Long Island? I think my biggest concern is the lack of intelligent informed advocates, elected or otherwise, who can speak on behalf of those in need and are willing to challenge the system if they have to. My question is: Is the quality of our leadership on Long Island and New York State inclusive? During the last few years on Long Island I still see it as a segregated community. Long Island has never elected a minority/woman county executive in either county and there still is not a lot of diversity in Albany either.

"Economic inequality is one of the major issues that still exists today. All of the issues (poverty, social justice, social action and access to health) all revolve around an individual/family's economic status/financial stability and viability.

Having been in both the public and private sector, I believe there is definitely a role for public/private partnerships in addressing some of these issues. As with any partnership, it depends on how clearly the goals are outlined between the parties in order for it to be successful. All parties have to be open to new ideas and be able to communicate in order to determine options that will help the entire community."

Robert Detor, LCSW, former President and Chief Executive Officer, Long Island Home.

Detor draws a parallel to changes in the health and behavioral health system to those undergone by hospitals in response to the Hill Burton Act, a U.S. federal law passed in 1946, during the 79th United States Congress. The law gave hospitals, nursing homes and other health facilities grants and loans for construction and modernization. In return, they agreed to provide a reasonable volume of services to persons unable to pay and to make their services available to all persons residing in the facility's area.

According to Detor, the health system went through dramatic changes in the 1960s with hospitals' establishment of health insurance and the adoption of the Medicare Program in 1965. These changes created a revenue stream for hospitals featuring a cost-based system where hospitals and their physicians could bill Medicare and insurance carriers for whatever they wanted regardless of the quality of care provided. Then, in the 1980s, in response to Medicare concerns about the increasing costs of health care, hospitals established a system of diagnostic related groups (DRGs) for Medicare patients. Under the DRG system, hospitals had to justify their costs, thus establishing a market-based system/competitive system to replace the cost-based one in operation since the 1960s.

In the 1990s, the State under Governor George Pataki, established a structure that protected hospitals, assuring them that insurance companies would make up for their losses, thus forcing hospitals to fight directly with insurance companies in the marketplace rather than fighting with Medicare for better rates. This changed forced hospitals to look at their costs and their health care outcomes measures. The basic purpose was to control costs and standardize health care outcomes. During the upcoming years, 27 Long Island hospitals closed while hospital systems developed such as SUNY/Stony Brook, Catholic Health System, Winthrop University Hospital, and North Shore/LIJ. These conglomerate systems could demand better prices from the insurance companies as they demonstrated better health outcomes and cost efficiencies.

This description of changes in hospital health care parallels what has happened to behavioral health, mental health, and drug and alcohol programs which had gone along with funding streams driving how their services are provided. In these community-based organizations, outcomes were not being measured with the result that these organizations were unable to justify better fees. In 1992, the federal Department of Health and Human Services began to ask states why there were such disparities between the rates for the behavior health services that they were providing regardless of their outcomes. Under the new Ambulatory Payment Groups (APG) system, the federal government began to determine the rates, per procedure, with the understanding that, providers could keep what they did not spend to deliver services. The response from the behavioral health care providers was to try to convince New York State that the APG rates were not sufficient with the state's response being that the "feds were non-negotiable." They felt that the APG system "would destroy community-based behavioral health care."

In response, in 2009, Detor certain that trying to convince the state to change its rates would be futile, proposed that the Long Island Behavioral Health Groups in Nassau and Suffolk Counties, undertake a study to determine if there was a more-efficient way to deliver behavioral health services within the APG fee schedule. Grants were secured from the Rauch Foundation and The Long Island Community Foundation to undertake the study. When the data was analyzed, a simulator was produced of a "modern day clinic." The major finding was that the amount of "face-time" between physicians and patients was the key determinate that drove up costs.

Detor and his colleagues proceeded to consider how Nassau and Suffolk counties, with twenty-two existing clinics, could respond to the study findings. The resulting discussions produced a proposal to reduce the number of clinics to six with three in a Nassau region and three in a Suffolk region. This could be done by psychiatric interventions being conducted deploying technological advances such as telemedicine and electronic communications among patients and psychiatrists. The result of this study was to change the way that behavioral health care clinics advocated to the state. Rather than begging to change the rates, providers began to ask for changes to adaptations to state requirements in the service deliveries. Detor basically said: "Let us do it to ourselves rather than waiting for the state to do it to us."

Detor reports that in 2014, New York State is changing from Medicaid to Managed Medicaid that included behavioral health services. Permissible services can include those provided by such paraprofessionals as peer counselors, ex-drug and alcohol abusers, etc. Under Managed Medicaid, the focus is on what the state considers "medical necessity," ie. when a person should be hospitalized and when they should be discharged. Insurance companies are in the position of deciding on medical necessity so they decide when to pay providers. These companies expect behavioral health clinics to provide the necessary network of services needed by their patients so it is essential that these services, both medical and social, be provided. The challenge is to demonstrate that the social components of behavioral health care are effective and drive down costs, a difficult thing to demonstrate since these services are often provided "on the fly," under pressure conditions and based on social and economic conditions present in the patient's life.

What the Behavioral Health Group observed during this period was that behavioral health interventions actually drive down medical costs because psychosomatic symptoms are observed and diagnosed early. These findings are potentially significant inasmuch as medical costs represent the major percentage of health care costs thus reinforcing the case that behavior health care should be made part of the regular managed care plan.

Detor is cautiously optimistic that such changes will occur as further evidence of behavioral health care benefits. His optimism is furthered since attending a recent conference "Access to Capital" where executives of the three largest proprietary hospital chains reported that they have gone into market-based behavioral health care. They have done so since behavioral health care went from a cost-based system to a market based one where the clinics take on the total risk of a population. Detor sees this as a significant sign these entrepreneurs understand the economic benefits to intervene early through behavioral health measures. The challenge is to convince managed care companies to really understand the benefits of comprehensive behavioral health care and translate it into actual dollars in order to change the configuration of care. Detor has concern that the companies, over the next few years, will "pocket the money" and then give back their contracts to the states.

Detor will continue his work trying to convince government to structure its contracts to measure changes in both medical and behavioral health care with financial incentives to reduce costs. "One day in a hospital," he says, "is the same as one month rent in a community-based apartment." To Detor, this means that community-based care is where the future lies.

Jane Devine, MPA, MA, former Suffolk County Legislator and former Suffolk County Commissioner of Consumer Affairs.

Devine strongly feels that politics is" the way you get things done" so she continues her involvement as a local and state Democratic committeeperson while also serving on the Huntington town Planning Board and the Suffolk County Water Authority Board.

Devine is also concerned about our future leadership since young people do not seem interested in government today. She wonders whether future nonprofit leaders will have the passion for social justice. Politics and lobbying are not dirty words to Devine. To her, government does not have to be heartless and uncaring. She sees some of the same problems today as she saw forty years ago; problems like homelessness, alcohol and drug addiction, and families being placed in motels with school districts resisting educating their children are still with us today.

Steve Englebright, MS, former Suffolk County Legislator and current New York State Assemblyman.

Englebright feels that long term care of the elderly should be one of the highest priorities on the state's agenda because the state will "go bankrupt." He is hopeful that, as state legislators begin to experience their own long term issues they will begin to act. "There is still time," he says. He wishes he was still chairman of the New York State Assembly Aging Committee so he could more forcefully push on the issues. The other important issue that he feels requires greater attention to the needs of suburbia is the need for affordable intergenerational housing on Long Island that he believes should be constructed above shopping centers and in downtown villages particularly ones where railroad access is present.

Ralph Fasano, MA, MED, CRC, Executive Director of Concern for Independent Living (Concern).

In 2012, Fasano presented testimony to the New York State Office for Mental Health at its Long Island Regional Hearing that reflects his current concerns and recommendations pertaining to the status of mental health services on Long Island. He expressed support for OMH's plan to focus on housing as a priority issue, indicating that safe, affordable housing with flexible services is the foundation for recovery. He further stated that: "Our experience has shown that congregate, supervised settings play an important role in the housing delivery system." Therefore, he urged OMH to support "permanent, supervised settings that offer privacy and onsite supports." He also believes there is need as well for a "more intensive supervised setting that can serve as a hospital diversion where people can receive the care they need without being in a hospital."

Fasano urged OMH to continue to strengthen funding for supportive housing programs in order to prevent the housing failures due to the inability to pay rent and the failure to take medications as prescribed. He urged that the program have a funding mechanism that funds the reasonable property costs that agencies incur, separate from the service costs. Fasano also pointed to the importance of expanding the availability of mental health services for the entire family.

Fasano spoke of the mental health housing crisis as being part of a larger affordable housing crisis that exists in many parts of New York State. He urged OMH to maximize the use of mainstream housing resources in order to close the gap between the need for housing and the availability.

Currently, Fasano reports that "Concern is working on numerous projects, all with hard deadlines that have been taking all of my attention. That being said, that is good news because OMH is providing us with funds to keep us busy developing housing. As discussed in my testimony, this funding allows us to leverage other funding to expand the housing that is available for people with psychiatric disabilities. In addition to the three adult homes that were converted into supportive housing we are now in the process of developing three more projects that will create opportunities for people to live in dignified housing with the supports they need."

According to Fasano, CONCERN's most recent project combines 50 units of supportive housing together with 73 units of generic affordable housing. This housing model allows people to live in an integrated setting much like any other housing complex but also have easy access to services located on site. Unlike the fierce opposition we have received for other housing developments, this project has widespread support, including the local civic associations. The total cost of this project will be around $40,000,000.

From a housing perspective, Fasano is very optimistic about the progress that has been made and the outlook for the future. He points to the fact that not too long ago, the majority of people with serious mental illness lived in hospitals to the present where less than 400 live in a state hospital. Thousands of housing options have been created in the community and more are on the way. Having a governor who used to be the Secretary of HUD has certainly helped us increase the resources for new housing. The Medicaid Redesign Team that Governor Andrew Cuomo convened came up with a major recommendation: Create more supportive housing that is geared to providing housing and services that will lead to reductions in emergency room and inpatient stays. This recommendation led to significant increases in funding for supportive housing (including the project mentioned above).

Fasano believes that by developing supportive housing alongside generic affordable housing we are not only providing what people with serious psychiatric disabilities need most but also meeting a major need for all of Long Island. He further believes that we have learned that organizations must be mission-based together with a commitment to use evidence based practices in guiding their activities. Board compositions should include people who are the intended benefit of services, family members and professionals. These members should be passionate about their work and should strive to make the organization be the best in its field.

In his own organization, Fasano has focused on housing and has avoided spreading out into other areas. Many organizations are tempted to "follow the money" which can lead to a lack of focus and expertise in any one area. Fasano believes that boards of directors should not only be "bean counters." People are needed on boards and in administration that understand finances and can guide the organization towards financial strength. The best intentions and the best mission-based group will not succeed unless the finances work. As nonprofit leaders, we need to be able to convince others that the work that we do is essential and benefits everyone. This is easier to do when the leader is passionate and knowledgeable about the work.

Rene Fiechter, Esq., Director, Community Affairs, Nassau District Attorney's Office and former Deputy Executive Director of EACINC.

"It is all about relationships but you also need to be nice to people. You need to have patience, says Fiechter, "Even a glacier moves slowly, stopping and then grinding ahead. You need to appreciate that the process of change is often slow."

He feels that a great deal of progress has been made in the relationship between nonprofits and government. They are "linked at the hip," he says, with many examples of collegial relationships unlike the old days when government was seen as the enemy.

"All these years later with 20/20 hindsight, clearly there was magic and mischief for which we owe much to a few dedicated, passionate, and selfless heroes."

"It is now forty years later and looking back I can see how it all worked out, how all of it was useful and, most of all, there were forces and people in my life that made the times, quietly, loudly, and profoundly amazing."

"To win the other side over, you need to figure out where they're coming from."

John Imhof Ph.D MSW, Master's in Health Care Administration and Education and Commissioner of Nassau County's Department of Social Services and an adjunct professor of Social Work at the LIU – Post.

Imhof feels he was destined to a social services career since his high school days when, at age 14, he served as president of Elmhurst's 110th Precinct Junior Civic Council, encouraging young people to get involved in community projects. He later served as a member of Elmhurst's Adult Civic Council and was president of the Queen's Newtown High School student government.

After graduating from St. John's University in 1966, Imhof taught American and European History. In 1969, after three students had died of drug overdoses, the school district formed a committee on drug education and created a new fulltime position, Coordinator of Drug Education, the first of its kind in the nation. Imhof was offered the position and accepted it. In that groundbreaking role, Imhof wrote a book on Drug Education for Teachers and Parents, produced an educational film strip series and conducted lectures around the county. In 1971, Imhof started a nineteen year stint at North Shore Hospital as Chief of the Drug Treatment and Education Center in the Department of Psychiatry. He went on to other positions becoming administrative director of Mental Health Services, assistant chairman of Psychiatry for Addiction Treatment Services and as the North Shore – Long Island Jewish Health System expanded, Imhof became vice president for Behavioral Health Services, a position he held until joining Nassau County government in 2003.

In recalling the evolution of community-based services prior to 1985, Imhof describes a "well-intentioned, good-hearted system being put in place with a funding structure that, to this day, plagues nonprofit agencies and the constituents they serve." Imhof continues: "The result was a proliferation of small programs with policies that virtually forced organizations to falsify reporting information in order to continue their funding. Many organizations did not survive while the state did nothing to consolidate its funding mechanisms. Local turf issues prevailed while each non-profit's constituency needed to mobilize political support among state legislators to insure their programs' survival. Regretfully, this state of affairs continues today with little promise of change."

Thus, Imhof feels "Since the 1960s maintained four separate billion dollar agencies - Department of Health (DOH), Office of Mental Health (OMH), Office of People with Development Disabilities (OPDD) and the Office of Alcoholism and Substance Abuse Services (OASAS) – each having many repetitive and duplicative services forcing community nonprofits to seek funding from each of the state agencies rather than the State seeking to consolidate and/or simplify the funding processes."

According to Imhof, the other major change that occurred during the 1980s and 1990s was the professionalization of the behavioral health field amidst fierce competition for state funding. The beginning of fiscal reductions resulted in dozens of community-based agencies throughout the county having to eventually go out of business, with today only seven or eight strong comprehensive program remaining, all the while each of them still competing to this day for shrinking State and local dollars."

Further complicating the funding and survival struggle is the fact that most major agencies are reluctant to seek mergers and affiliations with each other for fear of losing their identifies and, in some cases, the leadership positions of one or more agencies.

Finally, Imhof favors further professionalization of the community-based agencies and would like to see more of them seek accreditation, which would be a symbol of assurance and quality to the public

Looking to the future, Imhof believes that nonprofits have to "stop looking to government for funding and enhance fund-raising and seek more grant opportunities. Unless nonprofit agencies start employing and adapting business principles, they will be unable to stay in existence."

While he sees social work education today as very advanced with studies in nearly every field of practice he believes the "tradeoff" has been a dearth in foundational studies about social work history, community social work, administrative and business leadership practices, and policy development. As a social work educator himself, Imhof sees today's students more focused on where they can find employment and not focusing towards possible career advancement opportunities into social work leadership positions.

Imhof bemoans the fact that respect for society's major institutions - government, religious, law enforcement, and education - has diminished dramatically as a result of decades-long incidences of official corruption, misconduct and scandals among our leaders. "Regretfully the level of cynicism today is very great. Capitalism is derided, all politicians are viewed as manipulative and crooked, while law enforcement continues to struggle with retaining credibility in many culturally diverse communities," says Imhof, disappointedly. "We seem to be losing the spirit of community involvement, government participation and volunteerism. People get their news from social media and cable news and rush to judgment without thoughtful analysis. Hundreds of thousands of Americans fought and died for the defense and protection of our liberties and democracy, yet why does less than 50% of the electorate turn out to vote in local and national elections?" He questions where the outrage has gone about what is happening in America. "We seem to be losing our sense of purpose, our national direction and the values that have been characteristic of America since our nation's founding."

As a result of our economic downturns, there is also a new emerging class of poverty consisting of individuals who were formerly in the middle class yet no longer able to afford the higher costs of living and dealing with declining wage levels across the country. Increasingly, people cannot afford to live on Long Island and are often forced to work two and three jobs just to get by. As evidence, Imhof reports that ten percent of Nassau's residents receive Medicaid benefits, 45,000 residents receive SNAP benefits (i.e., food stamps) and there have also been a consistently high number of applications for temporary assistance. Those in need represent the full-spectrum of racial, ethnic and cultural diversity.

With respect to social work education, Imhof has witnessed a reduction in the number of seasoned professionals willing to serve as field instructors, which he finds troubling. "Students need more mentors to be available in clinical and leadership training programs. More internships are needed to help students not lose sight of the idealism that characterized the history and meaningfulness of social work. Mentors can help students recognize the gains that have been achieved through struggle, perseverance and activism. Imhof believes strongly that practicioners have a responsibility to their profession to find the time to help students in training. As DSS commissioner, he serves as mentor to a number of students each year and has insured that the Department of Social Services remains a learning laboratory as well for students in the health and human service professions, including social work. He encourages leaders of health and human services programs to expand their own training and internship opportunities for the students of the future. "I know everyone is very busy," says Imhof, "but in our own professional development there were dedicated people took the time to guide us in our own personal and professional development. In my opinion, all social workers practicing today have a responsibility to give some of that time back to the social workers of the future."

Imhof urges social workers and activists to be aware of self-preservation issues, of complacency and the importance of taking steps to take care of one self in order to avoid burnout, depression, anxiety, and alcohol and drug dependency. He urges practitioners to take steps to insure that they emotionally and physically replenish themselves as they deal with complex and challenging problems on a day to day basis.

Dave Kapell, BA from Harvard's Kennedy School of Government and MPA and president and principal broker of Kapell Real Estate and consultant to the Rauch Foundation.

Dave Kapell's story provides insights about life and social progress on Long Island's East End since World War II ended. It tells the story how a person with entrepreneurial skills and a commitment to social justice can effect change.

Referring to his early education, Kapell attended the Dalton School in Manhattan and the Riverdale Country School in the Bronx. He says: "At the time, I wasn't a good student and college material". As a joke, at a school assembly, one of his friends put up Kapell's name for class treasurer. After preparing and presenting a speech, to his surprise, he was elected. After completing his schooling, Kapell had a five-year career traveling around the nation as a touring musician. Afterwards, he managed various restaurants in New York City and, in 1979, moved to Greenport with his wife to become a supervisor in the village's community development office as well as a code enforcement officer. In 1981, he opened up a small real estate agency and antique store that he continues to own today.

By way of history, in the mid-1600s, a group of colonists from New Haven, Connecticut crossed Long Island Sound and settled in the township of Southold, which includes what is now the Village of Greenport. Over the course of its long history, Greenport has been known by several different names including Winter Harbor, Stirling, and Green Hill. At a public meeting in 1831, the name Greenport was officially adopted. Because of its deep and protected harbor, Greenport became a major whaling port between 1795 and 1859 and enjoyed a bustling shipbuilding industry as well. By the mid-1800s, the menhaden fishing industry was in full swing and employed thousands of people. The Long Island Railroad arrived in 1844 and was a driving force in the development of Greenport and the North Fork as local farmers used the railroad to ship their harvest to markets. Greenport became a huge oystering center during the first half of the 20th century and at one time there were over a dozen oyster processing plants in town. During WWII the shipyards in Greenport thrived on production of small vessels for the US Navy. When the war ended, the shipyards closed eliminating several thousand jobs. The village fell into a severe depression that continued until it turned its attention towards tourism and developed into a vibrant destination for visitors from all over the world. In 2011, Forbes magazine named Greenport one of the prettiest towns in the United States.

Kapell describes much of Greenport's housing when he arrived in 1979 as blighted and depressed. As code enforcement officer, he enforced village building codes which had not been done before and was, thus, controversial. He was able to correct most of the severe housing conditions. He also was able to secured $5M of federal community development funding. A junk yard was purchased and converted into the site of a seventeen-unit affordable housing development. The village worked in partnership with Bessie Swann, director of Community Action of Southold Township (CAST) to form the North Fork Housing Alliance previously known as the Greenport Housing Alliance. Together, they rehabilitated existing housing units and built new housing.

Kapell served as a village trustee from 1983-1987. As a village trustee, he found himself in the midst of a controversy being discussed by trustees in "hush-hush" behind closed door conversations. The subject was a proposal by one of Greenport's prominent businesses to relocate from the downtown area to a parcel owned by the village. Kapell was the only trustee who opposed the land sale. Because of his stand he "took a pounding for four years from the other trustees," says Kapell. Ultimately, the land sale deal was defeated because Kapell, with the help of a number of residents and a skilled attorney, discovered a 1929 village board resolution designating the parcel as parkland which a municipality cannot sell without an act by the state legislature.

After serving as a trustee, Kapell served as chairman of the village planning board from 1990-1991. In 1994, the village mayor was forced out of office during a controversy concerning the village police department that was subject to a grand jury investigation by the Suffolk County District Attorney due to allegations of complicity of drug dealing, corruption and malfeasance in office. Kapell knew that taxes were the major issue for the voters so he ran for mayor with a platform that focused on reducing local taxes by abolishing the village police department and taking advantage of the services of the Southold town police department. The village police chief supported Kapell's candidacy assuming like others that, like other politicians, Kapell would not do what he said he would do during a campaign. The village police chief was shocked at Kapell's commitment to his campaign promises. He was subjected to personal threats and harassment including anti-Semitic remarks. The controversy was resolved when residents voted overwhelmingly to abolish the village police and transfer policing to Southold town.

In 1994, after he was elected as Greenport's mayor Kapell helped revitalize the village into a tourist destination for visitors and young families. He expanded affordable housing units, created a park, a carousel, an ice rink, a power plant, and instituted community patrols in red berets. Perhaps most significantly, under Kapell leadership, Greenport relaxed requirements for two-family housing conversions and made it possible to develop residential uses on upper stories and in accessory buildings in the village's commercial district, thus making for more efficient use of the existing housing stock and creating housing for year-round residents to support local businesses. To generate public support for these and other initiatives, Kapell played the role of community organizer, recruiting people who would benefit from the initiatives to attend public hearings, thus assuring that there was balanced conversation of the proposals. Kapell emphasized that the initiatives would serve to make Greenport a diverse community both and would enable more young people and families to afford to remain in Greenport. The end result was a clear consensus in favor of the changes that Kapell proposed.

One battle that Kapell wasn't able to win was his 1994 effort to expand the village's physical boundaries. He says that it was as if he was proposing "Armageddon." The then-supervisor strongly opposed the measure reflecting the common public attitude that, as Kapell says: "People do not like people different from them living next door or above them. It all has to do with property values. Bias and discrimination on Long Island are real. When push becomes shove, people refuse to change." He describes the town of Southold as disinterested in Greenport. He points to social and economic bias as the underlying cause of the town's treatment of Greenport.

It is Kapell's belief that Long Island can address the very serious socio-economic challenges it faces but it needs "courageous public officials and people like Nancy Douzinas of the Rauch Foundation who have the intellect, the time, resources and the ability to generate the debate and move a progressive agenda further without concern for their personal economic security. He feels that change is going to happen due to Long Island's demographic growth and its fixed housing stock so something is going to give. Kapell believes that more rapid change will take place only if public officials are willing to take risks.

In looking towards the future, Kapell is an optimist. He discounts arguments that the economic boom that resulted after World War II with its tremendous opportunities for returning GIs to find employment and purchase housing, was a "glitch" and will not repeat itself. He is confident that we will soon work ourselves out of the national recession and the severe slump in local housing. As things loosen up, Kapell projects that public officials will be willing to spend money again in social betterment projects so now is a good time to talk with legislators to cultivate relationships. When asked how best to deliver housing services to the public, Kapell feels that government and the nonprofit sector are "systemically inefficient" so he feels that the for-profit sector can more effectively deliver most of the needed housing.

Lee Koppelman, Ph.D., Director and Leading Professor, the Center for Regional Policy Studies, the State University of New York at Stony Brook. (See Chapter V for an extensive profile of Dr. Koppelman's career).

When considering advice to provide to nonprofit organizations, Koppelman urges them to advocate for their social issues in economic terms.

Lawrence Levy, Executive Dean, the National Center for Suburban Studies at Hofstra University and a former Senior Editorial Writer and Chief Political Columnist for Newsday.

When presented with the list of progressive social policies and programs highlighted in Part V "Suburban Trail-blazing" that have been developed on Long Island since World War II, Levy is not surprised at the list of accomplishments. He feels that "suburbanites, and that includes Long Islanders, are more moderate and tolerant than they are often given credit for. They have always been willing to tax themselves to near the breaking point to fund programs they feel are important and that includes social services. As our National Suburban Poll has indicated, they are willing to spend tax dollars on the young, poor, sick and aged and they are reluctant to lay off public workers to balance the budget. For all the discrimination and segregation that persists today, there is still a good strong heart that bleeds on Long Island."

Levy views suburbanites as evolutionary in their conservatism. "They're open to new ideas and change but change takes time. It' is as if they need to get used to it and will accept change as long as they do not feel it will affect their overall quality of life. They're also sensitive to the needs of the sandwich generation to care for dependent elders. "

Levy is, therefore, optimistic that suburbanites will continue to evolve. As more and more of them experience the need to house their children and parents on Long Island, they will change and begin to accept the need to change zoning regulations that limit the amount of higher density housing. They will do so out of their own self- interest. Levy points to Paul Pontieri, the village's mayor, as an example of what can be accomplished by a skillful politician who worked over many years to transform the village into a diverse, vibrant community.

Andrew Malekoff, LCSW, Chief Executive Officer and Executive Director of the North Shore Child and Family Guidance Center. The following article *"It is not reform when it hurts the poor"* was written by Malekoff and published in the *Albany Times Journal*, July 7, 2009.

> In the past 25 years, the mental health system has seen many changes. From a system in New York State that consisted primarily of outpatient clinics, community hospitals, state hospitals, and residential treatment facilities, a continuum has evolved which now also includes family support, day treatment, a variety of in-home community support services, community residences, mobile crisis intervention, and respite care. Many of these services were originally funded with the reinvestment dollars saved from the 1990's reduction in state hospital beds. The largest of these programs, Home and Community Based Services (HCBS) Waiver and Intensive Case Management, are Medicaid-driven.

> Nevertheless, parents still find that there are major gaps in our service system. Even with the available community support services, children with mental illness and their families continue to need good, often intensive, outpatient clinical services. The onset of managed care resulted in hospitals discharging children earlier, often before they are sufficiently stabilized to return home. Mental health outpatient clinics are then left with the task of trying to provide adequate clinical care to these needy and often high-risk youths, but with highly inadequate rates of financial support from insurance companies and government funds.

> More low- and middle-income families than ever are in need of low-cost, high-quality community-based mental health care. Yet in New York State continued access to care is assured only to children and families with Medicaid and Medicaid Managed Care insurance coverage. This leaves a significant number of children in the lurch. Here is a true story to illustrate.

About 25 years ago I was swimming in the ocean in Long Beach, NY, and someone pointed to a group of girls that had drifted towards the jetty. The girls must have been pulled out by the undertow and were unnoticed by the lifeguards. I swam to them. When I arrived, there were three little girls; one looked about nine-years-old. The others, who were crying and holding on to the older girl, appeared to be six or seven. The older girl was trembling and barely in control of her emotions. I wrapped my arms around the three of them and said, "Hang on." Finally, the lifeguards arrived and took over. I swam to shore and went back to my beach chair. When I recall this encounter, I realize that the four of us were strangers who spent maybe 90 seconds together. I said only two words to them: "Hang on." Ninety seconds, two words and 25-years and I still think about them often. We were so close that I could see their freckles.

Now, let us consider another scenario. Try to imagine me swimming out to the three girls. Imagine if, instead of telling them to hang on, I treaded water at a safe distance and asked them if they had Medicaid insurance. Imagine if they answered, "No Mister." And, if I then said to them, "Sorry, girls," and turned my back on them and swam to shore.

This is the situation that we now face as New York State has made a dramatic departure from its responsibility to make sure that our most vulnerable citizens—our children—get community-based mental health care, regardless of their family's economic status. They expect us to ignore middle-class people and working poor overboard with no life preservers. I see nothing to suggest that the State's proposed Regional Centers of Excellence will change this.

The American reality today is 1 out of 5 children has a serious emotional disturbance and more children suffer from psychiatric illness than from autism, leukemia, diabetes and AIDS combined. Seventy-five percent of all serious mental illness occurs before the age of 24; and 50% before the age of 14. Yet, only one out of five children who have emotional problems receives treatment from a mental health specialist. Unfortunately, the mental health system has become largely Medicaid-driven.

For example, my agency, at any given time, sees over 75% of children who do not have Medicaid or Medicaid Managed Care. It is a constant struggle to provide what is needed for the majority of our clients who are either uninsured or underinsured middle class and working poor families. In Nassau County, and I suspect elsewhere, there are community-based outpatient mental health programs that have closed their doors, have been taken over by larger corporate entities with no community roots, have transformed their operations into per-diem factories with little capacity for dealing with complex or crisis situations, or have decided to turn away all clients who do not have some form of Medicaid.

When I raise the problem of inadequate access to care, I am advised by government officials that the marketplace – meaning private practitioners– would take care of children without Medicaid or Medicaid Managed Care. This belies reality, which is that (1) a great many private practitioners do not accept commercial insurance; and, (2) among those private practitioners who do accept commercial insurance, most are unwilling or ill-equipped to address the highly-complex, crisis-oriented needs of children with serious emotional problems. The reality is that only quality community-based children's mental health organizations with salaried employees and interdisciplinary teams and dedicated time for staff supervision are capable of providing the labor-intensive quality of care necessary to address the mental health needs of children with serious emotional disturbances and their families.

What is more, for those children who need a longer period of hospitalization, Sagamore Children's Psychiatric Center has been the answer for the children on Long Island. Unless another alternative is developed as part of the Regional Centers of Excellence planning (i.e. dedicated long term beds supported by OMH in nonprofit community hospitals), these children will be dramatically underserved. Queens and the Bronx are not viable alternatives for most families. For seamless transitions back to community, the children should be in the community; not in a distant community that would make transportation, visits, home passes, and attending meetings impossible for some families.

The increasingly swinging doors of the community-acute care hospitals, because of insurance limitations, are not able to keep kids long enough to stabilize them in many cases. So, kids are being discharged to a community with inadequate supports. As many sister agencies have stopped accepting this population, our agency has become a major landing point for these kids, as seen by our increasingly active triage and emergency service. And, the kids who really need a hospital have already experienced intensive community based services and have had at least one or multiple hospitalizations and emergency room visits which did not work.

With our current community system, and inability to provide an adequate level of outpatient clinical care without losing money, we cannot support these kids. We need all levels of care, including a children's psychiatric hospital as a local part of the continuum. But, we also need more well-supported and expanded outpatient services. Waiver slots, intensive case management and coordinated children's service initiative are all good, but these kids still require clinical care, and often not just once a week.

In conclusion, thinking back to my Atlantic Ocean memory, it is a story that is about more than me and three little girls. It is about all of us and the thousands of children that community-based mental health agencies across New York State guide safely to shore every year, and offer them the chance to see a brighter day. To do this we need to provide ready access to quality mental health care for all children who need it. To ensure universal access for all children in New York State, regardless of socio-economic status, requires a commitment from the state to enhance local assistance. When agency, client, community, and government work together and contribute collectively we all win. Then, and only then, can we refer to any entity formed on behalf of children with mental health problems as a "center of excellence."

Jim Morgo, MA, President, Morgo Private Public Strategies and a former Chief Deputy Suffolk County Executive, Suffolk County Legislator and former president, the Long Island Housing Partnership.

Since I have been on LI (1971), the major issue affecting all social need categories has been and remains the major issue is the wealth disparities among LI's many towns and hamlets. This disparity affects every other issue.

The relationship between nonprofits and government has sputtered. On the federal, state and local levels, there have been efforts to fund economic revitalizations of low-income communities. These efforts begun in the 1970s continue today with efforts by the state's Regional Economic Development Council, for example, to revitalize low-income hamlets in both counties as one of the current examples. Various public sources of funds on all levels-from the local to federal-to private funding sources helped by the federal CRA legislation that encourages bank investments in low-income communities have continued since the 1970s until the present. I now know it is impossible to revitalize communities by government efforts alone. "On the ground" community/civic allies are necessary. A major problem is that such groups often do not collaborate well with similar groups in the same community.

There were several public hearings involving the attempted revitalization of the North Amityville corner at which different community groups competed to the detriment of the overall efforts. These hearings were not unique. I saw similar hearings within and without of low-income communities. When the larger town surrounding the low-income community was involved, often racial fears inhibited progress.

Morgo offers the following pieces of advice to social advocates:

Progress is made on the ground. Theories do not result in progress. Block-by-block revitalization does.

Do not be involved in party politics. Have your for-profit partners get involved for you.

David Okorn, MS, Executive Director of the Long Island Community Foundation.

Due to the increasing demands on nonprofit leaders to have business skills, he feels that "we need not only people with skills in finance, real estate, human resources, and accounting but also people who understand individual, family, and group dynamics. You need both."

Evelyn Roth, former Suffolk Deputy County Executive, Director, Federation Employment Guidance Services (FEGS)/Long Island Division and Commissioner, Department of Services for the Aging, Town of North Hempstead.

Roth sees the nonprofit sector going through a sea change in which social welfare funding is critically needed. "Increasingly it is going to be among these types of community and home-based services," she says. "Technological advances are enabling more and more frail, older adults to remain in their homes much longer so we need to support these programs," she continues. Despite the value and success of Project Independence, there is not enough government support for these programs.

In Roth's view, "We are turning into a nation that does not seem to care but it is deeper than that. The guy who used to support government aid for the needy is having trouble paying his own mortgages. His taxes are rising while his income is not. There is not much energy left to worry about others."

In thinking about social activism today, it strikes Roth interesting that "so many social activists continue to pursue their causes beyond their working years, throughout their lives." The question for Roth is: "Who is going to join nonprofit boards in the future? She has concerns that boards are increasingly made up of business interests who are there to raise funds and network. "The money is important, but you have to wonder what is going to happen to these organization's services without consumer advocates," says Roth.

And, with regard to today's entrants into social work practice, Roth is concerned with the trend toward private clinical practice where one can earn a good living, with fewer entering social work careers with the goal of social activism; of reforming public policy.

Cindy Scott, former Executive Director, the Coalition Against Child Abuse and Neglect (CCAN) and current Executive Director of the Safe Center.

CCAN has always provided community and professional education programs to professionals and the community to help people identify and report child abuse and neglect. Onsite children's mental health services began in 2007. The program provides trauma focused (both long term and short term) modalities for children who have experienced the trauma of child abuse. The newest program, which began in 2014, is Safe Harbor, a program to identify and provide services to sexually exploited children. "These are truly some of the most vulnerable victims in our community. TSCLI will coordinate these cases as they are identified in the county, will provide the necessary mental health services to these victims and provide training on this issue to professionals and the community to help identify victims and how to refer them for services," Scott says.

"We helped to establish the case conferencing process and the investigative process" says Scott. The logical next step for CCAN was establishing Nassau's Child Advocacy Center (CAC) in 1998. As part of the co-located CAC model use by CCAN, police, CPS, District Attorney medical personnel were housed in CCAN's prior offices in Garden City. "The mission of the CAC is to reduce the trauma for victims of child abuse by providing them with a child-focused environment and timely delivery of treatment and services during the course of the investigation," says Scott. "The CAC model also enhances the collection of evidence for effective criminal prosecution and improved service planning in child protection proceedings." The Nassau CAC is one of 41 throughout New York and is supported through a combination of State and County and private funds. Almost simultaneously, CCAN began providing other direct services for victims of abuse and their families. "The rest has been a natural evolution," explains Scott. "As we started working with clients, we kept seeing greater needs for different and specialized services." The Child Victim Advocate Program offers assistance to children and non-offending family members as they go through the investigative and legal process. Advocates provide referrals to services, explain the legal process, and accompany the child and family members to court, police, medical and therapy sessions. "We are there to ensure that the family is taken care of while the investigation is happening. Maybe it is getting them some food, explaining what is going on and telling them what will happen next. Sometimes it is just holding the child's hand." After the initial investigation and legal proceedings, CCAN offers a number of services to assist children in recovering from the trauma of sexual or extreme physical abuse. Project Kidz Talk is one program designed to address the sense of isolation and loss of self-esteem from which child victims and their families suffer.

Scott says: "I have learned it is the "long game" that is important when wanting to create change. Things take much longer then we expect initially when we want to create change but it is important to "stay the course." Also, collaboration is much more work for us then if we worked independently. However, I believe the product we create with collaboration is always far better for our clients."

"We pull together non-offending family members and the child victims," says Scott. "We start with a family style dinner and then break up into groups - kids by age and a parent support group. "The combination of individual treatment for the child and a group work experience really helps with the healing process," Scott continues. "We have had kids who walked in and said, 'Wow, I am not the only one this has happened to'." Kids and families come together once a week. "We have one night for English-speaking families and one for Spanish-speaking families," says Scott. The support structure is also valuable for non-offending family members who may also have been isolated from friends and other family due to the circumstances surrounding the abuse. "Sometimes if a child accuses a father or other relative, the rest of the family may not believe the allegation and turn against the child and the mother," says Scott. The program typically serves approximately 25 families per week. "Some families come for a session or two. Others can be with us for years. It is totally voluntary and at no cost, as are all our services."

Walter Stockton, Chief Executive Officer and founder, Independent Group Homes for Living (IGHL)

IGHL's board of trustees is comprised of a group of dedicated members of the community. The mission of IGHL is to provide programs, services and support for people with developmental disabilities so they can realize their full potential as human beings and contributing members of their community. IGHL currently operates residential homes, day habilitation programs, and family support services with an $80M budget. Currently, the agency has 1,600 employees serving over 1,000 people annually. IGHL operates fifty group homes, seventeen day programs, a school and a nursing home, and a family support network.

Stockton describes major changes that have occurred in recent years in state funding of services for disabled people. In the 1970s, the state dramatically began to reduce the residency of people with disabilities in state institutions by funding the establishment of community-based group homes. This not only made sense from the perspective of providing services in the least restrictive environment, it also saved state taxpayers millions of dollars. Recently, the state began to change its focus away from funding group homes and outpatient clinics to services provided in home settings.

In addition, the New York State Office for People with Developmental Disabilities (OPDD) (previously called OMRDD), the primary funder of IGHL's programs, cut IGHL and other larger OPDD agencies', rates substantially. The situation forced the agencies to expand their fund raising activities to offset these cuts in state aid. Stockton could see that this wasn't a long range solution to the situation. He could see that the state was committed to cost containment regardless of what is best for IGHL's clients.

The situation was further exacerbated with the arrival of managed care in recent years with its capitated rates. Stockton and other providers of services funded by OPDD decided that they needed to be proactive, to make the best of what was felt to be the best of a bad situation. Initially, the agencies planned to establish the Alliance of Long Island Agencies Serving People with Developmental Disabilities solely of the twenty-eight Long Island agencies but decided that the substantial amount of funding required would be prohibitive for such a small number of agencies so it was decided to find partners around the state to participate. The Alliance also set out to find a managed care partnering company. Emblem Health Care was selected because it has the necessary $50M in reserves for such an enterprise and will cover the Alliance's upfront costs. The Alliance also hired a prominent law firm to assist the organization to set up and begin the necessary rate negotiating with the state.

Bringing together the agencies into the Alliance has produced consolidations and efficiencies but far from the amount necessary to offset the state rate reductions and the changes in the types of services it is willing to pay for. "Over 70% of our costs are for personnel costs so any cuts necessarily come from reductions in the quantity and quality of client services," Stockton regretfully says. "And not only are they cutting costs but they're imposing more onerous regulations than ever before along with unfunded mandates. It is clear to the Alliance's members that the Governor's fiscal advisors on the Capital's second floor are only concerned about the bottom line including nonprofit executive salaries, which now, do not permit any agency staff members to earn more than $199K." Stockton feels that these changes will result in "less-qualified staff. It means that you do not need to have a Social Science Degree to run an agency anymore. Business Degrees are what are necessary. It is very discouraging." For Stockton, a lesson learned is "if you are going to contract with the state, do not count on anything. It will change."

Looking back over a 40+ year career, Stockton feels "It was great. There was a time when I could dream up a new program idea and call the state and they would say "Do it." "It was never boring. You had varied responsibilities. It was a time to learn, to negotiate, and to work with others to make improvements. It was a challenging and creative time. At the time, the agency directors could blend the work's required fiscal and programmatic elements without compromising service delivery. Today, that is no longer possible."

Charles Russo, Esq., MA, Chairman, Hope House Ministries and Long Island Homeless Coalition and Partner, Russo, Karl, Widmaier & Cordano, PLLC.

Russo describes the problem with nonprofits that they have been put into a competitive game for funding, and, instead of working together, they work apart.

For further information about Charles Russo, visit Part III.

Paul Sabatino II, former Counsel to the Suffolk County Legislature and Chief Deputy County Executive.

Since 1985, the sources of funding for nonprofits proliferated at state, federal, and local levels. Local elected officials became more comfortable and proficient in dealing with the funding of multiple entities and multiple programs.

With the proliferation of new nonprofit entities at the local level, the politics of personality has all- too frequently taken precedence over the merits of the actual problems being addressed. This, in turn, has resulted in proposals for spending designed to meet a politically- predetermined level of governmental funding, as opposed to proposals that define a problem, present a solution, and request an amount of funding necessary to achieve an explicitly described goal.

The reality is that the rising tide of a booming national economy in the 1980s and 1990s did more to mitigate social distress and deal with local social needs than all of the proposals made by those individuals driven by the politics of personality and political connection

The truth is that there is a great myth about spending at the local level on Long Island. Everyone, both Republican and Democrat, repeatedly stated over the years that they would cut taxes by cutting waste, fraud, and abuse in town and county government. Although it is generally true that Republicans claimed to be against expanding funding for social programs, this was more of a political principle and platform that applied more to elected state and federal officials than to local elected officials. The budget cuts or budget proposals took place at the state and federal level, if at all. Again, the rhetoric has a tendency to overtake the reality. In general, it is fair to say that the rhetoric describing the level of cuts or savings in programmatic funding for social programs at the local level vastly exceeded the reality.

Betty Schlein. a Feminist and former Long Island Representative to Governor Hugh Carey.

The ERA failure in New York State in 1975 was where we met the real opposition. To encourage women to run for office we worked with the Women's Political Caucus. It was the time of the pill, the sexual revolution, Roe v. Wade and battles for enforcement at local hospitals. Demonstrations were held frequently. The effort to end sexual violence, rape and misogyny goes on to this day as does the fight to end discrimination and for economic equality.

For further information about Betty Schlein, see her profile in Part III.

David Sprintzen, Ph.D., Professor Emeritus of Philosophy at Long Island University and co-founder, The Long Island Progressive Coalition (LIPC).

Sprintzen offers the following thoughts about nonprofits and the political climate:

- Nonprofits are so heavily dependent on government that they cannot take an effective advocacy role.
- Long Island is a difficult place on which to get traction on things. There are no centers around which people can organize.
- You have to know how to respect people and treat them respectfully even when you differ.
- Over the past forty years, there has been a systematic defunding of the federal government. States have been squeezed while localities cannot raise taxes. The end result has been the shrinkage and privatization of services. The corporate share of the federal budget has been reduced dramatically as has the top tax brackets imposing higher taxes on the middle-class. The results of this dilemma force an organization into a quandary: Where do you put your time and effort, money and resources.

For further information about David Sprintzen, see his profile in Part III.

Lisa Tyson, Director of the Long Island Progressive Coalition (LIPC)

Reflecting on the organizing work that LIPC does, Tyson says "it is easy to be discouraged in this work. You are going to fail." At these times, she recalls the words of Winston Churchill: "Success consists of going from failure to failure without loss of enthusiasm." Tyson says that many of the young people she hires and who volunteer are passionate but get frustrated with the disappointments they experience as change agents. "They want things to be perfect and find it difficult to compromise their ideals," she says.

Tyson views compromises as often necessary and that change is incremental. She also feels that having a larger staff does not necessarily produce more and better results. "It is what you do with what you have and the relationships you have," Tyson says. When asked what part of her work she find most challenging, she says "it is the supervising of staff and how to create a positive and lasting climate to enable the work to be done."

LIPC has built a lot of political influence and power over the years with a very small staff," she continued. She points to the Living Wage Bill in Nassau County as a battle won as well as the work to stop the construction of high occupancy vehicles on Long Island's major highways and approval of an affordable housing bond issue in East Hampton as examples of battles won. But what Tyson loves most in her work are efforts to change the views of elected officials, the building of coalitions that stand together, the forming of trusting relationships, and helping people find jobs. "Give me these challenges any day!" says Tyson.

Rick Van Dyke, LMSW, former CEO, Family Service League (FSL)

"History repeats itself. Conditions may change but responses can be similar and innovation and passions are what much of our efforts were about and should be fostered as ways in which leaders should behave and act."

Part VII

The Influence of the Media

It is unlikely that the substantial work described in these pages to fight for progressive social policies and social welfare programs could have been done if it were not for the significant role played by the media, especially *Newsday* and the *Long Island Press* and most- recently *News12 Long Island.*

Newsday

The story of social action and social enterprise on Long Island since 1945 would not be complete if recognition were not given to *Newsday* for its significant role promoting a better quality of life for all Long Islanders. The newspaper often published stories that revealed hidden truths about social injustice, corruption, the consequences of poverty, and the needs of special populations.

My research reminds me of *Newsday's* coverage and editorial positions over the decades including many articles about social issues especially racism in public policy, education and housing; the presence of poverty amidst plenty; the deinstitutionalization of Long Island's state mental hospitals; the need to reform our treatment of people in our jails and children's shelters; the resistance of many neighborhoods to the location of group homes for at-risk populations, the homeless, the aged, and the mentally ill; the consequences of a drug culture, especially on the young; and the threat presented by the AIDS crisis and the dangers of breast cancer.

Newsday's reporting of social trends and issues reflect concern for people who are often forgotten by the larger society. Their editorial advocacy was heavily influenced by David Laventhol in the 1970s who wanted an informed and active citizenry. He initiated stories that exposed corruption by public officials in land scandals and became concerned regarding drug abuse on Long Island. In "The Heroin Trail," investigative reporter Robert Greene tracked heroin from Turkish poppy fields to Long Island neighborhoods and resulted in increased public attention to drug abuse and a Pulitzer Prize. Later, *Newsday* published a 12-part series "Long Island at the Crossroads," examining the region's economic malaise and lack of a unified leadership structure, issues that remain today.

Newsday's (now retired) Bob Keeler won the Pulitzer Prize for a series on a church with a mission of protecting new immigrants. Lawrence Levy was a Pulitzer Prize Finalist for editorials on how local tax policy punished the poor. Keeler recalls the time period:

> When they are doing their job right, newspapers can force bureaucracies to change their unfeeling and unfair behaviors," said Bob Keeler, a retired *Newsday* reporter, editor and editorial writer. "I often cite the example of a system set up by the Suffolk County Department of Social Services for distributing applications for aid. Only the first X-number of people who showed up at the Bay Shore office could get applications. That meant that people felt the need to get there long before the office opened, in the pre-dawn hours. Once I wrote about it, the department backed away from that policy. That is the kind of change that newspapers can bring about, by shining the light of public attention on places where public attention might not otherwise go: welfare offices, prisons, homeless shelters, to name a few.
>
> On a more global scale, I think back to the Pulitzer Prize that my former *Newsday* colleague Roy Gutman won in 1993 for revealing the existence of the death camps in Bosnia-Herzegovina. Roy's stories actually saved lives, and I know someone whose life was saved. Still, *Newsday* has not always been a positive force. I think back to an editorial that appeared when people were protesting the whites-only covenant in Levittown. That editorial criticized the protesting organizations harshly as 'Communist-dominated or Communist-inspired,' instead of saving all its righteous indignation for the covenants themselves. But by and large, *Newsday* has been a voce for positive change on Long Island.[1]

Marilyn Goldstein, a reporter at *Newsday* during the 1966-1995 period, regards this time as the Golden Age of *Newsday* in particular and of serious newspapers in general. She recalls that:

> Twenty-four hour TV news and political talk radio were in their infancy. Most TV news was limited to half-hour local broadcasts. And *CNN* was taking its baby steps in 1980. Then came Watergate and the Pentagon Papers and newspapers were expanding, not dying, and reporters became stars. *Newsday* was up there with the *Washington Post, The New York Times* and the *LA Times* changing, expanding, and modernizing. The large center section featured what is called 'soft news.' Part 2, was created to cover social issues with space for in-depth features produced by some of *Newsday*'s best writers, and

special pages to focus on current social issues like the environment, consumer affairs, religion and other emerging movements.

By the 1960s a response from *Newsday* like the one in the editorial on the whites-only covenant incident in Levittown mentioned previously by Bob Keeler would have been inconceivable. *Newsday* had by then had taken a leadership role in covering the progressive movements of the era, when they were still unpopular – racism, feminism, gay rights to name a few.

Newsday played an important part in the early days of the Women's Movement through its broad and frequent coverage. In 1967, when other media were still making jokes about the Women's Lib, I was tapped to cover the movement as a serious and potential society-changing entity. Sure, the very early coverage was relegated to the Women's Page (which *Newsday* soon replaced with the Part 2 feature section) but as the movement's impact grew, particularly with so many positive legal decisions and broad political involvement, it got more and more serious attention in the news, arts and sports sections as well as in feature sections. In the late 1960s, I knew of only one other reporter in the U.S. covering the Women's Movement as a beat.

We reported previously rarely covered areas such as no-fault divorce and equitable distribution of assets in divorce settlements, early coverage of heretofore unmentionable battered women, of course employment, abortion rights, women's emergence in politics, child care and other legal and social issues and gave editorial support for passage of the Equal Rights Amendment.

The strong coverage of this new social phenomenon accelerated interest among Long Island women, and offered a forum for their novel ideas and organizations. Long Island became one of the strongest communities in the nation promoting women's rights, with a large, well-recognized NOW chapter that developed strong political clout. It was also the geographic genesis of several important law suits, including winning a case against the Nassau County Police, which had stricter educational requirements for women than for the men entering their Cadet Academy and another allowing pregnant teachers to continue to work through their pregnancies and retain their jobs after taking a maternity leave. The New York State College in Old Westbury College was the seat of a major women's publishing house and an early proponent of Women's Studies, and both counties started sending women to local and state legislatures.

Ironically, as the coverage became more serious, the female staff formed the *Newsday* Women's Caucus in, I think, 1972, and ultimately filed a Title VII sex discrimination suit against their own employer. The suit was settled several years later with the promise of parity for women in story assignments, wages equal to the male staff with similar experience and talent, and promotions of women into management and senior reporting positions The company followed thorough, slowly but surely, appointing women to positions as photographers and editors; opening opportunities for them as columnists, sports writers, on investigative teams; advancing them to national and international news coverage and management positions.

Newsday had already, and without the pressure of a lawsuit, promised similar improvements for the minority employees. The changes were soon obvious to staff and readers and continue today."[2]

Lawrence Levy, who worked at *Newsday* for 31 years before going to Hofstra to run the National Center for Suburban Studies recalls:

As a reporter, editorial writer or columnist, whenever I proposed any piece with a social or racial justice theme, it was like pushing on an open door," said "I was given more than a year to work on a series of articles with Joye Brown, Edna Negron and Mike Alexander about the gentrification of Long Beach in the 1980s which saw thousands of poor and former mental patients lose their homes. That was an incredible commitment of resources, one that I would bet few other newspapers would have made. I was allowed to spend months on series – in both the news section and alter on the editorial page - about a property tax system that disproportionately burdened relatively poorer and mostly minority homeowners far more than others. And months on works about a state school aid system that punished poor school districts while rewarding rich ones. I could go on and on but I cannot remember a single time when I came to my editors – whether it was Jim Klurfeld on the editorial page or Howie Schneider in news – and was told not to pursue a "good" story about people in need. I never once heard – true or not – that we should not do it because our relatively conservative, suburban readers did not care. We cared. It was part of Newsday's DNA, our core mission. And I was very proud to be part of it." [3]

Newsday's Community Affairs Department's programs address many of Long Island's important social needs including:

- Future Corps' student community service programs are profiled year-round encouraging young people to be active citizens.

- Scholar-Artist Awards honors Long Island's artistically accomplished high school students throughout the school year.

- Marching Band Festival exhibits the talents of thousands of high school band students.

- *Newsday* Charities helps at-risk children and families on Long Island by raising funds through public campaigns – Kids Campaign and Help-a-Family. Every dollar donated is matched 50 cents on the dollar by the McCormick Foundation.

- Kids Campaign raises funds to help kids in need while the Help-a-Family helps Long Island families going through tough times. [4]

The Health and Welfare Council of Long Island awarded *Newsday* its 2014 Hagedorn Award for Philanthropy in recognition of its long-term commitment to improving the lives of disadvantaged Long Islanders by funding nonprofit organizations that provide vital programs in the areas of hunger, housing, child/youth education and child abuse prevention/treatment.

The Long Island Press

The following introduction to David Starr's important role in newspaper coverage of social action on Long Island is written by Karl Grossman, a full professor of journalism at the State University at Old Westbury and recipient of awards for investigative reporting including the George Polk, Generoso Pope, James Aronson and John Peter Zenger Awards, worked for the Long Island Press in the 1960s and 1970s.

"An element of the story of the development of social, educational, and health systems in Nassau and Suffolk involves the work of my former editor at the *Long Island Press* who is still, although 92 years of age, working, sharp as always, Dave Starr.

"Starr was not just the long-time senior editor of the *Long Island Press* but from Jamaica (Queens) was the Senior Editor of the entire Newhouse chain of 26 papers and the *Newhouse News Service*, a Washington-based news operation.

"Dave felt that a major role for a newspaper editor is to promote social, educational, cultural development in the area the paper services. Indeed, the last expose I wrote at *The Press* was a weeklong series about how Long Island was underserved in SUNY seats because of the way SUNY was structured originally on the skeleton of the former teachers colleges -Owego, Oneonta, etc. - upstate and because Long Island had, other than the then two-year agricultural college at Farmingdale, it had gotten short-changed. The series emphasized that even with Stony Brook, Farmingdale and Old Westbury, the number of SUNY seats on Long Island for Long Island high school graduates was a fraction of the ratio of SUNY seats upstate for high school graduates upstate. This was done by me in coordination with Stony Brook University President John Toll, the Stony Brook administration and Dave Starr.

"Starr, who started as editor of *The Press* in 1940 as a copy boy working his way through college, became its associate editor in 1953 and senior editor of the Newhouse papers in 1966. He had his hand in all sorts of stuff in Nassau and Suffolk before *The Press* went out in 1977 but I venture to say that in terms of social, educational, cultural promotion on Long Island, the work of Dave Starr at *The Press* might have been the equivalent of what *Newsday* did. In any event, it was close. It is rare for an editor to take the position that the development of social, educational, cultural institutions is a top priority but that has been Dave's thing."

The following description of the Long Island Press was written by David Starr. Starr served as national editor of the entire Newhouse chain as well as the fellow behind the Newhouse News Service, a Washington-based operation.

"The *Long Island Press* always considered itself a crusading newspaper, and its primary mission, for many years, was to create free colleges for its readers. *The Press* launched a campaign in the early 1930s to a get a free four-year city college in the New York City borough of Queens, its hometown. It argued long and loud that New York City had created a free four-year college for talented boys in 1866 in Manhattan, a free college for girls in The Bronx in 1870, and a coed college in Brooklyn in 1930. The only large borough left out was Queens. The Press enrolled politicians, civic leaders, educators and foot-soldiers to march, many times, on City Hall. Finally, *The Press* campaign bore fruit in 1937, when Queens College opened on a 20-acre campus in Flushing next to Willow Lake, where Mayor Fiorello LaGuardia had his summer City Hall.

"My wife Peggy and I were among its first beneficiaries. In June 1938, I enrolled at Queens College instead of making an hour-long trek to City College in Manhattan. I got a job at The Press as a weekend copy boy in 1940 and have worked for the same company ever since. In 1946, Governor Tom Dewey formed a state commission to study the need for a state university. He appointed to it Dr. Paul Klapper, president of Queens College and one of America's best-known education professors. I had gotten to know Dr. Klapper when I was editor of the campus student newspaper and he asked me to travel to early commission meetings with him as his secretary / companion. *The Press* let me do that on company time.

"The State University was officially created in 1948. I was named executive editor of the *Nassau Daily Review Star,* a small daily, in 1949 and immediately started a campaign to open a university branch in Nassau County. The Review-Star had a substantial circulation in Hempstead town adjoining Queens County and I was happy, as a brand new young editor, to take up the cudgels for a new college for readers.

"I followed the pattern that had been set by *The Long Island Press.* I met with the Nassau and Suffolk delegation in the state legislature, with all the other local elected officials, with businessmen and educators, with civic associations.

"But there was considerable opposition. There were private colleges in Nassau and Suffolk who did not enjoy the notion of a free education--- free at the beginning, anyway. *Newsday* barely mentioned its competitor's campaign, even after it passed the legislature. Alicia Patterson felt a public college simply wasn't needed. In the fall of 1954, the managing editor of *The Press* and I traveled to Albany to try to persuade Governor Averill Harriman to sign the bill. He met us in his dimly lit office while he gulped down supper, and then mumbled that Nassau and Suffolk did not need a public college. The private ones were just fine, thank you. It was elitism at its baldest.

"It did not matter, and I knew it. With powerful Long Islanders in the state legislature, led by Assembly Speaker Joseph Carlino of Rockville Centre and Perry Duryea of Montauk, the outcome was predictable. They just rolled their eyes and overrode Harriman's veto.

"When it came time to actually name sites for the new campuses, Nassau was ready. The legislature first approved a site in Oyster Bay as a State University College. It opened at the lovely Planting Field Fields estate in 1957 and relocated and moved four years later, as a full-fledged University Center, to Stony Brook, where philanthropist Ward Melville had donated a 400-acre campus.

"The Long Island Press also enthusiastically covered and promoted the formation of LI Jewish/North Shore Hospital. I was a founder, together with Len Hall, Judge Bernard Meyer and David Kadane, chief counsel of LILCO and a board member of the United Way of Long Island." [5]

News12 Long Island

The following profile was provided by Patrick Dolan, President of News 12 Networks and News Director of News 12 Long Island.

"News12 Long Island is the local news service for the 3 million residents of Nassau and Suffolk counties providing local news and information about its counties, townships and neighborhoods. Over the years, *News12 Long Island* has conducted a number of town hall meetings on a range of topics including: "Shoreham Power Plant"(to build or not to build),"What is in the Water" (water quality and issues), "Long Island's Changing Portrait" (diversity and racial issues), "The Long Island Sound" (pollution, jurisdiction, energy potential), "Broadwater", "Testing the Limits" (standardized testing), "Illegals on Long Island" (immigration, day laborers).

"News12 Long Island has also provided the most comprehensive election coverage arguably than any other station in the country. For years, the station did local debates for nearly all the elections exposing the audience to candidates they never would have met otherwise." [6]

Channel 21/Public Television

Since its first broadcast in 1969, public media station WLIW21, an affiliate of WNET, has served Long Island with arts, education and public affairs programming on-air and online. As the fourth most-watched public television station in the nation, WLIW21 is viewed by approximately 3 million people each week throughout New York City's five boroughs, Long Island, Westchester, New Jersey, and Connecticut. [7]

Channel 55

The origins of channel 55 date back to 1967. For a period of years, the station featured a daily newscast and other local programming including a political talk show called *Focus on Long Island*. [8]

Telecare Television

Since its inception in 1969, when founded by Monsignor Thomas Hartman of the Diocese of Rockville Centre, *Telecare* began as a local diocesan station and has become the foremost source for quality, faith-based television throughout the tri-state area and beyond. For many homebound and hospitalized, *Telecare* is their only conduit through which to celebrate their faith. *Telecare* also provides parochial schools with religious educational materials created for every grade level-from kindergarten through 8th grade. [9]

Other Print Media

In addition to the two major daily newspapers that circulated on Long Island, *Newsday* and the since-closed *Long Island Press*, there are a rich array of weekly newspapers in Nassau and Suffolk - an extraordinary number. Some of the weeklies, including *The Southampton Press, The East Hampton Star,*

Shelter Island Reporter, Sag Harbor Express, East Hampton Press, News-Review of Riverhead and *Suffolk Times*, have been recognized as the best weekly newspapers in New York State in their respective circulation groups in the annual contest of the New York Press Association. Several have also received major national recognition. Long Island weeklies have been civic-minded and remarkable in their journalistic initiatives. In addition to the community weeklies, other Long Island weekly publications have included *The Long Island Catholic, Suffolk Life* and the weekly *Long Island Press*.

Notes: Part VII

1. Robert Keeler, *email correspondence of November 5, 2014*
2. Marilyn Goldstein, *email correspondence of December 30, 2014*
3. Lawrence Levy, *email correspondence of November 5, 2014*
4. Information obtained from: www.newsday.com
5. David Starr, *email correspondence of October 15, 2014*
6. Patrick Dolan, *email correspondence of August 12, 2014*
7. Information obtained from: www.wliw.com
8. Information obtained from: www.longisland.com
9. Information obtained from: www.telecaretv.org

Part VIII

Racism and the Civil Rights Struggle

The National Backdrop

"In August 1955, Emmett Till, a fourteen year-old from Chicago, visited relatives in Mississippi. He and several other boys stopped at a local grocery store for some candy after a long day of picking cotton. While at the store, Till allegedly whistled at a white grocery store owner's wife. A few days later, after Roy Bryant, the store owner, returned to town and learned of the event, Bryant and his half-brother J.W. Milam made plans to "teach the boy a lesson." Bryant and Milam kidnapped Till, and then brutally beat, mutilated and shot him before dropping him in the Tallahatchie River. While Bryant and Milam were arrested for the murder, the all-white Mississippi jury took just over an hour to acquit the two. Mamie Till Bradley, Till's mother, held an open casket funeral in Chicago, so mourners could see how her son had been mutilated. Even so, Bryant and Milam later boasted about the murder in a *Look* magazine interview, since double jeopardy protected them from retrial.

"In December 1955, Rosa Parks, a member of the NAACP made civil rights history when she refused to relinquish her seat to a white passenger on a public bus. After she was arrested, the Montgomery black community launched a bus boycott, led by Reverend Martin Luther King, Jr., the recently elected president of the Montgomery Improvement Association. The boycott ended just over one year later on Dec. 21, 1956 when the city buses were finally desegregated.

"The social and political unrest of the civil rights movement characterized and defined the decade of the 1960s. From the March on Washington for Freedom and Jobs in 1963 led by Dr. Martin Luther King, to the televised police assaults on blacks in Birmingham, Alabama, with police dogs and water hoses, to the bombing of a black Birmingham church that killed four young girls, to the murders of civil rights workers Chaney, Goodman and Schwerner in Mississippi, the decade became a testament to the social, political and economic realities of violent and deep-seated racial hatred. In 1964, the massive Mississippi voter registration drive, "Freedom Summer" principally organized by Fannie Lou Hamer for the Student Nonviolent Coordinating Committee, increased black registered voters from 7% to 67% of those eligible in the five years. Hamer went on to become the vice chair of the Mississippi Freedom Democratic Party and attended the 1964 Democratic convention in Atlantic City where she made an impassioned speech to the delegates and the American public.

"Three weeks in March of 1965 marked the height of the modern civil rights movement, culminating in the Selma-to-Montgomery March for voting rights. On "Bloody Sunday," March 7, 1965, some 600 civil rights activists marched east on U.S. Route 80 out of Selma. They had traveled only six blocks to the Edmund Pettus Bridge when state and local lawmen attacked them with billy-clubs and tear gas and drove them back into Selma. Martin Luther King, Jr. led a "symbolic" march to the bridge two days later on March 9. Civil rights leaders then sought court protection for a third, full-scale march from Selma to the state capitol in Montgomery; Federal District Court Judge Frank M. Johnson, Jr. ruled in favor of the demonstrators. Two weeks later, on Sunday, March 21, around 3,200 marchers set out for Montgomery, walking 12 miles a day and sleeping in fields. Their ranks had swelled to 25,000 by the time they reached the capitol on Thursday, March 25. Less than five months later, President Lyndon Johnson signed the Voting Rights Act of 1965." [1]

"The civil rights movement can be defined as a mass popular movement to secure for African Americans equal access to and opportunities for the basic privileges and rights of U.S. citizenship. Although the roots of the civil rights movement go back to the 19th century, the movement peaked in the 1950s and 1960s. African American men and women, along with whites, organized and led the movement at national and local levels. They pursued their goals through legal means, negotiations, petitions, and nonviolent protest demonstrations.

"The civil rights movement centered on the American South, where the African American population was concentrated and where racial inequality in education, economic opportunity, and the political and legal processes was most blatant. Beginning in the late 19th century, state and local governments passed segregation laws, known as Jim Crow laws, and mandated restrictions on voting qualifications that left the black population economically and politically powerless.

"African Americans throughout much of the South were denied the right to vote, barred from public facilities, subjected to insults and violence, and could not expect justice from the courts. In the North, black Americans also faced discrimination in housing, employment, education, and many other areas. But the civil rights movement had made important progress, and change was on the way.

"The 1954 U.S. Supreme Court decision Brown v. Board of Education of Topeka, Kansas ushered in a new era in the struggle for civil rights. The Supreme Court ruled unanimously in *Brown v. Board of Education* that racial segregation in public schools was unconstitutional. This landmark decision outlawed racial segregation in public schools. Whites around the country condemned the decision, and in the South such white supremacist groups as the Ku Klux Klan and the Citizens' Council organized to resist desegregation, sometimes resorting to violence. A primary target of supremacist groups was the National Association for the Advancement of Colored People (NAACP). Over the course of decades the NAACP had filed a procession of court cases, including Brown, and had assumed the lead in the national struggle against segregated education. The oldest established national civil-rights organization, the NAACP also played an important role at the local level, where blacks across the South organized branches to combat discrimination in their communities.

"Many southern political leaders claimed the desegregation decision violated the rights of states to manage their systems of public education, and they responded with defiance, legal challenges, delays, or token compliance. As a result, school desegregation proceeded very slowly. By the end of the 1950s, less than 10 percent of black children in the South were attending integrated schools.

"The pace of civil rights protests rose sharply in response to the Supreme Court's decision. Martin Luther King, Jr., led a boycott that ended segregated busing in Montgomery, Alabama. In 1957, National Guard troops under orders from President Dwight D. Eisenhower enforced the desegregation of Little Rock Central High School in Arkansas. But, even after Little Rock, school integration was painfully slow, and segregation in general remained largely untouched.

"In February 1960, four black college students sat down at a Woolworth's lunch counter in Greensboro, N.C., and asked to be served. They were refused service, and they refused to leave their seats. Within days, more than fifty students had volunteered to continue the sit-in, and within weeks the movement had spread to other college campuses. Sit-ins and other protests swept across the South in early 1960, touching more than sixty-five cities in twelve states. Roughly 50,000 young people joined the protests that year.

"By the 1960 presidential campaign, civil rights had emerged as a crucial issue. Just a few weeks before the election, Martin Luther King, Jr., was arrested while leading a protest in Atlanta, Georgia. John Kennedy phoned Coretta Scott King to express his concern while a call from Robert Kennedy to the judge helped secure her husband's safe release. The Kennedys' personal intervention led to a public endorsement by Martin Luther King, Sr., the influential father of the civil rights leader.

"Across the nation, more than 70 percent of African Americans voted for Kennedy, and these votes provided the winning edge in several key states. When President Kennedy took office in January 1961, African Americans had high expectations for the new administration.

"But Kennedy's narrow election victory and small working margin in Congress left him cautious. He was reluctant to lose southern support for legislation on many fronts by pushing too hard on civil rights legislation. Instead, he appointed unprecedented numbers of African Americans to high-level positions in the administration and strengthened the Civil Rights Commission. He spoke out in favor of school desegregation, praised a number of cities for integrating their schools, and put Vice President Lyndon Johnson in charge of the President's Committee on Equal Employment Opportunity. Attorney General Robert Kennedy turned his attention to voting rights, initiating five times the number of suits brought during the previous administration.

"President Kennedy may have been reluctant to push ahead with civil rights legislation, but millions of African Americans would not wait. Eventually, the administration was compelled to act. For decades, seating on buses in the South had been segregated, along with bus station waiting rooms, rest rooms, and restaurants. In May 1961, the Congress of Racial Equality (CORE), led by James Farmer, organized integrated Freedom Rides to defy segregation in interstate transportation. Freedom riders were arrested in North Carolina and beaten in South Carolina. In Alabama, a bus was burned and the riders attacked with baseball bats and tire irons. Attorney General Robert Kennedy sent 400 federal marshals to protect the freedom riders and urged the Interstate Commerce Commission to order the desegregation of interstate travel.

"In 1962, James H. Meredith, Jr., an African American Air Force veteran, was denied admission to the University of Mississippi, known as "Ole Miss." Meredith attempted to register four times without success.

"Long telephone conversations between the president, the attorney general, and Governor Ross Barnett failed to produce a solution. When federal marshals accompanied Meredith to campus in another attempt to register for classes, rioting erupted. Two people died and dozens were injured. President Kennedy mobilized the National Guard and sent federal troops to the campus. Meredith registered the next day and attended his first class, and segregation ended at the University of Mississippi.

"In the spring of 1963, Martin Luther King, Jr., and Rev. Fred Shuttlesworth launched a campaign of mass protests in Birmingham, Alabama, which King called the most segregated city in America. Initially, the demonstrations had little impact. Then, on Good Friday, King was arrested and spent a week behind bars, where he wrote one of his most famous meditations on racial injustice and civil disobedience, "Letter from Birmingham Jail." Meanwhile, James Bevel, one of King's young lieutenants, summoned black youths to march in the streets at the beginning of May. Birmingham City Commissioner Eugene "Bull" Connor used police dogs and high-pressure fire hoses to put down the demonstrations. Nearly a thousand young people were arrested. The violence was broadcast on television to the nation and the world.

"Invoking federal authority, President Kennedy sent several thousand troops to an Alabama air base, and his administration responded by speeding up the drafting of a comprehensive civil rights bill.

"Governor George Wallace had vowed at his inauguration to defend "segregation now, segregation tomorrow, and segregation forever." In June 1963, he upheld his promise to "stand in the schoolhouse door" to prevent two black students from enrolling at the University of Alabama. To protect the students and secure their admission, President Kennedy federalized the Alabama National Guard. And on June 11, the president addressed the nation.

"Kennedy defined the civil rights crisis as moral, as well as constitutional and legal. He announced that major civil rights legislation would be submitted to the Congress to guarantee equal access to public facilities, to end segregation in education, and to provide federal protection of the right to vote.

"In August 1963, more than 200,000 Americans of all races celebrated the centennial of the Emancipation Proclamation by joining the March on Washington for Jobs and Freedom. Key civil rights figures led the march, including A. Philip Randolph, Roy Wilkins, Bayard Rustin, and Whitney Young. But the most memorable moment came when Martin Luther King, Jr., delivered his "I Have a Dream" speech from the steps of the Lincoln Memorial.

"Later that fall, the comprehensive civil rights bill cleared several hurdles in Congress and won the endorsement of House and Senate Republican leaders. It had not been passed, however, before November 22, 1963, when President Kennedy was assassinated. The bill was left in the hands of Lyndon B. Johnson. Before becoming vice president, Johnson had served more than two decades in Congress as a congressman and senator from Texas. He used his connections with southern white congressional leaders and the outpouring of emotion after the president's assassination to pass the Civil Rights Act as a way to honor President Kennedy.

"Provisions of the legislation included: (1) protecting African Americans against discrimination in voter qualification tests; (2) outlawing discrimination in hotels, motels, restaurants, theaters, and all other public accommodations engaged in interstate commerce; (3) authorizing the U.S. Attorney General's Office to file legal suits to enforce desegregation in public schools; (4) authorizing the withdrawal of federal funds from programs practicing discrimination; and (5) outlawing discrimination in employment in any business exceeding 25 people and creating an Equal Employment Opportunity Commission to review complaints. Passed on July 2, 1964, the Civil Rights

Act was a crucial step in achieving the civil rights movement's initial goal: full legal equality." [2]

"Congressman John Lewis, in looking back, feels that "there have been unbelievable changes for the better in politics and in the economy. But back in the Sixties, people had a sense of hope. I think we have lost that. Something died in America in 1968, and we have not been able to bring it back. Many of us still believe that good and right will still prevail, but we do not have the same spirit."

"Another important character of the 1960s was Andrew Young who served as Dr. Martin Luther King's Chief of Staff. In reflecting back to the late 1960s and the Black Power movement militancy, Young says that "we did not pay much attention to them...they were all talk. They really did not do anything. They resented us as old ministers with families who were still getting most of the press." According the Brokaw, Young was "far more concerned about the push to get Dr. King involved in the antiwar movement and the social problems of the cities in the North." Young felt that "we had more than enough to do at home; that Dr. King would undermine public support for the civil rights agenda he was also advancing." [3]

"In 1965, Mexican American civil rights activist César Chávez and the National Farm Workers Association (NFWA) led California grape-pickers in a strike to demand higher wages. Phillip Veracruz and Mariano Laya Armington, two Filipino farm workers involved with the Agricultural Workers Organizing Committee, along with the NFWA, organized the Delano grape strike to get higher wages. In 1966, Chávez and supporters marched from Delano to the state capital at Sacramento, and called for Americans to boycott grapes in support of farm workers. The strike, which lasted five years, garnered national attention about the plight of the mostly Mexican migrant workers and their exploitation. The effort resulted in the first major labor victory for U.S. migrant workers.

"In similar movements in South Texas in 1966, United Farm Workers-formerly NFWA-marched to Austin, Texas, in support of melon workers and UFW workers' rights. In 1969, Chávez and UFW members protested growers' use of illegal immigrants as strikebreakers by marching through the Imperial and Coachella Valley to the Mexican border. The UFW organized strikes and boycotts in the early 1970s to get higher wages from grape and lettuce growers. Chávez led a boycott in the 1980s to protest toxic pesticide use on grapes. Chávez' strike and boycott efforts resulted in signed bargaining agreements protecting farm workers. In 1965, riots erupted in Watts, a black

Los Angeles neighborhood. In 1967-68, riots occurred in Detroit, Newark and other major cities, some in response to the assassination of Martin Luther King in Memphis in April 1968. In 1968, anti-war protests disrupted the 1968 Democratic National Convention in Chicago as opposition to the war in Vietnam grew."

"In the U.S., blacks, Mexicans, Chinese and Japanese immigrants were targets of discrimination in employment and property ownership. African Americans lost their homes through foreclosures during the 1930s and 40s, many of them victims of fraud and deception. In the South, many blacks were victims of exploitative tenant-sharecropper systems that kept them in perpetual debt." [4]

Racism on Long Island

Long Island's history of social justice and social programs cannot be understood without an understanding of the impact that racism had on their development. It dates back hundreds of years.

Racism's history is recorded by Hofstra University's Alan J. Singer's curriculum guide that was named an "exemplary social studies program" by the National Council for the Social Studies at its 85th annual conference.

"Prior to 1898, Nassau County was part of Queens County. According to the 1698 census its population was 3,565 people including 199 enslaved Africans. One of the largest and best documented slave holdings was Lloyd's Manor where Jupiter Hammon, an African American preacher and poet was enslaved. In 1775, as Long Islanders prepared for a possible attack by British forces, a list of slaveholders in the town of Hempstead was assembled. It included Benjamin Hewlett, George and Cornelius Rierson, William and John Cornell, Hendrick and Thomas Hendrickson, Thomas and Sarah Seamons, Samuel, Daniel, and Jacob Searing, and John, Jacob, and Thomas Hicks.

"Eastern Long Island was settled by English farmers from New England and also by English planters from the Caribbean who used it as a source of raw material and foodstuffs for plantations in Barbados where they employed enslaved African labor to grow sugar cane. One of the earliest settlers on Shelter Island was Nathaniel Sylvester. In a 1680 "disposition" to his will, Sylvester listed twenty enslaved people, "Six men; five women; six girls; three boys. Tamero, his wife Oyou and their four children; Black John and his daughter Prescilla; Negro J.O. and his wife Marie; Negro Jenkin; Jaquero, his wife Hannah, and their daughters; Tony, his wife Nannie, and their four daughters; and Japhet and his wife Semnie." Other slaveholders on the east end were John Budd, John Conkling, Benjamin Horton, John Swazey, and John

Tooker of Southold, Thomas Jessup, James Herricke, and Peregrine Stanborough of Southampton, Stephen Hand of East Hampton, and Richard Smith of Smithtown. According to a 1698 census, 20% of the 2,679 people living in Suffolk County were enslaved Africans, three-quarters of whom lived on farms with three or fewer slaves. Perhaps the best know African enslaved in Suffolk County was Venture Smith, who published his memoirs in 1796. Smith was born in Africa, probably in current day Ghana, enslaved as a boy, and transported to Barbados. He was shipped to Rhode Island and sent to Fisher's Island, off of the coast of Long Island. When he was twenty-two years old, he married and attempted to escape from bondage. He eventually surrendered to his master, but was permitted to earn money to purchase his freedom and the freedom of his family.

"While post-World War-II white people settled on Long Island, their black counterparts found extremely limited housing options often r rental apartments in commercial and business districts. If you were white and poor, you could buy a home according to your ability to afford the mortgage. If you were African-American, whether poor or not, your housing choices were further limited by overt and covert racism and limited to certain communities such as Hempstead, Roosevelt, New Cassel, Central Islip, Brentwood, Wyandanch, North Amityville, Gordon Heights, and to specific sections of other communities like Glen Cove, Freeport and Riverhead. Black families could not afford to live a middle class life style including mortgages, cars, and a variety of appliances." [5]

Author's Reflection

Most racism in post-World War II Long Island can be described as insidious, not as blatant as William Levitt's restrictive covenant. I recall how my parents and their all-white Mineola neighbors felt when a white family, upset with their neighbors, threatened to sell their home to blacks. Their attitudes reflected the popular feelings that home values would decline and that it was better for people "to live with their own kind." White people also had strong feelings that their children's schools should not be integrated. There was also an underlying fear that Long Island would become urbanized with traffic congestion and the crime associated with city life. It was no surprise that local elected officials and members of boards of education were voted into office on platforms that purported to protect a suburban quality of life.

"The civil rights movement of the 1950s and 1960s is generally portrayed as a struggle to end racial segregation in the southern part of the United States, especially the deep southern states of Mississippi, Alabama, and Georgia. However, an important part of the civil rights struggle was fought in the north, including in several Long Island communities where terrorism and discrimination were used to maintain racial segregation. Many of the problems that confront Long Island today are a result of the inability of Nassau and Suffolk counties to resolve issues related to racism and social justice over twenty-five years ago.

"Historians tend to identify organizations like the Ku Klux Klan with the south, but clandestine racist groups existed on Long Island from the 1920s through the 1960s. In the decade after World War I, Long Island was a major site of a resurgent Klan that tried to intimidate recent Catholic and Jewish immigrants to the United States. Some local historians estimate that in the mid-1920s, over 20,000 Long Island residents were Klan members, including the Freeport chief of police and three Suffolk County Republican Party chairmen. In 1922, the Klan burned a cross in a Catholic and Jewish neighborhood of Freeport and in 1924, 6,000 Klansmen marched through the town. In 1928, an estimated 8,000 people were at a cross-burning in Wantagh.

"Paul W. F. Linder, a real estate developer from Malverne who was President of the Homeland Corporation, was also the Great Titan of the New York State Klan. Because of his role in the development of Malverne, a street and an elementary school were named after him. In July 1926, a Klan fair called a Klorero was held in Mineola and it was attended by thousands of Long Island residents. A fund-raising journal published in conjunction with the festivities recorded donations from hundreds of Long Island businesses, organizations, and individuals, including the Women's Welfare League of Suffolk County, the Bellmore Press, the Northport Observer, the Hempstead Sentinel, the Oceanside National Bank, the Lindenhurst Police Department, and the First Reformed Church of West Sayville.

"Even though the Klan fell into eclipse in the 1930's, racial intimidation continued, and it was increasingly aimed at Long Island's Black population. In towns like Amityville, Central Islip, East Meadow, and Setauket, groups tried to intimidate African American residents by defacing property with hate symbols and through cross burnings. African American groups countered these attacks by intensifying their campaigns against racism and by demanding increased police protection.

"Frequently during the 1960's, Black residents of Long Island felt that police officers were more inclined to harass than to protect them. In January 1966, Newsday reported charges by CORE that alleged police brutality in the arrest of a man from Hempstead. On July 29, 1966, the New York Times documented an incident in North Amityville where Suffolk police blocked the main roads leading into this predominantly African American community after a series of incidents following an outdoor rally whose aim was to improve community-police relations. At the rally and in the article, African Americans accused police officers of regularly using abusive language, including the term 'nigger.'

"Actions by white officials often frustrated young Blacks and incited rioting. In an unusually violent episode in 1966, Black youths in the Carleton Park section of Central Islip responded to what they considered police harassment of an African American man by assaulting the two police officers.

"Much of the racial conflict on Long Island had economic roots. Real-estate brokers exacerbated racism for their own economic gain. Brokers profited from the fears of white people. According to the New York Times, in the early 1960s they began "a strong campaign of 'block-busting' or inducing scare selling" in Port Jefferson, Freeport and East Meadow.

"In many towns, white residents opposed racially integrating schools or allowing Black teachers to teach their children. In 1957, the NAACP charged that many Black education students from New York City public colleges were being discouraged from applying for jobs on Long Island.

"Efforts to expose discrimination against African American teacher candidates were part of a larger struggle against job discrimination. Throughout this period, civil rights groups pressured large businesses on Long Island to hire African Americans. According to a Newsday article from January, 1963, "The Long Island effort to combat discrimination in hiring practices is part of a large-scale campaign by C.O.R.E. in the Metropolitan area. The organization is currently organizing a boycott by shoppers against the products produced by Sealtest Foods, a large dairy firm."

"Campaigns by the Congress of Racial Equality against job discrimination set off sharp conflict on Long Island and stirred up opposition in the white community. When Lincoln Lynch, the head of the Nassau County chapter of CORE, targeted the Franklin National Bank for its failure to hire employees from minority groups, he was charged with forcing companies to hire employees based on their race. A Newsday editorial accused Lynch of "sowing the seeds of disunity" and provoked an exchange of letters involving Lynch and other community activists. Despite these criticisms, CORE's activism successfully forced companies to end discriminatory hiring practices.

"Four years later, Lynch and CORE were again in the news as they led the campaign to integrate the all-white Hempstead Volunteer Fire Department. While the leading proponents of the civil rights movement on Long Island during the 1960s were CORE and the NAACP, churches, either acting independently or in coalition with these groups, also played a major role in the struggle. Local religious leaders were influential as mediators between civil rights activists and opponents of racial integration, organized groups like the Huntington Township Committee on Human Rights and the Freeport Community Relations Council, appealed to the individual morality of members of their congregations, brought together people from different racial and ethnic backgrounds, and participated in protests and meetings.

"An important figure on Long Island during this period was the Reverend Walter P. Kellenberg, the Roman Catholic Bishop of Rockville Centre. In an article in the *Hempstead Beacon*, Kellenberg declared, 'The principle and most difficult problem facing our country and each of its citizens today is the struggle for Civil Rights. The Declaration of Independence states what is also an incontrovertible fact of Christian teaching - that all men are created equally. But the problem of unequal treatment amongst men is really a moral one. For this reason it is necessary that each individual examine his own conscience in matters of interracial and social justice.'

"Despite gains during the Civil Rights movement of the 1950's and 1960's, most African American children in the United States continue to attend segregated and unequal schools. Nationally, three-fourths of all Black children attend schools that are 90% minority, and this situation is acute in the nation's largest cities.

"This pattern is replicated in Long Island's public schools, where the failure to create stable, racially integrated communities during the 1960s, has produced a checkerboard pattern of racial segregation and unequal school funding. In Nassau and Suffolk Counties, residents of poorer, predominantly minority communities often pay higher property tax rates, but because of an unequal distribution of commercial establishments and differences in property values, less money is spent on the education of their children. For example, in primarily white, relatively affluent, Hauppauge, residents pay an average of $2,100 in school taxes on houses assessed at $60,000, while the district spends $13,300 to educate each child. However in Brentwood, where 65% of students are either African American or Latino/a, residents pay an average of $3,000 in school taxes on houses assessed at $35,000, but the district spends only $9,700 per child.

"In his book, *Out of Our Past: The Forces That Shaped Modern America,* historian Carl Degler described the post-Civil War era in the United States as a "Dawn Without Noon" for African Americans. The end of slavery promised so much, but Reconstruction delivered so little. In many ways, the struggle for civil rights on Long Island in the 1950's and 1960's repeated this pattern. High hopes for change were dashed by stiff opposition from white opponents of integration and the deep roots and tenacity of institutional segregation and racism." [6]

Personal Accounts of Long Island Civil Rights Leaders

The following material represents an effort to acknowledge and chronicle a number of important Long Island civil rights leaders of the 1960s and 1970s. There were many more.

Accounts of Kenneth Anderson, Leone Baum, James Couch, Hazel Dukes, David Kadane, Lincoln Lynch, Irwin Quintyne, Leroy Ramsey, David Salten, Joyce Louise Spencer Insolia, Joyce Moore Turner, W. Burghardt Turner, and Ralph Watkins, are included in Part III, Exemplary Community Leaders and Grassroots Organizers. They are based on recollections by relatives, colleagues and archival information.

Some of the leaders that I wished to profile have died and, therefore, were unable to tell their stories personally. They include: Diana Coleman, James Davis, Audrey Jones, Farrell Jones, Reverend Earl Jordan, Lorenzo Merritt, and Jame Rice.

Other Long Island civil rights leaders' stories are described within the book's specific organizational stories. These include: Dean Frances Brisbane, Marvin Colson, John Kearse, Mel Jackson, Helen Martin, Marge Rogatz, Delores Quintyne, Bessie Swan, and Hugh A. Wilson. In addition, the story of Suffolk Housing Services and its director Janet Hanson provides a description of the struggle for fair housing on Long Island.

Other civil rights leaders who made significant contributions but whom I could not reach include the following: Joel Becker, Clayton Chesson, Lamar Cox, Jim Europe, Van Dyke Johnson, Florence Joyner, Betty Miller, John Moscow, Reverend William Rambo, Sam Raskin, Eugene Reed, James Rice, Albert Seay, Lloyd Sergeant, Camille Smith, Larry Smith, Ann and Delano Stewart, Moe Tandler, Reverend Reginald Tuggle, and Herman Washington.

Notes: Part VIII

1. Information obtained from the RACE Traveling Exhibit, the Museum of Minnesota website:
   www.understandingrace.org/history/society/civil_rights.html.
2. Information obtained from the Social Welfare History Project: Civil Rights Movement, (John F. Kennedy Presidential Library and Museum). www.socialwelfarehistory.com/eras/slaverycivilrights.
3. Tom Brokaw, Boom! Voices of the '60s and Today (Random House, 2007).
4. Information obtained from the RACE Traveling Exhibit, the Museum of Minnesota website:
   www.understandingrace.org/history/society/civil_rights.html.
5. Information obtained from Alan J. Singer's website:
   www.hofstra.edu/alan_j_singer.
6. Severin Cornelius, "Origins of the Long Island Civil Rights Movement," website: hofstra.edu/alan_j_singer.

Part IX

Unfinished Business

Overview

On a clear day, flying at 35,000 feet over the lengthy expanse of Long Island, I see both Montauk Point and Orient Point, Fire Island's beaches, the center moraine of hills, the Pine Barrens, North Shore's bluffs, the wetlands, bays, and inlets that make up this beautiful land. In between the shores, I see the villages and the roads and railroad that connect them amidst trees, houses, and businesses. The view from above gives me a sense of the big picture and how people and the environment are connected and dependent on one another.

Writing this book has given me a similar broad overview, in this case of social reform on Long Island over the past seventy years. It is been a wonderful journey. It is given me the opportunity to better understand this period of Long Island history and the challenges that community activists faced. I came to further appreciate what they accomplished. The journey provided me a wonderful opportunity to get to know people I knew only by reputation as well as renew acquaintances with people I knew and worked with in the past.

You will recall from the book's introduction that the inspiration to write the book came from my reading about the Progressive Era in the United States as described in Doris Kearns Goodwin's *"The Bully Pulpit."* [1] The book motivated me to try to inspire others through writing about progressive action in post-World War II Long Island featuring virtually unknown characters. Indeed, my interviews and research inspired me to write the book towards the culmination of my 50-plus year career in the social work and social action field. It is my hope that it will inspire others to continue or expand their public service work and advocacy especially in behalf of disenfranchised people.

It is clear that nonprofit organizations were formed for a variety of reasons based on the motivations of their lay and professional leaders. Some were formed due to their founders':

- Religious convictions
- Political or philosophical aspirations either as individuals, groups, or organizations
- Desire for status as part of plans to seek further public office

- Desire to create networking opportunities for themselves
- Personal or family experiences with illness or struggle
- Concerns for social justice
- Views regarding how to change society for the better
- Concern for the welfare of a local community's well-being (health/safety/youth/aged, etc.)
- Identification with one or more of the social movements of the 1960s and 1970s, during their formative years between ages 16 and 25.

Organizations were formed in a variety of ways:

- Lay people without professional aid often as a result of personal experiences or in response to social concern.
- A professional that brings lay people together to form an organization.
- The result of the work of a coalition of organizations.
- An existing organization established and spun-off as a separate, independent nonprofit.

Alexis de Tocqueville praised Americans for their enterprise to create problem-solving organizations. After visiting the United States he remarked about the American people:

> The political associations that exist in the United States are only a single feature in the midst of the immense assemblage of associations in that country. Americans of all ages, all conditions, and all dispositions constantly form associations. They have not only commercial and manufacturing companies, in which all take part, but associations of a thousand other kinds, religious, moral, serious, futile, general or restricted, enormous or diminutive. The Americans make associations to give entertainments, to found seminaries, to build inns, to construct churches, to diffuse books, to send missionaries to the antipodes; in this manner they found hospitals, prisons, and schools. If it is proposed to inculcate some truth or to foster some feeling by the encouragement of a great example, they form a society. Wherever at the head of some new undertaking you see the government in France, or a man of rank in England, in the United States you will be sure to find an association. [2]

The pioneers and leaders portrayed in the book addressed Long Island's challenges both from charitable and philanthropic perspectives. The difference between the two, as defined by Benjamin Sockis in The Chronicle of Philanthropy is that philanthropy addresses causes while charity addresses "palliatives" and "sentimental impulses." The article suggests that both charity and philanthropy seek a fairer distribution of essential survival resources but in different ways. It also suggests that the early history of modern American philanthropy indicates it may be possible to seek more charity and the end to charity with equal vigor; that the imperatives of charity and philanthropy can both guide a single institution; that there is ample space for each in the human heart. [3]

Within this conceptual framework, Long Islanders involved in social welfare did some philanthropy and much charitable work. What I see as I look at the Long Island described in these pages are many positives and areas of concern for the future for social welfare and social action organizations. The lay people portrayed who created new social institutions shared similar values emphasizing civic responsibility and social justice. Many were involved during the 1950s-1960s, having lived during the Great Depression and witnessed the positive impact that the federal government had in lifting the country out of the Depression and winning World War II. They, therefore, saw government as a positive force. They felt that an economic safety net was needed to protect citizens from unemployment, sickness, and poverty in old age and other social ills. They were optimists about America's future and confident that all problems could be solved through hard work, determination, and community organizing.

In *Confronting Suburban Poverty in America,* Elizabeth Kneebone and Alan Berube report that "nearly fifty years of federal policies and programs to help alleviate poverty and promote economic opportunity in lower-income places have achieved real progress. They have contributed to reductions in racial segregation and childhood hunger and to increases in affordable housing supply and quality, local commercial activity, and educational attainment." They view suburban poverty as facing considerable challenges and lacking what they call "the prerequisites for success – concentrated target populations; high-capacity, financially stable local government and nonprofits; market-based momentum; and the ability to orchestrate investment across dozens of siloed programs and policies." They point to emerging leaders and innovators who are trying to tailor approaches to suburban challenges. Certainly, Long Island has its share of such leadership. [4]

Some of the lay people described in the book grew up in New York City as social reformers. They were civic-minded and willing to dedicate part of their time, talents, connections, and personal resources to address the social conditions of concern to them as Long Island grew in size and changed socio-economically and racially. Without their willingness to get involved, little of what was accomplished could have happened.

The people described on these pages are a microcosm of thousands of other compassionate, civic-minded people. Long Islanders volunteer to put out fires and respond to medical emergencies. They donate food and clothing to religious institutions and social agencies to relieve human suffering when an environmental crisis occurs. They support programs such as Island Harvest,

Long Island CARES, The INN, Maureen's Haven, the Long Island Council of Churches, and many others. They help build homes with Habitat for Humanity and Rebuilding Together. They join hands with the Long Island Volunteer Center to meet their needs for volunteers.

Some of the lay people were not only concerned about Long Island's future, they were also people of means. Some of them established charitable foundations to support the development of social agencies and organizations. Of particular note, are the Veatch Program of the Unitarian Universalist Congregation at Shelter Rock, the Horace and Amy Hagedorn Foundation, the Rauch Foundation, the Long Island Community Foundation and the Sandy River Charitable Foundation. Many other smaller family foundations were also established, usually directing their support to specific hospitals, educational institutions, and other direct service organizations. Other people directed their charitable giving through the United Way of Long Island.

The social welfare professionals portrayed in the book were often a generation younger than the lay people who formed nonprofit organizations. These Master's Degree-holding professionals were part of a generation of idealists born during and after World War II who questioned authority, encouraged inquiry and dissent, and disdained racism. They had a strong sense of personal responsibility to be directly involved in addressing social problems with little concern for their personal aggrandizement and job security, and had a willingness to learn what they did not know as they went along. Some were risk-takers wherever they chose to intervene, whether in nonprofit organizations, governmental departments, academia, or in elected offices. They had a common set of values, the values of the National Association of Social Workers' Code of Ethics. *(See Appendix)*

Both the lay people and professionals interviewed especially look back fondly to the 1960-1985 period when they pioneered social programs, seeing the period as one when there was federal, state, and local support to create new programs. They recall inspirational national leaders like President John F. Kennedy, Dr. Martin Luther King, Jr., Robert F. Kennedy, and Caesar Chávez, who instilled optimism in them. They recall bipartisan congressional actions that created major advancements in social welfare.

The professionals worked together with the lay people to design direct service programs that responded to changing demographics, environmental concerns, equal opportunity for women and other minorities and changing socio-economic conditions. They dramatically expanded health care, mental health services, and substance abuse services. As the state closed two of the three Long Island state institutions for the mentally ill and sharply downsized the third, they insisted that the former patients be provided with community-based services and became advocates for these services.

They recognized that working families needed affordable, quality child care and created programs for infants, toddlers, preschoolers and school-age children. They understood that people with disabilities needed a wide variety of community-based programs and services and supported programs for them, persevering and producing concrete results in the formation of new organizations and advanced needed social legislation. They look back at those times as a "renaissance," a progressive period of innovation and creativity that flourished.

Community activists were also concerned about the health and safety of Long Islanders. They organized themselves to preserve farmlands and open spaces, establish public parklands, protect the Island's delicate pine barrens and wetlands, and successfully fight against the operation of nuclear power plants amidst powerful financial and media interests. Their work produced significant legislation and the participation of a group of environmental activists that reformed Suffolk County government.

Organizational leaders became more sophisticated in seeing the connections between their work with individuals and the systems impinging on their constituents' welfare. They cultivated and established relationships with elected and appointed officials as well as the media. They fought frequent battles against anti-government attitudes regarding public social spending for the poor and disenfranchised.

Alliances and networks were built that generated new individual, foundation, and corporate support for direct service programs. Educational curricula were reformed in our universities to train social workers to better serve their constituencies. Organizations successfully competed with other regions of the nation for state and federal grants. In many cases, previously described in Part V (*Suburban Trailblazing*), they designed new program and policy innovations that other suburbs replicated. They did all this in a spirit of healthy competition with little rancor or public scandal.

The substantial work completed during the past seventy years covered the entire spectrum of both charity and philanthropy. Those involved should feel a sense of pride in this body of work. On the other hand, for this writer, there is one major shortcoming, and that is that little was done to cultivate and produce new leadership in behalf of social causes. I base this view on the scarcity of graduate social workers who ran for political office. At the national level, social workers have made inroads, with two U.S. senators and seven congressmen currently in office. [4] To the best of my knowledge, the only Long Island social workers who were elected to a county, state, or national office are state assemblywoman Patricia Eddington, state assemblywoman Earlene Hill Hooper and county legislator Jack Eddington. Andy Casazza ran for a State Assembly seat in the late 1960s but lost his bid to replace Robert Wertz. Other than those four, no others have tried to bring their generic skills into the political arena.

This is not to say that social welfare advocates did not impact many public policies but most of their work was done in the roles of counselor, broker, mediator, and researcher - not as advocate or change agent. The change agents and advocates who entered politics came primarily from careers in education, business and law - not from social work or the other social sciences.

It should be noted, that despite the thousands of lay and professionals involved in this work over the decades, my research in *Newsday's* archives of news stories about individuals and nonprofit organizations and my personal experience in the field revealed very few stories of corruption, scandal, nor claims of the misuse of public funds or charitable contributions. That this is the case in an industry that represents approximately 15 percent of Long Island's economy stands as testimony to the honesty and integrity of the people in the field.

Moving Forward with Unfinished Business

The interviewed organizational leaders express great concern about the future, especially about Long Island's economy and environment. They feel it'is likely that Long Island families and individuals already burdened with high taxes, housing, and utility costs will face even more difficult times with the greatest burden on the middle class. Their concerns may be shared by Long Islanders in general.

An August 2014 national survey of Americans, including a disproportionate percentage of suburbanites, suggests the uncertainties felt in suburbia. The survey, conducted by Princeton Survey Research Associates International for the National Center for Suburban Studies at Hofstra University, reports that: "The mood in America's suburbs is unsettled in the summer of 2014. Some signs of recovery from the Great Recession are unmistakable, such as rising real estate prices. But suburbanites still see their overall personal finances as weak and voice growing concerns about problems where they live: unemployment, local public education, and crime." [5]

The leaders point to the dramatic decline in federal aid to Long Island that has denied Long Island the resources to seriously address the region's structural problems and the jobs that such aid would produce especially for lower income people. Indeed, federal aid shows signs of further declines in the near term based on political battles in Washington. David Sprintzen, co-founder of the Long Island Progressive Coalition (LIPC), describes the past forty years as a period in which "there was a systematic defunding of the federal government causing states to be squeezed while localities could not raise taxes. The end result has been the shrinkage and privatization of services. The corporate share of the federal budget has been reduced dramatically as has the top tax brackets imposing higher taxes on the middle-class." The results of this dilemma, Sprintzen says, has "forced organizations into a quandary: Where do you put your time and effort, money and resources?" [6]

Martin R. Cantor, CPA, director of the Long Island Center for Socio-Economic Policy at Dowling College has conducted a number of studies regarding Long Island that help to portray key economic changes that impact Long Island today. In one of these studies Cantor says:

> Long Island once had prime military contractors such as Fairchild-Republic, Eaton, Sperry, Haseltine and Grumman Corporation. Today, it has none. This contraction has led to manufacturing workforce reductions, which continue today, impacting much of the region's less skilled and less educated workers. At the same time, influenced largely by the globalization of economic events, the demand for more skilled and more educated workers has been growing in Long Island's high technology industries, and in the growing financial and banking sector,

> So, according to Cantor, "the mystery of what Long Island is to become is yet before us. To be sure, the requirements to succeed in the global economy are much more complex than what was required for success in the economy and society during the heady days after the end of World War II, when returning veterans found their way here and built America's first suburb. How Long Island succeeds, and what it will look like, will be very dependent on how Long Islanders adapt to the constant changes in the global economy; how we accept our newest residents; and how we understand the economic potential of communities of color and the importance of economic equality and opportunity. [7]

Economists suggest that Long Island's economic challenge today is to reduce heavy reliance on service industries and expand opportunities in small business innovations and technology and increase investments in infrastructure, especially in affordable rental housing located near transportation hubs. They also urge steps be taken to provide educational and training opportunities that produce a workforce whose skills match the needs of the changing environment.

Millennials who became unemployed after the Great Recession and cannot find affordable housing to enable them to leave their parents' homes are also a group for social welfare advocates to target to support reform measures. Cantor provides insights into the importance of Millennials to Long Island's future:

Having the Millennials remain is critical because they are Long Island's future middle class, with much of this new middle class creating a demand for housing. Over 90 percent of responding Millennials live with their parents or relatives, or rent apartments, with nearly the same percent of Millennials planning to purchase their own home. This future market for housing will sustain local housing values and cannot be allowed to leave. Something young people through their responses predict they will. [8]

It has been well-documented that the suburbs are changing. The suburban stereotype of uniformly prosperous, financially stable, politically-conservative voters is no longer the case. A 2012 survey conducted by the National Center for Suburban Studies at Hofstra University, suggests that continued progressive reform in the suburbs may be possible. The survey indicates that "a majority of suburban voters support higher taxes on the wealthy and government action to 'substantially reduce' income disparity." The poll showed suburbanites more supportive of social spending, especially for the elderly, than of tax cuts. "44 percent of survey respondents reported living paycheck to paycheck; 73 percent said they had lost a job or knew someone who had; and 43 percent said they or someone they knew had lost a home. Two in five suburbanites, 40 percent, say they live paycheck to paycheck always or most of the time. More than half of suburbanites, 51 percent, now fear they will not have enough money to live on when they retire. That is an increase of eight percentage points since 2008. [9]

According to Michael Zweig, an economics professor at Stony Brook University and head of the Center for Study of Working Class Life, a family of four requires an annual income of $90,000 in order to survive on Long Island due to its high cost of living. [10]

The Long Island Index reports that the recovery from the Great Recession is being experienced mostly at the top end of the economic spectrum, while the bottom 10 percent of households continues to experience income declines." [11]

Lawrence Levy, executive dean of the National Center for Suburban Studies at Hofstra University feels that Long Islanders, are more moderate and tolerant than they are often given credit for and have been willing to tax themselves to near the breaking point to fund programs they feel are important, and that includes social services. He points to a national suburban poll that the center conducted as indicative that Long Islanders are willing to spend tax dollars on the young, poor, sick and aged and are reluctant to lay off public workers to balance the budget. For all the discrimination and segregation that persists today, Levy feels there is still "a good strong heart that bleeds on Long Island." Levy views suburbanites as evolutionary in their conservatism. "They're open to new ideas and change, but change takes time. It is as if they need to get used to it and will accept change as long as they do not feel it will affect their overall quality of life. They're also sensitive to the needs of the sandwich generation to care for dependent elders. Levy is, therefore, optimistic that suburbanites will continue to evolve. As more and more of them experience the need to house their children and parents on Long Island, they will change and begin to accept the need to change zoning regulations that limit the amount of higher density housing. They will do so out of their own self- interest. Levy points to Paul Pontieri, the mayor of Patchogue, as an example of what can be accomplished by a skillful politician who worked over many years to transform the village into a diverse, vibrant community. [12]

Today, nonprofit leaders have a greater appreciation than they had fifty years ago that true institutional changes often take decades to implement. The hopes and dreams of the War on Poverty, the civil rights movement, the women's movement, and other social reforms initiated in the 1960s and 1970s have produced definite gains but much is yet to be done. The interviewed organizational leaders also understand that social progress comes and goes with no guarantees. Dr. Louise Skolnik reminds us that constructive institutional changes may be implemented during one political administration but discontinued in the next federal, state, or local election cycle. She reminds us that there are no guarantees in social welfare work.

Paul Sabatino II, former counsel to the Suffolk County legislature and a former chief deputy county executive, feels that Long Island politicians should not be stereotyped by their party affiliations and urges an understanding that "There is a great myth about spending at the local level on Long Island. Everyone, both Republican and Democrat, repeatedly stated over the years that they would cut taxes by cutting waste, fraud, and abuse in town and county government. Although it is generally true that Republicans claimed to be against expanding funding for social programs, this was more of a political principle and platform that applied more to elected state and federal officials than to local elected officials. The budget cuts or budget proposals took place at the state and federal level, if at all. Again, the rhetoric has a tendency to overtake the reality. In general, it is fair to say that the rhetoric describing the level of cuts or savings in programmatic funding for social programs at the local level vastly exceeded the reality." [13]

The interviewed nonprofit leaders and social justice advocates recognize that many advances have been made to address social justice issues and social program development but they recognize that Long Island continues to be one of the most racially-segregated regions in the nation. The vast majority of blacks and other minorities live in a handful of hamlets while working in low-paying jobs, face racial discrimination in housing, and black children attend schools that are disproportionately provided with fewer resources. After all the battles for civil rights years ago, Long Island's white majority appears willing to accept institutional racism in education, housing, employment, and the legal system as givens. Otherwise, how does one explain the facts of poor test scores among black students or black arrests and incarceration rates being so much higher than among whites?

Dean Frances Brisbane of the School of Social Welfare at Stony Brook feels that activists are better prepared and organized today to fight racism. She feels that young people will not let people get away with racist agenda. Brisbane describes racism today with a black president as worse that it was fifty years ago. [14]

Attorney Jamir R. Couch says her biggest concern is a lack of intelligent, informed advocates who can speak on behalf of those in need and willing to challenge the system when necessary. Marge and Peter Rogatz see racism as "pervasive, stubborn, difficult to eradicate and not well understood by many otherwise sophisticated people in the human services." [15]

Richard Koubek, Ph.D., chair of the Suffolk County Legislature's Welfare to Work Commission and community outreach coordinator for Long Island Jobs with Justice, crystallizes the overall challenge facing reform-minded Long Islanders:

> One of the challenges facing suburban Long Island today is rethinking how we define ourselves. Literally the 'mother of America's suburbs,' Long Islanders are stuck in the myth that we are a refuge from the urban decay that drove millions of people out of the inner cities after World War II. In fact, we were never as pristine as this myth would have us. Pockets of poverty, often solidified by deep racial prejudices built into the very fabric of our real-estate system, have existed from the day that Levittown barred the sale of home to African Americans in the late1940s. Today, according to a recent Brookings Institute study, US Census data, and the Welfare to Work Commission of the Suffolk County Legislature, poverty is growing at a faster rate in the suburbs than in the center cities and, surprisingly, there are now more people living in poverty in the suburbs than there are in the cities.

> The challenge ahead for social justice advocates is to persuade Long Islanders that they are not, and may never have been, the suburban Eden they thought they were, walled off from the people and problems that 'plague' inner cities. A good part of this awakening needs to be a recognition that suburban political, social and economic institutions have contributed to the isolation of poor and vulnerable people and the perpetuation of their problems here on Long Island. Exhibit A is, of course, our deeply segregated public schools founded on their segregated neighborhoods that cement class and racial disparities.

> Challenging the very premises that define us as a suburb will not be easy. We literally believe we live in Garrison Keillor's satirical Lake

Wobegone "where all the women are strong, all the men are good looking, and all the children are above average." For example, most white middle-class Long Islanders, dazzled by the fact that we are among the ten wealthiest suburbs in America; have trouble accepting the fact that our true poverty level is 200 percent of the Federal Poverty level, or almost $50,000 a year for a family of four. Using this measure drawn from our high cost of living, the Long Island poverty rate soars from the official federal definition of about 6% to almost 20 percent of the population. And, on close examination - such as checking the number of children on reduced price and free lunches in public schools - poor families can be found in just about every suburban community. This explains why over 300,000 or 10% of Long Islanders visit a food pantry every year to help make ends meet." [16]

These circumstances challenge concerned people to continue the struggle for social justice despite the absence of the inspirational national leaders and role models during the 1960s.

The profiled leaders provide much thought and suggestions for current and future leaders.

<u>Less Idealism and Increased Cynicism</u>

Many interviewees see a higher level of cynicism with a lower sense of purpose existing today on Long Island. Many interviewees also expressed the feeling that, in the past, a group of committed people could work together to achieve a great deal. Today, this sense of optimism is not felt as strongly.

Perhaps the greatest reasons for increased cynicism are two-fold. On one hand, nonprofit leaders and their direct service staff are disillusioned as they witness the emotional, social, and economic impacts on individuals and families of governmental retrenchments. They are frustrated by their reduced ability to provide services and advocate in behalf of vulnerable populations and society's apparent lack of interest in the needs of their clients. In some cases, morale is low, especially where programs have been totally eliminated and funding cuts have resulted in service reductions and staff layoffs. The threat of further service reductions looms heavily over much of the sector as needs grow and services are reduced.

Secondly, the level of optimism has been negatively affected since society, through its public policies, shows little recognition of the important role the nonprofit sector plays in alleviating pain and suffering as well as the sector's substantial positive economic impact in the overall economy.

Cynicism has further increased as organizations have been expected to do more with less without being provided the necessary funding to implement the changes expected of them. Since many nonprofit services are mandated by federal and state policies, leaders feel that the state is acting in loco parentis to many of its citizens thus neglecting their responsibility to address the needs of the service providers who address the needs of the most vulnerable citizens.

The Regulatory Environment

Most of the social welfare organizations described in the book focus on treatment of behavioral and psychological conditions and the alleviation of short-term suffering. They do so in compliance with contractual requirements with different levels of government. With so much required of them in terms of regulations and record-keeping, nonprofits have paid little attention to institutional change through political action. Interviewed leaders appear ready to be held more accountable, to be more accountable to federal and state regulatory agencies, with more focus on outcome measures. They feel, however, their ability to do so is greatly impacted by the lack of administrative staff support that they received in government contracts. For these reasons, many organizations are seeking regulatory reforms.

Arthur Gianelli, former CEO/President of Nassau Health Care Corporation and CEO of NuCare urges social service organizations to seek new sources of funding through Perferred Provider Systems (PPS) to the extent they work to transform the way Medicaid patients are cared for addressing the social determinants of health. Many nonprofits are uncertain about this funding path unsure how it will impact their agency financially. They see PPS as Medicaid-centric, ignoring the needs of children and families that do not have Medicaid. Whether the old government sources will open up again may be a long shot. However, what they can do is take on more of a role in pressuring commercial insurers to raise their rates. Otherwise, clinics may continue to close and perhaps be taken over by larger institutions who restrict access to those with Medicaid only raising the question of where private paying people who need a community-based clinic can get the affordable care they need.

Some leaders are excited and challenged by the changing face of the social welfare field and welcome the entry of for-profit providers into social and health care services. They see private investments in the field as filled with opportunities to serve more people. They feel that many nonprofit programs will not survive in the new environment and feel that they should merge or affiliate with larger, more-sophisticated entities with the financial, technological, and human resources to compete in an increasingly-competitive world. They feel that mission and profit do not have to be necessarily at-odds with one another, believing that, in today's funding environment both nonprofits and for-profits abide by the same state and federal regulations and accountability measurements resulting in little practical difference between the sectors.

They feel that mission and profit do not have to be necessarily at-odds with one another, believing that, in today's funding environment both nonprofits and for-profits abide by the same state and federal regulations and accountability measurements resulting in little practical difference between the sectors. They point out that Wall Street investors are showing interest in entering the behavioral health field as the beginning of a trend towards private sector confidence that they can meet their investors' expectations and customers' wishes while complying with increasing and ever-changing government regulations.

Funding Challenges

Many interviewees question where the resources will come from to sustain current social welfare services let alone expand them. There appears little doubt that it will not come from a dramatic increase of corporate and other philanthropic support to a level that begins to address current less or future Long Island needs. And, as many of the interviewees said, as long as Long Island's taxes remain high, residents may continue to object to spending tax dollars to alleviate social problems whether those dollars come from Washington, Albany, Mineola, or Hauppauge.

Leaders point to an increasingly un-level playing field where only larger organizations prevail, leaving smaller organizations in the lurch struggling to survive. Today, there are few opportunities to seek funding to address growing needs or expand successful existing programs. The number of organizations unable to spend time away from their contract obligations and fearful of negative sanctions may result in fewer advocates pursuing system changes and time spent community organizing, developing lay leadership, preparing testimony, and other similar activities.

Some interviewees urge nonprofits to seek independent means of financial support, perhaps from young Long Islanders such as those employed in Wall Street firms who benefited substantially from the Great Recession of 2008. Generational research suggests that Millennials who grew up in the 1980s in diverse environments often hold progressive views and may support social reform efforts with some of their largess.

Nancy Rauch Douzinas, president of the Rauch Foundation, urges charitable foundations to become long term investors in key organizations that they believe in and to work with other foundations and other sectors such as government, business, and labor. She also urges funders to invest in organizational capacity to develop management and communication skills and to remain open to new and creative ideas. [17]

David Kapell, a real estate broker and consultant to the Rauch Foundation, is confident that Long Island will soon work itself out of the national recession and the severe slump in local housing. As things loosen up, he projects that public officials will be willing to spend money again in social betterment projects. So, he feels that now is a good time for nonprofits to cultivate relationships with elected and appointed officials, foundations and business leaders. [18]

Sandy Feinberg, former director of the Middle Country Public Library, points to "ongoing funding as a constant concern as well as developing a sustainable model that is not too dependent on the whims of funders. They're tantamount for success as is the critical importance of working in partnership to achieve a goal that would not be attainable alone," say Feinberg. [19]

Governance Issues

Many interviewees question whether the growing number of nonprofit board members representing business corporations who joined boards in the past ten years to help organizations raise funds and network will also serve as consumer advocates as they have done in the past. All interviewees agree that board members are needed who understand finances and can guide organizations towards financial strength. Concern is also expressed about the criteria future board members will use when making the most important decision board members must make: whom they employ as leaders of their organizations.

Ralph Fasano, CEO of Concern for Independent Living, believes that board compositions should include people who are the intended benefit of services, family members and professionals and that these members must be passionate about their work and strive to make their organizations the best in their fields. Fasano urges organizations not to simply "follow the money" which can lead to a lack of focus and expertise in any one area. [20]

David Okorn, executive director of the Long Island Community Foundation, believes that nonprofits not only need board members with skills in finance, real estate, human resources, and accounting, but also people who understand individual, family, and group dynamics. [21]

Staffing Challenges

Interviewees urge organizational leaders to demonstrate to their board members and funders that the social work profession has unique skills to assess individual, group, and family dynamics-as well as skills to change institutional policies that are contrary to the best interests of those served. They believe that social workers are uniquely qualified to analyze and structure government and private sector contracts for services as evidence-based practice becomes the norm. They urge leaders to take steps to convince others that their organization's work is essential and benefits the society-at-large.

There is a great deal of concern about the trend towards private clinical practice where professionals can earn a good living while fewer people enter social science careers with the goal of social activism or instituting reforms in public policy. If few young people consider such careers, the nonprofits may have great difficulty finding qualified people with the necessary skills and motivation to do more than administer increasingly complex contractual obligations where federal and state government and for-profit entities require strict adherence to defined metrics as the top priority.

The future for direct-service social workers appears bright, especially in the fields of health and mental health, disabilities and criminal and juvenile justice. Steps need to be taken to encourage young people to enter social welfare organizations to assume leadership positions during their careers. Otherwise, programs will be lead by executives whose only priority is efficiency and bottom line results with little understanding of how best to serve people or advocate for needed institutional changes in behalf of their constituents. What may result is an acceptance of policies developed by federal and state government and for-profit entities with limited opportunities or knowledge how to reform these systems.

John Imhof, commissioner of Nassau's Department of Social Services points to social work education today as very advanced with studies in nearly every field of practice. He believes, however, the "tradeoff" has been a dearth in foundational studies about social work history, community social work, administrative and business leadership practices, and policy development. As a social work educator himself, Imhof sees today's students more focused on where they can find employment and not focused on career advancement opportunities in social work leadership positions. [22]

Andrew Malekoff, executive director of North Shore Child and Family Guidance Center expresses real concern for the future employment of the many social workers and their ability to provide quality, mission-driven services in the behavioral health field. He said:

> More and more community-based behavioral services agencies are using fee-for-service staff that is cheaper as there is little expense for fringe benefits. It also helps to offset the deficits generated by the state and county's failure to adequately support these services. Community-based behavioral health services are, by and large, Medicaid-driven. Consequently, individuals and families who are uninsured or underinsured are out of luck if agencies and private practitioners do not accept their insurance or if they cannot afford to devote the labor-intensive work necessary for quality of care for high risk individuals and families. By hiring fee-for-service staff community-based agencies are moving from a mission-driven model to a factory-style-conveyor-belt-piece-work operation. None of this bodes well for social

workers in this field who are interested in working for a mission-driven local organization, for consumers who are seeking a quality of care that includes crisis availability and a systems orientation or for the communities in which they live and work.[23]

Charles Russo, president of the Long Island Homeless Coalition feels that agencies may be very good at diagnosing personal problems but they often ignore other treatment alternatives. He urges organizations to develop effective ways to work with specialized populations by employing former drug and alcohol addicted people and seeing them as legitimate service providers.[24]

Some of the leaders, however, do not share these staffing concerns and see a new renaissance of creative opportunities in the employment for social workers and others who have both business skills and generic interpersonal skills. They view their colleagues who continue to rely heavily on government assistance as engaging in an anachronistic process. They feel that nonprofit leaders can no longer rely on government purse strings and must create new revenue streams if they are to survive. They feel that new leaders will come forth challenged to develop creative ways to address the new funding realities through employment in nonprofit organizations, the creation of for-profit companies or social enterprises created by nonprofit entrepreneurs.

The other concern that many interviewees expressed is about salary levels especially of direct service workers. Interviewees indicate that the starting salaries of beginning social workers, for instance, has remains the same today as they were twenty-five years ago, between $35K to $50K. These salaries do not enable most people to afford Long Island's high cost of living, and discourage long-term employment in the field, and increase the likelihood of supplementary employment, private psychotherapy practices, and pursuing higher salaried positions with their employer or elsewhere. They also may discourage much involvement in social justice and advocacy work.

Dean Frances Brisbane speaks with enthusiasm about the future of social work and its place in social change and social justice. She is optimistic that young people will stand up and fight reactionary forces over-and-over again. She indicates this optimism is present among schools of social work across the nation. In support of her views, Brisbane reports that many the children of the school of social welfare's early years are following their parents' path in pursuing social welfare careers. She also points to young peoples' activism in the Occupy Wall Street movement and the heavy participation of young white people in Ferguson, Missouri after the recent fatal shooting of Michael Brown an unarmed black teenager during 2014. She feels that today's youth will not take the racism that her generation accepted. She also sees the substantial activism of many faith-based organizations and the NAACP as reasons for optimism.[25]

In a recent article published in the News in Review section of the *New York Times,* Isabel Wilkerson, author of *The Warmth of Other Suns: The Epic Story of America's Great Migration* and a former national correspondent and bureau chief for *The New York Times,* provides historical insight towards racism in America today:

> "If the events of the last year have taught us anything, it is that, as much progress has been made over the generations, the challenges of color and tribe was not locked away in another century or confined to a single region but persists as a national problem and require the commitment of the entire nation to resolve." [26]

Certainly, Wilkerson's observation rings true here on Long Island which remains one of the most racially-segregated regions of the nation.

<u>Suggested Reform Measures</u>

As indicated in Part V, *Suburban Trailblazing,* Long Island has produced more than its share of progressive social reform measures. There is no reason to believe that it will not continue to do so.

But things have changed a lot in the past thirty years. Organizations are mostly funded and regulated by government who expect them to focus on micro-level interventions of people individually, in families or in small groups. Funding for mezzo level interventions to create changes in task groups, teams, organizations and network service delivery receive some support while macro level interventions addressing social problems in community, institutional and societal systems receive little support. Macro advocacy primarily involves efforts to assure institutional survival and negotiate reasonable terms with their funders. As long as this continues, little will change, presenting the sector with a very uncertain future. Most efforts to macro level issues have been funded by The Veatch Program, the Rauch Foundation, the Long Island Community Foundation, the Sandy River Charitable Foundation, and the Hagedorn Foundation. The Hagedorn Foundation, however, has announced its plans to discontinue operations at the end of 2017 thus causing uncertainty as to how many of its grantees will be able to continue their work.

Many leaders of the past urge future leaders to take steps to educate elected officials, making their proposals in economic terms as well as humanistic ones. Despite growing economic disparities and homelessness and hunger, many of Long Island's elected officials are reluctant to advocate for necessary state and federal resources to address documented current problems and their future implications. Elected officials need to be convinced that suburban poverty is a greater problem than they may have imagined, a problem that requires that they do something that they have been unwilling to do: raise taxes for new investments in education, mental health, and community-based children, youth, and family services. This can be completed through survey research projects.

Another point to be made by advocates is that the nonprofit sector is an economic driver that employs thousands of tax-paying people whose job it is to assist other tax-payers to enter and remain in the workforce. Its purchasing power is substantial, both through its employees' purchases as well as through nonprofit organizations' purchases of goods and services from other sectors.

In pursuit of educating and swaying elected officials regarding their voting behavior on any particular issue or program, interviewees recommend that advocates present themselves with open minds not stereotyping or pre-judging elected officials based on their party affiliations or positions on other issues. Advocates need to figure out where politicians are coming from, treating politicians respectfully, listening carefully to what they have to say. Ultimately, it is a relationship and trust-building process where nonprofit leaders demonstrate their knowledge and skills and their ability to build lasting relationships.

Jim Morgo, former Suffolk County chief deputy county executive, Suffolk County legislator, and former president, of the Long Island Housing Partnership, urges continued advocacy towards what he believes to be the major issue affecting all social need categories, the wealth disparities among Long Island's many towns and hamlets. He wants to see greater efforts to revitalize communities outside of government through community/civic alliances. He sees a major issue that such groups often do not collaborate well with similar groups in the same community. [27]

One action that advocates should support is federal legislation, some currently with bipartisan support in both the U.S. Senate and House, to protect and strengthen Medicare and Social Security for the long haul. They should also work with federal legislators for passage of affordable long term care insurance and universal early childhood education programs that have demonstrated effectiveness in preparing children for future success.

Other critical national issues that need advocates are changes to the way elections are financed and progressive reforms of our tax policies, campaign financing and immigration policies, which directly impact low-income people especially those who are also members of minority groups. Continued vigilance is also necessary concerning women's reproductive rights and other constitutionally-protected rights.

Generations United (GU) urges advocates to challenge the common refrain in the media about coming conflict between young and old, as rising numbers of "greedy geezers" purportedly spell disaster for future generations. Instead of leading to a war pitting "kids vs. canes," GU believes that collaboration across generations is possible, natural and essential. In particular, the organization is convinced that the vast and growing human capital present in the older population can be rallied to strengthen the education and development of young people, particularly children growing up in poverty. Long Island advocates might well take this advice. [28]

The aging of Long Island's population demands greater public attention. Advocates of all political stripes are needed to develop grassroots community organizations that help people age in place where the vast majority wish to remain in their later years. Successful models exist modeled on the Beacon Hill Village program in Boston or the Parish Social Ministry program at Our Lady Queen of Martyrs in Centerport. These programs rely heavily on volunteers and, sometimes, modest membership fees. In communities where residents are aging in significant numbers, other service models need to be developed and require advocates. In the Town of North Hempstead and the Town of Huntington, Neighborhood Natural Occurring Retirement Community (NNORC), are operated by Federation Employment Guidance Services (FEGS) while the Mid Island Y Jewish Community Center's NNORC in Plainview operates two NNORC programs. Other nonprofit agencies could provide assistance to local groups to dramatically expand these programs. The state office for aging provides technical assistance for these purposes. In addition, young people need to be able to afford to live on Long Island. Older people also need to be able to remain on Long Island near their families. Middle class families, sometimes "sandwiched" between caregiving for children and elderly parents, need to earn enough income to be able to remain here. An intergenerational coalition that is organized around cross-generational issues of the bookend generation of younger and older people is needed and may be a key to Long Island's future prosperity. Such an effort is needed-calling upon all sectors of the economy to work together. [29]

Impact investing may also warrant the attention of reform-minded Long Island social activists. Through impact investing, foundations and other institutional investors who currently support charitable activities may be willing to invest some of their endowment funds in social causes that have the potential of a return of capital instead of seeking purely monetary return. Foundations often hold endowments that are managed to protect or grow their principal while only spending the legally required 5 percent annually for charitable purposes. Nonprofits may find interested partners at foundations open to this concept that is taking hold in other regions of the nation. Long Island foundations are likely to have billions of dollars in such endowments. Nonprofits that set up for-profit arms and benefit corporations can help them tap into this funding. [30]

The latest issue of the *Nonprofit Times* reports that five New York City funders have announced a collective effort to make flexible, high-impact capital available to nonprofit organizations working with and on behalf of low-income New Yorkers. Through providing secured and unsecured loans, loan guarantees, and equity and equity-like securities, they seek to help these organizations increase their impact while offering the potential for some amount of financial return. Hopefully, Long Island funders will consider such projects. [31]

Richard Koubek offers another important strategy for reformers:

> One vehicle for unlocking our suburban myopia is the faith community-On the forefront of charitable works for years, as demonstrated in this book- the faith community also has the scriptural and historical resources to help their members understand that charity is not enough to care for their neighbors in need-The Jewish, Catholic and Protestant traditions are replete with calls for justice, that is, for addressing the underlying causes of the hunger, homelessness and other social ills that their charitable works address. Mobilizing this sleeping giant will not be easy because most clergy understand that their congregants do not want to hear such challenges to their "suburban dream." But there is a growing cadre of lay and clerical leaders willing to issue the challenge.

> Pope Francis is setting such a tone for the Roman Catholic and even larger religious world. And there are pockets here on Long Island-such as the progressive Jewish Community Relations Council, Catholic parishes such as Our Lady of the Miraculous Medal Church in Wyandanch, or the progressive Long Island Council of Churches, already willing to issue the call for people of faith on Long Island to move from charity to justice. So too, the AMOS Project of Long Island Jobs with Justice (AMOS is an acronym for 'A Movement of Solidarity') is bringing together a 'coalition of conscience' made up of progressive labor, faith and community-service leaders working to address the systemic injustices on Long Island-such as low-wages, the exploitation of undocumented immigrant workers or the lack of a viable public transportation system that largely serves working-poor people." [32]

Current and future nonprofit leaders and social activists owe a great deal to those who paved the way for them, perhaps especially the early ones whose contributions are described in the book. Their stories should inspire everyone to move forward to assure that future generations of diverse people will be able to live and prosper together. The pioneers had a deep-seated belief that Long Island could overcome its challenges. Their work is testimony to the resiliency, industriousness and generosity that exists on Long Island.

History suggests that changing public attitudes and reforming suburban institutions often takes decades to accomplish and is filled with challenges, disappointments and struggles. History also demonstrates that much larger international, economic and political forces have significant impacts on the social welfare scene. It also shows that we have little control over them. Suburbs like Long Island were shaped due to the need for affordable housing, a basic human need and an essential element of a democratic society. That need continues to exist today.

In 2014, the technology and creative models to provide affordable housing, public transportation systems and other basic human needs exist. Implementing them would enable Long Island to develop into a much-more livable place for future generations. But the disparity between rich and poor and white and black must also be addressed. What is needed is public and private people of imagination and boldness to find the resources needed, organize themselves and implement their ideas. Otherwise, Long Island will continue to move towards being a vast sprawl of exclusionary living and social disintegration conditions rather than the realization of the American dream. Smart growth projects currently underway in Glen Cove, Hempstead, Huntington Station, Wyandanch and the Ronkonkoma Hub show promise for the future. More such projects are needed.

Long Island nonprofits need to more successfully tap into the resources of individual donors who give five times as much as all foundations combined. They should also consider conducting more research to determine how much good a given program accomplishes (in terms of lives saved, lives improved, etc, per dollar spent. Foundations should also consider GiveWell.org's strategy that focuses on finding the best giving opportunities possible.

Nonprofits are challenged to do a better job convincing business corporations to contribute to their causes. Over the past ten years, even through the ups and downs of a violent economic cycle, contributions as measured by percentage of pretax earnings have dropped in charitable giving nationally, now comprising only about 6 percent of private sector donations and only a little more than 1 percent of the $1.5 trillion charitable economy. [33]

Academic institutions need to train professionals for administrative positions in the skills to hold political and bureaucratic systems accountable to consumers. They need to prepare people for leadership positions in the communities they serve with fundraising and community organizational skills to work with social and economically diverse populations. The days of trail-blazing are over but the challenges are no less great. Today, one needs much more that the desire, motivation, and perseverance to survive, you need competence in every-changing skill sets.

In speaking of the importance of the nonprofit sector, Robert A. Scott, Preident of Adelphi University, says:

"Our society functions well when the three sectors function well. Business takes risks and can generate profits needed for taxation and donations. Government is intended to provide a safety net for times of travail, preserve order through uniformly administered laws and provide for the common defense. The third sector, the nonprofit sector initiates functions that often are too small, too local, or too new for either business or government to take on. It seeks neither profit nor order in pursuing its mission, which often challenges business and government to be more mindful of the needs of humanity." [34]

Reformers must continue to do their part to keep hope alive, stirring the pot with inspirational passion, facts, concerns, challenges and questions. The body of social welfare and social action knowledge that has been accumulated by our fore bearers is as relevant today as it was years ago. The struggle must continue to not only treat symptoms of individual problems but address underlying causative factors. Reformers need to remain optimistic about the future and build on the many achievements of the past not getting disappointed when what we know doesn't become public policy due to political considerations.

I consider myself extremely fortunate to have lived during this period of life when hope was palpable and change was in the air. The opportunity to have known and associated with people over the decades of similar values and concerns is a gift that I am deeply grateful for. It has been a wonderful ride that I would gladly do over again. I look forward to the continued growth of an economically, ethnically and racially diverse Long Island where all children will live and prosper with equal opportunity for all.

Notes: Part IX

1. Doris Kearns Goodwin, The Bully Pulpit: Theodore Roosevelt, William Howard Taft and the Golden Age of Journalism (Simon & Schuster, 2013).
2. Alexis de Tocqueville, Democracy in America, Volume II, Second Book; Influence of Democracy on the feelings of the Americans.
3. Benjamin Sockis, "Today's Problems Call for Reviving Charity – and Eliminating the Need for It" (The Chronicle of Philanthropy, October 19, 2014).
4. Elizabeth Kneebone and Alan Berube, Confronting Suburban Poverty in America," (Brookings Institution Press. 2013). P. 95.
5. Lawrence Levy, interview with author, Garden City, NY, October 1, 2014.
6. David Sprintzen, Ph.D., interview with author, Hicksville, NY, April 7, 2014.

7. Martin R. Cantor, CPA, "Economic Benefits of Diversity: Untapping the Potential of Long Island's Black Community" (Long Island Institute for Socio-Economic Policy at Dowling College, 2008).
8. Martin R. Cantor, CPA, "Long Island's Young People: Why They Will Continue to Leave Long Island" (DestinationLI, June 2014).
9. Lawrence Levy, interview with author, Garden City, NY, October 1, 2014.
10. Information obtained on university website: www.stonybrook.edu/workingclass.
11. Information obtained on foundation website: www.longislandindex.org.
12. Lawrence Levy, interview with author, October 1, 2014.
13. Paul Sabatino II, email correspondence of May 1, 2014.
14. Frances Brisbane, Ph.D., interview with author, August 29, 2014.
15. Jamir Couch, Esq., email correspondence of October 6, 2014.
16. Richard Koubek, "Struggling in Suburbia: Meeting the Challenges of Poverty in Suffolk County" Suffolk County Legislature's Welfare to Work Commission, 2012.
17. Nancy Rauch Douzinas, interview with author, July 18, 2014.
18. David Kapell, interview with author, August 19, 2014.
19. Sandra Feinberg, email correspondence of November 15, 2014.
20. Ralph Fasano, email correspondence of October 7, 2014.
21. David Okorn, interview with author, July 29, 2014.
22. John f, Ph.D., interview with author, August 20, 2014.
23. Andrew Malekoff, email correspondence of April 17, 2014.
24. Charles Russo, interview with author, April 12, 2014.
25. Frances Brisbane, Ph.D., interview with author, August 29, 2014.
26. Isabel Wilkerson, "When Will the North Face Its Racism?" (New York Times, January 11, 2015).
27. Jim Morgo, email correspondence March 24, 2014.
28. Information obtained from agency's website: www.gu.org.
29. Evelyn Roth, interview with author, August 21, 2014.
30. Judith Rodin and Margot Brandenburg, A Guide to Impact Investing and an Activist's Memoir (Wharton Digital Press, 2014).
31. "SeaChange Capital Partners Announces New Fund to Make Program-Related Investments in New York City," (New York Nonprofit Press, December 2014).
32. Richard Koubek, email correspondence of November 15, 2014.
33. Ken Stern, "Why Don't Corporations Give to Charity?" (Philanthropy New York, August 2013).
34. Robert A. Scott, "The Third Sector: Long Island's Misunderstood Economic Engine," (Keynote Address, Long Island Business Development Council and Hempstead IDA, March 31, 2015).

Appendix

i. Advisory Committee

Rev. Beresford Adams, Pastor, Faith Baptist Church,

Kenneth Anderson, former NAACP leader and Suffolk County Human Rights Commissioner

Dr. Ruth Brandwein, professor emerita and former dean, School of Social Welfare at Stony Brook University and former Commissioner, Suffolk County Department of Social Services

Leone Baum, former deputy director, Nassau Economic Opportunity Commission

Andy Casazza, former commissioner, Human Services/Town of Huntington

Arline Cohen, major gifts officer, Philanthropic Leadership Group, UJA Federation

Miriam D. Couch, National Coalition of 100 Black Women, Suffolk County Chapter, Inc., charter member

Marvin Colson, clinical associate professor, School of Social Welfare at Stony Brook University

Dr. Richard Dina, former president and CEO, Family and Children's Association

Dr. Harvey Farberman, professor, School of Social Welfare at Stony Brook University

Rene Fiechter, assistant district attorney and director, Community Affairs, Nassau District Attorney's Office and former Education and Assistance Corporation executive

John C. Gallagher, former chief deputy county executive and police commissioner of Suffolk County

Karl Grossman, columnist and professor of journalism, Media & Communications, State University of New York at Old Westbury

Jean Kelly, executive director, The Interfaith Nutrition Network

Nancy Marr, community activist in North Bellport

Diana O'Neill, executive director, Long Island Volunteer Center

Rev. Dr. Katie Roche, founder and executive director, Rainbow Chimes International School for Early Education

Msgr. Peter Ryan, former executive director, The Smith Haven Ministries

Ron Roel, president, Roel Resources and former Newsday Editor

Evelyn Roth, former Suffolk County deputy county executive, former executive director, FEGS/L.I., and former commissioner, North Hempstead Department of Services for the Aging

Charles Russo, Esq., Russo, Karl, Widmaier & Cordano, PLLC, founder and chairman of the board, Hope House Ministries and board chairman, Long Island Coalition for the Homeless

Betty Schlein, feminist and former assistant to Gov. Hugh Carey

Dr. Louise Skolnik, professor emerita, Adelphi University School of Social Work and former deputy commissioner of Nassau County Department of Social Services

Sy Symonds, former YMCA of Long Island executive

Rick Van Dyke, former CEO, Family Service League, Inc.

Tom Williams, former CEO, Cornell Cooperative Extension of Suffolk County and former executive director of Brookhaven Youth Bureau and the Suffolk Community Council

ii. In Memoriam

Salvatore Ambrosino

Myron Blanchard

Joan Boden

Clive Chilton

Diana Coleman

Ruth Corcoran

James W. Couch

Matt Crosson

John J. Foley

Robert W. Green

Horace Hagedorn

Joan Imhof

Owen Johnson

Reverend Earl Jordan

Gerard Leeds

David Kadane

Pearl Kamer

Helen Kaplan

John L. Kearse

Wilbur Klatsky

Lee and Ed Lawrence

Gerard Leeds

William J. Lindsay

Lincoln Lynch

Kathy Maul

Robert Cushman Murphy

Anne Mead

Helen McIntyre

May Newburger

Dan Panessa

Catherine Papell

Reverend H. David Parker

Maxine Postal

Irwin Quintyne

Leroy Ramsey

William C. Richards

Beulah Rothman

Priscilla Redfield Rowe

David G. Salten

Alonzo Shockley

Mildred Steinberg

Leon "Jake" Swirbul

Martin Timin

Paul Townsend

Caesar Trunzo

Burghardt Turner

Joseph Vigilante

Phyllis Vineyard

Henry Viscardi

Gloria Wallick

Ralph Watkins

iii. Patrons

Gregory Blass

Karen Boorshtein

Ruth Brandwein

Francis Brisbane

Lucille Buergers

Miriam D. Couch

Jane Devine

Richard Dina

Nancy Rauch Douzinas

Rene Fiechter

Dana Friedman

Norman Goodman

Steve Held

John Imhoff

Jean Kelly

Larry Kennedy

James Kirby

Lilo and Gerard Leeds

Peter Levy

Nancy Marr

Lillian McCormick

Nawrocki Smith LLP

Dr. & Mrs. Peter O'Neill

Vera Parisi

Katie Roche

Jill Rooney

Evelyn Roth

Michelle Santantonio

Janet Schaberg Walsh

Walter Stockton

Middle Country Library Foundation

Joan Saltzman

Richard Schaffer

Betty Schlein

Cynthia Scott

Martin Seitz

Marcia Spector

David Starr

United Way of Long Island

Rick Van Dyke

Tom Williams

iv. Contributing Writers

Ken Anderson

Leone Baum

Ruth Brandwein

Richard Dina

Lucille Gluck

Karl Grossman

Bob Keeler

Lawrence Levy

Peter Levy

Nancy Marr

Evelyn Roth

Louise Skolnik

Tom Williams

v. Long Island Demographic Profile Charts

Source: United States Census Bureau

1945 POPULATION OF BOTH NASSAU AND SUFFOLK COUNTIES: 776,894

Estimated 1945 population by county:
Nassau County   520,519
Suffolk County   256,375

NASSAU COUNTY DEMOGRAPHICS										
Year	Total Population	Med. Age	% White	% Black	% Hispanic	% Other	% 65+	% 0-17	% Poverty	Percent College Grad	Median Fam. Inc
1950	672,765	31	97	NA	NA	NA	NA	NA	NA	21	NA
1960	1,300,171	31	97	3	NA	NA	6	NA	NA	NA	NA
1970	1,428,838	31	95	5	NA	NA	8	NA	4	17	NA
1980	1,321,582	34	88	7	3	2	11	26	5	24	$26091*
2012	1,349,233	41	64	12	15	8	16	22	6	41**	$97,409

SUFFOLK COUNTY DEMOGRAPHICS										
Year	Total Population	Med. Age	% White	% Black	% Hispanic	% Other	% 65+	% 0-17	% Poverty	Percent College Grad	Median Fam. Inc
1950	276,129	36	95	NA	NA	NA	NA	NA	NA	12	NA
1960	670,213	30	94	5	NA	NA	9	NA	NA	NA	NA
1970	1,124,950	26	95	5	NA	NA	8	NA	6	12	NA
1980	1,284,231	30	87	6	5	2	9	32	7	18	22359*
2012	1,499,273	40	71	8	17	4	14	23	6	32**	$87,778

* 1979 **2010
NA: NOT AVAILABLE
PERCENTS ARE ROUNDED

vi. Commonly Used Long Island Nonprofit Acronyms

Association for Children with Learning Disabilities ~~~ ACLD
Association for Fundraising Professionals of Long Island ~~~ AFPLI
Association for Help to Retarded Children ~~~ AHRC
Bellport Area Community Action Coalition ~~~ BACAC
Bellport Hagerman East Patchogue Alliance ~~~ BHEP
Big Brothers Big Sisters of America ~~~ BBBSA
Catholic Youth Organization ~~~ CYO
Central American Relief and Education Center ~~~ CARECEN
Coalition Against Child Abuse and Neglect of Nassau County ~~~
    CACANNC
Coalition Against Domestic Violence ~~~ CADV, CAST
Community Development Corporation of Long Island ~~~ CDCLI
Community Development for Youth ~~~ CDY
Community Programs Center of Long Island ~~~ CPC
Congress of Racial Equality ~~~ CORE
Early Years Institute ~~~ EYI
Economic Opportunity Council ~~~ EOC
Family and Children's Association ~~~ FCA
Family Service League ~~~ FSL
Federation Employment Guidance Services ~~~ FEGS
Friends of the Arts ~~~ FOTA
Habitat for Humanity International ~~~ HHI
Haven House Bridges ~~~ HHB
Independent Group Homes for Living ~~~ IGHL
Jewish Community Centers ~~~ JCC
League of Women Voters ~~~ LWV
Long Island Community Foundation ~~~ LIPF
Long Island Council of Churches ~~~ LICC
Long Island Gay Lesbian Bisexual Transgendered Services Network ~~~
    LIGLBT Network
Long Island Housing Partnership ~~~ LIHP
Long Island Mentoring Partnership ~~~ LIMP
Long Island Progressive Coalition ~~~ LIPC

Long Island Volunteer Center ~~~ LIVC

Long Island Volunteer Enterprise ~~~ LIVE

Mental Health Association of Suffolk ~~~ MHAS

National Association for the Advancement of Colored People ~~~ NAACP

National Association of Puerto Rican and Hispanic Social Workers ~~~
  NAPRHSW

National Association of Social Workers ~~~ NASW

National Center for Suburban Studies ~~~ NCSS

Natural Occurring Retirement Community ~~~ NORC

Neighborhood Naturally Occurring Retirement Community ~~~ NNORC

North Shore Child and Family Guidance Center ~~~ NSCFGC

Peconic Community Council ~~~ PCC

Planned Parenthood of Nassau County ~~~ PPNC

Planned Parenthood of Suffolk County ~~~ PPSC

Stewards of Our American Resources ~~~ SOAR

Suffolk Community Council ~~~ SCC

Suffolk County Coalition Against Domestic Violence ~~~ SCCADV

Suffolk County United Veterans ~~~ SCUV

Suffolk Network Against Teen Pregnancy ~~~ SNAP

United Cerebral Palsy ~~~ UCP

United Jewish Appeal/Federation ~~~ UJA/FED

United Way of Long Island ~~~ UWLI

Urban League ~~~ UL

Victims Information Bureau ~~~ VIBS

Voluntary Organizations Active in Disaster ~~~ VOAD

Young Men's Christian Association ~~~ YMCA

Yours Ours Mine ~~~ YOM

vii. Long Island Volunteer Hall of Fame Inductee Honor Role

2011 INDUCTEES

Children and Youth Services—*Patricia D'Accolti*, Children's Sport Connection

Education— *Nancy and Rod Zuch*, The Morgan Center

kEmergency Services—*Nancy Lynch*, Pet Safe Coalition

Family Support—*Glenda White-Hills*, Millennium Sistahs

Health—*Nancy Leupold*, Support for People with Oral and Head and Neck Cancer

Homelessness—*Larry Hohler*, Hope Children's Fund

Philanthropy—*Dan Connor*, The Gladiator Fund

Seniors—*Sister Jeanne Andre Brendel, O.P.*, Harvest Houses (run by The Emmaus House Foundation)

Special Needs—*Dr. Deborah Benson*, Common Ground Alliance

Next Generation Award in Emergency Services—*Simeon Melman*

Next Generation Award in Leadership—*Benjamin Jake Kornick*

Next Generation Award in Visionary Philanthropy—*Christopher Yao*

Lifetime Achievement Award in Volunteerism—*Jay Steingold*

Inspirational Service Award—*Victoria Ruvolo*

2010 INDUCTEES

Children & Youth Services — *Jill Rooney*, Harbor Child Care

Cultural Arts — *Valia Seiskaya*, Ballet Education and Scholarship Fund, Inc.

Education — *Maida Cherry*, Assoc. of Prof. Volunteer Administrators

Environment — *Richard Schary*, Friends of Massapequa Preserve

Family Support — *Janet Walerstein*, Child Care Council of Suffolk

Health — *Colette Coyne*, Colette Coyne Melanoma Awareness Campaign

Homelessness — *Robert McMillan*, Long Island Housing Partnership

Philanthropy — *Ralph and MaryAnn Napolitano*, Jay's World Childhood Cancer Foundation

Special Needs — *William Heiser*, William Heiser Foundation for the Cure of Spinal Cord Injuries

Lifetime Achievement Award in Volunteerism — *Jack Sullivan*, Abilities

Next Generation Award for Historic Preservation — *Rachel Obergh*, Nunley Carousel Restoration: Pennies for Ponies

Next Generation Award for Leadership-*Charles Sharkey*

2009 INDUCTEES

Children & Youth Services — *Marcia Spector*, SNAP Long Island

Environment — *Steve Corbett*, Floral Park Conservation Society

Family Support — *Vera Rivers*, Central Nassau Club - National Association of Negro Business and Professional Women's Club

Health Services — *Michael Nolan*, Hospice of the South Shore now known as Hospice Care Network

Health Advocacy — *Mitch Shapiro*, Foundation for Sight and Sound

Homelessness — *Teresa Kennedy*, Mercy Center Ministries

Philanthropy — *Jill Palmeri*, The Andy Foundation

Special Needs — *Frank Krotschinsky*, Suffolk Independent Living Org.

Lifetime Achievement Award in Volunteerism — *Shirley Katz*, The Retreat

Next Generation Youth Award for Education — *Jennifer Zwilling,* Youth Ambassador Program at Tourette Syndrome Association

Next Generation Youth Award for Leadership — *David O'Connor*

Next Generation Youth Award for Visionary Philanthropy — *Samantha Malis*, 1>0

2008 INDUCTEES

Children & Youth Services — *John White*, Project Challenge

Cultural Arts — *Joysetta and Julius Pearse*, Dr. Martin Luther King, Jr. Birthday Celebration Committee of Nassau County

Environment (Preservation) — *Robert Alvey*, Garden City Bird Sanctuary

Environment (Animals) — Sybil Meisel, PAWS (Pioneers for Animal Welfare Society)

Family Support — *Lillian Julien*, COPE (Connecting Our Paths Eternally)

Health — *Lorraine Pace*, Breast Cancer Help (Healthy Environment for a Living Planet)

Homelessness — *Kenneth Batchelor*, Habitat for Humanity of Suffolk

Hunger — *Ann and Phil Gribbins*, Floral Park Conservation Society Giving Garden

Seniors — *Leonard Sandel*, FOSSI (Friends of Senior Services, Inc.)

Special Needs — *Nina Eaton*, United Cerebral Palsy of Suffolk

Lifetime Achievement Award in Volunteerism — *William Tyree*, SCO Family of Services

2007 INDUCTEES

Children and Youth Services — *James Boisi*, Mentoring Partnership of LI

Education — *Fred Breithut*, School-Business Partnerships of Long Island

Emergency Services — *Tim Jaccard*, AMT Children of Hope Foundation

Environment — *Anna Hunninghouse*, Little Shelter Animal Rescue & Adoption Center

Family Support — *Rhoda Finer*, InterAgency Council of Glen Cove

Health — *Robert Donno*, Gift of Life

Health/Substance Abuse — *R. Brinkley Smithers*, Long Island Council on Alcoholism and Drug Dependence

Homelessness — *Sister Aimée Koonmen, O.P.*, Bethany House

Hunger — *Aimée Z. Holtzman*, rock CAN roll

Seniors — *John J. (Jack) Flatley*, Long Island State Veterans Home

Special Needs — *Judith S. Bloch*, Variety Child Learning Center

Lifetime Achievement Award in Volunteerism — *James W. Reed*

2006 INDUCTEES

Children and Youth Services — *Cindy Pierce Lee & Marjorie Chaplin*, Child Abuse Prevention Services

Cultural Arts — *Dr. Hiao-Tsiun Ma*, Children's Orchestra Society

Emergency Services — *Mr. & Mrs. Henry P. Davison*, American Red Cross in Nassau County

Environment — *Janine Dion*, Pet Peeves

Family Support — *Luke Smith*, Society of St. Vincent de Paul

Health — *Marion Terry*, African-American Health Education and Development Fund

Historical Preservation — *Thomas Roberts III*, Fire Island Lighthouse Preservation Society

Homelessness — *Patricia Shea*, MOMMAS House

Mental Health — *Dr. Davis Pollack*, Clubhouse of Suffolk

Philanthropy — *Betty Schlein, Suzy Sonenberg & Barbara Strongin*, Long Island Fund for Women & Girls

Special Needs — *Lisa Gatti*, Pal-O-Mine Equestrian

Lifetime Achievement Award in Volunteerism — *Sol Goldstein*, Rebuilding Together, Long Island,

Lifetime Achievement Award (honorary) — *Diana O'Neill*, Long Island Volunteer Center

2005 INDUCTEES

Children and Youth Services — *Dr. Carol Carter, Patti Kelly Barker & Dr. Tamara* Pelosi, Sunshine Center

Cultural Arts — *Boris Chartan*, The Holocaust Memorial & Educational Center of Nassau County

Education — *Mother Anselma Ruth*, Molloy College

Environment — *Sallie Ruppert*, Volunteers for Wildlife

Family Support — *The Honorable Hope Zimmerman*, Mothers' Center Hicksville, National Association of Mothers' Centers

Health — *Heather Buggee*, Splashes of Hope

Mental Health — *Irving Berkowitz*, Federation of Organizations

Hunger — *Syd Mandelbaum*, Rock and Wrap it Up!

Homelessness — *Peter Barnett*, Nassau-Suffolk Coalition for the Homeless

Philanthropy — *Marty Lyons*, The Marty Lyons Foundation

Seniors — *Paul Arfin*, Community Programs Center of Long Island

Special Needs — *Al Eskanazy*, ASCENT: A School for Individuals with Autism

Lifetime Achievement Award in Volunteerism — *Marc Blitstein*, AHRC-Suffolk Chapter

Lifetime Achievement Award in Volunteerism — *Thomas Cruso*, United Way of Long Island

2004 INDUCTEES

Children and Youth Services — *Jerry & Fern Hill*, Timothy Hill Children's Ranch

Cultural Arts — *Sharon Lippman*, Art Without Walls

Education — *Delores Smalls*, Association of Black Women in Higher Education

Emergency Services — *David Kilmnick*, Long Island Gay & Lesbian Youth

Family Support — *Geraldine Sheridan*, Dress for Success Brookhaven

Health & Mental Health — *John Theissen*, John Theissen Children's Foundation

Homelessness — *Cosco Williams*, Wyandanch Homes & Property Development Corp.

Philanthropy — *Lillian McCormick*, Family & Children's Association Port Washington Group Home

Seniors — *Anne Mead*, Retired & Senior Volunteer Program in Suffolk County

Special Needs — *Donald Mitzner*, Adults & Children with Learning and Developmental Disabilities

Lifetime Achievement Award in Volunteerism — *Sheila Johnson Page*, Newsday Community Affairs

2003 INDUCTEES

Children and Youth Services — *Jean Forman*, Coalition on Child Abuse & Neglect

Cultural Arts — *Faye Raymon*, Township Theatre Group

Education — *Diana Freed*, Education & Assistance Corporation (EAC)

Emergency Services — *Rev. John Paul Hankins*, RESPONSE of Suffolk County

Environment — *Nancy Manfredonia*, Long Island Greenbelt Trail Conference

Family Support — *Barbara Allan*, Prison Families Anonymous

Health & Mental Health — *Beatrice Cohart*, North Shore Child & Family Guidance Center

Homelessness — *Sr. Mairead M. Barrett*, OSU, New Ground, Inc.

Hunger — *Harry Chapin*, Long Island Cares - The Harry Chapin Food Bank

Philanthropy — *Elizabeth Gere Byrnes*, Junior League of Long Island

Seniors — *Angela Koenig*, Doubleday Babcock Senior Center

Special Needs — *Helen Kaplan*, AHRC Nassau Chapter

2002 INAUGURAL INDUCTEES

Children and Youth Services — *Gloria Wallick*, Rosa Lee Young Childhood Center

Cultural Arts — *Catherine Davison*, Nassau County Museum of Art

Education — *Joan Imhof*, Long Island Volunteer Center

Emergency Services — *Beverly Merkinger, Dr. Sherry Radowitz, & Arlene Siegelwaks,* Nassau County Coalition Against Domestic Violence

Environment — *Paul Stoutenburgh*, North Fork Environmental Council

Health & Mental Health — *Lyn Jurick*, Ronald McDonald House of Long Island

Homelessness — *Michael Moran & Patricia O'Connor*, Interfaith Nutrition Network

Hunger — *Linda Breitstone*, Island Harvest

Seniors — *Janet Walsh*, Long Island Alzheimer's Foundation

Special Needs — *Dr. Caryl Bank & Dr. Barbara Feingold*, The Hagedorn Little Village School

viii.   Health and Welfare Council of Long Island Award Recipients

Since 1980, the Health and Welfare Council of Long Island has recognized leaders in the social welfare sector who have made significant contributions to the field. They are recognized here as well.

<u>The Sandy Lenz and Jim Harnett Community Service Award</u>

In 1979 the Health and Welfare Council established its first community service award in memory of former Board member, President and long-time advocate for the poor, Sanford V. Lenz. We memorialize Sandy not only for his concrete contributions in the development of a Long Island Human Service network, but also for the manner in which he expressed his love and concern for all people. The community service award was re-named in 2010 in memory of Jim Harnett. Known as the ultimate caregiver, Jim shepherded the care of thousands of Long Islanders in his role as President/CEO of Family & Children's Association.

Luke Smith St. Vincent de Paul 1980
Sal Ambrosino Family Service Association 1983
Clive Chilton Action Council of Central Nassau 1984
Jim Shuart Hofstra University 1985
Joe Barbaro Catholic Charities 1986
Bill Warner LI Federation of Labor 1988
Vera Rivers National Council of Women 1989
Len Clark N/S Law Services 1990
Bob Ellis St. Vincent de Paul 1992
Marge Rogatz Community Advocates 1993
John Gilmartin Catholic Charities 1994
Richard Dina Children's House 1995
Ann Irvin Nassau County Youth Board 1996
Judy Bloch Variety Pre School Workshop 1997
Greta Rainsford Saltzman Center, Hofstra 1998
Donna Kass LI Coalition for National Health 1999
Helen Martin BHEP 2000
Horace Hagedorn Hagedorn Family Foundation 2001
Suzy Sonenberg LI Community Foundation 2002
Evelyn Roth FEGS 2003
Jean Kelly The Interfaith Nutrition Network 2004
Robert Detor South Oaks/Broadlawn 2005

Cindy Scott Coalition Against Child Abuse and Neglect 2006
Tom Goodhue Long Island Council of Churches 2007
Lawrence Raful Touro Public Advocacy Center 2008
Gerard McCaffery MercyFirst 2009
James Harnett Family & Children's Assoc. 2010
Michael McClain Suffolk Community Council 2011
Karen Boorshtein Family Service League of Long Island 2012
Mary Lou Jones, South Shore Family and Guidance2013
Robert A Scott, PhD, President, Adelphi University 2014

The David Kadane Memorial Award for Advocacy

In April of 1991, Long Island lost a long-time advocate for the poor with the
death of former HWCLI president David Kadane. The Health and Welfare
Council board of directors chose to honor the memory of this leader by
establishing the David Kadane Award. The award is given to an individual
who best exemplifies David's tenacious advocacy for justice.

Debi Zaiff Family Service Association 1991
Robin Sparks N/S Law Services 1992
Sadie Hofstein Mental Health Association of Nassau 1993
Ada Goldberg Nassau League of Women Voters 1994
Pat Dolan News12 1995
Jean Forman Coalition on Child Abuse 1996
Peter Visconti 5 Towns Community Center 1997
Robert Pierce Long Island Council of Churches 1998
Janet Walerstein Child Care Council of Suffolk 1999
Gloria Wallick Child Care Council of Nassau 1999
Ann Mallouk Planned Parenthood of Nassau 2000
Chris Reimann Office of Presiding Officer Suffolk Leg 2001
Sandy Oliva Nassau Coalition Against Domestic Violence 2002
Joseph Smith Long Beach REACH 2003
Jamie Bogenshutz YES Community Counseling 2003
Rose Guercia L.I. Health Access Monitoring Project 2004
Fred Scaglione New York Non Profit Press 2005
Patrick Young CARECEN 2006
Ann Sullivan ACORN 2007
Str. Margaret Smyth North Fork Hispanic Apostolate 2008
Paul Pontieri Mayor of Patchogue 2009
Joye Brown Newsday 2010
Connie Lassandro Nassau County Office of Community Development 2011
Vivian Viloria-Fisher Suffolk County Legislature 2012
Daniel Altschuler, Long Island Civic Engagement Table 2013
Philip M. Mickulas, LCSW, President/CEO, Family and Children's 2014
Lifetime Achievement Award: Congresswoman Carolyn McCarthy 2014

The Hagedorn Award for Philanthropy

In June of 2003, the Health and Welfare Council of Long Island's board established the Hagedorn Award for Philanthropy to honor Horace and Amy Hagedorn for their extraordinary generosity and vision in assisting Long Island's health and human service community.

Amy Hagedorn 2003
Horace Hagedorn 2003
John Miller 2004
Abraham Krasnoff 2005
Nate Berry 2006
Linda Landsman 2007
Ann Mallouk 2008
Suzy D. Sonenberg 2009
LI Unitarian Universalist Congregation at Shelter Rock 2010
Long Island Fund for Women & Girls 2011
Mazon: A Jewish Response to Hunger 2012
Robin Hood Foundation 2013
Newsday Charities 2014

ix. United Way of Long Island Award Recipients

HENRY D. PEARSON, JR. MEMORIAL FUND

1986 - Adrian Cabral (Health & Welfare Council of Nassau)

1987 - Salvatore Ambrosino (Family Service Association)

1988 - Patricia A. Nocher (American Red Cross, Suffolk Chapter)

1989 - Hamilton Banks (Economic Opportunity Council of Suffolk)

1990 - Reinhardt Van Dyke (Family Service League of Suffolk)

1991 - Sadie Hofstein (Mental Health Association of Nassau)

1992 - Percy Abrams (United Jewish Ys of Long Island)

1993 - Clive Chilton (Health & Welfare Council of Nassau (posthumously)

1994 - Gladys Serrano (Hispanic Counseling Center)

1995 - Dick Dina (Children's House)

1996 - Judy Bloch (Variety Pre-Schooler's Workshop)

1997 - Renee Pekmezaris (Nassau-Suffolk Health Systems Agency)

1998 - Gloria Wallick (Child Care Council of Nassau)

1999 - Barbara Hadel (Doubleday Babcock Senior Center)

2000 – Helen Martin (Bellport, Hagerman, East Patchogue Alliance)

2001 – Jack O'Connell (Health & Welfare Council of Long Island)

2002 – Evelyn Roth (FEGS)

2003 – Marsha Spector (SNAP Long Island)

2004 – Diane Merceica (South Fork Community Health Initiatives)

2005 – Barbara Bartell (Central Nassau Guidance & Counseling)

2006 – Tracey Lutz (The Retreat)

2007 – Sandy Oliva (Nassau Coalition Against Domestic Violence)

2008 – Kathy Rosenthal (F.E.G.S. Health and Human Services)

2009 – Rick Van Dyke (Family Service League of Suffolk)

2010 – Herb Ruben (Peninsula Counseling Center)

2011 – Janet Walerstein (Child Care Council of Suffolk)

2012 – Jim Dilts, (Society of St. Vincent de Paul)

2014 – Pam Johnston (Victims Information Bureau of Suffolk)

x. Suffolk County Community Council Awards

Woman of the Year

2005 -- Michelle E. Di Benedetto

2006 -- Sandra Feinberg

2007 -- Linda Howard Weissman

2008 -- Kay Kidde

Man of the Year

2006 -- Dr. Aldustus Jordan

2007 -- Michael L. Nolan

2008 -- Ernest G. Canadeo

Long Island Advocate of the Year

2005 -- Dr. Davis Pollack

2007 -- Mary Lou Beldy

2008 -- Lauren Terrazzano (posthumously awarded)

Long Islander of the Year

2003 -- Jim Morgo

Lifetime Award for Social Justice

2010 -- Ruth Brandwein

xi. Association of Fund Raising Professionals – Past Honorees

2014 – 1987 Outstanding Fundraising Executive

Rebecca Chapman

Marcie Rosenberg

James R. Rennert, CFRE

Sherry L. Friedman

Alan J. Kelly, CFRE

Jaclynne M. Jacobs

Barry Cosel-Pieper, CFRE

Ruth Del ColRobin S. Amato, CFRE

Randi Shubin Dresner, CFRE

Theresa Regnante

Sharon Markman, CFRE

Anthony E. Childs

Marsha Gittleman

Anita Fishman

Marie A. Palagonia, CFRE

Robert Mottola

John P. Renyhart, CFRE

Helen Fleshler, Ph.D.

Linda Howard Weissman

Wells B. Jones, CAE, CFRE

Ira Latinsky, CFRE*

George T. Holloway

Stephen M. Levy, CFRE

C. William Kimbell*

Jack J. Sage, CFRE

Rochelle M. Lowenfeld

Frank L. Regnante

Outstanding Corporation

Alure Home Improvements

Farrell FritzCapital One Bank

GEICO – Region II

MSC Industrial Supply Co.

CA, Inc.

ClearVision Optical

VerizonBank of America

Bethpage Federal Credit Union

FedExKeySpan

Astoria Federal Savings

North Fork BankNewsday

Roslyn Savings Bank

EABMarcum & Kliegman

First Long Island Investors, Inc.

KPMG Peat Marwick, LLP

Fleet Bank

Allstate

CablevisionCitibank

Grumman Corporation

Outstanding Fundraising Volunteer

Andrew Kover

Marge Rogatz

Jane Schwartz

Ann Dorman Adler

Frank Pelliccione

Mindy B. Alpert

Greg Demetriou

Theresa Brucculeri

Janine Dion

Wendy Chaite, Esq.

Maria Telesca

Roslyn D. Goldmacher

Rosamond Arthur Dean

Catherine A. Jansen

Mitchel Shapiro

Robert Kammerer

Angela Koenig

Michele Siben

Irving Klein

Marilyn Proferes

Alfred W. Levy

Harvey Granat

Peggy Teufel*

Ronnie Renken

Lyn Jurick

Walter Oberstebrink

Mary Ann Meyer*

Horace Hagedorn Outstanding Philanthropist

Susan & Matteo Bevilacqua

Karen & Frank Boulton

The Quinn Family

Joseph Mancino

Robert Donno

Lillian Barbash

Abe Krasnoff*

Amy Hagedorn

John D. Miller

Agnes and John* Funk

David Ochoa & Myrka Gonzalez

John A. Danzi

Maurice Barbash

Rita & Frank Castagna

Gerard & Lilo Leeds

Cynthia Marks

Horace Hagedorn*

Robin and John* Hadley

Martha Farish Gerry

Joan R. & Arnold A. Saltzman

Joseph Gurwin*

Robert S. Boas*

Tita* & Joseph Monti*

Gilbert Tilles*

Gilbert Tilles Award

Dave Widmer

Terrie Magro

Nancy Mazzola

Marian Conway

Ann McDermott-Kave

James Meyer

Rauch Foundation

The Heritage Group

Christopher Smithers Foundation

Ronnie Renken

Suzy D. Sonenberg

J. Stanley Shaw and Family

The God Squad Stephanie

Joyce Kahn

James J. Smith*

B. Strongin & G. Friedlander*

The Fay J. Lindner Foundation

Betty Schlein

LI Community Foundation

Terry and Paul* Townsend

Leaders of Tomorrow Award

Rae Specht

Brooke DiPalma

Maggie Moran

Sarah Connor

Kyle OrentKyle,

Ryan & Sean Habe

Nicholas Farano

Samantha Scoca

Dylan Cruthers

Jennifer Zwilling

Andrew Alderman

* Deceased

xii.   Past Honorees: Long Island Progressive Coalition

*Sylvia Aaron *Air America Radio *Eric Alexander *Barbara Allen *Alliance for Quality Education Youth Committee *Joe Alvarez *Rich Amato *Elizabeth Archeson *Sondra Bachety *Minna Barrett *Steve Bellone *Congressman Timothy Bishop *Melissa Bishop-Morgan *Carol Bissonette *Reverend Geoffrey Black *Pat Blanco *Myron Blumenfeld *Robert Boehm *Patricia Bowden *Ruth Brandwein *Robin Brazley *Fred Brewington *Jimmy Brigagliano *Father Bill Brisotti *Reverend Canon *Cecily Broderick-Guerra*April Brown-Lake *Olga Browner *Barbara Buehring *Maryann Calendrille *David Calone *Lenny Canton *Daniel Cantor *Florence Capers *Scott Carlin *John Carter *Sandy Chapin *Clive Chilton *Jean Christie *Sammy Chu *Lillian Clayman *Roger Clayman *Hugh Cleland *Ben Cohen *Diana Coleman *Jon Cooper *Lauren Corcoran-Doolin *Julie Dade-Howard *Reverend Noelle Damico *Fanny Davis *Circulo De La Hispanidad *Rosemarie Deering *Robert De Luca *Mary Dewar *Randi Dresner *NYS Comptroller Tom DiNapoli *Michael D'Innocenzo *Arthur Dobrin *Al Dorfman *Jean Duncan *John Durso *Jeannette Edelstein *Steve Engelbright *Stuart & Lynn Epstein *Magarita Espada *Adrienne Esposito *Tony Ernst *Ernie Fazio *Mark Finkel *Elisabeth Fiteni *Elsa Ford *Ellen Frank *Bob Frankum *Cecily Frankum *Helen Fitzgerald *Ruth Gaines *Reverend Ryland Gaines *Michael Gendron *Senator Kirsten Gillibrand *Jessica Glynn* *Angela Gonzalez *Amy Goodman *Gordon Greenfield *Mort Greenhouse *Jack Gremse *Dr. Rosemarie Guercia *Melodie Guerrera *Andreas Guilty *Jim Guyette *The Hagedorn Foundation *Michael Harrington *Fred Harrison *Marge Harrison *Ed Hernandez *Jan Hickman*George Hochbrueckner *David Hunter *Dick Iannuzzi *Glenda Jackson *Bob Keeler *Anne B. Kellett *Jack Kennedy *Councilwoman Connie Kepert *Charles Kernaghan *Steve Kraft *Dr. James Krivo *Kirk Kordeleski *Richard Koubek *Andrea Libresco

*Dal LaMagna *Nick LaMorte* Dale LaRocca *Marsha Laufer *Neal Lewis *Assemblyman Charles Lavine*Ann & Gene Lopez *Joe Lorintz *Michele Lynch *Timothy Lynch *Tony Macagnone *Laura Mallay *Jean E. Mannhaupt *MCCAP Committee *Serge Martinez & Hofstra Law Clinic *Bob Master *Ernesto Mattace, Jr. *Kevin McCarrick *Risco Mention-Lewis *Paul Merkelson* Ruth Messinger *Carol Miller *Gerry Mooney *Elizabeth Moseman *Bert Napear *Owen Neill *Jack O'Connell *Luis Olivera* Michael O'Neill *Ben Orr *Elsie Owens *Judy Pannullo *Vera Parisi *Dr. David Parkinson *Bill Pickering *Jan Pierce *Viola Pitts *Sonia Placio-Grottola *Debra Pofeldt *Maxine Postal *Peter Quinn *Philip Ramos *Bob Ralph *Fran Reid *Marge Rogatz *Jimmy Rogers *Amparo Sadler *Jeremy Samuelson *Richard Schary *Betty Schlein *Brian Schneck *NYS Attorney General Eric Schneiderman *Senator Charles E. Schumer *Martin Schwartz *Isabel Sepulveda de Scanlon *Don Shaffer *Vic Skolnick *Charlotte Sky *George Siberon *Katharine Smith *Pastor Mack Smith *Robert Smith *Cheryl Smyler-George *Carrie Solages* Dan Steiger *Joy Stein*Ron Stein * Fred Stelle *Delano Stewart *Robert Summerville *Honorable Thomas Suozzi *Assemblyman Bob Sweeney *Kathryn Szoka *The Workplace Project *Delores Thompson *Barbara Treen *Luis Valenzuela *Pauline Velazquez * Unitarian Universalist Congregation at Shelter Rock & Its Veatch Program *Vivian Viloria-Fisher *Lucius Ware *Herman A. Washington *Susan Weisman * William Winpinsinger * Pat Young *Barbara Zeller*

xiii. Forty Eyes: Common Vision Lessons Learned

The following lessons learned are culled from oral interviews from twenty Long Island nonprofit executive directors gathered and assembled in a 2010 monograph "Forty Eyes: Common Vision" written by Richard P. Dina, DSW and Craig S. Fligstein, LCSW. The project was funded by the United Way of Long Island. Its findings follow this book's lessons. As you will see, there is a good deal of overlap with those reported by the social activists profiled in the book. The full monograph is available at the United Way of Long Island. Contact Craig Fligstein at: craig@unitedwayli.org

- Passion for the Work: The strongest message that comes through is the belief that a passion for human service work is absolutely necessary to be an effective executive.
- Personal Credibility: The perception by others of how nonprofit organizational leaders are viewed cannot be underestimated.
- Multi-Tasking: The executive director must be able to wear many hats at the same time and be both a leader and a manager.
- Advocate: The executive must serve as an advocate with and for people served by the agency.
- Working with Staff: Most executives feel that handling personnel issues is the hardest part of their jobs.
- Educational Preparation for the Field: The majority of executives felt that a Social Work Degree with a concentration in community organization is the best preparation for the field.
- The Role of Organization's Leader: The executive must serve as the face of the agency finding the right balance between being an educator, advocate, and team-builder.
- Working with a Board of Directors: Executives must have a clear appreciation and understanding of the crucial role of the agency's board of directors and forge a partnership among the executive and the board.
- Mistakes and Disappointments: The most commonly-stated are: Not to be a "know-it-all" executive and to keep questioning and learning; not to make quick, knee-jerk decisions and keep an open mind; serve as a "servant" leader; attract the best possible staff and do not accept sub-par compensation for you and your staff; and do not shy away from fund raising

xiv. National Association of Social Workers Code of Ethics

Summary

The NASW Code of Ethics is intended to serve as a guide to the everyday professional conduct of social workers. This Code includes four sections. The first Section, "Preamble," summarizes the social work profession's mission and core values. The second section, "Purpose of the NASW Code of Ethics," provides an overview of the Code's main functions and a brief guide for dealing with ethical issues or dilemmas in social work practice. The third section, "Ethical Principles," presents broad ethical principles based on social work's core values that inform social work practice. The final section, "Ethical Standards," includes specific ethical standards to guide social workers' conduct, and to provide a basis for adjudication.

The Code identifies core values on which social work's mission is based, summarizes ethical principles that reflect the profession's core values, establishes a set of specific ethical standards that guide social work practice, and provides the basis on which the public can hold a practitioner accountable.

Summary of Principles

1. Social worker's primary goal is to help people in need and to address social problems.

2. Social workers challenge social injustice.

3. Social workers respect the inherent dignity and worth of the person.

4. Social workers recognize the central importance of human relationships.

5. Social workers behave in a trustworthy manner.

6. Social workers practice within their areas of competence, and develop and enhance their professional expertise.

Ethical standards are articulated under social workers' ethical responsibilities to clients, to colleagues, in practice settings, as professionals, to the social work profession, and to broader society.

The National Association of Social Workers is the largest organization of professional social workers with 155,000 members. It promotes, develops, and protects the practice of social work and social workers. NASW also seeks to enhance the well-being of individuals, families, and communities through its work and its advocacy. A professional social worker has a Degree in Social Work and meets state legal requirements. Professional social workers practice in many settings including family service agencies, child welfare, community mental health centers, private practice, schools, hospitals, employee assistance programs, and public and private agencies. Professional social workers are the nation's largest group of mental health services providers.

About the Author

Paul Arfin holds a Bachelor's Degree in General Business from Adelphi College (1962) and a Master's Degree in Social Work from Adelphi University's School of Social Work (1970). He has served as executive  director of several Long Island nonprofit organizations since 1970. During his fulltime work career, he founded Suffolk County's first youth center; established Long Island's first interpersonal dispute resolution center; and its first corporate-supported intergenerational day care center. He founded the YMCA of Long Island's Family Services Division and the Community Programs Center of Long Island, where he served as executive director for twenty two years.

Arfin served as president of the New York State Adult Day Services Association and is a recipient of the Association's Pioneer Award. He was inducted into the Long Island Volunteer Hall of Fame and received an "An Art of Caring Award" from former Governor George Pataki. He was also recognized by the Long Island Business Partnership with a "Sixty-over-Sixty" award for his community service.

From 1980 to 2002, he served as founding executive director of The Community Programs Center of Long Island (CPC), a nonprofit that operated three large intergenerational day care centers and Head Start programs. During this period, he earned support from numerous business corporations and government agencies.

After retiring from fulltime employment in 2002, Arfin founded Intergenerational Strategies, a nonprofit organization, the intergenerational studies center at Dowling College, and a Long Island chapter of the Social Enterprise Alliance. In addition, he assisted Family Service League and Family and Children's Association to establish HomeShare Long Island matching older adult homeowners with people needing affordable rental housing.. During this period, he also served as New York State coordinator for Generations United's Seniors4Kids and as an instructor at Hofstra University and Dowling College where he designed and taught courses in nonprofit employment and volunteerism to baby boomers.

In 2005, Arfin chaired the Suffolk County Executive's Commission on Creative Retirement authoring a report consisting of numerous specific action recommendations that were later implemented by the legislature due to the leadership of County Legislator Steven Stern.

Over the years, Arfin has written numerous articles published in *Newsday*, and the *New York Times* on family, aging, intergenerational and social enterprise issues. He has served as a consultant to numerous nonprofit organizations. He is the author of *Portrait of a Peace Corps Gringo,* the story of his growing up in Mineola, Long Island during the 1940s and 1950s; his decision to join the Peace Corps in 1963; his cherishd experiences as a community development worker in rural Colombia; and how his Peace Corps' years affected the rest of his life.

His Master's thesis, written in 1970, *Characteristics and Values Differentiating Alienated and Service-Oriented Youth* portrays the tenure and social turmoil of the late 1960s in America.

Arfin lives in Hauppauge, NY with his wife of 47 years, Karen. They love to travel, read books, eat great food and spend time with family and friends. They feel fortunate that their two daughters, Sari and Liza and son-in-law Jeremy and two granddaughters Daviel and Mira, live in the area to enrich their lives.

The author can be contacted at: paularf@optonline.net

Additions to Index

Due to technical reasons, the following names of people and organizations were inadvertently omitted from the Index. The author expresses his apologies.

Index